THE FAR RIGHT IN WESTERN AND EASTERN EUROPE

Edited by
Luciano Cheles
Ronnie Ferguson
Michalina Vaughan

Longman
London and New York

Longman Group UK Limited,
Longman House, Burnt Mill,
Harlow, Essex CM20 2JE, England
and Associated Companies throughout the world.

Published in the United States of America
by Longman Publishing, New York

First published 1991
Second impression 1992
Second edition 1995

ISBN 0 582 238811 PPR

British Library Cataloguing-in-Publication Data
A catalogue record for this book is available from the British Library

Library of Congress Cataloging-in-Publication Data
A catalogue record for this book is available from the Library of Congress

Set by 7 in 9.5 Times
Produced by Longman Singapore Publishers (Pte) Ltd.
Printed in Singapore

CONTENTS

LIST OF CONTRIBUTORS

Stephen K. Carter lectures in the Faculty of Human Sciences of London Guildhall University. His research centres on Russian intellectual and political history and post-Communism. His publications include *The Politics of Solzhenitsyn* (Macmillan, 1977), *The Political and Social Thought of F. M. Dostoevsky* (Garland, 1989) and *Russian Nationalism – Yesterday, Today, Tomorrow* (Pinter, 1990). He is currently interested in the Teaching and Learning Technology Programme as applied to teaching Russian history at first degree level.

Luciano Cheles is Senior Lecturer in Italian Studies at Lancaster University, and has been a Visiting Lecturer at the University of Lyons 2 (1994–95). His research has focused on the relations between visual arts and politics. He has been curator of various exhibitions, including *Extreme-Right Propaganda and Counter-Propaganda* and (with Ronnie Ferguson) *Art and Propaganda in Fascist Italy*. He has published *The Studiolo of Urbino* (Penn State Press, 1986), and several articles on the propaganda of Italian parties and on Renaissance political frescoes. His co-edited volume *The Art of Persuasion. Political Communication in Italy, 1945–1995* (Manchester University Press) is forthcoming.

Roberto Chiarini is Professor of Politics in the Faculty of Political Science at the University of Milan. He has published studies on liberalism (*Giuseppe Zanardelli*, Franco Angeli, 1987), on Fascism (*L'armonia e l'ardimento. L'ascesa del Fascismo nella Brescia di Augusto Turati*, Franco Angeli, 1988), and on neo-Fascism, (*Da Salò a Piazza della Loggia*, Franco Angeli, 1983), as well as on history and politics more generally (*Fini e fine della politica*, Franco Angeli, 1990). He writes regular columns for daily newspapers (*Il Sole-24 ore* and *Il Giornale di Brescia*) and periodicals (*Storia contemporanea* and *Il Ponte*).

David Childs is Professor of German Politics at Nottingham University. He is a member of the executive committee of the Anglo-German Association, and was chairman of the Association for the Study of German Politics, 1981–86, and secretary, 1986–88. His publications include *The GDR: Moscow's German Ally* (Unwin Hyman, 1986), *Germany on the Road to Unity* (The Economist Intelligence Unit, 1990), *Germany in the Twentieth Century* (Batsford, 1991), and twelve other works, as well as numerous contributions to books, journals and newspapers. He is currently working on a major study of the German far right.

António Costa Pinto lectures in Modern European and Portuguese History in the

Department of Sociology of the *Instituto Superior de Ciências do Trabalho e da Empresa*, Lisbon. He has been a researcher at the European University Institute, Florence (1986–89) and a Visiting Professor of Modern European History at Stanford University (1993–94). He has recently published *Salazar's Dictatorship and European Fascism. Problems and Perspectives of Interpretation* (Columbia University Press, 1995) and *Os Camisas Azuis. Ideologia, elites e movimentos fascistas em Portugal, 1914–1945* (Estampa, 1994).

Guy Desolre lectures in European Social Policy at the Free University of Brussels. He has been an official at the International Labour Office, Geneva, and an expert on social affairs for the EEC. He has published several books on workers' control, trade union policy and labour law. He co-edits the yearbook *L'année sociale* and currently works for the Senate of Belgium.

Martin Durham is a Senior Lecturer in Politics at the University of Wolverhampton. He has worked on British Fascism, the New Right, and 'pro-family' and 'pro-life' movements in Britain and the United States. He is author of *Sex and Politics. The Family and Morality in the Thatcher Years* (Macmillan, 1991).

Roger Eatwell is Senior Lecturer in Politics at the University of Bath. Recent publications relevant to neo-Fascism include 'Towards a New Model of Generic Fascism', *Journal of Theoretical Politics*, April 1992; 'Why Has the Extreme Right Failed in Britain', in P. Hainsworth (ed.), *The Extreme Right in Europe and the USA* (Pinter, 1992); R. Eatwell and A. W. Wright (eds), *Contemporary Political Ideologies* (Pinter, 1993); 'Why Are Fascism and Racism Reviving in Western Europe?', *Political Quarterly*, July 1994; and *Fascism* (Chatto and Windus, 1995).

Sheelagh Ellwood is Research Analyst for the Iberian Peninsula at the Foreign and Commonwealth Office, London. Prior to joining the FCO, she lived and worked for many years in Spain as a freelance researcher and writer. She is the author of *Prietas las Filas: Falange Española de las JONS, 1933–1983* (Crítica, 1983), *Spanish Fascism in the Franco Era* (Macmillan, 1987), *The Spanish Civil War* (Blackwell, 1991) and *Franco* (Longman, 1995).

Ronnie Ferguson is a lecturer in the Department of Italian Studies at Lancaster University. He was educated at the Universities of Glasgow and St Andrews, and has published on the Renaissance and on language and society in modern Italy. He has co-organised, with Luciano Cheles, exhibitions on Fascist art and propaganda and on the 1984 Euro-elections. He is the author of *Italian False Friends* (Toronto University Press, 1994) and *Angelo Beolco (Ruzante), 'The Veteran' (Parlamento de Ruzante) and 'Weasel' (Bilora)* (Peter Lang, 1995).

Gerry Gable is the editor of the monthly international anti-Fascist magazine *Searchlight* and founder of Searchlight's research service. He is a television producer and researcher, and has made several documentary programmes about the far right. He also lectures, writes and broadcasts widely. He lives in London, and has travelled and worked extensively abroad, researching and covering stories in his specialist fields of Fascism and organised crime since 1961.

Christopher T. Husbands is Reader in Sociology and Academic Audit Adviser at the London School of Economics and Political Science. He has researched widely on the extreme right and racist politics in a number of West European countries and in recent years has published contributions concerning France, the Federal Republic of Germany, Belgium, The Netherlands and the United Kingdom. He is also interested in the politics of immigration in Western Europe, especially variations in responses to different immigrant groups, as well as in the politics of political asylum.

Jill Irvine is Assistant Professor of Political Science at the University of Oklahoma. Her research interests centre on state-building and nationalism. Her most recent publication is *The Croat Question. Partisan Politics in the Formation of the Yugoslav Socialist State* (Westview, 1993).

Douglas Johnson was educated at the Royal Grammar School, Lancaster; Worcester College, Oxford; and the Ecole Normale Supérieure, Paris. He was Professor of Modern History at the University of Birmingham before becoming Professor of French History at University College, London, in 1968. He is author of several books on French history.

Vassilis Kapetanyannis is Press Officer at the Greek Ministry of Information. He lived in London for fifteen years where he worked for the BBC, and at the Embassy of Greece as Press Attaché. He read politics and economics at Athens University and holds a Ph.D. in politics from Birkbeck College (University of London). He has contributed extensively to Greek and foreign periodicals, and to books on Greek politics and international affairs. He regularly writes political analyses and book reviews for the leading Greek daily paper *Kathimerini*, and edits the foreign pages of the fortnightly political and cultural review *Anti*.

Jaroslav Krejčí studied law and economics in Prague. Due to his particular life experience, his research, teaching and writing were concerned mainly with various forms of sociocultural pluralism and with social dynamics. He is, at present, Emeritus Professor at Lancaster University and is involved in academic work in the Czech Republic. His most recent books are *Czechoslovakia at the Crossroads of European History* (Tauris, 1990); *The Civilizations of Asia and the Middle East Before the European Challenge* (Macmillan, 1990); *The Human Predicament: its Changing Image* (Macmillan, 1993); *Society in a Global Perspective* (SLON, Prague, 1993); and *Great Revolutions Compared. The Outline of a Theory* (Harvester Wheatsheaf, 1994).

Anthony D. Smith is Professor of Sociology at the London School of Economics and President of the Association for the Study of Ethnicity and Nationalism (ASEN). He has published several books on ethnic identity and nationalism, including *Theories of Nationalism* (Duckworth, 1971 and 1983), *Nationalism in the Twentieth Century* (Martin Robertson, 1979), *The Ethnic Revival* (Cambridge University Press, 1981),

The Ethnic Origins of Nations (Blackwell, 1986) and *National Identity* (Penguin, 1991). He also holds a doctorate in the history of art, with special interests in patriotism and neo-classicism.

Michalina Vaughan was born in Poland and educated in France. She read law, politics and sociology in Paris, gaining a *Doctorat en Droit (d'Etat)* and the diploma of the Institute of Political Studies. She taught sociology at the London School of Economics (1959–72) and at Lancaster University (1972–87), where she is Emeritus Professor. Her publications include *Social Conflict and Educational Change in England and France (1789–1848)* (Cambridge University Press, 1971) and *Social Change in France* (Martin Robertson, 1980). She currently works for the European Commission in Brussels.

LIST OF ILLUSTRATIONS

ACKNOWLEDGEMENTS

We are grateful to the following for permission to reproduce copyright material: the National Gallery of Ireland for the painting *Ecce Homo* by Titian, Plurigraf s.p.a. for the picture of the *Pietà*.

FOREWORD

In the late 1980s, when we undertook to assess the prospects and/or the threat of the far right, Europe was still divided by the iron curtain, symbolised by the Berlin Wall. At the time the volume, entitled *Neo-Fascism in Europe*, appeared in 1991, barriers between West and East were only just coming down. It was therefore assumed that our focus should be on Western and Southern Europe, where Fascism as an ideology had originated and still inspired varying degrees of nostalgia among disaffected groups. By Europe we meant seven countries (Italy, Germany, Spain, Portugal, Greece, France and Britain), all of which belong to the European Community/Union, and all of which, with the exception of Britain, had historical experience of Fascist (or at least *fascisant*) rule.

However, in the 1990s history is moving – and is being rewritten – fast. Both the map and the mood of Europe have changed. The reunification of Germany exemplifies the redrawing of political borders, as does the disintegration of the former Yugoslavia. The access of the far right to the Berlusconi government in Italy illustrates popular disenchantment with traditional ruling elites, a phenomenon echoed by the growing acceptance of nationalism in Russia. In order to take account of what appears to be an irreversible historical change, the fall of the Soviet Empire, it is now mandatory to define Europe more widely. Hence the addition of Poland, the CIS and the former Yugoslavia to the volume. Belgium has also been deemed worthy of inclusion, owing to the unusually important role there of the linguistic divide.

Although any second edition is at risk of being considered a mere rewrite and update, the pace of change made it imperative for us to adopt a more ambitious approach. Out of the eighteen chapters which comprise this volume, nine are wholly new. J. Krejčí's 'Neo-Fascism – West and East' and A. Smith's 'The dark side of Nationalism' provide a broad conceptual framework. As already mentioned, four additional countries have been included (chapters by Anita Prazmowska, Stephen Carter, Jill Irvine and Guy Desolre). In addition, three earlier contributors, Christopher Husbands, writing on East as well as West Germany, Gerry Gable, analysing the current structure and status of British neo-Fascism, and Roger Eatwell, looking at the ways neo-Fascists have sought to rewrite Fascist history, produced new texts. All the others have expanded their chapters to cover the recent evolution in the countries or areas they discuss. The extent to which they have had new ground to cover varies with the impact of external pressures (e.g. the Macedonian issue for Greece) or of internal ones (e.g. election results) on the far right. We are confident that no effort has been spared to reflect prevailing trends accurately and to predict alternative scenarios without either undue pessimism or complacency.

In Europe, 'we have been taught to take evil seriously' (Sartre). We can at least attempt a diagnosis, even if we cannot offer a cure.

Luciano Cheles
Ronnie Ferguson
Michalina Vaughan
January 1995

Chapter 1

NEO-FASCISM – WEST AND EAST
Jaroslav Krejčí

The terms Fascism and neo-Fascism are classic concepts derived from the name of one political movement and one political party, the name chosen by the founders of that party themselves. In the introduction to the first edition of this book the generic usage of this term was discussed with reference to the right–left political spectrum where various instances of militant nationalism could be described as neo-Fascist. A possible extension of this term to the political movements outside Europe was taken into account. In this, the second edition, I would like to focus on a conceptual analysis of the occurrence of political activities that can be classified as neo-Fascist, and of their causes. Since the first edition in 1991 a lot has happened and the empirical material for a comparative analysis has become substantially richer.

Let us start with a tentative definition: neo-Fascism is a phenomenon that has become politically and sociologically significant in the 1980s and 1990s. As in the original, classical Fascism, the essence of neo-Fascism lies in a political orientation extolling the value and position of one's own ethnic grouping (the nation) to such an extent that, as a rule, the following policies emerge:

1. Within one's own political framework (the State) those belonging to other ethnic groupings (or *ethnies*) have to be either fully assimilated or treated less favourably, that is, discriminated against or possibly even evicted.
2. Territories outside the borders of one's own state that are settled by the fragments of one's own ethnic grouping have to be incorporated into the political framework (i.e. the State) of the *ethnie* to which they culturally belong but from which they are detached politically; to achieve this, any kind of pressure or enforcement is considered legitimate.
3. All those who belong to the ethnic nation irrespective of class and social status should be united in the endeavour to promote the power and glory of that nation which also should be purified of any evils caused by foreign or cosmo-politan elements. Discipline and firm leadership are considered the main prerequisites of success.

The *ethnie* may be identified, alternatively or cumulatively, by common language, common religion, common descent and/or common historical memory. A specific life-style may be the most conspicuous mark of separate identity. The attitude

1

towards other *ethnies* may be graded according to racial and/or cultural criteria.

A few examples may illustrate the point. Cyprus is divided between two communities which differ by language, religion, descent and partly also by historical memory. Ulster's two communities do not differ by language but by descent, religion and historical memory. Bosnia's three communities differ merely by religion and historical memory, and only partly by language, the extent of difference being a bone of contention between them.

In all the above mentioned communities, policies are being pursued which, in terms of our definition, can be described as neo-Fascist. How does this square with the fact that there were prolonged periods during which these communities lived side by side quite peacefully? A similar contrast can be observed with respect to other cases of neo-Fascism throughout Europe. A tentative definition may be followed by a tentative explanation.

There are some sociopsychological dispositions towards intolerance and disrespect towards the people of another, different, community. These dispositions, are more often than not, latent; they come to the surface in exceptional, more or less sporadic, outbursts of enmity. In particular situations, however, these dispositions may give rise to prolonged aggressive behaviour in large segments of the population. It may be assumed that a latent disposition is prompted to militant action by certain contingencies.

The sociopsychological dispositions can be summarised under five headings. The first of them can be described as the homogeneity preference. People tend not to be fond of anomalies. Extremes may meet and variations may be pleasant but there are certain limits to such openness. These limits vary according to the circumstances. Three levels of communication, or thresholds of socially accepted contacts, with aliens may be distinguished: (1) business and employment relations (*commercium*), (2) sociability (*comensalitas*), and (3) nuptiality (*connubium*). It may be assumed that if the last level of socialisation is practised on a large scale, the homogeneity preference is not operative, as far as the particular people are concerned. There may be a wide range of varieties in this respect, but in the present epoch, the ethnolinguistic, ethno-religious and party-ideological differences are most frequently viewed as obstacles to the required homogeneity. Ethnicity is mentioned in this context in order to indicate that both the language and the religious affiliation are 'inherited' rather than acquired. Nevertheless fanaticism on the part of the converted may also play a significant role.

Another sociopsychological disposition to a Fascist-type orientation is the superiority complex which may often be an overcompensation for the opposite – an inferiority complex. The overcompensation may vary with respect to time, geographical region, or social strata within a particular community; a strong, militant, national consciousness may be shared by only a fraction of the population.

The third disposition is the wish to bring all the kin into the common fold. 'One sheepfold and one shepherd' is the appropriate metaphor. It implies not only unity but also a firm authoritarian leadership before which all the 'sheep' might be equal. Security, in its many-faceted aspects of real life, may be considered as the advantage derived from such an arrangement.

A particular case of insecurity that may be singled out as a special sociopsychological disposition towards Fascist or Fascist-like orientation is, as Michalina Vaughan puts it in this volume, 'an instinctive resistance of the "small man" to socioeconomic change'. It is the distaste of the traditionally minded lower middle class towards the encroachments of big business and finance upon their way of earning a living.

Finally, there is a disposition towards admiration of strength and heroism which may develop into the cult of violence. This motivation need not be related to a particular political aim. As we are experiencing now, the phenomenon of gratuitous violence may permeate the whole society. But in such an atmosphere, its politicisation may become easier and may find a widespread positive response.

Homogeneity preference in combination with the desire for 'all the kin into a fold' fosters populist attitudes among the elites: its combination with the superiority complex and with admiration of strength may develop positive attitudes towards enforced solutions. There are three alternative forms of this drive: (1) mandatory assimilation of the minorities, (2) their eviction, (3) their annihilation. The last two alternatives are also known as ethnic cleansing.

As is well known, Italian Fascism preferred linguistic assimilation, in line with how the French and English, at an earlier date, behaved towards their ethnic minorities. German Nazism considered assimilation as a privilege for the racially acceptable minorities; others, racially less good but still worthy of survival, were to be evicted; finally, the racially unacceptable were to be annihilated ('the final solution').

A wider perspective

It is worth stressing that neither enforced assimilation nor eviction is a modern phenomenon. According to the principle *Cuius regio, eius religio* (whose the country, his the religion, i.e. whoever rules the land determines its religion) mandatory assimilation (enforced religious conversion) combined with the eviction of those who refused conversion, became a widespread policy in the Europe of the sixteenth and seventeenth centuries. Burning heretics at the stake, which had started much earlier, was a kind of final solution.

The *Reyes Católicos* and their successors in Spain undertook an extraordinarily thorough cleansing of infidels as an act of piety. Muslims and Jews were expelled even if they had converted to Catholic Christianity; for who could believe the sincerity of a conversion achieved under duress? Later, purity of blood (*limpieza de sangre*) was also required as a safeguard of genuine conformity. Did not the Old Testament, in Ezra 10 : 2–5 and elsewhere, provide a respectable paradigm for such a purification?

Only when religious beliefs were becoming less sincere and ethnic consciousness replaced loyalty towards religious denominations did the policy of assimilation and eviction shift to an ethnolinguistic basis. In 1755, British eviction of the French Acadians from what, after 1714, became New Brunswick and Nova Scotia seems to be the first instance of this type of cleansing. Between 1848 and 1948 the drive toward ethnolinguistic homogeneity gathered momentum. Changing political frontiers to match ethnolinguistic borders and *vice versa* became the leitmotif for many political movements and government policies. The German *Befreiungskriege*, the Italian *Risorgimento*, the Balkan wars and the two world wars, all contributed to the reduction of the number of people living outside their ethnic (one nation) states. At the beginning it was done mainly by changing the borders; later the enforced large-scale transfer of populations played a greater role. During the Second World War about half a dozen small nations were displaced by Stalin, and Germans from beyond the border (*Volksdeutsche*) were settled in areas from which the Slavic population had been evicted. At the end of, and immediately after, the war about twelve million Germans fled or were expelled from the Central European and Baltic countries, and from the territories annexed by Poland and the Soviet Union. Instead of *Cuius regio eius religio,* homogeneity preference now followed the principle that each nation has to have its own state, and that each state has to embrace only one nation. The strong ones, however, felt themselves entitled to grab more land than was inhabited by their kin. Classical Fascism was born in that atmosphere.

The Bolshevik revolution in Russia and the formation of the USSR brought yet another type of homogeneity preference to the forefront. It was the uniformity of political ideology. It was like *Cuius regio eius religio* except that emigration was no longer allowed. 'The Fatherland' became the denotation of the first and, on account of its power, also the core country of a particular social system uniting various *ethnies.* Religion was to be eradicated. The other-worldly eschatology was to be replaced by a planned outcome for history.

In order to make conformity more acceptable, the aspirations of various peoples of the Russian empire for some kind of self-assertion were to be respected as legitimate. The Soviet Communist attempt at resolving the nationality question, however, eventually turned out not to be successful. The basic idea was sound: to transform the Russian empire into a multi-ethnic federation in which each individual nationality (*ethnie*) should have a certain scope for self-determination. Four grades or levels of autonomy were devised. The criteria were, mainly, the size of the population, the level of cultural development and the geographical position. Individual *ethnies* were granted territories, each named according to the respective nationality and styled according to the degree of autonomy, from the broadest to the narrowest, as follows: union republic, autonomous republic, autonomous region, and autonomous area.

During the seventy years of existence of the Soviet Union quite a few significant changes occurred both in the number and level of these geopolitical units. Occasionally, also, a new demarcation was made. In 1990 there were, altogether, fifteen union republics – the constituent members of the Union. Within their borders there were twenty autonomous republics, eight autonomous regions and ten autonomous areas. As there were many territories with ethnically mixed populations, the border was to be drawn rather arbitrarily but, as can be checked by reference to the territorial breakdown of nationality statistics, smaller nationalities were treated more favourably; they were allocated a larger share of the ethnically mixed areas.

In a federal state, officially bound together by an international ideology, (Marxism–Leninism was the philosophy of the state), it was supposed that the national consciousness of individual *ethnies* would be preserved, as a secondary loyalty bond, within the confines of the more comprehensive Soviet patriotism. Yet in a rigid dictatorship there was limited scope for spontaneous fitting into a wider international loyalty. The pressure enforcing ideological uniformity provoked opposition which, however, because of ruthless oppression, remained latent.

In a situation where the largest nation, the Russian, constituted more than half of the total population of the Union, and was the undisputed leader in the whole complex, it was quite natural that Russian ethnolinguistic patriotism should become the dominant element secondary to the all-Union patriotism identified with loyalty to the Soviet socialist system. The two patriotisms became almost indistinguishable. The patriotisms of the non-Russian nations, however, were carefully monitored lest they should upset the official unity imposed by the big brother. The Armenians, whose geographical position and historical experience made their nationalism a comparatively reliable partner for that of the Russians, were perhaps the only nation to be given more generous leeway. The closely knit nature of the Communist Party must be borne in mind. It ruled from the centre in Moscow, without regard to the federal structure of the state.

The right of the Union republics to secede from the USSR, declared in the constitution, was limited by so many prohibitory conditions that any use of this right had to wait until the Communist domination collapsed. As this collapse was preceded, or accompanied, by loss of credibility in the Soviet system and its ideology, something else had to be found to provide a new integrative idea. In Russia itself the old pre-1917 dilemma re-emerged in full vigour: to Westernise, to embrace a pluralistic system with capitalism and parliamentary democracy as its main institutional parameters, or to keep aloof and cultivate the native tradition.

Both alternatives lay in waiting. The Westernising alternative was given the first chance, but its leading agents, from Gorbachev to Yeltsin, were not up to the task of pushing it through. On the one hand, they did not elaborate an appropriate strategy, and on the other, they refrained from using force which, in Russian conditions, was necessary to break through the inertia. At the time of writing, fortune is smiling upon the *narodniki* with their wide spectrum, from the peaceful and idealist, to the militant and often imperialist hue. There are many nuances within the latter alternative that can rightly be classified as neo-Fascist and the reader will get a further glimpse of them in Chapter 12.

A few words are needed here about the situation in the former Soviet Union as a whole. In some areas, such as the Baltic and Caucasus regions, as well as the Ukraine, particularly in its western parts, we witness a return to the ethnolinguistic nationalism of an earlier epoch; in others, such as Central Asia and the Volga region, there is an upsurge of a new nationalism awakened by the secular education of the Soviet era that partly replaced, but also fragmented, the earlier religious loyalty which was common to various Muslim peoples.

Stalin's policy of generous demarcation of the territories assigned to the smaller nations left a great number of other nationals, in particular the Russians, beyond the borders of their own republics, even if they were settled in compact territories alongside the border. This is particularly the case of Kazakhstan, which already at the time of its constitution as a union republic (in 1934) contained more than one-third Russians and Ukrainians in its population. Since then their proportion has considerably increased. Still more generous was the transfer in 1954 of the predominantly Russian-inhabited Crimea from Russian to Ukrainian jurisdiction.

In the Soviet Union dominated by Russia, all this was of no great concern, but as soon as the Union became fragmented into its constituent parts (the union republics) such anomalies began to cause problems. Apart from that, there are many areas where people of different *ethnies* rub shoulders with one another, and as the bond of ideological homogeneity imposed from above disappeared and another one has failed to take its place (neither the Western philosophy of human rights nor any other ideology is in a position to achieve such a takeover) the ground is ripe for another bond of integration; nationalism gets an opportunity to step into the breach.

Supporting Communist policies through an appeal to nationalist feelings became general practice wherever the Communists achieved power. The case of Poland, discussed in Chapter 13 of this volume, provides a conspicuous example. The Yugoslav Communists likewise, under Tito, after the falling out with the Communist leadership of the USSR, had recourse to nationalist feelings. Their nationalism, however, was a composite one; it was based on ethnolinguistic affinity, but it can be surmised that its main unifying force was the menace from abroad. As soon as the danger of interference by the Soviet Union disappeared, there began to surface the weakness of a hybrid politico-economic system, unable to bridge the staggering gap between the rich and poor regions, and then the artificial, composite patriotism dissolved into its constituent parts in which not so much the language, as religion and political history, became the most divisive factors. The Romanian and Bulgarian Communists became fervent nationalists only in the latter stages of their rule, but – by way of compensation – their practices became particularly drastic.

Contingency and the West

My review of the sought-after homogeneity has already revealed some circumstances in which the lack of homogeneity, in combination with the other sociopsychological dispositions, led to the endeavour to overcome it by means which may be described as neo-Fascist.

Now we have to review in more detail the contingencies leading to the activation of these and other latent sociopsychological dispositions. Schematically, these contingencies may be summarised under the following headings:

1. Loss of security: breakdown of law and order.
2. Humiliation: offended pride.
3. Collapse of the established system of beliefs.
4. Relative deprivation, either diachronic (with respect to an earlier period), or synchronic (with respect to other countries abroad).
5. Irritation resulting from contrasting life-styles, possibly based on contrasting codes of behaviour.
6. Disputed border: one side longing for its change, the other concerned with the threat to its preservation.
7. Leadership losing popularity looks for a target towards which people's discontent could be directed.
8. Finally, a sense of frustration may be added as a general characteristic of the prevalent mood.

As is well known, Italian Fascism was born in an atmosphere of frustration and relative deprivation. The aftermath of the war, during which many became much poorer and a few much richer, was marked by widespread social unrest, by the lack of law and order and, within the 'political class', by disappointment with the peace treaties that did not award Italy its allegedly proper share of the spoils of war.

The more virulent Nazism in Germany was nurtured by a series of misfortunes. The humiliation of military defeat, loss of territory and reparation payments, repeated economic disasters – after the hyperinflation of the early 1920s came the big crisis of the 1930s – and, last but not least, the 'toothless' Weimar Republic, unable to preserve law and order, all produced an accumulated sense of dissatisfaction and frustration. On top of that there surfaced the almost ubiquitous and often latent envy directed towards successful minorities with their roots in another race and culture with cosmopolitan leanings. Combined with offended pride and a superiority complex, it fostered the quest for vengeance which eventually gave rise to the policy aimed at annihilating the scapegoat for the nation's failures.

The Spanish *Falange* and the lesser Fascisms throughout Europe were born of a similar mixture of causes. The most frequent contingencies causing the emergence of the Fascist movement were offended pride, relative deprivation in which the current situation was contrasted either with an idealised past or with the experiences of a more fortunate neighbour, and disagreements over state borders which left some conationals outside the flock.

The appearance of Fascist-type movements after the Second World War is due to an extended spectrum of contingencies. Some of these, almost unknown in Europe before the war, began to play a dominant role. While after the First World War Fascism was born of rivalry or hostility between autochthonous peoples, after the Second World War the winding up of colonial empires and the economic boom in Europe opened the gates of several European countries to immigration from other parts of the world. The former colonial powers, in particular the United Kingdom and the Netherlands, felt obliged to offer refuge to their erstwhile colonial subjects, in particular to those who, because of their loyalty to colonial masters, became the objects of discrimination or even persecution by the rulers of the newly independent states. France, with her lesser density of population and lower birth-rate, had already been, long before the First World War, a country which welcomed immigration from poorer countries whose population lent itself easily to assimilation. Although assimilation is still favoured by the French authorities, the increasing influx of immigrants from Algeria and other former colonies affected by rapid population growth and economic stagnation makes this policy increasingly difficult to implement, in particular as the religious self-consciousness of the Muslims has experienced a spectacular revival. Unlike the French, the British and Dutch are ready to accept cultural diversity and have started to consider their societies as multi-cultural. At the grass roots, however, the people's attitude does not always follow this paradigm.

The unprecedented need for an expanded workforce in the 1960s led to the employment of 'guest workers' from other European countries. West Germany became the most conspicuous case. After recovering from the ravages of war, the Federal Republic experienced the boom to such an extent that not only could it absorb twelve million Germans expelled from their former homes in the east, but it could also employ several million guest workers, particularly from Yugoslavia and Turkey. The latter, most of them wanting to stay, constitute a new cultural element in a Germany which is reluctant to award them its citizenship.

As long as they intend to stay, the immigrants do not mind accepting the language of their host countries, but they are also keen to preserve their cultural heritage in which their different ethnic, or rather racial, origin was indissolubly linked with a particular religion. The fact that they do not settle on a compact territory frees the host country from any problems of borders. However, the fact that they are more different from the people of the host countries than any earlier ethnic minority has become a new contingent factor in the arousal of the desire for homogeneity.

Differences in appearance and behaviour are the core of the matter. Economic rivalry is, as a rule, a secondary factor. The immigrants came to fill the gap in the labour supply for menial jobs which the domestic work people ('the natives') were not interested in taking up. The newcomers were mainly of working age and thus contributed more to the social insurance funds than they took out of them. According to a report in the *Rheinischer Merkur* of 20 October 1992, for instance, in 1989 foreigners' contributions made up 7.8 per cent of the revenues of the old-age pensions fund, whilst the same group participated only to the extent of 1.9 per cent in the benefits of the funds.

Yet images are often more to the forefront of people's minds than the facts. When the boom turns to recession, such images may be inflated out of all proportion. Furthermore, the late 1980s and the 1990s brought a new kind of immigrant to Western Europe. They were no longer invited guest workers but desperate refugees from countries affected by extreme poverty and the ravages of war. Decrease in the demand for foreign workers together with the increase in the numbers of asylum seekers began to create a new contingency for outbursts of xenophobic feelings.

Uneasiness became evident even among the Swiss, otherwise outstanding as an example of inter-ethnic coexistence, and accustomed to regulate their labour market by controlling access to a large number of foreigners to work in the country (in the early 1970s one in four among the wage earners and one in six among the resident population was a foreigner). *Überfremdung* (too many foreigners) became the slogan of those whose latent homogeneity preference was now being prompted to action. Yet the two popular initiatives seeking to limit the numbers of foreigners in the country (referendums in 1974 and 1977) ended in rejection by about two-thirds of the Swiss nationals participating in the vote.

In Switzerland, as in other countries with large numbers of immigrants (Belgium and Sweden may be mentioned as particularly favourably disposed towards their guest workers), majority opinion appears to be tolerant towards the new minorities. *Überfremdung*, however, has become a sensitive issue in which the sociopsychological dispositions conducive to neo-Fascist orientations are acquiring new strength.

In Western Europe, the traditional issues which can lead to neo-Fascist attitudes and activities are limited to a few areas. At stake is either long-lasting ethnic rivalry within the country, such as that between the Dutch and French-speakers in Belgium (on the double-track far right in that country, see Chapter 16), or inadequate auton–omy (political status), such as the case of the Basques, divided between Spain and France. The cases of Ulster and Corsica may also be mentioned in this context. Most situations where similar hostilities might arise were more or less satisfactorily resolved by granting to the ethnic minority an appropriate degree of autonomy. Catalonia in Spain and also South Tyrol in Italy may be mentioned as examples. This, however, does not mean that even in these instances some marginal elements could not take action of a neo-Fascist type.

Contingency and the East

The main area where the traditional type of Fascism is finding fertile ground is that part of Europe where the demise of the Communist regime has left a gap for the development of national consciousness. To find a satisfactory form and level for its legitimate expression is the crux of the matter.

The fall of the Communist regime and the end of the Cold War created a new, complex contingency for a possible revival of a Fascist type of orientation and action. Whereas the two Communist regimes that unashamedly pursued neo-Fascist policies, the Romanian and Bulgarian, were toppled and, at least in Bulgaria, the movement towards greater ethnic tolerance seems to be widely shared, by contrast the successor states of the USSR and the former Yugoslavia have evidenced wide currency for nationalism of a Fascist type. Although, up to now, such nationalism is more often than not promoted with the help of the ballot, the preservation of the latter method for solving political conflicts cannot be taken for granted. Hitler, too, came to power as a result of democratic elections.

The case of Yugoslavia is particularly complex. Its backbone was, ethnolinguistically, a common nationality, namely Serbo-Croat. This was, however, torn apart to form three ethnoreligious groups, each of which acquired, in the course of its turbulent history, the flavour of a particular civilisation. From the ninth century onwards, Latin and Greek Christianity fought out their prolonged struggle for territorial demarcation in the region. Not all the people, however, were happy with these two alternatives. Some, particularly those in Bosnia, preferred to turn to the heresy of Bogomilism and, after the Ottoman conquest in the fifteenth century, to Islam. The three hundred year struggle between the Austrian Habsburgs and the Ottoman Empire for dominance in the Danube basin created a closely watched 'military border', a divide which could not but accentuate the cultural differentiation of Croats and Serbs who, under other circumstances, might have developed into a single nation by any definition.

The shift from religious to ethnic loyalties that, from the late eighteenth century, began to change the sociocultural profile of Western Europe, eventually reached all corners of Central Europe and also found an echo in the Balkans. Attempts to unite the Serbs and the Croats of all creeds and to strengthen this union with yet another Roman Catholic Slavic nation, the Slovenes, culminated after the First World War. In 1918 a new constitutional monarchy with the existing Serbian dynasty at the helm, the Kingdom of the Serbs, Croats and Slovenes, was brought into existence. When, however, within eleven years its parliament began to degenerate into a kind of battle field, King Alexander I took over as an absolute monarch supported by the mainly Serb officered army. Changing the name of the country to Yugoslavia (South Slavia), he abolished all the historical names of individual regions, and introduced instead provinces with new boundaries and names based upon those of rivers in the style of post-Revolutionary France. The assassination of the king by Croat nationalists on his visit to France in 1934, and five years later a stillborn attempt to appease the Croats by granting them autonomy within their quite broadly demarcated settlements, were the hallmarks of the precarious existence of the composite nation-state of Yugoslavia.

The Second World War subjected Yugoslavia to a mortal blow; the ultra-Fascist Croat regime, installed with German support and including also the whole of Bosnia and Herzegovina, embarked on a genocidal cleansing of its land aimed at the non-Croat, mainly Serb, population. This was an outright negation of the earlier tendency promoting the idea of a fellowship of all southern Slavs. Surprisingly, after the terrible devastation of the war in which three different groupings fought each other, one including the Germans, Italians and Croat Fascists, another the Serbian nationalists, and the third the Communists of all ethnic groups in the country, the concept of Yugoslavia was still surviving. It was taken up by the Communists who, under Tito's leadership (himself half Croat, half Slovene), after the ruthless suppression of radical nationalists both on the Serbian and Croatian sides, managed to recreate Yugoslavia as a federation of not only the Serbs, Croats and Slovenes, but also of other formerly officially unrecognised *ethnies*, such as Macedonians and Yugoslav Muslims. Bosnia-Herzegovina was resuscitated within its traditional borders and, furthermore, Montenegro's identity was acknowledged. The linguistic and cultural rights of all other *ethnies*, such as Albanians and Hungarians, were respected. The latter two could even enjoy some share in provincial administration, those of Kosovo and Voivodina respectively. But all these beneficial arrangements could be kept in operation only so long as the charismatic dictator was in charge and a foreign military power (the Soviet Union) continued to present a common threat to all Yugoslav *ethnies*.

When Tito fell out with Stalin the Yugoslav regime began to relax. Not only did the economy become gradually more liberal, but also the centralised structure of the Communist Party was replaced by a federal one. After Tito's death a collective leadership took over supreme power. Communist leaders in the individual republics, within the federation, were quick to realise that their position, shattered by economic failures, might be strengthened by turning nationalist. Gradually this tendency began to prevail and the outcome was the dramatic dissolution of the federation. As the borders of individual republics did not always correspond to the borders of the respective *ethnies*, and in many areas the drawing of a just border was not even possible, there was enough ground for claims and counter-claims with respect to the borders of the successor states. The tragic consequences are well known.

From where the wind blows

The danger that the Yugoslav syndrome may spill over to other countries has often been discussed in the media. As there are other disputable borders in the area the danger has to be taken seriously. This is especially the case with the Albanians and Hungarians, who are in command of significantly smaller geographical areas than those in which they are living. The treatment of their minorities in the neighbouring states does not everywhere correspond with internationally accepted principles, the upholding of which would make the status quo more acceptable to these minorities.

Neo-Fascist orientation and practices have ample opportunity to spread in such a situation. Assimilation of, and discrimination against, ethnic minorities on the one hand, and the call for change of the ethnically unfair border on the other, are the main stimuli for neo-Fascist orientation to take action. Both these policies are most vigorously and also ruthlessly pursued by the Serbian side in the present conflict.

Enforced evictions of minorities are an echo of policies pursued in the Second World War and in its aftermath, but which in the Balkans have quite a few precedents in earlier wars of this century. Also the heightened sensitivity (or even nervosity) with respect to possible (or merely imagined) irredentist policies emerging as a response to close constraint of ethnolinguistic minorities, continues to be a particular 'Fascistogenic' feature peculiar to the European South-east. Greece's reaction to the mere name and symbols of the Yugoslav successor state – Macedonia – a reaction shared by wide strata of the population, is a case in point.

All this concerns issues in which militant nationalisms, or their accentuated forms – neo-Fascisms – confront each other. If there is any distinguishing mark between these two labels, it is the amount of violence and the extent of coercion which individual parties or factions are ready to use in order to promote their aims. Coercion presupposes authoritarian leadership, possibly that of a dictator, and a propensity to violence often leads to terrorism. Economic causes may play an important role as irritants which make the situation more tense, or as accelerators which precipitate political crisis. Economic conditions may also differentiate the level of involvement of various social groups in the process. But the fronts are drawn mainly in accordance with the intensity of nationalist feelings and with what may be called the authoritarian–populist disposition. There are types of people who prefer soldiering under firm leadership, which makes them feel that they, too, are strong and firm.

Confrontation between such 'armies' is certainly a serious threat to peace. However, is it possible that these 'armies' could make common cause? The potential for such a development does indeed exist. The far-right groupings of various West European nations already cultivate friendly and mutually supportive contacts. As the radical nationalists of this kind are racially, rather than ethnolinguistically orientated, they sometimes pose as determined defenders of the purity of European culture, a culture the very spirit of which they fail to understand. Perhaps for this reason they remain a marginal phenomenon, although they can be a source of considerable disturbance.

More weighty are the mass movements and political parties whose neo-Fascist orientation is disguised by a respectable veneer of participation in the democratic process, such as the *Alleanza Nazionale* (the *Movimento Sociale Italiano* being its core member). In early 1994 they reappeared, as a result of free elections, in Italy's governmental coalition. They claim that they are not Fascists any longer, but even if the possibility of such a mutation cannot be excluded, some noises on their part already bear witness to the contrary. A call for restoration of the pre-war borders, which were anything but just in an ethnic sense (the majority population in the areas claimed being either Croat or Slovene), and the pretext that the state with which the existing border was negotiated does not exist any longer are unmistakable marks of a Fascist orientation.

The main prop to neo-Fascism, however, has emerged in Russia. It happened under

11

the deviously cryptic name of the 'Liberal Democratic Party'. Its leader may be 'a caricature of a patriot' as Solzhenitsyn put it, but the electoral success of this party is alarming. Of grave concern also are Zhirinovsky's tentacles reaching over the borders to similarly oriented people and movements abroad.

It may be worthwhile to recollect that something similar has been seen before. Sixty years ago, an attempt was made to bring all Fascist parties together in order to find out how far they could cooperate. In 1934 they met at the international Fascist congress in Montreux. In those days no faction was ashamed to call itself Fascist; there was a whiff of novelty in this name, connected with a dream of a new type of society which would be created by a new generation imbued with virile virtues. However, eventually not much came out of the prospect of *Fascismo universale*. It was *Realpolitik* that eventually brought about the German–Italian Axis, with a few adjoint satellites in the neighbourhood.

Is the present time ripe for a similar attempt? In contrast with the 1930s, there is now no longer the bogey of Communism which helped pre-war Fascism to spread; furthermore, the neighbouring nations, where the germs of neo-Fascism are likely to flourish, are mutually hostile rather than friendly; thus there seems to be little scope for a neo-Fascist International. At worst, there might emerge a kind of axis, though one not geographically continuous. To determine the outcome, developments in Russia are crucial. If the pragmatists there win the day, there will be no axis, if they lose, we may see a bizarre development. Let us hope that this is merely a bad dream.

Chapter 2

THE DARK SIDE OF NATIONALISM: THE REVIVAL OF NATIONALISM IN LATE TWENTIETH CENTURY EUROPE
Anthony D. Smith

The revival of ethnic nationalism in late twentieth century Europe, though not unexpected, has occasioned considerable sadness and revulsion. Somehow, it had been thought that nationalism, though still a potent force elsewhere, had run its course in Europe and that only pale reminders of its former power would trouble the peripheries of the continent. Not only has its revival – some would say, survival – brought bitter ethnic conflicts in its train in Ireland, the Basque country, the former Yugoslavia and elsewhere; it has also forced us to reconsider all those evolutionary theories of the supersession of nations and the ascent of humanity to more inclusive and higher-order political associations, so dear to progressive politicians and intellectuals.

What has been particularly disturbing about this latest wave of nationalist movements is its apparent tendency to bring in its train more dangerous and sinister tendencies such as violent xenophobia, neo-Fascism, racism and anti-Semitism. These phenomena had never disappeared, even from the most civilised and democratic European states; but episodes like Poujadism, the Notting Hill race riots, historical revisionism and Holocaust denial seemed to be isolated, lacking coherence and the power of self-renewal.

The appeal of ethnic nationalism

The danger today is that a certain kind of nationalism has given these multifarious, and often competing, tendencies and movements an aura of legitimacy and a staying power that springs from its own more abiding appeal.

This appeal is multi-faceted. Nationalism, which may be defined as an ideological movement for attaining and maintaining identity, unity and autonomy for a human population, some of whose members deem it to constitute an actual or potential 'nation', offers a vision of the world, a symbolism and language for grasping it, and a set of ideals and aspirations for frustrated and ambitious individuals and groups. The vision is one of a plurality of nations, each with its own character and destiny, each aspiring to freedom and security, each demanding and receiving loyalty and solidarity from its members, in a world of commensurable but unique nations. The symbolism and language offer concepts and means for understanding the world through self-discovery and self-expression and authentic experience, and through ideals and aspirations of autonomy and individual freedom, a self-realisation achieved by unity and belonging and self-sacrifice for the nation.[1]

But how shall we understand the concept of the 'nation'? Here we must distinguish at least two quite different visions, the one civic and territorial, the other ethnic and genealogical. In the first conception, the nation is regarded as primarily a territorial community, whose members are citizens subject to common laws and institutions and united by a mass, public culture which also acts as a 'civil religion'. This was clearly the conception of the French *patriots*, at least in the initial stages of the Revolution, and more generally it has predominated in much of Western Europe to this day. A second, quite different vision of the nation, however, gained a powerful following in Central and Eastern Europe from the early nineteenth century onwards. Here the nation is viewed as a community of descent, whose members are related by fictive kinship ties to a putative ancestor through a potent myth of origins, nativistic history, a vernacular, folk culture and a populistic political ethos. This is not to say that, for example, territory – the 'homeland' – fails to figure prominently, or that members are not citizens, in the second, ethnic conception of the nation, but these components of the first conception are firmly subordinated to other ethnic elements. Conversely, we can find the elevation of native history and the vernacular in the civic conception, but these are again subordinated to its basic civic and territorial component.[2]

These two different, if overlapping, visions of the nation continue to shape the social and political direction of many European states to this day. Together, they fill up the 'nationalist conceptual space' in a manner that leaves little or no room for other, looser conceptions or discourses of the nation. The idea that nations may be 'plural' rather than culturally homogenous, that an overarching public sphere of unified culture and polity may encourage a multiplicity of minority, but institutionalised ethnic cultures, has made little headway in Europe. Despite attempts to institute multi-cultural education, this markedly contrasts with the immigrant societies of North America, Argentina and Australia. The fundamental European conceptions of the nation, which grew out of historic ethnic and social experiences, seem to preclude the possibility of moving to other, more culturally tolerant and politically experimental visions.[3]

It is the ethnic vision that has for some time underpinned a majority of Europe's nationalisms and it continues to do so, especially in Eastern Europe. The appeals of these specifically ethnic nationalisms lie in their ability to translate a much older and widespread type of community, what the French call *ethnie*, into modern terms, in such a way that they unite and mobilise popular aspirations, making them consonant with the needs of modern territorial statehood. Ethnic nationalisms make the nation the mould and measure of the state, and view nations in turn as the modern political forms of pre-modern *ethnies*. In this way, they appear to provide a transition to modern forms of community and polity. Herein lies their powerful, widespread and, many would say, insidious appeal.

Ethnies and exclusiveness

Why is it customary to denigrate ethnicity and attribute to ethnic nationalisms many of the world's contemporary evils? Several scholars, such as Hans Kohn, Elie Kedourie and Eric Hobsbawm, have drawn a sharp dividing line between the two kinds of nationalism, claiming that ethno-linguistic types of nationalism have had a pernicious and destabilising effect in the modern world. Hobsbawm, in particular, has poured scorn on the divisive ethnic and linguistic nationalisms which flourished in Europe between 1870 and 1914 and which have surfaced again in recent years, as the peculiar locus of the 'lower examination passing classes'. He goes on to claim that modern global developments – the international division of labour, transnational companies, great power blocs, mass communications and the like – have passed them by and made them irrelevant, if not yet obsolete.[4]

Such views grossly misunderstand the nature of ethnic ties, and the continuing power of ethnic nationalisms in the modern world. They also present a one-dimensional understanding of their consequences, which can only add to the dangers they may pose.

How shall we understand the nature of ethnicity? If ethnicity signifies the quality of adhering to an *ethnie*, then this term refers to a specific type of community, shaped by its historical culture. We may define an *ethnie* as a 'named human population with myths of common ancestry, shared memories and culture, an association with a homeland and a measure of (at least, elite) solidarity'. *Ethnies* may be, and often are, related to given nations, but the two concepts should not be confused, despite a measure of overlap. A 'nation' may, on one level, be understood as a particular historical development in the direction of a mass political, legal and territorial transformation of the *ethnie*, and can therefore be defined as a 'named human population sharing common myths and memories, a mass, public culture, an historic territory, a common economy and common legal rights and duties for all members'.[5]

Ethnic ties have been common throughout history in all continents, as have sentiments of ethnocentrism. They have been, like any social or cultural phenomenon, subject to fluctuations and changes, to schism and union, formation and dissolution. On one level, we may view these ties and sentiments as a recurrent form of community among human beings, on another as a collective cultural resource, on yet another as a source of political power and military action. *Ethnies* and ethnocentrism have formed part of the mosaic of social, cultural and political formations in Europe since Roman times, if not earlier, and some medieval historians claim that they constituted one of the bases for early medieval kingdoms and states.[6]

Ethnies continue to play a vital role in contemporary European culture, society and politics. This has been amply demonstrated by Jaroslav Krejči, who focuses on the linguistic aspect which has played so prominent a role in Europe. Of course, ethnicity is only one of several forms of association and sources of power; in Europe, it has been challenged, sometimes moulded, by other forces, notably the modern state and collectivist ideologies. Its resurgence today, however, reminds us of the recurrent role it has played in successive epochs, including the ways in which ethnic bonds and sentiments have furnished the bases for repeated waves of nationalist movements and national separatisms.[7] Yet closer inspection reveals that many of today's leading civic nations were built up initially around what we may term 'ethnic cores' – France, the Netherlands, Sweden, Spain and Britain among them. Even the United States, site of the great experiment in constructing a 'plural nation', was founded by settlers carrying with them a specific set of memories, traditions, myths and symbols of chosenness and providential destiny, yet able to assimilate waves of ethnically different immigrants.

These examples reveal that the power of ethnicity is not directed to any one set of ends, but can be used to shape a variety of ends. It is not even true that *ethnies* are inherently exclusive. Catalonia furnishes a good example of an ethnic culture that is assimilatory and inclusive, and its ethno-linguistic nationalism has, on the whole, been open and peaceful, even under oppressive circumstances; and the same could be said for Czech nationalism.[8]

At the same time, we cannot deny the many examples of exclusive ethnic nationalism; and the question is why, given the ambivalent neutrality of ethnicity and *ethnies* in this regard, so many ethnic nationalisms should turn exclusive and even violent.

Towards the purification of culture

The nationalist answer to this question is clear enough: state oppression and exploitation generate protest and necessitate struggle and counter-violence. However, not all oppression has been met by violent struggle – as not only the Czech and Catalan, but also the Norwegian and, to a lesser extent, the Finnish cases make clear.

Another suggestion is that an open, democratic and peaceful movement is typical of *ethnies* with advanced economies relative to the state's core; that it is the resentment of relative deprivation that breeds violent ethnic nationalism. Yet here, both Spain and the former Yugoslavia provide counter-examples: the economies of Catalonia and the Basque lands, Slovenia and Croatia, were 'overdeveloped' relative to the respective state's core, Castile and Serbia, yet while the Catalan and Slovene movements remained relatively open and generally peaceful, the Basque and Croat nationalisms became exclusive and ultimately turned to violence.[9]

Perhaps, then, we should look to the patterns of ethnic migration for an explanation of these exclusive tendencies, as so many contemporary commentators assume? But here too Catalonia offers a counter-example: it took in many immigrants, mainly from the south, and assimilated them into the Catalan community through the agency of the Catalan language.

Linguistic assimilation may provide us with a clue to our problem. What was it that was common to the Catalans and the Czechs, as well as to the Norwegians and, to a lesser extent, the Finns? Broadly speaking, we may say that these were linguistic nationalisms; though ethnic history, of course, has also played a key fertilising and deepening role, as it has done for all ethnic nationalisms – perhaps all nationalisms. Nevertheless, in these and other cases, language has been the supreme cultural resource, uniting and mobilising the community at all levels. What we have been witnessing is a movement of 'vernacular mobilisation', of mass mobilisation into the vernacular culture through the agency and expressive function of an indigenous but modernised language. Or, in the terms proposed by Gellner, a transition from an oral 'wild' or 'low' culture to a literate 'garden' or 'high' culture.[10]

There are two aspects to the connection between linguistic nationalism and exclusiveness. The first is the assimilatory or exclusive power of language itself, something that has to do both with its intrinsic nature and difficulty, and with the attitudes of those who use it as a political resource. The second is the degree to which language is the key or only cultural resource. Broadly speaking, where language is the main resource and has the power to assimilate newcomers, the course of linguistic nationalisms is likely to be relatively smooth. However, where language is rivalled by other cultural resources (religion, customs, territory, 'race'), different factions are likely to arise within the nationalist movement, as occurred in Germany, with new and more radical versions of the designated community – the nation-to-be. Successive factions may seize on alternative cultural resources and offer radical redefinitions of the *ethnie* as the basis for its status as a nation.[11]

We can now trace the main stages by which ethnic nationalisms with multiple cultural bases or resources can become exclusive and violent. First there is the stage we have mentioned, of vernacular mobilisation, which is common to all ethnic nationalisms. In order to mobilise the mass of the designated population, culture must be treated as a political resource, it must serve political ends and underwrite and explain social usages. The 'politicisation of culture' can also be found among the more peaceful linguistic nationalisms, but here it is not controversial; there is only one main resource which serves to unite and define the designated population.

However, where there is more than one such resource, and conflict ensues between rival nationalist interpretations (and parties), then the politicisation of culture entails the elevation of one or other cultural base or resource as the standard of that culture, the definer of the authentic ethnic experience and culture. Nationalists outbid each other to lay down more stringent tests of what shall count as the 'genuine' article of culture and the 'true' embodiment of that culture. In such circumstances, we begin to witness that familiar phenomenon of ethnic nationalism, the 'purification of culture'.

This third stage, the purification of culture is, however, also that of the exclusion of outsiders. The cosmopolitan corruption of authentic culture is, *ipso facto*, the defiling intrusion of alien communities and individuals. The process may commence with the purification of language, but where there are rival definitions of the nation, it usually ends with the purification of the community.

Nationalism and neo-Fascism

Of course, it cannot be claimed that exclusive tendencies in so many ethnic nationalisms are simply the function of multiple cultural resources and conflicting definitions of the nation. To such cultural sources of exclusiveness, we must add several geopolitical factors: the frequent lack of congruence between *ethnies* and state borders, the temptations of ethnic irredentism in adjacent states, the political uses of ethnic rivalries for competing states in a regional system, and the superimposition of other belief systems, religious or secular, on different versions of ethnic nationalisms.

Nevertheless, the logic of cultural redefinitions, crucial to the vernacular mobilisation of popular ethnic cultures, goes a long way to explaining the exclusive and xenophobic tendencies of many ethnic nationalisms. Very few of these nationalisms have escaped such tendencies, which can sometimes be found even within the more civic varieties of nationalism.

However, should such exclusive and violent tendencies be equated with the revival of Fascism? By 'Fascism' I understand a militaristic movement of obedience to the state and worship of the Leader, carried by a cult of violence for its own sake and an ethic of brutality. (To this Nazism added other racial and rabidly anti-Semitic dimensions, along with a belief in agrarian colonisation in lands seized by force whose inhabitants were to be enslaved or exterminated.) There have indeed been cases in the past where a divided ethnic nationalism took extreme forms and in part embraced a Fascist philosophy, as with Codreanu's Legion of the Archangel Michael in Romania. The question is whether any of the latterday ethnic nationalisms approximate to the Fascist philosophy.[12]

The closest approximations can be found in France and Germany, where the language of ethnic nationalisms masks a more strident redefinition of the nation in terms of racial criteria, using the strong feelings of some strata against immigrants of very different religions and cultures as a vehicle of ethnic exclusion. There are undoubtedly other movements – in Hungary, Poland, Russia and elsewhere – where older anti-Semitic prejudices and motifs are combined with authoritarian ethnic exclusiveness. Most of these groupings are small, but they represent a clear sign of the dangerous, dark side of ethnic nationalism.

We should be careful not to equate such nationalisms with neo-Fascist movements. This is neither analytically nor politically helpful. Ethnic nationalisms have different roots and outlooks from those of Fascism. Indeed, historically, Fascisms have often emerged in the wake of ethnic or civic nationalisms failing to attain their stated goals. At the same time, the ambivalence and exclusiveness of those ethnic nationalisms with their rival cultural resources and unsatisfied geo-political goals may lend themselves to an uneasy alliance with, or even cooptation by, the more sombre forces of neo-Fascism and neo-Nazism.

Without the popular power and tenacity of ethnic nationalism, in turn, the various neo-Fascist and neo-Nazi movements would be less threatening to liberal and democratic states. The enormous appeal of a politics of identity, which ethnic nationalisms appear to satisfy as well as generate, has tended to outflank the older politics of class and ideology. This provides fertile ground for radical collective self-definitions which fortify those within even as they exclude those outside the ethnic ramparts. On this view, identity and exclusion feed on each other, even as (perhaps because) social and economic pressures move us towards a more plural type of society and state.

Given the continuing resilience of ethnic nationalisms in Europe and outside, and the internal logic of such nationalisms no less than their geo-political consequences, we can expect a troubled first century of the new millennium in which the dark side of nationalism shadows the promise and fulfilment of its ideals.

Notes

1. W. Connor, 'A nation is a nation, is a state, is an ethnic group, is a . . .', *Ethnic and Racial Studies*, No. I (4), 1978, pp. 377–400; A. D. Smith, *Theories of Nationalism*, Duckworth, London, 1983 (1st edn 1971).

2. H. Kohn, *Prelude to Nation-States: the French and German Experience, 1789–1815*, Van Nostrand, Princeton, 1967; A. D. Smith, *The Ethnic Origins of Nations*, Blackwell, Oxford, 1986, ch.6.

3. But see R. Samuel (ed.), *Patriotism: The Making and Unmaking of British National Identity*, Routledge, London, 1989; H. Bhabha (ed.), *Nation and Narration*, Routledge, London, 1990, ch.16.

4. E. Hobsbawn, *Nations and Nationalism since 1780*, Cambridge University Press, Cambridge, 1990, chs. 4 and 6; see also E. Kedourie, *Nationalism*, Hutchinson, London, 1960.

5. Smith, *The Ethnic Origins*, cit., ch.2; idem, *National Identity*, Penguin, Harmondsworth, 1991, ch.1.

6. J. Armstrong, *Nations before Nationalism*, University of North Carolina Press, Chapel Hill, 1982; S. Reynolds, *Kingdoms and Communities in Western Europe, 900–1300*, Clarendon, Oxford, 1984, ch.8.

7. J. Krejči, 'Ethnic Problems in Europe', in S. Giner and M. S. Archer (eds), *Contemporary Europe, Social Structures and Cultural Patterns*, Routledge and Kegan Paul, London, 1978, pp. 124–71; A. W. Orridge, 'Separatist and Autonomist Nationalisms: The Structure of Regional Loyalties in the Modern State', in C. H. Williams (ed.), *National Separatism*, University of Wales Press, Cardiff, 1982, pp. 43–74.

8. P. Sugar and I. Lederer (eds), *Nationalism in Eastern Europe*, University of Washington Press, Seattle, 1969; S. Payne, 'Catalan and Basque Nationalism', *Journal of Contemporary History*, No. 6, 1971, pp.15–51.

9. M. Hechter and M. Levi, 'The Comparative Analysis of Ethno-Regional Movements', *Ethnic and Racial Studies*, II (3), 1979, pp. 260–74.

10. E. Gellner, *Nations and Nationalism*, Blackwell, Oxford, 1983, ch.3; see also B. Anderson, *Imagined Communities: Reflections on the Origins and Spread of Nationalism*, Verso, London, 1983.

11. G. Mosse, *The Crisis of German Ideology,* Grosset and Dunlap, New York, 1964; D. Conversi, 'Language or Race? The Choice of Core Values in the Development of Basque and Catalan Nationalism', *Ethnic and Racial Studies*, XIII (1) 1990, pp. 50–70.

12. E. Weber, 'The Men of the Archangel', *Journal of Contemporary History*, I, 1966, pp. 101–26; A. D. Smith *Nationalism in the Twentieth Century*, Martin Robertson, Oxford, 1979, ch.3.

Chapter 3

THE ITALIAN FAR RIGHT: THE SEARCH FOR LEGITIMACY
Roberto Chiarini

Post-Fascism and the right

There is every reason to believe that the 1990s will offer the Italian right a historic opportunity to break free from its fifty-year history of insignificance and political exclusion. In the Italian context, 'right wing' has always meant the undemocratic right – a movement not only without an electoral base and any organisational potential, but one which, above all, lacks legitimacy. That is why no party, apart from the neo-Fascists, has ever been keen on calling itself right-wing for fear of this delegitimation. The result of this has been that Italy is the only Western democracy since 1945 not to have had an openly right-wing party, apart, that is, from the Italian Social Movement [*Movimento Sociale Italiano*, MSI]. And it is no coincidence that this party has never come anywhere near the electoral success enjoyed by right-wing parties in the other Western democracies. The MSI's electoral strength settled down at around 4 to 5 per cent, ranging from a minimum of 1.9 per cent in the first general election in 1948 to a high point of 8.7 per cent in 1972 at the climax of its 'law and order' offensive against the student protests of 1968 and the trade union protests of 1969. Even in the 1950s, when there were two monarchist right-wing parties (Alfredo Covelli's National Monarchist Party [*Partito Nazionale Monarchico*, PNM] and Achille Lauro's Popular Monarchist Party [*Partito Popolare Monarchico*, PPM]), their results were much the same. The right remained undemocratic and never broke through the modest ceiling of 12 to 13 per cent.[1]

Why the MSI survives but is marginalised

Both the persistence of the neo-Fascist phenomenon and its limited importance need to be explained. The reasons are to be sought in both national and international factors linked to the post-war political settlement.

A first, general, point is that the allied victory against Nazism and Fascism was, above all, an ideological one. While it brought into being a new set of international power relationships, the war also bankrupted Nazism and Fascism as viable ideologies. The

Table 3.1 Votes obtained by the MSI in the elections for the Chamber of Deputies, 1948–92. The 1989 figures refer to the European Parliament elections.

Year	Votes	%	Year	Votes	%
1948	526,670	1.9	1976	2,238,339	6.1
1953	1,582,567	5.9	1979	1,930,639	5.3
1958	1,407,550	4.8	1983	2,511,487	6.8
1963	1,570,232	5.1	1987	2,282,212	5.9
1968	1,414,036	4.5	1989	1,915,596	5.5
1972	2,894,722	8.7	1992	2,103,692	5.4

two great powers, the USA and the USSR, in spite of the Cold War, were united in their determination not to allow any renewal of the far right in Europe. At most, in the short term, they could be occasionally accommodating (e.g. with the Colonels in Greece), but in the long term they stuck to a hard line. What happened to right-wing regimes already in power was, in this context, symptomatic. The Salazar dictatorship in Portugal and the Franco regime in Spain failed to survive the death of their founders, despite their apparently deep roots.

All this meant that the extreme right's strongholds were wiped out and suggested that right-wing radicalism had no future. The unconditional surrender of Hitler's Germany and of the Italian Social Republic [*Republica Sociale Italiana*, RSI] – the puppet regime set up by Mussolini in Northern Italy after he had been deposed by the Monarchy in 1943 – is what undermined the future of the extreme right. The deaths of the *Führer* and the *Duce* also had a symbolic impact. Military defeat made the association of right-wing extremism with blood, death and destruction inevitable. The myths held dear by the right (nationalism, colonialism and racism) as well as its political and ideological heritage (elitism, authoritarianism, corporatism and anti-parliamentarianism), were totally discredited. The extraordinary appeal of the right between the wars seemed impossible to recapture.[2] The extreme right could only stand by, powerless, as moderates were drawn irresistibly towards the centre. The unification of the middle classes, carried out by the totalitarian regimes of the right, survived but was no longer available to form the right's social backbone.

The prospect of an irreversible decline in capitalist society and the liberal state, which loomed on the horizon of the immediate post-war period, was soon dispelled, and economic growth became the foundation on which a consumer society was built and on which political democracy was consolidated. The parties of the far right, which had staked everything on the hope of crisis and conflict, were thus drained of their sustenance. This went to the parties of the centre or of the moderate left which aimed at maintaining the favourable economic trend by shrewdly managing political and social conflict.

There were two further factors which handicapped any grouping associated with the totalitarian/authoritarian tendencies of the right. First of all, in reaction to the repression exercised by Fascism against political parties and trade unions, there was now a deeply-felt appreciation of the rights and freedoms guaranteed by the State to both individuals and associations. As Juan Linz has observed, 'everybody understood that an authoritarian government not only meant the removal of rights from left-wing politicians, trade unions and peasant protest movements; it also meant they were taken away from large sections of the middle classes and even from the upper classes'.[3] Democratic governments and organisations derived strong legitimation from this public realisation. Secondly, the credibility of right-wing radicalism was undermined in the post-war period by the absence of any authoritarian model. There was no country able to provide an example like Fascist Italy in the 1920s and Nazi Germany in the 1930s. Franco's Spain, Salazar's Portugal and even the Greece of the Colonels were museum specimens rather than credible models of an endangered species. If moderate Western public opinion tolerated them it was because they seemed the most suitable type of regime for smoothing the way of these late-joiner countries towards democracy. Even regimes with greater ideological pretensions, like Pinochet's Chile, could not be viewed as permanent solutions to a country's problems, but only as a stop-gap bulwark against communism.

In Italy's case there were additional factors which discouraged a revival of neo-Fascism. To begin with, whereas Mussolini's regime could count on having a monopoly of all the political resources of a totalitarian state (from press, radio and education, right down to leisure organisations), neo-Fascism had to learn to compete, on equal terms, for the electorate's support.

Secondly, the right discovered that it lacked a social base. While it had never enjoyed a natural relationship with any class or social group, it had, now, even lost the capacity to represent the middle classes which had supported Mussolini. This unifying and protective function was taken over by political Catholicism. The Catholic lay organisation *Azione Cattolica* had been the only non-Fascist organisation able to operate legally in Mussolini's Italy, so that, after the war, the newly formed Christian-Democrat Party [*Democrazia Cristiana*, DC] was able to take advantage of the vast network of branches that had been set up over the years. Ultimately, political Catholicism had two great advantages. The Church–State rift which, since Italian unification (1860–70), had excluded Catholics from political life had been healed. In addition, the Church benefited from being perceived as the only true representative of institutional continuity in the country. This was especially the case since the monarchy had been largely discredited (after the king fled Rome in the wake of the Armistice signed with the Allies on 8 September 1943) and the country had suffered a constitutional crisis, one that was not resolved fully even when the referendum of 2 June 1946 established the Republic.[4]

What contributed most to curtailing the extreme right's capacity to make an impact – while, paradoxically, helping to strengthen its Fascist identity – were the discriminatory measures taken against it by the Italian State. The Republic came into being as a system explicitly hostile to, and hence incompatible with, any survival of Fascism. The Constitution left no political space for any successor to Mussolini's National Fascist Party [*Partito Nazionale Fascista*, PNF]. The democratic parties formed the so-called *arco costituzionale* (constitutional spectrum), which was intended as an alliance guaranteeing the anti-Fascist nature of the State. The corollary was that the shadow of suspicion also fell over the political area adjacent to neo-Fascism so that the rigid equation 'right = Fascist' was born and, with it, two implications. As far as the party system was concerned, it meant that no conservative party could win office. It also led, inevitably, to right-wing groupings identifying themselves more strongly with Fascism. Pride in being different brought them to look upon the Fascist experience as the fundamental ingredient of what it meant to be right-wing. At the same time, it supplied the moral strength to withstand the onslaught of anti-Fascist measures in the immediate post-war period, and to resist the temptation, when these ceased, to become integrated within the democratic system.

However, while this constant backward glance towards Fascism undoubtedly benefited the Italian extreme right after the war, it also cost it dear. The nostalgia for the rural and provincial Italy of the 1920s and 1930s prevented it from noticing how the country was being transformed by the 'economic miracle' of the 1950s and 1960s. While it talked of 'moral' and 'spiritual' values, the country at large was adopting the materialistic language of the consumer society. While neo-Fascism proclaimed the failure of the free-enterprise economy (and the need to overcome individual and sectional interests for the sake of the national interest) and of tolerant democracy (in the name of a hierarchical system), mass, democratic society was thriving all around it. The right's inability to understand, at the deepest level, the social and economic mainsprings of Western capitalist society led to its exclusion, to all intents and purposes, from the most influential collective experiences in contemporary society, such as trade unions, the education system, the mass media and culture.

But these considerations bring us back to our original query: how is it that the right's cultural and political exclusion did not lead to its withering away or even to its complete disappearance from the political scene? Undoubtedly, it had deep roots, but a further factor needs to be taken into account, that is, the Italian electoral system. The Italian system of outright proportional representation which came into effect in 1946, and which has not been modified since, has encouraged a proliferation of parties – even allowing those like the MSI, with fairly low-level electoral support, to survive.

The beginnings of neo-Fascism in Italy

The most difficult years for the extreme right were, obviously, those immediately after the war. It was ostracised not only morally and politically, but legally too. Those young people caught carrying arms at the fall of the Salò Republic ended up in internment camps. The most important Fascist officials were arrested, or took refuge abroad, or lay low in Italy (thanks, in some cases, to a blind eye being turned by the authorities). People suspected of having belonged to the defunct PNF were handed over to the *tribunale dell'epurazione* (de-fascistisation tribunal), set up to try those who abetted Fascism in a major way.

Therefore the problem for ex-Fascists, in the short term, was not how to make a political mark again, but how to survive. There were numerous abortive attempts by the right to bring together its depleted forces,[5] but there were clearly only two ways forward and each had serious drawbacks. It could either set up a full-blown neo-Fascist organisation which would fall foul of the law or, more prudently, it could adopt a convenient cover within a legitimate political party and wait for better days. This was the situation which obtained until 28 June 1946 when a political amnesty was granted, as a symbol of reconciliation, upon the proclamation of the Republic. Both options were explored. Some underground groups were formed, the most important being the Revolutionary Action Fasces [*Fasci di Azione Rivoluzionaria*, FAR], which was openly faithful to Fascism. The main strategy, though, was to operate in a more limited fashion, under the umbrella of the *Uomo Qualunque* (UQ) party.

The *Uomo Qualunque*, literally 'man in the street', was an organisation founded by an oddball character, Guglielmo Giannini, a political outsider with an extraordinary flair for understanding and expressing the average Italian's frustration with the State. The UQ's main targets were the parties, held up as perverse power structures whose only purpose was to perpetuate the rule of the politicians over the people. The party's initial popularity derived from that of its eponymous newspaper, cleverly used by Giannini to attack, in trenchant and often vulgar language, the credibility of the new, post-Fascist Italy. After the Liberation, UQ decided to face the voters, and changed from a movement to a party. In the elections for the Constituent Assembly in June 1946, it obtained 5.3 per cent of the vote. Four months later, in the local elections, it improved its position significantly. It performed sensationally in the main cities of Southern Italy, achieving 20.7 per cent in Rome, 19.7 per cent in Naples, 46 per cent in Bari (in alliance with the Monarchists and the conservatives of the Italian Liberal Party [*Partito Liberale Italiano*, PLI]), 34.6 per cent in Foggia, 47 per cent in Lecce, 34.6 per cent in Catania (with the Liberals) and 24.5 per cent in Palermo.[6]

Two main features have characterised the Italian extreme right since these earliest elections: a mostly Southern base and a predominantly clientelistic nature. The deep-rooted presence of a Catholic sub-culture in the North-East, and of a left-wing one in the Centre, together with the country's ready adoption of democratic values brought about, first of all, by the resistance to Nazism and Fascism and, second, by the activities of the major parties, jeopardised the chances of the right in these parts of Italy. The right-wing vote cannot therefore be treated as a reaction to a strong swing to the left. The areas where Socialists and Communists were strongest (notably in Emilia-Romagna) did not correspond to those where the extreme right achieved its best results. Similarly, in the industrial, mostly working-class areas of the North, modern social conflicts did not spark off a bourgeois mobilisation of an anti-democratic nature. It was, on the contrary, from the very heart of the South that the extreme right drew its votes. Here, limited industrialisation kept political relations dependent mostly on basic social ties – the family and the 'clan'.[7] This society was reluctant to be represented by parties such as the Communists and Socialists, which derived (and still derive) their support directly from the work-place or, indirectly, through class-based loyalties. At the same time, it could identify only in part with the DC which did not have, here, the sort of network of associations which the Catholic movement established in the North. It was the extreme right which took advantage of the clientelistic character of political relations that prevailed in the South. Its continuous polemic against *partitocrazia*, the domination of political parties in national life, made it especially appealing to local notables envious of the competition of the big parties. In other words, the future of the extreme right was tied to the aspirations of a largely pre-modern society. In the long run, however, its electoral base was likely to decrease, with the advance of capitalism and consumerism – these being factors which depersonalise human relations and so undermine the clientelistic structure of political relations. Its chance of reversing the downward slide was not subject to its willingness to play the rules of modern mass democracy and represent a specific class; it depended on its ability to exploit the sporadic discontent of the classes most exposed to the effects of the unbalanced modernisation which had taken place in southern Italy since the 1950s. This modernisation led to the traumatic overthrow of the old rural world, the loss of the young through emigration, chaotic urbanisation (e.g. in Naples, Palermo, Catania), the growth of an 'underground economy' and of jobs of a precarious and marginal nature, and to the huge and unjustified rise of a commercial and white-collar middle class which relied on the protection and favours handed out by the political powers that be. Simplifying a little, it could be said that, in the early 1950s, the MSI's mostly southern electoral base appealed to the economically as well as culturally deprived classes and to factory workers, tended to represent the urban middle classes employed in tertiary activities in the 1960s,[8] and was closely associated with the phenomena of urbanisation and underdevelopment, and in particular with those seeking employment for the first time, in the 1970s.[9]

The birth of the MSI

The Southern base and the clientelistic nature of the UQ vote, in essence, are the structural features that the neo-Fascists inherited when they decided to start an autonomous party. Soon after being given freedom of political action by the general amnesty, they officially entered the political arena. Though the UQ provided a useful screen to shelter them from the storm of de-fascistisation measures, it could not become their permanent home. It suited the neo-Fascists while it refused to distinguish between Fascism and anti-Fascism, but was no longer acceptable when it claimed that 'the anti-Fascists of today are yesterday's Fascists'. Besides, UQ and neo-Fascists held

Table 3.2 Distribution of MSI voters by geographical-political areas

	1948 %	1953 %	1958 %	1963 %	1968 %	1972 %	1976 %	1979 %	1983 %	1987 %
Industrial area	12.7	16.3	17.9	18.6	19.3	18.9	18.4	19.8	21.4	23.0
Traditionally Christian Democrat ('White') area	6.4	8.2	10.8	8.8	8.6	6.8	7.2	7.4	7.6	9.9
Traditionally Socialist-Communist ('Red') area	11.3	14.2	15.5	14.8	14.2	11.0	11.0	11.7	12.3	14.0
Southern area	53.1	41.1	41.2	43.8	47.7	46.7	46.5	46.6	44.8	39.6
Islands	16.5	20.3	14.6	14.0	13.2	16.9	16.9	14.5	13.9	13.5

Source: P. Ignazi, *Il polo escluso. Profilo del Movimento Sociale Italiano*, Il Mulino, Bologna, 1989.

N.B. The geographic-political areas named here include the following regions:

– Industrial area: Piedmont, Lombardy, Liguria
– 'White' area: Trentino Alto Adige, Veneto, Friuli Venezia Giulia
– 'Red' area: Emilia-Romagna, Tuscany, Umbria, Marches
– Southern area: Latium, Abruzzi, Molise, Campania, Calabria
– Islands: Sicily, Sardinia

different conceptions of politics and the State.[10] With the slogan the 'administrative state', the UQ advocated – without actually formalising it – a watered-down version of the 'minimal state', that is, the liberal conception of the State that makes its presence felt as little as possible and makes way for civil society, which it considers to be the only force capable of achieving progress. The neo-Fascists, on the other hand, wanted to exhume the 'ethical state', that is, a state capable of determining not only political and economic objectives, but the moral ones of the individual and of society as well. Clearly, the 'partnership' could not last very long.

The *Movimento Sociale Italiano* was started on 26 December 1946. All its founding fathers – starting with Giorgio Almirante – were figures in one way or another associated with the RSI. They all felt, therefore, an absolute need to refer to Fascism, and in particular to its most intransigent sides. Even the party's programme echoed, explicitly, themes dear to historical Fascism: the fundamental role of the nation (a role that was not supposed to be superseded by that of the individual, as the liberals advocated, nor by that of class as the Socialists insisted); the workers' state intended as the promoter of a complete partnership between employees and employers; Catholicism as the State religion; foreign policy as a form of nationalist ostentation or even as a civilising mission for the Italian nation.[11]

The first move the party made was to refute the Peace Treaty and the institutional and political set-up which came out of the war. Its intention was, in the first place, to delegitimise the new republican state. It also helped to preserve a collective identity for the MSI, by distinguishing it from all the parties of the 'constitutional spectrum', and by turning it into a magnet for the clandestine neo-Fascist 'groupuscules' scattered about the country. The rejection of the conditions imposed on Italy by the Allies, and the attacks on *partitocrazia* stem from the MSI's conception of the nation as a superior political value, overriding all other interests – be they those of the individual, of the unions and even of the parties – in order to establish the only true interest, that of the national Community. The colonial losses and the failure to retain the disputed territories around Trieste were considered to have damaged the political unity of the nation just as much as the intrusion of the parties in the daily life of the citizen.

The MSI's attacks on the post-war political settlement reflected its intention of discrediting the ruling class of the new State, and was thus intended to invalidate the anti-Fascist arguments on which it was based. The rejection of the guiding role which the two victorious super-powers had taken upon themselves offered the chance to argue in favour of an unlikely 'third way' – a way that was allegedly different from, and superior to, both capitalism and communism, because it was capable of avoiding their shortcomings: extreme individualism in one case, and out-and-out State control in the other.

A strong ideology was, after all, an essential resource for a movement that was discredited in the eyes of the outside world and was searching for an uneasy internal unity. The MSI had, in fact, to fight two battles: one for its own survival, against the Committee for National Liberation [*Comitato di Liberazione Nazionale*, CLN]; the other to convince the scattered neo-Fascist forces that they should abandon the temptation to go underground, and should organise into a party. These were the two fronts on which battle was engaged, and from which the MSI emerged victorious. The out-and-out appeal to the Fascist idea was not enough for the FAR to survive the political stranglehold that was suffocating it. The stigmatisation of the MSI by the anti-Fascist parties succeeded in marginalising it but not in eliminating it altogether. In the parliamentary elections of 1948, the MSI secured 1.9 per cent of the vote – a modest result if set against the high ambitions the party had nurtured, but an encouraging one considering the polarisation (DC *vs* Socialist/Communist alliance) that characterised the election campaign, the modest organisational resources of the party, and the left's attacks on it. The very fact of entering Parliament and local councils forced the MSI to moderate its ideology, which conflicted too markedly with that of other parties. Besides, its arrival on the public political stage occurred precisely at the time when the anti-Fascist discrimination was being succeeded in Italy by an anti-Communist one which led, in the spring of 1947, to the expulsion of the Socialists and Communists from the government, and to the establishment of a DC-dominated centre government. The credentials which the neo-Fascist right could boast of with regard to the defence of 'Christian Civilisation' and the fight against Bolshevism were not inferior to those of the centre. The MSI was thus offered the chance to overcome the isolation to which it has been condemned, provided it underplayed the much-vaunted 'difference' that opposed it to its potential allies (DC and Monarchists). The growing southern base also worked to the party's advantage. Suffice it to say that the six deputies and the one senator who were elected in 1948 all represented southern constituencies. The outlook was encouraging, but risky. The creation of a broad anti-Communist front meant, in the short term, the achievement of ideological legitimation and, in the long term, the widening of its sphere of influence beyond the circle of former Fascists unable, or unwilling, to adapt to a mass democracy. The overtures to the monarchists and to the DC had a price, though, one which the hard-liners were not prepared to pay: the watering-down of the party's ideology, in the name of a 'holy alliance'. The stormy debate on this question absorbed the MSI's energies throughout the early 1950s, and led it to seek an anti-Communist alliance encompassing Monarchists, Liberals and Christian Democrats.

Moderates and hardliners

At first the MSI chose a compromise position. It supported the policy of dialogue and, soon after, one of overt cooperation with centre-right parties at local level. As early as the autumn of 1947, its Rome city councillors played a decisive role in the election of the Christian Democrat mayor Aldo Rebecchini. In the local elections of 1951–52, the MSI achieved reasonable results, and obtained seats on many city councils, including such major Southern centres as Naples, Salerno, Foggia, Bari and Lecce. In Sicily, it comfortably exceeded its national average of 1948, and its regional deputies were able to exercise a decisive influence over this important semi-autonomous region. On national issues, however, the MSI pursued a policy of uncompromising opposi-tion. The event that best exemplifies this attitude was the party's vote against Italy's membership of NATO.[12] Behind the apparent intransigence, however, some changes were taking place. Almirante, whose leadership was viewed as an obstacle to a more effective policy of alliances with right-wing and centre parties, stepped down in 1951 and was succeeded by Augusto De Marsanich who was favourably disposed to the idea of a pact. Shortly afterwards, an agreement with the Monarchists was signed with the local elections of 1951–52 coming up. A shift in the MSI's attitude to NATO also took place at the end of 1951. Even the party's political *modus operandi* began to follow that of the other parties. The MSI shed, almost completely, its tendency to rely on anti-democratic and clandestine forms of political activism. A series of affiliated organisations was set up. These included the Italian Confederation of National Workers' Unions [*Confederazione Italiana Sindacati Nazionali Lavoratori*, CISNAL], the National Welfare Association [*Ente Nazionale di Assistenza*, ENAS] and the University Front for National Action [*Fronte Universitario di Azione Nazionale*, FUAN].

Strong internal opposition to the new line did not discourage the party from pursuing it. In fact, the appointment of Arturo Michelini to the leadership in 1954 confirmed and reinforced the victory of the moderate wing of the party. Moreover, the MSI was encouraged – in a way even forced – not to make a U-turn by the political situation of the time. At the end of the first parliamentary term, in fact, the DC prepared itself to deal with the growing strength of the right – a strength which emerged clearly after the local elections of 1951–52 – by means of two manoeuvres: firstly, by replacing the proportional representation system with one which apportioned two-thirds of the parliamentary seats to the party, or coalition of parties, that obtained more than 50 per cent of the vote, and secondly, by passing the so-called Scelba Law, named after the Home Affairs minister who championed it. This added a clause to the Constitution, which prevented the disbanded PNF from being re-formed. The new electoral system was intended to re-create conditions favourable to a political polarisation between centre and left: it warned conservative public opinion that a vote for the right was tantamount to a wasted vote which could indirectly benefit Socialists and Communists. The second manoeuvre threatened the very existence of the MSI in that it urged voters not to support a party on the fringes of the law. Faced with such measures, De Marsanich's party had no choice: it had to moderate its anti-system stance or fall foul of the law.

The MSI and the unstable centre government

The DC's strategy turned out to be only partly successful. While it prevented a completely legitimated right-wing force from developing, the DC did not succeed in winning an outright majority for its centrist coalition with the Liberals, Republicans and Social Democrats. The period of *centrismo stabile* (stable centre-party government), gave way to that of *centrismo instabile*. Having trebled its vote since 1948 (it now stood at 5.9 per cent), the MSI, with its 29 deputies, was in a position to exert a pivotal influence on a governmental coalition. This was especially the case as the DC was unwilling – or unable – to choose between right and left and was therefore forced, willy-nilly, to construct governments dependent on the non-belligerence or even the complicity of part of the opposition. Besides, the DC's middle position between the extremes of left and right was not always self-evident. Whenever Communist pressure mounted, the Christian Democrats did not hesitate to rely on MSI and Monarchist support. They never went so far, though, as to disregard the underlying premise of the Italian political system: the central position of the DC between two delegitimated extremes. While the central position was thus justified by the presence of the two opposing anti-system parties (MSI and Communists) it also, paradoxically, required the destabilising threat, which they posed, to continue. The most precarious moment for this balancing act was reached in 1953 when the DC openly discussed setting up a right-wing ticket in Rome to prevent the capital falling into the hands of the Socialists and Communists. This was the so-called 'Sturzo operation', named after the priest Don Sturzo who, in 1919, set up the first Catholic political party in Italy, the Italian Popular Party [*Partito Popolare Italiano*, PPI]. This move was supported by powerful Catholic lay groups such as the *Comitati civici* (Civic Committees), an organisation with a widespread network which actively mobilised public opinion in defence of values and institutions like the family and the school, as well as by influential sections of the Church, such as the Roman Curia and many bishops. It was only stopped from embracing the rightist option by its coalition partners who threatened to bring down the government.

Collusion between the government and the right was a regular feature of the Republic's second parliamentary term. First the Pella government (1953), then that of Zoli (1957) took advantage of MSI support. Furthermore, the second President of the Republic, Giovanni Gronchi, was elected in 1955 with the help of MSI votes.[13] In order to take full advantage of this situation, the MSI silenced those within its ranks who wanted it to be an anti-system party (in 1956 the 'diehards' of Pino Rauti's New Order [*Ordine Nuovo*, ON] left the party). In every way possible it endeavoured to take on the mantle of the one and only true defender of the system. It took to the streets in 1953 and 1954 to defend the right of Trieste to be Italian. It entered the schools to take on young left-wingers, using an aggressive, no-holds-barred style. It went out of its way to seek violent confrontation with Socialist and Communist activists during election campaigns or strikes. In the South, especially, it strengthened its ties with Monarchists and Christian Democrats in local government. All it needed to complete its 'long march through the institutions' and achieve full legitimation was a foothold in government.[14]

The trial of strength during the Tambroni premiership

Its big opportunity came midway through 1960 when the Tambroni government was formed. To the disappointment of the DC, the 1958 general election had failed to solve the basic problem of stabilising the centre ground. The result was particularly bad for the right. Both Monarchist parties declined, as did the MSI (it only received 4.8 per cent of the vote). A centre-left government, which would draw the Socialists into the majority, was now on the agenda, in spite of residual resistance within the DC and in spite of the continuing attempts by the MSI leaders to minimise the importance of this shift. The Prime Ministerial mandate given to Fernando Tambroni – who was not one of the DC's top men – has to be seen as part of the normal Italian practice of putting off difficult political decisions; this involves setting up deliberately transitional governments, led by secondary figures, whose job is simply to keep government ticking over. However, a crisis was sparked off when the MSI vote in parliament was decisive in clinching the vote of confidence for the new government, and was officially accepted by the Prime Minister. The DC saw that its whole central position was being undermined. The country now appeared to identify with the left which was revitalised by the appeal to anti-Fascism. There were some ten deaths in street clashes. The political price of MSI support was too heavy. Tambroni fell and his demise showed that a right-wing solution to the problem of governmental instability could only compromise the DC's linchpin policy of mediation between the extremes. This gave the green light to a centre-left solution.

For the MSI, the failure of the Tambroni operation was not simply a setback. It meant that the Michelini policy, based on the party gradually integrating into government, was in ruins. After ten years of painfully slow progress towards full legitimation within the party system, the MSI stood isolated, excluded and also empty-handed. The commitment of the centre-left coalition partners (Christian Democrats, Socialists, Social Democrats and Republicans) to exclude the Communists on the left and the Monarchists, Liberals and MSI on the right from central and local government, destroyed, in the space of a few months, all the gains put together by the MSI since the early 1950s. Michelini survived but without a policy for the future, especially after the elections of 1963 (giving the MSI a meagre 5.2 per cent) confirmed his inability to channel the disgruntlement of moderate public opinion, whose votes went to the Liberals. In the subsequent period, the MSI stepped up the viciousness of its attacks but remained impotent. In fact, its hold on society appeared to be crumbling. Symptomatic of this was the fact that its student movement, the FUAN, lost its position of dominance at Rome University, a traditional neo-Fascist stronghold. For the right as a whole a difficult and uncertain period of policy rethinking had opened up.

In the previous fifteen years the MSI had, in effect, come to represent all neo-Fascist opinion. Now, with the party drifting, new faces appeared[15] and its whole position was rethought. It ceased looking exclusively back towards its Fascist past and became more sensitive to developments on the world stage. The parochial horizons of the extreme right were now broadened to take in the economic, technological and political struggle going on between East and West. (This confrontation was no longer the direct one of the Cold War but the indirect one of 'peaceful coexistence', and its focus was decolonisation.) The extreme right saw 'peaceful coexistence' as a Trojan horse, part of a Communist plot based both on supporting and, thereby, taking over national liberation struggles (from Algeria to Cuba and from Latin America to Vietnam) and on subtly undermining democracy by working quietly on the hearts and minds of Western public opinion.[16]

In this perspective, the centre-left in Italy seemed to be a national version of this worldwide Communist plot. Far from staunching the drift to the left, it was seen as surrendering to Communism. Under the umbrella of democracy, the Italian Communists appeared to be gaining important footholds everywhere: in the press, in schools and among intellectuals, not to mention trade unions. They were about to prepare a very gradual takeover under the gaze of a public opinion lulled into complacency by the rules of the democratic game. The extreme right's process of taking stock was complicated by its realisation of the profound changes brought about in Italian society by the post-war 'economic miracle'. A traditional agricultural and provincial society was disappearing, while consumerism was rampant. In this climate, the right's most clearly held values (the defence of religion, love of country, attachment to the family and respect for authority) were drained of their potency. It could only appeal to what it called 'the Nation's vital forces', that is, the upper echelons of the army, of the Civil Service and, in general, of the anti-Communist establishment.[17]

These new aspirations and, in parallel to them, the search for an audience sympathetic to the extreme right's new message meant appealing to sectors of the population not traditionally associated with neo-Fascism. This was the period, too, when the so-called 'invisible government' (*governo invisibile*), became a major factor in Italian politics. This term is used to describe all the power centres in the country (the various state agencies, the secret services, important elements in the economic and financial sectors) not operating in an openly democratic way, but trying, instead, to run the country in the absence of an official government able to safeguard their own vital interests.[18] The effect of all this was to alter the relationship between neo-Fascism and the world of anti-democratic subversion in general. Their aims were the same – attacking democratic institutions – but their methods differed. While the official extreme right was content to adopt a more hard-line opposition to the centre-left governments, the subversive groups were formulating a ruthless plan of attack on state institutions. They had recourse to covert actions (i.e. terrorist attacks which they did not claim responsibility for) in order to create a climate of fear in the country and, thus, build the foundations for a right-wing backlash. This was the so-called 'strategy of tension' (*strategia della tensione*). Above all, the relationship between the extreme right and the State was changed. Before this, there had indeed been a relationship of connivance and sometimes there had been cover-ups. For instance, the MSI's frequent attacks on symbols and institutions of the Resistance, and even its thuggish attacks on trade union demonstrations, had often been tolerated or even encouraged by the police. But now there was an unexpected shift of emphasis. Right-wing plots and coups were being hatched within the state itself, while the neo-Fascist forces were simply instruments. It is now known that, in the summer of 1964, during a trying period following the government's resignation, the doomsday scenario of a suspension of political and trade union freedoms was brought forward. This was based on a plan drawn up by General De Lorenzo, Commander of the *carabinieri.*

The 'vital forces' of the nation against the 'Communist plot'

It later emerged during judicial enquiries that, within a year, the union between those elements in the secret services favourable to a *coup d'état* and those forces, both old and new, on the subversive right had focused on a plan of 'revolutionary war'. This was drawn up at a conference held on 3–5 May at the Parco dei Principi hotel by the 'Alberto Pollio' Institute for Historical and Military Studies. Its diagnosis of a Communist threat looming over the West called inevitably for a mobilisation of all the 'vital forces'. Two important points emerged from this response to the 'Communist threat'. First, the conference's call for a guerrilla counter-offensive let no room for an extreme-right party to operate above board. Second, the need to respond effectively to the challenge meant acting ruthlessly, even if this entailed violating the basic tenets of democracy and having open recourse to political violence.[19]

The scenario outlined at the Parco dei Principi conference stands out as a disconcerting prelude to the strategy-of-tension years about to hit the country. The call to mobilise had the effect of revitalising the whole sector of groups and organisations which rejected the policy pursued by Michelini's MSI, and which were determined to go for a radical alternative to the system. *Ordine Nuovo* aimed to become the focal point for all those forces which were no longer willing 'to obey the orders of the MSI "moderates" '. National Vanguard [*Avanguardia Nazionale*], the group founded by Stefano Delle Chiaie in 1960, burned its bridges with the party and its 'sterile and purely backward-looking' policy, and launched into action on the basis of a plan of anti-democratic subversion.[20] The MSI itself, as the 1960s came to a close, was preparing itself to face up, in the appropriate way, to the convulsive period which began with student protests and which immediately descended into a spiral of political violence. The first bomb in the strategy of tension exploded in Milan on 12 December 1969.

Giorgio Almirante's *strategia del doppio binario* (two-pronged strategy)

In 1969, Michelini was succeeded by Giorgio Almirante. The change in leadership brought about the so-called *strategia del doppio binario*. The new party secretary put an end to the policy of dialogue with the DC: it had proved to be such a handicap to the MSI that, in the 1968 elections, it polled a mere 4.5 per cent of the vote. Instead of the accommodating approach of the previous years, Almirante advocated a grander and more vigorous one that might enable the party to take advantage of the troubled social and political situation of the early 1970s. His ambition was to turn the MSI into a truly autonomous right-wing force, free from the conditioning influences of the governing parties, and thus to abandon the tactic of offering tacit support to the latter in return for clientelistic favours. The aim now was directly to undermine the central role of the DC. This role was already under threat from the crisis of the centre-left coalition, and the ensuing political instability, from the mass demonstrations of the student, feminist and trade union movements (which were intent on taking over from the parties the function of representing the country) and from the accompanying radicalisation of the political struggle. Almirante attempted to exploit the country's quest both for law and order and for change. He aimed to bring together the conservative middle classes of the North (e.g. the 'silent majority' of Milan, tired of the student unrest and trade union mobilisation of 1970–71) and the lower classes of the South (the demonstrators of Reggio Calabria who rebelled against the authorities' decision not to grant the city regional-capital status in 1971).

The new strategy proved immediately successful. In the local elections of 1971, the MSI vote rose to 13.9 per cent. Even better scores were achieved in the South. In Sicily, support for the party grew from 6.6 per cent in 1967 to 16.3 per cent, and was particularly strong in Palermo (19.5 per cent) and Catania (27 per cent). In Rome, too, the MSI nearly doubled its vote (from 9.3 to 15.2 per cent). Once again, as had happened before with the rise of the *Uomo Qualunque* and the Monarchists, the DC ran the risk of having its traditional base eroded by the right, and its hegemonic role in the political system weakened.

32

To increase its impact as an opposition force, the MSI tried to rally under its wing the entire right. It merged with the Monarchist Party (the new party was given the name MSI – National right [MSI – *Destra Nazionale*, MSI-DN]) and, in 1972, drew to its ticket personalities potentially attractive to the conservative middle classes, such as the former general De Lorenzo and the former NATO admiral Birindelli, as well as the hardliners of *Ordine Nuovo*, who had earlier been readmitted into the party fold. The outcome of the whole operation was very successful but not decisive. The MSI polled 8.7 per cent of the vote – its best general election result yet and one that placed the party neck-and-neck with the Socialists, in third position, after the DC and the Communists. However, it failed to unseat the DC from its central position. Another onslaught was attempted in 1974, by campaigning, together with the DC, and in competition with it, in favour of the abolition of the divorce law. This too ended in failure: the entire anti-divorce vote amounted to no more than 40.9 per cent. These results paved the way for the government's opening up to the Communists, which occurred after the early general election in 1976. The MSI vote dropped to 6.1 per cent (in the regional elections of 1975 it had already polled a mere 6.4 per cent). The MSI's hopes for a shift to the right brought about by years of political violence, terrorism and chronic political instability, vanished. Instead of acquiring full legitimacy through its own strength, the party found itself even more isolated. In this way, the tide turned against the MSI in the second half of the 1970s. The right-wing constellation could no longer identify solely with this party. A number of splinter groups jeopardised the party's very unity. The following parliamentary term saw a split in the party and the birth of a new group called National Democracy [*Democrazia Nazionale*, DN] which succeeded in halving the number of MSI deputies. This group accused Almirante of failing to turn his party into a democratic parliamentary one, and tried to establish in Italy a respectable right-wing party of the type found elsewhere in Western Europe. The attempt proved unsuccessful. The DC's unwillingness to respond to the overtures of DN led to the latter's total isolation. None of the breakaway deputies were reelected in 1979.

The radical right's ambiguous relationship with the MSI – one which wavered between rivalry and complementarity – also went through a critical period. The years in question saw the establishment of the 'governments of national solidarity', so called because they were intent on recreating the spirit of solidarity with which the democratic parties had, together, first fought against Fascism, then founded the Republic. These governments were formed in 1976–78, with the PCI's decisive external support, the first time this had happened since the party was ousted from government in 1947. They marked the end of a phase that saw the secret services covering up plots and coups. Though the details are still unclear, these plots and coups involved blatantly neo-Fascist organisation such as Stefano Delle Chiaie's National Vanguard and Valerio Borghese's National Front [*Fronte Nazionale*, FN], militantly nationalistic organisations like Carlo Fumagalli's Revolutionary Action Movement [*Movimento di Azione Rivoluzionaria*, MAR], and Amos Spiazzi's Wind Rose [*Rosa dei Venti*].[21]

The State's offensive against what was left of the remaining radical right groups was countered by a strategy of violence devised by Franco Freda: this sought to attract those forces, of both right and left, which aspired to destroy the existing order. Judge Vittorio Occorsio, murdered in 1976, was one of the victims of this strategy. Political activism no longer aimed to overthrow the democratic regime. It now consisted of terrorist attacks devoid of any political aim, whose sole purpose was to strike at some of the hated symbols of the 'system' – a procedure known as 'armed spontaneity' (*spontaneismo armato*).

This strategy was based on two facts. First, it was realised both that there was no hope of convincing the 'renegade' MSI to adopt a revolutionary stance and that the *coup d'état* scenario had led to the strengthening rather than the destabilisation of the system. Second, there was the arrival on the scene of a new generation of activists with no historical memories of Fascism. Their commitment tended to be personal and existential, rather than ideological or political. It grew, first and foremost, out of a need to assert themselves. They had an instinctive solidarity, on the ground, with anyone who was anti-system: from Italian left-wing terrorists operating as loners, to the Palestinian Fedayeen, and from the Argentinian Monteneros to the IRA. Their 'armed propaganda' which preached the slogan 'Let's build action' left the task of putting together a new consensus to the language of violence. The Armed Revolutionary Nuclei [*Nuclei armati rivoluzionari*, NAR] had no strategy, while Third Position [*Terza Posizione*, TP] hesitated between the 'armed spontaneity' option and a strong hierarchical structure.[22] In other words, the situation was a very fluid one reflecting the Italian right's crisis of political confidence.

A further warning light that the extreme right was in disarray was the setting up of the New Right [*Nuova Destra*, ND] movement, in the wake of the *movimento del '77* (a youth protest movement born in 1977, which transcended political ideologies and was mostly interested in the fulfilment of subjective aspirations). The ND shared with the French *Nouvelle Droite* a marked preference for ideological and cultural positions related to the idea of commitment within civil rather than political society. As a starting point, it wished to distance itself from all the right's previous stances – both illegal and legal.[23] At the same time it set out to rethink the right's cultural paradigm, in an attempt to free it from its sterile backward-looking position and to prepare it for the challenge of the future.

The challenge of democratic legitimation

The loss of representativeness of the whole of the right would not in itself have been wholly negative for the MSI if, in the meantime, there had been the prospect of new areas of influence for it within Italian society and/or new tactical openings for it in the political arena. Instead, paradoxically, at the very time when its legitimacy was ceasing to be called into question by the system, the MSI, like a bird kept for years in a cage (the cage of anti-Fascism), found flight awkward and did not know which direction to take; it remained attached to the familiar, confined spaces where it felt more at ease with itself.

The re-integration of the MSI into the political system was taking place without the party facing up to its ideological Bad Godesberg. This was helped along, quite simply, by the general climate of political deradicalisation which characterised Italian politics in the 1980s. By 1985 the process was virtually complete. Almirante's party was no longer discriminated against in party-to-party dealings or on parliamentary committees. Slowly but surely, anti-Fascism and anti-Communism were on the wane. The drop in the ideological temperature did not, however, mean that there was a reduction in ideological distance.[24] In other words the system of exclusion of the political extremes was still in operation, although in weaker form. The three political poles were still underpinning the system, with the centre, unchallenged, at the forefront. The right continued to be discriminated against, the only difference being that this discrimination was based not so much on its absence of legitimacy, but rather on the political distance separating it from the other parties.

For its part, the right, with its established position as polar opposite to Communism slipping, was being called upon to rethink the identity and strategy upon which it had constructed its fortunes (both positive and negative) in the post-war period. The forty-year-long opposition to the 'regime of the parties', considered to be an incarnation of the Communist strategy of conquering Italian society, was being recycled as opposition to *partitocrazia*. The MSI's fundamental rejection, from the beginning, of the parliamentary Republic was no longer perceived as a challenge to the democratic order which had arisen from the ashes of Fascism. It became, instead, the more legitimate demand for 'reform of the state' in the direction of a presidential system.[25] Of course the MSI has not deserted its position as champion of right-thinking conservatism. That is why it continued to back the demand for 'law and order' expressed by conservative public opinion, and raised the spectre of capital punishment. At the same time, however, it took up some of the so-called post-industrial issues, such as quality of life, the environment and citizenship. In its relationship with other parties it made some attempts to break out of its isolation, but with little success. In 1978 it announced the birth of the Euro-right (along with the Spanish *Fuerza Nueva* and the French *Parti des Forces Nouvelles*). This announcement came to nothing. On several occasions it made overtures to Craxi's Socialist Party, but, here too, it failed to implement a convincing alliance strategy. As a result, the MSI was slow to express its new policy stance. This led to confusion outside the party and a lack of cohesion within it.

After the death of the founding father and leader Almirante (1988), the MSI seesawed between falling back defensively on its neo-Fascist identity (under Gianfranco Fini 1988–90, and again from July 1991), and leaping forward 'beyond the right', propelled by claims to a national-revolutionary culture (under Pino Rauti 1990–91).[26] The party seemed unable to put together a strategy to relaunch itself. It was even unsure whether to entrust its fortunes to that battle which had revitalised the various right-wing parties in all other European countries: the battle against Third World immigration.[27]

Instead of playing the anti-foreigner card, the MSI, under the leadership of its ideologist Rauti, put its money on the risky anti-racism card. Its thinking on this matter was wildly ambitious: it used the exodus of migrants from poor countries of the South to relaunch the idea of the 'third way'. Mussolini's old aspiration of constructing an alternative to capitalist plutocracy and Bolshevik collectivism was revived: it took the form of a scheme to oppose the interests of multi-national capitalism in the West and state capitalism in the East, with the 'great proletarian' civilisation of the 'European Nation'. This civilisation was to act as a mediator for the countries of the Third World. In other words, the MSI used the international

North/South issue to finalise the victory of the countries defeated in 1945 and sacrificed to the Yalta settlement imposed by the victors. This meant no measures to put a stop to immigration from Africa. The Italian right was said never to have been colonialistic, even at the time of the war in Ethiopia. It was supposed, simply, to have been 'Africanist', that is, to have taken on the role of civiliser and liberator, not conqueror, as was the case with Britain and France.[28] Clearly, this was an abstract policy which did not reflect the views of MSI activists and voters, and deprived the party of the rich pool of xenophobic votes. Thus, instead of unleashing the energies of the right, 'deghettoisation' paralysed it. In ten years, the right had completely squandered the votes it accumulated in the early 1970s. The 8.7 per cent of 1972 fell to 6.8 per cent in 1983, to 5.7 per cent in 1987, to 5.5 per cent in 1989 (European elections), and to as little as 3.9 per cent in 1990 (local elections). Instead of reaping the long-cherished benefits of its achieved legitimisation, the right – like the ex-Communist left – saw its problems grow. Asked to come out into the open after acting in the shadows for nearly fifty years, it had to reveal its bluff.

The MSI remained an ambiguous party fluctuating between past and present, suspended between its Fascist identity and the wish to conform to the values of the 'new politics'.[29] It was an unresolved condition which corresponded to the political culture of the MSI – a ragbag of Fascist, revisionist and modern ideas, much criticised by the party's own officials as well as by its voters.[30]

A survey carried out in 1991 among the members of the *Fronte della Gioventù*, the youth movement of the MSI, showed that 88 per cent of them considered Fascism a historical 'model' to follow (even though 62.5 per cent rejected dictatorial solutions), 49.5 per cent branded democracy as a 'lie' (an additional 33.5 per cent viewed this term as 'ambiguous'), while 66.5 per cent and 64 per cent respectively saw no contradiction in their brief in elections and referendums. These young people did not think that the white race was superior (69.5 per cent), but considered immigration to be a problem (98 per cent). Finally, a large majority (73 per cent) viewed themselves as belonging neither to the right nor to the left.[31]

On the other hand, a survey carried out among Italian voters, also in 1991, in general confirmed that the party had not lost its traditional features. The MSI remained essentially a right-wing party (41 per cent of supporters placed themselves to the extreme right of the spectrum, with a progressively smaller percentage as they neared the centre); it was predominantly southern (61.7 per cent of all votes came from the South), urban (35.2 per cent of voters lived in towns with more than 100,000 inhabitants), and male (men made up 65.8 per cent of all votes). As far as education is concerned, MSI voters clustered themselves at either end of the spectrum: 35 per cent had a school qualification, and 10.9 per cent no education whatsoever (in this respect, they came third behind the DC with 18.2 per cent, and the PCI with 15.1 per cent).[32]

The MSI's attempts to rejoin the political mainstream – at risk because of the party's still incomplete overhaul of its own culture – began to succeed at the end of 1993, thanks to the tactical nimbleness of its leaders. Even the party's unchanging nature was turned into a resource.[33] The MSI's golden opportunity came simultaneously in the shape of the crisis of the First Republic and in the reform of the electoral system (actually strongly opposed by the party) which marked the passage from a proportional representation to a first-past-the-post system in both local and national elections. The discrediting of the governing class – hit by arrest warrants – seemed to bear out a traditional theme of MSI propaganda: the corrupt nature of the party-dominated Republic born out of the ashes of Fascism. It also fatally undermined the political centre, which was now reduced to a ruin abandoned by its electorate. With the passing of this new electoral law, the right was thus able to break out of its ghetto status. This created a polarising momentum which swept away the centre and breathed new life into the extremes of the political spectrum. On 21 November 1993 the MSI came top in the first round of the local elections in both Rome and Naples with 31 per cent and 31.2 per cent respectively – and its success was almost, but not quite, crowned, by the election of its candidates (Fini and Alessandra Mussolini) as the cities' mayors. Fini then grabbed his chance. With an early general election in the offing, he launched, just over one month later, the National Alliance (*Alleanza Nazionale*, AL) – a right-wing grouping open to the centre, in which he quickly submerged Almirante's party. Blackshirts and Roman salutes vanished. Fascism was consigned to the 'judgement of historians'. The old watchwords of the 'alternative to the system', of 'going beyond liberal capitalism and social-communism' in the name for a corporatist and social 'third way', and of the 'historic and political continuity with the Fascist movement' – watchwords which had in fact been strongly reiterated at the Rimini conference of 1990[34] – were forgotten. In their place came unreserved praise for the market (freed from all administrative restraints), for individual initiative (to be encouraged by tax relief on investment), for an ostentatious rediscovery of previously neglected values like 'freedom, democracy and solidarity', and for a rejection of 'any form of dictatorship or totalitarianism' and of 'any form of racism or discrimination'.[35] Only time will tell if this policy overhaul is cosmetic and opportunistic or, instead, the first step towards a complete integration into the democratic fold. It often happens that political parties are spurred into change not by internal dynamics but by an external challenge. For the time being the new AN grouping can boast a very flattering success in the General Election of 27–28 March 1994 (13.5 per cent in the proportional part of the vote for the Chamber of Deputies, 105 deputies and 43 senators). This result, opening the doors of government to the extreme right, within an openly right-wing coalition, has brought to a conclusion the 'long march through the institutions' begun by Almirante's MSI in that far-away December of 1946.

Translated by Ronnie Ferguson and Luciano Cheles

List of abbreviations

AN	*Alleanza Nazionale* [National Alliance]
CISNAL	*Confederazione Italiana Sindacati Nazionali Lavoratori* [Italian Confederation of National Workers' Unions]
CLN	*Comitato di Liberazione Nazionale* [Committee for National Liberation]
DC	*Democrazia Cristiana* [Christian-Democrat Party]
DN	*Democrazia Nazionale* [National Democracy]
ENAS	*Ente Nazionale di Assistenza* [National Welfare Association]

FAR   *Fasci di Azione Rivoluzionaria* [Fasces of Revolutionary Action]
FN   *Fronte Nazionale* [National Front]
FUAN   *Fronte Universitario di Azione Nazionale* [University Front for National Action]
MAR   *Movimento di Azione Rivoluzionaria* [Revolutionary Action Movement]
MSI   *Movimento Sociale Italiano* [Italian Social Movement]
MSI-DN   *Movimento Sociale Italiano-Destra Nazionale* [Italian Social Movement – National Right]
NAR   *Nuclei Armati Rivoluzionari* [Armed Revolutionary Nuclei]
ND   *Nuova Destra* [New Right]
ON   *Ordine Nuovo* [New Order]
PDUM   *Partito Democratico di Unità Monarchica* [Democratic Party of Monarchist Unity]
PLI   *Partito Liberale Italiano* [Italian Liberal Party]
PNF   *Partito Nazionale Fascista* [National Fascist Party]
PNM   *Partito Nazionale Monarchico* [National Monarchist Party]
PPI   *Partito Popolare Italiano* [Italian Popular Party]
PPM   *Partito Popolare Monarchico* [Popular Monarchist Party]
PR   *Partito Radicale* [Radical Party]
RSI   *Repubblica Sociale Italiana* [Italian Social Republic]
TP   *Terza Posizione* [Third Position]
UQ   *Uomo Qualunque* [Man-in-the-street Party]

Notes

1. G. Galli, *Il difficile governo*, Il Mulino, Bologna, 1972.
2. K. V. Beyme, 'Right-wing extremism in post-war Europe', *West European Politics*, XI, (2), pp. 3–6.
3. J. Linz, 'Legittimazione ed efficacia di governo', *Mond Operaio*, XLII, 1989. p. 116.
4. R. Chiarini, 'Neofascismo e destra eversiva in Italia nel secondo dopoguerra', in *Storia dell'età presente. I problemi del mondo dalla 2a Guerra Mondiale ad oggi*, Marzorati, Milan, 1984, vol. I, pp. 907–11.
5. P. G. Murgia, *Il vento di Nord. Storia e cronaca del fascismo dopo la Resistenza (1945–1950)*, Sugarco, Milan, 1975.
6. S. Setta, *L'Uomo Qualunque, 1944–1948*, Laterza, Bari, 1975 (reissued in 1995).
7. L. Grazziano, *Clientelismo e mutamento politico*, Franco Angeli, Milan, 1974.
8. G. Galli (ed.), *Il comportamento elettorale in Italia. Un'analisi ecologica delle elezioni in Italia fra il 1946 e il 1963*, Il Mulino, Bologna, 1968, pp. 266 and 247–8.
9. B. Bartolini, 'Analisi ecologica del voto del MSI-DN alle elezioni politiche del 20 giugno 1976', *Rivista italiana di scienza politica*, IX, 1979, pp. 297–316.
10. E. Forcella, 'Dieci anni di neofascismo. La chioccia qualunquista', *Il Mondo*, 20 April 1954, pp. 13–14.
11. P. Rosenbaum, *Il nuovo fascismo, da Salò ad Almirante. Storia del MSI*, Feltrinelli, Milan, 1975, pp. 55–60.
12. S. Finotti, 'Difesa occidentale e Patto Atlantico: la scelta internazionale del MSI (1948–1952)', *Storia delle relazioni internazionali*, I, 1968, pp. 85–124.

13. G. Mammarella, *L'Italia contemporanea (1943–1985)*, Il Mulino, Bologna, 1985, pp. 209–62.

14. G. De Luna, 'Neofascismo', in F. Levi, U. Levra and N. Tranfaglia, *Il mondo contemporanco. Storia d'Italia*, vol. II, La Nuova Italia, Florence, 1978, pp. 780–84.

15. D. Barbieri, 'Notizie sulle nuove organizzazioni che animano il cosmo nero a partire dagli anni sessanta', in *Agenda nera. Trent'anni di neofascismo in Italia*, Coines, Rome, 1976.

16. Various Authors, *La guerra rivoluzionaria*, Proceedings of the conference organised by the *Istituto 'Alberto Pollio'*, Volpe, Rome, 1965, pp. 262–4.

17. R. Chiarini and P. Corsini, *Da Salò a Piazza della Loggia. Blocco d'ordine, neofascismo, radicalismo di destra (1945–1974)*, Franco Angeli, Milan, 1983, pp. 213 ff.

18. G. Galli, *La crisi italiana e la destra internazionale*, Mondadori, Milan, 1974, pp. 32 ff, and A. Del Boca and M. Giovana, *I 'figli del sole'. Mezzo secoto di nazifascismo nel mondo*, Feltrinelli, Milan, 1965, pp. 203–21.

19. For a detailed analysis of the connections between radical right and state institutions, see G. Flamini, *Il partito del golpe*, Bovolenta, Ferrara, 1981, vol. I, pp. 3 ff.

20. On *Avanguardia Nazionale* and other extra-parliamentary right-wing groups of this period. see, 'La destra eversiva', in F. Ferraresi (ed.), *La destra radicale*, Feltrinelli, Milan, 1984, pp. 62–71.

21. G. Flamini, *Il partito del golpe*, cit., vols II and III, *passim*.

22. F. Ferraresi, 'La destra eversiva', in F. Ferraresi (ed.), *La destra radicale*, cit., pp. 78–96.

23. M. Revelli, 'La nuova destra', in Ferraresi (ed.), *La destra radicale*, cit., pp. 119–214.

24. This point is argued by P. Ignazi, *Il polo escluso. Profilo del Movimento Sociale Italiano*, Il Mulino, Bologna, 1989, pp. 220–21, which develops a concept by G. Sartori, 'Pragmatismo e ideologia in Italia e Stati Uniti', *Rivista italiana di scienza politica*, X (1), 1981, pp. 137–46.

25. S. Sechi, 'Da Salò alla rebubblica presidenziale', *MondOperaio*, July 1986, pp. 56–64.

26. G. Tassani, 'The Italian Social Movement: from Almirante to Fini', in R. Nanetti and R. Catanzaro (eds), *Italian Politics – A Review*, vol. IV, Pinter, London, 1990, pp. 124–45.

27. P. Ignazi, 'Nuovi e vecchi partiti di estrema destra in Europa', *Rivista italiana di scienza politica*, XXII (2), Aug. 1992, pp. 293–333.

28. R. Chiarini, 'La protesta anti-immigrati nel mercato politico-elettorale', in J. Petersen (ed.), *L'emigrazione tra Italia e Germania*, Lacaita, Manduria-Bari-Rome, 1993, pp. 185–97.

29. L. Cheles, ' "Dolce Stil Nero"? Images of Women in the Graphic Propaganda of the Italian Neo-Fascist Party', in Z. G. Barański and S. W. Vinall (eds), *Women and Italy*, Macmillan, London, 1991, pp. 64–94; idem, ' "Nostalgia dell'Avvenire". The Propaganda of the Italian Far Right between Tradition and Innovation', in this volume, pp. 41–90.

30. See the results of the research carried out on those taking part in the MSI conference held at Rimini 11–14 May 1990. These are commented on by P. Ignazi, 'The changing profile of the Italian Social Movement', in P. H. Merkl and L. Weinberg (eds), *Encounters with the Contemporary Radical Right*, Westview, Boulder, CO, 1993, pp. 75–92.

31. Though the survey was carried out by a publication politically close to the MSI (*Proposta*), and though the sample of interviewees was not homogeneous, the results are quite indicative. See G. A., 'C'era una volta il neofascismo', in *Segnavia*, No. 2, June 1991, p. 17.

32. This data, which originates from the Sociology Department of the University of Milan, has been computed and kindly been made available to me by Stefano Draghi. The survey is part of a research carried out by the *Osservatorio Politico* group, coordinated by Renato Mannheimer, Alberto Spreafico, Giacomo Sani and Giuliano Urbani.

33. M. Tarchi, 'Il MSI vuole governare? Abbandoni l'anticapitalismo', *L'Indipendente*, 25 Nov. 1993.

34. See the various motions put forward at the conference, in particular: 'Going Beyond', 'Unitary Commitment', 'New Perspectives within Continuity' and 'Moving forward with the Right'.
35. Gianfranco Fini at the Rome conference of the MSI (28 Jan. 1994). See G. Battistini, 'E Fini sponsorizza Berlusconi-premier', in *La Repubblica*, 29 Jan. 1994. See also idem, 'Nasce la Cosa grigia e aspetta il Senatur', *La Repubblica*, 23 Jan. 1994, p. 4.

Chapter 4

'NOSTALGIA DELL'AVVENIRE'. THE PROPAGANDA OF THE ITALIAN FAR RIGHT BETWEEN TRADITION AND INNOVATION*

Luciano Cheles

In April 1970, not long after his election to the leadership of the *Movimento Sociale Italiano* (MSI),[1] Giorgio Almirante (1914–88) stressed at a party conference the need to change the image of his party: 'If the Communists have won the war of words, we have so far lost it. . . . We, of all people, must beware of representing Fascism in a grotesque way, or at any rate, in an outdated, anachronistic and stupidly nostalgic way.'[2] Almirante, who had been a close associate of Mussolini in the Italian Social Republic (*Repubblica Sociale Italiana*, the Nazi-backed state founded by the Duce in northern Italy, with headquarters in the resort of Salò, shortly after he was deposed by the king in 1943), aimed to make his party look modern, law-abiding and respectable in order to widen its appeal and end its isolation.

On becoming leader, Almirante attempted to unite the two main factions of the MSI: the intransigent one (of which he had been the main exponent in the 1950s and 1960s), and the moderate one, which cultivated a policy of *inserimento* (gradual integration).[3] In the early 1970s, he officially projected an image of non-violence, but in practice tolerated, and even encouraged, street agitation, in the hope that a climate of social disorder would lead to a right-wing backlash.

Almirante's preoccupation with party image and his ability at transforming it will not seem surprising if we consider his past experience in the field of 'political persuasion'. He was in fact, in 1944–45, Cabinet Chief in the Ministry of Popular Culture (*Ministero di Cultura Popolare*, irreverently nicknamed MINCULPOP), whose activity was almost exclusively concerned with the organisation of the regime's propaganda machinery.[4]

The change in the party's image took various forms. Fascist trappings and rituals (e.g. the black shirts and the Roman salute) were discouraged, and its language updated. In the early 1980s, emboldened by the legitimation that other parties were beginning to bestow upon the MSI, as a result of the deradicalisation of political conflict in Italy and a more widespread attempt to 'historicise' Fascism, Almirante embarked on high-profile public relations activities. He got himself invited to well-publicised social occasions (such as gala performances and exhibition openings), went on a visit to the United States (where he lectured at a number of universities), and arranged an audience with the Pope. Clearly, the purpose of all this was to

41

persuade the general public that he was no different from any other political personality. In June 1984, he surprised everyone by visiting the headquarters of the Communist Party in Rome, where the party leader Enrico Berlinguer was lying in state, in order to pay his last respects.[5]

In this essay, I intend to focus largely on the MSI's image during the Almirante period as expressed by one type of activity only: poster production. I shall examine the new images that the MSI devised in order to appear respectable, and attempt to prove that frequently, beneath a veneer of modernity, lay hidden nostalgic themes.

It should be noted at this point that, contrary to the practice of other political parties in Italy, the MSI produced its propaganda internally, instead of entrusting it to outside agencies: the graphic artists who designed the posters were also party activists.[6] This meant that the party could exercise total control over its publicity, and include whatever allusions to Fascism it thought fit.[7]

Before looking at the new propaganda, it is worth considering two posters that well typify the old approach, and which Almirante would have described as 'outdated, anachronistic and stupidly nostalgic'. They were both produced for the regional elections of 1970. The first depicts, in the foreground, a man surrounded by Italian tricolours, his index finger pointed at the onlooker (Fig. 1). In the second, a man clutching the Italian flag rescues another man whose imploring hand we see in the foreground (Fig. 3). Both posters are strongly dependent, both stylistically and thematically, on the graphic propaganda of the Fascist period. The photographic realism – a style the general public was and is especially predisposed to respond to, since it is the one used by many of the popular media (e.g. cinema, television, photo-romances, adventure comics)[8] – allows a more effective rendering of the men's athletic build, foreshortened gestures, and crumpled shirts and flags. The values that these posters evoke are those typical of Fascist ideology: the cult of virility, courage, action and patriotism.[9]

The first poster's direct source is quite likely to be one issued by the regime around 1935 as part of its campaign for economic self sufficiency (Fig. 2). A number of similarities support this view: the three-quarter leftward turning of the men's torsos, with their unusual left-handed pointing gestures; the peremptory, three-word slogans ('AIUTATECI A DIFENDERVI!' [Help us defend you!] and 'ACQUISTATE PRODOTTI ITALIANI' [Buy Italian goods]); and their italicised lettering – the latter being very uncommon in MSI propaganda. It is worth noting that the finger pointed at the observer is a motif which recurs especially in wartime recruitment propaganda (its early prototype is Alfred Leete's well-known Lord Kitchener poster of 1914), and lends the two posters militaristic overtones. Equally martial is the slogan 'AIUTATECI A DIFENDERVI'.

As for the second poster of the MSI, it too might have been inspired by a Fascist one: that featuring a *squadrista* thug rescuing a drowning Italy from the perilous waters of Bolshevism, which was produced in 1922 to celebrate the near-failure of the general strike of July and August (Fig. 4). If this picture is not actually a direct source, the two posters undoubtedly share the typically Fascist fixation with heroic deeds.[10] The apocalyptic, rather than rationally argued, slogan of the MSI poster – 'CON NOI PRIMA CHE SIA TROPPO TARDI' (Join us before it's too late) is an appropriate complement to the dramatic image, and recalls the desperate tone of the propaganda of the besieged Salò regime.[11]

Figure 4.1   'Help us defend you!'   MSI poster produced for the 1970 elections.

Figure 4.2 'Buy Italian goods' Fascist poster, c. 1935.

Figure 4.3 'Join us, before it's too late' MSI poster produced for the 1970 elections.

Figure 4.4 'Who saved Italy? fascism did!!' Poster produced by the Fascist Party in 1922 to celebrate the near-failure of the general strike of July–August.

After 1970, posters so blatantly reminiscent of those of the Fascist period were rarely produced.[12] The MSI, in fact, went out of its way to disguise its identity. To do so, it did not hesitate to plunder from the visual codes of ideological traditions quite different from its own, if it considered them capable of triggering positive associations. Hence the adoption of images drawn from Renaissance iconography and, paradoxically, from the visual propaganda of the radical left. We will begin by considering examples of the latter type of borrowing.

Left-wing images were often copied especially by the youth wing of the MSI, the *Fronte della Gioventù*. Let us take, for example, the recruitment poster of 1983 (Fig. 5). It depicts a group of young people demonstrating. The bottom section of the poster is a photograph, while the upper one is a stylised drawing featuring the outlines of six rows of people, together with a superimposed left-wing-sounding slogan: 'CO-STRUIAMO NELLE SCUOLE L'ALTERNATIVA CULTURALE PER CO-STRUIRE NEL PAESE L'ALTERNATIVA AL SISTEMA' (Let's build an alternative culture in the schools, in order to build an alternative system in the country). The section of the poster that is of greatest interest is the stylised image, for it is almost certainly based on a Cuban poster of the late 1960s (Fig. 6). Instead of the demonstrators, we see in the latter a tractor ploughing the earth from which words expressing the ideals of Castro's revolution sprout ('work ethics', 'worth', 'honesty', etc.), but the visual conception is the same, as the wavy strips and superimposed irregular lettering show. The idea of the outline of tightly knit rows of people – suggesting unity and solidarity – is derived from a well-known May 1968 poster. It is worth remarking that the neo-Fascist poster looks at first more left-wing than its Cuban source, on account of the dominant use of red and the very presence of the demonstrators. Only on closer inspection do we notice in the photograph the tricolours and the black banners, one of which carries the slogan 'DALLE SCUOLE, DALLE CITTÀ, SPAZZIAMO VIA IL COMUNISMO' (Let's rid our schools and our cities of Communism).

Equally inspired by the left is the poster produced by the *Fronte della Gioventù* in 1979, which depicts the riot police clubbing a demonstrator, and carries the caption: '345 detenuti di destra per motivi ideologici. NO ALLA REPRESSIONE DI REGIME. VEGLIA PER LA LIBERTÀ' (345 right-wingers detained for political reasons. Say no to the repression of the regime. Guard your freedom) (Fig. 7). The image is strongly reminiscent of those which the radical left has been using since 1968, in its press and posters, to denounce the violence of the State against its militant activists, and which were in turn inspired by a celebrated May 1968 poster (Fig. 8). Red is again the dominant colour, and it is worth noting that 'NO ALLA REPRESSIONE DI REGIME' echoes the French students' slogan 'Non à la répression'.

Let us also briefly look at a poster brought out in 1985 by the Italian Confederation of National Unions of Workers [*Confederazione Italiana Sindacati Nazionali Lavoratori*, CISNAL], the trade union affiliated to the MSI, to celebrate May Day (Fig. 9). In this case, the left-wing imitation concerns, first of all, the very nature of the festivity. Its commemoration by the MSI, which began in 1970 (a year after Almirante became leader of the party), is all the more surprising if we consider that the Fascists had banned it from their calendar of celebrations in 1924, to replace it with the *Festa del*

Lavoro (Labour Day). This was made to coincide with the date of the mythical foundation of Rome (21 April) to give the commemoration a 'constructive' and optimistic character, rather than the polemical one of the socialist May Day.[13] As for the picture used, the motif of the factory whose chimney coincides with the number one of May 1 is an adaptation of yet another May 1968 poster (Fig. 10).[14]

The aping of the visual language of the left is not entirely surprising. Cuban graphics and those of May 1968 enjoyed considerable popularity among young people, especially in the late 1960s and in the 1970s, partly because they were the product of movements which had fired their imagination, and partly on account of their originality. They became cult images, appreciated beyond the circles of those who shared their actual political messages.[15] The MSI's appropriation of these icons – as indeed of the jargon of the radical left, the so-called *sinistrese* (leftese),[16] and of such socialist festivities as May 1 and Women's Day – was essentially an attempt to project an up-to-date and youthful image.[17] It is worth adding that, in the 1980s (and early 1990s) the MSI put itself forward as the interpreter of social protest (protest against *partitocrazia*, i.e. the excessive power of Italian political parties, consumerism, unemployment, etc.). In particular, the *Fronte della Gioventù* made some overtures to left-wing youth.[18] The adoption of leftist modes was intended to facilitate such a dialogue.

The imitation of the left could serve a negative function too: that of making it difficult to distinguish between right-wing and left-wing propaganda, and thus emptying the latter of its radical content.[19]

Some left-wing graphics were appropriated by the MSI because their aggressiveness made them equally suitable to diametrically opposite ideological ends. A good example is the *Fronte della Gioventù* poster of the late 1970s featuring a fist crushing a 'Communist' snake (Fig. 11); it is clearly based on a Cuban poster of 1962 marking the ninth anniversary of the beginning of Castro's guerilla campaign against the Batista dictatorship (Fig. 12).

Let us now consider the MSI's use of Renaissance art as a source for its propaganda. The prestige enjoyed by this visual tradition made it a code suitable for expressing, in an acceptable manner, unpalatable messages. The imagery chosen tended to be of a religious nature. Clearly, this enabled the MSI to address itself to a wider audience – the type of audience which, consciously or unconsciously, reacts to it with awe, on account of their Catholic upbringing.

The first poster we shall examine was produced in 1980 as part of a campaign to introduce the death penalty for drug-trafficking (Fig. 13). It features the naked torso of a dead man lying on an unidentifiable object. His head is tilted backwards, while his right arm hangs down prominently across the lower half of the picture. The slogan beneath it reads: 'CHI TI DÀ LA DROGA TI DA LÀ MORTE. FIRMA CON NOI PER LA VITA' (Those who give you drugs give you death. Sign our petition if you want life). Now, it is not difficult to recognise in this figure the Christ of Michelangelo's Vatican *Pietà* (Fig. 14). The drawing is rudimentary (the right arm's connection to the torso and the torso itself are anatomically dubious), but it is clear that the author's intentions are 'artistic' rather than simply illustrative, as the use of hatching, its incompleteness (which gives it the appearance of a preparatory sketch), and the conspicuous presence of the author's signature indicate. The allusion to the *Pietà* has

Figure 4.5 'Let's build an alternative culture in the schools in order to build an alternative system in the Country', Recruitment poster of the youth league of the MSI, 1983.

Figure 4.6   Cuban poster promoting community values, late 1960s.

Figure 4.7 '345 right-wingers detained for political reasons. Say no to the repression of the regime. Guard your freedom' MSI poster protesting against the State's 'repression' of right-wing activists 1979.

Figure 4.8   May 1968 poster.

Figure 4.9   'May Day 1985: Work for everyone, so that it may become everyone's celebration'   Poster produced by CISNAL, the trade union affiliated to the MSI.

Figure 4.10   May 1968 poster.

Figure 4.11   'Stop Communism before it's too late!!!'   Poster produced by the youth league of the MSI, late 1970s.

Figure 4.12   Cuban poster commemorating the 9th anniversary of the beginning of Castro's guerilla campaign against Batista's dictatorship, 1962.

precise functions: it aims to hit the viewers both emotionally and 'artistically', to prevent them from considering lucidly the gravity of the proposal being put forward. The identification of the drug addict killed by an overdose with Christ also seems to imply that the enormity of the crime justifies a punishment as extreme as the death sentence.[20]

The slogan too needs to be commented upon, since, like the picture, it serves a mystificatory function. The text strikes one especially on account of its symmetrical structure, based on two equations linked to each other through a relation of opposition: drugs = death *versus* we (MSI) = life. This structure is emphasised by the spatial arrangement of the slogan. The two sentences are placed on different levels in the left-hand and right-hand sides respectively of the lower section of the poster. Each sentence is in turn split into two parts occupying two lines, in such a way as to draw attention to the key-words of the equations: 'drugs', 'death', 'we' and 'life'. The slogan also features a number of interrelated phonic effects: the alliteration of the 'd' in 'CHI TI DÀ LA DROGA', that of the 't' in 'MORTE' and 'VITA', that of the 'm' in 'MORTE' and 'FIRMA', and the anaphoric repetition 'TI DÀ'. Such rhetorical and structural virtuosities aim to solicit a consensus based on effect rather than argumentation.[21] The antithetical structure of the slogan also fulfils a euphemistic function. It idealistically opposes life to death, yet in actual fact demands that whoever causes death should be punished by death.

The iconography of the Passion occurs, in less obvious form, in a poster on the subject of terrorism, brought out in June 1974, just after the terrorist attack in *Piazza della Loggia* in Brescia, to refute accusations that the MSI was implicated (Fig. 15). It features a man in shirt sleeves, whose hands are crossed at the front and handcuffed, while his head is bowed. The colour of the plain background is red, no doubt to imply that it is because of Communist accusations that he had ended up in gaol. The caption reads: 'PUÒ ACCADERE ANCHE A TE!' (It can happen to you too!). The posture of the figure is based on the traditional iconography of the *Ecce homo*, which in fact depicts Christ with his hands tied and his head tilted forward (Fig. 16).[22] The reference to this episode of the Passion serves to present the MSI as a defenceless victim of persecution. The religious metaphor ultimately fulfils a euphemistic function, since there is no doubt that the party's denial of all involvement in the massacre would hardly have appeared credible if stated explicitly. The *Ecce homo* image, like the *Pietà* one in the previous poster, is, finally, also an implicit celebration of sacrifice – a theme dear to Fascist rhetoric.[23]

The placard round the protagonist's neck, with the writing 'ANTI-COMUNISTA', is also worthy of comment. It confirms that the picture is not purely realistic, but includes a symbolic dimension, since wrong-doers are no longer pilloried. The detail is a likely reference to the way the supporters of the Salò regime were humiliated after its fall, that is, to the ritual of exposing them to public insult with placards inscribed 'FASCISTA', 'AUSILIARIA' (i.e. member of the women's militia), etc. (Fig. 17). This reference to the past is probably intended to hint at the continuous persecution to which, allegedly, the extreme right has been subjected since the war.

The practice of including motifs which discreetly allude to the Fascist period, with the intention of establishing an uninterrupted link with it, recurred frequently in the

Figure 4.13 'Those who give you drugs give you death. Sign our petition if you want life' MSI poster calling for the introduction of death penalty for drug traffickers, 1980.

Figure 4.14 Michelangelo's *Pietà* (Vatican). Reproduced by kind permission of Plurigraf, Terni.

Figure 4.15 'It can happen to you too!' MSI poster produced shortly after the terrorist attack in *Piazza della Loggia* in Brescia, 1974.

Figure 4.16 Titian, *Ecce Homo* (National Gallery of Ireland, Dublin).

propaganda of the period under consideration, as the examples which follow will show.

We shall begin by considering a poster of 1970 depicting two men and a young woman walking arm in arm before a red, white and green rainbow (a less overtly patriotic version of the Italian flag) (Fig. 18). The subject matter of the poster is far from obvious. Umberto Eco has argued that the young woman represents her gender, while the two men stand for the middle class and the working class, and hint at the party's cross-class appeal and corporativism – hence their linked arms. Yet this explanation is unconvincing, because the two male figures' clothes do not denote specific professions or classes. The key to the interpretation of the poster is provided by the slogan 'NOSTALGIA DELL'AVVENIRE' (Nostalgia for the future), which asserts the MSI's intention of projecting itself into the future while drawing inspiration from the past,[24] as well as by the source of the composition. The latter is undoubtedly a propaganda postcard of the Salò Republic featuring two marines and an auxiliary of the submarine and motor-torpedo force 'X MAS' (as the badge with the Roman number "X" she wears indicates) (Fig. 19). We must conclude that the MSI poster was intended as a tribute to the last few months of the regime. Given Almirante's position in the MINCULPOP, it is likely that the idea of seeking inspiration from the war postcard originated directly from him. To him may also be ascribed the slogan 'NOSTALGIA DELL'AVVENIRE', since he used it in a party rally in April 1970.[25] The poster has a more overt meaning too. The figures probably represent two generations: the man in the middle stands for the older one, as his formal clothing indicates; while the young woman in a miniskirt and the man in jeans and casual jacket stand for the younger one. In a word, the three-some, who walk cheerfully with linked arms, and whose composition has been modelled on the war postcard, are the very embodiment of the slogan: they stress the continuity with the past and the perennial relevance of Fascist ideals.

Before examining other posters incorporating allusions of a nostalgic nature, it should be remarked that, ever since its foundation in 1946 by veterans of the Salò Republic, and in spite of the fact that the Constitution forbids the reorganisation of a Fascist party and the defence of Fascism, the MSI has revered and mythologised the *Ventennio*. Indeed, this cult is at the core of the party's identity.[26] It is worth recalling that the very acronym 'MSI' was devised because the first letter, as well as standing for 'Movimento', corresponded to Mussolini's famous monogram, while the remaining two, 'SI', were the qualifying initials of the *Repubblica Sociale Italiana*.[27] More recently, in 1986, the MSI chose to begin the celebration of the fortieth anniversary of its foundation with a rally entitled 'Italia domani' (Italy tomorrow) which was held at the *Teatro Lirico* in Milan – the very premises where Mussolini made his last speech on 16 December 1944. In his keynote address, Almirante alluded to the 'historic' significance of the location and stressed his party's loyalty to its roots. 'The past', he remarked, 'is embodied in our present and projects us into the future.'[28]

The party acronym and the event at the *Teatro Lirico* provide irrefutable evidence that the MSI delighted in referring to its origins. However, unlike these two instances, and as the *Ecce homo* and *Nostalgia dell'avvenire* posters suggest, the allusions to Fascism presented in the propaganda of the Almirante period aimed at the general

Figure 4.18   'Nostalgia for the future'   MSI poster produced for the 1970 elections.

Figure 4.19   Propaganda postcard of the Salò Republic, 1943–45.

Figure 4.20   MSI poster showing Almirante talking at a party rally in Rome, 1983.

Figure 4.21   Mussolini addressing a crowd from the balcony of *Palazzo Venezia,* Rome.

public tended to be covert, being addressed mostly to the initiated. The posters we are about to consider confirm such a view.

The Fascist past was frequently evoked through the way the leaders were portrayed. A poster of 1983 features Almirante in the foreground before a large audience (Fig. 20). The aim is to recall one of the canonical images of the *Ventennio*: that of the Duce haranguing one of his *adunate oceaniche* (or 'ocean-like gatherings', as the cheering crowds were hyperbolically referred to by the media) from the balcony of *Palazzo Venezia* in Rome (Fig. 21). It is an image which the Luce newsreels and the press (all of which was party-controlled) had popularised in the 1930s and 1940s.[29] All parties like to show that their leaders are charismatic, and it is undoubtedly true that the most effective way of doing so is by photographing the political figure together with the crowd from the place where he or she is standing. However, the iconography of the leader addressing a mass audience is so charged with Fascist connotations that in Italy no party other than MSI would have considered using it in a form of political communication as public as the poster. Similar representations of leaders occasionally appear in the press and promotional publications of other parties, but when they do, care is always taken to differentiate them from their Fascist counterpart – for instance by portraying the figures in unusual or informal attitudes, rather than in severe, dignified and rhetorical poses, and also by making it quite clear that the leader is speaking from a platform.[30] In the poster under consideration, Almirante too is speaking from a platform, but the photograph has been taken or cropped so as to give the impression that he is addressing his audience from the more exalted heights of a balcony.

Just like the ceremony marking the fortieth anniversary of the MSI's foundation, held, as we have seen, in the very premises where Mussolini delivered his last speech, the party's printed publicity alluded at times to specific events of the Fascist period. Let us consider a *Fronte della Gioventù* poster of 1974 inviting the public to vote 'yes' in favour of the abolition of the divorce law, in a referendum held on 12 May (Fig. 22). It sports the reiterated phrase 'ALT AL COMUNISMO' (stop Communism) printed in red, with a superimposed large, black 'SI' in the middle, complemented below by the explanatory phrase, printed in smaller characters: 'ALL'ABROGAZIONE DELLA LEGGE FORTUNA' (to the repeal of the Fortuna law).[31] This layout recalls that of a giant billboard which the Fascists erected in 1934, on the facade of *Palazzo Braschi*, the party's national headquarters in Rome, to urge people to vote 'yes' in a plebiscite for or against the list of new deputies proposed by the Great Council for the following parliamentary term (Fig. 23)[32] Here, it is the 'SI' that is reproduced in repeated form, while pride of place is ascribed to a stylised effigy of Mussolini. That the similarity between the two posters is not coincidental is shown by another poster produced by the MSI for the same occasion. It depicts a large 'SI' over which the following slogan has been printed: 'I COMUNISTI VOGLIONO FARE DEL REFERENDUM UN'ARMA PER IMPORRE IL LORO INGRESSO AL GOV-ERNO. GLI ITALIANI DEBBONO FARE DEL REFERENDUM UN PLEBI-SCITO CONTRO IL COMUNISMO' (The Communists want to use the referendum as a weapon to impose their entry into the government. The Italians must use the referendum as a plebiscite against Communism) (Fig. 24). Given that the word *plebiscito* is no longer used in Italian in this sense, we must conclude that the aim was

59

Figure 4.22 Poster produced by the youth league of the MSI to urge people to vote 'YES', i.e. in favour of the abolition of the divorce law, in the referendum of 1974.

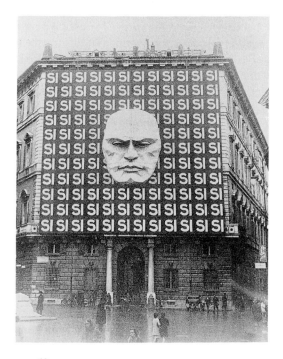

Figure 4.23 Fascist billboard on *Palazzo Braschi,* Rome, urging people to vote 'YES' , i.e. in favour of the list of parliamentary candidates proposed by the regime, in the plebiscite of 1934.

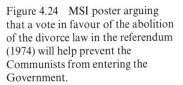

Figure 4.24 MSI poster arguing that a vote in favour of the abolition of the divorce law in the referendum (1974) will help prevent the Communists from entering the Government.

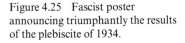

Figure 4.25 Fascist poster announcing triumphantly the results of the plebiscite of 1934.

to establish a wishful parallel with the plebiscite of 1934, when the 'SI' amounted to 96.25 per cent of the total vote – a result achieved partly through vote-rigging and systematic intimidation. The parallel was also appropriate because in both 1934 and 1974 the Communists campaigned for a 'no' vote (they could have advised people to abstain in 1934). The very fact that the referendum on divorce was taking place exactly forty years after the plebiscite must have been seen by the MSI, out of some kind of number mysticism, as a good omen. A final confirmation that the MSI poster just described contains a reference to Fascism is provided by the three-dimensional letters 'SI' with serifs: these have been copied from the poster produced by the Fascists to announce triumphantly the results of the plebiscite, and featuring a photomontage of Mussolini (Fig. 25).

An allusion to Fascism, albeit a generalised one, is also present in another anti-divorce poster. This features a young, modern and unconventional family; the woman wears a miniskirt, while the man sports a beard (a sign of anti-conformism, at the time) and carries a little girl on his shoulders (Fig. 26). Clearly, he is presented as an affectionate father – a far cry from the Rambo-like man depicted in a poster only four years earlier, urging the onlooker 'Help us defend you!'. The couple walks with a playful, synchronised gait. Now, it is precisely this last detail which lends itself to a second interpretation: it is in fact tempting to suggest that it is a reference to the goose step (Fig. 27). It should also be noted that the criss-crossing of the legs evokes the letter 'M', Mussolini's monogram; and, if we combine the 'M' with the 'SI' we obtain the acronym MSI.[33]

The next two posters we shall examine deal with the issue of terrorism. The first, dated 1975, depicts a *carabiniere* standing to attention before the tricolour (Fig. 29) – a picture quite probably inspired by the standard armed forces recruitment posters of the 1950s and 1960s.[34] A gun is pointed at his head by a 'Communist' (as the hammer and sickle on his cuff indicates). We naturally sympathise with him, not only because he is the defender of the nation's law and order, but because he is being treacherously attacked by the terrorist. However, a detail strikes one as odd: the military helmet. It is unexpected because it is not generally worn in peace-time. Its martial overtones are confirmed by the facial features of the *carabiniere*, which, on closer inspection, look familiar: the fleshy lips and prominent jaws recall Mussolini's legendary profile. The portrait of the *carabiniere* is in fact a fairly accurate copy of one of the official war portraits of the *Duce* (Fig. 30). It is arguable that the aim was to establish an implicit parallel between the execution of Mussolini by the Partisans in 1945, and the murder of representatives of law and order perpetrated by left-wing terrorists in the 1970s. The parallel also suggests, perhaps, that the violence and social anarchy which shook Italy in that decade is the direct consequence of the termination of Mussolini's 'firm' leadership.

The second poster we will focus upon was produced in 1970. It depicts a mother sheltering her child from the menacing hand of a 'red' terrorist (as the colour of his hand indicates). The text reads: 'LA DONNA TI DÀ LA VITA, IL TERRORISMO LA TOGLIE. CON LE DONNE DEL MSI–DN, CONTRO IL TERRORISMO' (Women give you life, terrorism takes it away. Join the women of the MSI–DN to combat terrorism) (Fig. 31). Like the poster urging the introduction of the death penalty and featuring a *Pietà*-like image, examined earlier, this one has a Manichean structure that inevitably presents a distorted view of reality. Women, the life-givers, are contrasted to death-bringing terrorists. This opposition is underlined by the visual arrangement of the first sentence: the text has been split into two parts, and each placed at opposite ends of the picture, near the detail it refers to. The claim that left-wing terrorism kills innocent women and children is gratuitous and meant to elicit facile outrage: 'Red' terrorists, in fact, tended to aim at specific targets (e.g. members of the establishment). Just as false is the idea, implied in the opposition, that terrorists are always male, as indicated by the examples of the Red Brigade terrorists Barbara Balzarani and Natalia Ligas, and of the member of the Armed Revolutionary Nuclei [*Nuclei Armati Rivoluzionari*, NAR] Francesca Mambro, who is serving a life sentence for her involvement in the Bologna Station massacre of 1980. But it is the picture that interests us most; this is because it has been copied from the poster of Salvatore Samperi's film *Cuore di mamma*, a political parable on contemporary violence and the breakdown of all values, whose main characters are a woman fascinated by all sorts of terrorism, and her three children, two of whom, budding Nazis, play sadistic games (Fig. 32).[35] The film poster must have appealed to the graphic artist of the MSI because the younger child featured in it wears an SS helmet (for obvious reasons, this detail has been excluded from the political poster). It is likely that the film itself impressed the artist, on account of its apocalyptic message (and perhaps for its extreme violence too). That the MSI should choose to proclaim the firm anti-terrorist stance of its women's caucus by secretly quoting from the poster featuring Samperi's sadistic heroine is disconcerting. At best it could be assumed that the quotation was intended as a generic reference to the party's origins, and not as a celebration of Nazism and terrorism. It should be noted that a period of ten years separates the MSI poster from its source; so in this case too, the allusion could not have been recognised by the general public, but is likely to have been known only to the party hierarchy and their immediate entourage.

The above is not the only example of the technique of appropriating and adapting a picture originally devised to deal critically with the subject of Fascism, in order cryptically to celebrate the *Ventennio*. Another is provided by a recruitment poster of the *Fronte della Gioventù*, dating from 1986, which carries the slogan 'IL TUO FUTURO LO PUOI COSTRUIRE SUBITO. CON NOI.' (You can build your future *now*. With us) (Fig. 33). It depicts the group's logo (a black hand clutching a torch with a tri-coloured flame) repeatedly, and so arranged symmetrically as to produce, depending on how one looks at it, an alternating horizontal effect or a diagonal pattern. The idea is very likely to have been borrowed from the specifically designed cover of a book by Adolfo Mignemi, entitled *Immagine coordinata per un impero. Etiopia 1935–36.* (A Corporate Image for an Empire. Ethiopia 1935–36), published by Gruppo Editoriale Forma, Turin, in 1984 (Fig. 34). This work deals with the propaganda produced by the regime to justify and promote the Ethiopian campaign, and intersperses official images arguing that the Italians were bringing civilisation to a backward country, with pictures of massacres carried out by the invaders. The book's implicit aim is to explode the myth that Italian imperialism was more 'humane' that its British and French counterparts. The reiterated motif on the book's cover (a motif also featured full-page, once) is actually a Blackshirt giving the Roman salute, rather than a torch; however, the general visual conception is the same. It

Figure 4.26 'Say yes to the family, say yes to life' Anti-divorce poster produced for the referendum of 1974.

Figure 4.27 Goose-stepping soldiers.

Figure 4.28 MSI poster produced for the local elections of 1972.

Figure 4.29 'For law and order, against violence'   MSI poster denouncing 'Communist' attacks against the police forces, 1975.

Figure 4.30   Wartime official portrait of Mussolini.

Figure 4.31 'Women give you life, terrorism takes it away. Join the women of the MSI–DN to combat terrorism' Poster produced by the women's caucus of the MSI, 1979.

Figure 4.32   Film poster for Salvatore Samperi's *Cuore di mamma* (Mother's heart), 1969.

Figure 4.33 'You can build your future *now*. With us'   Poster produced by the youth league of the MSI, 1986.

Figure 4.34   Cover design of Adolfo Mignemi's volume *Immagine coordinata per un impero. Etiopia 1935–1936* (published in 1984), which critically investigates the nature of Fascist propaganda during the Ethiopian campaign.

Figure 4.35 'Mussolini, man of the people' MSI poster commemorating the centenary of Mussolini's birth, 1983.

Figure 4.36 Poster produced by a self-styled 'Centre de Propagande anti-Bolscévique (sic), Genève', c. 1983.

should also be noted that the two motifs are not dissimilar: the man's black shirt is paralleled by the black, torch-clutching hand, and his outstretched arm is vaguely echoed by the rightwards-bending flame. The formal analogy with the youth group logo enables the latter to strengthen the poster's secret allusion to the book on the Ethiopian campaign – an allusion that points synecdochically to the Fascist period as a whole.

Not all the nostalgic references in the propaganda of the MSI of the Almirante period were expressed in concealed form. Some posters unambiguously celebrated Fascism. However, these were intended for purely internal consumption: they were used to decorate the walls of party branches and, presumably, the homes of some of the activists. Two posters, both featuring Mussolini, provide good examples of this genre. The first, issued in 1983 to commemorate the centenary of the Duce's birth, carries the caption 'MUSSOLINI UOMO DI POPOLO' (Mussolini, man of the people) (Fig. 35). The second poster, dating from around the same time and officially produced by a self-styled 'Centre de Propagande anti-Bolscévique (*sic*), Genève' (as a credit in small print along the left-hand margin of the poster declares), has a quotation from one of Mussolini's speeches/writings: 'Dovete sopravvivere e mantenere nel cuore la fede. Il mondo, me scomparso, avrà bisogno ancora dell'idea che è stata e sarà la più audace, la più originale e la più mediterranea ed europea delle idee. La storia mi darà ragione.' (You must survive and keep faith alive in your heart. The world, after I have gone, will still need the idea that has been and will be the most daring, the most original, and the most Mediterranean and European of all ideas. History will prove me right.) (Fig. 36).[36] It should be noted in passing that, though the poster commemorating Mussolini's centenary was not, as far as I am aware, posted up in public spaces, the actual commemorative events that were organised were given considerable visibility by the MSI. This proved feasible thanks to their 'cultural' nature. The main events were in fact a colloquium bearing the academic title of *L'Italia tra le due Guerre* (Italy between the Wars), which was held at the Castel Sant'Angelo, one of the leading sights of Rome, and twenty smaller conferences, organised in several cities along an *itinerario mussoliniano*.[37]

The logo that was devised for these commemorations is worth commenting on. It features a triple dove motif coloured red, white and green, whose outline echoes Mussolini's monogram (Fig. 37). This logo is yet another example of the MSI's opportunistic appropriation of the graphics of the contemporary left, and of its urge to refer to its own roots. Not only has Mussolini been associated with the symbol which alludes to the peace movement, but the incorporation of the doves into the letter 'M' is a cunning adaptation of a similarly designed Fascist motif, featuring, however, a different kind of bird – the imperial eagle (Figs 38, 39).

Posters with fairly explicit allusions to Fascism, evidently directed at the converted, did occasionally make a public appearance, but only in carefully selected locations: usually in the immediate proximity of party branches, where the activists were able to cast a vigilant eye and to ensure that they were not torn or defaced by indignant passers-by.[38] A good example of this type of propaganda is the poster brought out by the *Fronte della Gioventù* in 1985, featuring two youths with their right arms raised (Fig. 40). Though the picture is far from sharp (it is based on a much-enlarged photographic detail), there is little doubt that the white, amorphous blot to the left is

Figure 4.37 Logo of the MSI's commemorations of the centenary of Mussolini's birth, 1983.

Figure 4.38 Mussolini addressing a crowd. Location unknown, 1930s.

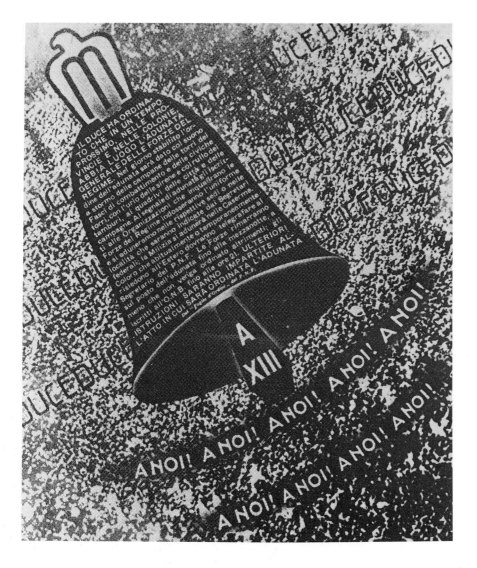

Figure 4.39 'A NOI!' (Roughly: 'We are the people') Fascist photo-montage, 1935.

the open palm of a Roman salute. In order to temper the strong Fascist connotations of the picture, the graphic artist has superimposed on the youths' arms an extended text that could equally well have featured on a poster or tract of the radical left:

FARE FRONTE:
• Per una cultura aldilà dei vecchi schemi
• per la sperimentazione e la creatività didattica
• per la partecipazione studentesca diretta
• per superare la burocrazia dei Decreti Delegati favorendo forme spontanee di rappresentanza

(LET'S STAND TOGETHER:
• for a truly innovative type of culture
• for pedagogic experimentation and creativity
• for direct student participation
• to defeat the bureaucratised staff–student–parent committees, and replace them with spontaneous forms of representation)

In conclusion, the MSI propaganda of the 1970s and 1980s underwent great transformations. The macho-militaristic images of direct Fascist inspiration were replaced by others borrowed from a number of 'alien' sources, such as Renaissance iconography and the fashionable graphics of the radical left, principally in the hope that they might make the party more acceptable. When, as was frequently the case, Fascist images or images alluding to the Fascist period were used, they were manipulated and camouflaged in order to look 'innocent' and contemporary to a general audience. The MSI's urge to refer to its origins, and the practice of doing so in a coded, even esoteric, form, require some general comments.

The cult of the past is one of the features that best characterises the extreme right. Most parties – indeed most societies – consider the past as a model for the present, but their devotion to tradition tends to be accompanied by the awareness of a need for innovation and change. The right, on the other hand, obsessed as it is by its quest for stability and by its dissatisfaction with the present, clings to its roots resolutely.[39] The MSI's veneration of Fascism should also be ascribed to the violent suppression of the movement, and in particular to Mussolini's tragic end. 'Martyrdom' inevitably leads to mythologisation.

The realisation that the party needed to project a modern image if it was to survive, and the Italian Constitution's ban on the reorganisation of Fascism frustrated the MSI's urge to declare its unwavering devotion to past ideals. Hence the creation of visual propaganda incorporating two levels of meaning: an overt one, aimed at the public at large, respectable and above board, and a hidden one, nostalgic in tone, intended essentially to fulfil an existential need (the proud self-declaration of the party's identity), but also to reassure the *cognoscenti* that, in spite of what appearances suggest, Fascism had not been repudiated.

Some of the nostalgic allusions are so outrageous (e.g. the goose step in the poster of 1974, and the portrait of Mussolini in that of 1975), that it is tempting to treat them as typically Fascist acts of bravado. They challenged the Constitution and attempted

Figure 4.40 'For student counter-power' Poster produced by the youth league of the MSI, 1985.

to prove that they could make a mockery of a mightier opponent on its own ground.[40]

As already noted, the hidden references to Fascism of the MSI were intended for very small audiences. Those in the *Nostalgia dell'avvenire* poster, and in the poster featuring the *carabiniere* standing to attention may have been recognised by some war veterans, but the allusions to the plebiscite of 1934, incorporated in the anti-divorce poster (which, it should be recalled, was produced by the *Fronte della Gioventù*, and thus aimed at a generation born *after* the fall of Fascism), and to Samperi's film in the anti-terrorism poster, are esoteric to the point that only the party cadres could possibly have been aware of them.

The existential need to affirm one's identity and the bravado spirit only partly account for this surprising approach to propaganda. The taste for 'secret' messages should also be connected to the party's generally circumspect attitude to the 'outside world' – an attitude resulting from its past marginalisation.[41]

The propaganda output of the post-Almirante period is, generally speaking, considerably blander than anything that has been examined so far. The demise of Communism, which led to the weakening of ideological conflict, and the MSI's eagerness to project a respectable image do not entirely explain the nondescript character of the posters. The MSI's abandonment of its distinct persuasive approach, mainly based, as we have seen, on the use of politically and emotionally charged figurative languages borrowed from various sources, is on a par with the process occurring in other parties with strong visual traditions (the Communists and the Christian Democrats in particular) for some time.

The practice of 'secretly' alluding to Fascism also virtually disappeared from the MSI graphic propaganda of the late 1980s and early 1990s. It would be rash to interpret this as a sign of the party's desire to turn over a new leaf. It is worth recalling that the present leader, Gianfranco Fini, first appointed Party Secretary in December 1987, was Almirante's heir apparent. The 'declaration of intent' Fini presented to support his own candidature at the special congress held in Sorrento argued that 'Fascism was a part of the history of Italy and the expression of permanent values'.[42] As for Pino Rauti, who led the MSI from January 1990 to June 1991, he is steeped in the ethical and political culture of the Salò Republic. It is tempting to suggest that after 1987, the MSI no longer considered it necessary to make subtle allusions to its origins because the increasingly relaxed and 'tolerant' political climate allowed it to come out into the open. The triumphal launch, in 1992, of Alessandra Mussolini – a failed starlet who had hitherto shown no interest in politics – was the most striking expression of the party's new unabashed attitude to the outside world: while her glamorous looks were intended to suggest 'modernity', her genetic make-up proclaimed the MSI's unremitting allegiance to Fascism.[43] The huge and much-publicised rally in the centre of Rome, called in October 1992 to protest against corruption, *partitocrazia* and fiscal policies, provides further evidence that the MSI was not above parading its identity: thousands of demonstrators, many of them wearing black shirts, raised their arms in a Roman salute and chanted '*Duce! Duce!*' as they passed beneath the balcony of *Palazzo Venezia,* while Alessandra Mussolini, in a move calculated to capture media attention, shouted '*Grazie, nonno!*' (Thanks, granddad!).[44]

This new 'confidence' probably explains why, occasionally, posters with strong Fascist overtones of the type that only a few years earlier would only have been for

Figure 4.41   Poster produced by a youth group close to the MSI to advertise a three-day event on 'Rome and the many ways of being patriotic', 1993.

internal consumption enjoyed a more public life. One such poster is that produced in 1993 by a youth group close to the MSI, called *Comunità nel Territorio* (Community in the Land)[45] to advertise a 'Festa delle comunità nazionalpopolari' (Festival of national-popular communities). This three-day event, which took place in Rome's Castel Sant'Angelo, bore the title of *Roma e i tanti modi di dire patria* (Rome and the many ways of being patriotic).[46] The theme of Rome, one especially dear to Fascist and neo-Fascist mythology,[47] led the graphic artist to illustrate the poster with a picture of fully armed, muscular Roman soldiers, in the macho-heroic style that typified some of the propaganda of the pre-Almirante period (Fig. 41).

Interestingly, the MSI's launching of *Alleanza Nazionale* (AN), an allegedly modern, moderate and democratic right-wing grouping open to the centre, early in 1994,[48] has resulted in a return to the earlier practice of including subtle references to Fascism in the printed propaganda. An examination of the posters produced for the March 1994 parliamentary elections – the first of the Second Republic – shows a recurrent use of the Roman salute, in variously disguised forms. This most Fascist of all signs appears quite clearly (though, strangely, it has gone totally unnoticed) in the poster featuring the leader of AN himself (Fig. 42). The square incorporating Fini's portrait is cut diagonally into two parts. The upper 'triangle' is filled by a portion of the European flag – a gratuitous element that must have been included to enhance the status of the party. As for the lower part, the background features an arm that incongruously extends from Fini's left shoulder. The detail is not immediately recognisable because it is blurred, and because the area beneath the elbow and that between the inner curve of the arm and the left side of Fini's face have been filled in with amorphous elements whose likely aim is to confuse the ordinary viewers, in turning their attention away from the outrageous detail. That the 'raised arm' behind Fini's back should be interpreted as a Fascist salute, rather than viewed as a totally incidental and innocent element of the background, is indicated by the fact that the full picture is not a single photograph, but a collage. Only this proposed interpretation of the arm could justify the distracting presence of incongruous additions.[49]

Another AN poster which, arguably, features a disguised Roman salute is that which advertised Fini's election rally in Milan (Fig. 43). The picture features Ignazio La Russa – the local party leader – holding up Fini's right hand in an attitude of anticipated electoral triumph.[50] Because this gesture is extremely unusual in Italy in a political context, it is reasonable to suggest that it was intended to allude to Fascism.

A similar coded meaning may be proposed for the rhetorical gesture which Franco Servello makes in the election poster advertising his candidature for the Senate (Fig. 44).[51] The open hand that clumsily emerges from the foreground is too striking a motif to be unintentional.

To lend further support to these interpretations, it is worth pointing out that raised arms and open hands do not feature in the posters produced by other parties for the same elections.[52] In fact, arms and hands are very rarely shown in Italian political posters. Only the head and shoulders of the candidate are usually visible. When their arms are also depicted, they are crossed (i.e. arranged in a 'neutral' position), or associated with items connoting specific qualities: for instance, a book indicates that the candidate is an intellectual, and a dog suggests a trustworthy person, as well as an animal lover.[53]

Figure 4.42 'A Right ready to govern. At last. To rebuild Italy' *Alleanza Nazionale* poster produced for the 1994 parliamentary elections, featuring the party leader Gianfranco Fini. 'finalmente' is a pun.

Figure 4.43 'The New Italy is growing' *Alleanza Nazionale* poster produced during the 1994 parliamentary election campaign to advertise Gianfranco Fini's party rally in Milan. Fini is featured with Ignazio (Benito) La Russa, the local party leader.

Figure 4.44 'A safe choice' *Alleanza Nazionale* poster (first on the left) promoting the candidature of Franco Servello for the parliamentary elections of 1994.

The revived practice of disguising references to Fascism in the graphic propaganda clearly conflicts with AN's claims that it is a modern and 'respectable' right-wing party. These allusions are, in fact, a direct consequence of the 'transformations' undergone by the MSI. Forced to shed all outward signs of Fascism, after the electoral pact formed with Silvio Berlusconi's *Forza Italia* and Umberto Bossi's Northern League, and yet unwillingly to sever its links with Fascism, AN could only assert its identity by stealth.[54] The tension is not just between tradition and innovation, but between assertiveness and secretiveness.

Notes

* I wish to express my gratitude to the Italian Institute in London, whose financial support made the research for this chapter possible. I must also thank the staff of the Library of the *Istituto Gramsci* of Bologna, and Dr Fausto Sacchelli in particular, for their invaluable assistance.

1. On the MSI, see Roberto Chiarini's chapter in this volume, as well as: P. Ignazi, *Il polo escluso. Profilo del Movimento Sociale Italiano*, Il Mulino, Bologna, 1989; G. Tassani, 'The Italian Social Movement: from Almirante to Fini', in R. Nanetti and R. Catanzaro (eds), *Italian Politics – A Review*, Vol. IV, Pinter, London, 1990, pp. 124–45; F. Sidoti, 'The Extreme Right in Italy: Ideological Orphans and Countermobilisation', in P. Hainsworth (ed.), *The Extreme Right in Europe and the USA*, Pinter, London, 1992, pp. 151–74; P. Furlong, 'The Extreme Right in Italy: Old Orders and Dangerous Novelties', *Parliamentary Affairs*, XLV(3), 1992, pp. 345–56. In January 1994, the MSI launched *Alleanza Nazionale,* about which see below.

2. The full text of the speech was published in the *Secolo d'Italia* (the party's official newspaper) on 7 April 1970, p. 3.

3. The MSI hoped to win power by making the ever-weaker governments of the Christian-Democrat Party dependent on its support.

4. Ph. Cannistraro, *La fabbrica del consenso. Fascismo e mass media*, Laterza, Bari, 1975, pp. 326–33.

5. On the MSI's attempts to modernise its image in the 1980s, see especially G. Rossi, 'C'eravamo tanto odiati. Almirante spiega cosa è cambiato tra MSI e governo', *La Repubblica*, 11 Nov. 1983, p. 4; P. Franchi, 'In fondo, a destra . . .', *Panorama*, 17 Feb. 1989, pp. 47–52; C. Incerti, 'Giovanni delle bande nere', *Panorama*, 21 April 1985, pp. 62–3; S. Messina, 'MSI, la possibilità di essere normale', *La Repubblica*, 10 June 1987, p. 10. As far as the linguistic updating is concerned, see: M. Dardano, *Il linguaggio dei giornali italiani*, Laterza, Bari, 1981, 2nd edn, pp. 270–80; M. Revelli, 'Panorama editoriale e temi culturali della destra militante' and O. Calabrese, 'I linguaggi delle destre', in *Fascismo oggi. Nuova destra e cultura reazionaria negli anni ottanta*, special issue of the *Notiziario dell'Istituto Storico della Resistenza in Cuneo e Provincia*, No. 23, June 1983, pp. 51, 57–8, 63 and pp. 126–7 respectively. The party's modernisation also concerned its internal organisation: see Ignazi, *Il polo escluso*, cit., pp. 140–2.

6. I owe the information that the MSI relied on its activist artists to the kindness of Signora Sala of the party's Propaganda Department in Rome, who also explained to me that the poster designs were often chosen from entries submitted to specially organised competitions. The obvious danger of such a system is that of unprofessionalism. This was implicitly recognised in 1986 by the then official in charge of the publicity of the party, Domenico

Mennitti, in an unpublished paper, 'Il Partito e la sua immagine', delivered at the conference of the MSI, held in Taormina. While calling for greater professionalism in the presentation of political messages, and drawing attention to the need for a 'corporate image', Mennitti also strongly argued against the dominant tendency to commission party publicity from commercial advertising agencies, on the ground that politics should not be sold to the public like a brand of washing powder. Such 'purist' views have a familiar ring, of course. They were shared by the Italian Left (the Communist Party in particular) until the mid-1970s, and by the British Labour Party until the early 1980s.

7. It is true that, as Dominique Memmi has shown in *Du récit en politique. L'affiche électorale italienne*, Presses de la Fondation Nationale des Sciences Politiques, Paris, 1986, pp. 96–7, 100–1, parties which rely on advertising agencies work closely with them anyway, and have the final say in the designs. However, a collaboration of this nature might have proved problematic if attempted by the MSI. It is arguable that the party preferred to turn to its own propagandists because it might have found it difficult, or at least embarrassing, to convince an 'outsider' to devise publicity that referred to Fascism and, as with one of the posters analysed below, even Nazism.

8. See A. C. Quintavalle, 'Il modello', in M. G. Lutzemberger and S. Bernardi (eds), *Cultura, comunicazioni di massa, lotta di classe*, Savelli, Rome, 1976. p. 25.

9. A. C. Quintavalle (ed.), *Nero a strisce. La reazione a fumetti*, University of Parma, 1971; U. Eco, 'Fascio e fumetto ('Eja, Eja! Gulp!)', in *Il costume di casa*, Bompiani, Milan, 1973, pp. 183–93.

10. The MSI poster (as well as its possible source) lends itself to being analysed in the light of the scheme of standard narrative functions which Vladimir Propp identified in folktales. The sequence of events that are condensed in the picture may be expressed as follows: There is a danger (Communism), and a defenceless being (Italy) has fallen victim to it. However, a hero, whose special powers derive from his talisman-like flag (Fascist ideology), rescues him, thus triumphing over Evil. It is worth noting in passing that the Christian-Democrat propaganda of the Cold War period was similarly structured. See A. C. Quintavalle 'La fiaba "manifesta" ', in D. Audino and G. Vittori (eds), *Via il regime della forchetta. Autobiografia del PCI nei primi anni '50 attraverso i manifesti elettorali*, Savelli, Rome, 1976 (unpaginated). Mythical stories of the type just outlined have an easy appeal. The general public is favourably predisposed to them not only through its familiarity with the fairy-tale tradition, but because much of the mass culture too (the popular weeklies, commercial cinema, comics, etc.) is constructed along the same lines. See A. C. Quintavalle (ed.), *La bella addormentata. Morfologia e struttura del settimanale italiano*, University of Parma, 1972.

11. On the propaganda of the Italian Social Republic, see G. Vittori (ed.), *C'era una volta il Duce. Il regime in cartolina*, Savelli, Rome, 1975; R. Guerri, *Manifesti italiani della Seconda Guerra Mondiale*, Rusconi, Milan, 1982; Various Authors, *1943–45. L'immagine della RSI nella propaganda*, Mazzotta, Milan, 1985. Interestingly, the same apocalyptic approach has been used by the British extreme right. A National Front poster of 1983, featuring a map of Britain made up of a photo-montage of aggressive-looking black people, carried the slogan 'WHILE THERE'S TIME'. Clearly, the similarity with the MSI slogan was not due to direct influence, but to both parties' isolation – a condition that led them to adopt a persuasive strategy based on hyperbole and doom-mongering in order to attract attention.

12. Macho imagery more or less disappeared from MSI propaganda. When it recurred, it was always tempered by graphic stylisation. See, for instance, the poster dated *c.* 1975 which accuses the government of 'stealing' and squandering tax-payers' money. It depicts a simply drawn, literally square-chested 'hunk' pulling out his empty pockets to show that he has

been fleeced by the State. For an illustration, see O. Calabrese (ed.), *Italia Moderna. IV, 1960–80: La difficile democrazia*, Electa, Milan, 1985, p. 57.

Though heroic and military themes no longer featured in pictorial form in the posters, they recurred in the slogans. See, for instance, the following: 'PER LA TUA SALVEZZA, IL NOSTRO CORAGGIO' (For your salvation, you need our courage), 1972; 'IL VOTO DEL 15 GIUGNO È IL VOTO DELLA SALVEZZA' (The vote of 15 June is the vote of salvation), 1975; 'SALVARE LA SCUOLA DAL COMUNISMO' (Save the schools from Communism), 1976; 'ELETTORE ANTICOMUNISTA, LA DC TI TRADISCE. VOTA A DESTRA E GLIELO IMPEDIRAI' (Anti-Communist voter: the Christian Democrat party is betraying you. Vote for the Right to prevent it.), 1976; 'LA DC SI ARRENDE AL COMUNISMO. LA DESTRA MAI!' (The Christian Democrat Party is giving in to Communism. The Right will never do that!), 1979; 'CARLO ALBERTO DALLA CHIESA. ASSASSINATO DALLA MAFIA, TRADITO DAL REGIME. GLI ITALIANI TI VENDICHERANNO' (Carlo Alberto Dalla Chiesa. Murdered by the Mafia, betrayed by the regime. The Italians will avenge you.), 1982. (Dalla Chiesa was the prefect of Palermo.)

13. M. Massara, C. Schirinzi and M. Sioli, *Storia del Primo Maggio*, Longanesi, Milan, 1978, pp. 119–214. In spite of its abolition by the Fascists, May 1 continued to be commemorated clandestinely. See L. Casali, 'Il Primo Maggio proibito, 1923–1943', in G. D. Donno (ed.), *Storie e immagini del 1° Maggio*, Lacaita, Manduria–Bari–Rome, 1990, pp. 113–138.

14. For a few other examples of MSI posters inspired by left-wing graphics, see L. Cheles, '"Dolce Stil Nero"? Images of Women in the Graphic Propaganda of the Italian NeoFascist Party', in Z. Barański and S. Vinall (eds), *Women and Italy. Essays on Gender, Culture and History*, Macmillan, London, 1991, pp. 75–79, 85–88, Plates 20–27.

15. On Cuban graphics and their cult, see esp.: D. Sterner (ed.), *The Art of Revolution*, Pall Mall Press, London, 1970 (with an excellent introduction by Susan Sontag); D. Kunzle, 'Uses of the Che Poster', *Art in America*, September–October 1975, pp. 66–72. On the graphics of May 1968, see M. Rohan, *Paris, '68. Graffiti, posters, newspapers and films of the events of May 1968*, Impact Books, London, 1988.

16. The widespread prestige enjoyed by *sinistrese* during the years of social unrest was due to its association with the student and trade union movements, considered at the time as the intellectual and political vanguards. On *sinistrese*, see especially P. Violi, *I giornali dell'estrema sinistra*, Garzanti, Milan, 1977; M. A. Cortellazzo, *Il linguaggio dei movimenti di contestazione*, Giunti-Marzocco, Florence, undated [1980]; A. Martin and M. A. Cortellazzo, *Il linguaggio politico-sindacale*, Giunti-Marzocco, Florence, undated [1980]. For the MSI's borrowings from the jargon of the left, see Dardano's, Revelli's and Calabrese's works, cited in note 5, above.

17. The need to modernise the party's image by imitating the left, whose language had achieved a hegemonic position, is implied in Almirante's statement of 1969, quoted at the beginning of this chapter. The term 'language' may be extended to cover all forms of political communication.

18. See P. Ignazi, 'Il MSI partito della protesta', *Il Mulino*, XXXVII, 1988, pp. 633–51, and *idem, Il polo escluso*, cit., pp. 197–238.

19. In December 1975, the MSI's misappropriation of left-wing phrases prompted a students' organisation in Padua to denounce the practice and its mystificatory aims with a poster. See M. A. Cortellazzo, 'Note sulla lingua dei volantini', *Versus. Quaderni di studi semiotici*, X, 1975, p. 77. It is worth noting that a similar manipulative technique had been used by Mussolini, who, originally a Socialist, was quite familiar with Marxist jargon. See P. Agosto, 'The Language of Mussolini', *The Italianist*, I, 1981, pp. 60–1. The appropriation of left-wing commemorations by the extreme right has a most notable precedent in Hitler's proclamation of May Day as a national festivity, in 1933. By obliging workers to take part

in the spectacular parades stage-managed by Goebbels together with the Nazis, he effect-ively transformed a revolutionary day of class struggle into one of class collaboration. See U. Achten, *Illustrierte Geschichte des 1. Mai*, Asso Verlag, Oberhausen, 1985, pp. 262–77, and U. Achten, M. Reichert and R. Schultz, *Mein Vaterland ist international. Internationale illustrierte Geschichte des 1. Mai, 1886 bis Heute*, Asso Verlag, Oberhausen, 1986, pp. 57–8, which also reproduces (p. 57) a satirical photomontage by Heartfield showing Goebbels applying a false bushy beard to Hitler's face to make him look like Marx. To mention a more recent example of appropriation, it will be recalled that on the eve of the French presidential elections of 1988, Le Pen brought forward the *Front National*'s traditional Joan of Arc festivities (23 April) by eight days in order to celebrate May 1 in competition with the left. See *Le Monde*, 2 May 1988, pp. 1, 6 and 16.

20. Michelangelo's *Pietà* had been used before in Italian political propaganda, for equally manipulative ends. A Christian-Democrat poster of 1957 commemorating the anniversary of the Liberation (25 April) depicts a Madonna-like woman mourning the semi-naked body of a young partisan lying across her lap. An extended caption urges the public not to forget that it owes its liberty to her son's sacrifice, and calls for all-out opposition to 'Communist dictatorship'. The aim of this thinly disguised *Pietà* image and its complementary text is clearly to deny the Communist Party its hegemonic role in the anti-Fascist resistance struggles. For an illustration of the poster, see C. Dané (ed.), *Parole e immagini della Democrazia Cristiana*, Broadcasting & Background, Rome, 1985 (unpaginated). The Christian Democrats used to rely fairly systematically on Christian iconography for propaganda purposes. They virtually abandoned this practice in the late 1950s, when they realised that the rapid secularisation of Italian society had considerably weakened the persuasive power of such images, and revived it briefly only during the campaigns for the referenda on divorce and abortion to give them a crusade-like character. See L. Cheles, 'L'uso delle immagini rinascimentali nell'iconografia del manifesto politico', in R. Varese (ed.), *Letture di storia dell'arte*, Il Lavoro Editoriale, Ancona–Bologna, 1988, pp. 49–50. Only the MSI continued to believe in the political effectiveness of religious imagery.

21. Inevitably, one is reminded of Mussolini's high-flown rhetorical style, about which see especially G. Lazzari, *Le parole del fascismo*, Argileto, Rome, 1975; A. Simonini, *Il linguaggio di Mussolini*, Bompiani, Milan, 1977; E. Leso, M. A. Cortellazzo, I. Paccagnella and F. Foresti, *La lingua italiana e il Fascismo*, Consorzio Provinciale di Pubblica Lettura, Bologna, 1977; P. Agosto, *La semantica del potere*, Ph.D. thesis, Sheffield City Polytechnic, 1980; K. Ille, *Politische Sprache im Dienst der Gewalt. Untersuchungen zu Production und Rezeption faschistischer und neofaschistische Texte,* Ph.D. thesis, University of Vienna, 1980.

 It is interesting to note that, in his conference paper 'Il partito e la sua immagine' (see note 6 above), Mennitti stated quite candidly that in political communication *impressione*, which was 'by its very nature tied to the emotional sphere of the unconscious', was just as important as *convincimento*, which was 'based on the rational logic of argumentation'. Mennitti's dichotomy seems to echo that expressed by Mussolini in a celebrated interview with Emil Ludwig, when he argued that, in addressing the masses, one should bear in mind that the 'mystical' element was as essential as the 'political' one. See E. Ludwig, *Colloqui con Mussolini*, Mondadori, Milan, 1965, p. 131. Mennitti, incidentally, has of late become Silvio Berlusconi's political adviser and staff coordinator. See G. Quaranta, 'Nati con la camicia. Nera', *L'Espresso*, 22 April 1994, p. 52.

22. On the iconography of the *Ecce homo*, see L. Réau, *Iconographie de l'art chrétien*, Presses Universitaires de France, Paris, 1957, vol. II, pp. 459–60.

23. On the Fascist ethos of sacrifice, which derives precisely form the Christian dialectic of death and resurrection, see M. A. Ledeen, *The First Duce. D'Annunzio at Fiume*, The Johns

Hopkins University Press, Baltimore, 1977, pp. 19–20, 202–3; G. L. Mosse, 'The Poet and the Exercise of Political Power: Gabriele D'Annunzio', in *Masses and Man. Nationalist and Fascist Perceptions of Reality*, Howard Fertig, New York, 1980, pp. 92–7. See also: U. Eco, 'La voglia di morte', in *Sette anni di desiderio. Cronache 1977–1983*, Bompiani, Milan, 1983, pp. 123–5. It should be noted that not all the Christian imagery which the MSI uses is centred on the Passion; some of the posters aimed at a female audience rely on Renaissance representations of the Virgin. See L. Cheles, ' "Dolce Stil Nero"? ', cit., pp. 69–71, Plates 8–10, 12, 13.

24. This past–future dialectic parallels Mussolini's exaltation of the Roman past, and his call to imitate it in order to achieve future greatness. See: N. Tranfaglia, 'Il capo e le masse. L'esempio di Mussolini', in *Labirinto italiano. Il fascismo, l'antifascismo, gli storici*, La Nuova Italia, Florence, 1989, p. 51. On the Roman myth during Fascism, see below, note 47.

25. See *Il Secolo d'Italia*, 7 April 1970, p. 3.

26. The reverence I am talking about is of a general, mostly emotional nature. The question of the MSI's actual ideological and cultural debts to Fascism is in fact quite complex, because of the faction-riven nature of the party, and, of course, of Fascism itself. See D. Cofrancesco, 'Le destre radicali davanti al Fascismo', in P. Corsini and L. Novati (eds), *L'eversione nera. Cronache di un decennio (1974–1984)*, Franco Angeli, Milan, 1985, pp. 57, 134; M. Revelli, 'La RSI e il neofascismo italiano', in P. P. Poggio (ed.), *La Repubblica Sociale Italiana, 1943–45* (proceedings of the Brescia conference, 4–5 October 1985), Brescia, 1986, pp. 417–30; P. Ignazi, 'La cultura politica del Movimento Sociale Italiano', in *Rivista di Scienza politica*, XIX, 3, 1989, pp. 431–65.

27. The genesis of the party's name was described by Alfredo Cucco, a former member of the National Directory of the Fascist Party and an under-secretary in the Salò Republic, in the preface to A. M. La Grua's *Lo Stato Nazionale del Lavoro nella vocazione del MSI*. The relevant passage is quoted in Revelli, 'La RSI e il neofascismo', cit., p. 424.

28. For Almirante's speech at the *Teatro Lirico,* see *Il Secolo d'Italia*, 28 Jan. 1986, pp. 1, 3. Mussolini's last speech was especially close to the MSI leader's heart. In an interview he described it as 'one of his most beautiful'. See F. Nirenstein, 'Almirante – una vita vista da destra'. *Epoca*, 5 Feb. 1987, p. 98.

29. On the ritual of the speech from the balcony, which originated from D'Annunzio, and its iconography, see: M. Isenghi, 'Iconografia della stampa fascista', in *Intellettuali militanti e intellettuali funzionari. Appunti sulla cultura fascista*, Einaudi, Turin, 1979, pp. 176, 179; G. L. Mosse, 'Public Festivals: The Theatre and Mass Movements', in *The Nationalization of the Masses*, Howard Fertig, New York, 1975, pp. 109–10; M. A. Ledeen, *The First Duce*, cit., pp. 3, 8; N. Tranfaglia, 'Il capo e le masse', cit., pp. 41–53.

30 It should be noted that MSI leaders were represented formally in the party's propaganda; their actual behaviour at party rallies also tended to be stiff and solemn. See P. Leone, *Lo spettacolo della politica*, Editoriale Bios, Cosenza, 1987, p. 117.

31. Fortuna was the Socialist MP who introduced the divorce Bill. On the referendum, which the MSI fought alongside the Christian Democrats (an opportunity it was eager to seize in order to come back to the political arena as a legitimate political force), see M. Clark, D. Hine and R. E. M. Irving, 'Divorce – Italian Style', *Parliamentary Affairs*, XXVII, 1974, pp. 333–58.

32. On the plebiscite of 1934, see R. De Felice, *Mussolini il duce. I. Gli anni del consenso, 1929–1936*, Einaudi, Turin, 1974, pp. 311–13.

33. A pun not unlike that on the anti-divorce poster was featured on a poster produced for the local elections of 1972 (Fig. 28); here the 'M' in 'DESTRA NAZIONALE MSI' was coloured differently so that the party's name could be read as the slogan 'DESTRA

NAZIONALE MSI, SI' (say 'yes' to Destra Nazionale MSI).' (The phrase 'Destra Nazionale' was added to the name of the MSI in 1972, when the Monarchists were incorporated into the party.) The opposition too has exploited the punning possibilities afforded by the acronym. An alternative magazine of the early 1970s, *Ca Balà*, urged its readers to 'neutralise' neo-Fascist grafitti by modifying the letters 'MSI' daubed on walls into 'MNO'. See the illustrations in R. Cirio and P. Favari (eds), *L'altra grafica*, Bompiani, Milan, 1972, p. 142.

34. By the early 1970s, the military-men-standing-to-attention motif looked pathetically out-dated on account of its unabashed patriotism; hence its replacement with pictures stressing the armed forces' high-tech equipment and training. Clearly, it is precisely this patriotic quality that made it so appealing to the MSI. On the theme of the serviceman standing before the flag and its 'lay' use, see Roland Barthes's *Mythologies*, Paladin, London, 1973, pp. 116 ff.

35. On this film, see G. Grazzini, *Eva dopo Eva. La donna nel cinema italiano*, Laterza, Bari, 1980, pp. 118–19.

36. Both types of posters were offered to me in a number of MSI branches I visited in 1985.

37. Giuseppe Ciarrapico's introduction to the proceedings claims that 'the *Castel Sant'Angelo* meeting was characterised by papers following a strictly historical approach', while the other conferences were 'dominated by the contributions of right-wing intellectuals and politicians, who wished to reconstruct the life and works of Mussolini motivated by scholarly rather than propaganda purposes'. See *Mussolini nel centenario della nascita*, Ciarrapico Editore, Rome, 1985, p. 9. However, apart from the contributions of two serious historians, Renzo de Felice and James Gregor, who were no doubt invited so that they could bring prestige and academic respectability to the events, the proceedings are totally apologetic and hagiographic.

38. The more remote the location of the party branch, the greater would be the density and 'hardness' of the posters on public display. In Bologna, for instance, such posters were to be found on the walls of *vicolo Posterla*, a long and narrow side-road, half-way along which were the offices of the MSI. In spite of its central location, the party exercised such 'control' over it that in the politically troubled 1970s, it was practically a no-go area.

39. As the political philosopher Norberto Bobbio has put it:

> The sense and cult of tradition are [for the extreme right] a constant, passionate and emotionally-felt rather than rationally-justified reference to the past – a past that must be relived and in which one must mirror oneself. Little it matters if this is the kitsch Roman empire of the Fascists with their massed legions, the crude blood and soil communities of the Germanic peoples, or quite simply the *ancien régime*. Every reactionary right has its own past – a past more or less remote, mythical or historical, one that has to be recovered, restored, pointed out as a model, and to which one must remain loyal; loyalty to tradition is an unfailing element of the declarations of principle and the rhetoric of the ideologues and the propagandists of the radical right. . . . The revolutionary left, on the other hand, places its trust in great transformations, in rebirth and in renewal, not in the revival of ancient virtues, but in the creation of a new man. The former looks backwards to find its Golden Age, the latter forward. . . . Whoever seeks consolation and salvation in tradition starts from a ruthlessly critical analysis of the present, interpreted as an age of decadence.

('Per una definizione della destra reazionaria', in *Fascismo oggi*, cit., p. 31.) For detailed accounts of the extreme right's attitudes to tradition, cf. esp. D. Cofrancesco, 'La tradizione come archetipo e i suoi usi politici', *Il politico*, XLI, 1976, pp. 209–36; *idem, Destra e sinistra*,

Bertani, Verona, 1984, pp. 45–54. See also J. Le Goff, 'Il peso del passato nella coscienza collettiva degli italiani', in F. L. Cavazza and S. R. Graubard (eds), *Il caso italiano*, Garzanti, Milan, 1979, pp. 534–53; *idem*, entry 'Passato/Presente', in *Enciclopedia*, Einaudi, Turin, 1980, X, p. 502–8.

40. One is reminded of D'Annunzio's flight over the enemy capital of Vienna to drop Italian propaganda leaflets (Ledeen, *The First Duce*, cit., pp. 1–2), and of the much publicised exploits of the *maiali*, the frogman-guided torpedoes that sank the British battleships *Valiant* and *Queen Elizabeth* in the port of Alexandria, in December 1941.

41. On the MSI's diffidence towards the outside world and its cult of secrecy, see Ignazi, *Il polo negato*, cit., p. 291, n. 51.

42. Tassani, 'The Italian Social Movement', cit., p. 30. For Fini's biography, see G. Locatelli and D. Martini, *Duce, addio. La biografia di Gianfranco Fini*, Longanesi, Milan, 1994.

43. On the promotion and rise of Alessandra Mussolini, see L. White, 'Mussolini in a mini marches on Rome', *The Sunday Times*, 9 Feb. 1992, p. 3; E. Vulliamy, 'Fighter for the Grand-Fatherland', *Week-End Guardian*, 22–23 Feb. 1992, pp. 4–7; and F. Rocco, 'The Mouth from the South', *The Independent on Sunday*, 28 Nov. 1993, pp. 5–9.

44. O. La Rocca, 'Camicie nere in piazza – il MSI torna a sfilare', *La Repubblica*, 18–19 Oct. 1992, p. 6.

45. Roberto Chiarini kindly informs me that the group in question belongs to Pino Rauti's faction within the MSI. The poster was made available to me by the main Florence branch of the MSI.

46. The poster, also bears the words 'HOBBIT '93', which of course allude to Tolkien. This author has, since the mid-1970s, been revered by the youth wing of the MSI. Drawing on the counter-culture of the 1960s, and inspired by the far-right philosopher Julius Evola (once described by Almirante as 'our own Marcuse, only better') and his follower Rauti, the New Right in particular has sought in his work the visionary knowledge, esoteric realities and alternative cosmologies it wished to oppose to the materialism of the modern age. Woodstock-style gatherings called *Campi Hobbit* were organised in 1977, 1978 and 1980 at Montesarchi (near Benevento), Fonte Romana (near L'Aquila) and Castel-camponeschi (also near L'Aquila) respectively. *Hobbit '93*, however, is likely to have been a much more sober event, as the prestigious venue and patriotic theme indicate. For the Italian far right's interest in Tolkien, see: M. Revelli, 'La nuova destra', in F. Ferraresi (ed.), *La destra radicale*, Feltrinelli, Milan, 1984, pp. 131, 188–89; R. Griffin, 'Revolts against the Modern World, *Literature and History*, XI, spring 1985, pp, 101–23. (esp. pp. 103–106 and 112–17).

47. In order to encourage the Italians' patriotic feelings, Mussolini frequently recalled the achievements of classical civilisation. The regime was keen to present itself as the continuator of the traditions of ancient Rome. On the cult of *Romanitas* during Fascism, see especially D. Cofrancesco, 'Appunti per un'analisi del mito romano nell'ideologia fascista', *Storia contemporanea*, I, 3, pp. 383–411; C. Cresti, *Architettura e Fascismo*, Vallecchi, Florence, 1986; P. Bondanella, 'Mussolini's Fascism and the Imperial Vision of Rome', in *The Eternal City. Roman Images in the Modern World*. University of North Carolina Press, Chapel Hill, NC, 1987, pp. 172–280; R. Visser, 'Fascist Doctrine and the Cult of Romanità', *Journal of Contemporary History*, XXVII, 1992, pp. 5–22; E. Gentile, *Il culto del Littorio*, Laterza, Bari, 1993. On the myth of Rome in MSI propaganda, see L. Cheles, 'The Italian Far Right: Nationalist Attitudes, and Views on Ethnicity and Immigration', in A. C. Hargreaves and J. Leaman (eds), *Race, Ethnicity and Politics in Contemporary Europe*, Edward Elgar, London, 1995.

48. On Alleanza Nazionale, see G. Battistini, 'Nasce la Cosa grigia e aspetta il Senatur', *La Repubblica*, 23 Jan. 1994, p. 4; A. Longo, 'Lo "strappetto" di Fini: "Siamo anti-totalitari"',

La Repubblica, 21 May 1994, p. 6; C. Valentini, 'Alleanza Nazionale: la componente "storica" del Polo delle Libertà', in P. Ginsborg (ed.), *Stato dell'Italia*, Il Saggiatore – Bruno Mondadori, Milan, 1994, pp. 677–81.; P. Ignazi, *Postfascisti? Dal Movimento Sociale Italiano ad Alleanza Nazionale*, Il Mulino, Bologna, 1994.

49. It is worth mentioning that, when in October 1992 thousands of MSI activists demonstrated in Rome saluting Fascist style, Fini, asked to comment, professed embarrassed disapproval. See La Rocca, 'Camicie nere', cit.

50. La Russa is a close associate of Fini's and supported his candidature in the leadership contest of 1987. Cf. Tassani, 'The Italian Social Movement', cit., p. 130. On La Russa, whose middle name, Benito, was tactically concealed during the election campaign, see Quaranta, 'Nati con la camicia. Nera', cit., p. 52.

51. On Servello, a follower of Almirante's and one of the protagonists of neo-Fascist activism in the turbulent 1970s, see Tassani, 'The Italian Social Movement', cit., p. 130; and A. Padellaro, 'Insomma, sei fascista o no?', *L'Espresso*, 13 May 1994, p. 60.

52. At least not in those which I saw and photographed in the cities I visited during the election period, namely: Cagliari, Pisa, Bologna, Ferrara, Venice and Milan.

53. The representation of Italian politicians and aspiring politicians in posters is partly dependent (mostly unconsciously) on the Renaissance portraiture tradition. Hence the preference for the half-length portrait format, and the use of props connoting status in fuller portraits. I shall be dealing with this topic in detail in a separate essay. On Renaissance portraiture, see especially E. Castelnuovo, 'Il significato del ritratto pittorico nella società', in R. Romano and C. Vivanti (eds), *Storia d'Italia. I documenti*, V, 2, Einaudi, Turin, 1973, pp. 1042–84; P. Burke, 'The Presentation of Self in Renaissance Portraiture', in idem, *The Historical Anthropology of Early Modern Italy*, Cambridge University Press, Cambridge, 1987, pp. 150–67.

54. Despite Fini's assurances, and those of Prime Minister Berlusconi, whose government, formed in May 1994, includes five ministers from the far-right camp, it is hard to believe that AN is a fully democratic party. The MSI's 'transformation' has occurred too suddenly to be sincere. It has not preceded by an internal debate – a practice it would be only legitimate to expect from a party proclaiming to have embraced democracy. Nor has there been any serious attempt to renew its parliamentary intake: 95 per cent of the MSI MPs who served in the outgoing parliament were fielded as AN candidates; the few 'new faces' came almost exclusively from the old ranks of the MSI. See C. Valentini, 'E sotto, la camicia nera', *L'Espresso*, 25 March 1994, pp. 72–74. AN's reluctance to repudiate its past is indicated by Fini's ambiguous description of his new party as 'post-Fascist', as well as by the claims – made *after* the elections had taken place – that Mussolini was the greatest Italian statesman of the twentieth century, and that Fascism was, until 1938 (i.e. before Mussolini signed the pact with Hitler), 'mostly good'. See M. Sheridan, 'Learning to live with Il Duce', *The Independent*, 11 April 1994, p. 17; and A. Longo, 'Fini ricade nel vizio del "fascismo buono" ', *La Repubblica*, 4 June 1994, p. 4. Especially significant – and disturbing – is AN's half-hearted attempt, made in May 1994, to legitimate Fascism by proposing that the clause in the Italian Constitution forbidding the reorganisation of a Fascist party be repealed (this proposal was withdrawn shortly after having been signed by all AN MPs, including Fini). See A. Longo, 'La tentazione di Alleanza Nazionale', *La Repubblica*, 17 May 1994, p. 7.

Chapter 5

THE EXTREME RIGHT IN SPAIN: A DYING SPECIES?*
Sheelagh Ellwood

In 1985, the European Parliament set up a Committee of Inquiry into the Rise of Fascism and Racism in Europe. Two members of the Committee visited Spain to collect material for their research. They were surprised (and disturbed) to find that the related phenomena of racism and Fascism seemed to arouse little interest among Spaniards.[1] Both Spain's recent history and her future objectives seemed to be at variance with such indifference. Only ten years earlier, Spain had emerged from forty years under the autocratic, anti-democratic rule of general Franco, whose regime had once been the ally of Hitler and Mussolini and was known to have sheltered the erstwhile followers of these dictators. It was difficult, too, to understand how Spaniards could assume that the reappearance of Fascism in Europe had no implications for them at a time when their country aspired to be an integral part of Europe and, indeed, was then on the verge of becoming a member of the EEC. In the following pages, we shall look at some possible explanations for these apparent paradoxes. We shall also try to answer a question which springs inevitably from them: is there a solid basis for the optimistic assessment Spaniards implicitly make of their country, as being a Fascist-free zone? In order to broach these questions about today's Spain, we must first look briefly at the origins of the extreme right there, in the first third of the present century.

The roots of the rabid nationalism, ultra-authoritarian attitudes and disdain for parliamentary democracy as a political system which characterise the Spanish extreme right today go back to the collapse of the Spanish empire in the latter part of the nineteenth century. Later, in the 1920s and, especially, in the 1930s, the feelings of resentment and fear harboured by the middle classes against what they saw as, on the one hand, an inefficient political class and, on the other, the threat of an increasingly organised and vocal working class, began to crystallise into political movements which claimed to defend conservative interests against both liberalism and Communism. At a time when Fascism was rapidly gaining ground elsewhere in Europe, similar movements made their debut in Spain. What was ultimately to be the longest-lasting of the Spanish Fascist organisations, Spanish Phalanx (*Falange Española*, FE), was created in 1933, the year that Adolf Hitler became Chancellor in Germany. Unlike its German and Italian counterparts, however, FE remained a minority organisation. Its numbers were increased and its social base broadened slightly in early 1934, when it joined forces with another Fascist group, the Committees

91

for National Syndicalist Attack [*Juntas de Ofensiva Nacional-Sindicalista*, JONS], but the new party, the Spanish Phalanx of Committees for National Syndicalist Attack [*Falange Española de las JONS*, FE de las JONS] was still unable to attract a nationwide, mass following.

When a military coup was staged in July 1936 to oust the legitimately elected government of the day, FE de las JONS joined the insurgents. For the duration of the Civil War to which that coup led, the party backed its political commitment to the anti-democratic cause with men, women, arms and propaganda. I have examined elsewhere the role of FE de las JONS during the Spanish Civil War.[2] For the purposes of the present discussion, the importance of the War lay in the fact that it enabled the party to pass from being a political nonentity to occupying a position of state power as a source of ideological legitimation and structural organisation for the military regime born in and from the war. On 19 April 1937, the leader of the insurgent armies and self-styled head of the Spanish State, general Francisco Franco, issued a decree which amalgamated all the rightist political organisations supporting the military enterprise. Franco himself assumed the leadership of the new party, which was called Spanish Traditionalist Phalanx of Committees for National Syndicalist Attack [*Falange Española Tradicionalista y de las Juntas de Ofensiva Nacional-Sindicalista*, FET y de las JONS].[3] This unwieldy title indicated that it was the extreme, rather than the moderate, brand of rightism which was to provide the organisational and ideological framework of the Franco regime.

Because the ideological bases and political structures of Francoism remained unchanged throughout the thirty-nine years that the Franco regime lasted, this hybrid, quasi-single party survived, formally intact, to the end. In social, economic and cultural terms, however, Spain changed a great deal in the course of those years and when Franco died, on 20 November 1975, barely six months elapsed before a Law of Political Associations was introduced which set the stage for dismantling the single party and legalising a democratic, pluralist, political system. In fact, behind the official facade of FET y de las JONS, only the Traditionalist and Falangist sectors of the old party retained the ideological positions and physical existence they had had prior to April 1937. The other parties had disappeared as organised groups, and their Catholic conservatism had been transformed by their ideological heirs into positions sufficiently progressive to cause their advocates to be referred to as the Franco regime's 'tolerated opposition'. By the time the Law of Political Associations was passed, in June 1976, Traditionalism was largely confined to the northern province of Navarre and to Seville, in the south, whither its followers had withdrawn to winter quarters in 1939, on realising that Franco's victory in the Civil War was not going to bring a monarchical restoration in the person of their Pretender.

As for the *Falange*, a tendency to internal fragmentation inherent in the pre-Civil War party had re-emerged after Franco's death and, by 1976, there were four rightist groups each laying claim to the original title, *Falange Española de las JONS*. These were the Spanish National Front [*Frente Nacional Español*, FNE]. Authentic Spanish Phalanx [*Falange Española (auténtica)*, FE(a)], the National Syndicalist Coordinating Committee [Junta Coordinadora Nacional Sindicalista, JCNS] and a group without a name, made up of notoriously violent right-wingers whose leader was the chief of another extremist group, the Warriors of Christ the King (*Guerrilleros de Cristo Rey*).

Each claimed to be the direct descendant of the party founded in 1933 and accused the others of having 'betrayed' the original doctrine by their collaboration with the Franco regime.

The question of which group might legitimately call itself *Falange Española de las JONS* was finally resolved in October 1976, by the assignation of the title to the FNE. In fact, it mattered very little what these groups called themselves, for their style and their discourse were the same as they had been forty years earlier and everyone recognised them as remnants of an anti-democratic past. They still wore the navy blue shirt and yoke-and-arrows symbol adopted by the *Falange* as its uniform in 1933; they still sang the Falangist anthem, 'Face to the Sun' (*Cara al sol*); and they still rejected traditional rightist anathema, such as Basque and Catalan nationalism or Marxism. Indeed, in 1977, during the campaign for the first democratic elections since 1936 – in which the Falangists participated despite their openly admitted contempt for parliamentary democracy – they based their appeal on the idea that their tenets were as valid in the 1970s as they had been in the 1930s, on the grounds that they had not been applied, simply usurped, by the Franco regime.

This ingenious argument found little response in the Spanish electorate. Taken as a whole, the extreme right polled less than 1 per cent of the total number of votes cast on 15 June 1977.[4] Its nearest rival, the conservative People's Alliance [*Alianza Popular*, AP] obtained 8.21 per cent of the vote, while the Spanish Socialist Workers Party [*Partido Socialista Obrero Español*, PSOE] accounted for 29.21 per cent, and the winning centre-right coalition, Democratic Centrist Union [*Unión de Centro Democrático*, UCD], took 34.74 per cent.[5] Between them, FE(a), and two of the groups which had participated in the JCNS, Independent Spanish Phalanx [*Falange Española (independiente)*, FE(i)] and the José Antonio Doctrinal Circles [*Círculos Doctrinales José Antonio*], polled 40,359 votes.[6] The main extreme rightist group, the '18 July' National Alliance [*Alianza nacional '18 de julio'*], having adopted a line which defended, rather than reneged on, the Francoist heritage, received 64,558 votes, which represented 0.36 per cent of the total.[7] Not one of the extreme rightist candidates was elected to either of the two parliamentary chambers. These results made it abundantly clear that, whether or not it presented the defence of Franco's memory as part of its programme, the extreme right had no appeal for a majority of people who identified with the idea of a modern, democratic, Europeanist future, not with ideologies which they associated with a repressive and outmoded past.

The results of fresh general elections, held two years later, in March 1979, appear, at first sight to belie this statement, for while the Socialist, Communist and centrist parties each made only slight advances, the extreme right increased its poll from 0.6 to 2.2 per cent of the total vote. In the wake of the 1977 débacle, the *Círculos Doctrinales* had joined forces with FE de las JONS as National Union [*Union Nacional*, UN], which polled 379,463 votes, or 2.1 per cent of the total.[8] Blas Piñar López, leader of the third group integrated in the National Union, New Force [*Fuerza Nueva*, FN], was elected for Madrid. In fact, these results did not reflect a real shift to the right so much as a 'settling down' of the electoral panorama after the 'novelty' of the 1977 poll. Many of the dozens of tiny groups which had put up candidates in 1977 did not run again in 1979, and regional parties played a role in 1979 which they had not played in 1977. Most significantly, the conservative vote went down in 1979 by 2 per cent on the

1977 figure. Very probably, the votes gained in 1979 by UN (274,546) came largely from the 500,000 lost by AP.[9]

That conservatism in general and extreme conservatism in particular had few supporters in post-Franco Spain was shown by two key – and not unrelated – events which occurred in the 1980s: an attempted *coup d'état*, in February 1981, and a socialist victory at the polls, in October 1982.

From the point of view of the present discussion, it was not the coup itself, but its failure and, particularly, popular reaction to it that were important. It is very difficult to say whether there was any civilian involvement in what appeared to be an operation organised and executed solely by officers from the army and the paramilitary police force, the Civil Guard. No civilian connections emerged in the subsequent trial, beyond the minor role played by a former employee of the Francoist trade union system, notorious for his ultra-rightist political views, Juan García Carrés.[10] Without concrete evidence, it would be equally difficult to estimate how much sociopolitical support the coup would have had if it had been successful. However, the reaction of the majority of the armed forces, of the political parties and of the Spanish people suggested that such support would have been minimal. An enormous demonstration, held in the centre of Madrid (and in other cities all over Spain) on the night of 27 February, three days after the coup had been definitively aborted, showed that, in general, people actively wanted peace and democracy.

In the light of the very real sense of danger generated by those events, and of the strong emotional response they provoked, it is easy to understand that, when general elections were held in October 1982, there was a massive swing towards the Socialist Party as an emphatic gesture of dissatisfaction with the internal squabbles of the governing centrist coalition and of disaffection from everything associated with a return to the past. The PSOE landslide did not reflect a conscious *ideological* choice on the part of the majority of the electorate, so much as a deeply felt desire for change, for newness – new faces, new ideas, new policies. And that was what the PSOE promised, with its electoral slogan 'Socialism is freedom. For change'.

The total discredit of the old order was clearly reflected not only in the results of the October 1982 election, but also in those of the June 1986 poll. In 1982, the largest of the extreme right-wing groups, the coalition UN, polled a mere 100,899 votes in the whole of Spain.[11] In the light of this result, its leading candidate, Blas Piñar, announced the dissolution of his own party, New Force, on 20 November 1982 – the seventh anniversary of Franco's death. A few months later, in February 1983, the veteran right-winger and former Francoist Minister, Raimundo Fernández Cuesta, announced his resignation as president of FE de las JONS. In spite of the UN's poor showing in 1982, FE de las JONS presented candidates on its own ticket when the next elections were held, in June 1986. As in 1977, 1979 and 1982, the 1986 electoral platform of FE de las JONS was based on the alleged validity of the original, 1930s Falangist concepts. Their result – 32,663 votes, or 0.16 per cent of the total – was consistent with the 40,000-vote ceiling registered by *Falange* purist options in previous years.[12]

At this point, it is possible to answer two of the questions raised at the beginning of the present chapter: why did Spaniards feel uninvolved with respect to the possible existence of neo-Fascism in the Spain of the 1980s and why were they so uninterested in the problem of its growth in Europe? The answer to the first part of the question was that no one was interested in the extreme right because it scarcely existed; and it scarcely existed because no one was interested. In a situation of free political competition and at a time when both the popular mood and the historical moment were overwhelmingly in favour of democracy, reactionary, anti-democratic options attracted only minimal electoral support from a die-hard minority of urban, middle-class voters fearful of the 'chaos' Francoism had taught them democracy would bring and hostile to any change which might endanger social and economic privileges acquired during the Franco regime. On account of its organisational and electoral weakness, the extreme right was not perceived even as a *potential* threat to the new, democratic order.

With respect to Europe, where, by contrast, neo-Fascism clearly did exist, there were two main reasons for Spanish unconcern. First, forty years of Francoist isolation had contributed to a lasting feeling that what went beyond the Pyrenees had nothing to do with Spaniards. Second, and partly as a result of this, the fact that the autochthonous breed of Fascism appeared to be a thing of the past made people think that, whatever was happening elsewhere, it couldn't happen in Spain and, therefore, there was no need to take any notice of it.

We come, now, to the third of our initial questions: is it correct to assume that Fascism in Spain is a dying species? If we consider electoral results as 'solid' evidence and, in the case of post-Francoist Spain, there is no reason to doubt their reliability, then the immediate answer is, as we have seen, that there *is* some basis for that assumption. However, the fact that people did not *vote* for the extreme right's candidates does not of itself necessarily imply its disappearance as a sociopolitical force, not least because electoral statistics tell only part of the story. They do not, for example, tell us anything about the rightist groups which did not participate in electoral contests.

It is difficult to give an accurate and detailed account of the extra-parliamentary right in terms of the social composition, size, internal structure or economic resources of its components. In the first place, reliable, verifiable data are not available from published sources.[13] In the second, the fact that the extreme right is not averse to the use of physical violence against those to whom it takes a dislike leads one to be wary of carrying out one's own, first-hand research. Nevertheless, on the basis of the few sources which are accessible and of personal observation in Spain, and bearing the methodological difficulties in mind, it is possible to sketch an outline of what these groups are and how they operate.

The first thing to note is their tendency to extreme fragmentation: in 1984, it was estimated that as many as 400 groups existed throughout the country.[14] Occasionally, they appear to have a certain capacity for organising propaganda campaigns. Such is the case of the Spanish Committees [*Juntas Españolas*, JJ.EE.], centred in Madrid; or Spanish Statement [*Afirmación Española*, AE], said to be run by a Spanish publisher (Alberto Vasallo de Number) and to have some thirty high-ranking army officers among its members.[15] More typically, however, ultra-rightist groups in Spain are little more than tiny nuclei of adolescents. They have little material or organisational infrastructure and few activities other than spraying graffiti on walls, shouting abuse in front of cinemas showing films they disapprove of and participating in decreasingly attended demonstrations on Francoism's commemorative dates. Their message is essentially backward-looking. For some, the central figure is Franco; for others it is the founder of *Falange*, José Antonio Primo de Rivera or one of the other pre-war Falangist leaders. For all, the external paraphernalia, the lexicon, the iconography and the ideological content are culled from the 1930s regardless of the fact that the Falangist yoke and arrows painted on walls, the protests against 'reds' and 'Masons', the blue shirts and Roman saluting seem anachronistic in post-Francoist Spain. Indeed, the impression these groups give is that the Spanish extreme right is ahistorical.

In addition to these small groups, there are also a series of larger nuclei, for which the smaller ones can, of course, always serve as a recruiting ground.

The organisation which shared with FE the title of the Francoist party, the Traditionalist Communion [*Comunión Tradicionalista*, CT], cannot, strictly speaking, be considered Fascist, on account of its monarchical principles, its profound Catholicism and its non-revolutionary character. Nevertheless, its extreme conservatism, rabid anti-Marxist, anti-democratic postures and corporativist economic ideas make it eligible for inclusion on the extreme right of the political spectrum. Towards the end of the 1960s, and after a series of internal schisms, CT split into a progressive sector of a social-democratic nature, and an ultra-conservative sector. The latter has proven connections with Italian and Latin-American extreme rightist organisations and has, on occasions, used violence against the social-democratic sector. It participated in the 1977 elections as part of the '18 July' National Alliance, but has not taken an active part in contemporary politics since then.

Until its dissolution in 1982, the paradigmatic ultra-right group was New Force (*Fuerza Nueva*), differentiated from FE de las JONS by the former's greater readiness to use physical violence as a political instrument, by its more overtly Catholic integrist nature, and by its tendency to invoke Franco, as well as Primo de Rivera, as its hero-figures. FE de las JONS stalwarts often accused New Force of making illegitimate use of the Falangist blue shirt, while New Force considered the Falangists, at best as 'softies' and, at worst, as undercover leftists.

The leader of New Force, Blas Piñar, is the only person on the extreme right who could be classified as a charismatic leader. By profession a solicitor, Piñar has always cultivated the suave elegance of the aristocratic Primo de Rivera, usually besuited and with the slicked-down hair characteristic of the FE de las JONS founder, although, at close quarters, Piñar in fact bears a closer resemblance to the 1950s leader of Argentinian *justicialismo*, Juan Domingo Perón, than to Primo de Rivera. Like both of them, Piñar's capacity for impassioned haranguing totally commands the awe and the fervour of his devotees. One of the latter wrote of him in 1977:

> Gentlemen, we must take our hats off to Blas Piñar. Always consistent, faithful and loyal to the same ideas, immaculate in his political practice... That's why he attracts masses of young people and fills the People with enthusiasm ... Blas Piñar has never sucked off the teat of the previous régime[16] ... He unmasks the sanctimonious Christian Democrats, lashes the reds with his tongue and stands up to all the Francoists who are traitors to Franco.[17]

Even so, Piñar is not given to making outrageously provocative public statements in the style of the French extremist, Jean-Marie Le Pen.

Yet Piñar has never been able to act as a rallying point for the whole of the extreme right. The reasons may well be historical, rather than ideological. In spite of his strong personal connections with the Castilian city of Toledo, where he was born in 1918, Piñar was not in the habit of attending the annual ceremony to mark the anniversary of the time when, during the Spanish Civil War, Francoist troops entered Republican-held Toledo and rescued the remains of a contingent of anti-Republicans who had been besieged in the city's fortress (the *Alcazar*) for two months. Piñar's presence at the fiftieth anniversary commemoration, in September 1986, caused considerable irritation among the 'regulars' who, it need scarcely be said, could not be suspected of left-wing sympathies.[18] Surprisingly, too, given the importance attached by the extreme right to the Civil War, Piñar has never used his past to legitimate his position as a political leader. On the contrary, he prefers to elude references to the past. The reason is clear, though rarely stated: on the day of the anti-Republican rising, 18 July 1936, Piñar was in Madrid. However, he did not return to Toledo (where his father was shortly to be among the besieged defenders of the *Alcazar*), nor did he enlist as a rebel volunteer. Instead, young Blas took refuge, first, in the Finnish, then, later, in the Panamanian legations, remaining in the latter until the end of the war in 1939.[19] This was hardly a convincing start for an aspiring *caudillo*. Seriously handicapped in the eyes of his extreme rightist clientele by his lack of a good Civil War curriculum, Piñar distracts attention from the short-comings of the content of his claim to political authority by carefully orchestrated attention to its form. His catastrophist arguments and the vehemence of their delivery are designed to secure the kind of irrational, unquestioning allegiance commanded by such oratorial marathon-runners as Hitler, Mussolini, Castro or Stalin.

New Force always maintained good relations with South American and European rightist groups. Chilean and Argentinian *ultras* were frequently to be seen at its meetings, and the Italian group *Ordine Nuovo* was a regular attender at New Force's annual rally, on 20 November, the anniversary of Franco's death. It has been suggested, too, that, in spite of being disbanded in 1982, New Force continued to receive financial support from foreign sources.[20] Certainly, the group continued to maintain, as its meeting place, two adjacent flats in the centre of Madrid and to publish a fortnightly magazine, also entitled *Fuerza Nueva*.

On a much smaller and more 'discreet' scale than New Force is a group which, though not explicitly a political organisation, indoctrinates its members with extreme rightist ideas and organises them as a para-military commandos against the day when their 'Security Corps shall be a great army . . .' after the style of 'the guards of imperial Rome or the army of Napoleon'.[21] Registered as a cultural organisation, *Nueva Acrópolis*, is known to be a Naziphile organisation whose central offices are in Brussels and which has branches in thirty-four countries. In Spain, it was reported in 1985 as being active in twenty-seven of the country's fifty-two provinces and as having about 1,000 members, most of whom were below the age of 30.[22]

Much closer to European neo-Fascism in both style and ideology than any of the groups mentioned so far is the group Spanish Circle of Friends of Europe [*Círculo Español de Amigos de Europa*, CEDADE]. Originally founded in West Germany in 1965, by a group of German, Italian and Spanish Fascists, CEDADE was established in Barcelona in 1966 as 'an entity of Europeanist character, which would act as the spokesman for the sentiments of Spanish youth'.[23] In 1973, a branch was opened in Madrid. Between them, these two cities account for about 1,000 of the 2,500 members CEDADE was reported to have in Spain in 1985.[24] With Spain as the centre of its operations, CEDADE has created subsidiaries in various Latin American countries, in France and in Portugal.

CEDADE takes its ideological inspiration directly from German National Socialism, and is differentiated from other Spanish rightist groups by its less insistently Falangist character, its overt anti-Semitism and its Europeanist stance, which sees European unity as a cultural and racial issue, rather than a political or an economic one. CEDADE has organised a number of summer camps and congresses in Spain, although its proposed Congress of European Youth, planned for 1974, was ultimately prohibited. In recent years, CEDADE has not been very visible in terms of public meetings, proselytising campaigns, press statements or other newsworthy activities. Nevertheless, the group maintains an office in the centre of Madrid and has a stand at the large book-fair held annually in Madrid, offering mostly Nazi literature and music cassettes. It also publishes a magazine – *CEDADE* – and is capable of organising *ad hoc* propaganda campaigns. When Spain formally resumed diplomatic relations with Israel in 1986, CEDADE pasted up anti-Jewish posters, and when the news of Rudolf Hess's death was announced in August 1987, CEDADE instantly papered Madrid and Barcelona with propaganda in his favour. These four activities, together with the relatively high quality of the design, paper and printing of the group's propaganda indicate an economic capacity superior to that of all the other groups, with the exception of New Force.

A French magazine, *Article 31*, wrote of CEDADE in 1985: 'The public activities of CEDADE are almost certainly no more than the visible tip of the iceberg. Does CEDADE serve as a coordinating and documentation centre for European Nazi movements? What logistic support might it have provided for "black" terrorism?'[25]

Those questions might equally be asked of all extreme right-wing groups in Spain. The answers are fragmentary and the evidence often circumstantial. Nevertheless, in recent years there have been numerous reports in the Spanish press of links between individuals known to militate in, or to sympathise with, Spanish ultra-rightist groups and international terrorist networks. The Bologna station massacre of 1980, for example, and the Milan–Naples train explosion of 1984, are alleged by Italian legal authorities to have been prepared in Spain, with Spanish explosives, by members of the Italian rightist organisations, *Ordine Nuovo, Avanguardia Nazionale* and *Movimento Sociale Italiano*, operating from Madrid, Barcelona and the south coast, and in collaboration with a Spanish group called International Revolutionary Action Groups [*Grupos Revolucionarios de Acción Internacional*, GRAI].[26] Similarly, right-wing extremists wanted for terrorist actions in Italy are known to live, or to have lived, in Spain and are often suspected of having taken part in other terrorist actions there. Carlo Cicuttini, resident in Spain from 1972 onwards and responsible for the organisation of *Ordine Nuovo* outside Italy, is alleged to be implicated in the massacre of five left-wing lawyers in Madrid in January 1977.[27] He and Giuseppe Calzona, resident in Spain since 1974 and implicated in the murder of an Italian Communist (Alfio Oddo) in Monza, are reputed to be confidants of the Spanish police and to have taken part in operations against the Basque separatist organisation, ETA, in collaboration with two Spanish counter-terrorist organisations, the Spanish Basque Battalion [*Batallón Vasco-Español*, BVE] and the Anti-terrorist Liberation Groups [*Grupos Anti-terroristas de Liberación*, GAL], in turn said to be linked to Spanish police intelligence services. Elio Massagrande, founder member of *Ordine Nuovo* was arrested in March 1977, on the discovery of an illegal arms factory in the centre of Madrid. Others involved were *Avanguardia Nazionale* terrorist, Stefano delle Chiaie, and the leader of the Spanish *Guerrilleros de Cristo Rey*, Mariano Sanchez Covisa.[28]

A more outlandish and, in some ways, more unnerving manifestation of right-wing extremism was the revelation, in May 1986, of meetings between a Spanish Army officer, Colonel Carlos de Meer, and the Libyan leader, Colonel Gaddafi. De Meer was president of a clandestine group formed in the summer of 1985, called the Coordinating Committee of National Forces [*Junta Coordinadora de Fuerzas Nacionales*], composed of nineteen autonomous rightist groups. De Meer evidently travelled to Tripoli in January 1986, to negotiate Libyan financing to the tune of some £4.5 million, for the creation of a new right-wing party.[29] What, at first sight, appears to be a case of a strange bed-fellows makes more sense when we remember that De Meer's activities coincided with a period in which the situation in the western Mediterranean had become extremely tense on account of the deterioration in relations between the USA and Libya. This, together with Gaddafi's declaration, on 11 April 1986, that all cities in southern Europe might be considered military targets, and the presence of several US military bases on Spanish soil, perhaps led the Coordinating Committee of National Forces to believe that its members and the Libyans could become fellow-travellers for purposes of subverting the existing order on Europe's south-western flank. Certainly, indications exist of Arab assistance for extreme rightist groups in Europe. In this connection, the implications of Spain's geographical proximity to North Africa, and the potential utility of having willing collaborators in Spain, are self-evident.

Disturbing though such activities are to anyone with democratic sensitivities, they are, nevertheless, beyond the bounds of legality, and judicial mechanisms exist to pursue and suppress them. Society is not entirely defenceless against them. Thus, the Madrid arms factory was dismantled, De Meer was arrested and expulsion orders were issued against some of the Italian *ultras*.[30] Neo-Fascism is far more dangerous when it operates within the bounds of legality, for then democracy can find itself threatened by its own belief in the right of all law-abiding citizens freely to express their opinions. It is difficult to say whether or not this was taken into consideration by the Spanish extreme right. The fact remains, however, that when, in the autumn of 1986, New Force reappeared, it did so with the express intention of playing the parliamentary system according to the system's own rules.

After disbanding as an aggressively anti-liberal, anti-democratic party in 1982, New Force went to ground by converting itself into a 'study centre', the Centre for Social, Political and Economic Studies [*Centro de Estudios Sociales, Políticos y Económicos*, CESPE], with little or no external projection. When it re-emerged, four years later, it had adopted a new, more respectable look, abandoning the rabidly anti-European stance which, until then, had always been one of the hallmarks of the extreme right in Spain. It had also adopted a new name – National Front [*Frente Nacional, FN*] – which gave it immediately recognisable connotations of similar groups in other European countries. Indeed, at the constitutional meeting of the new party, Piñar was accompanied by the (then) secretary general of the Italian MSI, Giorgio Almirante, and by a delegate from the French *Front National*, Jean-Marc Brissaud.[31]

The idea of returning to the political arena arose in May 1986. In June of that year, as a result of another conservative defeat at the polls, the decision was taken to create the *Frente Nacional*.[32] An open-air rally in July provided an insight into what were to be the party's composition and aims. The event constituted an almost surreal meeting of old and new waters. To begin with, the date chosen – 18 July – was also that of the 50th anniversary of the rising which initiated the Spanish Civil War. Most of the old paraphernalia was still present, too: the blue shirts, the New Force badges, Spanish flags with Franco's crest on them, stalls selling cassettes of right-wing favourites and bronze busts of Franco. Even so, the two young men in full Falangist regalia were in an anomalous minority, and when a group of spectators tried to sing the Falangist anthem, they were rapidly silenced by the rest of the audience. The most significant change, however, was that the speakers, although as impassioned as ever, no longer harped on the Francoist past so much as on an ultra-Catholic future.[33]

When, on 1 March 1987, the new party held its first congress as such, its president, Piñar, spoke of the need to construct 'the Europe of Christianity' as a means to entering 'an epoch of prosperity and development'. In ethical terms, he said, this meant the rejection of 'abortion, euthanasia, and the corruption of youth', and the promotion of 'the institution of marriage' and the family. Politically, it meant unity between the countries of southern Europe, to protect themselves from the 'destruction of [their] economy to the benefit of that of the countries of northern Europe', and the 'recuperation' of 'absent Europe' – the countries of the Communist bloc.[34]

In spite of giving the crisis of 'liberal conservatism' as one of the motives for creating *Frente Nacional*, Piñar was emphatic in his rejection of the notion that his party would 'pull the chestnuts out of the fire' for Spanish conservatism.[35] As if to underline this, he announced that the *Frente Nacional* would not participate in the next domestic elections – local and regional government elections, set for June 1987 – but would only put up candidates for the elections to the European Parliament, also to be held in June 1987.

Behind the apparent paradox of a *Frente Nacional* deliberately eschewing participation in domestic politics, lay two hard realities, which Piñar undoubtedly included in his calculations. In the first place, as the party's own electoral track record showed and the crumbling state of AP confirmed, the right in Spain was on a serious down-swing. In an electoral system based on proportional representation, the *Frente Nacional* stood very little chance of success in domestic elections. The elections for Strasbourg, by contrast, would be fought on the basis of a single, nationwide constituency. This maximised its chances of amassing sufficient votes to obtain at least one Euro-MP. The second factor was that election to the European Parliament would not only provide the moral, political and strategic advantages of having an important international platform from which to broadcast the *Frente Nacional* ideology, it would also mean receipt of European parliamentary funds. In so far as it would be part of the extreme rightist parliamentary group formed by French, Italian and Greek members, the Spanish *Frente Nacional* would be eligible for a share of the monies available to all groups. An ironic situation indeed: the temple of European democracy financing groups committed to the destruction of democracy itself.

The closing event of the *Frente Nacional* electoral campaign, on 8 June 1987, was attended by Jean-Marie Le Pen and Nino Tripodi, president of the *Movimento Sociale Italiano*. Their interest in Piñar's candidacy was not simply one of ideological solidarity. The precarious existence of the European Right parliamentary group would be shored up if Piñar were elected, since it would thereby increase its three-country representation (the minimal requirement to form a parliamentary group in Strasbourg) to four. In the event, the *Frente Nacional* obtained only 123,000 votes in the whole of Spain and, consequently, Piñar was not elected.[36]

Did this mean, then, that the threat of neo-Fascism had been definitively routed in Spain? Certainly, the conditions which had favoured the growth of Fascism in industrialised, Western European countries in the past were not present in Spain in the 1980s. For example, there was no racial or religious element, readily utilisable as a scapegoat 'explanation' for massive unemployment. Parts of the Spanish economy were undeniably in crisis, following the recession which affected the whole of Spain's economy in the 1970s. These, however, were mostly in the primary sector, such as mining, shipbuilding or steel-making. By contrast, the secondary and tertiary sectors were well on the way to recovery by the second half of the 1980s, and it was these which employed the middle classes to whom the extreme right has traditionally directed its appeal.

Politically, too, the erstwhile clientele of the extreme right did not feel itself threatened by the left as it had done in the 1930s. On the contrary, the anarchist left was a very marginal force, and the Communist left, though experiencing a resurgence of popular support from 1986 onwards, still lagged far behind the PSOE in terms of parliamentary seats and access to power. For its part, the PSOE had abandoned its explicitly Marxist positions for reformist centrism, while the conservative right was also intent upon presenting itself as a centre-rightist option. An observation made by Stuart Woolf with regard to 'traditional' Fascism seems relevant in this respect: 'Where no Bolshevik threat existed, it was difficult for a Fascist movement to act as a rallying-point of reaction, for the space had already been occupied by the politically powerful and socially respectable forces of the right.'[37]

Against this background, the situation of the extreme right in the 1980s was similar to what it had been in the first half of the 1930s: it was destined to remain marginal as long as the classes with most economic and political influence retained confidence in the ability of the parliamentary system to protect their interests by maintaining the existing political status quo. Unlike the majority of its extreme-rightist brethren, the *Frente Nacional* understood the changes which had occurred from 1982 onwards, and updated its analysis of the contemporary political and economic situation accordingly. Speaking in 1986 of what he termed the 'Fabian socialism [now] in power' in Spain, Piñar said:

I don't think Communism is the great threat to Spain ... Today, there is no conflict between Fabian socialism and means-of-exchange capitalism (money). On the contrary, socialism is the great political instrument of money and money capitalism offers all its enormous strength . . . Money supports the installation of Fabian socialism in the countries of the west.[38]

Recognising the futility of 1930s-style revolutionary appeals (e.g. to nationalise the banking system) at a time when the centres of economic, financial and military power were satisfied with the policies of the Socialist government, the extreme right in Spain no longer tried to compete with the 'politically powerful and socially respectable forces', so much as to ride on their coat-tails. In this light, it becomes comprehensible that the veteran Falangist and close friend of Piñar, José Antonio Girón, should publicly pass favourable judgement on the leaders of the PSOE,[39] while Piñar preferred the consolidation of his international image to lambasting the government of the day at home.[40]

Towards the end of the 1980s, the stagnation of Le Pen's appeal in France, and the death of Almirante in Italy had a dampening effect on the hitherto buoyant spirits of the *Frente Nacional*, which was not offset by the triumph of the neo-Nazi *Republikaner* Party in the West Berlin regional elections of January 1989. The elections to the European Parliament held in June 1989 dealt a further blow to extreme right-wing hopes of revival in Spain. While the *Republikaner* gained six seats in Strasbourg and the French *Front National* held on to its existing ten seats, their Spanish comrades not only failed, as in 1987, to secure any seats, but also lost ground in terms of the number of votes they received. The *Frente Nacional* polled 59,783 votes, 63,016 less than two years earlier, while *Falange Española der las JONS* collected a mere 23,500 votes, which was 500 fewer than in 1987. In the light of this trend, the *Frente Nacional* did not put up any candidates for the general elections held four months later, on 29 October. FE de las JONS candidates did stand, but polled less than 50,000 votes. Had *Frente Nacional* run, *Falange*'s share of the poll would have been even smaller.

Surprisingly, given the continual decline in electoral support for the extreme right, the poor showing of its representatives in the European and general elections of 1989 did not lead to this disappearance of its political organisations. It did, however, make them withdraw to lick their wounds and reconsider their position. Little change was subsequently visible in the line followed by FE de las JONS, which remained convinced of the eternal relevance of its founder's doctrine. *Frente Nacional*, however, seemed to retreat from its relatively outward-looking stance of the mid-1980s into an obsession with what it regarded as 'Spain's problems': declining standards of law and order, divorce, abortion, lay education, regionalism, Communism, Socialism, liberalism, elections and democratic government in general. In short, as *Frente Nacional* constantly lectured its followers, their struggle was against 'the system'. This message, which harked back to the crisis-stricken 1930s, struck few chords at the end of a decade, the 1980s, which, for most Spaniards, had been characterised by political stability and economic prosperity. By the turn of the decade, however, that picture was beginning to change as the recession which gripped the whole of Europe also began to affect Spain. By 1993, the Spanish economy was showing negative growth, and 2.26 million people (17.4 per cent of the workforce) were registered as unemployed. Moreover, the Socialists, in power since 1982, were deeply and publicly divided over questions of party strategy and organisation, and their leader, Felipe Gonzalez, was widely rumoured to be physically and spiritually tired of party politics. In theory, the circumstances might thus have appeared more favourable for extreme rightist candidates in the June 1993 general election than they had four years earlier.

In practice, the outcome was almost identical, with *Frente Nacional* presenting no candidates and FE de las JONS achieving only a few thousand votes.

The key factor in the failure of the extreme right to capitalise on the atmosphere of deepening economic crisis and increasing social and political discontent which preceded the election was the concomitant growth in popular and political support for the main conservative party, the People's Party [*Partido Popular*, PP]. Having portrayed itself in the late 1980s as a straightforward conservative party, this direct descendant of Manuel Fraga's AP had, under the leadership of José Maria Aznar, progressively recast itself in a centre-rightist mould. The results of the 1993 general election showed that the PP had successfully carried with it not only the bulk of its traditional voters, but also part of the PSOE electorate. What had *not* happened was a shift to the extreme right by people disillusioned with democracy. In the light of recent developments in Italy, where the collapse of the political centre, represented by the Socialist and Christian-Democratic parties, had fostered the resurgence of more extreme right-wing options, the ability or otherwise of the PP to consolidate and re-tain its position as popular champion of moderate conservatism becomes especially significant.

Certain events and political trends in other European countries might lead the outside observer to expect in Spain an upsurge in extreme rightist activity linked to immigration. Certainly, there has been a marked increase in the number of racist attacks (some of which have caused fatalities) over the last five or six years. However, although people of known extreme rightist affiliation or sympathies have been in-volved, there is no evidence to suggest that such incidents have been organised by any particular rightist group. It is equally true that immigration, particularly from North Africa, has risen considerably since 1985. Here, too, there is little evidence of a well-orchestrated campaign of extreme rightist condemnation. On the contrary, the attitude of *Frente Nacional* is highly ambiguous (though no less insidious for that), never rejecting immigrants outright, but claiming that the crux of the matter lies in the question of numbers, while eluding the provision of a clear definition of what, in their view, constitutes an unacceptable number. A range of factors help to explain why Spain's extreme right has not followed in the footsteps of some of its partners in the European Union. In the first place, sheer numbers do have a bearing: in Spain, the immigrant population constitutes less than 2 per cent of the total, which is far less than Belgium (9 per cent), France (8.2 per cent), Germany (6.5 per cent) or the UK (4.3 per cent). With over two million people unemployed, it is simply not plausible to argue that 500,000 immigrants have caused Spanish redundancies. Second, there is no tradition of racism on the extreme right in Spain; with one exception, none of its constituent groups are white supremacist (although all are ultra nationalist). Third, since 1985, Spanish immigration policy has actively sought to exercise strict control over conditions of entry and residence for non-Spanish and, particularly, non-EU nationals.

The one exception referred to above is CEDADE, whose long-standing claims to Europeanist positions may, at first sight, appear to be in tune with the current thinking of groups at many different points on the political spectrum. CEDADE's Europe, however, is not that of the single currency, the single market or the regions, but of the races, with the Aryan race taking pride of place. As a supposedly cultural organisation,

CEDADE has never taken part in elections. However, it was reported in the autumn of 1993 to be considering conversion to party status, presumably in order to participate in the 1994 European elections.[41] One can only speculate as to the motives behind such a change, since there is no reason at present to think that CEDADE would fare any better at the polls than *Frente Nacional* or FE de las JONS. It would be difficult to make domestic political capital out of its one area of notable success – as principal European printer and distributor of neo-Nazi literature and propaganda in German. Even the most ardent supporter of Catalan nationalism would probably find repellent CEDADE's claim that Catalans are ethnically different from other Spaniards.[42]

Considered only in national terms, the extreme right in Spain does not currently possess the strength to overthrow democracy. Today, however, neo-Fascism must be viewed as an international phenomenon, whose significance lies in its capacity to undermine the principle of democratic coexistence, rather than in its practice in any given geographical area. Its tactics – from within and without – are those of interconnecting sapper commandos, which do not require a complex infrastructure or a mass following. As we have seen, there are many such groups in Spain, some of them fully attuned to the international networks in which money, arms and influence circulate. It may be that, within the frontiers of Spain, there is no immediate cause for alarm. Spain, however, is in Europe; and in Europe, there can never be room for complacency.

List of Abbreviations

AE	*Afirmación Española* [Spanish Statement]
AP	*Alianza Popular* [People's Alliance]
BVE	*Batallón Vasco-Español* [Spanish Basque Battalion]
CEDADE	*Círculo Español de Amigos de Europa* [Spanish Circle of Friends of Europe]
CESPE	*Centro de Estudios Sociales, Políticos y Económicos* [Centre for Social, Political and Economic Studies]
CT	*Communión Tradicionalista* [Traditionalist Communion]
FE	*Falange Española* [Spanish Phalanx]
FE(a)	*Falange Española (auténtica)* [Authentic Spanish Phalanx]
FE de las JONS	*Falange Española de las Juntas de Ofensiva Nacional-Sindicalista* [Spanish Phalanx of Committees for National Syndicalist Attack]
FE(i)	*Falange Española (independiente)* [Independent Spanish Phalanx]
FET y de las JONS	*Falange Española Tradicionalista y de las Juntas de Ofensiva Nacional-Sindicalista* [Traditionalist Spanish Phalanx of Committees for National Syndicalist Attack]
FN	*Frente Nacional* [National Front]
FN	*Fuerza Nueva* [New Force]
FNE	*Frente Nacional Español* [Spanish National Front]
GAL	*Grupos Anti-terroristas de Liberación* [Anti-terrorist Liberation Groups]

GRAI   *Grupos Revolucionarios de Acción Internacional* [International Revolutionary Action Groups]

JCNS   *Junta Coordinadora Nacional Sindicalista* [National Syndicalist Coordinating Committee]

JJ.EE.   *Juntas Españolas* [Spanish Committees]

JONS   *Juntas de Ofensiva Nacional-Sindicalista* [Committees for National Syndicalist Attack]

PAN   *Partido de Acción Nacional* [National Action Party]

PCE   *Partido Comunista de España* [Spanish Communist Party]

PP   *Partido Popular* [People's Party]

PSOE   *Partido Socialista Obrero Español* [Spanish Socialist Workers Party]

UCD   *Unión de Centro Democratico* [Democratic Centrist Union]

UGT   *Union General de Trabajadores* [General Workers' Union]

UN   *Unión Nacional* [National Union]

Notes

* The opinions expressed in this contribution are the author's own and should not be taken as an expression of official Government policy.

1. Personal conversation in Madrid, April 1985, with Geoffrey Harris and Glyn Ford, members of the European Parliamentary Committee of Enquiry into the Rise of Fascism and Racism in Europe.
2. S. Ellwood, 'Falange Española, 1933–1939: from Fascism to Francoism', in R. M. Blinkhorn (ed.) *Spain in Conflict*, Sage, London, 1986, pp. 206–23.
3. The word 'Traditionalist' came from the title of the second-largest para-military force in the Francoist camp, the Traditionalist Communion [*Communión Tradicionalista*, CT]. Politically, it was a monarchical organisation dating from the nineteenth century, that supported the cause of a branch of the Bourbon royal family which contested the legitimacy of the reigning branch's claim to the Spanish throne.
4. J. J. Linz, 'Il sistema politico spagnolo', *Rivista italiana di scienza politica*, III, 1978, p. 372; Various Authors, *Historia de la transición*, Diario 16, Madrid, 1984, vol. II, p. 466.
5. *Historia*, cit., p. 466.
6. *Informaciones*, Madrid, 18 June 1977.
7. *Historia*, cit.; Linz, *Rivista italiana*, cit., p. 372, gives 0.21 per cent. The '18 July' National Alliance was a coalition of the following rightist groups: New Force [*Fuerza Nueva*, FN], FE de las JONS, CT, Confederation of Combatants [*Confederación de Combatientes*] and National Action Party [*Partido de Acción Nacional*, PAN].
8. *El País*, 3 March 1979, pp. 10–13, and 21 Nov. 1982 p. 18; J. Rodríguez Aramberri, in F. Claudin (ed.), *¿ Crisis en los partidos politicos?*, Dedalo, Madrid, 1980, p. 130; *Historia*, cit., p. 580.
9. *Historia*, cit., p. 580.
10. In July 1980, García Carrés participated with lieutenant colonels Tejero and Más Oliver in a meeting at which the idea of a *coup d'état* was mooted. At a further meeting of army officers, in January 1981, Garcia Carrés was asked, as a civilian, to leave. He was ultimately sentenced to two years for 'conspiracy to military rebellion'. Juan García Carrés died in 1986.
11. *El País*, 21 Nov. 1982.

12. Author's computation, from data in *El País*, 23 and 24 June 1986.
13. The mouthpiece of the extreme right, *El Alcazar*, was resuscitated as a weekly paper in 1987, after almost a year in abeyance as a daily. It devoted itself almost exclusively to acid criticism of current social and political events. Rightist publishing houses, such as DYRSA or Fuerza Nueva, tend to publish historiographical material such as memoirs or accounts of the Spanish Civil War, or works on the theory of Fascism, but not accounts of the composition and activities of present-day groups.
14. *Tiempo*, 26 Nov. 1984, p. 34.
15. *Tiempo*, 3 Nov. 1986, p. 32.
16. In spite of the fact that Piñar had held a number of official posts during the Franco regime, such as National Councillor of the Movement, National Councillor for Education and Director of the Institute of Hispanic Culture.
17. A. Royuela, *Diccionario de la ultra derecha*, Dopesa, Barcelona, 1977, pp. 15–16.
18. Personal observation, Toledo, Sept. 1986.
19. Anon. 'Vida de Don Blas', *Cuadernos para el diálogo*, 26 March 1977, pp. 21–22.
20. *Tiempo*, 26 Nov. 1984, p. 31.
21. From the *Nueva Acrópolis* 'Leader's Manual', quoted in *Tiempo*, 13 May 1985, p. 40.
22. Ibid.
23. J. Mota, *Hacia un socialismo europeo*, Ediciones Bau, Barcelona, 1974, back cover.
24. 'La Cedade', *Article 31*, VII, 1985, p. 14.
25. Ibid.
26. *Tiempo*, 13 May 1985, p. 10.
27. Ibid. Members of New Force were subsequently tried as the active perpetrators of the Jan. 1977 'Atocha massacre'; see *Diario 16*, 15 March 1977, pp. 16–17.
28. *Tiempo*, 13 May 1985, p. 12.
29. *Tiempo*, 3 Nov. 1986, p. 32.
30. *Diario 16*, 10 June 1987, p. 10.
31. *El País*, 27 Oct., 1986, p. 18.
32. Blas Piñar, in *Diario 16*, 3 March 1987, p. 12.
33. Personal observation at the *Frente Nacional/Fuerza Nueva* rally in El Escorial (Madrid), on 18 July 1986.
34. *Diario 16*, 2 March 1987, p. 7.
35. Personal observation at the *Frente Nacional/Fuerza Nueva* rally in El Escorial, on 18 July 1986.
36. *Diario 16*, 11 June 1987. The party spokesman, Luis Villamea, immediately issued accusations of fraudulent dealings at the polls and threatened to take the matter up with the European Parliament, for, he said, 'in Madrid alone we have more than 40,000 voters'. In fact, the official figure was absolutely consistent with successive electoral results for the extreme right since 1977, with the exception of 1979, discussed above.
37. S. J. Woolf, Introduction to S. J. Woolf (ed.) *Fascism in Europe*, Methuen, London, 1981, p. 7.
38. Blas Piñar, personal interview, Madrid, 17 October 1986.
39. In an interview published in *Interviú*, 29 July 1987, pp. 16–19, Girón said of President González that he is 'a man who is full of good intentions, who always tries to resolve problems by the most agreeable means. He seems fairly moderate.' Likewise, PSOE vice-secretary general, Alfonso Guerra, was considered by Girón to be 'an alert and agile man, who has to play the villain of the piece, which doesn't mean he *is* a villain'.
40. See, e.g., the report of Piñar's guest-of-honour appearance at the 'Red, White and Blue Festival', organised by the French *Front National* at Le Bourget in Aug. 1987, in *Fuerza Nueva*, No. 945, 12–26 Sept. 1987, pp. 12–15.

41. *El País*, 14 Oct. 1993, p. 22.
42. *El País*, 26 Nov. 1993, reported an all-party proposal in the Catalan parliament rejecting extreme rightist propaganda activities in Catalonia, and urging the Catalan President to press central government to clamp down on them in Spain as a whole.

Chapter 6

THE RADICAL RIGHT IN CONTEMPORARY
PORTUGAL*
António Costa Pinto

The neo-Fascist manifestations which have recurred periodically in European countries since 1945 have had no Portuguese equivalent as yet. For anyone supporting a
restricted definition of Fascism, and hence of neo-Fascism, it would hardly make sense
to discuss this theme in Portugal. The concept of radical right is therefore to be
preferred since it enables us to cover a wider spectrum closer to the reality investi-
gated.[1] If we dealt only with the emergence of neo-Fascism, we would be confined to
the tiny groups and intellectual circles set up in the early 1960s. These found no
expression in the political spectrum either under the New State [*Estado Novo*, EN]
created by Salazar in the 1930s, or under the democratic regime.

In investigating the Portuguese case, it is therefore important not to lose sight of
the different realities covered by those two concepts. This is all the more necessary
since the debate about the political nature of Salazar's regime is far from closed. In
addition, some specific characteristics differentiated that regime from its European
counterparts in the inter-war years. This fact had important consequences for the
legacy left to the democratic regime after 1974.

The second point refers to chronology. On 25 April 1974, a military coup, which
rapidly turned into a revolutionary process, ensured the transition towards, and later
the consolidation of, a democratic regime, and the irreversible fall of the EN. Both
Iberian dictatorships had survived the demise of European Fascism, and 1945 had not
caused any significant break in the nature of either. Yet the downfall of the Axis caused
some changes in the political system and a rapid downgrading of some institutions
associated with Fascism. This was probably more true of Portugal than of Spain, and
it was the starting point for the emergence of a minority located to the right of the
EN, which, from then on, called itself an 'organic democracy'.

Until Salazar's political death in 1968, neo-Fascism and some nuclei of the radical
right in Portugal defined themselves as a trend aimed at purifying the regime. The
figure of the leader was always spared. With the advent of the dictator's successor,
Marcello Caetano, who supported various reformist attempts in the last years of the
authoritarian regime, some trends emerged which demarcated themselves from the
new political power. They were the origin of the radical right groupings which were
active in Portugal after the transition to a democratic regime. Hence their genesis from
1945, still under the EN, must be covered in a brief introduction.

The legacy of the 'Estado Novo'

A populist radical right has not been part of Portuguese political culture in the twentieth century. There were political movements similar to *Action Française* at the beginning of the century, but the elitism of their ideology was hard to combine with a populist strategy for political action. Though present in the ideological field, they never went beyond an elitist type of intervention.[2] The very short dictatorship of Sidonio Pais (1918) might have brought about such a constitution. However, the regime which imposed itself in the wake of a military dictatorship (1926) – Salazar's EN – always resisted that temptation.

There may be legitimate doubts about the relationships of causality between the ups and downs of radical right movements in contemporary Europe, and the historical Fascisms of the inter-war period. Yet it remains true that one of their legacies to post-war democratic regimes is an embryonic neo-Fascism. Even in countries where native Fascism only shared power thanks to enemy occupation, as in France, the more or less episodic emergence of this type of movement has remained a constant. Italy provides a clear example of this, while in Germany it was only an antagonistic electoral system which blocked its rapid reappearance after the Second World War. It was not so in Portugal.

Unlike other regimes of the 'Fascist period', Salazar's did not leave to posterity, after its fall, the symbols, organisation, ideology and human support capable of feeding a neo-Fascist party.[3] One component of Francoism was a native Fascism which ultimately acknowledged him as head of the movement. In post-authoritarian Spain a neo-phalangism was possible, though it remained marginal. In Portugal it was impossible to introduce a neo-Fascist practice based on the abolished regime.

Though it shared some features and underwent the influence of Fascism, the EN differed from it in a number of basic aspects. Historically, it emerged from a military dictatorship, introduced in 1926 after a coup which abolished a liberal republic. It was not based on a Fascist-type party (which did not exist during the crisis and the downfall of liberalism). The single party of the regime – the National Union [*União Nacional*, UN] – was created in 1930, from above and through a decisive intervention of the state apparatus. The corporative institutions, inspired by Italian Fascism, were tempered by the 'Social Catholicism' from which the dictator originated. In practice they were mere appendages of the state machinery, without life of their own or autonomy. Furthermore, the regime – unlike its Fascist counterparts – did not rely on the intense political mobilisation of the population.

It was at the height of the military dictatorship, when Salazar was emerging as a major candidate for the post of Prime Minister, that a Fascist party, the National Syndicalism [*Nacional Sindicalismo*, NS], headed by Rolão Preto, was set up.[4] There was a leadership contest and the NS was repressed, indeed outlawed, in 1934. The following year, an attempted coup against Salazar resulted in the exile and persecution of its leaders. The single party was also created to oppose this native Fascism. It was, in addition, intended to provide representation in a parliament which met infrequently, merely to ratify the decisions of the executive. It sank into lethargy until the end of the Second World War.[5]

The threat represented by the Second Spanish Republic and the start of the Civil War in that neighbouring country induced a shift towards Fascism in the regime. Salazar allowed the formation of the Portuguese Legion [*Legião Portuguesa*, LP], which sent volunteers to fight beside Franco, as well as a paramilitary organisation, Portuguese Youth [*Mocidade Portuguesa*, MP]. Both provided a Fascist political backing to the regime in the second half of the 1930s, but they remained under the strict domination of the state. MP was under the direct rule of the Ministry of Education and the LP was controlled by the army. There was no linkage with the party which was merely an institution of the regime, without any effective powers.[6]

Anticipating a new international situation after the defeat of Fascism, the regime prepared a cover-up operation in 1944. The single party was resurrected to ensure a 'certain victory' in the general and presidential elections, in which the opposition was allowed to participate. It took advantage of those brief interludes to denounce the dictatorial nature of the regime, until its fall in 1974.[7]

In the post-war period, the EN came to define itself as an 'organic democracy' and endeavoured, without too much difficulty, to conceal the outward signs of its association with Fascism. The paramilitary organisations, the MP in particular, acquired a more 'former-student' and 'sporting' character. The *Secretariado de Propaganda Nacional* (Secretariat for National Propaganda), entrusted with organising mass demonstrations throughout the 1930s, and led by António Ferro, an intellectual extrovert and admirer of Mussolini, changed name and leader. It acquired a more anodyne image as a promoter of 'tourism and information'. The LP, downgraded since 1939, when Franco won the Spanish Civil War, vanished from the streets and went into decline.

In the unfavourable international climate of 1945, Salazar was able to secure the survival of his regime. This he owed to his neutrality during the war, to his military concessions, to Britain and the United States and to the rapid onset of the cold war, which gained him the recognition of the new international community (Portugal joined the UN and NATO at the end of the decade).[8] However, changes at the level of institutions and of decision-making machinery proved very limited. There were no basic changes in 1945, as far as the authoritarian nature of the regime was concerned. It was only when Salazar was replaced by Marcello Caetano, in 1968, that a series of reforms took place, and that part of the political elite associated with the old dictator was removed.

Some of the characteristics which demarcated the EN from European Fascism may account for the fragility of the Portuguese radical right on the eve of the regime's fall.[9] The main one, no doubt, was the minimal autonomy of party institutions in relation to the state. One author rightly concluded that 'the truth about the way Portugal was governed from 1930 to 1974 was (that it was) an administrative state'.[10] Apart from administration, the little that existed disintegrated over time, if only for lack of functions, as the regime – once established – did not attempt any extensive or intensive political mobilisation. Political militancy was weak and participation in the single party or the paramilitary organisations remained limited since, from the inter-war period, but more explicitly after 1945, the regime promoted depoliticisation. Salazar never sponsored any ideological or mobilising organisation, even when confronted with a colonial war in the early 1960s.

One of the subtlest ideologists of Portuguese neo-Fascism, writing in the short exile to which he was forced by the transition to democracy, wrote that Salazar:

> was, in spite of everything, a sceptic about the potential of others. He was not a Fascist, but a reactionary and, as Drieu taught, they are polar opposites. He did not believe in popular energies, in the permanent revolution, in that collective sense of national mystique, perhaps manufactured by propaganda, but possibly the great moving-force of peoples. Salazar preferred the force of circumstance, of common sense, of routine.[11]

This statement anticipated how difficult it would be to find in the collapsed regime an ideological and political basis for neo-Fascist practice. However, until 1974, the figure of the Leader was never challenged.

The first properly neo-Fascist nucleus, demarcated from the native radical right entrenched in some institutions such as the old LP or the official press, was founded in 1959 around the review *Tempo Presente*.[12] It was a group of young intellectuals who, faced with the ideological and political decrepitude of the regime, and in the wake of presidential elections in which an opposition candidate (one General Humberto Delgado, with a governmental background and a military man to boot), achieved considerable popularity, sought to revive the 'Fascist' wing of the regime.

Though of marginal importance, politically, this group started the intellectual revival of the Portuguese radical right. The neo-Fascism to which they gave foundations and substance developed through the 1960s. The start of the colonial war gave them some governmental support. It also gave them a 'political struggle' with which they wanted to mobilise the energies needed to preserve the empire, threatened by African liberation movements. They started various university nuclei, such as the Young Portugal movement [*Movimento Jovem Portugal*, MJP], the Front of Nationalist Students [*Frente de Estudantes Nacionalistas*, FEN] and the National Revolutionary Front [*Frente Nacional Revolucionária*, FNR].

Tempo Presente linked itself explicitly with Fascism, that 'unforgettable revelation of our youth'.[13] Contrary to the domestic and defensive radical right, the group embraced modern aesthetic values. It sought to deprive opposition intellectuals of their overwhelming monopoly in the cultural field.[14]

The main political themes of the review revolved round a critique of the 'enemies within'. The main one, the real *bête noire* of the 1960s, was the Catholic world, in which youth organisations and groups of intellectuals were beginning to break away from the dominant orthodoxy.[15] This movement, which was later legitimised by Vatican II, gave rise to a Catholic Opposition centre. A second theme focused on the 'technocrats', associated with the moderate economic boom of the 1960s. They were accused of lacking any ideological scruples and of defending European options incompatible with a multi-continental Empire. These accusations became sharper when the old dictator was replaced, and the sector associated with the Empire lost important positions within the state machinery.

The beginning of the colonial war in 1961, and its extension to several fronts in later years, provided the small neo-Fascist group with a leitmotif. It also ensured the support of various institutions, worried by the growth and the politicisation of the student movement, which was the main target of conscription. However, in this last struggle of the regime, Salazar – consistent with the total distrust he had always shown since the 1930s – did not rely on any large-scale mobilisation of 'refascistisation'. Once the control of the armed forces had been secured, by purging them of waverers, the war was hardly mentioned by the media, except for rare 'confrontations' with 'terrorists' from outside. This applied until the situation deteriorated dramatically in the early 1970s. For the neo-Fascists, 'it was a war without heroes or rather one in which heroes were hidden or concealed', without any encouragement of 'the cult of those who were fighting'.[16]

As for the political organisations proper, they were always very limited and exclusively linked with the student milieu, in which they had the secret support of the Ministry of Education, the political police and the old LP. Their appearance was nearly always merely part of a counter-propaganda strategy used by official bodies since 1945, when opposition organisations began to engage in semi-legal activities. Such was the case of the Patriotic Academic Front [*Frente Académica Patriótica*, FAP] which was active in the late 1940s but served merely as a mouthpiece for government propaganda.[17]

The previously mentioned Young Portugal Movement, founded in 1961, enjoyed more autonomy.[18] Its leaders wished to create a party which would conform to the organisational ideal type of the 1930s. They even managed to contact the old NS leaders to show their loyalty to the old principles of intransigent Fascism. In the meantime, some of them had moved a long way away and allied themselves to the 'democratic opposition', as was the case of Rolão Preto.[19] The MJP would be succeeded by the National Revolutionary Front [*Frente Nacional Revolucionária*, FNR] in 1966.[20]

Defining itself as a movement of young students and workers, the FNR did not hesitate to criticise the thirty dangerous years in which the regime itself promoted the 'apoliticisation of youth', with results which were all too obvious, as mobilisation for a colonial war coincided with the ageing of the ruling elite.[21]

In the ideological sphere, this group endeavoured to blend the European neo-Fascist themes of the 1960s with an updated version of National Syndicalist principles, defined as the Movement's official doctrine.[22] From the 1930s emerged the Fascist heroes, such as the Romanian Codreanu and the Spanish José António, from the 1960s Maurice Bardèche, Blas Piñar and the whole international panoply of the most virulent, dogmatic and 'revolutionary' sector of European neo-Fascism. In France, as groups proliferated on the far right, contacts with Pierre Sido's *Jeune Nation* movement were made.[23] In Italy this happened with the more radical faction of the *Movimento Sociale Italiano*, the splinter group *Ordine Nuovo*.[24]

Created as the university students' movement became more politicised, after the academic crisis of 1962, the MJP had a brief existence. Its main leaders were called up to serve in the colonial war. In 1964, the FEN, which has already been mentioned, was created to fill the space thus vacated. The following year it became known by taking part, together with the LP, in the attack on the Portuguese Writers' Association.[25] A less clandestine existence was led by the FNR, which was based in the universities of Lisbon and Coimbra, where it organised meetings and action against the student movement.[26] More atuned to the ideological renewal of the French group

Europe-Action, of whom Zarco Moniz Ferreira was the correspondent in Portugal, the FNR appeared more future-oriented, and no longer considered NS as its official ideology.[27] This is not an exhaustive list of Portuguese neo-Fascists groups in existence until 1974. The model adopted, however, was that of the study group, linked with universities rather than the political party.[28]

Although it often shared the same editorial and thematic space with young neo-Fascism, the indigenous radical right was associated with a different generation and with ideological and cultural references much more closely related to traditional Portuguese anti-liberalism. Its programme expressed the resistance of a cultural and political universe which had been in decline since 1945. It was against the world of the United Nations, 'born with its back turned to God' as a strange alliance between 'American plutocratic utilitarianism and the militant atheism of communism'.[29] Its political expression did not extend beyond the publication of reviews such as *Agora* and *Resistência.*[30]

In the editorial team of *Agora*, in its early phase, old names of the 1930s reappear, mainly the National Syndicalists who accepted Salazarism.[31] Its journalistic activity was limited to saying what diplomatic caution prevented the mainstream press from being open about. Catholic dogmatism, anti-cosmopolitanism and nationalist isolationism against a 'world in chaos': these central values of the Salazarist universe were asserted against the 'enemies within' and the pernicious influence of fashions from outside. The performer Cecilia Meireles, who 'sings what the people sing no longer', was contrasted positively with the Beatles[32], and the poet António Sardinha with Arthur Miller, the 'communist Jew', or Sartre, 'wrongdoer of literature and homosexual'.[33] On the eve of the dictator's removal, *Agora*, in a special issue on Fascism, published statements by representatives of various generations who had kept the ideological flame of the radical right burning during the long authoritarian regime. Nevertheless, all of them were politically marginal in relation to Salazarism.[34]

The removal of Salazar in 1968 and the coming to power of Marcello Caetano did not provide favourable ground for the continued support or the benevolent neutrality of official bodies. Supported or covertly tolerated in the last years of Salazarism, the neo-Fascist nuclei foresaw the difficult problem of succession in a dictatorship bound up with the charismatic figure of its leader. Salazar, always respected, was secretly accused of lacking firmness, but any queries about his successor elicited a reply which announced problems: 'After him, nobody.'[35]

It was under the reformist experiment of Salazar's successor that both the radical right and the neo-Fascists openly distanced themselves from the authoritarian political power, sought alternative leaders and even called for coup attempts.

As the single party was reorganised under *Marcelismo*, as the liberalising sectors acquired an autonomous organisation, as censorship eased and as some opposition figures began to return home, the radical right dissociated itself from the leadership of the regime. It became known by public opinion, with its own spokesmen in the National Assembly and with the support of some Salazarist barons.

Nuclei such as Social Studies Circles VECTOR [*Círculos de Estudos Sociais VECTOR*] claimed the purity of the EN and set up a national network.[36] Symbolically, the first meeting of that organisation took place in 1969 at Fátima. Apart from the left, which then had more access to the media, its enemies were the reformists and the technocrats associated with Caetano. Some figures from that milieu became known in the struggle with the 'liberals' in the National Assembly.

While *Resistência* represented the hard nucleus of Salazarism, *Política*, created in 1969, was the voice of neo-Fascism.[37] Neither the ideology nor the names changed much from what had existed in Salazar's last years.[38] The only novelty was its organisation and its acknowledgement as a political trend, detached from power.[39]

In those years, a close association was forged between some opponents of Caetano's candidacy as a successor to Salazar, for example, the former Minister of Foreign Affairs, Franco Nogueira, and these groups. Later, just before the downfall of the regime, this stance was adopted by members of the armed forces, such as General Kaúlza de Arriaga, who was capable of launching a *pronunciamento* against Caetano, in the context of the crisis unleashed by General Spínola.

The radical right and the transition to democracy

Some specific features of the transition to democracy, such as the lack of compromise with the old regime's elite and the 'anti-Fascist' radicalism of 1974–75, deeply affected the overall political realignment of the Portuguese right. For the radical right this new situation was devastating, both politically and organisationally, but ideologically as well.

In the first two years, while political parties were set up and the new constitution was approved, the radical right was affected by a number of electoral prohibitions, political *saneamentos* (purges) and party bans. Hence, any quick reconversion of the elite of Salazarism or – at the outset – of the groups discussed here was impeded.[40]

It was under pressure from strong social and political movements led by the left and the extreme left, and in the shadow of illegality, that the two parties which stood for the centre-right and the right in the general election of 1975 were formed.[41] The adverse conjuncture in which they began life was made obvious both by the political programmes of the centrists and the social democrats, on the one hand, and by their own choice of leaders with no active political past under the old regime. Drawing up a balance sheet of those years, a Portuguese neo-Fascist got close to the truth when he stressed, years later, that these factors involved both parties in adopting 'programmes to the left of their leaders, who were to the left of militants and voters'.[42]

In the context of the transition to democracy in Southern Europe in the 1970s, the *saneamento* movement, which started immediately after the coup and developed throughout 1975, was a singularity of the Portuguese case.[43] Although it was ultimately rather limited, as was the whole process of 'defascistisation' after the Second World War, it still had significant consequences in that it prevented a rapid readjustment by most of the old regime's political personnel.

The first measures of the National Salvation Junta [*Junta de Salvação Nacional*, JSN], presided over by General Spínola, were directed towards a rapid and straightforward purge programme. The former President of the Republic and the Prime Minister, together with some ministers, were exiled. The paramilitary and the police groups (the political police and the old anti-Communist militia, LP), who attempted

114

resistance, were dissolved and a part of their elite entourage arrested. The single party, the official youth organisation and other institutions from the Fascist era were also dissolved. The Armed Forces Movement [*Movimento das Forças Armadas*, MFA], which led the coup, proposed to retire sixty generals, the majority of whom had participated, some time before, in a public demonstration of solidarity with the old regime.[44]

The first legislation on *saneamento* included the demise of the civil service and the loss of political rights of all presidents of the republic, ministers, national leaders of the single party and of the LP. At the local level, the clandestine and semi-legal opposition to the old regime – particularly the Portuguese Democratic Movement [*Movimento Democrático Português*, MDP], a front organisation connected with the Communist Party [*Partido Comunista Português*, PCP] – occupied the majority of the town councils and expelled their previous leaders. The old corporative unions were occupied by the workers, the majority of whom were affiliated to the Communist Party. The pressure of left-wing political movements and the effect of 'liberation' prevented any action which could have permitted the survival of the institutions and the national political elite of the dissolved regime, against the initial wish of Spínola.

The first policy declarations of the left-wing parties were, in general, fairly cautious as far as *saneamentos* were concerned. The Socialist Party asked in its first communiqué for 'the removal of all those directly involved in the previous government'. The Communists also made rather moderate declarations. Nevertheless, the first *saneamentos* occurred in various sectors, and the demands for purges were part of the first workers' strikes. In the Universities of Lisbon and Coimbra, lecturers and staff who had cooperated with the former regime were denied entrance by students' unions.

In response to these spontaneous movements, the provisional government issued the first regulations on civil servant *saneamentos*, creating an inter-ministerial re-classification committee in order to bring to justice those who might reveal behaviour 'contrary to the established order after 25 April 1974'.[45] This committee functioned until 1976 and the legislation was reviewed several times, thus revealing the radicalisation of the political situation. At the beginning of 1975, the legal text itself referred to the previous regime as 'Fascist regime' and the behaviour of civil servants before the revolution became subject to *saneamento*.[46]

After Spínola's overthrow, the anti-capitalist thrust of events provoked a second wave of purges. Individual *saneamentos* were encouraged. The nationalisation of the most important firms and the expropriation of the great landowners were called for. These two groups were considered the supporters of the previous regime by the two main agents of the second part of the process – the PCP and the ultra left-wing groups, which dominated the Portuguese revolution until the end of 1975. Purging and anti-capitalism were strictly connected in the second period.

In February 1975, the official reports on the purge process declared that 12,000 citizens were involved.[47] Between March and November 1975, this figure must have significantly increased, since, by 25 November 1975, when the purge movement was suspended, this number was approximately 20,000, if we consider all types of punishments: from the simple transfer to dismissal from work.

The proponents of the purge process were many and varied. If we exclude the first measures of the JSN immediately following the coup, it was, however, essentially the PCP and the small but influential extreme left parties which led the movement.

The demands for purges were often led by workers' commissions independent of the unions, and organised according to place of work (the so-called *Comissões de Trabalhadores*) where the PCP had to share control with the extreme left parties. Most of the 'wildcat purges' were implemented by these committees which occasionally escaped the control of the PCP bureaucracy.

In general, the purge movement did not keep to clear strategies and coherent patterns, being extremely diverse from sector to sector. The concept of 'collaborator' changed during the period of 'exception'. In 1974, the first purge movement was based on a strict concept of collaboration, but in 1975, with the burgeoning anti-capitalist wave, a number of traditional attitudes held by industrialists were considered as symbols of the old regime.

The purge deeply affected the top cadres of Salazarism, most of whom went into exile or retreated into political silence without giving much symbolic commitment to the reorganisation of the radical right at the time.

The young neo-Fascists, unaffected by the initial measures of purge and exile, since they had not exercised any eminent political functions under the former regime, were the first to initiate the creation of resistance parties, within the new legal order. These included the Progress Party [*Partido do Progresso*, PP], whose headquarters were ransacked and which was dissolved on 28 September, after the departure of General Spínola, as well as the Liberal Party [*Partido Liberal*, PL], and the Portuguese Nationalist Movement [*Movimento Nacionalista Português*, MNP]. Only the Christian Democrat Party [*Partido de Democracia Cristã*, PDC], survived this first offensive and achieved legal status, after having been prevented from contesting the first elections in April 1975. However, it is rather unclear whether the early PDC really did belong to the radical right. In fact this tiny party, which for many years was the only electoral contender representing the far right, went through very diverse phases and never united the main elements of that sector.[48]

After the party's dissolution, following the fall of Spínola, some nuclei began a clandestine struggle in 1975, as part of a major anti-Communist offensive.

At the beginning of 1975, the radicalisation and the shift to the left gave way to several organisations that played an important political role in the centre and north of the country during the so-called 'hot summer' of 1975.

As already suggested, the situation changed in this period. The occupation of land in the south began; the great economic groups were nationalised; important company directors left the country; and even the Catholic Church lost control of its official broadcasting station. The latter was occupied by workers and journalists and turned into the mouthpiece of the revolutionary left.

Thus were created the conditions for the political fulfilment of one of the main themes of the ideological discourse of the radical right since the turn of the century: capital (Lisbon) versus province, Catholic north versus 'red' south.

The theorisation of this dual political culture of Portugal was a constant element of Portuguese conservative and traditionalist thought: the hard-working Catholic north versus the Mozarabic south of the rural workers of the latifundia area and the urban world of Lisbon.

116

The anti-Communist political offensive of the summer of 1975 can only be compared to the anti-liberal social movements of the nineteenth century, even though hurried comparisons might lead to anachronism. However, we are clearly confronted with the first relatively successful mass mobilisation of the provinces since the middle of the nineteenth century. Local notables and Catholic churchmen played an important part in the movement, in the centre and north of the country.[49]

After his escape from the country, General Spínola created the Democratic Movement for the Liberation of Portugal [*Movimento Democrático de Libertação Nacional*, MDLP] which was connected with the Portuguese Liberation Army [*Exército de Libertação Nacional*, ELP], and led part of the movement. These organisations were largely dominated by right-wing military men, associated with the provincial elites, while the Church of Braga, the centre of the more conservative northern Catholic hierarchy of the country, provided connections with local notables. Financial support was forthcoming from northern industrialists and from some Western nations. The Spanish border and the police showed a collaborative neutrality. The hard core of the MDLP, created in Madrid in the mid-1970s, was formed by military men and the newly created ultra-right parties, which became illegal upon the fall of Spínola. However, some veterans of the colonial war led the operations. Alpoim Galvão, an army officer and veteran of the colonial war (he led the attack on Guiné-Conakry in 1970), recruited some military men and after dealing with Spínola, by that time in Brazil, created the movement.[50]

According to Galvão, the ELP was bringing together the more radical elements, who supported a return to the authoritarian regime, of which he did not approve. Nevertheless, there was cooperation between them. The ELP carried out several terrorist actions, bomb attacks and even political murders.

The ELP activities were of a classic political terrorism type. More important were the effective anti-Communist demonstrations, which usually led to the burning and pillaging of the PCP offices, and those of the MDP which still dominated part of the local administration.

The ELP, which has received little academic attention, relied on the decisive support of the Catholic hierarchy mainly in the north and particularly in the Braga diocese. A whole network of provincial parish priests did their utmost to link their anti-Communist activities from the pulpit with political demonstrations. It would be hard to describe the various clashes between the rural and provincial world, on the one hand, and the urban and working-class one, on the other, during the 'hot summer' of 1975, whether by referring to the social actors involved or from an organisational viewpoint. The truth remains that while in Lisbon a workers' demonstration besieged the Constituent Assembly, 50 kilometres north of the capital, on its rural outskirts, peasants beat up pickets and destroyed the headquarters of the PCP, after a demonstration of 'support for the lord bishop'.[51]

This whole dynamic process had an important impact in isolating the capital city, its industrial belt and the Alentejo region, shaken by strong radical movements. It was also in the north that organic links between the MDLP-ELP, the religious hierarchy and the local notables, closely associated with small business, made political action more effective.[52] It should be stressed that all this activity, including attacks on Communist headquarters in the centre-north of the country, took place with the support of local branches of the centre-right and Socialist parties.

In Lisbon it was the Socialist Party [*Partido Socialista*, PS], together with members of the armed forces belonging to the moderate left, who led the movement which came to a head on 25 November 1975. This date was crucial in containing the pre-revolutionary wave and in establishing a representative democracy. These sectors were the main recipients of large financial support from the West, mainly from the United States, which rapidly turned off the small tap available to Spínola and the MDLP.

The operational activities, terrorism included, of the MDLP and the FLP were mainly undertaken by soldiers or former soldiers. Some of them were arrested, but their connections with moderates during the 'hot summer' of 1975 and the promises made to many that everything would be forgotten, turned their trials into sensitive matters, dragging on for many years, and led to vendettas among the persons concerned.

The end of the revolutionary period and the gradual establishment of democracy from 1976 onwards led to the vanishing of illusions about an extreme right restoration, and even about the minimum programme on which any such organisation could be based. The return of exiles to Portugal, the growing press activity of those who had been 'plundered' in 1974–75, and the search for anti-Communist 'military heroes', ended without leaving any trace. Decolonisation, made worse by the inability to mobilise the *retornados*, marked the end of an era in the political culture of the radical right.

The reintegration process of purged individuals went forward between 1976 and the early 1980s. Based upon new legislation, the most rapid measures were taken in the economic sector, where the 'wildcat purge' had been strongest. The governments implemented a set of incentive measures aimed at the return of emigrés or purged managers, in a climate of economic crisis and negotiations with the International Monetary Fund. The law declared that the purge of citizens for political or ideological reasons, occurring between 1974 and 1976, was legally non-existent.

Within the civil service, new legislation invited purged people to apply for rehabilitation. The purge committees were dismantled, and a rehabilitation commission was set up, which worked until the 1980s and rehabilitated individuals in the majority of the cases presented. However, in the light of present knowledge it seems that 'reintegration' did not mean a return to former positions. For example, in the case of the armed forces, the old elite remained in reserve or retired. Because of complicated administrative processes, it took longer to reintegrate the victims of legal purges.

In the same period, an anti-leftist purge developed: militants from the extreme left and the PCP were dismissed from the media, state departments and public enterprises. This was particularly evident in the Ministries of Agriculture and Work, and in the nationalised banks where Communists had exerted a strong presence.

With the renegotiation of the pact between the democratic parties and the inheritors of the MFA, and the disappearance of military tutelage, some leading figures of the old regime returned to Portugal. The President, Tomás (who remained politically silent until his death), and some ministers returned from Brazil, and only Marcello Caetano was refused permission to return, and died in Brazil in 1980.

However, these figures were not associated with a possible future revival of the native radical right, and the old ministerial elite of Salazar died in silence. Exceptions prove this rule: only one ex-minister made a political career in the new democracy: Adriano Moreira, former Minister of Overseas Territories, who was deputy and general secretary of the right-wing Social-Democratic Centre [*Centro Democrático Social*, CDS] for a short period. Two reformist ministers of Caetano's were brought back into the fold: the Secretary of State for Corporations, who introduced the liberalisation of the unions before the end of the regime, and also the architect of the education reform.

The new political climate of 'political reconciliation', which characterised the end of the 1970s, influenced some processes connected with the inheritance of the old regime, for example, in the case of the members of the ex-political police.

Despite efforts by some military sectors to save the colonial branch of the political policy, the entire body was, after brief resistance, totally dismantled. In 1974, in an atmosphere of persecution, those who had not fled spent the two years of the period of exception awaiting trial. Their trials were already organised in accordance with the new political ethos. Consequently, those who had not taken advantage of conditional freedom to emigrate were lightly punished by military courts, which were especially lenient towards those with good military records.

Among the few who had been gaoled in Portugal since 1974 was General Kaúlza de Arriaga. A veteran of the colonial war, whose name was much mentioned by the extreme right in the last years of the regime, he created in 1977 the Independent Movement for National Reconstruction [*Movimento Independente para a Reconstrução Nacional*, MIRN], later renamed Party of the Portuguese Right [*Partido de Direita Portuguesa*, PDP].[53] This party was the last attempt to unify various fringe groups associated with the old regime. With a moderate programme, demarcated from the authoritarianism of the past and seeking to defend the interest of white settlers from the former colonies, this party fought the general election of 1980, allied to the PDC. It did not win any seats, despite an electoral system based on proportional representation which enabled the extreme left to be represented in parliament, during the transition period, with less than 2 per cent of the vote.

The failure of the MIRN, which was dissolved soon after, symbolically marked the end of an era. To the ideological trauma caused by the loss of the colonies, which generated an abundant literature of recrimination, corresponded a very moderate sociological trauma for those affected – at least by comparison with similar processes.[54] Obviously the relatively peaceful integration of the *retornados* was not only caused by the 'gentle ways' of the Portuguese or by the sustained provision of financial support by the State. Sociological characteristics of the white community in Africa, such as relatively recent settlement (and thus family ties in the metropolitan country) or direct emigration to other countries, in particular South Africa, cushioned the shock.

The end of the 1970s, with the gradual withdrawal of the military from the political arena, the consolidation of parliamentary parties, and the settling down of their electorate, ended any chance of political reconversion for some populist military figures, tempted to capitalise on the success of their anti-leftist action in 1975.

The Radical Right in the 1980s

It was in the cultural field that the most active groups concentrated their activities in the 1980s. The core of Portuguese nationalism, the multi-continental 'empire', on which the ideology of the extreme right had rested until the 1970s was irreversibly destroyed. An abundant cultural activity revolved around its reshaping in the context of the European option and of the attendant threats to Portuguese national identity.

Once again it was the – by now fewer – young neo-Fascist 1960s intellectuals who undertook the task. They were prompted by the belief that it 'would be more important, in the political sphere, to indoctrinate and influence the non-Marxist parties into moving to the right, and to support strongly the leaders and groups who favoured this trend, rather than to create autonomous rightist forces'.[55] Without repudiating their past heroes, they started a process of ideological revision and of separation from simple anti-democratic reaction. An example was provided by the journal *Futuro Presente*, where part of the neo-Fascists generation of the 1960s, in particular those who had not joined centre-right parties in the meantime, could be found.[56] This was far from dogmatic and militant neo-Fascism: it rather represented an attempt at doctrinal reformulation of the Portuguese right.[57]

This effort went on throughout the debate on the new geo-strategic location of Portugal, now stripped of its colonial possessions, and through the reassessment of the 'nation' as a concept. The themes of the European and American New Right were also introduced under a political system which had been dominated by socialist legacies since 1975.

Revealing a multiplicity of influences, the debate covered the contributions of North American neo-liberals and 'anarcho-capitalists', of sociobiology, of Alain de Benoist's *Nouvelle Droite* and of the classics of Portuguese traditionalism which were being revived. Classic themes from Lusitanian nationalist mythology such as the Discoveries and the 'Atlantic calling' inherited from the colonial empire, the problem of the Iberian peninsula and the Spanish threat, and the decadence caused by nineteenth-century liberalism, were invoked to legitimate a new conservative nationalism 'or a Nationalism conceived as a political doctrine in which the Nation State is . . . the first value to preserve and to defend in the temporal order'.[58]

From the late 1970s this cultural and ideological effort acquired various centres of development. Among them were the private universities founded by lecturers purged from the state universities in 1974, a new privately-owned press, the youth organisations of right-wing parties and also some foundations associated with them.

This rethinking of new ideological elements by the right and the attempt to overcome dogmatism were accompanied by a proliferation of cultural initiatives. Such initiatives relied on the cooperation of young neo-Fascists, traditionalist monarchists, Catholic fundamentalists, right-wing dominated students' associations and other conservative sectors which developed during the 1980s, sometimes under the patronage of universally respected figures.[59] The latter ranged from Franco Nogueira, old 'baron' of Salazarism and author of a monumental biography of the dictator, to distinguished historians and university professors.

Since the transition to democracy, the radical right has been characterised by an absence of leaders with even minimal public impact, by the extreme weakness and

Table 6.1 PDC/MIRN in national elections

Party	Year	Votes	%
PDC	1976	28,178	0.5
PDC	1979	65,417	1.1
PDC/MIRN	1980	20,489	0.4
PDC	1983	36,365	0.7
PDC	1985	39,675	0.7
PDC	1987	30,724	0.6
PDC	1991	—	—

fragility of party organisations, and by the drifting away of its cadres, as well as by an ideological crisis. The PDC has been virtually the only party to fight in every election, and its results are so modest, even in conjunction with Kaulza de Arriaga's MIRN-PDP in 1980, that no assumptions about electoral sociology can be drawn. Its results at the polls have ranged between 0.3 per cent and 1.1 per cent in general elections (see Table 6.1).

Prevented from standing in the first elections, deprived of any well-known personalities, and despised by ideological neo-Fascism, the PDC found a refuge in propaganda on behalf of former colonials.[60] As for the more ambitious but brief experiment of the MIRN, it appeared rather late in the process and was damaged, indeed literally destroyed, by the electoral alliance of right-wing parties. In the 1980s, new and rather fragmented organisations emerged, nearly always run by youngsters and devoid of electoral impact.

On the other hand, neo-Fascism survived, residually, in the cultural field, through depleted youth organisations, but without the symbolic presence of crowds in the streets, expressive propaganda, or electoral impact. Paradoxically, it was the gradual consolidation of the extreme right in the European Parliament in the second half of the 1980s, and the corresponding development of international structures which generated some unrest among the native radical right. Some European rightist leaders, Le Pen for example, visited Portugal and made some noise in the media. Organisations such as the National Force – New Monarchy party [*Força Nacional – Nova Monarquia*. FN-NM], created in 1989 through the merger of two youth organisations, can be connected with this trend.[61]

The same period witnessed the birth of other small, youth-based organisations with neo-Fascist political and ideological tendencies. Right at the beginning of the 1990s the National Action Movement [*Movimento de Acção Nacional*, MAN] attracted attention as the focus of the Constitutional Court's first public trial. MAN was linked to skinhead groups involved in the assassination of a young Trotskyite activist, and in 1993 its leaders were brought before the court under the constitutional pretext prohibiting the activity of any group espousing 'Fascist ideology'.[62] Their trial ran after that of the youths who had actually taken part in the events leading to the death of the above-mentioned youth. Beforehand, however, MAN had publicly disbanded but, given its visibility, this did not change the predominately inward-oriented and marginal character that neo-Fascism and the radical right had exhibited throughout the 1980s.

121

In the first article concerning the Portuguese ultra-right after the authoritarian regime, Tom Gallagher concluded: 'but one thing is certain: the time is still far off when the Portuguese ultra right will be as irrelevant as authoritarian rightist movements are currently in most liberal democracies'.[63] At the end of the 1980s, he came to a quite different conclusion.[64] The ultra-right seemed to be more irrelevant in post-authoritarian Portugal than in old liberal democracies like France and, certainly, Italy. Even compared to countries with transitions to democracy in the same period, such as Spain and Greece, the same conclusion applies.

Right and radical right – some prospective elements

Throughout the 1980s, Portuguese society grew away from the double legacy of the authoritarian regime and the revolutionary period of 1975. Some compromises between the largest right-wing and the largest left-wing party, the PSD and the PS, and Portugal's entry into the EC in 1986 (which only the Communist Party rejected) brought about significant changes in the country's economic and political landscape. In 1990, much to the surprise of public opinion, Portugal left the ranks of the 'underdeveloped countries' where it had been ever since the concept was invented. At least that was what the statistics of the international organisations said.

Portugal's entry into the EC, considered by the main parties as fundamental to the consolidation of democracy and the only possible choice after decolonisation, brought about a significant increase in foreign investments, an influx of subsidies for improvement to infrastructures and the reconversion of weak sectors such as agriculture.[65] At the internal level, the revision of the Constitution in 1989 eliminated the principle of nationalisation and agrarian reform, and the process of privatising the vast state sector was initiated.

Indices such as inflation and unemployment showed improvements between 1986 and 1991. The former dropped to 11.5 per cent in 1991 and the latter to almost full employment (4.5 per cent) in the same year. Of course, the negative effects of EC membership only began to be felt after 1991, with the progressive opening of the frontiers putting pressure on the weakest sectors of Portuguese industry and agriculture. It was, however, in this atmosphere of economic growth and unanimity about EEC membership, that the old quarrels inherited from 1975 disappeared with the 1989 revision of the Constitution.

Up to 1985, the successive governments produced by the elections were either minority or coalition governments. However, in 1987 the PSD, the largest centre-right party, obtained 51.3 per cent and was thus able to from the first one-party government, and the first to complete its mandate. In 1991, this majority was reconfirmed (see Table 6.2). The PSD's almost total occupation of the right, with the CDS fighting for survival without moving to the far right, literally destroyed even the smallest space for extremist representation.

The CDS, which during the process of transition and consolidation of democracy played an essential role in the 'democratisation' of an authoritarian sector of the Portuguese right more closely associated with Salazar's regime, has been the great 'victim' of the right-wing electorate's pragmatism, supportive of the strong, populist

Table 6.2 The right in national elections

Party	1975 %	1976 %	1979* %	1980* %	1983 %	1985 %	1987 %	1991 %
CDS	8.2	16.7	46.3	48.3	12.7	10.0	4.4	4.3
PSD	28.3	25.2			27.8	30.6	51.3	50.4

* CDS-PSD coalition.

leadership of Cavaco Silva, Secretary General of the PSD and Prime Minister since 1985. Since the departure of party leader Freitas do Amaral, the CDS has changed leadership and political strategy virtually every year. Given the 1993 recession, the possibility that it will take advantage of it to try to express a new protectionist nationalism and xenophobia should not be excluded.

Let us also analyse some of the variables that have been closely associated with the growth of radical right parties: a temporary representation of social groups threatened by the economic crisis and immigration.

Immigration from the ex-colonies, mainly from Cape Verde, was relatively low until the late 1980s: 50,000 in 1989, most of them Africans, representing 0.5 per cent of the population.[66] In spite of this, racist acts multiplied at the end of the decade and caused the first violent incidents involving groups of skinheads.[67] In recent years, some skilled migrants have entered the country, from Brazil for example, causing some signs of xenophobia in a society which had not known significant foreign communities. But these numbers rose considerably at the beginning of the 1990s, and indeed they were probably already much higher than the official statistics stated. According to the Interior Ministry, legal and clandestine immigration in 1993 amounted approximately to 250,000, close to 2.5 per cent of the country's population. In 1992 and 1993 the first violent confrontations with immigrants, mostly black Africans, occurred on the outskirts of Lisbon. However, although it is a potential element of growth for the extreme right, the immigration/racism factor is still comparatively insignificant.

The same cannot be said of the political attitudes of groups which have been negatively affected by EC membership. In 1991, a number of farmers' movements appeared, separately from their own associations; they were mostly dominated by the right-wing parties and protectionist movements. Portugal's obligation progressively to open her market may, as one author said, open a political space for a nationalist Poujadism.[68]

Towards the end of 1992, the situation favouring these movements was aggravated by the first signs of the economic recession that announced the end of the 'golden age' stemming from Portugal's entry into the EC in 1986. Examples can be seen, for instance, in the increase in violence in the agricultural and fisheries sectors, and with the initiation of import boycotts and occasional blockades. Highway roadblocks against imported pork and milk dumping began to be a common sight in the Portuguese political landscape. These events must, however, be treated as the effect of modernisation, rather than as a legacy of the old Salazarist authoritarianism.

Conclusion

There is an apparent paradox in that, after forty years of authoritarian rule, Portuguese democracy does not have to confront a neo-Fascist party (or a radical right party based on Salazarism as a positive model), of even minimal effectiveness. The nature of the regime partly explains this paradox. In fact, Salazarism always preferred 'non-political' institutions (administration) to 'political' ones (party), and can be characterised as a promoter of political demobilisation, repressing all autonomous manifestations of native Fascism. The process of transition and consolidation of democracy were not, for that matter, favourable to its appearance. What must be emphasised, however, is that while the 'New State' did leave behind an important legacy to the young democracy, it was not a neo-Fascist one. And it will be difficult to associate it with any possible future emergence of neo-Fascism in Portugal.

To disregard the chances of neo-Fascism as a legacy of the past does not amount to any forecast for the future. Movements of the far right have a potential in all industrial societies and Portugal is, obviously, no exception. Until the early 1990s, some of the factors associated with the growth of such movements did not exist in Portugal. Their usual functions as conveyor belts for popular aspirations were lacking, as they had no social base or support. There had been the wholesale return of white settlers caused by decolonisation. However, such factors as significant foreign immigration and its attendant popular xenophobia did not occur in Portuguese society.

The most important shifts on the radical right occurred at the cultural level after a profound crisis bought on by the transition to democracy and by decolonisation. Nevertheless, the right and centre-right parties have, until now, absorbed whatever potential for autonomous growth in the political sphere the extreme right may have had.

(Translated by Michalina Vaughan)

List of abbreviations

CDS	*Centro Democrático Social* [Social Democratic Centre]
ELP	*Exército de Libertação Nacional* [Portuguese Liberation Army]
EN	*Estado Novo* [New State]
FAP	*Frente Académica Patriotica* [Patriotic Academic Front]
FEN	*Frente de Estudantes Nacionalistas* [Nationalist Students Front]
FNR	Frente Nacional Revolucionária [National Revolutionary Front]
FN-NM	*Força Nacional/Nova Monarquia* [National Force – New Monarchy]
JSN	*Junta de Salvação Nacional* [National Salvation Junta]
LP	*Legião Portuguesa* [Portuguese Legion]
MAN	*Movimento de Acção Nacional* [National Action Movement]
MDLP	*Movimento Democrático de Libertação de Portugal* [Democratic Movement for the Liberation of Portugal]

MDP	*Movimento Democrático Português* [Portuguese Democratic Movement]
MFA	*Movimento das Forças Armadas* [Armed Forces Movement]
MIRN	*Movimento Independente para a Reconstrução Nacional* [Independent Movement for National Reconstruction]
MJP	*Movimento Jovem Portugal* [Young Portugal Movement]
MNP	*Movimento Nacionalista Português* [Portuguese Nationalist Movement]
MP	*Mocidade Portuguesa* [Portuguese Youth]
NS	*Nacional Sindicalismo* [National Syndicalism]
PCP	*Partido Comunista Português* [Portuguese Communist Party]
PDC	*Partido da Democracia Cristã* [Christian-Democrat Party]
PDP	*Partido de Direita Portuguêsa* [Party of the Portuguese Right]
PFN	*Partido Força Nacional* [National Force Party]
PL	*Partido Liberal* [Liberal Party]
PP	*Partido do Progresso* [Progress Party]
PPD	*Partido Popular Democrático* [Popular Democratic Party]
PPM	*Partido Popular Monarquico* [Popular Royalist Party]
PS	*Partido Socialista* [Socialist Party]
PSD	*Partido Social Democráta* [Social Democratic Party]
UN	*União Nacional* [National Union]

Notes

* The final version of this chapter was written when I was Visiting Fellow at the Center for European Studies of Stanford University. The paper was completed in Palo Alto in 1993 where I was a Visiting Professor of European History. I should like to thank Philippe Schmitter, director of the Center, and the Luso-American Foundation, which supported the Fellowship.

1. For an introduction to the application of these concepts to post-war political movements see K. V. Beyme (ed.) *Right-wing Extremism in Western Europe*, Frank Cass, London, 1988, pp. 1–18. See also P. H. Merkl and L. Weinberg (eds), *Encounters with the Contemporary Radical Right*, Westview, Boulder, CO, 1993.

2. *O. Intergralismo Lusitano* was the main ideological challenge to the liberal order at the start of the century. Created under the influence of *Action Française*, this traditional, corporatist and anti-liberal royalist movement inspired anti-republican plots, but never became a political party. See M. Braga da Cruz, 'O Integralismo Lusitano nas orígens do Salazarismo'. *Análise Social*, XVIII, No. 70, 1982, pp. 137–182 and A. Costa Pinto, 'A Formação do Integralismo Lusitano: 1907–17', *Análise Social*, XVIII, No. 72–74, 1982, pp. 1409–19.

3. For the interpretations of the 'New State' see A. Costa Pinto, *Salazar's Dictatorship and European Fascism. Problems and Perspectives of Interpretation*, Columbia University Press, New York, 1995.

4. On the National Syndicalists see A. Costa Pinto, *Os Camisas Azuís. Ideologia, elites e movimentos fascistas em Portugal*, Estampa, Lisbon, 1994.

5. On the single party of the EN see M. Braga da Cruz, *O Partido e o Estado nó Salazarismo*,

Presença, Lisbon, 1988, reviewed by the author in *Annales. Economie. Société. Civilizations*, XLIII, 1988, pp. 691–3.

6. On the MP and its origins see S. Kuin, 'Mocidade Portuguesa nos Anos Trinta: a instauração de uma organização paramilitar de juventude', *Análise Social*, XXVIII, 1993, pp. 555–88.

7. On the opposition to Salazarism see D. L. Raby, *Fascism and Resistance in Portugal Communists, Liberals and Military Dissidents in the Opposition to Salazar, 1941–74*, Manchester University Press, Manchester, 1988.

8. See F. Rosas, *Portugal entre a Guerra e a Paz*, Estampa, Lisbon, 1990, and N. Teixeira, *From Neutrality to Aligment: Portugal in the Foundation of the Atlantic Pact*, European University Institute, Florence, 1991.

9. See A. Costa Pinto, 'The "New State" of Salazar – An Overview', in R. Herr (ed.), *Portugal Democracy and Europe*, Institute of International and Area Studies, Berkeley, CA, 1993, pp. 73–106.

10. L. S. Graham, 'Portugal: The Bureaucracy of Empire', *LADS. Occasional Papers*, IX, 1973, p. 8.

11. J. Nogueira Pinto, *Portugal os anos do fim. A revolução que veio de dentro*, Sociedade de publicações economia e finanças, LDA, Lisbon, 1976, vol. I, p. 79.

12. This review was published from 1959 to 1961, and directed by Fernando Guedes. On this group see E. Lourenço, 'Fascismo e cultura no antigo regime' *Análise Social*, XVIII, Nos. 72–74, pp. 1431–36.

13. A. José de Brito, *Tempo Presente*, No. 10, Feb. 1960, p. 12.

14. Its most prolific ideologist was A. José de Brito, still active in the 1980s. Always a self-confessed neo-Fascist, he taught philosophy in a private university in Oporto, while publishing in the extreme-right press. His most interesting work, as far as Portuguese neo-Fascism in concerned, is *Destino do Nacionalismo Português*, Verbo, Lisbon, 1962.

15. See, for instance, the article by C. de Mello Beirão, *Tempo Presente*, No. 4, 1959, pp. 76–84.

16. Nogueira Pinto, *Portugal*, cit., p. 122.

17. Its organ was the *FAP – Deus. Patria. Familia.* which denounced opposition activities, and supported the politics of the government.

18. As did the National Syndicalist Portuguese Youth [*Juventude Portuguesa Nacional Sindicalista*]. It published *Ataque*, which appeared on and off in 1961–62, as well as the ideological journal *Ofensiva*, which was clearly inspired by JONS, the matrix of Fascism in neighbouring Spain.

19. Z. Moniz Ferreira contacted the NS leader to seek his support. At the time, Rolão Preto, who had been actively involved with the candidacy of Humberto Delgado, belonged to the royalist opposition, which later presented 'independent' candidates and created the Popular Royalist Party [*Partido Popular Monarquico*, PPM] after the fall of the EN.

20. The national organ was *Frente*, which first appeared in October 1965.

21. *Ataque*, Nos. 6–8, Oct. – Dec. 1962, p. 1.

22. Z. Moniz Ferreira, 'Nacional Sindicalismo', *Ataque*, No. 13–14, May–June 1963, p. 4.

23. On the *Jeune Nation* movement see P. Milza, *Fascisme français – Passé et Présent*, Flammarion, Paris, 1987, pp. 224–371.

24. See F. Ferraresi (ed.), *La destra radicale*, Feltrinelli, Milan, 1984, and *idem*, 'The Radical Right in Post-War Italy'. *Politics and Society*, XVI(1), March 1988, pp. 71–119.

25. J. Morais and L. Violante, *Contribuicão para uma cronologia dos factos económicos e sociais – Portugal 1926–1985*, Livros Horizonte, Lisbon, 1986, p. 185.

26. See the manifesto of the organisation in *Frente*, No. 5, April 1966, pp. 4–5.

27. *Europe-Action* was published until 1963, and anticipated some of the themes of the *Nouvelle Droite*. See Milza, *Fascisme*, cit., pp. 328–31.

28. See e.g., the review *Itincrário*, first published in March–April 1965, more cultural than ideological, and *Movimento Vanguardista*, founded in 1969, which made repeated attacks on Caetano.

29. *Agora*, 8 Jan. 1966, p. 12.

30. *Agora*, No. 1, 18 Feb. 1961; *Resistência*, No. 1, 1968.

31. To begin with, its first director, Raul de Carvalho Branco, and various contributors, such as Neves da Costa. In 1967, *Agora* became the mouthpiece of the neo-Fascist faction, as it attracted former leaders such as Valle Figueredo and Jaime Norgueira Pinto.

32. *Agora*, 20 Oct. 1965, p. 3.

33. *Agora*, 28 Aug. 1965, p. 3 and 26 Feb. 1966, p. 5.

34. See J. Nogueira Pinto, 'Fascismo 67' *Agora*, 4 Nov. 1967, p. 13.

35. J. Valle Figueiredo, in *Frente*, No. 6, July 1966, p. 1.

36. *Resistência* continued to be published after 1974 with remarkable regularity.

37. Edited by J. Nogueira Pinto; the first number appeared in November 1969.

38. The most notable names being Lucas Pires and José Miguel Júdice, in Coimbra. The latter wrote a preface, from a neo-Fascist perspective, for the Portuguese edition of José António Primo de Rivera's writings. See J. M. A. Júdice, *José António Primo de Rivera*, Cidadela, Coimbra, 1972, pp. 11–51.

39. On the various factions, from the royalists to the neo-Fascists, see A. Valdemar (ed.), *Ser ou não ser pelo partido único*, Arcadia, Lisbon, 1973.

40. For an introduction to the *saneamentos* (literally 'cleanings out'), the political purges after the fall of the regime, see A. Costa Pinto, 'Dealing with the Legacy of Authoritarianism: Political Purge and Radical Right Movements in Portugal's Transition to Democracy (1974–90s),' in S. U. Larsen *et al.* (eds), *Modern Europe After Fascism, 1945–1980's*. Columbia University Press, New York, 1995.

41. These were the Popular Democratic Party [*Partido Popular Democrático*, PPD] – later Social Democratic Party [*Partido Social Democrático*, PSD] – and the Social Democratic Centre [*Centro Democrático Social*, CDS].

42. J. Nogueira Pinto, 'A direita e o 25 de Abril' in M. Batista Coelho (ed.), *Portugal: O Sistema Politico e Constitucional, 1974–87*, Instituto de Ciências Sociais, Lisbon, 1989, p. 203.

43. On this subject, see G. O'Donnell and P. C. Schmitter, *Transitions from Authoritarian Rule. Tentative conclusions about uncertain democracies*, Johns Hopkins University Press, Baltimore and London, 1986.

44. P. C. Shmitter, 'Liberation by *Golpe*', *Armed Forces and Society*, II, Nov. 1975, pp. 5–33; D. Porch, *The Portuguese Armed Forces and The Revolution*, Croom Helm, London, 1977. On the military in twentieth-century Portugal, see M. Carrilho, *Forças Armadas e mudanças politica em Portugal no século XX*, Imprensa Nacional, Lisbon, 1985; J. Medeiros Ferreira, *O Comportamento Político dos Militares. Forças armadas e regimes políticos em Portugal no séc. XX*, Estampa, Lisbon, 1992.

45. See Decree-Law No. 277/74 of 25 June 1974, *Diário do Governo*, 1st Ser., No. 146, p. 744.

46. See Decree-law No. 123/75 of 11 March 1974, *Diário do Governo*, 1st Ser., No. 59, p. 375.

47. *O Século*, Lisbon, 27 Feb. 1975, p. 6.

48. See the book of one of its first leaders, an army officer who held governmental posts under the second provisional government and who followed Spínola in exile; S. Osório, *O equivoco do 25 de Abril*, Intervenção, Lisbon, 1975.

49. This contribution will not cover one aspect of extreme right activity, namely the development of separatist movements in the Atlantic islands, particularly in the Azores.

50. On the ELP/MDLP see A. Galvão, *De Conakry ao MDLP-Dossier secreto*, Intervenção, Lisbon, 1976; P. de Abreu, *Do 25 de Abril ao 25 de Novembro – Memória de um tempo perdido*, Intervenção, Lisbon, 1983.

51. On this see a case study by M. Espirito Santo, *Comunidade rural ao norte do Tejo (estudo de sociologia rural)*, Instituto de estudos para o desenvolvimento, Lisbon, 1980, pp. 199–214.
52. For a detailed description see P. de Abreu, *Do 25 de Abril*, cit., pp. 144 ff.
53. On the formation of MIRN see K. de Arriaga, *No Caminho das soluções do futuro*, Edições Abril, Lisbon, 1977.
54. See, e.g., the book by the former minister for Overseas Territories, S. Cunha. *O Ultramar a nacão e o 25 de Abril*, Atlantida, Lisbon, 1977, and A. Moreira. *A Nação Abandonada*, Intervenção, Lisbon, 1977. For some factual information on the decolonisation and the *retornados*, see Grupo de pesquisa sobre a descolonização portuguesa, *A descolonização portuguesa – aproximação a um estudo*, Instituto Amaro da Costa, 2 vols., Lisbon, 1979–82.
55. Nogueira Pinto, 'A direita', cit., p. 206.
56. No. 1, 1980, edited by Nogueira Pinto.
57. See J. Nogueira Pinto, 'Direita em Portugal-notas para uma autocrítica e projecto', *Futuro Presente*, Nos. 9–10 (2nd edn), 1982, pp. 10–16.
58. See J. Nogueira Pinto, 'A direita e as direitas – algumas questões prévias', *Futuro Presente*, No. 7 (2nd edn), 1981, p. 11.
59. It would be pointless to list them exhaustively. In the second half of the 1980s, literally dozens of magazines, associations, etc. mushroomed. See, e.g., *Portugueses/revista de ideias*, first published in December 1987, whose early issues reveal a variety of ideological influences. For the international affiliations of these groups see C. Ó. Maoláin, *The Radical Right. A World Directory*, Longman, London, 1987, pp. 229–33.
60. This is the only reference made in its party political broadcast in the elections for the European Parliament of 1989.
61. The party claimed in 1989 that it had 1,200 members.
62. See *Expresso*, 26 June 1993, p. 11.
63. T. Gallagher, 'From Hegemony to Opposition: The Ultra Right before and after 1974', in L. S. Graham and D. L. Wheeler (eds), *In Search of Modern Portugal. The Revolution and its Consequences*, The University of Wisconsin Press, Madison, WI, 1983, p. 97.
64. T. Gallagher, 'Portugal: the Marginalization of the Extreme Right', in P. Hainsworth (ed.), *The Extreme Right in Europe and the USA*, Pinter, London, 1992, pp. 232–45.
65. C. S. Costa, 'Cinco anos e meio de integração da Portugal na CEE: das dúvidas do momento de partida à autoconfiança reencontrada', in Various Authors, *Portugal em Mudança. Ensaios sobre a actividade do XI governo constitucional*, Imprensa Nacional, Lisbon, 1991, pp. 239–307.
66. European Parliament, *Relatório de Inquérito sobre o Racismo e a Xenofobia*, Luxembourg, 1990, pp. 67–68.
67. In Lisbon a young Trotskyist militant was killed, and in Oporto several attacks against black immigrants took place.
68. See M. Rebelo de Sousa, 'Seis anos-do Estado à sociedade', in *Portugal em Mudança*, cit., pp. 33–4.

Chapter 7

NEO-FASCISM IN MODERN GREECE
Vassilis Kapetanyannis

Introduction

The political history of modern Greece is marked by a legacy of conflicts, instability, polarisation and fragile legitimacy. Political processes and political development have been confronted by pressures from outside the parliamentary system. Until very recently, the military occupied a dominant position in the country's political and institutional setting, exercised undue influence over the political process, and showed little hesitation in interrupting and/or abolishing parliamentary institutions. It is no accident, therefore, that Greece has been seen as a 'praetorian society' affected by endemic political instability.

Western parliamentary institutions were imported into the country in the last century. The demise of Greek oligarchic parliamentarianism and the transition to broader forms of political participation and representation occurred at a time when industrial capitalism was very weak. In any case, its impact on the process of political development can in no way be compared with the effects of industrialisation on political institutions in Western Europe.[1]

The national schism of 1915, caused by the clash between the pro-Entente liberal Elefterios Venizelos and the Germanophile King Constantine, acquired the dimensions of a serious confrontation between throne and parliament, and marked the beginning of a series of military coups and counter-coups. The involvement of army officers in the party political affairs of the country was such that it can amply justify the claim that the military clientele of each political party became the arbiter of political disputes.[2] The first Greek Republic, established in 1924, was short lived. King George II was restored to his throne in 1934. This was a turning point in Greece's modern political history. Two years later, on 4 August 1936, a quasi-Fascist military dictatorship was imposed by General Metaxas with the King's full support and patronage.

The inter-war period

Inter-war Greece was still a predominantly agrarian society. In the main, the dominant class of peasant smallholders emerged from the distribution of the 'national lands',

129

the previously Turkish properties taken over by the Greek state.[3] Radical land reforms were effected, particularly after the Asia Minor disaster of 1922 (the defeat by the Turks).

Not only did these reforms accommodate the demands of the huge refugee population numbering approximately 1.2 million, which was driven out of Asia Minor, they also created a massive new stratum of smallholders largely dependent on state agencies for support and survival.[4] By 1930, Greece had irrevocably become a country whose smallholders constituted the main social class.[5]

On the political level, the two major bourgeois parties, the Liberals [*Filelefteroi*] of the charismatic Elefterios Venizelos (1864–1936) and the staunchly royalist People's Party [*Laiko Komma*, LK], commanded the loyalties of the peasantry, whereas the newly founded Communist Party of Greece [*Kommounistiko Komma Elladas*, KKE][6] was never able to make any significant inroads in the countryside. The peasants were kept firmly within the clientelistic networks of the two major parties which were fundamentally divided over the issue of the throne.[7] On the other hand, although the KKE's influence within the working class was very limited, industrial capitalism had made little advance in inter-war Greece.[8]

Moreover, Greek society was highly homogeneous from the linguistic, religious, cultural and national points of view. There was no foreign ethnic group in a dominant economic and/or cultural position to attract hatred from other social groups and be made a scapegoat for the country's social and political ills. The refugee problem did not provide a social basis for the growth of Fascist or extreme right-wing movements feeding on massive human misery or wounded nationalist feelings. Patriotism did not prove a vehicle for any Fascist movement. The fragile legitimacy of the political parties and political institutions played into the hands of the military, not of any would-be Fascist leader.

The period of the Republic (1924–1935) was a turbulent one. However, despite the serious economic crisis of 1932, and a degree of labour militancy led by the Communists, a Fascist movement was, again, virtually absent. General Metaxas's party of Free believers [*Elefterofronoi*, EL], for instance, had only two deputies elected in the 1932 general election, as against nine Communists, in a 250-seat parliament. A few right-wing organisations, inspired to some extent by National Socialist ideas, made their appearance during this period, but were rather insignificant in terms of both size and political impact.[9] These organisations[10] failed, also, to spark off any massive movement in support of Fascist ideologies and/or goals. However, pressure from military and monarchist elements was mounting. A new National Socialist organisation, the Panhellenic National Front [*Panellinio Ethniko Metopo*, PEM] made its appearance and was responsible for some acts of terrorism against the Communists in Athens.

The abortive pro-Venizelos military coup of 1 March 1935 was followed by an anti-Venizelos backlash. A rigged plebiscite on the issue of the restoration of the monarchy held in November 1935 produced, predictably enough, a 95 per cent majority, and King George II returned to the throne. New elections held on 26 January 1936 were, on the whole, conducted fairly under a system of proportional representation. However, the result was inconclusive. The Communist-dominated Popular Front held the balance of power in a hung parliament, and, despite an agreement with the Liberals, the two major parties finally gave their vote of confidence to Metaxas when he was appointed Prime Minister in April 1936.

The Chamber was not to meet again for ten years. A nation-wide general strike, proclaimed for 5 August, served as a pretext for Metaxas to secure the King's assent to the suspension of a number of key articles of the Constitution on 4 August.[11] The nightmare of the '4th of August' dictatorship had begun with little resistance.[12] Metaxas, a marginal political figure, was now invested with unlimited powers which he exercised until his death in January 1941.

The '4th of August' regime

Metaxas embarked on the reshaping of the Greek state and society. His basic objective was to establish a totalitarian state and to 'discipline' the Greek people by evolving the concept of the Third Hellenic Civilisation, a self-conscious imitation of Hitler's Third Reich. He aped many of the trappings of Fascism and Nazism. The regime tried to buy off the support of the workers and peasants by introducing labour and social legislation. Some of his chief ministers, such as the Press and Propaganda Minister Theologos Nicoloudes, never concealed their admiration for Fascist regimes, although, officially, the Greek regime shied away from such explicit references.[13]

The regime's anti-plutocratic, anti-capitalist and anti-parliamentary rhetoric failed to create any enthusiastic, large-scale political mobilisation in support of the dictator-ship. The style of government remained paternalistic and authoritarian,[14] but beneath the surface lay the brutal reality of oppression, persecution, systematic torture, censorship and terror. Resistance to the regime was ruthlessly crushed by the 'efficient' Public Security Minister, Constantine Maniadakis, with his notorious Special Security Branch. Lacking a political following, and having acquired some degree of autonomy *vis-à-vis* the king, Metaxas sought to obtain a power base of his own by setting up the National Youth Organisation (*Ethniki Organossis Neolaias*, EON) and the Labour Battalions (*Tagmata Ergassias*, TE), membership of which was compulsory. However, with Metaxas's death this Fascist youth movement, which had around 600,000 members, effectively collapsed.

During Metaxas's rule, a number of more or less serious military plots to overthrow him failed. The military were deeply divided, while a group of army generals was actively plotting with the Germans behind the scenes. The paradox was that, despite his ideological loyalties, Metaxas sided with the British and the allied camp against the Axis powers.

Occupation, resistance and civil war (1941–1949)

On the morning of 28 October 1940, Metaxas was presented with an ultimatum by the Italians which he instantly rejected. At that time Greece was the only country to have sided, of her own volition, with the Allies, when Britain stood alone.[15] The Greeks drove the invading Italians back, deep into Albania, and when the war was reduced to deadlock, Hitler decided to intervene in order to secure his southern flank in his preparations to invade Russia.

General Tsolakoglou, the Commander of the Western Macedonian front and one of the prominent figures of the pro-German military faction, surrendered his troop (without government authorisation) and singed an armistice in April 1941. He was soon to be rewarded when the Germans installed him as the first Quisling Prime Minister of Greece. The King and the government, headed by the banker Tsouderos, had already fled, first to Crete and, after its fall to the Germans, to Egypt.

Resistance to the occupation forces (Germans, Italians and Bulgarians) took on formidable proportions. The most powerful groups were the Communist-led and controlled National Liberation Front [*Ethniko Apelefterotiko Metopo*, EAM], founded in September 1941, and its military arm, the National Popular Liberation Army [*Ethnikos Laikos Apelefterotikos Stratos*, ELAS]. Despite the terror and horrifying reprisals of the occupation forces against acts of resistance, the movement quickly embraced the great majority of the Greek population. This occurred even though the Quisling governments had organised a number of Fascist and extreme right-wing collaborationist groups which assisted the Germans to defeat resistance in any possible way. The most notorious of these groups were the Security Battalions [*Tagmata Asfaleias*, TA].[16]

In the Middle East, new Greek military units were formed from remnants of the Greek army, under the aegis of the British Command. These units were highly factionalised along political lines. Pro-EAM elements had fomented mutinies in the unit stationed in Egypt, demanding the formation of a government of national unity in exile to be based on the Political Committee of National Liberation [*Politiki Epitropi Ethnikis Apelefterossis*, PEEA], the so-called 'Government of the Mountain', created by EAM in mid-March 1944. The mutinies were suppressed by the British, the units were purged of leftist elements, and large numbers of those involved were interned.[17]

During this period, many clandestine organisations were formed by officers. Most of them were right-wing, pro-royalist and anti-Communist. The most prominent and active of these organisations in the post-civil war era, the Sacred Bond of Greek Officers [*Ieros Syndesmos Ellinon Axiomatikon*, IDEA], originated in the Middle East during 1943–44. There were many other groups of lesser importance.[18]

A national unity government under George Papandreou, with the participation of EAM ministers in minor posts, was formed in the Middle East and landed in Greece in October 1944. Papandreou had the full support of Churchill who had previously secured a free hand in Greece under the Yalta agreement with Stalin. Early in December 1944, a bid for power by the Communists failed when the military tide turned with British intervention. In February 1945, a political settlement was reached. ELAS agreed to disarm.

However, the terms of the agreement were never to be implemented. The right-wing backlash and white terror followed. Collaborators were not brought to justice and were on the loose. Violence by right-wing bands and gangs, such as that of the notorious X (*Hi*), was widespread. This reign of terror paved the way for elections in March 1946. However, the left decided to abstain and thus excluded itself from parliament – with disastrous consequences. The slide towards civil war gathered momentum with the return of the King after a plebiscite in September 1946, the fairness of which is still very much in doubt.

In the winter of 1946–47, a fully fledged civil war broke out. The 'Democratic Army', the KKE's military arm, was to be led to defeat in 1949 by a variety of factors. The Americans, with the declaration of the Truman Doctrine in 1947, had replaced the British as the patron-power of Greece, and their influence over Greek affairs in subsequent years was to be enormous.[19] The civil war left a bitter legacy of bloody political divisions with lasting effects on the country's political system and political culture.

The post-civil-war state and military dictatorship (1949–1974)

After its victory, the right imposed a quasi-parliamentary regime. The 'repressive parliamentarianism'[20] was controlled by the triarchy of throne, army and the political right. Within this power bloc, the army played the dominant role, an important aspect of which was its political, ideological and, to a lesser extent, financial dependence on the United States.[21]

Beyond its own vast security apparatus, the Greek army was in a position to exercise direct or indirect control over the key 'civilian' intelligence and security services which, in fact, were heavily miltarised. Files were kept on the majority of the population[22] (between 80 and 90 per cent); in addition, there was a nationwide system of identity cards. These services became the centre of plots, counter-plots and military conspiracies. Moreover, the military were also in control of the Battalions of National Defence [*Tagmata Ethnikis Amynis*, TEA], which were officered, commanded and trained by the army. The threads connecting the Security Services with the 'parastate' organisations were also numerous. It seems that parastate organisations started to appear and proliferate, under legal or illegal covers, around 1957–58. This was the time of rising popular discontent expressed clearly by the electoral triumph of the left in 1958 which, under the banner of the United Democratic Left [*Eniaia Demokratiki Aristera*, EDA], became the major opposition party in parliament, against all odds.[23]

These parastate organisations were no more than rubber-stamp associations, with few members in most cases, recruited mainly among the petty criminal and political underworld. They were used as an instrument for doing the 'dirty work' so that official state organs could, publicly, keep their hands clean. They were also used in other provocative actions and, more openly, in student politics.[24] Their obscure existence came into broad daylight with the assassination of the left-wing MP Gregoris Lambrakis,[25] in Thessaloniki, in May 1963.

Generally, the term 'security state' seems appropriate to define the post-civil war state both in legal, political and ideological terms. The dominant role of the army as a state institution was to be demonstrated in many crucial instances. Especially after 1958, more funds were allocated for psychological warfare and, in 1959, two more security agencies were added to an already overprotected state. Prisons were still full of political detainees, and places of internal exile for political opponents were to be found all over the country.[26] The public administration was purged, and the institutionalised practices of requiring certificates of 'civil loyalty' and of strict security screening were widespread. This regimentation of society required an enormous army of functionaries, estimated at nearly 60,000.[27]

The rise of George Papandreou's movement of democratisation in the early 1960s, which became known as 'the unyielding struggle', was to erode the regime's own sources of legitimacy. The landslide victory of the Centre Union Party [*Enosis Kentrou*, EK] in the February 1964 elections produced an overall majority in Parliament, broke the right-wing parties' monopoly of power and carried the promise of a democratic, reformist government.

However, the government was short-lived. With the active involvement of King Constantine II, Papandreou's government was toppled in 1965, and the country slipped into a protracted and deep political crisis having as its epicentre the political control of the armed forces. The crisis was 'resolved' by military intervention in April 1967. This time, a group of middle-ranking officers, acting more or less autonomously, abolished parliamentary institutions and established a military dictatorship which lasted for seven years.[28] The traditional political system[29] crumbled under the pressures of rapid economic development and intense and protracted political mobilisation.

The seven-year military dictatorship[30] did not fundamentally alter the status and role of right-wing ideologies in Greek society. The military conspirators who gravitated round Colonel George Papadopoulos, the leader of the 1967 coup, were now elevated to key ministerial posts. Their political ideas were crude, naive and extremely vague. Though the regime's ideology was *sui generis*, it left a residual sensation of much of it having been heard before. There is no doubt that, behind the changing rhetoric and verbiage of the main propagandists,[31] one can isolate persistent references to the ideological principles of Metaxas's regime, frequent religious overtones, a right-wing populist approach and crude anti-Communism. Among the most recurrent themes, were: national security, alleged social decadence and the need for the 'political re-education' of the Greeks who had lost their way in the jungle of modernity and irresponsible parliamentarianism.[32]

Members of the military junta maintained close links with the '4th of August Party'[33] [*Komma tis 4 Avgoustou*, K4A], named after the date on which Metaxas established his dictatorship in 1936. The fortnightly left-wing magazine *ANTI* carried numerous reports, between 1974 and 1977, documenting the various new parastate organisations created by the military regime, such as the National Movement of Young Scientists [*Ethniko Kinima Neon Epistimonon*, EKNE] and, more importantly, the relations between the Greek military regime, the K4A and 'New Order' [*Nea Taksi*, NT] with Italian far-right groups. It was reported, in this context, that Greece was a convenient hideout for Italian neo-Fascists like Elio Massagrande, deputy leader of *Ordine Nuovo*, or Clemente Graziani, leader of the organisation and of the International of neo-Nazism. It was also argued that the Italian fugitive neo-Fascists had made Greece their headquarters for organising a coup in Rome on 2 June 1974.[34] The assassination of Christos Mantakas, a Greek studying in Italy, in February 1975, led the Italian authorities to discover many vital clues about the activities of Italian neo-Fascists.[35]

However, the Greek colonels failed to legitimise their power[36] and obtain any mass support. The regime collapsed amid chaos and the national tragedy of Cyprus, invaded by Turkey in July 1974.

1974 to 1993

The transfer of power from military to civilian leadership under Constantine Karamanlis inaugurated an entirely new phase in Modern Greek politics. Karamanlis's gradualist approach to the serious problems that confronted him was evident in the timing of the measures he adopted. He defused the near-war situation with Turkey, formed a government of national unity and proceeded carefully in restoring civil authority over a demoralised and disintegrated military. His strategy succeeded in full.[37] He was also able to consolidate the new parliamentary regime and establish the most liberal political system in the post-war period. The KKE was legalised and could now compete on an equal footing with other political forces, despite its split.[38]

The new open, competitive and democratic regime successfully passed the test of functionality and stability[39] with the smooth transition of power from the conservative New Democracy [*Nea Demokratia*, ND] to a radical-socialist party, the Panhellenic Socialist Movement [*Panellinio Socialistiko Kinema*, PASOK], in October 1981, when the later's leader Andreas Papandreou won a landslide victory at the polls. The protagonists of the 1967 military coup were tried and sentenced to death, although the government rushed to commute their sentences to life imprisonment. In December 1974 a plebiscite on the divisive issue of the monarchy was held. Support for a republic soared to 69 per cent of the total vote.[40]

Since 1974, social, economic and, above all, political conditions have not been conducive to the creation and/or profileration of extreme right-wing groups. The collapse of the military regime, under the burden of its own incompetence and crimes, completely demoralised, confused and disorganised the far right. Although ND, under the leadership of Karamanlis, won the general elections of 1974 and 1977, the wave of radicalism sweeping the country appeared unstoppable. The charismatic Andreas Papandreou, who founded the PASOK in 1974, succeeded in leading the movement to power shortly after, by sweeping to victory in 1981 and by winning, convincingly, a second term in office in 1985 with an overall majority.

Meanwhile, the far right tried parliamentary tactics to make its voice heard. This does not mean that right-wing organisations had altogether disappeared from the Greek political map. Although, according to some sources,[41] nearly 150 groups, which were Fascist, royalist or associated with the military dictatorship, appeared during 1967–84, none survived for more than a few months. The K4A is still around and faithful to its National Socialism. Its influence, however, is insignificant.[42] Given the circumstances in which the military regime collapsed, it is not surprising that the extreme right of the political spectrum made a very poor showing in the first freely conducted general election of November 1974. The National Democratic Union [*Ethniki Demokratiki Enosis*, EDE] received no seats by scoring only 1.1 per cent of the total vote: 54,162 votes out of a total of 4,912,356. A more serious regrouping of the far right emerged in time for the 1977 elections. This was a new political formation, the National Camp [*Ethniki Parataxis*, EP], led by Stephanos Stephanopoulos, which won 6.8 per cent of the total vote (349,851 votes out of 5,129,884), and secured five seats out of a total of 300. Stephanopoulos had been Prime Minister in 1965–66 and a minister in several pre-1965 governments. The EP consisted of an assortment of right-wing revivalists of various shades, disenchanted with Karamanlis's policies, and of royalist diehards.

Although the EP did not manage to deprive ND of an overall majority in parliament, it nevertheless became a force to be reckoned with and a serious threat to ND's right flank. Although the new ultra-right formation emphasised that the monarchy was not an electoral issue, its deputy leader, Spyros Theotokis, was a prominent royalist.[43] The Camp, though, was soon to develop centrifugal tendencies.[44] Three of its five deputies defected in 1980 to support Karamanlis in his bid to become President[45] of the Republic, and the 'Party' disintegrated. Theotokis himself was invited to cooperate with ND and rejoined its ticket in the October 1981 elections. Subsequently, he won a seat on ND's national list.[46]

George Rallis, who succeeded Karamanlis in the leadership of ND, and in the premiership of the government, made some pre-electoral concessions to the far right in order to secure their withdrawal from the electoral contest, in the face of the growing threat of Papandreou's 'Marxist' PASOK, but to no avail. In the meantime, in 1979, the United Nationalist Movement [*Enomeno Ethniko Kinema*, ENEK] was formed. This organisation had Fascist, National Socialist and racist views, but made no particular impression upon the political scene. However, the standard for the disintegrated ultra-right was borne, in the 1981 election, by Spyros Markezinis, the puppet Prime Minister of Greece's military dictatorship in 1973, when the regime tried to 'liberalise' itself for a short time. The new right-wing party, called Progressive Party [*Komma Proodeftikon*, KP], was launched on 7 December 1979. It secured 1.4 per cent of the vote (77,465 votes out of a total of 5,670,941). The party won 1.95 per cent of the vote in the European elections which were conducted simultaneously and, thanks to the simple proportional representation system, it secured one of the twenty-four seats allocated to Greece in the European Parliament.

The difficulties of right-wing groups in consolidating a solid electoral base were exacerbated by the lack of any serious, stable leadership and organisation. It is not surprising, therefore, that another electoral formation, the National Political Union [*Ethniki Politiki Enosis*, EPEN], was hastily set up to contest the June 1984 European elections.

After a polarised campaign, EPEN managed to win 2.29 per cent of the vote (136,642 out of a total of 5,956,060) and elect one MEP, who joined the group of the European Right. EPEN made no secret of its ideological and political links with the protagonists of the 1967 military coup whose release from prison it had constantly demanded. It is characteristic that the former dictator Papadopoulos had secretly recorded a message which was played at a meeting of EPEN's founding members. In December 1984, Jean-Marie Le Pen hosted an Athens meeting of the Group of the European Right, which provoked violent protest demonstrations.[47]

Despite EPEN's initial relative success in regrouping the far right and gaining some publicity, the problems besetting this part of the political spectrum did not go away. ENEK scored only 0.03 per cent of the total vote in the 1984 European elections, while EPEN was unable to hold most of its votes gained. In the general election the following year it scored a poor 0.6 per cent and won no seats at all in the *Vouli*, the national parliament. Despite this setback, EPEN continues its activities today and publishes a weekly political newspaper, the *Ellinikos Kosmos* [Greek World] with a strong anti-

Communist line (circulation figures are not available). There are also a few other daily and weekly papers which disseminate extreme right-wing and totalitarian ideas with strong anti-Semitic overtones, but their circulation is insignificant.[46] The common denominator of all these publications, representing small far right-wing groups, is their anti-Communism, anti-Semitism and deep hostility towards democratic and parliamentary institutions.

In the general and European elections conducted simultaneously in Greece on 18 June 1989, the far right failed again to make any impression. EPEN, for instance, scored only 1.16 per cent of the total vote and lost its single seat in the European Parliament, whereas ENEK's share of the vote was a poor 0.23 per cent. EPEN took only 0.32 per cent of the vote in the general election.

In the electoral contests of November 1989 and April 1990, conducted amid political instability and bitter inter-party bickering, the far right electoral groupings failed once more to make any impression. Deputies of far right-wing persuasion had found refuge in the ND party which won the election by a whisker in terms of parliamentary seats (151 out of 300). This group of deputies tried occasionally either to force a pardon for the 1967 coup leaders on the government, or to openly pronounce their royalist views. However, it was 'discovered' that public opinion remained solidly behind its anti-junta and anti-royalist stance. A new electoral law[49] made it hardly possible for any extreme right political grouping to be represented in parliament. Indeed, in the October 1993 general election the National Party (*Ethniko Komma*, EK)-EPEN coalition scored a mere 0.14 per cent of the total vote. The governing party of ND suffered a devastating defeat and PASOK assumed again the reins of government by winning nearly 47 per cent of the total vote and a large majority in parliament. It is safe to conclude that the official far right has been virtually extinguished from parliamentary politics. However, this is not to say that the extreme right's potential to influence political opinion is nearly extinct.[50] The emergence of nationalistic feeling could well play into the hands of politicians eager to exploit and make political capital out of it. To see why, we have to ponder briefly on the nationalist tide that swept Greece following the dismemberment of Yugoslavia and the re-emergence of the so-called 'Macedonian' problem.

The nationalist tide

The disintegration of Yugoslavia has added a new element to the instability of the Balkans, unleashing powerful centrifugal forces in the post-Communist era. An area which in the nineteenth century earned the reputation as the powder keg of Europe, due to the explosion of nationalism and the intervention of the great powers, is now beset by bitter ethnic conflict upsetting old delicate balances and having important implications for European security. The legacy of 500 years of authoritarian Ottoman rule, the lack of any strong democratic traditions and institutions, autocratic Communist rule, deep historically rooted ethnic rivalries and outside intervention in the crisis are considered the most crucial factors which have contributed to the present turmoil and the resurgence of nationalism and chauvinism.

Greece, although not a part of the Balkan conundrum and bloody conflict, has been deeply concerned. Developments in the area have affected its domestic politics in various ways. The revival of Greek nationalistic sentiment, albeit of a defensive character, of latent xenophobia and racism are a direct consequence of the Balkan turmoil.

In the first place, the near-collapse of the economy and the breakdown in social order in neigbouring Albania, where a substantial Greek minority is established in the southern part of the country (Voreios Epirus), has created a major refugee problem, as hundreds of thousands of desperate Albanians have fled across the border to Greece. Neither financial assistance nor investment have provided, for the moment, an incentive for prospective refugees to stay at home. The flood of Greek and Albanian refugees has aggravated social and economic problems in Greece and polarised public opinion. Official statistical data grossly underestimate the total number of economic refugees in addition to the Pontiac Greeks from the ex-Soviet Union who are heading for Athens and other parts of the country. However, it is estimated that more than half a million illegal economic refugees are now in Greece seeking jobs and a better life. Albanians are the most numerous, compact and visible group. They not only put a serious pressure on an already depressed labour market, with a nearly 9 per cent indigenous rate of unemployment, particularly in the construction sector, but also display a highly criminal profile. Serious criminal offences both against persons and property have increased by 25 per cent in Athens in the last three years. The media seized on the opportunity to portray 'foreigners' as persons with a higher criminal propensity, giving prominent coverage to offences involving Albanians. However, the proportion of serious criminal offences committed by 'foreigners' is usually very low, belying stereotypes and prejudices widely held among the common people. It is not accidental that opinion surveys indicate widespread sentiments of latent xenophobia and racism. Nevertheless, there have been no ugly racial incidents against foreigners and no serious mass reaction. Greek society is still tolerant enough to accommodate hostile feelings and/or to learn to live with people carrying different cultures and ways of life. This is not to say that, given an aggravated social and political situation, the 'foreigner' could not be made into a scapegoat for society's ills. However, apart from some minor public incidents instigated by small far-right groups like the 'Golden Dawn' [*Chryssi Avghi*], with explicit Fascist slogans, no major non-left political party has tried to publicly make political capital out of the situation or endorsed a policy openly hostile to refugees. Moreover, no political group emerged to focus exclusively on social issues related to the presence of 'foreigners', or to formulate a political platform on which a separate political identity could be based.

The issue remains submerged, but could burst into the open given a combination of economic deterioration and perceived threats against the alleged 'purity' or 'unique-ness' of Greek culture and way of life. Besides, tension with Albania over the treatment of the Greek minority could well invite counter-measures and reprisals with the blessing of public opinion.

The Albanian problem has been overshadowed by the 'Macedonian' problem which has fanned dormant Greek national sentiment. It serves no useful purpose to outline here the historical roots of the problem.[51] What is important is that the move by the new republic, which has emerged as from the ashes of the Yugoslav Federative Republic of Macedonia, to be diplomatically recognised as a separate state under the name of 'Republic of Macedonia', has caused considerable concern in Greece. Without doubting the right of the new state to exist as a buffer zone, both against aspirations of a 'Greater Albania' and a 'Greater Bulgaria', and against the spread of the war in Bosnia to the south, Greece has strongly objected to the move. It has demanded that the neighbour country stop usurping its historical heritage, cease using hostile propaganda and historical symbols regarded as Greek in its flag, eliminate references in its Constitution to annexing neighbouring provinces and stop monopolising the Mace–donian name in the denomination of the State. The name of the state has been seen not only symbolically but as a vehicle of Slavic Irredentism, reviving bitter memories of the late 1940s when during the occupation and the ensuing civil war Yugoslavia and Bulgaria tried unsuccessfully to annex parts of Greek Macedonian lands.

The issue is a deeply emotional one in Greece and has mobilised mass support both domestically and among the Greek communities abroad. It could have been resolved in 1993 when it was brought under the mediation of the United Nations, and a negotiated settlement was imminent, if the government of Skopje had been less intransigent and the Greek government more determined to reach a compromise. However, the then Prime Minister Constantine Mitsotakis, with a one-seat majority in parliament, mounting economic problems, PASOK's vigorous opposition, and growing dissent from within his party ranks, could not afford to make major concessions. Eventually, early in September 1993, his government was toppled from within when members of his parliamentary party close to his ex-Foreign Minister Antonis Samaras deserted the ranks, forced his resignation and caused his subsequent defeat at the October polls.

Samaras had already launched his own political movement cum party, the Political Spring [*Politiki Anoixi*, PA], on an uncompromisingly nationalistic political platform. Given the indications that Greek citizens were becoming disillusioned with mainstream political parties, Samaras sought to portray himself as a new, renovating force in Greek politics breaking its duopolic mould and abolishing old political mores and practices. He managed to win 4.9 per cent of the vote and 10 seats in parliament.

Such is the strength of national feelings that not even a PASOK commanding a comfortable majority in parliament dares to ignore them. The broad range of substantive and theoretical issues related to nationalism, which has been one of the most powerful – and perhaps also of the most destructive – forces shaping the course of Balkan history as well as the history of other peoples, will not be addressed here. The mental construction of nations as 'imagined communities'[52] is a long, painful and sometimes very bloody one.

For the time being, the nationalist tide and issues of nationalistic ideologies are integrated into the dominant political discourse and confined to major political parties. No strong leader or personality has emerged as yet to exploit a potentially receptive social and political base in terms of neo-Fascist policies and ideologies. Needless to say, nationalistic hysteria and ethnocentric political manoeuvring can be potentially explosive, upsetting not only the political scene but the very alignment of political forces. It can also be politically and diplomatically self-destructive. Opportunities for far right ideologies and political formations are looming around the corner.

Conclusions

It is characteristic of the post-1974 era in Greek politics that, once eradicated from State bodies or made redundant, extreme right-wing ideologies ceased to play a political organisational role by rallying all groups under their banner and giving them cohesion. Once discarded from the mainstream of Greek politics by no longer being at the core of conservative ideologies, right-wing extremism found its 'proper' dimensions. Stripped of this ideological mantle, it became confined to small groups. Despite their temporary electoral revival in 1977, they never constituted a real challenge either to the conservatives as a political party or to the government of the day.

From a *social* point of view, Greece is not so polarised as to create and reproduce marginalised sections of the population living under extremely harsh conditions and thus vulnerable to right-wing ideologies. So far, social conditions in the country have not created any dynamics of mass discontent which could be easily exploited by extreme right-wing groups. The economic system, the pattern of capitalist development and property relations have not produced a large stratum of dispossessed people, nor a large agricultural and/or industrial proletariat which could be potentially mobilised by Fascist groups or constitute the social basis of such a movement. There is no tradition of Poujadism in Greece. Old and new petty bourgeois economic and social strata usually register their protest by voting for the major political parties, and not by supporting extreme political movements and/or forming their social backbone. It must be stressed that Greek political parties are multi-class formations in many respects: in the social composition of their membership, in their electoral support and in their policy making. When in opposition, they promise everything to everybody; when in government, they are characterised by strong bureaucratic, clientelistic practices, and display exceptional skills in satisfying sectional, particularistic and corporatist demands, as well as in coopting social groups into the power bloc. These functions and practices of the political parties do not leave much room for the development of right-wing extremism. However, whereas under present conditions the Greek ultra-right groups do not have the capabilities of mass recruitment and political mobilisation, and, more generally, conditions are not such as to make this feasible, there is always the possibility of some growth given the new circumstances shaped by the flood of refugees and nationalistic propaganda. Nationalistic feelings may well be linked to, and/or incorporated into, neo-Fascist political and ideological discourses of various shades.

It hardly needs stressing here that the authoritarianism and racism within all extremist movements of the right tend to overlap, and their re-emergence in the Greek case cannot logically be ruled out. Although the challenge of neo-Fascism is far more serious in other European countries than it is in Greece, it would be unwise to underestimate a dangerous movement which is using extra-parliamentary action, mass mobilisation and the very democratic institutions and political-electoral processes in order to destroy them.

List of Abbreviations

EAM	*Ethniko Apelefterotiko Metopo* [National Liberation Front]
EDA	*Eniaia Demokratiki Aristera* [United Democratic Left]
EDE	*Ethniki Demokratiki Enosis* [National Democratic Union]
EEE	*Ethnikistiki Enosis Ellados* [Nationalist Union of Greece]
EEK	*Elliniko Ethnikosocialistiko Komma* [Greek Nationalist Socialist Party]
EK	*Enosis Kentrou* [Centre Union]
EK	*Ethniko Komma* [National Party]
EKM	*Ethnikosocialistiko Komma Makedonias Kai Thrakis* [National Socialist Party of Macedonia and Thrace]
EKNE	*Ethniko Kinima Neon Epistimonon* [National Movement of Young Scientists]
EL	*Elefterofronoi* [Free Believers]
ELAS	*Ethnikos Laikos Apelefterotikos Stratos* [National Popular Liberation Army]
EN	*Ethniki Nemesi* [National Nemesis]
ENA	*Enosis Neon Axiomatikon* [Union of Junior Officers]
ENEK	*Enomeno Ethniko Kinema* [United Nationalist Movement]
EON	*Ethniki Organossis Neolaias* [National Youth Organisation]
EP	*Ethniki Parataxis* [National Camp]
EPEN	*Ethniki Politiki Enosis* [National Political Union]
ERE	*Ethniki Rizospastiki Enosis* [National Radical Union]
EYP	*Ethniki Epiressia Pliroforion* [National Intelligence Service]
FS	*Foititiko Somatio* [All Student Union]
IDEA	*Ieros Syndesmos Ellinon Axiomatikon* [Sacred Bond of Greek Officers]
KKE	*Kommounistiko Komma Elladas* [Communist Party of Greece]
KP	*Komma Proodeftikon* [Progressive Party]
K4A	*Komma tis 4 Avgoustou* [4th of August Party]
KYP	*Kratiki Epiressia Pliroforion* [State Intelligence Service]
LK	*Laiko Komma* [People's Party]
ND	*Nea Demokratia* [New Democracy]
NT	*Nea Taksi* [New Order]
PA	*Politiki Anoixi* [Political Spring]
PAO	*Pnevmatiki Ananeotiki Ormi* [Intellectual Renovating Momentum]
PASOK	*Panellinio Socialistiko Kinema* [Panhellenic Socialist Movement]
PEEA	*Politiki Epitropi Ethnikis Apelefterossis* [Political Committee of National Liberation]
PEM	*Panellinio Ethniko Metopo* [Panhellenic National Front]
PK	*Patriotiko Kinema* [Patriotic Movement]
SAN	*Syndesmos Axiomatikon Neon* [Association of Young Officers]
SEKE	*Socialistiko Ergatiko Komma Ellados* [Socialist Workers' Party of Greece]
TA	*Tagmata Asfaleias* [Security Battalions]
TE	*Tagmata Ergassias* [Labour Battalions]
TEA	*Tagmata Ethnikis Amynis* [Battalions of National Defence]
XA	*Chryssi Avghi* [Golden Dawn]

Notes

1. N. Mouzelis, *Politics in the Semi-Periphery. Early Parliamentarism and Late Industrialisation in the Balkans and Latin America*, Macmillan, London, 1986.
2. Th. Veremis, 'The Greek Army in Politics, 1922–1935', Ph.D. thesis, Trinity College, Oxford, 1974.
3. K. Vergopoulos, To *agrotiko zetema sten Hellada* [The agrarian question in Greece], Exantas, Athens, 1975.
4. G. Mavrogordatos, *Stillborn Democracy: Social Coalitions and Party Strategies in Greece, 1922–1936*, University of California Press, Berkeley, CA 1975.
5. According to the 1928 Census, 88 per cent of the heads of agricultural businesses owned their land.
6. The Socialist Workers' Party of Greece [*Socialistiko Ergatiko Komma Ellados*, SEKE] was founded in 1918. In 1920, the party joined the Third International and, in 1924, changed its title to the Communist Party of Greece.
7. N. Mouzelis, *Modern Greece. Facets of Underdevelopment*, Macmillan, London, 1978.
8. G. Coutsoumaris, *The Morphology of Greek Industry and A Study in Industrial Development*, Center for Economic Research, Athens, 1963.
9. Y. Andricopoulos, 'The Power Base of Greek Authoritarianism', in *Who Were the Fascists?*, Universitets Forlaget, Bergen-Oslo, 1980, pp. 568–84.
10. Andricopoulous, ibid., mentions the following: the Nationalist Union of Greece [*Ethnikistiki Enosis Ellados*, EEE], which had its headquarters in Salonica, where an 80,000-strong Jewish community was based; the Greek Nationalist Socialist Party [*Elliniko Ethnikosocialistiko Komma*, EEK]; the anti-Semitic National Socialist Party of Macedonia and Thrace [*Ethnikosocialistiko Komma Makedonias Kai Thrakis*, EKM], and the tiny All Student Union [*Foititiko Somatio*, FS]. This list was drawn up by the British Embassy at the request of the Foreign Office, and despatched on 4 May 1934.
11. Two days earlier the King had rejected an offer by the two major parties in parliament to form a coalition government.
12. S. Linardatos, *Pos Ftassame sten 4e Avgoustou* [How We Reached the 4th of August], Themelio, Athens, 1965.
13. S. Linardatos, *H 4h Avgoustou* [The 4th of August], Themelio, Athens, 1966. See also, 'H 4h Avgoustou', To *Vima*, special issue, 3 Aug. 1986, pp. 15–34.
14. R. Clogg, *A Short History of Modern Greece*, Cambridge University Press, Cambridge, 1979. See also 'The Fourth-of-August Regime', *Journal of the Hellenic Diaspora*, Nos. 1 and 2, 1986, pp. 53–112. The 'hybrid nature' of the regime, which took inspiration from, and aped, Western European models of Fascism and National Socialism, is rightly stressed by Constantine Sarantis, 'The Ideology and Character of the Metaxas Regime', in R. Higham and Th. Veremis (eds), *Aspects of Greece 1936–40: the Metaxas Dictatorship*, Eliamep – Vryonis Center, Athens, 1993, pp. 147–177.
15. C. M. Woodhouse, *Modern Greece: a Short History*, Faber and Faber, London, 1966 (4th edn.).
16. A. Gerolymatos, 'The Security Battalions and the Civil War'. Paper presented at the Conference on the Greek Civil War, University of Copenhagen, 1984.
17. H. Fleischer, 'The Anomalies in the Middle East Forces, 1941–44', *Journal of the Hellenic Diaspora*, special issue on Greece, 1940–1950, Autumn 1970, pp. 5–36.
18. For example, the pro-Fascist National Nemesis [*Ethniki Nemesi*, EN], the extreme royalist Union of Junior Officers [*Enosis Neon Axiomatikon*, ENA], the right-wing Association of Young Officers [*Syndesmos Axiomatikon Neon*, SAN], or others known only by their acronym like the PAN and the EE.

19. L. Wittner, *American Intervention in Greece, 1943–1949*, Columbia University Press, New York, 1982.

20. N. Mouzelis, 'Capitalism and Dictatorship in Postwar Greece', in *New Left Review*, No. 96, 1976, pp. 57–80.

21. V. Kapetanyannis *Socio-Political Conflicts and Military Intervention: The case of Greece, 1950–1967*, Ph.D. thesis, Birkbeck College, University of London, 1986.

22. During the parliamentary debate on a new bill about the State Intelligence Service [*Kratiki Epiressia Pliroforion*, KYP], renamed National Intelligence Service [*Ethniki Epiressia Pliroforion*, EYP] in January 1984, figures of between 12 and 30 million files were officially mentioned. According to some reports, they could well number 35 million. See *ANTI*, No. 252, 20 Jan. 1964, pp. 11–13.

23. J. Meynaud, *Les forces politiques en Grèce*, Etudes de Science Politique, Lausanne, 1965.

24. A. Lentakis, *Neo-facistikes organoseis neolaias* [Neo-Fascist youth organisations], EDA, Athens, 1963.

25. The Lambrakis affair was dramatised in the film 'Z' by K. Gavras, named after the book by the Greek novelist Vassilis Vassilikos.

26. N. Alevizatos, 'Les institutions politiques de la Grèce à travers les crises: 1922–1974,' Unpublished Ph.D. thesis, Université de Droit, d'Economie et de Sciences Sociales de Paris, Paris II, 1977.

27. K. Tsoukalas, *The Greek Tragedy*, Penguin, Harmondsworth, 1969.

28. J. Meynaud, *Rapport sur l'abolition de la démocratie en Grèce*, University of Montreal, 1967.

29. K. Legg, *Politics in Modern Greece*, Stanford University Press, Stanford, CA, 1969.

30. C. M. Woodhouse, *The Rise and Fall of the Greek Colonels*, Granada, St Albans, 1985.

31. In April 1970, the publication of *Politiki Agogi* [Political Education], written by Th. Papakonstantinou, sometime Minister of Education in the regime, was announced. The book was widely distributed and used as a school textbook. George Georgalas, the regime's chief spokesman, published in April 1971 his *Ideologia tis Epanastaseos* [Ideology of the Revolution], which was given wide distribution. Savas Konstantopoulos, editor of the pro-regime newspaper *Elefteros Kosmos* [Free World], was another 'theoretician' of the dictatorship. George Papadopoulos himself has published seven volumes of *To Pistevo mas* [Our Creed] to state his 'case'.

32. R. Clogg, *The Ideology of the Revolution of 21 April 1967*, in R. Clogg and L. Yannopoulos (eds), Greece under Military Rule, Secker and Warburg, London, 1972.

33. The 'K4A' was founded in 1960 by Costas Plevris, who has openly propagated National Socialist ideas. The organisation was particularly active between 1960 and 1967 in Thessaloniki, during the students' mobilisations. The emblem of the organisation (the two axes) was identical to that of the Italian neo-Fascist organisation *Ordine Nuovo*. According to *ANTI*, No. 62, 8 Jan. 1977, p. 26, splinter groups like that of P. Dakoglou, nicknamed '*Achaioi*' [Achaeans], were fanatical supporters of Brigadier Dimitri Ioannides, Commander of the notorious Greek military police which had tortured many of the victims of the junta during the dictatorship. Ioannides was responsible for the coup which overthrew Papadopoulos in 1973, and was, behind the scenes, the strong man of the new military regime until its collapse in July 1974. After the fall of the military regime, Dakoglou's group was renamed Intellectual Renovating Momentum [*Pnevmatiki Ananeotiki Ormi*, PAO]. Another splinter group of 'K4A', led by A. Dedrinos, was also renamed Patriotic Movement [*Patriotiko Kinema*, PK]. See *ANTI*, No, 62, 8 Jan. 1977, p. 25.

34. *ANTI*, No. 19, 17 May 1975.

35. *ANTI*, Ibid.

36. Th. Veremis, 'Greece: Veto and Impasse, 1967–74', in C. Clapham and G. Phillip (eds), *The Political Dilemmas of Military Regimes*, Croom Helm, London, 1985, pp. 27–45.

37. N. Diamandouros, 'Transition to, and Consolidation of Democratic Politics in Greece, 1974–1983. A Tentative Assessment', *West European Politics*, VII (2), 1984, pp. 50–71.

38. V. Kapetanyannis, 'The Making of Greek Euro-Communism', *Political Quarterly*, L (4), 1979, pp. 445–60. See also *idem*, 'The Communists', in K. Featherston and D. Katsoudas (eds), *Political Change in Greece: Before and After the Colonels*, Croom Helm, London, 1988, pp. 120–55.

39. Th. Couloumbis and R. Yannas, 'The Stability Quotient of Greece's Post-1974 Democratic Institutions', *Journal of Modern Greek Studies*, Dec. 1963, pp. 359–72.

40. R. Clogg, *Parties and Elections in Greece*, C. Hurst, London, 1968.

41. *Decapenthimeros Politis*, Nos. 67–68, Dec. 1984, pp. 34–41.

42. European Parliament, Committee of Inquiry into the Rise of Fascism and Racism in Europe, *Report on the Findings of the Inquiry*, Luxembourg, 1985.

43. Theotokis was elected deputy for Corfu with Karamanlis's ND in 1974. However, he was soon to express his strong disagreement with the party's neutral stand in the constitutional plebiscite that followed on 8 Dec. 1974, and ended the monarchy by a two-to-one vote. He resigned his seat four days later.

44. See *ANTI*, No. 106, 26 Aug. 1978, pp. 2–11.

45. Karamanlis was elected President on 5 May 1990 in the third and final parliamentary ballot by receiving 183 votes, three more than the minimum required.

46. Theotokis died in Athens in 1988 at the age of 79. See his obituary in *The Times*, 9 Sept. 1988, p. 18.

47. See *The Times*, 5 Dec. 1984, p. 6. Le Pen visited Greece again in Sept. 1988. The government spokesman said then that he was a *persona non grata* for the Greek government.

48. *Stochos* [Target], for instance, is an eight-page broadsheet weekly full of anti-Slav, anti-Moscow, anti-Jewish propaganda, and is extremely racist and chauvinistic. *Elfteri Ora* [Free Hour] is a six-page daily paper with an eight-page Sunday edition. It hosts the views of Costas Plevris, the leader of the 'K4A', and of other right-wingers. It is strongly anti-Communist and anti-Jewish. Its circulation is very low, around 1,500 copies daily (Nov. 1988), in the Athens-Piraeus area.

49. Law 1907/1990 stipulated a national 3 per cent threshold for a party to qualify for any seats at all.

50. See P. E. Dimitras, 'Greece: The Virtual Absence of an Extreme Right', in P. Hainsworth (ed.), *The Extreme Right in Europe and the USA*, Pinter, London, 1992.

51. Among the voluminous bibliography, see D. Dakin, *The Greek Struggle in Macedonia, 1897–1913*, Institute for Balkan Studies, Thessaloniki, 1966; E. Kofos, *Nationalism and Communism in Macedonia*, Institute for Balkan Studies, Thessaloniki, 1964; E. Kofos, 'National Heritage and National Identity in Nineteenth- and Twentieth-Century Macedonia', in M. Blinkhorn and Th. Veremis (eds), *Modern Greece: Nationalism and Nationality*, Sage-ELIAMEP, Athens, 1990.

52. See B. Anderson, *Imagined Communities. Reflections on the Origin and Spread of Nationalism*, London, 1983. See also E. Gellner, *Nations and Nationalism*, Blackwell, Oxford, 1983 and E. Kedourie, *Nationalism*, Hutchinson, London, 1983.

Chapter 8

NATIONALISM AND THE EXTREME RIGHT IN THE FORMER YUGOSLAVIA*
Jill A. Irvine

All the countries of Eastern Europe have experienced dramatic and unpredictable political consequences as a result of the fall of Communism, perhaps none more than the former Yugoslavia. Much attention has been paid to the outbreak of war and its devastating impact upon the population of this area. While it is clear that extreme nationalism has been a major cause of the conflict, there has been little systematic analysis of the political role of neo-Fascism and the extreme right. How have the forces of the extreme right affected the conflict among Yugoslavia's various national groups? More importantly, how are they likely to affect the future political development and reconstruction of its successor states?

A brief overview of the extreme right in the former Yugoslavia will provide the framework for addressing these questions. It focuses on Serbia-Montenegro and Croatia, since these areas constitute the most populous political units of the former Yugoslavia and are directly involved in the current wars of secession, and because the extreme right has developed under different circumstances in Slovenia and Macedonia.[1] It begins by examining the ideologies and political programmes of the major right-wing political parties in Serbia and Croatia, the Serbian Radical party [*Srpska radikalna stranka*, SRS] and the Croatian Party of Rights [*Hrvatska stranka prava*, HSP]. Exploring the ways in which these parties define themselves can shed light on important differences and similarities with other European neo-Fascist and extreme right groups. In seeking to explain the reasons for the growth of the extreme right in the former Yugoslavia, this chapter examines the historical roots of extreme right movements and their emergence after 1989. While the extreme right draws upon historical roots in Serbia and Croatia, it is also deeply embedded in the current circumstances of political transformation and war. Consequently, the chapter investigates the current socioeconomic, military, and political contexts of ultra-nationalism and concludes with a discussion of its likely future role. Although the extreme right has been a potent force in Serbia and Croatia, it has proved vulnerable to pressure and cooptation by the ruling parties in these areas, the Socialist Party of Serbia [*Socijalistička partija Srbije*, SPS] headed by Slobodan Milošević and the Croatian Democratic Union [*Hrvatska demokratska zajednica*, HDZ] headed by Franjo Tudjman, both of which indicate strong ultra-nationalist tendencies.

Figure 8.1 Former Yugoslavia, April 1993 (Washington DC, United States Central Intelligence Agency).

Ideology of the extreme right

The difficulty of classifying extreme right and neo-Fascist movements and parties has been the subject of much discussion and has prompted long terminological disputes. This problem is also evident in the newly emerging study of extreme right movements in Eastern Europe and the former Soviet Union.[2] While recognising the vital importance of clarifying concepts and developing classification schemes of the extreme right, such a task is outside the scope of this chapter. Nevertheless, the discussion that follows will attempt to place the current extreme right in the former Yugoslavia within a larger framework, distinguishing it in important ways both from historic Fascism and from current neo-Fascism in Western Europe.

'The politics of identity' is a phrase that can be aptly used to describe political life in much of Eastern Europe today. Rapidly changing social and economic conditions coupled with the loss of legitimacy and authority by the previous regimes have resulted in a crisis of political legitimacy and identity.[3] While political life in the industrial democracies of Western Europe and the United States centres primarily around instrumental and economic questions (questions about 'how much?'), in Eastern Europe since 1989 politics has revolved largely around questions concerning the basic shape and character of the political community (questions such as 'who belongs?' and 'to what kind of state?'); in this setting the expressive and symbolic aspects of politics are emphasised.[4]

This preoccupation with the most basic questions of political identity is both cause and effect of the potency of extreme nationalism and the rise of the extreme right in Eastern Europe. Socialism has been discredited and it has proved difficult to achieve a liberal political consensus in Eastern Europe. In these circumstances, extreme nationalism has proved particularly conducive to solving the crisis of political identity.[5] It does this through a profoundly anti-liberal perspective which places the source of an individual's value and meaning within the context of the national community. As this view was expressed by Ivan Vekić a leader of the extreme right in Croatia: 'The most immoral act is to be free of an obligation to the community'.[6] As students of historic Fascism have frequently pointed out, extreme nationalism – centred on the idea of an organic community based on nation, race, blood or soil – provides a link from the individual to the larger political community or state.

According to extreme right ideology, the strengthening of the nation, which is seen to be in a constant struggle for survival with other nations, is the main object of political life. In order to survive, however, a nation needs its own state, or at the very least to be able to put the resources of the state to work for its particular national purposes.[7] Therefore, an essential part of the neo-Fascist ideology is the 'sacralisation' of the state, a belief that, as an expression or reflection of one's own nation, it is the highest political end.[8] Historical Fascism sometimes displayed a more universal, revolutionary perspective, or at least a dedication to expanding the Fascist state's dominion over the widest possible territory. Current neo-Fascism and the extreme right have eschewed this expansionist perspective in favour of what might be called the doctrine of 'Fascism in one country', and their main preoccupation has been to achieve the 'pure' nation-state based on national exclusivity.

If the foremost goal of neo-Fascists is to create or maintain a state which offers full membership to only one nation, the practical implications of this goal have differed in the recent contexts of Western and Eastern Europe. In Western Europe, where nation-states are more fully established, extreme nationalism is often directed against outsiders – immigrants who migrated to these countries in large numbers in previous decades. Neo-Fascists seek to keep the nation-state free from 'contamination' by these 'outsiders'.[9] In Eastern Europe, where state and nation have seldom corresponded, the problem since 1989 has been one of creating such states, either by redrawing borders to include conationals excluded from the state, or by denying full rights to minorities residing within the state. The forcible removal of other nations has also been used, as attested by the 'ethnic cleansing' employed in the former Yugoslavia. Geo-politically, the creation of nation-states often means a struggle 'for survival' against neighbouring states and their sponsors which are viewed as encroaching upon the legitimate state aims of the nation in question. In other words, while the extreme right in Western Europe is primarily concerned with closing borders, in Eastern Europe it is often concerned with redrawing them. In both halves of Europe, however, racist and hostile propaganda toward national groups perceived as threats or competitors are essential tools in the struggle to achieve these goals.

Although creating a sense of collective identity through the nation-state is of foremost importance in extreme right ideology, certain domestic political and economic arrangements are also part of its programme. Unlike traditional Fascism, which rejected parliamentary democracy as corrupting and weakening the nation, neo-Fascism and the extreme right in the current European context often seek to work within this system. Consequently, they have affirmed their support for a multi-party system and the most important procedural aspects of democracy such as contested elections, the rights of free association and a free press. Nevertheless, while these groups nominally accept the democratic framework, they often act in ways that undermine it, for example resorting to violence to achieve their goals, or branding as national traitors those who do not share their views. While they may seek particular institutional reforms that will further their political aims (such as proportional representation), extreme right groups in Eastern Europe do not see strengthening or maintaining democracy as a main priority.

In terms of the economy, traditional Fascist ideology emphasised a third way between capitalism and Communism, usually through a corporatist system of linkages between labour and capital. Neo-Fascism and the extreme right have generally looked more favourably upon capitalism, though in its more benign form of the full welfare state. In Western Europe this has meant a determination by right-wing extremists to prevent those who are not 'real' Germans or French from enjoying the economic benefits of the welfare state. In Eastern Europe, ultra-rightists have tended to support a gradual transition to a market economy with significant state intervention in the economy in the foreseeable future.[10] This position has in some cases brought them into an alliance with former Communists, many of whom have simply switched their allegiance from Communist to extreme right parties. While the reasons for this alliance are more complex than their similar positions on the economy, the 'red–brown' condominium is, in any case, an intriguing feature of the extreme right in Eastern Europe today.

The political programmes of the extreme right in Serbia and Croatia reflect the general ideological positions of neo-Fascism and the extreme right outlined above. Extreme nationalism lies at the heart of the ideology embraced by the SRS and the HSP, and their leaders have been vociferous in articulating 'essential' national aims. Their positions on political pluralism and tolerance for minorities, institutional reform, the treatment of former Communists and the transition to a market economy have been less clearly articulated, and the two parties have not always adopted similar positions. Like other European neo-Fascist and extreme right groups, they differ in essential ways for historical Fascism, chiefly in their acceptance of parliamentary democracy and the market economy. They also differ in significant ways from their counterparts in Western Europe in the character and implementation of their nationalist agenda.

The main spokesman for the extreme right in Serbia is Vojislav Šešelj, leader of the

SRS. Šešelj's strong hold over his own followers and his ability to attract a wide measure of support from non-party members has contributed significantly to the growth of the extreme right in Serbia since 1990. (The adulation in which Šešelj is held by his followers is revealed by a Radical Party leader's description of his first meeting with him: 'For the first time I talked to a man who was more elevated and more powerful than I am. Then it became clear to me how it is for other people to talk to me. Before me was a true politician and a true Serb. Great, strong, all powerful. Powerful in his words, thoughts and behaviour.')[11] Šešelj, who was the youngest person to be awarded a Ph.D. in Communist Yugoslavia, was derided by the press after the collapse of Communism in 1990, which characterised him as a disappointed man and a frustrated academic. Nevertheless, his frequent and flamboyant appearances on television, his imprisonment under the Communist regime (Šešelj had gone from Communist hardliner to nationalist dissident in the 1980s), his commanding presence and his quick, acerbic wit had earned him a certain amount of notoriety, if not respect, at the beginning of the post-Communist period.

Šešelj has been instrumental in defining and articulating the views of his party, whose foremost political objective he describes as the defence of the Serbian nation through the creation of a strong Serbian state. According to him, Serbs are engaged in a struggle for national survival, against neighbouring nations like the Croats and, indeed, the entire world. Šešelj's rhetoric is bellicose and Messianic. Describing Serbs alternately as a chosen and a persecuted people, he exhorts them to remain true to their character as a strong 'warrior people',[12] and to refuse to relent in the current 'war of nerves'.[13] Šešelj warns that their struggle for national liberation may take ten, twenty, even thirty years, but that ultimately Serbs will emerge victorious, with their nation intact and their state reconstructed.

The state that Šešelj has in mind is a Great Serbian state taking in Serbia, Montenegro, Macedonia and large portions of Bosnia-Herzegovina and Croatia.[14] Šešelj envisions that the creation of such a Serbian state will involve the destruction of the Croatian one, which will be reduced to 'as much as one can see from the tower of the Cathedral in Zagreb'.[15] Croats, whom he characterises as a 'cowardly', 'spoiled' and 'unhistorical' people,[16] will be expelled from the new Serbian state, in a 'retaliatory move', and other minorities will be permitted to stay only if they 'do not question Serbia's national integrity and interests'.[17] Denouncing the old Yugoslav state 'as the worst possible alternative facing Serbs', he warns repeatedly of the dangers of Western, especially American, attempts to resurrect such a state.[18]

In addition to the political dangers facing Serbs, Šešelj warns of such genetically corrupting influences as inter-mixing with neighbouring nations. According to him, this is a process by which the Serbian genetic essence has flowed into the Croatian national corpus, or has been Muslimised.[19] The extreme to which some of these racist ideas have been carried can be seen in the recent proposal by a well-known Serbian artist, Milić Stanković, that a Ministry of the Procreation of Serbs be established to produce genetically pure Serbs.[20] It is ironic that Šešelj himself has been accused of not being a true Serb, but rather a Catholic Croat whose ancestors converted to Orthodoxy in order to gain employment.[21] In any case, the Radicals have contributed greatly to creating an atmosphere in which the judgement of an individual according to ethnic and national criteria has become an accepted feature of public discourse.

Although domestic political and economic concerns are secondary in the Radicals' thinking, they have become more important components of their political programme. From the outset, the Radicals have proclaimed their support for a multi-party system and parliamentary democracy. Šešelj has vehemently denied any intention of using violence to achieve his political goals and has denounced other opposition parties for encouraging street demonstrations. He currently supports a republic because he objects to Prince Aleksandar who has given 'too much praise to Slovenian and Croatian democracy'.[22] (Born in Britain in 1945 shortly after his father, King Peter II, fled Yugoslavia, Aleksandar is now seeking to return to the country and establish himself as monarch.) Šešelj has also called for certain institutional reforms such as proportional representation (a favourite position of non-ruling parties in Eastern Europe).[23] Nevertheless, his main concern is the consolidation of public order, and he has vowed to strengthen the police force (which he characterises revealingly as the most important public institution) if he comes to power. Moreover, Šešelj has shown himself to be unwilling to work with other opposition parties, whom he frequently brands as 'traitors' or 'agents for the German Intelligence Service'.[24] Radical deputies have also shown a predilection toward violent and obstructionist tactics in parliament.[25]

Šešelj's Radicals and Milošević's Socialists initially agreed about the need for a gradual transition to a market economy, though Šešelj criticised Milošević on occasion for the slow move toward privatisation. During 1993, however, Šešelj displayed an increasing willingness to champion social causes, which he charged the Milošević government of having ignored. Calling on the government to introduce a massive public works programme to alleviate the problem of unemployment, Šešelj also advocated improved health benefits and expanded educational programmes.[26] When pressed to present more concrete ideas for the organisation of the economy, however, his ideas bordered on the fantastic. In an interview with the Belgrade weekly *NIN* at the beginning of 1992, Šešelj proposed that the government should 'turn all of Serbia into a duty-free zone; why not offer all our factories to the Japanese for a song?'[27] In any case, material concerns are secondary to the Radical message, which emphasises that Serbs must hold out even if sanctions last for twenty or thirty years.

Although Šešelj has denied vehemently that the Radicals have anything in common with right-wing extremists in Croatia, their views are often mirror images of one another. The main spokesman for the extreme right in Croatia is the young Dobroslav Paraga, leader of the HSP. Paraga is a former law and seminary student who spent most of the 1980s as a dissident to the Communist regime. First imprisoned in 1980 for passing out a petition calling for the freeing of all political prisoners in Yugoslavia, Paraga subsequently brought charges against the state for cruel and inhumane treatment in the notorious Communist prison, Goli Otok. His frequent testimony to the US Congress and to Western leaders about political repression in Yugoslavia further consolidated his reputation as a champion of human rights. Ironically, Paraga has used this reputation to lend respectability to his right-wing group and cause.[28] An intelligent-looking, articulate man, he also has a predilection for creating tough-looking images, such as giving interviews behind a desk with rocket launchers perched on top. Nevertheless, in contrast to Šešelj, he has been unable to project an appeal beyond his party's own supporters and he has failed to generate wider electoral support. Since extreme right parties tend to rely heavily on charismatic personalities for their success, this lack of a commanding personality has weakened the extreme right in Croatia.

Paraga also sees Croats as engaged in a struggle for their national survival against enemy nations like the Serbs and a frequently hostile world. The HSP leader champions the creation of a Great Croatian state 'encompassing its historical and ethnic borders', that is, including significant portions of Serbia and all of Bosnia-Herzegovina; the HSP slogan in the 1990 elections was 'Croatia to the Drina (River)'. According to Paraga, Croatia is one of those states which 'under natural law are moving toward the formation of independent national states'.[29] In order to accomplish this state-building objective, Paraga insists that the war with Serbia must end in 'total defeat' in which 'nothing is left of Serbia except Belgrade and its surroundings'.[30] Arguing that Bosnian Muslims are mostly Muslimised Croats, Paraga insists that Bosnia-Herzegovina and Croatia are 'the same soil, the same blood, the same nation' and that they must be united in a common state.[31] While Paraga maintains that the structure of the new state (federal or not) must be decided by plebiscite, he also emphasises that this state will be 'for only one people living in Croatia, the Croats'.[32] Like Šešelj, Paraga sees Yugoslavism as a 'cancer' on the body politic, and he harbours deep suspicious of what he fears is an American policy of creating a Serbian 'gendarme' in the Balkans.[33]

Paraga and the HSP define their programme largely in relation to the inter-war Ustasha Fascist movement and the Ustasha-controlled Independent State of Croatia [*Nezavisna Država Hrvatska*, NDH] from 1941 to 1945 (see below). HSP supporters openly endorse the Ustasha regime, often wearing a U on their caps and donning the black shirts of the Ustasha paramilitary forces. Paraga has insisted repeatedly that there was nothing Fascist about the Ustasha regime.[34] According to him, the NDH represented the wishes of the majority of the population for independence from the Serbs and was the legal embodiment of the continuity of the medieval Croatian state. Although he condemns the 'few' racial laws that were promulgated by the Ustashas, he denies that there was systematic racial or national persecution by the state: 'I would never say that Serbs were persecuted (in the NDH) simply because they were Serbs'.[35] Moreover, Paraga and the HSP have indicated their willingness to adopt some repressive Ustasha policies such as the creation of an autocephalous Croatian Orthodox Church.[36] However, Paraga, who possesses a highly developed ability to adapt his message to his audience, has shown signs of toning down his rhetoric on the Ustasha state in recent months, even as the wave of enthusiasm for Ustasha iconography and symbolism that swept Croatia after the outbreak of war in 1991 appears to be subsiding slowly.

The HSP, like its counterpart in Serbia, has pledged its support for parliamentary democracy. Indeed, Paraga has campaigned tirelessly against what he claims are massive human rights abuses by the Tudjman regime. In contrast to the Radicals in Serbia, who until fairly recently maintained a kind of alliance with Milošević's Socialists, the HSP has been an implacable foe of the Tudjman regime which it condemns as 'Fascist' and undemocratic. Nevertheless, Paraga has stopped short of extending this human rights campaign to Serbs in Croatia, arguing that a 'Serbian problem' does not exist in the Croatian state. To a large extent, Paraga's defence of democracy appears to be aimed at curbing various legal and illegal moves taken against the HSP by the Tudjman regime. At the HSP's first party congress in the spring of 1991, the use of violence to achieve the party's political goals was abandoned reluctantly after a great deal of internal dissension.[37]

The HSP supports the transition to a market economy, but its economic views remain a relatively undeveloped part of its programme. It has been highly critical of the HDZ's economic programme, charging the ruling party with 'neo-Communist views' and with corruption in carrying out its privatisation programme. Nevertheless, the HSP has maintained that all concrete measures for the transition to a market economy should be debated and implemented after the conclusion of the war in Croatia (which the HSP insists is nowhere near over).[38] Like the Radicals, the HSP emphasises that the main solution to all social and economic problems is the creation of a Great Croatian state.

A common feature of the ideologies of the extreme right parties in Croatia and Serbia (which they share with historic Fascism) is their relatively undeveloped character. Although both groups have clearly articulated national aims (the creation of a Great Croatian or Great Serbian state in which minority rights will be partially protected at best), they have failed to offer detailed programmes for solving pressing social and economic problems other than simply defeating the enemy. Indeed, the relative flexibility of the political ideology of these extreme right parties, coupled with the circumstances of the war, has allowed bandit groups to operate increasingly under their rubric. The breakdown of law and order and the rise of corruption in parts of the former Yugoslavia since the outbreak of war in 1991 often make it difficult to distinguish exactly where the extreme right leaves off and simple banditry begins.

Historical roots

The metaphor most frequently invoked in popular parlance when explaining the re-emergence of the extreme right in Eastern Europe and the former Soviet Union is that of a deep freeze in the Communist period followed by a subsequent thaw in the post-Communist period. According to this image, politics has simply picked up where it left off in 1939 or 1941, with Fascism and the extreme right playing their previously significant or insignificant role. This intuitively appealing popular notion is reinforced by the continuity of names adopted by extreme right groups, of actual personalities in a few cases, and of statements by the participants themselves. Nevertheless, while an examination of the current extreme right reveals some striking similarities with the inter-war period, there are also significant differences in the character of current ultra-nationalist groups and the political context in which they operate.

There are three important factors to consider when looking at the historical roots of extreme nationalism in the former Yugoslavia. The first is the original formulation of national ideologies, which constitute the heart of nationalist doctrine endorsed by extreme right groups. The second is the political strength and role of previously existing Fascist and ultra-nationalist organisations, which provide organisational forms to the extreme right. The third factor is the impact of the Communist period, the way in which it reshaped the national question and its legacies for the post-Communist response to it.

Croats and Serbs formulated fundamentally different national ideologies in the nineteenth and early twentieth centuries as a result of differences in the geographic distribution of their national populations and the political circumstances in which they found themselves. Croats faced the problem of creating a sense of national community from their disparate regions and dialects and of carving out political autonomy, if not independence, from Austro-Hungarian rule.[39] They faced an additional challenge from the large number of Serbs residing within the historical territory of Croatia in the crescent-shaped area along the borders with Serbia and Bosnia formerly known as the Military Frontier (*Vojna krajina*, today's Krajina region). Administratively autonomous until the late nineteenth century, this largely Serb-populated area of Croatia was used by the Habsburgs to create a military buffer against the Ottoman Empire. In the nineteenth century, Serbs in the Military Frontier became increasingly receptive to the emerging Serbian national ideology which sought to reunite them with a Serbian state. The challenge to national unification and independence posed by the Serbian population within Croatia became a major preoccupation of the Croat national movement.[40]

Although there was a strong strand of Yugoslav national ideology among Croats – a desire to unite with other South Slavs in a unified state – there also developed a national ideology which sought to establish an independent Great Croatian state. Ante Starčević was the first Croatian political leader to articulate such a political goal, although other political parties, such as the Croat Peasant Party [*Hrvatska seljačka stranka*, HSS], subsequently adopted political programmes based primarily on achieving Croatian national aims. Carrying the idea of 'Croatian state right' to its extreme, he contemplated a greater Croatia, including Bosnia, and refused to recognise the existence of any other South Slav nations besides the Bulgarians. Well aware of the difficulty posed by the large number of Serbs residing in historically Croatian territory, Starčević attempted to deny the historical validity of the existence of the Serb nation in Croatia, describing Serbs as 'beggars' and 'slaves'.[41] Together with Eugen Kvaternik, he established the Croatian Party of Rights which espoused an integral Croat nationalism with a markedly anti-Serb tone.[42] Although some of Starčević's followers adopted a more conciliatory stance toward Serbs in the years after his death in 1903, others joined the Pure Party of Rights, formed by Josip Frank in 1895, which continued to endorse as its main position an implacable hatred of Serbs.[43] The HSP, the main representative of the extreme right in Croatia today, considers itself the direct successor of Starčević's creation.

Serbs encountered different problems in the formation of their national ideology in the nineteenth century. In contrast to Croats, who faced the challenge of integrating the large Serb minority residing within Croatia's historic borders, they faced the challenge of large numbers of their conationals residing outside the borders of Serbia proper. Primarily assimilationist, they were concerned with retrieving their fellow Serbs across the border. The formation of an independent Serbian state in the early part of the nineteenth century reinforced this national ideology.[44] The Serbian political parties formed at this time shared similar views on Serbian national goals and relations with other South Slavs. The main political party, the People's Radical Party [*Narodna radikalna stranka*, NRS], formed by Nikola Pasić in the 1870s, believed that Serbia's primary task was to join Serbs living outside Serbia to their homeland primarily through territorial expansion. Less interested in the South Slav unity espoused by many Croats, the Radicals had few contacts with Slovenes and Croats and these were usually at the latter's initiative.[45] This vision of a Serbian state that would unite the entire Serb nation was uppermost in the minds of Serb politicians as they formed the new Kingdom of Serbs, Croats and Slovenes in 1918. The SRS, the main representative of the extreme right in Serbia today, is committed to realising these national aims.[46]

The national question continued to preoccupy Serbs and Croats in the inter-war period, and it fuelled support for the various Fascist and ultra-nationalist organisations which began to emerge soon after the formation of the new Yugoslav state. Nevertheless, although Fascism played a significant role in political developments in Yugoslavia from 1918 to 1945, it never established a strong social basis of support.[47] First, Fascism became associated with Germany and Italy, and there was strong sentiment against these powers in inter-war Yugoslavia. Second, and more importantly, the mainstream national parties, the HSS and the NRS, espoused many of the same national goals. Finally, the political apparatus remained relatively free of Fascist influences and was able effectively to repress these groups.

The most important of the several Fascist and proto-Fascist organisations in inter-war Yugoslavia based upon Serbian nationalism was the *Zbor* (Convention) movement of Dimitrije Ljotić, formed in 1934.[48] The *Zbor* sought to transform Yugoslavia into a highly centralised, corporatist state. Based on a strong leadership principle, it rejected multi-party competition and parliamentary democracy. Although it gained a foothold in Belgrade University, it did not attract widespread support and failed to win a single seat in the parliamentary elections of 1935 and 1938. Its counterpart in Croatia was the Ustasha-Croat Revolutionary Organisation [*Ustaša-Hrvatska revolucionarna organizacija*] which was formed in 1932 by Ante Pavelić, a former leader of the HSP. The Ustasha pledged to use all means, including terrorism, to fight for an independent Croatian state, encompassing Bosnia and Herzegovina, which would grant political rights only to Croats. In the 1930s Pavelić established a network of camps in Italy and Hungary in which to oversee the political indoctrination and military training of his national revolutionaries. The Ustasha gained support among the peasantry, particularly in the poor and nationally mixed regions of western Herzegovina, Lika, Kordun, Banija and Dalmatinska Zagora.[49] Ustasha supporters, along with their fellow travellers, the *Frankovci*, also established a stronghold at the University of Zagreb, where they became the largest student group in 1940.[50]

As the Second World War approached and Axis influence over Yugoslavia increased, Fascist political forces grew in strength. The regime of Milan Stojadinović increasingly took on Fascist trappings, with its own brownshirts, Fascist-style rallies (Stojadinović allegedly liked to hear the crowds chanting '*Vodja, Vodja*,' the equivalent of '*Duce, Duce*') and pro-Axis foreign policy. The outbreak of the war in 1941 brought a fully Fascist regime to power in the NDH, under the control of the Ustashas and backed by Germany and Italy.[51] Although it is difficult to measure the extent of support for the Ustasha regime, many Croats were undoubtedly sympathetic to Pavelić's demands for an independent Croatian state. (Archbishop Alojzije Stepinac was certainly not alone when he proclaimed the new state 'the hand of God in action.')[52] The Ustashas quickly promulgated racial laws against Jews, Serbs and Gypsies (Serbs were required to wear an armband with a P for *Pravoslavac*, meaning Orthodox) and launched a campaign of terror against Serbs.[53] A civil war ensued, with the Ustashas fighting the Chetniks (the traditional name given to Serbian fighters against the Turks and the main Serbian resistance group during the Second World War), and the Communist-led partisans fighting them both. It has left an indelible mark upon the political map of Yugoslavia. Extreme right groups in Croatia and Serbia today both define and justify their positions largely in relation to the Ustasha regime and the civil war of 1941–1945.

The Communists sought to heal the wounds of the civil war and resolve the national question by placing blame equally on the 'Serbian hegemonists' (for example, labelling King Aleksandar's regime 'monarchist-Fascist') of the inter-war period and the 'Croatian Fascists' of the NDH. By constructing a federal state which recognised national differences but centralised power in the hands of a unitary party, it initially hoped to follow the Soviet state model to harmony among Yugoslavia's various national groups. But the League of Communists of Yugoslavia [*Savez komunista Jugoslavije*, SKJ] vacillated between two models of one-part federalism, the highly centralised one adopted in 1945, which appealed largely to Serb national interests, and the decentralised version enshrined in the 1974 constitution (giving extensive autonomy to Serbia's autonomous provinces of Kosovo and Vojvodina and resulting in eight independent party leaderships within one nominally unified party), which appealed largely to Croat national aims. Fighting over these two federal models increasingly paralysed the party-state after Tito's death in 1980.[54] As the one-party system unravelled in the late 1980s, both Serbs and Croats denounced the bitter legacy of the Communist approach to *their* national questions. Both became convinced that they could not achieve their national aims within a federal Yugoslav state. Five decades of Communist rule had transformed rather than simply frozen conflicts among Yugoslavia's national groups.

Although by the end of the Communist period nationalist aims were endorsed more and more openly, there were important political differences in the evolution of nationalist politics in Serbia and Croatia. From the mid-1980s, Serbia saw the growth of popular political participation primarily focused on nationalist issues. Slobodan Milošević became an indisputably popular Communist boss by using populist tactics to articulate Serbian national grievances. Charging that Serbia had been weakened immeasurably by the Communist regime (and possibly by its association with the Yugoslav state), Milošević called for a reassertion of Serbian strength and control, above all over its two autonomous provinces of Kosovo and Vojvodina, but by implication also over Serbs living in the republics of Croatia and Bosnia-Herzegovina. In addition to mobilising popular support along national lines, Milošević united the opposition and party elites around him on a programme of achieving Serbian national aims. Before long, he began to call into question the very borders of the political units drawn up by the partisans which, Serbs have charged, had 'parcelised' and weakened Serbia. The Serbian question, or how to achieve the political unity of Serbs, now became the most pressing political problem in Yugoslavia. When Communism collapsed in Yugoslavia in 1990 (largely as a result of forces exerted in other republics and abroad), there was strong elite and popular agreement about the overriding goals of reuniting and strengthening the Serbian nation and state.

In the late 1980s, when the Serbian question was emerging as the most important political issue in Serbian politics, political life in Croatia was relatively calm, due in large part to the more repressive atmosphere there concerning the national question. In contrast to Serbia, where nationalist views were espoused by Communist party leaders, in Croatia such views were expressed mainly by non-Communists or ex-Communists, many of them victims of purges after the 1971 *maspok* (mass movement). During the 1980s, the Communist leadership was split between a hardline group gathered around Stipe Šuvar, who fought to stamp out expressions of 'national chauvinism', and a moderate but cautious group of reformers committed to 'staying the course' forged by the 1974 constitution. By the late 1980s, Croatian leaders, inside as well as outside the Communist party, began to express more openly nationalist views. Nevertheless, when the HDZ was formed in 1989 and announced its programme for achieving Croatian national aims, it was dismissed as an irrelevant, marginal element. The strong popular and elite agreement about the post-Communist political agenda characteristic of Serbian politics was not present in Croatia.

These circumstances preceding the collapse of Communism in 1990 in Yugoslavia created different conditions for the emergence of the extreme right in Croatia and Serbia during the multi-party elections that followed.[55] In Croatia, the HDZ, a centre-right, anti-Communist party, came to power with the Communist turned dissident, Franjo Tudjman, at its head.[56] In Serbia, the SPS – the Communist party renamed – won the elections, and Milošević continued his political dominance as Serbian president.[57] Despite these differences in the character of the post-Communist regimes, the ruling parties in both republics were firmly committed to achieving (what were ultimately mutually exclusive) national goals. However, Milošević soon proved less concerned than his counterpart in Croatia about being outflanked by the ultra-nationalist right and less willing to take harsh measures against it. As a result of his solid reputation as champion of the Serbian national cause, Milošević did not appear to feel threatened by the extreme right (except briefly during the period of heightened insecurity of the first post-Communist elections). In contrast, Tudjman had not forged a consensus around a nationalist political agenda nor had he established himself as a 'great national leader', the status often accorded Milošević in Serbia.[58] Consequently, Tudjman was in a weaker political position and more vulnerable to being outflanked by the extreme right. Hence he attempted from the outset to repress extreme right groups or to coopt them within his own party.

During the 1990 election campaign, extreme right leaders were active in promoting the views of their political organisations. Šešelj campaigned on behalf of his newly formed paramilitary organisation, the Chetniks. Announcing that he had been made *Vojvoda* (warlord) of the Chetniks by the oldest living Chetnik, Momčilo Djujić, in California, Šešelj pledged that his forces would fight for the rights of Serbs everywhere in Yugoslavia. Although the Chetnik Movement was the only political group officially banned from the 1990 elections, the extent of Šešelj's appeal was revealed when he received 100,000 votes in the presidential elections, or approximately ten times the number of his official supporters.[59] Shortly after the 1990 elections Šešelj agreed to take over the leadership of the SRS, on the condition that its followers renounce unequivocally a Yugoslav state, in favour of a Great Serbian state.[60] Šešelj pledged strong support for the Serbs in Croatia who were demanding autonomy from Croatia, his frequent travels to the Krajina region in 1990 and 1991 creating further strains in Serb–Croat relations. With the outbreak of war in Croatia in 1991, the SRS became associated with its hardline defence of Serbs living outside Serbia proper and the activities of its Chetnik forces. By the summer of 1991, Šešelj and his supporters were claiming 25,000 members for their ultra-nationalist party.[61]

The HSP was formed in February 1990 by Paraga and a group of associates living in Croatia and abroad. Declaring itself to be a direct continuation of the HSP formed in the nineteenth century by Ante Starčević, the new party pledged to fight for Croatian independence and sovereignty. The HSP quickly attempted to fold into its party those organisations and individuals like the Ustasha Youth that began to display neo-Fascist tendencies.[62] The HSP did not run in the elections of 1990, probably due to its lack of organisation and its unclear status as a legitimate player. Nevertheless, it quickly became a sharp critic of the Tudjman government, denouncing its negotiations with Belgrade over the future shape of Yugoslav federalism as an attempt to 'sell out' Croatian interests. The party also opposed the promulgation of the 1990 Croatian constitution and spearheaded a drive to gather signatures for a petition to the United Nations calling for Croatian independence. The HSP organised demonstrations, like the one in Zagreb in December 1990, which drew thousands of people in spite of the fact that it was banned.[63] Its membership, estimated at 18,000 at the end of 1990, grew to approximately 100,000 by the autumn of 1991.[64]

The socioeconomic context

The social bases of support for the extreme right in Croatia and Serbia is an extremely interesting question, to which only partial answers can be provided at this time. Support for ultra-nationalism and the extreme right has usually been associated with severe social and economic strains. Although class-based theories of historic Fascism and the extreme right have not proved tenable, it has been argued more convincingly that neo-Fascist and ultra-nationalist movements have attracted greater support when there is a severe economic and political crisis.[65] The current fears concerning the rise of the extreme right in Russia and elsewhere in Eastern Europe are based upon this assumption that continued economic hardship and social dislocation will increase its appeal. Evidence concerning the steady increase of support for the extreme right in Serbia would appear to support this view.

The economy of Serbia has been severely strained by the war and the international sanctions imposed in May 1992. The rate of inflation in the summer of 1993 was over 3 per cent a day. By December it had risen to approximately 2 per cent an hour. Unemployment stood at over 50 per cent and real wages fell by 90 per cent in two years; the average monthly salary in Serbia fell to under $10.00 a month. Rationing of basic foodstuffs was introduced in September 1993; in December the government announced it would begin providing bread to pensioners and other welfare recipients. By the end of 1993, it was estimated that more than 90 per cent of the population in Serbia was living below the poverty line. These economic hardships resulted in numerous social problems such as a rash of suicides among the elderly and a dramatic increase in crime.[66] Many young and educated Serbs, who might have provided a moderating political influence, simply opted to leave the country altogether; it is estimated that by mid-1993 Serbia had lost 200,000 of its citizens out of a population of 9,791,500.

As the economic situation has worsened and its impact has been increasingly felt by all sectors of the population, nationalist attitudes have strengthened. A recent study conducted by the Institute of Social Sciences in Belgrade found a strong correlation between increased financial anxiety and a rise in xenophobic attitudes. According to this study, fully three-quarters of the population of Serbia-Montenegro could be characterised as xenophobic by the autumn of 1992.[67] As the study's authors indicate, the worsening economic situation has increased xenophobic and nationalist attitudes instead of class conflict and divisions. In other words, the deteriorating economy is translating into political support for the extreme right.

Although the extreme right draws support from all social groups in Serbia, its adherents appear to be concentrated not in the villages, as has been frequently asserted in the press, but among blue collar workers. The majority of these workers live in suburbs and towns and have been hardest hit economically since 1992.[68] Villagers may be less likely to be Radical supporters because they still have access to basic foodstuffs difficult to procure in many urban settings and because Milošević's tight control of the press in the countryside has kept them firmly in his camp. Nevertheless, there is also a major concentration of extreme right supporters in Belgrade, indicating that even where the press is less controlled, rightist attitudes are increasing. Survey data indicate that the SRS and SPS draw from virtually the same electorate, many Socialists switching their allegiance to the Radicals out of frustration with the slow pace of achieving national goals.[69] This fact, combined with the Radicals' steadily growing popularity, appears to have made Milošević feel increasingly vulnerable to the Radicals' inroads on SPS support, and Šešelj increasingly covetous of expanding that support.

Croatia has also experienced a great deal of economic hardship and dislocation since 1990 related to the war and difficulties of shifting the economy to a market basis. With one-third of its territory under the control of the Serb minority, the capital and surrounding regions have been virtually cut off from the Dalmatian hinterland. In addition to the difficulty of losing its traditional market with the break-up of Yugoslavia, the war has disrupted or destroyed a great deal of Croatia's infrastructure. The vitally important tourist trade has slowed to a trickle. Croatia has also been forced to absorb a large number of refugees.[70] These economic difficulties have resulted in a rapid decline in the standard of living in Croatia since 1992; in 1993 the value of real wages fell to the mid-1960s level, and real household income to one-third of what it was in 1990. Inflation in mid-1993 was about 25 per cent monthly, with an annual rate of 1,000 per cent.

This economic hardship, however, has not translated into increased support for the HSP. Conscious of the possible future threat of sanctions, Croats appear reluctant to support groups whose actions they fear might invite such a fate. Moreover, in a country where integration with Western Europe is seen as an overriding economic and political goal, extreme right groups likely to invite censure from the West are suspect.[71]

Paraga's unyielding stance on pursuing maximum national goals and his aggressive rhetoric about renewing the war appear to have made voters wary of him. The HSP's relatively low support in the 1992 elections came primarily from members of the armed forces and the police, and from residents of towns and villages close to the recent fighting.[72] This profile of HSP support suggests that it is drawn from segments of the population concerned with a strong military and defence and from refugees and others whose lives have been completely disrupted by the war. Nevertheless, while the HSP has been unable to capitalise on the difficult economic situation, extreme right forces could capitalise on a renewal of fighting in Croatia, particularly if their paramilitary forces play a significant military role.

The military context

Historical Fascism has long been associated with the formation of paramilitary organisations and this has continued to be the case with current extreme right groups. These organisations have been formed for a variety of purposes: to provide training for youthful recruits, to bolster the party's quest for political power and, finally, to provide an elite corps for maintaining control once the ultra-nationalists are in power. As the extreme right has grown in Eastern Europe and Russia, it has spawned a variety of paramilitary organisations – for example, right-wing paramilitary forces played a significant part in the upheaval in Moscow in October 1993. Due to the war in the former Yugoslavia, such forces have played a particularly important role in the rise of the extreme right, and have been a crucial component in its success. The military gains of these forces in the recent wars has resulted in popular support for them and their political parties.

When war broke out after Croatia's declaration of independence in the summer of 1991, there was great confusion in organising Croatia's military forces. The newly formed national guard and the local police were pressed into service with inadequate weaponry and supplies. There was a huge gap in the military capacities of the country which the HSP's paramilitary force, the Croatian Defence Force [*Hrvatske obrambene snage*, HOS], succeeded in filling. Calling on volunteers to fight against the 'Serbo-Bolsheviks' at the front, the HOS quickly swelled to several thousand fighters in the autumn of 1991.[73] Military headquarters were set up in a baroque, eighteenth-century building in Zagreb's old town, with guards and sandbags outside and reams of ammunition inside. Money from the Croatian community abroad was used to purchase arms and equipment.

The HSP gained a great deal of political capital as it became associated with the activities of its paramilitary forces. Images of HOS blackshirts, U's (standing for Ustasha) carved on the stocks of their guns, soon became familiar sights on television screens across Croatia.[74] HOS posters picturing 'brawny, tattooed men in black uniforms, their arms upraised in a Nazi salute' and featuring the HOS slogan (an old Ustasha greeting) – 'Ready for the Homeland' – appeared on Zagreb building walls.[75] The HOS quickly earned the reputation as the most effective fighters in the field, especially during the defence of Vukovar where they held out for three months against well-equipped Serbian forces. Paraga's popularity soared when he charged Tudjman with failing to protect Vukovar and with having 'sold out' Eastern Slavonija.

Tudjman faced a difficult dilemma in his relations with Paraga and the HOS. As an old partisan general, Tudjman was well aware of the political dangers of a military resistance force, and he was determined to assert control over the HOS. But in the dire military situation Croatia faced in the autumn of 1991, he could little afford to weaken his most effective fighting force. Nor was it clear that he could disband the HOS even if he wished. The repeated warnings of the Croatian defence minister that militias outside the normal chain of command must be dissolved had little effect. Tensions were high in the field between local officials and national guardsmen, on the one hand, and HOS fighters, on the other; but the former were little inclined to challenge the latter.[76] When Tudjman had Paraga arrested in November of 1991 on charges of forming an illegal paramilitary group, thousands of HOS fighters poured into Zagreb demanding Paraga's release, which the government was forced to grant.[77] As long as the war continued, Tudjman's government was helpless to stop the activities of the HOS and the growing support for the HSP.

With the signing of the Vance plan in January 1992, however, Tudjman soon had his chance. One of his main priorities with the halt in the fighting was to reorganise and strengthen the army and to incorporate the HOS into it. During the next several months, the army made some headway in subsuming the paramilitary forces, though it often simply swallowed them whole. A ruling by Croatia's high court conceded that HOS militiamen could continue to wear their own insignia, thus allowing them, in some measure, to retain their separate identity.[78] Moreover, although the HSP agreed to place its fighters under the command of the regular army, it continued to solicit recruits for the war in Bosnia-Herzegovina. Although these forces were nominally under the control of the Bosnian president, they were in effect loyal to Paraga.[79] When the Tudjman government accused Paraga in the summer of 1992 of recruiting paramilitary fighters for the war, Paraga countered that the 'ruling party [was] afraid of HOS competition in Herzeg-Bosnia'.[80] (This accusation carried the double sting of questioning Tudjman's commitment to the defence of an independent Bosnian state, a position that was echoed increasingly loudly by other opposition groups.) During the summer of 1992, at a time when the integration of HOS fighters into the Croatian Army was ostensibly in full swing, the HOS was still estimated to have approximately 30,000 fighters active in Croatia and Bosnia-Herzegovina.[81]

In the months after the 1992 elections in which the extent of the HSP's political weakness was revealed, the government stepped up its campaign to eradicate the HOS as an independent military force. After a raid on HOS headquarters in September 1992, when the government allegedly discovered 500,000 DM worth of weapons, Paraga and three of his associates were charged with terrorism, this time by a military court; in June 1993 Paraga was arrested and brought to trial on these charges. The government simultaneously launched an 'anti-Fascist' campaign which appeared in part to be aimed at curbing the influence of HSP supporters in the military.[82] By the autumn of 1993, the government had succeeded largely in subsuming HOS forces into the Croatian army and, most importantly, in preventing the possibility of their use as a means of bolstering an HSP bid for political power.

In contrast to Croatia, where the strength of the paramilitary forces declined after

January 1992, in Serbia it increased steadily. When war broke out in the summer of 1991, the Yugoslav People's Army [*Jugoslovenska narodna armija*, JNA], which was in the process of being transformed into a Serbian and Montenegrin army, also found itself in a greatly weakened state. Although it had the advantage of inheriting most of the weaponry from the formerly well-equipped JNA, it suffered from low morale and serious human resources shortages; its ranks were depleted from desertions not only by Croats, Slovenes and Macedonians, but by Serbs and Montenegrins as well.[83] The reshaped JNA sought to rectify this situation by allowing the formation of 'volunteer units' which were supposed to be incorporated into the ranks of the regular army, but in fact were allowed to operate autonomously.[84] This decision gave some legitimacy to Šešelj's previously formed Chetnik units which quickly began to operate in areas where there was heavy fighting. Chetnik forces, estimated at about 15,000 men in the fall of 1991, soon gained a reputation as aggressive fighters for the Serbian cause.[85]

Šešelj and the SRS sought to use the successes of their paramilitary forces to their political advantage. Charging that the Yugoslav Army was failing to protect Serbs adequately, Šešelj pledged that his fighters would come to their rescue wherever they lived.[86] As *Vojvoda*, he stressed his control over the Chetniks' military as well as the Radicals' political operations. The Radical leader increasingly appeared in military guise, surrounded by gun-toting bodyguards; Radical campaign posters featured Šešelj in full combat dress striding, as one journalist put it, 'in mud and blood up to his knees on the battlefield'.[87] These ties between the SRS and the Chetniks were reinforced by the almost obligatory stint that Radical leaders performed in the 'volunteer units'. SRS leader, Toma Nikolić, described how when he joined the party, in order 'to demonstrate that he wasn't just all words about the Serbian cause', he joined a volunteer unit and fought in Bosnia-Herzegovina for over a year.[88] The paramilitary forces thus provided a training ground for Radical leaders and created a sense of community among its members. Most importantly, participation in the Chetniks and other paramilitary forces gave the Radicals a kind of legitimacy as war heroes that they would not otherwise have achieved.

In contrast to the situation in Croatia, where the Tudjman government persistently attempted to weaken the HOS and strengthen the regular army forces, Milošević initially made few efforts to curb the power of paramilitary forces in Serbia and Montenegro. Tensions between the paramilitary and regular army forces were high in the field at the outset of the war in Croatia, but they began to cooperate closely in the war in Bosnia-Herzegovina.[89] Despite their increasing power, Milošević failed to take any steps that would limit their role (let alone disband them altogether) until the autumn of 1993. Indeed, the quarrel between Yugoslav President Ćosić and Serbian President Milošević was reputed to have been at least partially a result of Ćosić's efforts to curb the power of paramilitary groups. Moreover, Milošević progressively weakened the Yugoslav Army by almost constant purges of the military leadership and by creating a rival police force that he considered more politically reliable.[90] Consequently, a strong military committed to subsuming the paramilitary forces did not emerge in Serbia. In any case, Šešelj was extremely well connected to the military leadership and was reputed to have as much influence over the army as Milošević himself.

While the SRS's paramilitary forces strengthened it politically, some detrimental effects of this association began to appear. By the summer of 1993, members of paramilitary forces increasingly became the targets of hostility expressed by the civilian population and the regular armed forces alike. Their growing power and particularly their perceived ability to enrich themselves through corruption and theft appeared to be provoking a backlash against the paramilitary forces and their political sponsors such as the SRS. The September 1993 uprising in Banja Luka against 'profiteers' indicated the extent of this hostility. Šešelj was also accused of amassing his own fortune (large enough to buy a television station) by corrupt means. The SRS leader took steps to dampen this criticism, pressuring officials in Krajina and the Bosnian Serb territory to stem popular dissatisfaction over 'war profiteering' by those associated with the Chetnik forces.[91] As tensions increased between Milošević and Šešelj in the summer and autumn of 1993, they both began to attack each other on this sensitive point.

When political conflict between Milošević and Šešelj erupted in September 1993 as a result of Šešelj's call for a parliamentary vote of no confidence, Milošević attempted to discredit Šešelj politically by attacking the activities of his paramilitary forces. Chetniks who only months earlier had been declared heroes by the regime-controlled press were now denounced as rapists, pillagers and morally corrupt recruits. More than twenty-five Chetniks, most of them regional SRS leaders, were arrested and jailed. While this campaign to discredit the Chetniks and the SRS appears to have had some success, it is not clear yet whether Milošević will break the power of the Chetnik forces or prevent their role in strengthening a possible future bid for power by their leader Vojislav Šešelj.

The political context

The HSP and the SRS are both committed to working within the democratic context, but their political success in doing so over the last three years has differed significantly. Although neither party participated in the elections of 1990, both signalled their intention to participate in the electoral process and to run in the elections of 1992. The results of these elections caught many observers by surprise; while the HSP performed much more poorly than expected, the SRS scored an unexpectedly large second place. The losses suffered by the Radicals in the December 1993 elections in Serbia indicate, however, that the SRS's electoral strength may prove to have been short-lived. Part of the explanation for these different electoral outcomes can be found in the more severe socioeconomic strains present in Serbia which have contributed to support for the extreme right. The end of the war in Croatia, and a diminution in the role of the HOS, can also partially explain the HSP's poorer than anticipated showing. Part of the explanation must be sought, however, in the differing political contexts of Croatia and Serbia. The interaction between the extreme right and other opposition parties and the regime can also account for their varied political success.

The critical turning point in HSP's political fortunes can be found in the 1992 parliamentary and presidential elections in Croatia. The HSP went into the elections confidently (publicly anticipating 35 per cent of the vote) with many foreign observers speculating about the large number of its 'hidden supporters'.[92] The party ran on a platform of continuing the war against Belgrade, expelling the UNPROFOR and establishing a Croatian state 'within its natural and ethnic borders'.[93] The HSP also continued its vigorous criticism of the Tudjman government during the campaign, charging it with corruption and 'treacherous' activities during the war. Despite its pre-election optimism, however, the HSP was placed fourth at the polls, garnering only about 7 per cent of the vote; Paraga received 5 per cent of the presidential vote. Although Paraga charged the regime with massive fraud (for permitting large numbers of foreigners to vote), polling data from shortly before the election suggested a similarly low level of support.[94]

There are several reasons why the HSP performed relatively poorly in the 1992 elections. First, in the months prior to the election, the regime attempted to weaken the HSP organisationally and politically in two ways: by harassment and repression, on the one hand, and by cooptation, on the other. From the outset of the war in Croatia when the popularity of the HOS and the HSP began to alarm the regime, Tudjaman took steps to weaken the HSP leadership. Charges were brought against Paraga repeatedly for his activities relating to the HOS. Moreover, several HSP leaders were killed under mysterious circumstances, including HSP vice-president Ante Paradžik, who was shot by police at a checkpoint outside Zagreb. Not only Paraga, but members of other opposition parties charged the regime with complicity in these crimes.[95] In the weeks before the campaign, Paraga was accused in the largely government-controlled press with being, among other things, 'a US agent who worked for Belgrade'.[96]

In addition to repressing the extreme right, Tudjman also attempted to coopt it. Tudjman had been one of the original initiators of 'revisionist' historical accounts of the NDH, and his attempt to paint it in a more favourable light must have found some sympathy among the extreme right. Moreover, the Croatian president was not adverse to adopting many of the symbols of the Ustasha state or attempting to rehabilitate some of its leaders.[97] In the spring of 1992, the HDZ incorporated into its ranks the Croatian National Committee, the successor to a group of the same name founded by Branimir Jelić, a close associate of Ante Pavelić; Committee leaders were given two places on the HDZ executive board.[98] Other former Ustasha leaders were nominated for government posts.[99] While this strengthening of the right wing in the HDZ caused Tudjman problems, as the unwieldy party was increasingly pulled between its right and left factions, it also allowed him to assert more control over the extreme right, at least part of which was now under his own roof.[100]

Finally, it appears that the HSP platform of expelling the UN forces and continuing the war was simply not appealing to a large portion of the electorate. Tudjman had campaigned on a platform of putting the war behind and getting on with the business of rebuilding the country. This strategy appears to have been successful, though the population has become increasingly frustrated since the elections with the stalemated military situation in Croatia. Moreover, in the months after the implementation of the Vance Plan, which resulted in the deployment of UN peace-keeping forces in Croatia, there was a sense that the Croatian army simply was not up to the task of continuing the war without more time to strengthen its forces. Supporting the HSP platform probably appeared to many to be a vote for an inevitable resumption of the war on terms that were not very favourable to Croatia.

Paraga attempted to recoup his losses after the 1992 elections, but without much initial success. In December 1992, he created the HSP Youth Group, which was aimed at retaining the political loyalty of demobilised HOS fighters. Although he announced that henceforth the youth group would 'form the kernel of the party', this attempt to revitalise the HSP had little discernible effect.[101] The HSP was also hurt by its failure to take part in the February 1993 elections, ostensibly because the electoral commissions were not formed on a multi-party basis. Its position was further weakened by the fracturing of the extreme right. In December 1992, a Croatian Pure Party of Rights [*Hrvatska čista stranka prava*, HCSP] was formed by Ivan Gabelica and Nedeljko Gabelica. The HCSP pledged to fight for an 'integral Croatia' and for 'the truth [to] be told about the NDH'.[102] Two other extreme right parties, the Croatian Democratic Party of Rights [*Hrvatska demokratska stranka prava*, HDSP] led by Krešimir Pavelić and the National Democratic League [*Nacionalna demokratska liga*, NDL] led by Ivan Vekić, threatened to form an alliance of the 'moderate right' that would counter what Pavelić described as HSP 'extremism'.[103] Throughout 1993, however, Paraga appeared unwilling or unable to unite the extreme right and assert his leadership over it.

The growing strength of the Croatian Social Liberal Party [*Hrvatska socijalno-liberalna stranka*, HSLS] of Dražen Budiša, (which was placed second in the 1992 elections and was running slightly ahead of the government in the opinion polls in 1993), and its adoption of increasingly hardline policies on the resumption of the war and the defence of a unified Bosnian state, probably siphoned off support from the HSP. The HSP cooperated with the Liberals in opposing Tudjman's support for the partition of Bosnia, a position which was extremely unpopular among a significant segment of the Croatian population. Paraga emphasised that his party was the first to denounce Mate Boban, the Croat leader in Bosnia-Herzegovina, and the first to warn against the influence of the 'Herzegovinian lobby' in Croatian politics. In return, the Liberals denounced government repression of the HSP and Paraga. Nevertheless, there was no formal cooperation between the two parties in 1993 nor did Praga display a willingness to join a moderate coalition of the opposition.

By the summer of 1993, the HSP's political position appeared irretrievably weakened, prompting Tudjman to launch a vigorous offensive against it. When Paraga returned from a trip to the USA in May (where he pleaded for support against what he alleged was a campaign of repression against the HSP), he was removed from his position on the Parliamentary Commission for Human Rights and charged by HDZ deputies with slandering Croatia. A vociferous campaign was launched against him in the press which portrayed the HSP as a party rent by factionalism and leadership splits.[104] Paraga's trial began two weeks later on his previous indictment by a military court which charged the HSP with plotting to 'seize civilian and military power in Croatia'. Although the trial ended in an acquittal in November 1993, Tudjman's effort to squelch the far right party appeared to have paid off. Despite the insistence by HSP leaders that the party was suffering from mere 'temporary' difficulties, its support appeared to have declined steadily.[105] Nevertheless, this decline in support for the HSP should not be confused with a decline of the extreme right more generally. Ultra-nationalists continue to find a hospitable environment within the confines of the ruling HDZ and the extent of their future political power remains to be seen.

In contrast with Croatia, where the HSP progressively weakened after January 1992, the SRS continued to gain in strength until its setback in the December 1993 elections. During the campaign for the December 1992 elections, the SRS ran on a platform of supporting Serbs outside Serbia proper; its campaign slogan proclaiming 'The Radicals are Throughout the Serbian Lands'. Presenting itself as a party of the 'moderate right', the SRS received 20 per cent of the vote to become the second largest party in Serbia, with 75 seats to the Socialists' 99 seats in the 250-seat parliament. And, in contrast to the HSP, the Radicals demonstrated a strong appeal outside their own membership; while the HSP received fewer votes than its claimed 150,000 members, the Radicals received ten times the number of votes of their estimated membership of 100,000.

In the months after the election, the SRS entered into a kind of unofficial coalition with the Socialists. Although Šešelj insisted that the Radicals were an opposition party, they remained much closer to the ruling SPS on most issues. Šešelj pledged shortly after the election that he would not form a coalition with the main opposition group, the Democratic Movement of Serbia [*Demokratski pokret Srbije*, DEPOS], and he continued to revile its leaders as traitors and agents of foreign powers. Milošević returned this goodwill, announcing in March 1993 that he esteemed the SRS leader more than any other because he has 'been consistent in expressing his political opinion'.[106] Indeed, until the summer of that year the president of Serbia had never been heard to utter a single unfavourable opinion of Šešelj.

The turning point in this unofficial alliance and in the Radicals' political fortunes came in the wake of Western pressure on Serbia in May 1993 to accept the Vance–Owen Plan. While Milošević expended valuable political capital to get the Bosnian Serbs to accept it, Šešelj remained implacably opposed, denouncing the plan as a Western 'deception'. When the Bosnian Serbs rejected the plan and the West abandoned its support for it, Šešelj's hand was strengthened considerably. Thereafter, he began to show signs of a willingness to challenge Milošević more directly, and his criticism of the ruling party's handling of the economy and foreign policy increased. SRS leaders in towns outside Belgrade began to admit openly that they no longer considered themselves junior partners in the red–brown alliance.[107] The Socialists retaliated by launching an 'anti-Fascist campaign' in which Šešelj was charged with profiteering and war crimes. When Šešelj formed a shadow cabinet at the end of August and threatened a vote of no confidence in parliament, a showdown seemed only a matter of time.

The denouement came in early October 1993 when Milošević dissolved parliament and called for parliamentary elections in December of that year. The Serbian president quickly launched a frontal attack against the Radicals, arresting numerous regional party leaders for their alleged criminal activities. Šešelj was subjected to a barrage of charges in the press including corruption, terrorism and even treachery to the Serbian cause. Moreover, Milošević attempted to fracture the extreme right by supporting paramilitary leader turned politician, Željko Ražnjatović (Arkan) and his new Serbian Unity Party [*Srpska partija jedinstva*, SPJ]. As the election results indicated, these efforts paid off. While the Socialists improved their margin of support, securing 123 seats in the Serbian parliament (up from 101 the previous year), the Radicals dropped in popularity, winning only thirty-nine seats (down from seventy-five the previous year).[108]

Nevertheless, the Radicals' loss of support in the elections does not necessarily mean the demise of the party or the eclipse of the extreme right in Serbia. Šešelj has shown himself to be an adept and popular politician in the past and he may yet prove a match for Milošević. Moreover, the fact that the SRS was placed third in the elections despite an intense media campaign against it indicates that Šešelj and his party may continue to attract significant support in the future. Milošević's attempts to fracture the extreme right were largely ineffectual since the SPJ failed to win a single seat in parliament, though Arkan himself appears to have some popular appeal. Finally, it is important to remember that the SPS itself has consistently maintained its popularity through its advocacy of an ultra-nationalist political agenda. Indeed, while a full examination of the SPS has been outside the scope of this chapter, it can be characterised in many ways as an extreme right or neo-Fascist party.[109]

Conclusion

Since the fall of Communism in 1989, and the political upheaval and euphoria in its wake, there has been a resurgence of the extreme right throughout Eastern Europe. This has also been the case in the former Yugoslavia where the break-up of the state and the resulting wars have been both a cause and effect of the politics of extreme nationalisms. Although extreme nationalism draws upon historical roots in Serbia and Croatia, it is also a product of the current political transformation and war. Social and economic upheaval have fuelled support for the extreme right in both areas, though there is evidence that the more severe deterioration of the Serbian economy has resulted in a more far-reaching growth of ultra-nationalism there. Moreover, the paramilitary forces of Serb and Croat extremists have contributed to the popularity of far right political parties. Although the ruling parties in both areas have taken steps to curb these forces, it is not clear how effective Milošević's belated moves in this direction will be.

Perhaps one lesson that can be learned from a study of the extreme right in Serbia and Croatia is the significant impact the regimes can have on undermining far right parties when they undertake this task. Both the SRS and the HSP have suffered serious setbacks since 1993 as a result of pressure from the SPS and the HDZ, which have skilfully manipulated the extreme right parties to their own political purposes. In Croatia, the HSP has been hounded by the ruling party into an increasingly peripheral position and the extreme right has become more fragmented. In Serbia, the Radicals suffered serious losses in the December 1993 elections due in large part to the harsh campaign against them by the ruling SPS. Thus, while the SRS, HSP and their leaders represent the main forces of the extreme right at the end of 1993, they may not continue their dominance of right-wing politics in the future.

The weakening position of the SRS and the HSP does not indicate, however, a diminishing of extreme nationalism in the former Yugoslavia. The ruling parties of Serbia and Croatia contain considerable ultra-nationalist elements within them (though there are admittedly important differences between the two parties and their leaders). The continued existence of the politics of extreme nationalism in various forms will undoubtedly make resolving the problems connected to the break-up of Yugoslavia more difficult. Whether more democratic forces can offer an effective political counterweight to the extreme right in the former Yugoslavia is arguably the most pressing political question in current Balkan politics.

List of Abbreviations

DEPOS	*Demokratski prokret Srbije* [Democratic Movement of Serbia]
HCSP	*Hrvatska čista stranka prava* [Croatian Pure Party of Rights]
HDZ	*Hrvatska demokratska zajednica* [Croatian Democratic Union]
HOS	*Hrvatske obrambene snage* [Croatian Defence Force]
HSDP	*Hrvatska stranka demokratska prava* [Croatian Party of Democratic Rights]
HSLS	*Hrvatska socijalno-liberalna stranka* [Croatian Social Liberal Party]
HSP	*Hrvatska stranka prava* [Croatian Party of Rights]
HSS	*Hrvatska seljačka stranka* [Croat Peasant Party]
JNA	*Jugoslovenska narodna armija* [Yugoslav People's Army]
NDH	*Nezavisna Država Hrvatska* [Independent State of Croatia]
NDL	*Nacionalna demokratska liga* [National Democratic League]
NRS	*Narodna radikalna stranka* [People's Radical Party]
SKJ	*Savez komunista Jugoslavije* [League of Communists of Yugoslavia]
SPJ	*Srpska partija jedinstva* [Serbian Unity Party]
SPS	*Socijalištička partija Srbije* [Socialist Party of Serbia]
SRS	*Srpska radikalna stranka* [Serbian Radical Party]

Notes

* For comments on an earlier draft of this chapter I would like to thank Melissa Bokovoy, Mark Brandon, Gary Cohen, Robert Cox, Carol Lilly and Misha Nedelj-kovich. My thanks also to Erich Frankland for his research assistance.

1. Although much of my discussion also applies to Montenegro, there are important political differences between Serbia and Montenegro that cannot be treated in this chapter. Therefore, I will focus primarily on Serbia.
2. For example, a recent paper on the current extreme right in Russia identified nine main ideological groupings on the right, each of which has several sub-groupings within it. Peter Reddaway and Catherine Dale, 'The Significance of Nationalism and Communism in Contemporary Russian Politics'. Paper presented at the annual convention of the American Association for the Advancement of Slavic Studies, Hawaii, November 1993.
3. G. Ekiert, 'Democratization Processes in East Central Europe: A Theoretical Reconsideration', *British Journal of Political Science*, XXI, July 1991, pp. 285–313.
4. G. Schopflin, 'Obstacles to Liberalism in Post-Communist Politics', *East European Politics and Societies*, V, winter 1991, pp. 189–94.
5. There has been much dispute about whether Fascism and neo-Fascism can be said to possess a coherent ideology. Robert Vivarelli, for example, argues that Fascism 'was not an intellectual movement with anything comparable to a doctrine'. Roger Eatwell and others such as Roger Griffin have argued convincingly for a definition of Fascism that places a coherent ideology at its centre. Thus for Griffin, 'Fascism is a genus of political ideology whose mythic core in its various permutations is a palingenetic form of populist ultranationalism'. Eatwell offers a definition of Fascism based on its 'spectral-synthetic' ideology which sees the essence of Fascism as a series of syntheses around four main themes: natural history, geopolitics, political economy and leadership, activism, party and propaganda. In any case, it is clear that while Fascism does have a discernible ideology,

it is one characterised by flexibility, which may be due, as Juan Linz suggests, to its latecomer status and the associated problem of defining its political space. See R. Griffin, *The Nature of Fascism*, Pinter, London, 1991; R. Eatwell, 'Toward a New Model of Generic Fascism', *Journal of Theoretical Politics*, IV, (2), 1992, pp. 161–94; and R. Vivarelli, 'Interpretations of the Origins of Fascism', *Journal of Modern History*, LXIII March 1991, pp. 29–43; J. Linz, 'Some Notes toward a Comparative Study of Fascism in Sociological Historical Perspective' in W. Laqueur, *Fascism. A Reader's Guide*, University of California Press, Berkeley and Los Angeles, 1976, pp. 3–121.

6. Foreign Broadcast Information Service (FBIS)-EEU-93-159, 30 March 1993, pp. 41–42; in *Danas*, 26 Feb 1993, pp. 20–21.

7. John Breuilly and others have pointed out that nationalism makes 'eminent sense' in the situations produced by the modern state, which declares itself the legitimate dispenser of political and economic goods. As the state expands its functions and capabilities, power over the state apparatus becomes the crucial goal of national movements. See J. Breuilly, Nationalism and the State, St Martin's Press, New York, 1982.

8. E. Gentile, 'Fascism as Political Religion', *Journal of Contemporary History*, XXV (2–3), 1990 pp. 229–51.

9. P. Hockenos, *Free to Hate. The Rise of the Right in Post-Communist Eastern Europe*, Routledge, London, 1993.

10. In Russia, neo-Fascist groups tend to be more opposed to capitalism, arguing that it is foreign in spirit. Groups like Russian Unity, therefore, advocate a third way between capitalism and Communism. For a treatment of this question see W. Laqueur, *Black Hundred. The Rise of the Extreme Right in Russia*, Harper Collins, New York, 1993, pp. 119–82.

11. N. Stefanović, 'Šešeljevi mali mravi' [Šešelj's Little Ants], *Duga*, April 10–23 1993, pp. 15–16.

12. ' "Dann nehmen wir alles", Spiegel interview mit dem serbischen Tschetnik–Führer Vojislav Šešelj' ['Then We'll Take Everything', Spiegel interview with the Serbian Chetnik leader Vojislav Šešelj] *Der Spiegel*, 5 Aug. 1991, pp. 124–26.

13. V. Šešelj, 'Dići ću ustanak protiv Miloševića'. [I Will Launch an Uprising Against Milošević], *Duga*, 8–21 May 1993, pp. 84–87.

14. According to Šešelj the borders of the new state will stretch from Karlobag on the Adriatic coast, north through Karlovac and east to Virovitica and the Hungarian border.

15. 'If this is not enough for the Croats,' he adds, 'then we will take everything'. *Der Spiegel*, 5 Aug. 1991, pp. 124–26.

16. Ibid.

17. FBIS-EEU-91-200, 16 Oct. 1991, pp. 42–43.

18. Šešelj charged that 'the Americans have revived the Brezhnev doctrine of limited sovereignty'. According to Šešelj, the Americans are attempting to resurrect a Yugoslav state in order to counter German expansionism in the Balkans. S. Leković, 'Amerika protiv Hrvatske' [America against Croatia], *Duga*, 22 May–4 June 1993, pp. 91–93.

19. FBIS-EEU-93-043, 8 March, 1993, pp. 71–72; interview in *NIN*, 29 Feb. 1993.

20. D. Doder, 'Serb Artist's Procreation Proposal: Sign of the Times', *Boston Globe*, 30 Aug. 1993, p. 2. According to Doder, Stanković claims to have support from numerous Serb women who have told him they want to 'lie down beside a real Serb hero' and add more 'supermen' to the nation.

21. FBIS-EEU-93-043, 8 March 1993, pp. 71–72; interview in *NIN*, 29 Feb. 1993.

22. FBIS-EEU-92-031, 14 Feb. 1992, pp. 42–47; interview in *NIN*, 24 Jan. 1992, pp. 18–21.

23. *Der Spiegel*, cit., 5 Aug. 1991, pp. 124–26.

24. FBIS-EEU-92-124, 26 June 1992, pp. 27–28.

25. For example, in June 1993 SRS deputy Branislav Vakić hit SPS deputy Mihailo Marković in parliament, precipitating the demonstrations which resulted in the imprisonment of opposition leader Vuk Drašković.

26. Šešelj, *Duga*, 8–21 May 1993, pp. 84–87.

27. FBIS-EEU-92-031, 14 Feb. 1992, pp. 42–47; interview in *NIN*, 24 Jan. 1992, pp. 18–21.

28. In his testimony to Congress in May 1993, Paraga insisted that the HSP is an anti-Fascist party fighting against the 'Fascist' Tudjman regime. In his testimony Paraga stated: 'Nothing could be more damaging to the future of Croatia and the region as a whole than totalitarian philosophies of government such as ethnic purity and one-party rule.' *Congressional Record*, No. 76, 26 May 1993.

29. FBIS-EEU-92-1003, 28 May 1992, pp. 57–62; interview in *Slobodna Dalmacija*, 9 May 1992, pp. 10–11.

30. FBIS-EEU-92-149, 3 Aug. 1992, pp. 26–27.

31. FBIS-EEU-92-103, 28 May 1992, pp. 57–62; interview in *Slobodna Dalmacija*, 9 May 1992, pp. 10–11.

32. FBIS-EEU-92-149, 3 Aug. 1992, pp. 26–27.

33. D. Paraga and A. Paradžik, *Borba za Hrvatsku državnu nezavisnost* [The Struggle for the Independence of the Croatian State], Hrvatska Stranka Prava, Zagreb, 1991, p. 164.

34. *Danas*, 5 March 1991, p. 8; interview with Dobroslav Paraga.

35. FBIS-EEU-92-103, 28 May 1992, pp. 57–62; interview in *Slobodna Dalmacija*, 9 May 1992, pp. 10–11.

36. M. Čulić, 'Tko zaziva ustaštvo?' [Who is Hailing Ustashism?], *Danas*, 5 March 1991, pp. 7–9.

37. Ibid.

38. FBIS-EEU-93-112, 14 June 1993, p. 48; interview with Ante Djapić in *Danas*.

39. At the beginning of the nineteenth century, the Triune Kingdom was composed of the diverse regions of Dalmatia, Slavonia and Croatia proper (the area around Zagreb that was usually termed Inner Croatia or *Banska Hrvatska*). Croatia's marked regional flavour was expressed in a variety of dialects: the Kajkavian dialect spoken in the Zagreb region, the Čakavian in parts of the Croatian littoral and Dalmatia, and the Štokavian dialect everywhere else.

40. For a discussion in English of the Croatian national movement see I. Banac, *The National Question in Yugoslavia. Origins, History, Politics*, Cornell University Press, Ithaca, NY. 1984; and A. Djilas, *The Contested Country. Yugoslav Unity and Communist Revolution, 1919–1953*, Harvard University Press, Cambridge, MA, 1991.

41. For a discussion of Ante Starčević see M. S. Spalatin, 'The Croatian Nationalism of Ante Starčević, 1845–1871', *Journal of Croatian Studies*, XV, 1975, pp. 19–146; and G. G. Gilbert, 'Pravašvo and the Croatian National Issue', *East European Quarterly*, No. 1, 1978, pp. 57–68.

42. Although the Croatian Party of Rights advocated the establishment of an independent state, it more immediately supported a trailist solution within the framework of the Habsburg Empire.

43. While proclaiming Starčević as their leader, the *Frankovci* in fact reversed his policy of opposition to the Habsburgs and began to look to Vienna for protection from Hungary. They also renounced Starčević's aim of creating an independent Croatian state outside the monarchy.

44. Language and religion were the essential, through occasionally contradictory, elements of Serb national ideology. All Orthodox Slavs speaking the Štokavian dialect were considered Serbs who should be united within Serbia's borders.

45. For a discussion of the Radical Party during this period, see D. Janković, *Srbija i*

jugoslovensko pitanje, 1914–1915 [Serbia and the Yugoslav Question, 1914–1915], Belgrade, 1973.

46. As Šešelj put it to several representatives of the National Radical Party who asked him to take over its leadership in 1991, 'You Radicals created Yugoslavia, and you have the right to destroy [*rasturite*] it.' N. Stefanović, *Duga*, 27 Feb.–12 March 1993, pp. 15–16.

47. For a discussion of Fascism in inter-war Yugoslavia see D. Djordević, 'Fascism in Yugoslavia, 1918–1941', and I. Avakumović, 'Yugoslavia's Fascist Movements', in P. Sugar (ed.), *Native Fascism in the Successor States, 1918–1945*, ABC-CLIO, Inc., Santa Barbara, CA, 1971.

48. After failing to win electoral support, *Zbor* organised 'task groups' to fight the labour movement and political parties. Following a major clash with leftist students at the University of Belgrade in 1940, many of its leaders and members were arrested and the *Zbor* outlawed. After April 1941, it re-emerged as the Serbian Volunteer Corps, and it remained a dependable ally of German forces throughout the war.

49. For a social profile of Ustasha support, see B. Krizman, *Ante Pavelić i ustaše* [Ante Pavelić and the Ustasha], Globus, Zagreb, 1978, pp. 564–74.

50. For a discussion of the relationship between the *Frankovci* and the Ustashas, see Djilas, *The Contested Country*, cit., pp. 108–109.

51. For a description of this regime, see B. Krizman, *Ustaše i Trač i Reich* [The Ustasha and the Third Reich], Globus, Zagreb, 1983; and Djilas, *The Contested Country*, cit., pp. 103–27.

52. S. Nešović and B. Petranović, *AVNOJ i revolucija* [AVNOJ and Revolution], Narodna Knjiga, Belgrade, 1983, p. 18.

53. The actual number of Serbs who were killed has been the subject of acrimonious dispute among Serb and Croat scholars and publicists. For a recent discussion of this question in English see N. Pasic, 'In Search of the True Number of War Victims in Yugoslavia in the Second World War', *Serbian Studies*, No. 1, 1989, pp. 92–120.

54. For a discussion of these two federal models and how they affected post-1945 political development, see J. A. Irvine, *The Croat Question. Partisan Politics in the Formation of the Yugoslav Socialist State*, Westview, Boulder, CO. 1993, pp. 253–89.

55. In examining the emergence of the extreme right in the former Yugoslavia (and the rest of Eastern Europe) after 1989, it is useful to look at the character of civil society and method of popular mobilisation in the 1980s, and the contours of elite bargaining as it led to the dismantling of the party-state. It could be argued (though this remains largely an empirical question) that in those countries where political mobilisation took place largely along national lines (and this often coincided with weak civil societies) ultra-nationalist groups and ideologies were more likely to have wide appeal among the population. If this coincided with widespread elite agreement about the primacy of a nationalist political agenda, the extreme right was more likely to find a hospitable political atmosphere in which to pursue its goals. For a description of the relationship between the collapse of Communism and subsequent political developments, see D. Stark and L. Bruszt, 'Remaking the Political Field in Hungary: From the Politics of Confrontation to the Politics of Competition', in I. Banac (ed.), *Eastern Europe in Revolution*, Cornell University Press, Ithaca, NY, 1992. For a discussion of the importance of elite bargaining and agreement in the transition to democracy, see M. Burton, R. Gunther and J. Higley, 'Introduction: Elite Transformations and Democratic Regimes', in R. Gunther and J. Higley (eds), *Elites and Democratic Consolidation in Southern Europe*, Cambridge University Press, Cambridge, 1991, pp. 1–37.

56. The elections held in late April and early May 1990 in Croatia resulted in a clear defeat for the Communists and a secure victory for the HDZ. The HDZ won approximately 43

per cent of the vote, and in coalition with other centre right parties obtained 205 of the 356 seats of the Croatian parliament. The League of Communists of Croatia-Party of Democratic Change won approximately 27 per cent of the vote, and in coalition with other leftist parties took seventy-three seats in the parliament.

57. The elections in Serbia on 9 December, 1990 resulted in a huge victory for Milošević and the Socialist Party of Serbia, with the SPS winning 194 seats in parliament. The major opposition party, Serbia Movement for Renewal, took nineteen seats, and the remaining seats were divided among more than ten parties.

58. Tudjman possessed good credentials as a champion of the Croat national cause as a result of his role in the 1971 *maspok* in Croatia, and his writings and political activities on behalf of Croatian self-determination thereafter. For a description of Tudjman's intellectual evolution during this period, see I. Banac, 'Svšimo s odiljanjem od Hrvatske na ljevici', *Globus*, 10 Jan. 1990, pp. 4–5.

59. N. Stefanović 'Pretedent na vož da [Pretender to the Leader (Father of the Nation)], *Vreme*, 28 Dec. 1992, pp. 24–26.

60. At the time he took over its leadership, Šešelj insisted that the name of the party be changed from the National Radical Party to the Serbian Radical Party. See N. Stefanović, *Duga*, 10–23 April 1993, pp. 15–16.

61. FBIS-EEU-91-084, 1 May 1991, p. 48; interview in *Politika*, 22 April 1992, p. 8.

62. Čulić, cit., *Danas*, 5 March 1991, pp. 7–9.

63. Ibid.

64. Paraga estimated his party's membership at 100,000 in the autumn of 1991. See R. Moseley, 'Croatian Extremist Spoiling for Wider War', *Chicago Tribune*, 7 Oct.1991, p. 8.

65. Griffin, *The Nature of Fascism*, cit., pp. 208–35.

66. N. Stefanović, 'Abandon All Hope You . . .', *Vreme News Digest*, No. 102, 6 Sept. 1993, pp. 6–11.

67. 49 per cent of those polled said that their financial situation was worse than it had been the previous year, and 37 per cent believed that the following year would be much worse. At the same time, the study found that while 10 per cent of the population could be characterised as openly xenophobic the previous autumn, fully three-quarters of the respondents fell into that category that year. Another study by S. Branković from the Institute for Political Studies adapted claims from Hitler's speeches to local conditions in order to measure the extent of Fascist attitudes. His findings, according to this *Vreme* author, concur with the study discussed above. M. Milošević, 'A Barometer for Measuring Stubbornness', *Vreme News Digest*, No. 91, 21 June 1993, pp. 10–15.

68. This study by Dragomir Pantić created an index to measure extreme right attitudes among the populace in Serbia and Montenegro. Pantić discovered that those with the strongest right-wing orientation admire Šešelj and consider the SRS their first or second choice in an election. They support ethnic cleansing and the 'volunteer forces'. They believe that Yugoslavia is the best country in the world, and that it is a state for Serbs and Montenegrins only. According to this study, one third of the population is anti-radical, 31 per cent ambivalent and 38 per cent latently radical. Ibid.

69. Stefanović, cit., *Vreme*, 28 Dec. 1992, pp. 24–26.

70. *RFE/RL Research Report*, 2 (42), 1993.

71. Survey data indicate the high value citizens of Croatia place on 'Europeanism'. See M. Kasapović, 'The Structure and Dynamics of the Yugoslav Political Environment and Elections in Croatia', in J. Seroka and V. Pavlović (eds), *The Tragedy of Yugoslavia. The Failure of Democratic Transformation*, M. E. Sharpe, Armonk, New York, 1992, p. 38.

72. *Radio Free Europe News Briefs*, 15 June 1993.

73. According to an HOS commander interviewed in the autumn of 1991, the HOS had 30,000

to 40,000 soldiers in the field (T. Rogers, 'Going to War with a Camera', *Soldier of Fortune*, May 1992, p. 72). This is considerably higher than the figures Paraga gave in an interview in October 1991 in which he claimed that HOS had 2,000 soldiers at the front and 10,000 waiting to be deployed. R. Moseley, 'Croatian Extremist Spoiling for Wider War', *Chicago Tribune*, 7 Oct. 1991, p. 8.

74. B. Harden, 'Croats Field Militant Milities', *Washington Post*, 10 Oct. 1991, pp. 17, 31–33.

75. W. T. Vollman, 'Welcome to Hell', *Los Angeles Times Magazine*, 18 Oct. 1992, p. 19.

76. Rogers, 'Going to War with a Camera', cit., pp. 39–41, 72.

77. It was also suggested that Paraga was involved in a plot to bring down the Tudjman government.

78. FBIS-EEU-92-117, 17 June 1992, p. 28; interview in *Politika*, 4 June 1992, p. 10.

79. ' "Ein Morden wie in Sarajevo". Spiegel–Interview mit dem Croatischen Nationalisten Dobroslav Paraga' ['A Death Sarajevo-Style'. Spiegel–Interview with the Croatian Nationalist Dobroslav Paraga], *Der Spiegel*, 12 Sept. 1992, pp. 246–48.

80. FBIS-EEU-92-119, 19 June 1992, p. 18; in *Novi vjesnik*, 3 June 1992, p. 3a.

81. *Der Spiegel*, 12 Sept. 1992, pp. 246–48.

82. It also reflected a factional struggle within the HDZ. See J. Lovrić, 'Hoće li Srbi opet braniti i spasavati hrvatske partizane od ustaša?' [Will the Serbs Again Defend and Save Croatian Partisans from the Ustasha?], *Duga*, 10–23 April 1993, pp. 33–34.

83. A. Ciríc, 'Dangerous Liaisons', *Vreme News Digest*, No. 88, 1993, pp. 5–9. There was poor morale and difficulties in the reservists whose ranks were depleted by about 150,000. In October 1991, the Yugoslav papers published a terse item about the orders to accept volunteers in the JNA. According to Ciríc, however, such a decision had already been taken in July 1991. The organ of the JNA, *Narodna Armija*, wrote on 4 December 1991 that the 'Yugoslav public at large welcomed the idea about the volunteers with approval and therefore it should not be surprising that the idea is being very successfully realised.'

84. Ibid.

85. *Der Spiegel*, 5 Aug. 1991, pp. 246–48.

86. Šešelj criticised the Yugoslav Army which he claimed 'interferes only if Serbs fight against Croats'. Ibid.

87. N. Stefanović, *Vreme*, 28 Dec. 1992, pp. 24–26.

88. N. Stefanović, *Duga*, 27 Feb–12 March 1993, pp. 15–16.

89. Šešelj ordered the Chetniks to retreat if the army appeared because, according to him, 'there [were] still some old Communist commanders with prejudices against Chetniks'. See *Der Spiegel*, 5 Aug. 1991, pp. 124–26.

90. M. Vasić, 'The Final Purge', *Vreme News Digest*, No. 101, 30 Aug. 1993, pp. 1–4.

91. U. Komlenović and M. Vasić, 'The New Serbian Colony', *Vreme Digest*, No. 105, 27 Sept. 1993, pp. 14–17.

92. C. J. Williams, 'Rightists Gather Support to 'Spoil' Croatian Vote', *Los Angeles Times*, 28 July 1992, pp. 1, 4

93. FBIS-EEU-92-149, 3 Aug. 1992, pp. 26–27.

94. S. Engelberg, 'Croatian Leader on Defensive in Fight for Re-election', *New York Times*, 2 Aug. 1992, sec. 1, p. 14.

95. FBIS-EEU-92-189, 29 Sept. 1992, p. 35; in *Novi danas*, 31 Aug. 1992, p. 22.

96. Williams, 'Rightists Gather support', cit., pp. 1, 4.

97. For example, there was a move to name a street next to the Faculty of Philosophy after Mile Budak, who was a high-ranking member of the Ustasha regime. The vigorous protest of the Jewish community in Zagreb stopped this effort, though there are streets named after Budak in other towns in Croatia.

98. Čulić, *Danas*, 7 April 1992 pp. 7–10.

99. Tudjman has nominated at least two former Ustasha officials to government posts. He nominated Ivo Rojnica, former Ustasha commander in Dubrovnik, as ambassador to Argentina and Vinko Nikolić, who was an official in the Ustasha Ministry of Education, to a seat in parliament.

100. At the second HDZ convention in mid-October 1993, the party voted to maintain its unity, despite predictions that it might finally split into at least two separate parties. Analysts speculated that Tudjman had managed to maintain a tight grip on the party's right wing by preventing hardliners like Vladimir Šeks and Branimir Glavaš from gaining seats in the HDZ executive body. *RFE/RL New Briefs*, No. 43, 1993, p. 9.

101. FBIS-EEU-92-249, 28 Dec. 1992, p. 35.

102. FBIS-EEU-92-241, 15 Dec. 1992, p. 44.

103. FBIS-EEU-93-059, 30 March 1993, pp. 41–42; in *Danas*, 26 Feb. 1993, pp. 20–21.

104. Ž. Luburovic, 'Dobroslav Paraga, disident ili agent?' [Dobroslav Paraga, Dissident or Agent?], *Danas*, 4 June 1993, pp. 5–7.

105. While two years previously HSP demonstrations had drawn tens of thousands of participants, they were now generally agreed to be lacklustre affairs with only 200 or so participants.

106. N. Stefanović, *Vreme*, 28 Dec. 1992, pp. 24–26.

107. G. Jovanović, 'Sve bolji dani' [Better and Better Days], *Duga*, 10–13 April 1993, pp. 14–16.

108. The results of the Serbian parliamentary elections held on 19 December 1993, according to the official election results announced by election commission officials on 22 December, were as follows: the Socialist Part of Serbia won 123 seats, the main opposition coalition, namely the Democratic Movement of Serbia (DEPOS) 45 seats; the Serbian Radical Party 39 seats; the Democratic Party 29 seats; the Democratic Party of Serbia 7 seats; the Democratic Community of Hungarians in Vojvodina 5 seats; and the Coalition of Albanian Parties 2 seats.

109. For example, see I. Banac, 'Separating History from Myth: An Interview with Ivo Banac', in R. Ali and L. Liefschultz (eds), *Why Bosnia? Writings on the Balkan War*, Pamflateers Press, Inc., Stoney Creek, CT, 1993, pp. 156–157.

Chapter 9

THE CIS AND AFTER: THE IMPACT OF RUSSIAN NATIONALISM

Stephen K. Carter

When Lenin and the Bolsheviks seized power in the Russian Empire on 7 November 1917, the prospects for Russian nationalists seemed to be extremely poor. Lenin, as a convinced Marxist, believed in proletarian internationalism. The new Soviet state which emerged after the Civil War in December 1922 was a Union of Soviet Socialist Republics (USSR). However, at this early stage in Soviet history, the high tide of international working-class revolutions had receded, and under Stalin the Comintern rapidly became an instrument of Soviet foreign policy. During the social revolutions of the 1930s, any manifestations of nationalism were ruthlessly crushed, but after the Great Patriotic War (1941–45) Soviet ideology took on some characteristics which seemed akin to Russian nationalism. Only the Russians had successfully resisted the Third Reich, while many of the non-Russian republics such as Ukraine and Byelorussia and the Baltic States had been under German occupation. Under Nikita Khrushchev, there was a serious attempt to revitalise Soviet ideology, and all manifestations of nationalism, whether Russian, Ukrainian or any other variety, were dubbed 'bourgeois'. Khrushchev believed that national distinctions would disappear as Communism was approached, and he dreamed of a 'new Soviet man' and the merging (*sliyanie*) of nations. Khrushchev's successors were more cautious, and as Soviet ideology lost its appeal during the 'stagnation period' of Brezhnev, dissident writers revived the themes of Russian nationalism. The most prominent of these authors was Alexander Solzhenitsyn. Even in the official literature and in the other arts Russians tried to revive and depict their national heritage; this was particularly the case among the so-called 'countryside writers' (*derevenshchiki*).

Most Western sovietologists failed to notice the significance of these developments, believing as they did that Soviet institutions could achieve their own internal evolutionary reform. Thus Mikhail Gorbachev's *perestroika* (reconstruction) was greeted with enthusiasm by many who saw only that the Cold War would thereby come to an end. It was not generally recognised that the USSR itself might break up under the impact of *glasnost* (openness) and political reform. Gorbachev himself cannot be held directly responsible for this development, as he had sought to preserve part of the USSR with his Union Treaty of 1991. However, the attempted coup against Gorbachev in August 1991 precipitated the final collapse of the USSR as several former Soviet republics immediately proclaimed their independence in the last week of that month.

The political power of Boris Yeltsin was enormously enhanced by his courageous stance against the coup plotters in August 1991. As the power of Yeltsin waxed, so that of Gorbachev waned. It had been Gorbachev who had appointed the hardliners such as Dmitry Yazov, Gennady Yanaev, Valentin Pavlov, Vladimir Kryuchkov and Boris Pugo who had conspired to remove him from office under the false pretext of his ill-health. Did Gorbachev know about the plans to install a 'state of emergency', and did he even have some knowledge of the proposed 'State Committee for the State of Emergency' which was announced on 19 August? Gorbachev even made the mistake of trying to support the Communist Party as an agent of reform after his return from the Crimea, at a time when the country was recoiling from the Communist Party of the Soviet Union [*Kommunisticheskaya Partiya Sovietskogo Soyuza*, KPSS] as the instigator of the attempted coup. In any event, all those schemes which Gorbachev had in mind for the former USSR, including the proposed Union Treaty, were now dead. The stage was set for a much looser confederation of states, especially after the three Baltic states were recognised internationally in the aftermath of the coup. The Commonwealth of Independent States (CIS) was set up in December 1991, and Gorbachev resigned to be replaced by Yeltsin and his advisers as Head of the Russian Federation in the Kremlin. The USSR was no more, and the West hoped that the largest republic of the CIS, the Russian Federation, would now assume the major responsibilities of the former Soviet Union. These included a monopoly over nuclear weapons, control of the money supply within the rouble zone and the USSR's seat on the Security Council.

Why does the CIS seem to be an unstable political institution? The first reason is clearly that it was created in a great hurry without adequate preparation or consultation. This also means that the new democratic Russia came into being much too rapidly, like a premature birth. The new country, although gigantic, was based on arbitrary borders drawn up in the 1920s, and it possessed from the first a sickly constitution. Without the crucial 'oxygen' of Western aid and investment, without wise policies and firm government, the new quasi-state could hardly survive in its incarnation of December 1991. Russia's new environment, the CIS, was also still a very amorphous body without any kind of charter a year after its creation. All the constituent republics of the CIS had different agendas in 1991. While Russia wanted a permanent kind of association somewhat like the British Commonwealth, Ukraine regarded the CIS only as a civilised means of divorce, and viewed its own membership as temporary.[1] Belarus and the other eight republics that joined two weeks later each saw the CIS in a different light.

The problems of joint economic infrastructure, division of property and debts, and above all the organisation of the armed forces and nuclear weapons had not been adequately discussed. Citizenship questions often remained unresolved, particularly for Russian ethnic minorities in the 'near-abroad' (*blizhnee zarubezhye*), as the new republics were called. Russia wanted these expatriate Russians to have dual citizenship, but most non-Russian republics regarded this as unsatisfactory, fearing that Russians on their soil would have divided loyalties. The new republics lacked personnel, funds and experience to deal with independence while they faced all the problems we have come to associate with the collapse of Communism: namely, incipient mass unemployment, rapidly rising inflation, falling production, the collapse of traditional trading patterns and rising crime levels.

As in any confederation where one member is significantly larger than all the others, non-Russian republics feared the ambitions, and resented the influence, of Russia itself. This was exacerbated by the presence of the former Soviet army on their territory, in some cases (such as Moldova and Estonia) against the wishes of that republic. In its first year, the CIS lost one member (Azerbaidjan) and seemed about to lose another (Moldova). Although some republics, such as Kazakhstan and Uzbekistan, argue very strongly for closer cooperation, and many members now realise their mutual inter-dependence, the attitude of Ukraine and Moldova makes real cooperation difficult. The idea of a common economic space has failed, and foreign policy goals cannot be coordinated. The commander of the CIS forces, Marshal Yevgeny Shaposhnikov, proposed that the new republics try to align their military activities like NATO, but by December 1992 he admitted that this project was doomed. Customs barriers have been created between Ukraine and Russia, and other trade constraints have resulted in severe shortages of input to Russian factories. The division of former Soviet assets abroad has been disputed, particularly by Ukraine. No joint peace-keeping forces are yet in place to deal with the virtual civil war in Tadjikistan, or the disputes between Armenia and Azerbaidjan, in the Caucasus or in Moldova.

To summarise, we can say that the trend at present is towards increasingly bilateral relations between republics. Many shades of opinion in Russia, including the nationalists, are unhappy about this trend and Russia's general loss of influence in the region. As Stephen Foye of Radio Liberty has written: '. . . it was unclear at the end of 1992 whether the CIS represented the first step toward the consolidation of a new political order or merely another stage in the disintegration of the old'.[2]

In Russia itself, Yeltsin faced an extremely complex task. The new Russian government would have to dismantle the former Soviet Empire, including the withdrawal of troops and the apportionment of debt between the new independent states. Russia required a new and veritable economic miracle as it transformed itself into a capitalist economy, needing a radical privatisation programme, the abolition of subsidies, and macroeconomic stabilisation. Even more difficult would be the transformation of the 'dependency psychology' of three generations of Socialism, and the creation of a consensus among the population for really radical reform along Western lines. Russia needed to revive its national culture and religion, and to rediscover its true identity and history after the ravages of Communism, and without this process of rediscovery it was difficult to see how a genuinely Russian civil society could be created. Yeltsin and his team would have to transform the totalitarian society of the past into a Western-style multi-party democracy which was at the same time legitimate and stable. If any one of these objectives could be achieved in a five-year period, it would be miraculous.[3]

President Boris Yeltsin, with all his usual showmanship and panache, set about achieving not one of these objectives, but all of them at once. For example, he distanced himself from the totalitarian past by attempting to make the KPSS illegal in September 1991. He appointed 36-year-old Yegor Gaidar as his Prime Minister,

176

and instituted radical economic reforms including a free-market economy and a privatisation programme. Finally, he appointed as his Foreign Minister Andrei Kozyrev, who followed a Western-directed foreign policy in all areas, including condemnation of the Communist past, Serbian irredentism and Saddam Hussein.

However, the legacy of the former USSR created enormous inertia against these valuable and progressive reforms. To begin with, very few of the former republics of the USSR were convinced that Russia had abandoned its former imperial ambitions. The radical right or nationalist opposition often spoke openly of their desire to recreate the Union, and much pressure was, for instance, exerted against the Baltic states to rescind their new citizenship laws and to force them to treat their Russian minorities with more respect. Second, the territorial integrity of the Russian Federation itself was threatened by independence movements in Chechnya and Tatarstan. Yeltsin initially considered using force in Chechnya, but was dissuaded from this by the Russian parliament. Only a 'federal-type' Russian state would survive, so it seemed. However, such an arrangement was a far cry from the aims envisaged by the Russian national- ists, namely measures to create a new Russian State which would be unitary, 'one and indivisible'. In general, we can say that the problem of Russian statehood (*gosudarstvennost*) was quite unresolved at the end of 1992. Third, and most im- portantly, the balance of power between the executive and legislative branches of government remained undefined. This was a legacy of the Gorbachev era, for Gorbachev had created a 'working legislature' or Supreme Soviet in 1989 which was appointed by an elected Congress of Peoples' Deputies. In 1990, similar institutions were created in the republics, Russia included. These legislative bodies challenged the Power of the President as head of the executive, and forced him, at the end of 1992, to replace the free-market Prime Minister, Yegor Gaidar, with the former Communist economic manager, Viktor Chernomyrdin. Yeltsin was forced by the leftist and nationalist-inclined legislature, elected before the 1991 revolution, to compromise with the military–industrial complex, in order to gain time for the reform programme to be carried through.

Yeltsin seems to have made the same mistake as Gorbachev in that he tried to reform the political and economic systems simultaneously. He believed that the powers of the President and government were stronger than they were in reality. However, the Russian parliament, the VIIth Congress of Peoples' Deputies, soon disabused him of this notion in December 1992. As Peter Reddaway wrote in an article in *The Independent*:[4]

> He lost his Prime Minister, Yegor Gaidar, he lost his special powers, he lost the right to appoint key ministers without parliamentary approval, he lost his closest political allies by removing them from their posts . . . and he lost when he demanded a quick referendum on whether the people trusted him or the parliament.

Russia inherited a strong legislature from Gorbachev, but it has not used this power to pass progressive legislation and to further market reforms. Instead, the Russian parliament and its speaker Ruslan Khasbulatov competed destructively with the executive. The Congress did not systematically work to produce a new Constitution to replace the outdated 'Brezhnev' Constitution to suit its own requirements. The

Constitutional problem was eventually 'solved' only by force on 4 October 1993, and finally by a narrow referendum majority on 12 December of the same year.

The radical reform programme adopted by the Gaidar government in 1992 included abandoning price controls and subsidies, a sweeping privatisation scheme based on vouchers and private ownership of land. The reforms were similar to the shock therapy of the Balcerowicz plan applied to the Polish economy in 1990. However, Russia proved much less successful than Poland in achieving macroeconomic stabilisation, the control of inflation and the money supply, and a growth in supply-side provision of goods and services. The strength of the private sector remains dubious, while support for the continuation of reform is rapidly waning. Economic statistics at the end of 1992 made dispiriting reading. Inflation zoomed to 1,060 per cent, while there was a huge fall in production (minus 20 per cent), and wage inflation reached 650 per cent – a level well below that of inflation.[5] Many categories of the population fell below the poverty line, including old-age pensioners, academics, professionals on fixed rouble incomes and students. The fortunate few with access to foreign currency waxed exceedingly rich. Practically no Russian enterprise had been declared bankrupt at the end of 1992, but as smokestack industries cease to be viable, unemployment seems certain to escalate throughout 1994–95. Some republics, such as Ukraine, left the rouble zone in 1992, and others plan to follow. Economic conditions in Russia were so severe at the end of 1992 that 90 per cent of the population could have been experiencing serious economic hardship. In these conditions, Yeltsin's political power seemed to be under challenge and then under real threat throughout 1992, and especially in early 1993 until his referendum victory in April. In 1992 and 1993 the opposition parties attacked Yeltsin's close adviser Gennady Burbulis and in particular the youthful Gaidar, who had come into the government from outside the traditional *nomenklatura* circles. Yeltsin had cancelled local elections in the autumn of 1991, a decision which may have weakened the democrats who had earlier brought him to power. Repeatedly criticised by Vice-President Alexander Rutskoi, the new government was opposed by Communists and nationalists. The largest faction of Communists in the Congress was Russian Unity [*Yedinstvo*], while the Communists as a whole had the support of about 30 per cent of the deputies. Many varieties of Russian nationalists emerged in 1992. They will be discussed more fully in the second part of this chapter.

In October 1992 the National Salvation Front [*Narodnyi Front Spaseniya*, NFS] emerged, calling openly for Yeltsin's removal. At the same time, Ruslan Khasbulatov claimed that the Presidium of parliament should control the armed forces and state security. He also tried to muzzle the democratic press, such as the newspaper *Izvestiya*. Yeltsin responded by banning Khasbulatov's parliamentary guards and by issuing a decree to abolish the NFS. However, the deputies, who already had three years' experience, resented Yeltsin's threats to dissolve Congress and therefore struck back at presidential power in December 1992. As mentioned above, President and Congress were forced to compromise over the proposed referendum, and in January–February 1993 Khasbulatov tried to back off from holding one at all, arguing that it would split society and lead to 'civil war'. Meanwhile he went on an extensive tour of the provinces urging the local Soviets to resist presidential rule, and calling for a new Soviet-style democracy.[6] Khasbulatov also tried to gain the support of the Russian nationalists by accusing the Yeltsin government of selling national assets to the West. He managed to persuade the writer Alexander Prokhanov and Mikhail Astafiev (a leader of the NFS) to take up this theme.

In March 1993 the Eighth Congress attempted to seize power for the Presidium of parliament. It rejected power-sharing, cancelled the referendum, passed several amendments curtailing Yeltsin's powers and stated its support for the old constitution. The Presidium of parliament began to look very like the old Politburo, and all but one of its members were hardliners. On 20 March Yeltsin announced conditions of 'special' rule in a TV address to the nation. An emergency session of parliament, the Ninth Congress, threatened impeachment of the President, and Rutskoi declared his direct interest in the Presidency. While Yeltsin was away in the Urals mourning the death of his mother, the Congress backed away from impeachment and agreed to a referendum, while insisting on the right of Congress to set the questions and the terms on which they were convinced that Yeltsin would not win. For example, Congress insisted that no result would be valid if not supported by over 50 per cent of all eligible votes. The Constitutional Court ruled that this '50 per cent rule' would apply only to the last two questions relating to early presidential and parliamentary elections as these were constitutionally important matters. The first two questions, relating to support for President Yeltsin and his economic policies, were seen as political questions without bearing on the constitution.

The results of the referendum of 25 April surprised many observers in the West who had predicted a negative vote on Yeltsin's economic policies and a very low turnout. A 65 per cent turnout (69.2 million out of 107.3 million) confirmed the results shown in Table 9.1.[7]

Yeltsin reacted cautiously to his evident moral victory, but he did dismiss two prominent conservatives, Yuri Skokov, head of the Security Council, and Georgy Khizha, a representative of the military–industrial complex. The referendum was fairly conducted in the main, and additional questions were added in only three regions. Only Chechnya, already known for its unyielding separatism, failed to hold a referendum and in only one region (Tatarstan) was the turnout too low to be valid (20 per cent). In Ingushetia, Yeltsin gained a mere 2.4 per cent of the vote, but about half of the remaining autonomous regions and republics gave him more than 50 per cent. The opponents, such as Mikhail Astafiev of the NFS, claimed that Yeltsin's votes (39 million) were less than half of the total electorate (107.3 million), and therefore that the President had actually lost the referendum. However, most Russian politicians drew the opposite conclusion. Possibly the most balanced verdict on the referendum was given by Otto Latsis, a member of Yeltsin's Presidential Council. He argued that

Table 9.1 Results of referendum, 25 April 1993

Substance of question	% votes cast	% electorate
Confidence in President Yeltsin	58.7	37.3
Approval of economic reforms	53.0	34.0
Early presidential elections	49.5	31.7
Early parliamentary elections	67.2	43.1

'. . . many voters were not so much saying "yes" to the President and government, as "no" to the opponents of the renewal of Russia'.[8]

While the referendum result represented an almost miraculous reversal of Yeltsin's political fortunes, the West should remain cautious about the verdict of 25 April 1993. Firstly, if the economic promises made by the Yeltsin government to certain sections of the electorate were fulfilled, they would be highly inflationary. Secondly, the regional support for Yeltsin is very uneven. While the President did extremely well in Moscow and St Petersburg, the Urals, Northern Russia and the Pacific seaboard, he gained less than 50 per cent in most of European Russia south and west of Moscow, the Caucasus, Kaliningrad and those regions bordering Mongolia.[9] Thirdly, the constitutional and political crisis at the centre remains unresolved.

The fearsome dispute at the centre of power has gained much attention and comment in the West, but I believe that it is overshadowed by a much more elemental and fundamental process: the ongoing collapse of the Russian Federation itself. Dynamic centrifugal forces have afflicted the Russian heartlands themselves in the early 1990s. In theory, such forces should be easy to control because more than 80 per cent of the population of the Russian Federation are ethnic Russians. However, some of the inhabitants of the Russian north have begun to demand greater control of their mineral wealth and hard-currency earnings. Autonomous regions such as Tuva and Buryatia on the Mongolian border are gradually slipping away from the centre, while the whole North Caucasus region seems to be moving out of Moscow's orbit amid much bloodshed. Chechnya refused to sign the Federation Agreement in March 1992, while Tatarstan has adopted its own constitution. Tatarstan is important not only for its oil, but also because the mid-Volga region straddles the transport links between European Russia and Siberia. In February 1993, a new treaty granted Tatarstan greater autonomy than is allowed to other republics. Recently the Tatar parliament called for a new regional organisation called the Volga Confederation; if realised, this would give Tatarstan a border with Kazakhstan, thus reducing Russia's power over Tatarstan. In 1993 this republic was totally surrounded by Russian territory.

However, the most serious internal problem in Russia today is the breakdown of a uniform system of law coupled with an exponential rise of law-breaking activities. A recent paper by Paul Goble disclosed that Russia's eighty-eight *oblasts* (regions of local government) have passed around 14,000 regulations which directly contradict Moscow's legislation. The chairman of the Russian parliament's committee for nationalities openly admits that the Federation is in danger, '. . . because laws are not being observed, because there is a power crisis and economic reforms are not conclusive'.[10]

In 1991, although the world was horrified by the violent disintegration of Yugoslavia, it did not seem that such a thing could happen in Russia. Indeed Foreign Minister Kozyrev praised the CIS precisely because, in his opinion, it had obviated the possibility of a Yugoslav-style disintegration in the former Soviet Union and Russia. However, in 1993, in the face of economic and political disintegration, President Yeltsin proposed to establish democracy and the market economy by authoritarian methods. The nationalist and Communist oppositions have been wrong-footed by the referendum results and their own inept tactics, such as the violent demonstration in Moscow on 1 May when a policeman was killed. However, the

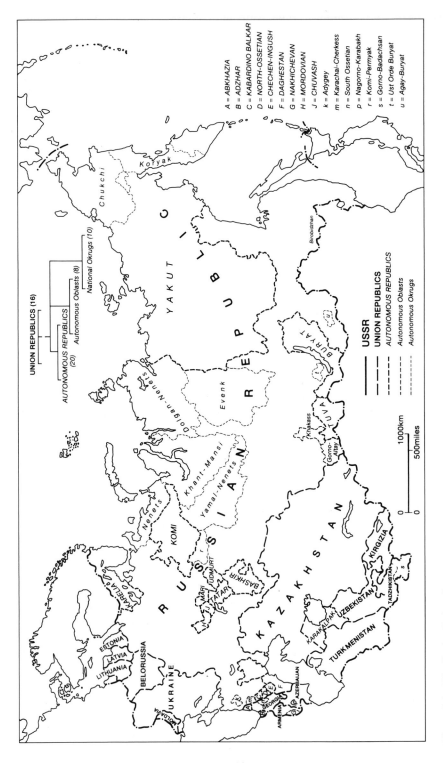

Figure 9.1 The Soviet Federation.

paralysis of power continued at the centre until October 1993. Anti-Western Russian nationalists are strong in many areas, and their political position could easily improve if public opinion were to turn against government incompetence and the ongoing disintegration of the state. 'Weimar Russia' may very well bring forward from a range of possible political actors a leader and a movement committed to imperial order and authoritarian solutions. In December 1993, this leader appeared to be Vladimir Zhirinovsky.

The prospects for Russian nationalists and neo-Fascists.

Russia is undergoing a period of revolutionary change in the 1990s. The reforms of Gorbachev started the process, but the really rapid destabilisation of the political system, the economy and the state were occasioned by the failure of the coup attempt in August 1991. Radical economic reform was initiated by the Yeltsin–Gaidar 'shock-therapy' of January 1992 in the context of political in-fighting between the Congress of Peoples' Deputies elected in 1990 and the presidential executive. An analysis of the parliamentary groupings in the Congress may not be particularly fruitful, as they represented a 'snapshot' of the political forces operative in Russia in 1990, before the revolution of August 1991.

The major political movements of the Russian Federation before 4 October 1993 could be divided into three: the revolutionary democrats who support change towards liberal democracy and the market while generally approving of the CIS; the Civic Union [*Grazhdanskii Soyuz*], which sought a more gradual pace of change in the economy, social-democracy and the protection of entrenched interests; and the Communists-Nationalists, who entirely reject the Yeltsin government and its reforms while seeking their own (different) versions of a new state corresponding to the territory of the USSR or even of the old Russian Empire. Some nationalists favour an isolationist, anti-Western Russian state within the borders of the Russian Federation, but this is generally a minority view. The following survey is based largely on the work of Vera Tolz, Wendy Slater and Alexander Rahr.[11] For the purposes of this chapter, I will deal only with the Communists-Nationalists.

In April 1992, a powerful bloc was formed in the Russian parliament consisting of 375 deputies (about 30 per cent) calling itself 'Russian Unity' [*Rossiiskoe Yedinstvo*]. It prefers the name 'red–white opposition', but democrats use the phrase 'red–brown opposition' suggesting a hint of Fascism. Although its members are united in violent opposition to Yeltsin, whom they accuse of being an agent of the West or even of a secret Judeo-Masonic conspiracy, the goals of Russian Unity are extremely diverse, ranging from the restoration of the planned economy and the USSR to monarchism. The term 'red–brown opposition' may indeed be applicable in an objective sense to a combination of National Bolsheviks and the authoritarian left of the nationalists. However, there are many Communists to the left of the National Bolsheviks, and many nationalist groups to the right of the Fascists.

A coalition between Communists and nationalists seems, at first sight, improbable, but two factors in particular united them in 1993: opposition to Yeltsin, the free market and 'Western' democracy; and fury at the collapse of the state. It is difficult to imagine that the Communists could really have a common cause with the nationalists in power. One gets the impression that the hard-line Communists view nationalist parties rather like the Stalinists viewed 'popular front' parties in Eastern and Central Europe after 1945. In other words, they seek genuine coalition only as a means to consolidate monolithic Communist unity at a later stage. However, the authoritarian (statist) nationalists do not seek the restoration of the old order. On the contrary, they seek to establish a new order (*poryadok*) after the democratic revolution. The Communists and their paramilitary demonstrations are a very useful disruptive force for the nationalists who know very well that Marxism-Leninism is a spent force in Russia.

The nationalist parties and movements should now be considered, since they covered a wide area of the political spectrum. The more moderate groups included the Constitutional Democratic Party [*Konstitutsionnaya Demokraticheskaya Partiya*, KDP] which advocates policies similar to the pre-revolutionary Kadet Party. The policies of the KDP should naturally coincide to some extent with those of the democrats, but like Pavel Milyukov in 1917, the KDP leader Mikhail Astafiev has 'statist' or even imperial aspirations, and in October 1992 he joined the NFS. The Russian Christian Democratic Movement [*Russkoe Khristianskoe Demokratischeskoe Dvizhenie*, RKDD] formed in April 1990 and led by Viktor Aksyuchits, rejected rapprochement with the Communists and originally tried to form links with international Christian Democracy. However, being based in Russian Orthodoxy rather than in Western Catholicism, the RKDD was always inclined towards Russian national values and Aksyuchits in particular is a Russian 'statist'. None of these leaders and parties managed to collect enough signatures in time to register for the December elections. Another significant Russian nationalist politician was Sergei Baburin, who gained a seat in December without specific party affiliation. More extreme was the Russian National Council [*Russkoe Narodnoe Sobranie*, RNS] founded in February 1992 and led by former KGB General Sterligov. It was a serious political organisation with a structure based on that of the former KPSS. Among its leaders were the nationalist writer Valentin Rasputin and Gennady Zyuganov who later joined the Communist Party of the Russian Federation [*Kommunisticheskaya Partiya Russkoi Federatsii*, KP-RF]. RNS was founded as a mass national-patriotic movement designed to revive Russian national statehood. It claims to have wide support in military and state security circles, and rejected both the revolutionary democrats and the Communists. The misnamed Liberal Democratic Party of Russia [*Liberalno-Demokraticheskaya Partiya Rossii*, LDPR], led by Zhirinovsky, was formed in 1990 and postured as a mass party. It does seem to have acquired many members in late 1993. This is a Fascist movement which seeks to restore the Russian Empire and even to extend Russia's sphere of influence to the Indian Ocean and the Mediterranean. Zhirinovsky has his own parliamentary grouping known as 'Zhirinovsky's falcons' (*Sokoli Zhirinovskogo*), but he also has links with the various 'Memory' (*Pamyat*) societies such as that led by Dmitry Vasiliev. These groups are well-armed and trained, but their neo-imperialist politics were not thought to be widely popular in October 1993. Zhirinovsky himself was dismissed by most political scientists, both in Russia and abroad, as a joker who need not be taken seriously.

The NFS was set up in October 1992, but was promptly banned by Yeltsin. However, on 12 February 1993 it was relegalised by the Constitutional Court.

Although boycotted by Aksyuchits and Sterligov and ignored by the hardline Communists, it was supported by the KP-RF, moderate nationalists and even parts of the Civic Union. Its political strength came from its association with Russian Unity in Congress and it was able to spread nationalist ideas through the extensive network of cadres in the KP-RF. The existence of the NFS seemed to indicate the widespread alarm felt by many sectors of the population at the instability of the democratic structures and the erosion of Russian national interests at home and abroad.

As the election results of 12 December 1993 have shown, it is entirely possible that in conditions of instability over a long period of time, the balance of political forces within the country may shift towards the nationalists. Why is Russian nationalism an ever more potent force in Russia in the 1990s? In one way, the answer to this question is obvious. Imagine that you are an adult Russian living in the former USSR. Since 1988 the following events have taken place. Firstly, the Soviet Empire suddenly collapsed and all the 'outer territories' in Eastern and Central Europe demanded immediate independence as from 1989, and the withdrawal of Soviet troops and administrators. Secondly, the USSR lost four of its constituent republics, and all Soviet troops and police officers were forced to withdraw within a short period of time, as nasty little civil wars broke out on the periphery of the country, unchecked by the overstretched international community. Then the remaining non-Russian republics declared independence from Moscow and were recognised by the UN. The political system in Moscow changed in a revolution which proclaimed a democratic Russian Republic. Several hundred thousand destitute expatriates have arrived in Russian cities. Among the expatriates were several thousand ex-servicemen and their families with their weapons, but with nowhere to live. Political and economic instability coincided with something close to hyper-inflation and incipient mass unemployment. The rouble became nearly useless for many transactions, and in practice only US dollars or other hard currency are really valuable. Savings, property values and pensions in roubles are very nearly worthless. Foreign travel has become virtually impossible. Inter-ethnic tensions have grown threatening and racist murders have become frequent. Property crimes, crimes of violence and homicide rates have escalated to levels well above those of the most dangerous US cities. Many citizens are trying to acquire small arms for self-protection. Such enormous changes in the status of a former superpower, accompanied by a catastrophic decline in economic conditions, resulted in a climate of change in peoples' attitudes, and these were not always favourable to the new freedom.

In an interesting article published in 1992, Leokadia Drobizheva argues that Russian patriotic movements had little influence on public awareness in the 1980s.[12] In answering the question, 'What is your motherland?', 70 per cent of all Russians, regardless of where they lived in the Soviet Union, said that the USSR was their motherland. In contrast, 80 per cent of Georgians and Uzbeks named their own republics.[13]

By the mid-1980s, declining economic conditions created more criticism from the non-Russian republics directed against the All-Union Centre (Moscow), which tended to be identified with Russia. At this point a Russian nationalist reaction was generated because Russians had also suffered from 'the system' which included negative discrimination against Russians. After 1985, *glasnost* and *perestroika* created 'an extraordinary growth of national movements and inter-ethnic conflicts'.[14] When autonomous regions of the Russian Federation such as Tatarstan, Tuva and Buryatia tried to acquire the status of Soviet republics, many Russians began to adopt a more belligerent stance. Russians living in these regions or in non-Russian republics began to form 'interfronts' in order to protect their communities. National-patriots developed a more strident tone, concerning themselves at first with ecological questions and the preservation of historical monuments, but later tending towards militancy in the form of *Pamyat* and other 'patriotic' societies. The liberal press attacked the *Pamyat* societies and their ideology was not popular at first.

In December 1989, a survey conducted by the Centre of Applied Sociological Research in Moscow claimed that only 5 per cent of respondents were prepared to 'struggle against non-Russians and cosmopolitans'. Nevertheless, patriotic societies proliferated and an incomplete list includes *Otechestvo* (Fatherland), *Rossiia Molodaya* (Young Russia), *Rossiiskoe Obshchestvo Spravedlivosti* (The Russian Society for Justice), and many *Pamyat* societies; the Russian Writers' Union (*Soyuz Russkikh Pisatelei*) also espoused their cause. These groups did not possess a homogeneous ideology, but it is significant that some groups started to speak of the army as a defender of Russian statehood.

Even in the time of Gorbachev, the 'Russian national idea' was beginning to have an impact on mass consciousness and public life. Gorbachev invited the nationalist writer Rasputin to join his Presidential Council. Yeltsin actively employed the idea of Russian sovereignty in his struggle for power. Forces opposed to *perestroika* also latched on to the national idea. By the end of the perestroika period, tensions between Russians and non-Russians had increased considerably. As Drobizheva summarises: 'according to polls at the end of the 1980s and expert data assessment, the proportion of Russians with ethnic prejudices had risen by more than 1.5 to 2 times'.[15] In many non-Russian republics, such as Estonia and Tuva, Russians began to feel extreme ethnic pressure. For a brief period, the defeat of the coup in August 1991 created a new feeling of pride in Russian achievements and hopes for democracy. However, the secession of Ukraine, Kazakhstan and Uzbekistan created a new ethnocentrism, fear and resentment in Russians by the end of the year. This helps to explain the deep hostility of many quite 'democratic' Russians towards separatism in Chechnya and Tatarstan. Drobizheva predicts that the decentralisation of the political system will only exacerbate ethnic tensions. However, she points out that migration problems and the status of ethnic groups outside the new national boundaries cannot be resolved without a democratic framework of cooperation between the post-Soviet states. She concludes that economic stabilisation and political democracy based on a new constitution are the only conditions under which the new Russian national ethnocentrism might recede.[16] Only the establishment of a genuine market economy and a democratic constitution can save the former Soviet Union from becoming an area of acute ethnic conflict.

Russians know that they have lost an empire. However, Russia's political elites differ profoundly in their desired policies for the future. The liberals and democrats find themselves in an unprecedented situation, since Russia has always exerted a powerful regional influence beyond its borders except during the 'Time of Troubles' (1605–1613) and during the Russian Civil War (1918–1921). These are hardly encouraging precedents, and the doctrine of democratic national self-determination is new to most Russians. How many Moscow politicians really take seriously the concept of an independent Belarus or Ukraine for the forseeable future? Vera Tolz[17] distinguishes between the democrats whom she terms 'Westernisers-Atlanticists', on the one hand, and 'Slavophile-isolationists' and 'Imperialist-unionists' on the other, She points out that both the latter groups are nationalists, and that they have some very extensive historical and intellectual capital on which to draw. Tolz implies that the last group are gaining in influence and that they wish to recreate the USSR or else establish a Russian-Muslim 'Eurasian' Union. It has been especially difficult for Russians to accept the position of an independent Ukraine. 'Kievan Russia' was the cradle of Russian civilisation and Russian Orthodoxy. Ukraine has been under Russian domination since at least the time of Catherine the Great in the eighteenth century. The dispute over the Crimea is particularly dangerous. Political scientist Liliya Shevtsova stated that, 'The amorphous . . . nature of Russia's statehood is not only dangerous for the process but also for the other states that were set up as a result of the disintegration of the USSR'.[18] Former presidential adviser Galina Starovoitova has drawn an obvious conclusion:

> One cannot exclude the possibility of [a Fascist period] in Russia. We can see too many parallels between Russia's current situation and that of Germany after the Versailles Treaty. A great nation is humiliated . . . many of its nationals live outside the country's borders. The disintegration of an empire has taken place at a time when many people still have an imperial mentality . . . All this at a time of economic crisis.[19]

Many Communists have favoured imperialist ideas as a way of solving the problem of Russia's statehood. They include such names as Colonel Viktor Alksnis, Sazhi Umolatova and Gennady Zyuganov (all of whom joined the NFS). Many of these are 'Eurasians', taking their ideas from conservative writers of the nineteenth century such as Dostoevsky. They also have a case when they point out that the Western-oriented foreign policy of the 'Atlanticists' carried out by Foreign Minister Kozyrev and President Yeltsin had produced very few practical results by 1993. The President himself has often been forced to accommodate the national-patriots and the military. For example, Yeltsin rescinded the withdrawal of Russian troops from the Baltic states on 29 October 1992, and dismissed his adviser Galina Starovoitova on 4 November.

Igor Torbakov has stated that the disintegration of the USSR has caused a profound psychological trauma since December 1991. 'The result has been a sharp upsurge of morbid nationalism.'[20] Although this nationalism is not new, it has become more prominent in the 1990s, first, because the collapse of the USSR also toppled Communist ideology and created and ideological vacuum; second, because restraints on freedom of expression no longer exist and therefore nationalist ideas can be propagated; and third, because the nationalists are gradually uniting their forces and 'liberal nationalism' is losing out. The nationalists see individualism, economic liberalism and democracy as being characteristics of the Atlanticist tradition, while authoritarianism, hierarchy and the primacy of the nation-state are characteristics of Eurasianism. Eduard Limonov, in his 'Manifesto of Russian Nationalism', has declared: 'everything that is good for my state is good for me. The state is above everything. Nothing matters but the state.'[21] Limonov also expresses the idea of a corporate state in his Manifesto, combined with a call for national revolution. As Walter Laqueur has concluded in his January 1990 Foreword to the Russian edition of '*Russia and Germany*': 'if the reformist party in the Soviet Union is forced into a serious retreat, right-wing ideologies will be in great demand'.[22]

Even President Yeltsin has had to make concessions to these hitherto unpopular ideologies. Zhirinovsky's LDPR has recently argued that the West should recognise the former Soviet Republics as a Russian sphere of influence. Obviously such claims must make non-Russian states in the region extremely uneasy. Meanwhile, the warning signs continue to mount. It is noteworthy that while meetings organised by the extreme right-wing opposition in 1991 attracted only a few hundred people, in 1993 they were attracting audiences of 10,000 or more.[23]

In Russia today, deteriorating economic conditions and a disintegrating social order have contributed to an exponential rise in crime rates. Statistics have been published since the *glasnost* period and show steep increases in property crimes, violence and homicide. Between 1991 and 1992 there was a 27 per cent increase in serious crime, while homicide rates in Siberia were 19.7/100,000 of the population compared with 9.2/100,000 in the USA. The average for the whole country was 12.5/100,000 in 1992.[24] Rutskoi has claimed that 40 per cent of the country's gross national product is controlled by the criminal mafia, and it is estimated that 25 per cent of all hard currency earnings find their way abroad into illegal bank accounts. Weapon smuggling is big business, and German police in 1992 intercepted more than a hundred attempts to sell radioactive materials. Preoccupation with crime levels has now become a major political issue. In May 1992, the Moscow polling organisation VCIOM conducted a survey of 2,000 residents in European Russia: 90 per cent said that crime levels were increasing; 74 per cent said that corruption was a serious threat to society, and felt that no one was safe any more.

In March 1993, the Public Opinion Foundation in Moscow stated that 30 per cent of respondents in their survey claimed that they or their friends had been victims of violent crime in the past year. Most importantly, support for a political system that could stem this rising tide of crime has increased considerably. When asked if they would prefer a political system that would provide more security in society or one which provided more freedom for individuals, the results in May 1991 were about 33 per cent for each kind of system (34 per cent were undecided). In October 1992 the results were 64, 19 and 17 per cent respectively.[25]

In mid-1993, there were at least 120,000 illegal residents in Moscow alone, and popular anger against illegals and criminal elements is growing. Chechens, Caucasians and others suspected of criminal activities faced ethnic hostility. Crime reporting in the Russian press is very sensational and feeds the impression that the country is badly governed. It is becoming clear that the poorly paid, corrupt police and the over-burdened judiciary simply cannot cope. Obviously, those who call vociferously for a restoration of law and order will tend to gain supporters under such frightening conditions.

Where does the Russian army stand? Stephen Foye has pointed out that the Russian Officers' Union is now challenging the military leadership. This reflects the declining authority of the High Command and the increasing vulnerability of the officer corps to political influences outside the military. 'The emergence of the neo-communist and ultra-nationalist Russian Officers' Union headed by Stanislav Terekhov appears to be symptomatic not only of a rising tide of political conservatism in the country but also of growing dissatisfaction with the performance of the current military leadership.'[26] The Officers' Union was registered as a public organisation in February 1992. In October, it joined the NFS and Terekhov called for the resignation of Yeltsin and Defence Minister Pavel Grachev. He also called for the restoration of the Soviet Union, rejection of the Strategic Arms Limitation Treaty (SALT-2) and an end to the disarmament process. Terekhov claimed a membership of 10,000–30,000 and wide support in the officer corps as a whole. He was dismissed from the service on 13 November, but in April 1993 the Military Court in Moscow ruled Grachev's order illegal. There is no established mechanism for civilian control over the military today, and pledges by the High Command to stay out of politics may be difficult to enforce. At least some sections of an admittedly very divided military might be amenable to the blandishments of conservative and nationalist politicians.

While the results of the April 1993 referendum gave Yeltsin a breathing space, it remained unclear in the autumn of 1993 whether he could win a new Russian constitution and a legislative majority which would allow him to stabilise a market economy in Russia. After the trials and tribulations of Russians since 1988, and especially since 1992, we know that Yeltsin does not have much time left. While it may seem inconceivable to observers living within the Western international economic system that Russia should reject the West, the threat of an imperial-nationalist putsch and a period of effective civil war cannot be ruled out. In this case the Russian Federation would become the centre of Yugoslav-style civil war in the area of the FSU, or it might become a neo-Fascist dictatorship. The consequences for Western Europe would be grave and there would be serious implications for the international community in the early twenty-first century.

What can the West do to influence the situation? Communications are a crucial contribution, and it was international reportage and communication which helped to defeat the August 1991 coup. Major television channels and newspapers should retain permanent staff in Russia, while offers of Western aid should be targeted at tele-communications systems. Radio Liberty, BBC, Voice of America and Deutsche Welle have a crucial role to play. A kind of 'Marshall Plan of the Mind' could expand cultural and business activities through such organisations as the BBC, Voluntary Service Overseas, the British Council, the Goethe Institut, the Institut Français and others. Coordination of Western European foreign policy seems crucial in view of its signal failure in Yugoslavia. The European Union can do much to help, by speeding up the process of integration and admitting its associate members to full membership. A security system for Europe, presumably within NATO or the West European Union, should also be established. Coordination of European policies with Washington and Tokyo are vital. Finally, an escalation of support for President Yeltsin seems likely to occur if his health permits him to stay in office.

Postscript: October–December 1993

Boris Yeltsin confronted the expected coup attempt by Communists and nationalists on Monday 4 October 1993. At the beginning of September, Yeltsin's political position again looked very weak. The Russian Congress of Peoples Deputies opposed nearly all the proposed presidential legislation and threatened to pass a budget which would have plunged Russia into hyper-inflation. On 21 September, the day after the Congress convened, Yeltsin dissolved it and called for a new parliamentary election on 12 December. The Constitutional Court under Valery Zorkin ruled Yeltsin's action unconstitutional and parliament voted to impeach Yeltsin, electing Alexander Rutskoi in his place. The deputies occupied the Russian White House. On 23 September, the parliamentary leadership split, and four constitutional court judges called for a review of the previous ruling. On 28 September, troops surrounded the White House, while a day later, Yeltsin issued an ultimatum to the deputies to leave the building by 4 October. Electricity and other essential services were cut off, but leaders of sixty-two out of the eighty-nine regional councils demanded that Yeltsin lift the siege of the national parliament. Parliament then rejected a compromise, proposed under the auspices of the Orthodox Church, to restore electricity in exchange for the surrender of weapons. Parliamentary forces obviously believed that there was support for their position among the general public, and that the army would never fire on the White House. Having appointed their own rival President, they also appointed a rival Defence Minister, Vladislav Achalov, and under the leadership of General Albert Makashov and Colonel Terekhov, the NFS and the Officers' Assembly had obviously made substantial provision for an armed uprising.

On Sunday 3 October, anti-Yeltsin demonstrators successfully pushed their way through Interior Ministry police cordons, and were urged on by a fanatical speech from Rutskoi to seize one of the offices of the Moscow mayor. They attempted to occupy the ITAR-TASS and *Novosti* press agencies, and, most importantly, they stormed the state television centre at Ostankino. Sixty-two people were killed, and a section of the Interior Ministry forces appeared to waver as Yeltsin and government leaders failed to react quickly. Deputy Prime Minister Gaidar made a courageous television appeal for support on the Sunday, but it was not clear during the course of the night that Rutskoi and Khasbulatov would be defeated. Only at 08.00 on Monday were troops and tanks loyal to Yeltsin in position around the White House. At 09.00 Yeltsin appeared on television vowing swift action to crush the 'Fascist–Communist mutiny', saying that there could be no mercy for those who had shed the blood of peaceful people. At 09.45 Yeltsin's troops stormed the Parliament building with tank and machine-gun support. An Interior Ministry official said that the first two floors of the building were quickly seized and at 09.50 Rutskoi appealed for talks with Yeltsin. Prime Minister Viktor Chernomyrdin offered to halt the attack if all the defenders gave up their weapons and came out of the building. Reports of a white flag of surrender at 10.00 caused one sector of fire to cease at 10.15, but firing continued intensively as Khasbulatov claimed he was ready for ceasefire talks, but not for surrender, at 11.20. Tanks fired incendiary shells at the thirteenth floor of the White House at 12.00, and smoke billowed out of the building, extending finally to all the remaining floors. After vainly seeking guarantees through mediation by Western ambassadors, Rutskoi and Khasbulatov surrendered with most of their supporters, and at 17.09 it was confirmed that the two leaders and several White House defenders had been captured.

At least fifty people were killed on the Monday, and hundreds were injured, some of them innocent bystanders. The local councils in Moscow were suspended that day, and on 5 October, two regional governors were sacked in a campaign to curb the powers of the regions. On 6 October press censorship was imposed on thirteen newspapers ranging from Fascist and Communist to the centre-left publication of the trade union movement, *Rabochaya Tribuna*, and the apparently independent *Glasnost*. Among the banned newspapers was the pro-parliament *Pravda*.[27] Although pre-publication censorship was lifted on 6 October, the Head of the State Office of the Media said that publications could be shut down under Emergency Regulations after one warning only. Editors were invited, but not compelled, to consult with the authorities about controversial matters. In addition, several parties and organisations were banned. The banned parties were: the Russian Party of Communists [*Russkaya Partiya Kommunistov*, RPK], the KP-RF, the Russian Communist Workers' Party [*Russkaya Kommunisticheskaya Partiya Trudyashchikhsya*, RKPT], the All-Union Communist Party of Bolsheviks [*Vsesoyuznaya Kommunisticheskaya Partiya Bolshevikov*, VKPB], *Pamyat* National-Patriotic Front [*Pamyat Natsialno-Patrioticheskii Front*,], the RNS and the NFS. Several organisations such as the Russian Officers' Union and the 'Shield' (*Shchit*) servicemen's union were also banned. The latter organisation supported military reform, and its demise suggests an attempt to eliminate all politicisation in the army. Zhirinovsky's LDPR escaped the ban, since he did not support Rutskoi and Khasbulatov.

Subsequently, the ban on the KP-RF and the Peoples' Party of Free Russia [*Narodnaya Partiya Svobodnoi Rossii*, NPSR], once led by Rutskoi, was lifted. When elections took place on 12 December, both the LDPR and the Communists (with their Agrarian allies) did well. Fanatics from the remaining banned parties such as *Pamyat* probably supported Zhirinovsky's LDPR. When Yeltsin called for elections to national and local parliaments he scrapped the Federation Council, which had hitherto been the main forum for regional leaders. Now that the central power had apparently been won, Yeltsin moved quickly to reinforce his authority in the regions. At last the terrifying process of regional fragmentation seemed to have been halted or slowed as a result of decisive measures in Moscow. Even the CIS seemed a little more robust as a result of the centralisation of power in Moscow. Georgia, riven by internal turmoil, joined the CIS on 8 October.

Accusations of 'Bolshevik'-style censorship[28] and authoritarianism have been made against Yeltsin's government, and certainly there are many dangers ahead for Russia in the new situation which obtained after 4 October. These dangers are listed briefly below.

Elections

At the time of writing, elections to many local *dumas* and a referendum on the Constitution have been held on 12 December 1993, together with elections to both houses of the national parliament. The Upper House, called the Federal Council, has 178 seats (two for each region of Russia) and the Lower House, the State Duma, has 450 seats, half of which are elected on a simple plurality system and half by proportional representation. Government ministers can stand for election. Russia's new constitution seems to owe something to the US Senate, the German *Bundestag* and the British House of Commons. The powers of the President, however, look remarkably like those of the French Fifth Republic. The self-consciously applied model may not be any one of these, but rather that of Stolypin's Third Duma elected on a restricted franchise in 1907.[29] It is interesting that the new State Duma will not meet in the ruined White House, which has been refurbished for presidential government. The new political parties included Gaidar's Russia's Choice [*Vybor Rossii*, VR], Shakhrai's Party of Russian Unity and Concord [*Partiya Russkogo Yedinstva i Soglasii*, PRYeS], Yavlinsky-Boldyrev-Lukin bloc (*Yabloko*), Travkin's Democratic Party of Russia [*Demokraticheskaya Partiya Rossii*, DPR], the Women's Party of Russia [*Zhenshchini Rossii*, ZhR], the Agrarian Party [*Agrarnaya Partiya*, AP], the KP-RF and Zhirinovsky's LDPR. Yeltsin himself refused to identify with any single party, but it seemed likely in November 1993 that the new governing coalition would be centre-right with strong media support. However, given the necessary speed in which the elections were held, and the shallow roots of all these new parties in Russian society, this outcome could not be guaranteed.

Dictatorial powers at the centre

Abuses of human rights have undoubtedly occurred, and may discredit the government, since many are certain to be detected. However, strong executive power at the centre may still be ineffective in the regions. Most importantly, the powers of the 'dictator' will not always be held by Yeltsin.

Regional dissent

As already pointed out, the regions of Russia became centrifugal during the period 1991–93. They will not easily give up their recently challenged political and economic power. A long period of struggle will weaken the State's fiscal resources and the rule of law, and may result in ungovernability. However, many recently antagonistic regions such as Novosibirsk and Chelyabinsk 'caved in' after the defeat of parliament, and some regions have voluntarily dissolved their local councils.

Loyalty of officers

It is possible that certain leading officers such as the Head of the Airforce, who supported Rutskoi, can be sacked; but it seems unlikely that Yeltsin and Grachev can dismiss every officer who supported the NFS and parliament. In December 1993, many Russian servicemen, including those who stormed the parliament on 4 October, voted overwhelmingly for Zhirinovsky.

Economic situation

This is still catastrophic, but some signs of improvement have recently appeared.[30] Yeltsin cannot now blame his opponents for failure. Even if the market reforms can still continue in 1994, the economy will deliver even lower standards of living for at least two years before any improvement can be noticed.

Political violence

Force was used to crush an important institution – parliament. The action itself was unconstitutional and technically illegal, but seemed at the time to be justified both politically and morally. However, the result has been to create an over-powerful presidential government, which might even be termed 'Tsarist', and sets an ominous precedent. Opponents who have been criminalised cannot be a 'loyal opposition'. Parts of the political oppositions in Russia may not accept the verdict of the electorate. In December 1993 the most likely candidate for Russia's dictator after 1996 is surely Zhirinovsky himself. The example of the Weimar Republic does spring to mind since it is clear that Yeltsin's new Russia will be unable to silence its internal critics and must use partially undemocratic methods to contain its anti-democratic opponents.[31]

Law and order

Much headway was made in Moscow against criminals such as some of the Caucasian street traders and illegal residents during the Emergency Regulation Period which was imposed after 4 October. Residents were asked to inform on their neighbours, an alarming reminder of a Stalinist tradition. However, one feels that the 'big' criminals will still continue to operate. Zhirinovsky's support for the police and his promise to 'crush' criminal mafias undoubtedly aided his election success.

Timetable for December 1993

Elections were held 'too soon' because Yeltsin had to capitalise rapidly on his advantage and the support of Western leaders was conditional upon timely elections. The timetable for elections and the drawing up of constituency boundaries, the formation of political parties and the adoption of candidates all occurred at breakneck speed. As a result, the outcome will always be contested by significant sections of society. Many of the international observers left Russia before the final results were announced, and the election broadcast was interrupted when it became clear that Zhirinovsky's party was gaining predominance.

Conclusion

By the end of 1994, Russia will have a new constitution and a highly centralised presidential political system. There will be many abuses of human rights, and a multi-party democracy of a genuinely democratic kind including a 'loyal opposition' is unlikely to emerge. Yeltsin himself will have to pay off political debts to the Ministries of Defense, the Interior and Security, although he can now afford to treat the regions more strictly than before. His government will be quite 'nationalist' because it will seek to steal some of the thunder from the former parliamentary opposition. The new Russian democracy will be very unlike Western models of multi-party democracy. It will probably seek to extend the influence of Russia over the CIS in both cultural and economic terms. There will be attempts to bully Western governments into denying NATO membership to Central and Eastern European countries, attempts which should be resisted for reasons outlined above. Naturally, in a democracy there can be no purges or prison camps and any press censorship can only be intermittent or partial. As Kerensky discovered in 1917, *Pravda* may not be so easily eliminated. The mental attitudes of several generations of Communism cannot be eradicated overnight, and great dangers face Russia and the world in the months and years ahead. Professor Geoffrey Hosking[32] has shown why there may be new conditions in 1993–94 which did not obtain in the previously revolutionary circumstances of 1917–18. In contrast to 1917, Russian society is not currently disturbed by chaotic class struggles and intense politicisation. On the contrary, the public now seems to be exhausted by the years of *perestroika* and the bloodletting of October 1993. Public opinion seems to blame the parliamentarians and excuses the President.[33] Russians appear to believe that the 'parliamentary experiment' has failed[34] and are now ready for a solution to the paralysis of decision-making at the centre. In establishing a new Russian Republic and a new Constitution, President Yeltsin may turn out to have been Russia's President de Gaulle.

Table 9.2 Party Representation in Russian State Duma elected Dec. 1993[35]

Name of party	Seats	Party lists	Constituencies
Russia's Choice	96	40	56
Liberal Democratic Party	70	59	11
Communist Party	65	32	33
Agrarian Party	47	21	26
Yabloko	33	20	13
Party of Russian Unity and Concord	27	18	9
Women of Russia	25	21	4
Democratic Party of Russia	21	14	7
Civic Union	18	0*	18
Other parties	12	0*	12
Independents	30	—	30
Elections declared invalid	6	—	6
total	450		

* Failed to overcome 5 per cent barrier.

However, the results of the December elections, shown in Table 9.2, suggest that Yeltsin's political gamble of October has failed.

Civic Union, led by Arkady Volsky and the Movement of Democratic Reform [*Dvizhenie Demokraticheskogo Reforma*, DDR] led by Anatoly Sobchak, failed to clear the 5 per cent hurdle. VR (Russia's Choice) is the largest single party in the State *Duma*. The electoral arithmetic suggests that unless there is an 'anti-Fascist bloc' for which Gaidar pleaded in desperation soon after the first results, President Yeltsin cannot get a stable and predictable legislative majority in the State *Duma*. Yeltsin must face an articulate parliamentary opposition from both left and right, and it is now clear from the results in the seats elected by proportional representation that at least 47 per cent voted against the market reforms while 23 per cent voted for Russian nationalism.

Under the new Constitution, passed by a small majority of those who voted, the President can form an administration whose members may, or may not, be legislators, and only the Prime Minister needs to be approved. Obviously Zhirinovsky and his party will be in opposition. However, he can form an 'alternative' government or shadow cabinet which will be able to criticise Yeltsin's government systematically from a position outside administrative responsibility. Assuming that Yeltsin will continue with the reforms with a slightly altered ministerial line-up, he can continue to govern under the new constitution, but *Duma* opposition and obstruction will be as persistent as it was during the time of the former Congress of Peoples' Deputies. In early 1994, the State *Duma* pardoned the 'criminals' of October 1993, including Rutskoi. Andrei Kozyrev and Anatoliy Chubais (Minister in charge of Privatisation) will be attacked constantly, if they are reappointed. Moreover, Zhirinovsky's party in the *Duma* now has much greater legitimacy than the deputies of the former Congress. It seems inevitable that policies articulated by Zhirinovsky will be followed in modified form by Yeltsin's government after 1994. Russia will be more assertive in the 'near abroad', such as Ukraine, Moldova and the Baltic states. Economic reforms will be slowed down and inflation is likely to spiral out of control.

How may we interpret these astonishing results? Clearly, the democrats were punished for their disunity. Opposition to market reforms was underestimated by the political class, so that democrats could indulge their differences in the belief that the case for a market economy had already been won. Political ambition among the democrats also played its part to the detriment of political unity. President Yeltsin did not endorse VR and stayed 'above' party politics in much the same way as President Hindenburg stayed above party politics in Germany in 1930. A certain contempt for the Russian working class and peasantry, who were living in an exclusively rouble economy, rendered the democrats' campaign ineffective, while Zhirinovsky's homely posters and electoral style seemed to speak more directly to the people. Affluent Westernisation and the influence of foreign advisers created complacency among democrats.

However, it cannot be proved that the 20–25 per cent of the Russian electorate who voted for Zhirinovsky agreed with his crazy plans for geo-political expansionism as outlined in his political tract *The Last Leap South*. A single extract from this semi-autobiographical text will serve to prove the point. According to Zhirinovsky, 'The last leap south, the arrival of Russia on the shores of the Indian Ocean and of the

Mediterranean – these really are the goals necessary to save the Russian nation.'[36] It is almost certain that Russian voters were given a selective slant on Zhirinovsky's programme, and were also partly entertained by his jokey television style. Nevertheless, LDPR propaganda did evoke a response from those sectors of the population for whom economic reform has been painful and to whom VR promised more blood and tears in the future. Economic humiliation has been compounded by the political humiliation of Russia itself and the constant retreat from empire in recent years. A protest vote is not yet a vote for Fascism. An interesting article by Vladimir Prokhvatilov claims that Russians voted less for Fascism and more for 'goulashism'.[37] Just as the population wanted to believe Khrushchev's promises of 'goulash Communism' in his Party Programme of 1961, so they had wanted to believe Yeltsin's promises of 'goulash capitalism' in 1992. Now the same wilful delusions had prompted the people to believe in 'goulash nationalism'. Russians have significantly preferred comforting, self-assertive lies to the harsh and self-denying truth about the inevitability of market reform. In so doing they have in one sense exercised their democratic right. The Russian people should perhaps note that in the event of a new State Committee for the State of Emergency, Zhirinovsky urges them to stay at home and not to protest.[38]

At the close of the twentieth century, a shadow hangs over Russia and its neighbours. It is the unmistakable shadow of Fascism and the threat of war. Modern communications may yet expose Zhirinovsky and his followers, this effectively eliminating his chances for the Presidency in 1996 or before. Yeltsin may still succeed in putting together a governing cabinet of ministers which can work intermittently with the State *Duma*. However, it is clear that Washington, the European Union, NATO and the Western European Union must now begin an urgent and thorough review of all previous policies with respect to Russia and the former Soviet Union. The intellectual history of Russian nationalism has yielded a bitter harvest in modern times. Before the 1917 revolutions, Russian Fascists called 'black hundreds' carried out pogroms and supported imperialist policies. In the 1990s, 'black hundredism' and nationalist revanchism have dramatically erupted into the body politic of the new Russia, and could develop into Fascism. Such an outcome would inevitably threaten the peace and stability of the entire world.

List of abbreviations

AP	*Agrarnaya Partiya* [Agrarian Party]
DDR	*Dvizhenie Demokraticheskogo Reforma* [Movement for Democratic Reform]
DPR	*Demokraticheskaya Partiya Rossii* [Democratic Party of Russia]
KDP	*Konstitutsionnaya Demokraticheskaya Partiya* [Constitutional Democratic Party]
KP-RF	*Kommunisticheskaya Partiya Russkoi Federatsii* [Communist Party of the Russian Federation]
KPSS	*Kommunisticheskaya Partiya Sovetskogo Soyuza* [Communist Party of the Soviet Union]

LDPR	*Liberalno-Demokraticheskaya Partiya Rossii* [Liberal Democratic Party of Russia]
NFS	*Narodnyi Front Spaseniya* [National Salvation Front]
NPSR	*Narodnaya Partiya Svobodnoi Rossii* [Peoples' Party of Free Russia]
PRYeS	*Partiya Russkogo Yedinstva i Soglasii* [Party of Russian Unity and Concord]
RKDD	*Russkoe Kristianskoe Demokraticheskoe Dvizhenie* [Russian Christian Democratic Movement]
RKPT	*Russkaya Kommunisticheskaya Partiya Trudyashchikhsya* [Russian Communist Workers' Party]
RNS	*Russkoe Narodnoe Sobranie* [Russian National Council]
RPK	*Russkaya Partiya Kommunistov* [Russian Party of Communists]
SNG	*Sodruzhestvo Nezavisimikh Gosudarstv* [Commonwealth of Independent States]
VKPB	*Vsesoyuznaya Kommunisticheskaya Partiya Bolshevikov* [All-Union Communist Party of Bolsheviks]
VR	*Vybor Rossii* [Russian's Choice]
ZhR	*Zhenshchini Rossii* [Women's Party of Russia]

Notes

1. *Radio Free Europe/Radio Liberty Research Report*, II, No. 1, 1993, p. 37.
2. Ibid., p. 45.
3. *Times Literary Supplement*, 13 March 1992, p. 10.
4. *The Independent*, 12 Jan. 1993, p. 17.
5. *RFE/RL Research Report*, cit., p. 47.
6. *Pravda*, 27 April 1993, p. 3.
7. *RFE/RL Research Report*, II, No. 21, 1993, p. 12.
8. *Izvestiya*, 24 April 1993, p. 2.
9. *The European*, 29 April–2 May 1993, p. 8.
10. *The Economist*, 30 Jan. 1993, p. 41.
11. *RFE/RL Research Report*, II, No. 20, 1993, pp. 16–25.
12. 'Perestroika and the Ethnic Consciousness of Russians', in G. Lapidus, V. Zaslavsky and P. Goldman (eds), *From Union to Commonwealth*, Cambridge University Press, Cambridge, 1992, pp. 98–113.
13. Ibid., p. 101.
14. Ibid., p. 102.
15. Ibid., p. 110.
16. Ibid., p. 111.
17. *RFE/RL Research Report*, I, No. 49, 1992, pp. 1–9.
18. L. Shevtsova, in Y. Afanasiev (ed.) *God posle avgusta, gorech i vybor.* [A year after August, Grief and Choice.], Politizdat, Moscow, 1992, p. 121.
19. *Ekho Moskvy*, 14 Oct. 1992, p. 4.
20. *RFE/RL Research Report*, I, No. 49, 1992, pp. 10–16.
21. *Sovetskaya Rossiya*, 12 July 1992, pp. 2–3.
22. W. Laqueur, *Russia and Germany: A Century of Conflict*, Transaction Publishers, New Brunswick, 1990, p. 27.

23. *RFE/RL Research Report*, II, No. 20, 1993, p. 46.
24. Ibid., p. 81.
25. Ibid., p. 84.
26. Ibid., p. 68.
27. *Nezavisimaya Gazeta*, 6 Oct. 1993, p. 2. The publications banned by the Ministry of Information were *Den, Glasnost, Krasnaya Presnya, Molniya, Nasha Rossiya, Pravda, Puls Tushina, Put, Rabochaya Tribuna, Russkoe Voskresenie, Russky Vestnik, Sovetskaya Rossiya* and *Soyuz Offitserov.*
28. *Izvestiya*, 6 Oct. 1993, p. 3.
29. *Nezavisimaya Gazeta*, 6 Oct. 1993, p. 2.
30. *The Economist*, 16 Oct. 1993, p. 50.
31. *The Independent*, 5 Oct. 1993, p. 3.
32. Ibid., p. 17.
33. *Rossiiskie Vesti*, 6 Oct. 1993. p. 1. 71 per cent trusted Yeltsin and Chernomyrdin, while 4 per cent trusted Khasbulatov and Rutskoi. (19 per cent trusted neither, while 5 per cent abstained.)
34. *Nezavisimaya Gazeta*, 5 Oct. 1993, p. 1.
35. *RFE/RL Research Report*, III, No. 2, 1994, p. 3.
36. V. Zhirinovsky, *Poslednyi Brosok na Yug* [The Last Leap South], Liberalno-Demokraticheskaya, Moscow, 1993, p. 3.
37. *Vek*, No. 49. 17–23 Dec. 1993, p. 3.
38. V. Zhirinovsky, *Liberal*, No. 10, 1993, p. 2.

Chapter 10

THE NEW RIGHT IN POLAND: NATIONALISM, ANTI-SEMITISM AND PARLIAMENTARIANISM
Anita J. Prazmowska

The upheavals of recent Polish history are reflected in the story of Polish nationalist and extreme right-wing movements, though frequently in unexpected ways. Discontinuity rather than continuity seems to characterise the course of the movements' most recent development. This is most starkly exemplified by the case of Bolesław Piasecki. He led the Polish *Falanga* – the pre-war Polish Fascist movement which appeared during the early 1930s – and subsequently headed the government-approved Catholic group *Pax* under Communist rule. As a result of this amazing *volte face*, neither the organisation which he led in the 1930s, nor he himself, have provided models for the new nationalist and neo-Fascist groups which emerged after the collapse of Communism. On the other hand, Józef Piłsudski, who staged a *coup d'état* in 1926 and afterwards implemented policies of national unity, had achieved a reduction in the effectiveness and popularity of right and centre parties. Yet in the 1990s Piłsudski became a role model for the best organised and most effective right-wing parliamentary party in present-day Poland, the Confederation of Independent Poland [*Konfederacja Polski Niepodłeglej* – KPN].

While thirty-five years of dictatorial Communist rule help account for that discontinuity and confusion, the meaning of right-wing and nationalist concepts has also changed in recent years. Immediately after the collapse of the Communist regime, and with the return to pluralist politics, the hitherto united opposition union *Solidarność* (Solidarity) gradually diversified into distinct parties and political organisations. Since the only common feature shared by the disparate social, political and professional groups which formed the *Solidarność* movement of the 1980s was opposition to the corruption of the Communist governments, the end of that regime led to the piecemeal emergence of more definite political objectives and, with it, of distinct political organisations. In the formative years of the 1980s and prior to the first free elections in 1991, nationalism was a common feature of all new parties. Nor was anti-Semitism confined to the extreme right wing.

In 1989 when it became possible for parties to register with the district court in Warsaw, a process which led to their legislation, 160 did so. After the October 1991 elections, twenty-nine parties obtained sufficient numbers of votes to secure representation in the Lower House, the *Sejm*. Such a proliferation of political parties did

not necessarily reflect genuine political diversity. Regional loyalties, shared professional experiences, doctrinaire divisions within *Solidarność* and personal loyalties
accounted for the establishment of so many separate organisations. Party political
programmes forged and publicised in the post-Communist Poland reflected an attempt to understand the political and economic failure of the past period as much as
a search for solutions to the difficulties experienced in the 1990s. Not surprisingly in
these circumstances, parties which participated in the 1991 elections focused on
patriotism, on the guilt of those who had cooperated with the previous regime, and
on Poland's capacity for economic reconstruction without assistance from historic
enemies – Germany and the Soviet Union. It was generally believed that parties would
have to persuade the electorate of their nationalism and of their determination to
defend the interests of the nation. Few parties – if any – were able to avoid using
nationalist and xenophobic slogans during the political battles of this time. In those
arguments the experiences of the inter-war period provided few useful solutions,
although they could be used as potent symbols, where necessary, to prove a given
party's commitment to national issues. The politically turbulent period of the 1920s
and 1930s offered easily recognisable names, even if their context was never fully
analysed. Those most frequently referred to and used by right-wing parties and
organisations were Roman Dmowski and Józef Piłsudski.

By the end of 1991 and the beginning of 1992, the small nationalist and neo-Fascist
parties and groups which had emerged earlier either vanished from the public eye or
became so insignificant that even their occasional publications were nearly impossible
to obtain outside their narrow circle of sympathisers. The Polish electorate was
becoming more sophisticated and clearly demanded from political parties more than
a commitment to the defence of national interests, in the narrowest meaning of the
phrase. In 1992 the debate shifted from fighting old battles, be it against the Russians,
the Germans or the Jews, to analysing the role of the World Bank and the European
Bank for Reconstruction and Development in helping to solve Poland's economic
problems. In common with other parties, nationalist and extreme right-wing parties
had to discuss the process of privatisation and emotive issues such as pension rights
and the role of the Church in the social and cultural life of the nation.

The inter-war years

The emergence of a new Polish state in 1919 dramatically changed the political debates
which had hitherto been taking place in Polish territories. The issue which had
previously dominated the programmes of all Polish parties and clandestine organisations was the right of Poles to have an independent state. Within each of the three
areas of partitioned Poland, a certain degree of integration had taken place with the
political parties of the partitioning state. Specifically Polish preoccupations were
viewed in the context of the issues facing the big empires. The autonomy of the Poles
within the Austro-Hungarian empire was a problem which related to the debate on
the nature of that empire. The emergence and the survival of a Polish socialist
movement in the German and Russian empires were historic developments which
forced the Poles to address themselves to the political systems of those empires and to

their relations with the respective socialist movements. Once Poland became independent, the problems of the ex-partitioning powers were no longer a factor in Polish
politics. Debates and, inevitably, also political programmes narrowed down and
focused on Poland. New ideologies emerged, and all already established parties had
to rethink their ideas. Thus most political debates in present-day Poland go back no
further than 1919, even if the years under partition act as a strong emotional factor
in stimulating nationalism.

The basic principles of Polish right-wing and nationalist ideologies had evolved
during the inter-war period. These had been honed during the search for a Polish role
in European politics. Ensuing economic and political instability created a fertile
ground for the proliferation of debates on the subject of Poland's internal and external
enemies. Not surprisingly, therefore, it was during the 1930s that these movements
captured the headlines and the attention of the people with simple solutions and
emotive appeals to unity in the face of perceived threats. In the 1990s the debates of
the 1930s acquired a new meaning. Present-day nationalists chose their symbols
selectively and with little regard for historic veracity. Roman Dmowski's nationalist
ideology, which strongly attacked the role of Germany in inter-war European politics,
and Józef Piłsudski who, epitomised strong executive control over weak and indecisive
parliamentarians, head the pantheon of past leaders much admired by present-day
right-wing and nationalist politicians. Notwithstanding frequent references to these
two men by contemporary leaders, present-day nationalists do not, in reality, seek
either to understand or develop further the ideologies of the inter-war period. They
merely use them to flag their own allegiance to what they perceive to be the key
achievements of the largely glorified recent past.

In the pantheon of past leaders, the most difficult one for Poles to come to terms
with is Bolesław Piasecki. His formative early years coincided with the political
disorientation caused by the Piłsudski coup in 1926. The nationalist right was confused
by his success and by the apparent popular support for this attack on the state. Support
for it was drained by the subsequent government's use of basic chauvinistic slogans
and by its successful appeal to national unity. Nevertheless the economic difficulties
of 1931 affected the middle class and déclassé intelligentsia, creating a ready pool of
support for more extreme movements. Warsaw University, where Piasecki enrolled
for a law course, was known as a centre of nationalist movements. There he joined
the Camp of Radical Nationalism [*Obóz Narodowo-Radykalny*, ONR]. In 1934 he led
an attempt to consolidate and rebuild the movement, initiated by the publication of
a strident new programme. The basic assumption of the ONR was that Polish state
and society were undergoing a crisis and were in need of rebuilding their institutions
and defining their objectives. The ONR economic programme was anti-capitalist. It
supported the nationalisation of industry and land reform as a means of securing the
control of land and Polish economic resources for the nation. According to this
programme, the new Polish state would, at last, represent the interests of Poles and of
some Slav minorities. Jews would be stripped of Polish nationality, and the ultimate
objective would be to exclude Jewish communities from Polish life. The role of the
state would be to represent the interests of the Polish nation. In pursuit of these
objectives, it would be granted extensive rights to govern on its behalf.[1] A few months
after the publication of the programme, the government used extensive emergency

laws, introduced after the Minister for the Interior had been assassinated by a Ukrainian nationalist, to imprison political prisoners without trial. Piasecki was arrested and interned at the notorious internment camp at Bereza.[2] On being released a few months later, Piasecki headed a break-away group of the ONR, naming it the *Falanga*.

In 1935 the *Falanga* launched a political offensive to mobilise youth and to prepare for a take-over. Piasecki had modelled himself on the Italian Fascist example, therefore considerable emphasis was put on posturing in uniforms and on violent attacks against perceived enemies, mostly Jews. Among the most notorious achievements of the *Falanga* were instigating the boycott of Jewish trade and creating 'ghetto' benches for Jewish students in the lecture rooms of the University of Warsaw.

Piasecki did not become a Polish 'Quisling' after the German occupation of Poland in September 1939, although he was not unwilling to cooperate with the Nazis. During the first weeks of occupation, tentative contacts had been established between him and some German officers. Nevertheless, in the absence of instructions from Berlin, these initial probings proceeded no further.

After the war Piasecki collaborated with the Communist regime in establishing a Catholic organisation which was loosely called *Pax*. Although the ideology and the actions of the *Falanga* still meet with approval from within certain sections of the nationalist movements, Piasecki's obvious opportunism after the war makes it impossible now for any party or organisation to claim affinity with his movement. His name and his ideological statements are never referred to. Instead, personalities who were less successful in organising the extreme right are cited by the contemporary right as their role models. However, the *Falanga*'s political programme is clearly one which most nationalist movements take as a model.

Roman Dmowski was one of the key ideologists of the Polish right and nationalist camp during the inter-war period. His formative political experiences had been in the Polish Congress Kingdom of the Russian Empire. As a result of these, he held the firm conviction that Poland should establish itself as a leading Slav state. His 'nationalist democratic' ideas were based on the conviction that democratic principles had weakened the Polish state in the eighteenth century and were thus directly responsible for its fall.[3] He therefore took the view that the role of the state was to represent the interests of the nation, and not of its citizens. Anti-Semitism was the logical corollary of these ideas. In that context he viewed 'Jewish influence' as cosmopolitan and anti-Polish.[4] An exception among the leading Polish ideologists of the time, Dmowski believed that Poland's historic enemy was Germany rather than Russia.

During the inter-war period Dmowski was a relatively insignificant political personality. He nevertheless remained the leader of the right-wing National Democratic Movement (*Narodowa Demokracja*, ND). Dmowski's party was the biggest loser after the May 1926 coup. Its leadership was bewildered by Piłsudski's unwillingness to share power.[5] In due course the landowners' and bourgeois vote moved away from the National Democrats and to the Piłsudski camp. This was caused by fear of Communism and social upheavals, but also by the regime's apparent ability to come to grips with the economic and political instability that had characterised the newly independent state. The fact that the Piłsudski regime was willing to forge mutually advantageous alliances and to make compromises with these powerful social groups, namely the landowners and industrialists, increased its hold over political life in Poland.

Dmowski nevertheless remained an important ideologist and spokesman of the right throughout the inter-war period. His ideas evolved towards identifying the Jews as the biggest threat to the newly independent Poland. In the early 1920s he seemed to show no interest in current political developments, dismissing parliamentary activities as irrelevant in view of the impending conflict between the Slav and Jewish races.[6]

Dmowski, though impressed by the achievements of the Italian Fascists and German Nazis, was loath to approve action on the streets. Nor did he seek a head-on confrontation with the Piłsudski regime, which was increasingly known as the *Sanacja* (moral renewal). As a result of this, the youth sections of the ND camp broke away in 1934 to form their own quasi-Fascist groups, over which the ND leadership had no control.[7] By the time of his death in January 1939, Dmowski's key achievement was acknowledged to have been formulating a nationalist ideology rather than leading the National Democrats to recovery.

In contemporary Polish history the person who epitomises the rule of a strong man, a patriot and father of the nation, who in his concerns was supposedly above the divisive preoccupations of parliamentary politics, is Josef Piłsudski. He would never have identified directly with any of the Fascist movements in Europe, though similarities do exist between some of the policies of his regime and the political programme of any European Fascist party. Paradoxically, though, his regime was identified with extreme nationalist policies and with the gradual destruction of parliamentary democracy. Neither Piłsudski nor the coterie which succeeded him would admit to these aims. The defence of national interests against the petty concerns of corrupt and unpatriotic parliamentarians was their avowed objective. Nevertheless, in order to achieve social and political stability, emergency laws were implemented. By these means political opposition, both left and right, was destroyed. In due course, laws limiting the rights of national minorities were introduced. This process was completed when in 1935 the Constitution was amended to strengthen the executive at the expense of the legislature. Henceforth the *Sejm* became irrelevant, and individual ministries, increasingly staffed by ex-military men, were run like private fiefdoms. This removed the pretence of democracy and replaced it with a veneer of unity and national salvation. Yet Piłsudski's regime cannot be classified as a Fascist one. It was essentially a military dictatorship. The illusion of government by a strong apolitical patriot, an image carefully cultivated after Piłsudski's death in 1935, seemed to suggest national consensus as a means of overcoming divisions, and the forging for Poland of a new role in Europe.

Piłsudski was, to a large extent, responsible himself for creating the myth of his apolitical, paternalistic attitude towards Polish politics. He considered the constitution of 1921 to have been wrong in so far as it had, as he believed, allowed the narrow sectional interests of petty politicians to stand in the way of national progress. He was, nevertheless, initially reluctant to launch a direct attack on democratic institutions and left the task of implementing constitutional changes to his subordinates. In 1921 and in 1935, when a first Polish constitution was approved and then when it was amended, he claimed to have had no interest in these matters. In reality he intensely disliked the 1921 Constitution which gave the *Sejm* the right to restrict presidential prerogatives.[8] After the 1926 *coup d'état* Piłsudski did not state openly that he wished to see the *Sejm*'s role curtailed. Nevertheless its functioning was restricted and disrupted by the activities of officers who clearly intended to discredit the politicians.[9] The regime turned a blind eye to officers intimidating deputies and disrupting the deliberations of the *Sejm*. Piłsudski was known to speak of the *Sejm* in pejorative terms, which led to suspicions that he had instigated these actions.

Since he did not formulate a clear political programme, nor openly state that he wished to see the destruction of democracy, Piłsudski can be seen as a patriot, only too willing to be called to the helm at a time of trouble. A carefully cultivated portrait of the Supreme Commander, shrouded in the myth of the victorious leader of the Polish defence against Bolshevism in the Polish–Soviet war in 1921, benefited the regime's objectives of undermining its opponents, who could thus be portrayed as narrow, corrupt and unpatriotic. Behind the scenes efforts were pursued to secure popular support without necessarily destroying the illusion of democracy. In 1927 Piłsudski approved the creation of a ruling party Non-Party Bloc of Cooperation with the Government [*Bezpartyjny Blok Współpracy z Rządem*, BBWR]. Ostensibly apolitical and intended to represent the interests of the nation, it was in reality a vehicle for retaining control of the institutions of power.[10] In 1937 General Śmigły-Rydz tried to resurrect the spirit of the Piłsudski era by creating the Camp of National Unity [*Obóz Zjednoczenia Narodowego*, OZN]. This organisation was supposed to re-establish links between the nation and the military authorities, while reinforcing the importance of the latter in Polish life. In reality it was no more than a vehicle for Śmigły-Rydz in his battles with his opponents within the ranks of the *Sanacja*. Thus all efforts made by Piłsudski's followers and successors to formulate an ideology were no more than attempts to legitimise the military's interference with civilian life. National unity, discipline and obedience were all invoked to justify political control and the continuing suppression of democratic rights.[11]

To those who in later years looked to the Piłsudski legend and to those who wanted to invoke for their own purpose the so-called heroic days of past unity, Poland's foreign policy appears to offer easy examples of lost greatness. The fact that both Piłsudski and his successors set Poland on an independent course and challenged French tutelage by re-establishing Polish–German relations, gives an easily comprehensible, if not entirely correct, impression that they were true patriots. The 1930s are thus seen as a time of international greatness, destroyed by German–Soviet military cooperation in 1939. The failure of the British and French governments to assist Poland directly only heightens the feeling that Piłsudski was a visionary who steered Poland towards recognition of its status as a 'Great European Power'.

Although Piłsudski did not take up the Jewish theme, his own ideas on the national issue were fairly conventional in so far as he believed that the state's role should be to pursue a policy of integration and assimilation of national minorities into Polish life. He does not appear to have displayed or formulated anti-Semitic views, although his government was, from the outset, associated with extremely brutal and arbitrary action against the Ukrainian population.[12]

Contemporary politics

During the period of Nazi occupation, Polish nationalist and right-wing parties and Fascist movements were granted no privileges or immunity by the German authorities. Their members were imprisoned and were as likely to be victims of arbitrary brutality as the whole of the Polish population. No attempt was made by the Nazi occupation forces to create a Polish administration. The defeat of the Nazis became the overriding objective of all opposition movements, and this facilitated the creation of the broadly based Home Army [*Armia Krajowa*, AK] which was loyal to the Polish government in exile. On the right of the Home Army were the National Armed Forces [*Narodowe Siły Zbrojne*, NSZ], whose ideology was anti-Nazi but also anti-Communist. In spite of the tragedy which befell the Jewish community, the NSZ continued to support anti-Semitic policies and were subsequently accused of having waged a fratricidal war against Communists and against Russian partisan units. The subject of the NSZ has been inadequately researched and remains a contentious issue because of suspicions that its members had been willing to reveal the whereabouts of Jews and political opponents to the Nazis.

The establishment of Communism in Poland created an entirely new situation. By 1948 all independent political organisations ceased to exist. Those which had not been forcibly disbanded were broken up and incorporated into the Communist movement. In December 1948 the Polish Workers Party [*Polska Partia Robotnicza*, PPR] absorbed remaining sections of the Polish Socialist Party [*Polska Partia Socialistyczna*, PPS] and formed the United Workers Party [*Polska Zjednoczona Partia Robotnicza*, PZPR]. This marked the beginning of a one-party state which survived until 1991.

Lacking mass appeal and fully aware of their inability to establish either a democratically elected Communist authority or a Communist-dominated genuine Popular Front government, the Polish Communists were obliged to espouse patriotic slogans. In 1945 the security of Poland's western frontiers was already emphasised, and it was repeated that its inviolability could only be guaranteed by the Red Army. In pursuit of popularity and legitimacy, the Communist regime, from the outset made use of nationalist slogans. Since public discussion of such issues was not permitted and the existence of politically diverse organisations was not tolerated, all open political debates were conducted only within the ranks of the PZPR. The result was that within the PZPR complex political battles continued to be fought. Extreme nationalist and anti-Semitic slogans, which in genuinely democratic societies would be associated with the extreme right of the political spectrum, were represented within the PZPR. These ideas were also used to attack opponents and to justify complex internal blood-lettings. This was particularly the case in 1968, though anti-Semitic views were apparent both before and after that date.

The purging of the Party and the attacks on prominent Jewish and other intellectuals which started in the spring of 1968 had all the characteristics of a neo-Fascist campaign, though it was led by the Communist Party. Its origins were complex. In the Arab–Israeli conflict of 1967 the Polish state sided with the Arab cause. Thus Jewish origins became easily associated with treason, or at least with potentially divided loyalties. In March 1968 a conflict between the artistic milieu of Warsaw and the authorities over increased censorship appeared to coincide with the emergence of a radical intellectual critique of the government and of its economic policy from within the University of Warsaw. The response of the authorities was to launch a full-scale attack on intellectuals.[13] What followed had both the appearance and the reality of an extreme right backlash. Leading personalities within the party conducted the attack on intellectuals, supposedly in the name of the workers and peasants. The media world in general and prominent personalities within the cultural life of the country were accused of having 'Zionist sympathies' – a cryptic but obvious reference to their Jewishness. Within the Central Committee of the Party, where the First Secretary Władysław Gomułka put up a feeble resistance to their campaign, Andrzej Werblan and Mieczysław Moczar attacked the Jews for having supposedly distorted the course of the party's progress in the early 1950s.[14] It was hinted that they had in some way acted against the interests of the nation. Moczar became particularly notorious for rabble-rousing speeches to the Association of Veterans and for a book, later turned into a film, which presented the establishment of Communism in Poland as the achievement of Polish patriots. Thus a distinction was being made between Jews and full-blooded Poles. Edward Gierek, the First Secretary of the Silesian district party organisation, pointed to the loyalty and patriotism of the Silesian miners in contrast to the opportunistic and unpatriotic intellectuals of Warsaw.

The result of the campaign, which rumbled on for a whole year, was that numerous Jews were stripped of their party membership, while those who were in the army, government employment, teaching and the media lost their jobs. Most were hounded out of Poland. The purge also affected non-Jews within and outside the party. The realignment which took place within the party apparatus was accompanied by an attempt to establish firmer control over all aspects of life in Poland. In particular, education was singled out as a means of affecting the composition of future professional elites. During the next year, reforms were introduced to enable children from working-class backgrounds and from the countryside to enter universities in larger numbers. In order to ensure that students did not develop contempt for manual labour, a period of compulsory mobilisation for male students was introduced.

In the late 1970s and early 1980s a vocal group was once more active within the closed ranks of the party. This was the *Grunwald* association, which espoused patriotic slogans and made virulently anti-Semitic statements. Though never influential, this group showed that the Communist party was able to accommodate within its ranks people who clung to such ideas.

The disintegration of the Communist regime and the granting of the right to form political associations made it possible for parties and groups to emerge under their own banners and with their own political programmes. Under Communist party rule the conventional meaning of the phrases 'left-wing' and 'right-wing' had been lost. It took a few years before organisations evolved their own structures and appealed to supporters on the basis of clear programmes. In the early 1990s radical and reactionary parties shared certain features and appeared to have objectives in common. The defence of the interests of the nation and support for the national economy were principles on which all agreed. Anxiety about the loss of national identity was also emphasised. Fears were expressed that the influence of the World Bank and of the European Union would in some way lead to the nation's dissolution, and to the loss of its economic, cultural and social wealth.

No party openly advocated secular policies. Topics like abortion and religious education in schools tended to offer opportunities for consensus rather than for politically motivated dissent. Support for the principles of parliamentary democracy and for political pluralism was accepted by all. What divided those parties which genuinely wanted to work within such a society from those who chose to speak of circumstances when they might have to put pressure on the (democratic) authorities, was the degree to which democratic principles were presented as vital, rather than conditional upon circumstances. Hence the terms 'nationalist' and 'neo-Fascist' have to be applied judiciously in contemporary Poland.

At the end of the 1980s a number of nationalist parties and organisations had appeared in Poland. By 1991 at least six had established themselves, advertising their existence by publishing their own newsletters. Yet they appeared unstable and lacked any coordinated policy. Within the next year some became notorious while others merely survived. None was able to obtain seats in the *Sejm*. Most of these organisations were dominated by distinctive personalities. Most nationalist parties harked back to the political thinking of Dmowski. Their political allegiance was signalled by the use of the word 'National' in their names, for example, the National Front, National Front 'Fatherland' Party, National Democracy, National-Democratic Front, Democratic-National Front.[15]

The National Front 'Fatherland' Party [*Stronnictwo Narodowe 'Ojczyzna'*, SN] is probably the most durable and best organised of the nationalist parties which derive their ideology from Dmowski. Its weekly newspaper *Ojczyzna* (The Fatherland) first appeared in March 1990, but by the summer of 1993 it had become a fortnightly with a clearly scaled-down format. Its staff openly admitted to the author that financial problems were the cause of the party reducing its activities. Whereas in 1991 the party produced leaflets to tackle the most recent economic scandals and grievances, thus giving the appearance of an organisation which was defending the interests of Polish people, by 1993 it was unable to prepare literature for the forthcoming elections.

At first, the nationalist parties tried to form a broad nationalist bloc, but to no avail. The most obvious failure of the nationalist movements to close ranks occurred during the elections of September 1993. In the run-up, they disagreed publicly and as a result failed to secure any seats in the *Sejm*. The SN initially concentrated on exposing the continuing historic German menace to the Polish nation. Its publications frequently raised the subject of what poses a threat to Poland. Dangers were identified as the loss of national identity, economic buyouts, nihilism and cultural demoralisation, cosmopolitanism and, finally, German and Jewish capital.[16] In 1990–91 the German threat was continuously referred to as the main one, but the perceived Jewish threat was discussed with equal prominence.

The SN suggested that the changes in property rights approved by the Bielecki government had enabled Jews and Germans to purchase Polish land and real estate. This was described as a failure of the government to be vigilant and thus a betrayal of national interests. The real and imagined Jewish and German wealth which would be used by both communities against Polish national interests was discussed extensively by the SN and its supporters.

The SN attitude towards the Catholic Church is fraught with ambiguities. The general view seems to be that the Church's identification with Polish nationalist causes is to be expected. Catholic organisations or individual priests suggesting a less dogmatic interpretation of the Church's role are viciously attacked. Maximilian Kolbe, the Polish priest who died in a German concentration camp and who was subsequently beatified by Pope John Paul II, is frequently quoted by the nationalists. His pronounced anti-Semitic views are cited to support the nationalist assertion that the role of the Church and of the state is to defend the nation and its interests against the Jews.[17]

The economic policy of the SN is defined as the defence of the nation's well-being. It is described as being neither in support of capitalism nor of socialism, but subservient to the needs of the Polish nation.[18] While a slow policy of privatisation is accepted as a necessity, protecting the welfare of peasants and workers is considered a priority. Unemployment is attacked as the main evil of modern society. The nationalists have also espoused green issues, suggesting that a healthy nation should live in harmony with nature.

The lack of unity between the nationalist and neo-Fascist organisations in Poland was the key source of their weakness during the 1993 elections. Under the new electoral law, individual parties needed to secure 5 per cent of the vote in order to gain parliamentary seats. If they formed electoral coalitions, they were required to poll 8 per cent of the total vote. During the run-up to the October elections the SN formed such a coalition with the Party of Polish Pensioners and a faction of the old Peasant Party. Both parties were small and insignificant with a very low public profile. Union with Bolesław Tejkowski's neo-Fascist party does not seem to have been considered. Most damaging to the nationalist and right-wing cause was the unwillingness of the Confederation of Independent Poland [*Konfederacja Polski Niepodległej*, KPN] to enter into electoral pacts with the nationalists.

Had the KPN been willing to act as a lynch-pin of the right-wing movement, it would undoubtedly have been successful. The reality is that ideological differences between the disparate nationalist movements and the KPN are too serious to be overcome. The KPN leader Leszek Moczulski has modelled himself on Piłsudski and his objective is a regime which would resemble the pre-war Polish government. He and his followers are committed to democracy and to upholding its institutions, though they would have wanted to see a strong presidency. Moczulski makes no bones about the fact that he believes that the President should have a strong political base in society, independent of the *Sejm*.[19] The KPN uses the term 'national interests' to describe the role of the state, though it is noticeable that in principle it is committed to respecting individual liberties and that there is little emphasis on national questions in its programme.

The KPN, as a Piłsudski-ite party, has shunned close association with the nationalist parties. It has had considerable success in attracting the blue-collar vote and that of various veteran organisations and associations. There has been a notable willingness of Moczulski's part to engage in demagogic street politics. There have been well-publicised blockades of roads in which the KPN strove to prove its military preparedness in a way reminiscent of the Piłsudski legionnaires of the 1920s. The organisation's headquarters in a very prominent crossroads of Nowy Swiat and Aleje Jerozolimskie in Warsaw have been the centre of intra-party brawls and displays of strength. In most cases the government security forces seemed reluctant to interfere.

The result of these has been that the KPN is, not entirely rightly, perceived to be a party of the disaffected.

In spite of this, the KPN's biggest successes have been in parliamentary politics, which accounts for its reluctance to enter into electoral agreements with extreme nationalist movements. During the 1991 elections the KPN secured 7 per cent of the vote and obtained forty-six seats. The party's leader confidently spoke of increasing the KPN's vote to over 60 per cent. He had pinned his hopes on a centre-right coalition, in which the KPN would capture the right-wing vote. As it turned out, his predictions were incorrect, as the KPN, which refused to enter into electoral pacts with any party, was barely able to secure the minimum required 5 per cent vote, and thus reduced its parliamentary representation to twenty-two deputies. These manoeuvres had prevented the nationalist parties from entering the *Sejm*. Unable to obtain sufficient votes on their own, they had pinned their hopes on electoral pacts which would have enabled them to do so on the KPN's tailcoats. After the elections in September 1993, the SN bitterly denounced the KPN, calling it somewhat inelegantly, 'A cow which lows a lot, but gives little milk.'

As a result of the September 1993 elections, the right-wing as well as the nationalist parties have been routed. Analysts of the election results suggested that there was considerable popular support for slowing down the process of privatisation, for greater state involvement in the economy and for financial restructuring of peasants' debt burden. Paradoxically, these were policies advocated by the nationalists, the right-wing and the left-wing parties. In the event, the electorate supported the ex-Communist left rather than the nationalist groupings. In a post-election reappraisal, the prominent weekly paper *Polityka* pointed out that the characteristic feature of the nationalist and right-wing movements of the inter-war period was a determination to forge unity. Thus the successive government parties, the BBWR and OZN, both tried to draw the *Falanga* and the National Democrats into alliances. Contemporary right-wing parties and nationalists moved in the opposite direction. On the eve of the 1993 elections they went to great lengths to cut the ground from under each other's feet and, as a result, failed to make an impact.[20]

The nationalist movement will continue as an extra-parliamentary force, though in all probability not one of much consequence. Its main weaknesses seem to be the lack of an ideology and, as *Polityka* pointed out, an apparent inability to analyse contemporary developments, to adjust to the politics of the time and to go beyond cheap slogans and religious chauvinism.

If the nationalist movement as a whole can be ignored, because of its self-imposed ideological and organisational limitations, such is not the case with the neo-Fascist movement which has emerged at the same time in Poland. These are political organisations which depend on rabble rousing and on the appeal for extra-parliamentary action on the streets. The movement and its leaders reject the intellectual and historic heritage of the past while addressing themselves deliberately to the fears and ills of the present. Two parties seem to fit the neo-Fascist mould, though both have distinct characteristics and appeal to different social groups. Yet they are both populist and have made heavy use of nationalist and anti-Semitic slogans.

The Polish Nationalist Union: The Polish Nationalist Party [*Polska Wspólnota Narodowa: Polskie Stronnictwo Narodowe*, PWN-PSN], led by Bolesław Tejkowski, is the best known party to claim openly and without reservation a clearly articulated and virulently anti-Semitic programme. It is also notable for advocating a change of the political legislature to strengthen executive bodies, even though it seems to want to implement this change through parliamentary means. According to the Polish Information Agency's list of registered political parties, in 1991 Tejkowski's party claimed to have a membership of 4,000. This figure may be misleading in more ways than one. Access to the leadership of the party is extremely difficult and its membership cannot be gauged. The party depends heavily on its appeal to skinheads and unemployed youths. Young men from industrial backgrounds have been heavily demoralised by the collapse of the employment and educational opportunities provided by the previous regime. They have gravitated towards nationalist organisations, although their support is transient and cannot be considered to constitute a permanent party membership.[21]

Tejkowski's supporters became notorious for their vocal demonstrations against the authorities, during which extreme anti-Semitic slogans were voiced. In 1991 and 1992 they were suspected of being behind attacks on the Jewish Historical Institute in Warsaw and other Jewish targets in Poland. Tejkowski has been referred for psychiatric investigation by the judge who presided over his trial for incitement to racial hatred. The judiciary was clearly reluctant to use existing legislation against other nationalist and neo-Fascist leaders. They were finally forced to order psychiatric investigations when Tejkowski appeared on television goading the authorities to detain him.

In 1990 Tejkowski declared that his party did not aim to replace 'foreign capitalism by an equally foreign socialism'. He was suggesting a third nationalist solution.[22] The starting point was the ideas of Roman Dmowski, although Tejkowski emphatically stated that he considered them only as the foundation for his new ideology. He declared that his would be a truly national, new and comprehensive programme for Poland. In its election manifesto of 1991 Tejkowski's party declared that the highest values were God, 'the Nation', the Family and the 'Creative Union' (presumably the corporatist state).[23]

Tejkowski's PWN-PSN is exceptional among Polish contemporary parties in attacking the Catholic Church. His key assertion is that the Papacy and the Polish Episcopate have been taken over by Jews. In December 1992 he disseminated a list of the key figures in the Catholic hierarchy who were Jews. This was truly formidable since it included most Polish archbishops and bishops. Father Henryk Jankowski, Wałęsa's confessor, was identified as being of German origin, by implication nearly as bad as being a Jew. But the most astounding assertion was made about the Pope. Tejkowski claimed that the takeover of the church by Jews dates back to the Second World War when Jewish children were hidden in monasteries. They were usually baptised and, according to Tejkowski, proceeded to become priests. He claims that this is how Karol Wojtyła became a Catholic priest.[24]

The PWN-PSN party's attitude towards the Jewish question is exceptionally shrill. The Jews would appear to be responsible for all the political and economic reverses of Poland's past. The idea of Jewish anti-Polish conspiracy is repeated continuously and incessantly in the party's publications and leaflets. The government and *Solidarność* are alleged to have been taken over by Jews, together with all other aspects of

Polish public life. The defence of the nation against this conspiracy is defined as the only aggressive aim of the movement. It is otherwise portrayed as peaceful in its objectives and seeking to encourage other nations to establish similar national unity. Tejkowski sees scope for cooperation between nations, whose right to existence is accepted by him as equal to that of the Poles.

Tejkowski's economic programme is based on the notion that Poland is a state with ample natural resources, whose full value will only be realised when Poland is no longer exploited by Jews and Germans. He supports state intervention in industry but believes that agriculture should be entirely in private hands. A great deal of emphasis is placed on the development of small crafts as a way of realising the nation's potential.

The party's social programme is confined to the usual defence of large families and of women's maternal and domestic role. There is a clear commitment to supporting the family as the organic unit of the nation.

The PWN-PSN party fielded candidates in the 1991 and the 1993 elections. In neither did it obtain a sufficient number of votes to enter the *Sejm*. However, this is obviously not the party's objective, since street demonstrations and the mobilisation of young unemployed men from the industrial areas of Central Poland continue to offer more opportunities for gaining support and quick publicity.

A notable feature of all nationalist and neo-Fascist movements has been their determination to assert their credibility by stressing links with the past. Disparate nationalist movements repeated their commitment to the traditions of Dmowski. All of them, even Tejkowski's neo-Fascist movement, have tried to draw parallels between present circumstances and the fate of Poland before the war, when they argue that the presence of a large Jewish community was a source of political weakness and economic instability. The Communist period is explained as the imposition of an alien ideology by Jewish agents. All nationalist parties call for an investigation which would weed out from politics and the media those supposedly foreign elements which have assumed control over key areas of Polish life. In this way the problems of the present day have been linked to the past. The nationalist preoccupation with the past is a weakness which they have not overcome. It has left the field wide open to new and entirely different interpretations of what should be done to save the Polish nation. In 1991 such a movement appeared, and in the course of 1992 its popularity increased rapidly.

In January 1992 a new political organisation was registered. Its most notable feature was the absence of an emphasis on past grievances. Its programme and objectives are strikingly simple and contemporary. *Samoobrona* (Self-Defence), whose leader is Andrzej Lepper, has one overriding aim: to attack the government for its neglect of agriculture and of the peasant. Initially *Samoobrona* was assisted by the Confederation of Independent Poland which, lacking a strong rural base, saw it as a way of mobilising the peasants. In due course the leaders of the two organisations fell out, and in the summer of 1992 Lepper and his coorganisers were excluded from the KPN's premises in a quasi-military action. The result has been that KPN and *Samoobrona* do not cooperate, and *Samoobrona* has been forced to develop its own distinctive political platform. Its leaders are politically inexperienced, and this is confirmed by the fact that they are mainly from outside Warsaw.

From the very beginning, Lepper's followers set out to make their mark on the streets and in the provinces, rather than within established institutions. During the summer of 1992 they organised road blockades to display their own power and, needless to say, the impotence of the authorities. Well-publicised marches to the capital and hunger strikes followed. The willingness of various deputies from established peasant parties and Christian movements to associate – albeit briefly – with *Samoobrona* in order to put pressure on the government to slow down the process of privatisation, gave them additional publicity. The party had no representation in the *Sejm*. Nevertheless, it has briefly been able to become an issue in the discussions taking place there. An expression of support for Lepper's economic aims by President Wałęsa was much appreciated by *Samoobrona*, although there has been an acrimonious and public exchange of letters since then. This suggests that Wałęsa, like other politicians, was not willing to stake his political reputation on supporting an organisation which had become too public and too embarrassing.

Lepper's approach to politics is unhindered by any ideological ballast. According to *Samoobrona*'s electoral programme, Poland should follow neither a capitalist nor a socialist path. It should not march in other countries' footsteps, but stick to its own, Polish path:

> We shall try to go straight ahead, in accordance with the laws of nature. That path will lead us to an 'organic system', in which a great variety of individual forms of human behaviour, and that also includes economic behaviour, will yield to the mechanics of integration and cooperation for the benefit of the whole society, the nation and the state.[25]

Samoobrona clearly avoids endorsing any detailed policy which might prove divisive. According to its electoral programme, it aims at integrating Poland and the Poles, while seeking to promote common sense and modernity. Though *Samoobrona* avoids any open references to the Jews as the source of all evil and exploitation, it is vehement in attacking the right of foreigners to purchase land. Since Lepper's supporters are mainly peasants, the fear that foreigners, especially Germans, will be able to purchase land after the break-up of state farms, dominates the party's economic programme. Banks, and foreign banks in particular, are singled out as the cause of social insecurity and economic instability. Peasants had been granted extensive loans during the Communist period and, since the collapse of Communism, had with reason come to doubt successive's governments' commitment to supporting agriculture. Anxiety about banks foreclosing on farm debts figures very strongly in Lepper's public statements and explains his short-lived appeal to other parties and political figures.

While *Samoobrona*'s leaflets and political programme remain strikingly simple, the analysis of the party's official advisers has provided additional information on its politics. Bohdan Poręba film producer responsible for a string of films on military and patriotic themes, was also the President of the anti-Semitic Grunwald faction within the Communist Party. Bożena Krzywobłocka was associated with the nationalist section of the Communist party, in particular with its ultra-conservative publication *Rzeczywistość(Reality)*. Other like General Stanisław Skalski and Edward Kowalczyk are distinguished war veterans, the former in the Polish air force in Britain, the latter in the Home Army. This line-up, as well as the party's veiled attacks on the

World Bank, the European Bank for Reconstruction and Development and Jacques Attali personally, have persuaded the public of the party's impeccable anti-Semitic credentials.

In the spring and summer before the last elections, *Samoobrona* was extremely confident of its national support. A figure of 300,000 registered members was referred to loosely, though this was never verified. The spectre of Lepper, an uncharismatic figure by all accounts, becoming a parliamentary deputy and obtaining parliamentary immunity while pursuing his street activities, was viewed with distaste.[26] The party entered into no electoral coalition and having failed to secure the required 5 per cent of the total vote, did not gain any seats in the *Sejm*. *Samoobrona*'s future popularity might be decisively affected by the fact that in the 1993 elections the two parties which secured the largest majorities and thus formed, together, the new government are the Polish Peasant Alliance [*Polskie Stronnictwo Ludowe*, PSL] and the Democratic Left Alliance [*Stronnictwo Ludowo Democratyczne*, SLD]. This hints at a slowing down of the privatisation programme, and a greater sensitivity to the peasant grievances which had been the source of the party's popularity.

Both Tejkowski's PWN-PLN party and *Samoobrona* have become notorious for their encouragement of street actions. In the case of Tejkowski's, his cooperation with groups of skinheads has led to violence. It is very difficult to ascertain whether the skinhead groups, an entirely new phenomenon in Poland, are directly linked with Tejkowski and Lepper's organisations or are merely coopted on the basis of tacit understandings. While the latter seems to be the case, there can be no doubt that skinheads have been attracted to nationalist and neo-Fascist organisations because of their well-publicised opposition to Germans and Jews.[27]

In 1992 they were associated with widespread attacks on Gypsies and clearly identifiable foreigners: African students, Romanian asylum-seekers and German tourists. In many ways the emergency of a skinhead sub-culture has been similar to that in other European countries. The best organised groups have been formed in areas of high unemployment. They see themselves as aiming at a renewal of the Polish nation, and therefore use symbols which relate to the distant past, a time of Polish greatness. Their organisations remain loosely linked, and the general suspicion is that they themselves are rarely responsible for organising major street actions. However, their participation has been welcomed by some political leaders; this was the case with Lepper, in the summer of 1992. Nationalist leaders have tried to assist them by providing premises, as Tejkowski did, or by encouraging them to publish broadsheets.[28] Cooperation between organised nationalist movements is nevertheless limited and one of the explanations offered is that the leadership of these movements is too old and too preoccupied with past battles to be able to link up ideologically with the young unemployed generation of the post-Communist period. Left to themselves, disparate skinhead groups are unlikely to form disciplined, and therefore effective, political pressure groups.

Whereas it appeared in the first years of genuine freedom from Communism that nationalist parties would have a decisive say in the future political life of Poland, the picture is not so pessimistic now. The growing maturity and sophistication of the electorate is a source of surprise to both outside observers and to Polish politicians. This maturity has been manifested by the different level of debates in recent elections.

During the presidential elections and the 1991 general elections, the political agenda of all parties and of all public debates was affected by the ever-present nationalist issues. The question of who was a Jew and who was a patriot was a matter of considerable importance. Political programmes, public debates and graffiti in the streets bore witness to the general preoccupation with these questions. In the 1993 elections, pensions, and the funding of educational and health systems were key issues. Attacks on political personalities and their failures tended to be more specific and related to their track record rather than to their perceived ethnic or religious affinities.

There is, nevertheless, a clear possibility that nationalist and neo-Fascist movements might still have a say. A feeling of national insecurity can still have a powerful impact on emotions. The growth of aggressive nationalism in Russia or in the Baltic states is capable of creating circumstances in which extreme nationalist pronouncements would find a ready audience in Poland. Likewise, economic disappointments, caused by insensitive and prejudicial decisions by the World Bank, the IMF or the European Community, might rob the present government of the opportunity to prove that cooperation with the West is the best way of achieving stability and full employment in Poland.

List of abbreviations

AK	*Armia Krajowa* [Home Army]
BBWR	*Bezpartyjny Blok Współpracy z Rządem* [Non-Party Bloc of Cooperation with the Government]
KPN	*Konfederacja Polski Niepodległej* [Confederation of Independent Poland]
ND	*Narodowa Demokracja* [National Democratic Movement]
NSZ	*Narodowe Siły Zbrojne* [National Armed Forces]
ONR	*Obóz Narodowo-Radykalny* [Camp of Radical Nationalism]
OZN	*Obóz Zjednoczenia Narodowego* [Camp of National Unity]
PPR	*Polska Partia Robotnicza* [Polish Workers Party]
PPS	*Polska Partia Socialistyczna* [Polish Socialist Party]
PSL	*Polskie Stronnictwo Ludowe* [Polish Peasant Alliance]
PWN-PSN	*Polska Wspólnota Narodowa: Polskie Stronnictowo Narodowe* [The Polish Nationalist Union: The Polish Nationalist Party]
PZPR	*Polska Zjednoczona Partia Robotnicza* [United Workers Party of Poland]
SLD	*Stronnictwo Ludowo Demokratyczne* [The Democratic Left Alliance]
SN	*Stronnictwo Narodowe 'Ojczyzna'* [The National Front 'Fatherland' Party]

Notes

1. A. Dudek and G. Pytel, *Bolesław Piasecki. Próba biografii politicznej* [An Attempt at a Political Biography], Aneks, London, 1990, pp. 38–9.

213

2. L. Blit, *The Eastern Pretender. The Story of Bolesław Piasecki*, Hutchinson, London, 1965, pp. 44–5.
3. R. Wapiński, *Roman Dmowski*, Wydawnictwo Lubelskie, Lublin, 1988, pp. 184–5.
4. Ibid., p. 203.
5. A. Garlicki, *Przewrót majowy* [The May Coup d'etat], Czytelnik, Warsaw, 1976, p. 324.
6. Wapiński, *Roman Dmowski*, cit., p. 299.
7. Ibid., pp. 376–77.
8. W. Jędrzejewicz, *Piłsudski: A life for Poland*, Hippocrene Books, New York, 1982, pp. 138–9.
9. Garlicki, *Jósef Piłsudski*, cit., pp. 507–11.
10. Jędrzejewicz, *Piłsudski: A life for Poland*, cit., pp. 259–60.
11. P. Stawecki, *Nastepcy Komendanta* [The Successors of the Commander], Wydawnictwo Ministerstwo Obrony Narodowej, Warsaw, 1969, pp. 148–51.
12. Jedrzejewicz, *Piłsudski: A life for Poland*, cit., pp. 248–9.
13. J. B. de Weydenthal, *The Communists of Poland. An Historical Outline*, Hoover Institution Press, Stanford University, Stanford, CA, 1978, p. 125.
14. Ibid., pp. 126–33.
15. I am especially indebted to Professor Szymon Rudnicki (University of Warsaw) for this information, and for allowing me to quote from a lecture given by him on the subject of contemporary Polish nationalist parties and anti-Semitism.
16. *Ojczyzna*, 31 March 1990, No. 0(1), p. 5.
17. *Ojczyzna*, 29 April 1990, No. 1, p. 3.
18. *Ojczyzna*, 9 Dec. 1990, No. 15, pp. 6–7.
19. E. Sochacka and T. Krasko, *Leszek Moczulski, Wygram tę Wojnę* [Leszek Moczulski, This War I Shall Win], Agencja Wydawnicza SENS, Warsaw, 1992, p. 60.
20. 'Bez Głowy' [loosely translates as 'Without a Thought'], *Polityka*, 18 Oct. 1993, No.38(1898), p. 7.
21. Most information concerning skinheads and extreme right-wing organisations in contemporary Poland has been provided by Mariusz Janicki of the weekly *Polityka* whose book on this phenomenon is due to appear in Poland shortly.
22. *Mysl Narodowa Polska* [Polish National Thought], Jan.–Feb. 1990, pp. 26–27.
23. *Myśl Narodowa Polska*, No. 5, July 1991, PWN-PSN Election Manifesto, p. 11.
24. PWN-PSN Statement, 12 Dec. 1992, pp. 1–4.
25. A. Lepper, *'Może, a więc musi być lepiej'. Materiaty programowe* ['It may be, therefore it must be better'. Policy Statement], June 1993.
26. 'Kosynierzy nowej generacji' [The New Generation of Scythmen], *Polityka*, No. 14(1874), 2 April 1993, p. 3. This title alludes to the peasants who joined Tadeusz Kosciuszko in his anti-Russian uprising in 1794.
27. 'Krzepa łysych' [The strength of the bold ones], *Polityka*, No. 51(1911), 18 Dec. 1993, p. 9.
28. Ibid.

Chapter 11

THE EXTREME RIGHT IN FRANCE: 'LEPÉNISME' OR THE POLITICS OF FEAR

Michalina Vaughan

The avatars of the extreme right

The dichotomisation of politics into right and left is an integral part of the Revolution's legacy to republican France. The full endorsement of the organising myths which underpin the regime is held to be the birthright of the left. In contrast, the ideological credentials of the right remain perennially open to challenge. The recent bicentennial celebrations highlighted yet again the divide between those who accept not only the Republic, but the Revolution as a whole (*en bloc*, in Clémenceau's words), and those whose acceptance is more or less heavily qualified. It is a moot point whether differences in values upheld by different sections of the right are of degree or kind. To stress the existence of a continuum from *centre-droite* to *extrême droite* is to hint at shared meanings or even at guilt by association. For instance, the disgrace of the Vichy regime was visited on the political right at the Liberation, regardless of the fact that Pétain's supporters were of diverse backgrounds and that de Gaulle in his youth had been a follower of *Action Française*, the monarchist organisation of Charles Maurras, so called after the daily paper published from 1908 to 1944.[1] An alternative approach consists in focusing on the plurality of *droites* and on the deep-seated ideological differences which demarcate them, as René Rémond has done in his class work *Les droites en France* (Aubier-Montaigne, Paris, 1982). In accordance with his terminology, the 'Orléanist' trend – closest to the centre – has always stood for parliamentary democracy, whereas its 'Bonapartist' counterpart has been populist, anti-parliamentarian and, to a degree, anti-capitalist. The former identified with the institutional structures of the Republic, the latter showed a readiness to adopt revolutionary means (albeit for reactionary ends). Thus, both accepted some elements of the tradition which the left tends to claim as its own. Yet a repudiation of the whole revolutionary past and of republican institutions was characteristic of the 'legitimist' minority, committed to the restoration of the monarchy and – at the beginning of the twentieth century – of Catholicism as a state religion. This extreme right became so politically disaffected as to opt out of any participation in republican institutions. Described as *émigrés de l'intérieur* (emigrants within their own country) – in an allusion to the emigration of aristocrats during the Revolution – the legitimists remained estranged

215

from mainstream society, contemptuous of the ruling elite and, by corollary, inclined to adopt a conspiracy theory of politics.

The tradition which they established by negating the legitimacy of post-revolutionary French institutions was cross-fertilised by a number of trends which emerged under the Third Republic, from the 1880s onwards. The exacerbation of nationalism by the defeat of 1870 stimulated the unrest which General Georges Boulanger attempted to exploit, and provided an environment conducive to the so-called Leagues of Barrès, Deroulède and Drumont. The latter exemplified the increasing connection between popular aspirations to revenge over France's enemies and the anti-Semitism which considered Jews as their agents. The Dreyfus case displayed how widespread these emotions were and added fuel to them. Furthermore, the exploitation of financial scandals involving republican politicians enabled the nationalist right not only to discredit the ruling elite, but also to denounce Jewish capitalist interests. This was a fertile breeding ground for a new blend of populism, based on a denunciation of both parliamentary democracy and bourgeois capitalism.[2] According to the analyses of Rémond, these stirrings fit in with the 'Bonapartist' right, of which Boulanger could be considered an exponent. However, he had to acknowledge that as nationalism moved to the right, it 'contaminated' even the royalists of *Action Française* with an element of the Jacobin legacy. In advocating rebellion against a Republic denounced as both insufficiently patriotic and too corrupt, its supporters became *contestataires*, increasingly willing to be defined as extremists. To the historian Sternhell, they were the heirs of a pre-Fascist radicalism of the right, which had openly advocated the use of violent means to effect sociopolitical change.[3] In the 1930s, this legacy was truly acknowledged when, despite their membership of a Monarchist association, the younger activists of *Action Française* described themselves as 'revolutionary conservatives'. To prove that they meant business, they entered into alliances with the Leagues, which drew on both nationalism and revolutionary syndicalism in an attempt to mobilise the crowds along lines reminiscent of Fascist movements in other Western-European countries. A new blend of political themes borrowed from the traditional right and of social themes from the left, the advocacy of violence, and even the terminology (for instance, Georges Valois's movement was called *Le Faisceau*, i.e. The Fasces) hint at Fascist leanings. This was plebeian company for the upper-class, intellectually sophisticated *Action Française*. It would be interesting to review in detail the debate between Rémond, who argues that the French rights (in the plural) retained their originality and that the Leagues merely made a lot of noise, but did little harm, and Sternhell, who detects a spread of Fascism from the mid-1920s.[4] The latter hypothesis distinguishes between the moderates (Rémond's *Orléaniste* right) and the populists, closer to the extreme left in their discourse and tactics. However, whether to use a label is really a semantic issue. Whether Fascist or merely *fascisante*, an extreme right existed as a mobilising force rather than a submerged trend. It made capital out of the economic recession in the 1920s, out of the fears which were rife among an ageing population, weakened by the losses of the First World War and out of the rumours about corruption and/or inefficiency in high places. The anti-parliamentarian demonstrations in Paris in February 1934 showed that their supporters could be stirred to action.

Since the French economy had not been affected as adversely, these outbursts could not be compared with the riots, born out of despair, which paved the way for Fascism in Germany. Moreover, national pride had been assuaged by victory – despite the price paid for it. Still, these events were significant to the extent that they inspired the extreme right with a new confidence in its ability to bring about a change of political regime. Characteristically, 6 February 1934, when a mob attacked the Chamber of Deputies, was described by the writer Robert Brasillach (later sentenced to death for collaborating with the enemy, and executed) as ushering in 'Year One of the National Revolution.'[5] It was, of course, no coincidence that the *Révolution Nationale* should have been proclaimed in 1940 by Pétain as the only means available for national regeneration. That defeat should have been received by some nationalists as a 'divine surprise' can only be understood because the rejection of modernity, construed as decadence, and of parliamentarianism, perceived as bankrupt, had permeated their thinking. Thus, the Vichy regime was born out of a collapse of national morale and of state institutions which had long been predicted by the extreme right. Some individuals – de Gaulle was a case in point – responded as patriots rather than as ideologists. Others attempted to apply the traditionalist blueprint, with the aid of some opportunists and of some believers in an 'understanding' between Pétain and de Gaulle.[6] For the first time since 1789, the chief objective of officialdom was to put the clock back; the modern industrial world was repudiated and secular society rejected. The authority principle was to be asserted in the state, at work and in the family. The return to the land, the reliance on religious values to buttress the family and transform education, all of these were well-known themes of the extreme right from the old days of *émigrés de l'intérieur*. The attempt to 'return France to the French' by implementing discriminatory legislation against Jews, Freemasons and *Français de fraîche date* (recently naturalised French) belonged to an agenda developed since the 1880s.[7] Although all these policies were repealed at the Liberation, they were to be heard of again, when their supporters reappeared on the political scene.

Buried with Vichy, reborn in Algiers

To begin with, the collapse of the Vichy regime drove the extreme right underground. In fact, the right seemed to have vanished altogether. *Pétainistes* went into exile or were tried, and sanctions involved (at the least) the loss of civic rights. Collaborators faced heavier sentences and, in some cases, got rough justice. Somewhat unfairly, the whole right seemed to be tarred with the same brush because its republicanism was suspect, even if its patriotism was not. Political credibility could only be regained by adopting protective covering, that is, joining a liberal or Christian-Democrat Party and participating in coalition governments, initially dominated by the left. Under the Fourth Republic, the moderates gained more and more votes, achieved majorities in Parliament and could finally acknowledge their true allegiance, thought they were not able to solve the Algerian crisis.[8] Hence, they were defeated by the nationalism of the extreme right, which acted as a midwife to de Gaulle's Fifth Republic.

After lying low for about a decade, supporters of the extreme right began to have an impact on French politics in the mid-1950s. Their first reappearance in Parliament occurred when Poujadism attracted the votes of the petty bourgeoisie, a traditional clientele of reactionary populists. The appeal of Poujade was to small-scale shop-keepers and tradespeople threatened by policies of economic rationalisation and by urban growth. The main plank of his platform was tax reform to benefit the self-employed.[9] It proved highly effective and, in 1956, his movement gained 11.6 per cent of votes cast and fifty-two seats in the National Assembly. One of the new MPs was called Jean-Marie Le Pen. A couple of years later, Poujadism had burnt itself out and Le Pen had quarrelled with Poujade. Still, its brief popularity bore witness to the persistence of 'a virus which France cannot eliminate'[10] – an instinctive resistance of the 'small man' to socioeconomic change, and hence, a vulnerability to demagogy.

The outbreak of yet another virus – nationalist extremism – was unleashed by the protracted process of decolonisation. Both in Indochina and in Algeria, aspirations to independence were ascribed to Marxist infiltration by army cadres responsible for control. Hence, a virulent anti-Communism spread among the officer corps and furthered their connections with Catholic fundamentalism. The lessons of *Action Française* were explicitly invoked to advocate the need for counter-revolutionary groups to 'save the fatherland' and to 'defend Christian Western civilisation'. From the creation of the Algerian National Liberation Front [*Front de Libération Nationale*, FLN] in 1954 to the demonstration of European settlers in Algiers on 13 May 1958, which brought de Gaulle back to power, the army activists became increasingly determined to take the law into their own hands. They advocated the *droit d'insurrection*,[11] the right to rebel, which was the legacy of those *contestataires* whose true ideological colours are the theme of the Rémond–Sternhell debate.

The cause of *Algérie Française* became the rallying cry of the extreme right under the Fifth Republic. Illegal organisations proliferated while de Gaulle ruled.[12] In fact, anti-Gaullism was their stock-in-trade. This bitter resentment was fuelled by memories of de Gaulle's refusal to grant a pardon to old Marshal Pétain (who died in gaol in 1951), but was mainly prompted by his 'betrayal of the army's trust' in having negotiated with the FLN. Thus, it had all the added resentment characteristic of family feuds. Army officers traumatised by the loss of Algeria, and *pieds noirs* (European settlers repatriated to a 'motherland' they hardly knew, and who were not always of French descent) became as determined to rewrite history as the legitimist *ultras* had been after the Revolution. The failure of the army coup in Algiers in 1961 drove underground the conspirators of the Secret Army Organisation [*Organisation de l'Armée Secrète,* OAS]. Some clandestine groups operated outside the law, for example, the Revolutionary Army [*Armée Révolutionnaire,* AR], while, on the margins of legality, the *Occident* movement attempted to organise protest. Dissolved in 1968 after an anti-immigrant demonstration, it spawned New Order [*Ordre Nouveau*, ON] in 1969. A number of strong-arm groups operated in the 1970s, for example, *Club Charles Martel, Groupe Delta, Honneur de la Police*, the students' *Groupe Union-Défense* (disbanded in 1973 to be reborn and connected in the 1980, with the Party of the New Forces [*Parti des Forces Nouvelles*, PFN] of which more later). The best known is the neo-Nazi Federation of National and European Action [*Fédération d'Action Nationale Européenne*, FANE], reborn as National and European Fasces [*Faisceaux Nationaux et Européens*, FNE] – a deliberate return to the terminology of the 1930s.[13] According to the European Parliament's Committee of Inquiry into the Rise of Fascism and Racism in Europe, 'the violent nature of these groups is real enough but their impact should not be overestimated'.[14] Although they have some international connections (e.g. ON with the Italian *Movimento Sociale Italiano* and the *Nationaldemokratische Partei Deutschlands*, and the FANE with like-minded German groups), they lack financial resources to such an extent that some of their criminal activities are 'fund-raising' burglaries. Others are attacks against individuals – mainly Algerians and Jews. In 1980, the peak of their 'form', commandos of the extreme right claimed over sixty such actions.

This is not to say that the extreme right refrained from legitimate political activities in the aftermath of the *Algérie Française* trauma. In the referendum of April 1962, intensive lobbying yielded 9.2 per cent of the vote. In the presidential election of 1965, the *Algérie Française* candidate, Tixier-Vignancourt, managed 5.2 per cent in the first round. He was sponsored by his own party, the Alliance for Freedoms and Progress [*Alliance pour les Libertés et le Progrès*, ALP] and by a network of support committees with a secretary general, the former Poujadist MP, Le Pen. Although the two men quarrelled and parted company, this was a kind of dress rehearsal for the coordination of anti-Gaullists, fundamentalists, self-confessed neo-Fascists and the so-called neo-pagans, later to be known as the New Right [*Nouvelle Droite*, ND]. The time was not yet ripe, but it was already apparent that a national organisation would be needed if the extreme right sought to be legitimated through the ballot box. Such an outcome was rendered difficult by the proliferation of small, often short-lived groups between which antagonism was sharp. Ideological heterogeneity was not the only obstacle to cooperation; the personality characteristics of individuals did not help, since they were often embittered or even unstable.

In the aftermath of 1968, which was widely perceived as a 'cultural revolution',[15] the intellectuals of the extreme right sought to make their ideas respectable through quasi-academic publications under the auspices of the Research and Study Group for European Civilisation [*Groupement de Recherche et d'Etudes pour une Civilisation Européenne*, GRECE].[16] Though it took nearly ten years for this *Nouvelle Droite* to be discovered by the media, its elitist discourse, its claims to be scientific and its emphasis on European culturalism were influential throughout the 1970s in rehabilitating a number of ideas previously held to be indefensible.[17] The New Right's strategy of intellectual rearmament was the polar opposite of commando activism, but continuity of personnel and, in substance (though not in form), of major tenets can be traced back to the OAS[18] and beyond. Despite clear differences, particularly in the appraisal of Christianity, between *Nouvelle Droite* and *Action Française*, both posited intellectual reform as a preliminary to societal change, and both fostered a climate of opinion in which right-wing extremism could thrive.

While the ND redefined metapolitics and the commandos pursued their 'cottage industry' of violence,[19] attempts to establish the extreme right on a party-political basis did not prosper. The electoral successes of the *Movimento Sociale Italiano* in Italy prompted members of ON to join with some of their former partners of the Tixier-Vignancourt campaign in setting up a new party, the National Front [*Front National*, FN] in 1972. This federation of groupuscules split, in no time, into rival parties and it was only a court order which granted to the faction led by Le Pen the right to be called FN, while the others became the PFN, led by Pascal Gauchon. Both before and after this split, the scores of the extreme right candidates were disastrous (1.32 per cent in the elections of 1973, and a mere 0.74 per cent for Le Pen, as presidential candidate, in the first round of the 1974 election).[20] Not a promising start, to say the least. The instability of the Front and its initial lack of appeal could be ascribed to its heterogeneity. It has been called *un fourre-tout idéologique* (an ideological hold-all) in which monarchists were cheek by jowl with revolutionary nationalists, neo-Poujadists cohabited with Catholic fundamentalists, the last Pétainists mixed with OAS veterans, disappointed Socialists joined renegades from the mainstream parties of the right and anti-parliamentarians of every variety met with tireless protesters.[21] Initially, it was no more successful than its 'terrible twin', the PFN.

From another groupuscule apparently doomed to obscurity, the FN rose to achieve credibility within a decade. By the autumn of 1983, it was capable of attracting over 10 per cent of votes in local elections.[22] This unexpected result can only be understood by reference to Le Pen's own rise to notoriety as a communicator and to his charismatic appeal (at least to a sizeable percentage of the electorate – fluctuating from over 10 to under 20 per cent). The image he projects and the skills he displays are as significant as the often contradictory messages he conveys. He has been eminently successful as a performer in gaining attention for his party and his programme. Therefore, it makes sense to discuss his *persona* first, his political philosophy next and finally to account for their appeal as expressed by voting behaviour.

The life and times of Jean-Marie Le Pen

The founder member of the FN could be considered exemplary to the extent that his background fits all the stereotypes of the extreme right.[23] The son and grandson of sailors, he was born in Brittany (in 1928), in the heartland of Catholic traditionalism. He was a war-orphan (*pupille de la nation*), and was educated by the Jesuits. If he is to be believed, he joined the *maquis* at the age of 16 and, allegedly, that is where he acquired his life-long hatred of the Communists, whom he accuses of trying to monopolise the Resistance movement. As a law student (registered in Paris – on and off – between 1947 and 1953), he was involved in anti-Marxist politics, and was even elected president of the student union (*Corpo de Droit*). In 1953, he volunteered to serve in Indochina with the Foreign Legion as a parachutist – though he actually worked on the forces newspaper when he got there. Back at the Law Faculty, he met Poujade, accompanied him to a rally of the Union for the Defence of Shopkeepers and Tradespeople [*Union de Défense des Commerçants et des Artisans*] held at Rennes, and extemporised an impassioned speech, on the strength of which he was asked to stand for parliament. Elected in a working-class Paris constituency in January 1956, he rapidly gained a reputation for the effectiveness of his vitriolic oratory. In particular, attacks on Mendès-France – alluding to a 'patriotic and quasi-physical repulsion' – were widely reprinted,[24] though often deplored as anti-Semitic.

Just as he was gaining a political reputation, Le Pen showed himself to be a man of action rather than a mere talker. He took six months' leave from parliament to rejoin his former regiment. He was sent to Suez first and then to Algeria (from September 1956 to May 1957). Back in parliament, he embraced the cause of *Algérie Française* with characteristic enthusiasm. By late 1957, he had left the Poujadists and sat as an independent. Re-elected in November 1958, he joined the group of *Indépendants Paysans* (going back to his Breton roots). In the elections of November 1962, his anti-Gaullism lost him his seat. So far, his extreme right credentials were impeccable. The only missing feature was that Le Pen had never belonged to OAS – a fact which did complicate relationships within the FN (Mark One) prior to the split of 1973.[25] Out of parliament, he remained politically active, especially in the Tixier-Vignancourt campaign. In order to overcome financial difficulties, he set up a company for the production of records bringing to life the history of the twentieth century, through speeches made by Lenin, Churchill and Stalin and by royalists and anarchists.[26] Out of some 140 such records, the public prosecutor picked on a medley of songs from the Third Reich and Le Pen received a suspended sentence of three months, as well as being heavily fined for infringing the legislation on war crimes (eulogised in the lyrics). This was not the first time he had been in trouble with the police: as a student, he was known to be a *baroudeur* (a 'hard man'), occasionally arrested for violence (e.g. in a Pigalle cabaret in 1948). Boys will be boys, of course, and it was always on record that when Le Pen lost one eye during a fight at an electoral meeting in 1957, it was to protect a Muslim friend (a supporter of *Algérie Française*). Somewhat less predictably, the police had to be called at Aix-les-Baines in 1951 to curb his aggressive behaviour in a church, where he had been refused communion while drunk. A trivial detail, maybe, but revealing a wild streak for which military life offered plenty of scope.

Lieutenant Le Pen was accused of having tortured a young Algerian of 19, arrested by the parachutists on 8 March 1957 and released on the 31st. A police report was drawn up at the plaintiff's request on the day after his release, but there was to be no prosecution. Its contents were first published in *Vérité-Libération. Cahiers d'information sur la guerre d'Algérie* in June–July 1962.[27] The reaction of Le Pen when asked about this aspect of his past during the now famous interview of 13 February 1984 (*L'heure de vérité* [The hour of truth] on the TV network *Antenne Deux*) was not to deny any facts, but to stress that the unit to which he belonged had been entrusted with a mission 'by a Socialist government' and acquitted itself of the obligations 'imposed by the military and political hierarchies of the time'.[28] It is the well-worn reasoning about 'obeying orders'. To the extent that there is abundant evidence of systematic reliance on torture during the Algerian war, Le Pen is not only defending himself, but his generation. Therefore, he may actually gain some support, at least among older voters as well as among the most fervent nationalists, unprepared to countenance any blemish on the army's good name. In addition, the younger age group may simply lack any interest in a remote past and may consider any criticism of Le Pen's early career as diversionary tactics intended to discredit him. Be that as it may, no harm appears to have been done to the FN by revelations about the less savoury episodes in its leader's career.

Yet by no means all of these episodes can be ascribed to war-time emergencies or to military discipline – which are certainly redeeming circumstances for authoritarian nationalists, who are the natural supporters of the FN. Paradoxically, Le Pen's record is far from reassuring in two spheres which have traditionally been of particular concern to the extreme right: firstly, religion and, secondly, the family. Both institutions, which loom so large in his rhetoric, provide constraints that are hardly compatible with his exuberance. FN rallies begin with a Latin mass, but its leader would not have a crucifix in his house, according to the revelations made by his estranged wife at the time of their divorce (*Le Matin* of 7 May 1987). Should this source of information seem unreliable, he is on record as saying that he would rather send his children on holiday to a Communist-run camp than to '*les curés*' (the priests).[29] A touch of anticlericalism is in the French tradition, but it is still somewhat unusual for a devout follower of St Joan of Arc[30] to set so little store by the sanctity of family life. Not only did Le Pen marry a divorcee,[31] but the marriage was dissolved nearly a quarter of a century and three daughters later, after a most acrimonious and unseemly divorce. In 1987 – the year he was being taken seriously as a candidate for the presidency of the Republic – his image was hardly enhanced by the comment that the mother of his daughters, if she needed money, could get employment as a charlady, or indeed by her retaliation (posing for *Lui* in an apron and no other garments). Hardly the behaviour expected of a pillar of Catholic traditionalism.

While this proneness to becoming involved in scandal must be an embarrassment to the more conventional milieux in which Le Pen recruits voters, two factors help to explain why it has not damaged him as much as might have been expected. On the one hand, he appears to have a gift for generating uncritical admiration. Thus, his considerable personal fortune was acquired through a controversial legacy[32] from an early recruit to the FN. As in the case of many charismatic leaders, he is expected to be somewhat 'larger than life', and his followers may well feel that ordinary standards do not apply. On the other hand, and more importantly, Le Pen's sympathisers do not conform to the pattern of the old-fashioned extreme right, respectful of established hierarchies and scathing about any sexual peccadilloes. His electorate tends to be both younger and, more often, male than that of the two main parties of the right in France – hence less influenced by religious beliefs. In each election, the Front has spread to working-class neighbourhoods from its initial bourgeois strongholds,[33] thus recruiting from among 'de-christianised' sections of the population. More will be said about this dual catchment area in connection with fluctuations in the FN's scores. At this stage, the point is that the vagaries of Le Pen's private life would not deter those voters to whom only the aspects of his message which relate to their own concerns are relevant and to whom the Catholic rhetoric does not matter. Precisely because the message is contradictory, the 'duality' of the Front's potential constituency can be explained.

Lepénisme

The political philosophy of the FN is largely reducible to Le Pen's writings and speeches. He is widely held to be a talented demagogue with undoubted debating skills, a love of rhetoric and a keen understanding of TV technique. However, it ought to be remembered that within his own following, he is taken seriously as an original thinker. He is 'master of the truth, guardian and supreme judge of orthodoxy, unfailing guide to action, visionary, prophet',[34] no less! Such enthusiasm is hardly shared by the occasional FN voter. At any rate, though, there is a widespread belief that Le Pen's discourse is at least consistent, and that he is prepared to face unpopularity, accusations about his past and media attacks in order to put his ideas forward.

Insofar as these ideas add up to a system, its cornerstone is nationalism. Le Pen claims to be part of a 'long chain',[35] dating back to *Action Française* and to its forerunners. Predictably, the approach is deterministic rather than voluntaristic. Belonging to the French people is achieved by linear descent. This birthright yields exclusive exercise of citizenship and priority in terms of access to scarce and valued resources such as social security benefits, housing and education. The principle of 'national preference' (*Les Français d'abord* – the French first)[36] is derived from the basic democratic principle of national sovereignty vested in the people and of which the state is a mere representative – and an undependable one at that. The common-sense justification of this exclusivity is derived from the analogy between the nation and the family. Once more, the *Antenne Deux* interview of February 1984 spelt out the common-sense view of proximity as a key to trust (the so-called 'concentric circles' approach to which Le Pen always returns: 'I like my daughters better than my cousins [*cousines*], my cousins better than my neighbours [*voisines*]; my neighbours better than strangers [*inconnus*], and strangers better than foes [*ennemis*]'[37] – the nearest and dearest being female, while outsiders and foes are male. No great knowledge of sociobiology is required to draw the conclusion that the preservation of a 'breed' is aimed at.

Concepts of natural selection are drawn upon by Le Pen in order to show that society cannot be based upon a concern for the weak. It must be gladiatorial or collapse:

'By granting privileges to the weak, by favouring them excessively in all respects, one weakens the social body as a whole. One does the very opposite of what dog and horse breeders do. I am not against relief for misfortune, e.g. for the handicapped, but nowadays we have almost got to the stage where handicap is promoted.'[38]

The analogy of 'dogs and horses' not only suggests that defective specimens . . . ought not to have been bred and that compassion for them should be kept within strict limits. . . . It also hints at the need to keep thoroughbreds uncontaminated by miscegenation.[39]

This pseudo-Darwinian approach – with the expected references to the survival of the fittest – is explained as a realistic acceptance of human nature. Its counterpart is an apocalyptic warning. To disregard nature is to accept defeat in the struggle for survival. The decadence which threatens the Western world as a whole, and French society in particular, derives from an egalitarianism contrary to the hierarchical principle enshrined in nature: 'The egalitarian movement which consists of levelling age groups, the sexes and peoples, is to be criticised in my view because it masks reality, which is based on inequalities. . . . The theme of equality strikes us as decadent.'[40] That age-groups, as well as the sexes, have natural roles is illustrated by the model of the family, in which the authority principle is fully vindicated. The legacy of the past is inseparable from these natural hierarchies and the future can only be made safe if they are buttressed or – if need be – restored. Conservatism (a defensive attitude) is linked with proposals for the protection of core values: the family, the rights of the people, national identity. These consist in preserving the health of the social organism by attacking the ills to which it is subjected. The organic analogy, which is so common in any discourse of the right, is fully developed in order to justify *Lepénisme* as a symptom of healthy nationalism: 'If to be reactionary is to react like an organism reacts when faced with disease, then yes, I am a reactionary. Not to be a reactionary, is to sentence oneself to death. It is to let the disease or the enemy take over.'[41]

The 'disease' is the weakening of the family and the drop in the birthrate which makes the inflow of immigrants and their large families increasingly threatening to an underpopulated country, likened to a house no longer filled. Immigration is 'a foreign invasion by osmosis',[42] admittedly peaceful, but whose long-term effects will be the same as the incursions of alien hordes, prepared to fight when denied bread, wine and women. The use of emotive analogies and value-laden vocabulary is analysed by Honoré,[43] who shows how family imagery (father, brother, patrimony, legacy, mother, son, generation, blood, love) is used when discussing the national identity of the French people and how threats to it are given sexual connotations (intrusion, rape, miscegenation, cuckolding, homosexuality, prostitution).

The genetic and cultural threat to national integrity must be resisted by a number of policies, some destined to protect the French family, and the mother in particular, others to curb abortions, and yet others to restrict the rights of immigrants, whether to the acquisition of nationality by birth on French soil or to family allowances. Ultimately, the top priority will be to challenge immigration, the blame for which is ascribed to the suicidal policy of French governments over the years, and to enforce 'national preference'. This would entail discontinuing any assimilation of foreigners to nationals by laws and regulations, expelling any immigrants who behave in ways 'unworthy of French hospitality', and gradually repatriating others. This drastic programme is justified by the logic of inbuilt inequalities. The Third World is not capable of the achievement which made the West what it is; the Muslims, and the North Africans in particular, are neither willing nor able to assimilate, nor are Africans. They are simply not deserving, they do not work hard enough, they would drag any society down. The fear of downward-levelling through miscegenation is compounded by that of contamination by alien value systems and life-styles. Despite the stress on differences, held to be natural and therefore valuable, there is no doubt that some ethnic groups are ranked higher than others in the hierarchy of *assimilables* (capable – or worthy – of being assimilated). Back to the concentric circles and the cousins preferable to the mere 'neighbours' – especially if they live 'next door' (across the Alps or the Pyrenees), rather than on the other side of the Mediterranean. Proximity is not only a spatial category, but a cultural one. This is where Christianity plays an important part as an intrinsic component of national identity. The Islamic immigrant is doubly alien, in cultural as well as ethnic terms, whereas the Spaniard or Portuguese shares with the French a religious dimension which can make assimilation easier. Once more, the concentric circles come into play, so that 'strangers' would be preferable to 'foes' (e.g. former dependents like Algerians).

To claim a share in the Christian legacy of the past is a prerogative of the right: 'The right seems to me to be philosophically linked with the natural order, with the Christian message, even though there are atheists on the right, and agnostics as well'.[44] While it is surely doubtful that 'the Christian message' conforms to 'nature', since its objective is to curb natural impulses, there is also a contradiction between the tribute paid to Catholic traditionalism and the strong materialist undertones of Le Pen's discourse. His commitment to 'popular capitalism' links freedom of choice to the possession of private property. The harshness of competition under capitalism – pilloried by the Poujade movement in its time – is accepted as a means of rewarding merit and effort. It is a prerogative of the family to pass a patrimony on from generation to generation, thus protecting individuals from the vagaries of the labour markets.[45] Hence, without property there is neither freedom nor security. The creation of wealth is the task of individuals, caring for their families and struggling for survival. The state should not interfere with this process, but should merely ensure that its citizens and their property are protected from any aggression. Its basic duties are 'to defend the Nation and its people, to maintain order, to dispense justice'.[46] It is this fundamental concern for order, for the assertion of authority and the control of delinquency, which reconciles the religious and the economic dimensions. When Le Pen asserts, 'I think that Monseigneur Lefebvre does a little of what I attempt to do in politics',[47] he highlights which aspect of Catholicism is closest to his own view. It is the punitive rather than the compassionate. The state must be more repressive because society must be 'cleaned up'. The pernicious elements to be sanctioned range from the unions (the socialist threat to economic freedom), to homosexuals and drug addicts (the physical threat of AIDS) and – last but not least – to immigrants (the alien threat to national identity). Although, in each instance, the arguments are presented by reference to the organic analogy (i.e. the dichotomisation of health and disease in society), religious justifications are also available (by reference to 'station in life', to procreation as a duty, and to the preservation of a Christian community from unbelievers). Whichever line is chosen, one feature remains unchanged: the endorsement of order, of state authority, of the law, of paternalism. In sharp contradistinction to the advocacy of economic liberalism (with an occasional dig at international trusts – no doubt a residue of Poujadism), there is a fierce rejection of libertarian values in both ethical and political matters.

For all its inconsistencies, the message is powerful, precisely to the extent that it is simplistic. It appears to invoke elementary common sense and to put forward obvious solutions (*y a qu'à* – nothing is needed but to . . .) to boldly defined problems. 'Everything comes from immigration. Everything goes back to immigration':[48] unemployment, 'invasion' of council housing by the minorities, overcrowding in schools, currency drain, rising crime-rate, even the spread of AIDS, all social ills can be traced back to the same root-cause, and therefore a simple remedy can be prescribed for all of them. The method is not exactly a new one. Le Bon's classic study of crowd psychology foresaw its success: 'Pure and simple assertion, unconnected with any reasoning and any proof, is a sure means of making an idea enter into the mind of crowds.'[49] The simpler the idea, the more readily acceptable it proves. The *Maghrébins* (North Africans) have merely taken over from the Jews as the alleged cause of all social ills. It could be said of Le Pen, as Barrès exclaimed about Boulanger, that it is the person rather than the programme in which people put their trust.

Le Pen's constituencies

The increased receptiveness of public opinion to Le Pen's discourse is correlated with a shift to the right, initiated by the backlash following 1968 and by de Gaulle's withdrawal from politics, since, without him, Gaullism was less and less a *rassemblement* (a rally). While power was uneasily shared in the 1970s by the nationalist/populists (not called *Chiraquiens* yet) and the 'Orléanists' (from Pompidou to Giscard), anti-egalitarian themes became more and more common. As the recession began to bite, public policies restricted immigration, at the time when the ND was propagating pseudo-scientific arguments in support of exclusion.[50] A growing sense of personal insecurity, linked with the presence of immigrants, and a demand for 'law and order' measures, appeared to peak towards the middle of the decade.[51] The extreme right was bound to capitalise on this upsurge of negative emotions and Le Pen could claim that he was daring to speak out on behalf of the common Frenchman, reduced to silence by the hypocrisy of the main parties (*le bande des quatre*, the gang of four – Gaullists, Giscardians, Socialists and Communists, all tarred with the same brush). Resistance to social change – which had accounted for the success of Poujade – served Le Pen equally well, but it no longer took the form of rejecting capitalism. It consisted in the *refus de l'altérité*, rejection of the 'other', the immigrant who is highly visible (by virtue of racial characteristics) and resistant to assimilation (by virtue of cultural background, and of religion in particular). The immigrant is 'the enemy within' (a familiar character in the demonology of the extreme right), denounced as a potential offender, as a drain on state resources and as a competitor (both on a tight labour market and on an inadequate housing market). All ethnic minorities, but Algerians in particular, are described as an uncontrollable demographic threat (through the high birth-rate and through miscegenation), and as a territorial threat (through the formation of ghettos).

The common denominator to which *Lepénisme* appeals is fear: 'Today the man who is of the right is he who instinctively feels threatened by others, by immigrants, by women, by children and, in general, by everything that is alien to him.'[52] The pervasiveness of this theme was exemplified by the setting up, under the auspices of the Gaullist party, of *Légitime Défense* as an association in 1978, of *Sécurité et Liberté* in 1979, and by the bulldozing, in 1979, of a refuge for immigrants at Vitry (by order of the Communist-dominated local authority). In such a climate of opinion, the extreme right necessarily exploited the widespread sense of insecurity[53] – hence Le Pen's definition of 'security as the first freedom' was particularly enticing. Even though this sense of insecurity receded gradually after the mid-1970s, the justification of immigrant labour as contributing to national prosperity could no longer be used.[54] This meant that the ethnic minorities could be construed as expendable. Furthermore, a Socialist majority could be more readily blamed for disregarding the national interest on ideological grounds, and the 'orthodox' right which used such arguments in opposition found itself pushed further into an anti-immigrant stance by the competition (*surenchère*) of the FN.

The turning point in the electoral scores of the FN occurred in 1983, after the decrease in the sense of insecurity. A number of other considerations must be taken into account to explain this upswing (which, in any case, is more marked for the FN than for Le Pen personally, thereby confirming his early charismatic effect).[55] Firstly, the introduction of proportional representation helped the minor parties, FN included, in the Euro-elections of 1984 and the general election of 1986. Secondly, local elections (at Dreux, Aulnay and in the Morbihan department in 1983) and Euro-elections are not as 'committal' as presidential or parliamentary ones. They provide an opportunity for expressing resentment at, and giving a warning to, the main political parties. Furthermore, they have a cumulative effect, in attracting the attention of the media and in convincing people that a vote for the FN would not be wasted in future. This appeared a good deal more credible in 1983, after a 16 per cent score in the local elections at Dreux, than in 1978 when the corresponding results was 2 per cent. Thirdly, the spread of conservative values affected the whole of the right in the 1980s, thereby prompting some Gaullist and even, occasionally, some Giscardian voters to support the FN.[56] This 'slide to the right' was favoured by the dissemination of new political themes (security/immigration) over which the traditional parties wavered. Consequently, the clear, if simplistic, position of Le Pen was increasingly contrasted with the inability of the political elite to confront the everyday problems of life in France. The less politicians are trusted and the less they are believed to be speaking the truth,[57] the more willingness there is to vote for 'the odd man out'. As the *état de grâce* – the period of indulgence towards the new Socialist administration – ended, and as new austerity policies were implemented, the hour of the FN appeared to have come. In the parliamentary elections of 1986, Le Pen was returned as MP for Paris – back in Parliament after 20 years (his 'traversée du désert' or period in the wilderness – an expression used by analogy with de Gaulle's exile in Colombey-les-Deux-Eglises under the Fourth Republic).

A number of data confirmed the new-found strength of the FN. From a (self-confessed) membership of 20,000 in spring 1984, it reached 50,000 a year later. Its score of 10.87 per cent in the Euro-elections of 1984 showed areas of considerable influence (e.g. 21.39 per cent in the Nice area, an average of over 19 per cent in the whole South-East, 14.53 per cent in the Paris area, 13.2 per cent in Corsica). These coincided with regions where the *pieds noirs* settlers are numerous and also where the presence of immigrants is keenly resented.[58] The South-East in particular – with its Italianate political tradition of clientelism and with well-established ties between local politicians and organised crime, for example, in Marseilles and Nice, has always been the neo-Fascist heartland. The same areas of concentration characterised the FN results in the local elections of 1985, where its candidates gained 8.8 per cent of votes cast. As it had put up no candidates in approximately a quarter of *cantons*, this apparent decline in relation to the Euro-elections was actually a consolidation, even a slight increase, in urban constituencies. In the general election of 1986, with its vote down to 9.8 per cent, the FN showed the same regional pattern (peaking in the South-East, with 22 per cent of the vote in the Marseilles area, and around Paris), but with a changing electorate. Its voters were becoming younger, less middle class and less likely to have voted previously for a party of the right; they were more pessimistic than the average about the role of their country in the world, about unemployment and about the future of the economy.[59] In addition, they were disenchanted with all political parties: predictably, nearly three-quarters of them voiced their dissatisfaction with the Socialists, but over half felt that way about the Gaullist–Giscardian coalition of the right. They tended to view the whole political class as corrupt: an opinion expressed by 71 per cent of them (as against 42 per cent of the French in general). Thus, the catchment area of the FN remained geographically circumscribed, but shifted downwards in the social scale and towards younger males.

That the intake of the FN should be young and predominantly male[60] is striking, since this distinguishes it sharply from the parties of the right, as does its relatively high intake of clerical and manual workers – even compared with the Socialist Party. This youthfulness of its activists means that they have no direct experience of the Vichy era or even of decolonisation. Some have transited through the *Occident* movement, but nearly half – in a sample dating back to 1978 – had no political past at all, a proportion which has certainly increased in the meantime. As a result, the 'complexes' of the past are shrugged off with greater ease than by older age groups. There is no hesitation in asserting extreme views, both in the valuation of authority and in that of the in-group ('the tribe' to be protected from outsiders).[61] The avowed motivation for supporting the FN is the dislike and fear of immigrants, linked with a concern for security. The two main themes of Le Pen's discourse are clearly echoed by his supporters, but in the reverse order – his emphasis being always on law and order, while his disparagement is not limited to ethnic groups, but extends to other 'undesirables', such as AIDS sufferers and homosexuals. These attempts to capitalise on 'moral panics' are better adapted to the nostalgia for the past prevalent among fundamentalists and other traditional supporters of the extreme right. They find less of an echo among the new constituency in which religious practice is low and views about sexual morality (about abortion in particular) are more emancipated than among supporters of the two main right-wing parties. A common antagonism, in both categories, towards established parties and towards politicians in general, is in tune with Le Pen's attacks against the 'gang of four'. The votes for him and his party are always protest votes, with a component of nostalgia dominant until 1986 and an element of anomie in the new, suburban lower-class strongholds, often formerly dominated by the Communist Party. By its very nature, this support is fluctuating and highly dependent on an emotional response to the leader.

Media exposure was therefore crucial to the creation of Le Pen's credibility as a candidate for the presidency of the Republic, and not only to the diffusion of his views. Attempts to tone down his message, in order to reassure a wider audience, occasionally gave way to a more spontaneous reaction. The first slip-up, the reference to the Holocaust as 'a point of detail' during an interview in September 1987, was damaging in so far as it revived fears about the extremism of the FN, even among some of its more 'respectable' supporters and sponsors.[62] A year later, the play on words: *Durafour crématoire* (from the name of the Civil Service minister Durafour and *four crématoire* or gas oven) was found distasteful even by FN leaders, so that the single MP the party boasted at the time, Yann Piat, was expelled for her criticism of Le Pen's 'barrack-room joke'. Yet neither his verbal infelicities, nor his matrimonial troubles did the presidential candidate any real harm. In the first round, in April 1988, he gained 14.4 per cent of votes, thus establishing a record for the extreme right and, apparently, managing to hold his different constituencies – neo-Poujadists, white-collar and suburban working class. He even widened his geographical base somewhat, especially in eastern France (where nationalism always had a strong hold), but with inroads in the South-West and in his own Brittany. The extent to which this was a protest vote was shown in the second round of the election, when over a fifth shifted their allegiance to Mitterrand, rather than supporting the candidate of the right, Chirac. The extent to which it was 'personalised', attracted by one man's charisma, was demonstrated in the general election of June 1987, when the Front went down from thirty-two MPs to one. The policy of electoral agreements with right-wing parties had occasionally served them, but had not delivered votes for FN candidates. Once more, it appeared to have been marginalised and the image of Le Pen to have deteriorated (according to *Le Monde*, 69 per cent of the French considered him 'a dangerous man' and 61 per cent a racist).[63]

Yet again, the Euro-elections showed that the FN had become a feature of the French political landscape. With 11.73 per cent of the vote, it gained ten seats in Strasbourg, achieved the third highest score of all parties (behind the orthodox right and the Socialists) and influenced, to a considerable extent, the political discourse of Giscard's right. The opportunity to be in the news again – when one of the new FN Euro-MPs was in the chair as Father of the House and caused an exodus in protest – was no doubt the first of many. Le Pen's ability to generate scandal is only exceeded by his zest for it and by his survival skills.

These skills have remained in evidence throughout the early 1990s. They have helped personalise the FN and legitimise it. Thus, under Socialist rule, some local authorities attempted to restrict access to their premises in order to prevent the FN from holding meetings there. In the run-up to the regional elections of 1992, Le Pen appeared repeatedly on television to complain that his party was denied free speech. The part of victim suited him to perfection. For the government, it was a no-win situation. The Interior Minister had to appeal for restrictions which were clearly counter-productive to be relaxed. As a result, Le Pen could pass for having campaigned to have democratic rights restored. From then on, mass meetings under FN auspices could proceed without interference, despite the potential threat to law and order. Incidentally, the annual parade on 1 May attracts approximately 10,000 participants as does the Whitsun pilgrimage to Chartres.

Before mass audiences, Le Pen, basking in the limelight, has increasingly tended to play the elder statesman, almost as if the leopard were actually beginning to change his spots. 'People say that [his] sophisticated new wife has tamed him – made him more elegant, less aggressive, more statesmanlike. But behind the well-tailored suits and erudite-sounding Latin phrases, the bully-boy still lurks. . . . His public performances are masterly,'[64] if occasionally marred by lack of restraint. This has sometimes been construed as a spontaneous outburst of verbal violence, revealing the man behind the mask. In fact each performance may be calculated to help demarcate the FN from the conventional parties of the right. Unlike the Italian MSI, the FN does not recognise trends in its midst, yet it aims to attract multiple associations pertaining to different extremist sub-cultures (e.g. *Pétainistes*, the former OAS internees).[65] While Le Pen's verbal infelicities have been shown to have a negligible impact on votes, they may well have helped widen his appeal to the far right. Over time the local bulletins issued by the FN in all parts of France have become more and more streamlined to achieve a moderate approach to emotive issues, including immigration. There is little scope for self-expression for the potentially antagonistic sub-cultures coexisting within the nationalist spectrum, from Catholic traditionalism to neo-paganism and from neo-liberalism to corporatism. Ideological controversy being kept to a minimum, the occasional expression of extremist tenets from the top may contribute to reinforce cohesion among the party's cadres.

Despite occasional splits, such as that of the team which published the monthly *Militant* and later became *Parti Nationaliste Français* (PNF),[66] and the withdrawal of comparatively moderate individuals,[67] the FN has endured. In this it differs from other groupings originating from the extreme right. It boasts an active membership of approximately 75,000 and is organised in each *départment*, as well as providing a framework of *cercles* for special interest groups, such as students, farmers and the military.

Le Pen's score in the presidential election of 1988 (i.e. 14.4 per cent) has never been achieved by his party, which gained 13.5 per cent of votes cast in the *cantonales* of March 1994.[68] The fact that the general elections of 1993 had not yielded a single parliamentary seat had been construed as highly damaging. However, the return to the traditional French 'two-round, first-past-the-post' voting system was bound (and intended) to harm small parties. Furthermore the two parties of the moderate right had borrowed extensively from Le Pen's rhetoric during the electoral campaign. Chirac's reference to an 'overdose' of immigrants was matched by Giscard d'Estaing's allusion to an 'invasion', which his follower Michel Poniatowski actually compared to the Nazi occupation. Similarly, during the referendum campaign on the Maastricht Treaty in September 1992, Le Pen's strictures against the *fédérastes* were matched by nationalist appeals for a 'no' vote from among both RPR and UDF leaders (Phillipe Séguin and Charles Pasqua, and Philippe de Villiers respectively).

The parties which make up the ruling majority have been poaching on FN territory. Luring voters by the promise of more restrictive policies on the naturalisation of immigrants, they have actually gained power. Yet they have done so at a time when the growth of unemployment can hardly be blamed on either the inflow of immigration or the Brussels bureaucracy. As public opinion begins to turn against the ruling coalition, neither the neo-Gaullists nor the Giscardians can claim to occupy the high moral ground. Such is the measure of Le Pen's success.

List of abbreviations

ALP	*Alliance pour les Libertés et le Progrès* [Alliance for Freedoms and Progress]
AR	*Armée Révolutionnaire* [Revolutionary Army]
FANE	*Fédération d'Action Nationale et Européenne* [Federation of National and European Action]
FLN	*Front de Libération Nationale* [National Liberation Front]
FN	*Front National* [National Front]
FNE	*Faisceaux Nationaux et Européens* [National and European Fasces]
GRECE	*Groupement de Recherche et d'Etudes pour une Civilisation Européenne* [Research and Study Group for European Civilisation]
ND	*Nouvelle Droite* [New Right]
OAS	*Organisation de l'Armée Secrète* [Secret Army Organisation]

ON   *Ordre Nouveau* [New Order]
PFN   *Parti des Forces Nouvelles* [Party of the New Forces]
PNF   *Parti Nationaliste Français* [French Nationalist Party]

Notes

1. On the political philosophy of *Action Française*, see J.-P. Apparu (ed.), *La droite aujourd'hui*, Armand Michel, Paris, 1979, pp. 117 ff.
2. C. Nicolet, *L'idée républicaine en France (1789–1924)*, Gallimard, Paris, 1982, p. 16, analyses the evolution of the nationalist right towards radicalism, nationalism and populism from the 1880s onwards. See also, Z. Sternhell, *La droite révolutionnaire (1855–1914)*, Seuil, Paris, 1978, who describes this tradition as pre-Fascist.
3. Z. Sternhell, *Neither Left nor Right*, University of California Press, Berkeley, CA, 1986.
4. For full information on this debate, see the earlier versions of Rémond's accounts of the right, i.e. R. Rémond, *La droite en France de 1815 à nos jours*, Aubier, Paris, 1954, and *La droite en France de la Restauration à la Cinquième République*, Aubier, Paris, 1963, as well as *Les droites*, cit. (which is a rejoinder to Sternhell, *La droite*, cit.).
5. R. Brasillach, *Les captifs*, Plon, Paris, p. 115.
6. The close relationship between the two, before the war, gave added verisimilitude to this assumption. Pétain was the godfather of De Gaulle's son, and it was to him that De Gaulle's book was dedicated.
7. R. Paxton, *Vichy France*, Barrie and Jenkins, London, 1972.
8. B. Criddle, 'France: legitimacy attained', in E. Kolinsky (ed.), *Opposition in Western Europe*, Croom Helm, London, 1987, pp. 108 ff, emphasises the importance of the Algerian crisis for relations between right and extreme right.
9. S. Hofman, *Le mouvement Poujade*, Colin, Paris, 1956.
10. A. Siegfried, *Tableau politique de la France de l'Ouest sous la Troisième République*, A. Colin, Paris, 1913, p. 495, quoted by Perrineau in N. Mayer and P. Perrineau, *Le Front National à découvert*, Presses de la Fondation Nationale des Sciences Politiques, 1989, p. 37.
11. Two authors of attempts on De Gaulle's life, Alain Bougrenet de la Tocnaye and Jean-Marie Bastien-Thiry, claimed this right. See Rémond, *Les droites*, cit., pp. 369 ff.
12. F. Duprat, *Les mouvements d'extrême droite en France depuis 1944*, Albatros, Paris, 1972, pp. 56 ff.
13. See J.-M. Theolleyre, *Les Néo-Nazis*, Messidor, Paris, 1982, and J. Algazy, *La tentation néo-fasciste en France*, Fayard, Paris, 1984.
14. European Parliament, Committee of Inquiry into the Rise of Fascism and Racism in Europe, *Report on the Findings of the Inquiry*, Luxemburg, 1985.
15. Rémond, *Les droites*, cit., p. 269.
16. P.-A. Taguieff, 'La stratégie culturelle de la Nouvelle Droite en France (1968–1983)' in R. Badinter *et al.*, *Vous avez dit Fascismes?*, Arthaud-Montalba, Paris, 1984, pp. 20 ff.
17. M. Vaughan, 'Nouvelle Droite: Cultural Power and Political Influence', in D. S. Bell (ed.), *Contemporary French Political Parties*, Croom Helm, London, 1982, p. 52 ff.
18. M. Vaughan, 'The Wrong Right in France', in Kolinsky (ed.), *Opposition*, cit., p. 276.
19. European Parliament, Committee of Inquiry, *Report*, cit., p. 39.
20. A. Rollat, *Les hommes de l'extrême droite: Le Pen, Marie, Ortiz et les autres*, Calmann-Lévy, Paris, p. 57.
21. Ibid., p. 7.
22. The two main sources – sharply contrasting in intent and approach – are the hagiographic

J. Marcilly, *Le Pen sans bandeau*, Grancher, Paris, 1984, and the highly critical E. Plénel and A. Rollat (eds), *L'effet Le Pen*, Le Monde – La Découverte, Paris, 1984.

23. J.-Y., Camus, 'Origine et formation du Front National', in Mayer and Perrineau, *Le Front National*, cit., pp. 20 ff.

24. See Marcilly, *Le Pen*, cit., p. 199.

25. Ibid., p. 28.

26. Ibid., p. 28.

27. Details in *Le Monde*, 14 Feb. 1984 (article by E. Plénel), p. 10.

28. 43 per cent of respondents in a SOFRES survey, conducted in 1985, believed that if he had actually been a torturer in Algeria, this would not disqualify Le Pen as a politician. See SOFRES, *Opinion Publique*, Gallimard, Paris, 1985.

29. J. Ferniot, *Pierrot et Alice*, Grasset, Paris, p. 28.

30. In the *Antenne 2* interview, Le Pen said that he 'voted for Joan of Arc' in the second round of the presidential election (of 1974). He wants the saint's day (8 May) to be a national holiday. See Marcilly, *Le Pen*, cit., pp. 147 ff, and p. 157.

31. Pierrette Lalanne was the former wife of a theatrical impresario (and friend of Le Pen, for whom she left her husband). Their marriage took place soon after he ceased to be an MP and she helped him launch his recording company.

32. In 1976, Mr and Mrs Le Pen inherited some thirty million francs from Hubert Saint-Julien Lambert, whose family were the biggest cement producers in France. Lambert – a nationalist writer on military matters – died aged 42, leaving his whole estate to the Le Pens. The Lambert family initially challenged this will, but the matter was settled out of court. See Plénet and Rollat, *L'effet Le Pen*, cit., pp. 229 ff.

33. See N. Meyer, in Meyer and Perrineau, *Le Front National*, cit., pp. 256 ff.

34. Le Pen supporter, quoted by P.-A. Taguieff, 'La métaphysique de Jean-Marie Le Pen', in Mayer and Perrineau, *Le Front National*, cit., pp. 173–4.

35. European Parliament, Committee of Inquiry, *Report*, cit., p. 38.

36. J.-M. Le Pen, *Les Français d'abord*, Carrère-Lafon, Paris, 1984.

37. Vaughan, in Kolinsky (ed.), *Opposition*, cit., p. 283.

38. Le Pen, in Apparu (ed.), *La droite*, cit., p. 175.

39. See Vaughan, in Kolinsky (ed.), *Opposition*, cit., p. 282.

40. Le Pen, *Les Français*, cit., p. 183.

41. Ibid., p. 176.

42. Marcilly, *Le Pen*, cit., p. 190.

43. J. P. Honoré, 'La hiérarchie des sentiments', in *Mots*, No. 12, 1986, pp. 129–57. In June 1989, at a special meeting of Euro-MPs of the extreme right from five countries, Le Pen reasserted that he had no objection to the presence of Portuguese immigrants in France, provided that 'national preference' applied to employment. See *Expresso* (Lisbon), 16 June 1989, p. 3.

44. Le Pen, *Les Français*, cit., p. 71.

45. Ibid., p. 140.

46. Ibid., p. 115.

47. J. Marcilly, *Le Pen*, cit., p. 106.

48. *Le Monde*, 12 June 1987, p. 6.

49. G. Le Bon, *Psychologie des foules*, 1895, quoted in G. Paicheler, *Psychologie des influences sociales*, Delachaux and Niestlé, Paris, 1985, p. 55.

50. G. Albet and M. Sajous, *Contrepoint, ou l'art d'être Républicain*, Proceedings of the third International Lexicology Conference, Ecole Normale Supérieure de St Cloud, Paris, 1984.

51. See data in Meyer and Perrineau, *Le Front National*, cit., pp. 70–1, about the peak of insecurity in 1975 (at 70 per cent of sample) and the drop to 59 per cent in 1984.

52. J.-M. Domenach, 'Des Transferts', in J.-P. Apparu (ed.), *La droite*, cit., p. 66.

53. R. Dulong and J. Léon, 'L'insécurité est-elle de droite?', in Albet and Sajous, *Contrepoint*, cit., emphasise the exploitation of cases of self-defence or of militia-creation by the extreme right, and stress its ambivalence towards the police.

54. G. P. Freeman, *Immigrant Labour and Racial Conflict in Immigrant Societies*, Princeton University Press, Princeton, N.J., 1979, pp. 280 ff.

55. In 1973, the average FN score was about 2 per cent, but Le Pen's own, in Paris's 15th *arrondissement*, was 5.2 per cent. Even in the parliamentary elections of 1981, when the FN barely reached 1 per cent, he achieved 4.4 per cent in the 17th *arrondissement*.

56. C. Yamal, 'Le RPR et l'UDF face au FN: concurrence et connivence', *Revue politique et parlementaire*, 1984, LXXXVI, No. 913, pp. 6 ff.

57. J. Charlot, 'La transformation de l'image des partis politiques français', *Revue française de science politique*, 1986, XXXVI, 1, pp. 5 ff.

58. 57 per cent of foreigners in France live in the three main areas of FN concentration, i.e. Île-de-France, Rhône-Alpes and Provence-Côte d'Azur (*Le Monde*, 15–16 Jan. 1984, p. 11).

59. H. Sofres, *L'état de l'opinion*, Seuil, Paris, 1988, p. 131 ff (The age-group under 35 was up to 43 per cent of the Front's electorate in 1987, according to a SOFRES poll; the lower-middle and working class was up to 61 per cent, and the percentage of those who were sympathetic to the two main parties of the right was down to 12 per cent – as against 31, 37 and 39 per cent respectively in 1984).

60. C. Ysmal, 'Sociologie des élites du FN', in Mayer and Perrineau, *Le Front National*, cit., pp. 107 ff.

61. J. Stoetzel, *Les valeurs du temps présent: une enquête européenne*, PUF, Paris, 1983, shows a greater sense of isolation and more dislike of interaction with people who do not share their views, as well as more worries about the future among supporters of the extreme right in all European countries.

62. *Le Monde*, 1 Jan. 1987, p. 6. One of the main providers of funds for Le Pen, *Causa*, an organisation of the Moon sect, gave warnings to Le Pen, through its representative Pierre Ceyrac, that anti-Semitic statements would have to be avoided.

63. *Le Monde*, 6 Jan. 1989, p. 8.

64. *The Economist*, 14 March 1992, p. 66.

65. J.-Y. Camus and R. Monzat, *Les Droites nationales et radicales en France*, Presses Universitaires de Lyon, Lyons, 1992, p. 105.

66. The *Militant* was first published in 1967 and became an FN organ in 1972. The split occurred in 1981 and the PNF was created in 1983. See Camus and Monzat, *Les Droites*, cit., pp. 254–5.

67. Namely: François Bechelot, the late Michel de Camaret, Gilbert Devèze, Olivier d'Ormesson and Jules Monnerot.

68. *Le Monde*, 22 March 1994, p. 3.

Chapter 12

THE NEW RIGHT IN FRANCE
Douglas Johnson

One day in February 1893, Xavier Rollin, who was a mason working in Paris, asked for a day off. He had, he said, to visit a relative who was ill somewhere in the suburbs. He was given his day off. But he did not turn up for work the next day, nor on subsequent days. After a week's absence, as one can readily imagine, his wife and his work-mates were extremely worried, and about this time, on a Sunday, a number of these same work-mates spent part of their leisure time visiting the morgue on the Île Saint-Louis. Whether this was a normal way of spending a Sunday afternoon or whether it was a special expedition arising from their anxiety concerning the missing Rollin, is not certain. But perhaps it does not matter. Among the corpses that had been fished out of the Seine or had been found on the public highway, and which were displayed to the public so that they could be identified, they recognised their friend. He had the same face, the same moustache, even in death, they thought, the same somewhat mocking expression which had characterised him in life. Deeply moved, they asked to see the clothes which the dead man had been wearing. They were shown the blue overalls that a worker normally wore; these, though, were covered with white plaster. There could be no doubt: it must be their friend.

When Madame Rollin came to see the corpse, she had no doubt either, and she tearfully identified her dead husband. Everything seemed sad, but simple. There was only one further formality to be gone through. The measurement of the corpse, and a comparison of these measurements with the official anthropometric records which the police kept. Presumably Rollin had a criminal record; and presumably the corpse also possessed a criminal record. At all events, the authorities asserted that in spite of the positive identification made by all those who knew Rollin best, the corpse could not be his. The shape of the corpse's ear did not tally with the records of Rollin's ear. And sure enough, a Rollin, who was alive but probably not well, emerged shortly from the prison where he had been held on a charge of drunkenness.

This is, one would have thought, a story which is amusing in its tragi-comedy rather than edifying in its suggestions. Many explanations could be given as to how the misunderstanding arose. The author of the anthropometrical system, Bertillon, has had a popular rather than a scientific reputation (in the *Hound of the Baskervilles* he is presented as a more impressive scientific investigator than Sherlock Holmes). The whole story may, in any case, be inaccurately represented. How extraordinary, then, that it should be presented as a key passage by Henri de Lesquen in his book *La*

234

Politique du Vivant, published on behalf of the *Club de l'Horloge*, an independent group of higher French civil servants and technocrats. The biological implications are made explicit. Individuals exist in all their physical originality. Socially they may be confused with someone else. Even within the intimacy of their family, confusion can exist. But scientifically each individual is different from any other person; one person is different from another. Julian Huxley is called in as a witness. Individual human beings are separated from each other by degrees which are as considerable as those which separate one part of the animal kingdom from another. There is, thus, a fundamental variation; there are, therefore, distances; there can arise hostilities and mutual incomprehension. But all these are based upon scientific reality. The social and political consequences are clear. To endeavour to treat human beings as if they were all alike is to start from a false premise. To suggest that people are born equal, or to aspire to some sort of equality, is to fly in the face of a sociobiological knowledge which was already illustrated in the days of Bertillon, but which has been more than confirmed by a great deal of subsequent investigation.[1]

This new point was not confined to the *Club de l'Horloge*, which tended to be an intellectual pressure group close to the sources of political power in France, especially Gaullist power and aspirations. It was founded in 1974 by a number of graduates of the *Ecole Nationale d'Administration* and of the *Polytechnique*, and took its name from the fact that its original meetings took place in a room at the *Ecole Nationale d'Administration* which contained a particularly ornate clock. It claimed to be independent of other intellectual groups and it distinguished itself from them in so far as its members both sought and achieved active positions in politics.[2] Nevertheless it had many similarities with the *Groupement de Recherche et d'Etudes pour une Civilisation Européenne* (known as GRECE) and with the various organisations and publications which became known as '*Nouvelle Droite*' [ND].[3] GRECE was founded in January 1968 by a small group of young men. Many of them had earlier been associated with a university students' organisation, the *Fédération des Etudiants Nationalistes* formed in opposition to the *Union National des Etudiants Français*, which allegedly, had supported the cause of the rebellion in Algeria from 1960 onwards, and with a number of not very successful periodicals such as *Les Cahiers universitaires*, *Défense de l'Occident*, *Europe Action* and *Valeurs actuelles*, which had all been accused of being Fascist and racist. More significant, perhaps, is the fact that through these activities, the founders of GRECE had established a link with earlier right-wing thinkers and leaders, such as Jacques Doriot, Pierre Drieu la Rochelle, Robert Brasillach and the Breton regionalists who had received Nazi support during the occupation. The years after 1965 saw the collapse of many of these right-wing endeavours, as, in the presidential election of 1965 and the general election of 1967, right-wing candidates had clearly failed. With the Algerian question settled once and for all and with *l'après Gaullisme* conspicuously on the agenda, a new start was necessary, and this was the reason for the creation of GRECE.

From 1968 onwards, GRECE shared the experience of many *clubs* which had, in a France dominated by Gaullism, become an accepted means of political discussion and expression. There were dissensions and rivalries among its members; individuals came and went; seminars and colloquia were held with varying degrees of success. But, gradually, progress was made. The review *Nouvelle Ecole*, which had circulated privately among members of the group, became public from 1969 onwards; the same happened to the review *Eléments*, from 1973; between 1975 and 1976, bulletins were circulated in military, medical and educational circles; in 1976 a publishing house, Copernic, was founded; and in 1978, with the launching of the Saturday supplement of the newspaper *Le Figaro*, called *Le Figaro Magazine*, some members of GRECE became known to a wide public. From June to September 1979, the *Nouvelle Droite* became the term by which this group of writers was known (contrary to their wishes), and they became the subject of considerable interest, with newspapers publishing an unprecedented number of articles and interviews concerning them.[4]

The first problem concerning the ND is to understand why it created such a sensation during the summer of 1979. Articles about these thinkers had been published earlier and had aroused little interest.[5] It appeared that a moment had come when there was a particular need to discover something new. There were the *nouveaux philosophes* (Bernard-Henri Lévy, Jean-Marie Benoit, Jean-Paul Dollé and, in spite of his denials, André Glucksmann), the *nouveaux historiens* (Georges Duby, Pierre Chaunu, Emmanuel Le Roy Ladurie, Jacques Le Goff), the *nouveaux économistes* (with Jean-Jacques Rosa), the *nouveaux sociologues* (with Evelyne Sullerot); there was, of course, the *nouvelle cuisine* and there was talk of *un nouveau romantisme*. It was suggested that all this stemmed from the discrediting of the old creeds. No one believed in Marxism or in the Soviet Union any more. The churches had little appeal. Since 1968, revolution seemed impossible. De Gaulle had no successor as the leader of the nation. Liberalism and capitalism were both uninspiring and unsuccessful. Since intellectuals detest a vacuum, something had to take the place of what was missing.

At the same time, the nature of the ND's presentation of ideas was attractive. Alain de Benoist was continually surveying the literature of the past, and his book, *Vu de droite*, which received a prize from the *Académie Française* in 1978, was a collection of reviews. When the public had the impression that they were being bombarded by publications and that they were saddled with an intolerable burden of past thinkers, it was very satisfying to have someone who was prepared to act as a guide. In this, Alain de Benoist resembled Bernard-Henri Lévy, except, it was said, that he appeared actually to have read the books which he was talking about.[6]

The French public is attracted towards superlatives. René Mayer was known as the richest and most intelligent man in the National Assembly. General Salan was the most decorated soldier in France. Raymond Barre was the finest economist in the country. And soon it was whispered that Alain de Benoist had the best private library in Paris. He was said to be capable of explaining, in simple terms, the most complicated ideas, and to bring to life a whole series of half-heard names, from Kant to Wittgenstein, from Hegel to Karl Popper. He was a reassuring figure when compared to the young intellectuals who had seemed so threateningly aggressive in 1968, or to the structuralists and their associates who were so incomprehensible at all times. Furthermore, such an 'encyclopédie vivante' was to be encountered in a glossy magazine (also containing articles about tourism and restaurants) which, in 1979, was distributed free.

There were two other features which aided the success of the ND. One was that they were not afraid of being associated with the word 'right'. Since the Liberation, no one wished to be classified as belonging to the right politically. No one, or hardly anyone, had claimed to be in that tradition or had willingly accepted being placed on the right-hand side of the hemicycle of the Assembly. Words like *centre* or even *centre-gauche* had been preferred. This sensitivity demonstrated that the normal aims of social democracy were shared by everyone within a framework of general consensus. By this, was meant the search for general prosperity, the demand for greater equality and the achievement of social and economic security. The fact that a group had appeared which did not accept these priorities, and which accepted a label which said so, was striking and unusual.[7] The other feature was that the ND was attacked as being dangerous. The very fact that they had received their greatest publicity through the newspaper *Le Figaro*, whose owner had, at best, an ambiguous attitude during the war, at worst an unpatriotic one, was sufficient to suggest that one was witnessing a revival of French Fascism. It was alleged that racist articles had appeared in early numbers of *Nouvelle Ecole*, and that while such manifestations had, then, been confined to a few isolated and unimportant groups, the fact that they could now achieve a mass circulation was a direct threat to democracy in France. There was, thus, a general denunciation of the ND. Even when writers were careful to say that they were observing not a French version of Hitlerism but a revival of the old, traditional and irrelevant right, it was emphasised that such a resurrection was disagreeable and unwelcome.[8] But the more the ND was attacked in these terms, the more it defended itself, the more it appeared in the public gaze and the greater the importance it assumed.

Naturally, other reasons were given to explain the success, or the scandal, of the ND. It was said to be an invention of the left. Embarrassed by the revelations of the Soviet gulag and by the supposed discrediting of Marxism, disappointed by the failure to bring about a union of the Socialists, Communists and Radicals and to win the elections of 1978, the left was quick to seize upon the opportunity of creating a scare. What *France-Soir* called '*la basse police intellectuelle*' of the left brandished the old monster of Fascism in order to give life to what was a strategy in a shambles and a cause which many thought of as lost.[9] The *Giscardiens*, then in power, were also believed to have an interest in magnifying the importance of the ND. They constantly sought to enlarge their support in the centre and they were only too pleased to suggest that they were liberals who had nothing in common with the right as exemplified by the ND and which they too viewed with hostility and apprehension. The man most directly responsible for bringing the ND into the public eye, the editor of *Figaro Magazine*, Louis Pauwels, explained in an interview what he considered to be the farcical nature of such exaggerations. He claimed that the ND hardly existed; that those who sought to make it appear as a sinister force had commercial motives, since they wished to attack the economic success then being enjoyed by his magazine. He denied that he was a member of GRECE or of the *Club de l'Horloge*, and he scorned the idea that his publication had accepted the ideas of the ND. However, such declarations did not put an end to the controversy (possibly because Pauwels had not been as explicit as he might have been: he did not mention his long-standing association with *Nouvelle Ecole* or the similarities between some of his own publications and those of the ND).[10]

One is obliged to conclude that there was a general fascination with the ND, both on the right and on the left.[11] It is conceivable that people were disarmed by the claim that GRECE was a laboratory of ideas and a centre for reflection, and that its leaders had no intention of leading an active political party. This may have coincided with the development of a certain public indifference to organised political parties. Alain de Benoist rejected any connection with a traditional right that was nationalist, militarist, religious, populist and, on occasions, racist and monarchist, and which sought to put crowds in the streets (as on 6 February 1934 in Paris) or deputies in the Assembly. He was amused, although in the long run irritated, by those foreign journalists who asked him how many parliamentary votes he controlled.[12] The only active political organisation which openly claimed any affinity with the ND was the *Parti des Forces Nouvelles* [PFN], the French branch of Euro-Right. It claimed that it had called for the formation of an ND as early as 1974, and that it had organised a forum with GRECE and with interested individuals (including Louis Pauwels) in that year. However, the leaders of the PFN, such as Pascal Gauchon and Alain Robert, had turned to Jean-Louis Tixier-Vignancourt as their leader and, with him, were then engaged in a rivalry with Jean-Marie Le Pen and the *Front National* for leadership of the extreme right. Its intellectuals, such as Yves Van Ghele, had been obliged to leave GRECE once they had become activists, militating in favour of the PFN. Its position, therefore, was confined to the statement that it and the ND were 'de la même génération' and 'de la même famille intellectuelle'.[13]

The discussion of whether the ND was a reincarnation of the old traditional right or not, or whether it was a camouflaged and coded post-war version of pre-war Fascism, has continued to be debated ever since the heady days of the summer of 1979. Some observers note that in a confidential memorandum it was determined to be prudent with regard to its vocabulary, but that, in spite of such precautions, one finds in its publications the essential mix of race-politics and race-science, and that its language is that of classical Fascism.[14] Raymond Aron, while being particularly anxious to be fair to Alain de Benoist and to avoid any suggestion that he was a National Socialist or a Fascist, nevertheless concluded that his manner of thinking and reasoning was often similar to that of the National Socialists and the Fascists.[15] René Rémond, the historian of the right in France, has observed a resemblance between the role of Charles Maurras in the *Action Française* and that of Alain de Benoist in the ND, a role which extends to their method of work, as well as to their vision of an active cultural group in conflict with a political establishment.[16]

Naturally, observers as sophisticated as Aron and Rémond were always well aware of the circumstances that cause the ND to be distinguished from any of its ancestors, whether French or not. Yet, it is true that Alain de Benoist has dominated his movement, as did Maurras. It is significant that both of them were more concerned with the cultural rather than with the political, and that both of them saw their work as something which had to be accomplished within a long framework of time. They both made a fundamental distinction between the day-to-day running of a society and the accepted political climate of that society. In 1979, Alain de Benoist was able to point out that the left had never been in power since the Liberation, but that the accepted political culture, whether it was expressed by intellectuals or by *instituteurs*, was dominated by the ideology and the assumptions of some sort of Marxism. In a manner which had been made familiar by Gramsci and by Althusser (two thinkers whom he claimed to admire), his object was to change the values and the assumptions of French society and to influence the prevailing ideological apparatus without having to gain any political victory, and without having to promote any institutional change. By constantly challenging old axioms, by bringing forward thinkers relegated to oblivion and by promoting ideas which were strongly in contradiction with certain values and principles that had been taken for granted, the ND sought to stake a claim and to be accepted. In this way, it is true that it can be compared to such figures as Maurice Barrès or Charles Maurras or to certain Fascist thinkers, all of whom challenged prevailing liberalism. But, it need hardly be said, this in no way makes it comparable to the *squadristi* or to the Brownshirts.

The challenge from the ND came essentially over three themes. Firstly, there was the rejection of equality. They argued that everyone must understand that people were not born free and equal. The study of primitive and ancient societies confirmed this. No community could take as its basis a purely arithmetical and theoretical equality, and no community should endeavour to construct such an equality. Secondly, there was the need for elites. Without a hierarchy, a society would have no sense of responsibility. A hierarchy classifies people according to their abilities and according to their tasks. Without this there can be no harmony. Thirdly the understanding of society depends upon science, that is to say sociobiology, rather than upon moral concepts. Human nature has an instinctive basis, however much this may be modified by social learning, and it is the genetic variety in the species which is vital for survival and for the success of the evolutionary process. In other words, what determines the nature of a society are the ethnic rather than the economic factors.[17]

It is not surprising that these simple ideas should have had a certain success. People had become cynical about the possibilities of achieving social equality. New elites were constantly being created and it seemed sensible to accept them. Contact with the Third World suggested that there were fundamental differences between groups, and it did not seem unreasonable to suppose that biology might some day be recognised as being as important in political life as economics.

There was nothing surprising, either, in the fact that the ND was hostile both to the Soviet Union and to the United States (it was this latter hostility which aroused the most disapproval from Raymond Aron). No intellectual movement in France in 1979 would have stated otherwise. What was more unusual was its opposition both to Christianity and to Marxism. The basis of this attitude has been explained by Alain de Benoist as being an attack on a senseless form of history. Christianity, or Judeo-Christianity as he has always preferred to call it, supposes that there was once a moment of ante-history, the Garden of Eden, which was destroyed by the original sin of Adam and Eve. There will also be a period of post-history when the Redeemer returns. Marxism, equally, supposes that there was once a time of primitive communism when people lived happily together. One day, though, they committed the fault of dividing up property and labour, and there developed a system of classes which set the exploiters against the exploited. But this will also come to an end when those most exploited succeed in dominating all society. Then, exploitation will cease, harmony will reign and the state will wither away. For Christians as for Marxists, humankind is dominated by a past, a present and a future, and has therefore lost its freedom and the possibility of self-creation. It is not simply the church, the chapel, the ghetto and the gulag which have to be rejected, as if they were bad examples of good ideologies. Christianity is the Bolshevism of ancient times, monotheism is totalitarianism, all attempts at imposing equality are equally stultifying and barren. The philosophy of the ND is that of a new anthropology. The human being is a defiant being, a creature of unlimited possibilities.

It is not surprising that these aspects of the ND were not appreciated by the readers of *Figaro Magazine* or were mentioned by those who sought to frighten liberals with the bogy of immediate Fascism. The insistence upon the values of paganism may have had a passing appeal for societies which found some attraction in the mysteries of Eastern religions, but this was hardly likely to be lasting. What was most challenging, and therefore least acceptable, was the ND's questioning of accepted ideas about progress. History, they claimed, was not a linear process; history was chaos. The world and the future will be what the human race wishes to make of them. None of the rules and laws which have been accepted as universal need be accepted at all. Everything is open to question. There is no reason why anyone should accept the cult of weakness and humility that was inaugurated by Christianity; no reason why the cult of egalitarianism should be derived from the supposition that people wish to satisfy their material needs in the same economic manner; no reason to accept the rule of some superman with outstanding intelligence or strength. But if history is chaos, history none the less exists. Just as animals have their sense of order, of defence, of territory, of gradation, so people live in groups which develop their instincts, differences, intuitions, beliefs and varied forms of rootedness. History may be chaos, but that is all the more reason to believe, with Nietzsche, that the future belongs to the person with the longest memory. History may be chaos, but that is all the more reason to believe in what exists rather than in what ought to exist. Universal and abstract concepts are names which have no corresponding realities.[18]

It could be argued that such a method of thinking is devastating in its destructiveness, and that if it ever, for a short time, achieved a certain popularity, however limited, it was because no one obeyed Alain de Benoist's advice that the texts of the ND should be carefully read and studied. But it must be admitted that there are other reasons why the vogue of the ND was short-lived. It was a phenomenon of the media, and as such was bound to be temporary, by definition. It was, as was pointed out at the time, a characteristic of Parisian intellectual life to take up a current of thought, to give it importance and then to drop it. There is a tendency in all cultural and political pressure groups, especially in France, for individuals to fall out and for organisations to divide and to sub-divide, and this has happened to the ND. Financial support, however discreet, is not necessarily permanent.

The political climate has also changed. The victory of the left in 1981 was in itself significant, but the progressive abandonment by French Socialists of many of their egalitarian ideas removed an issue from the debate that had existed in 1979. The preoccupation with modernisation, which became a fetish for the Socialists under Prime Minister Laurent Fabius, pushed the hostility of the ND towards the modernisation of life by machine into the background.[19] The emergence of the *Front National* as a political party which wins votes means that allegations of racialism and anti-Semitism are concentrated upon Le Pen and his supporters, and there are few commentators who wish to organise a theoretical discussion when an extreme right-wing party is active in day-to-day political affairs. The ND was not alone in suffering from this lack of attention. If in the 1970s a paper like *Le Monde* was publishing many articles on the ND, in the early 1980s it was publishing articles about 'the silence of the intellectuals', a silence which allegedly was common to all branches of political allegiance. It was believed that intellectuals had been so wrong in the past that they should sacrifice their right to comment and to explain.

The circulation of ND periodicals declined, although there is some uncertainty about the exact number of readers.[20] But while it has been argued that the journal plays a vital part in the intellectual life of the Fifth Republic, particularly in the field of experimental ideas, it has also been claimed that the very success of the ND periodicals meant that their decline was inevitable. Once an argument has been taken away from the periodical which sows ideas and is taken up in more general discussion and debate, then the journal has lost much of its *raison d'être*.[21]

If this is so, then Alain de Benoist and his associates appear to have learned a lesson, or at least to have adapted themselves to a changing situation. The idea of an intellectual elite becoming an influence on politics gives way to a preoccupation with culture, and essentially with European culture. A new journal, *Krisis*, enabled the ND to engage the cooperation of intellectuals who were invariably classified as being people with left-wing sympathies, such as Jean-Pierre Vernant, Jean Baudrillard and Oliver Mongin (the director of the centre-left review *Esprit*). Eclecticism was the order of the day. *Krisis* announced that it would be on the left, on the right, at the heart of matters and in the middle of the world; and this included members of GRECE and the *Club de l'Horloge* who were associated with the extreme right. More directly connected with right-wing extremism, and with ideas denying or questioning the existence of war-time German gas-chambers, were certain members of the editorial board of *Nouvelle École*. It was also noted that Alain de Benoist was the director of a series published by Pardès, which included works on 'revolutionary traditionalists' (such as Oswald Spengler and Werner Sombart) but which also devoted works to the Italian Fascist Julius Evola and to the Nazi racist Hans Günther. He was also collaborating with the Italian publisher Roccia di Erec, whose director was the leader of the Italian New Right, Marco Tarchi.

Doubtless, the ND could have continued to attack universalism (especially as represented by Judeo-Christianity), individualism and bourgeois liberalism, sharpening these traditional themes with a denunciation of America, Brussels and its attempts to impose a uniformity upon the different countries of the European Community and the long-term effects of the Treaty of Versailles.[22] But there came a change in the intellectual climate of France.

Whether this change came about because there was an ideological vacuum, or whether it was forced upon intellectuals by the discovery of certain historical realities (the history of Vichy) or of public concern (immigration), there was a concentration on such issues as the nature of the nation and the nature of racism. In particular, there was alarm at the prospect of those who had always been considered left-wing, consorting with those who were assuredly right-wing.[23] There was a sense of alarm that certain influential thinkers held ambiguous positions on the subject of race and racism.[24] It was in October 1987 that the former editor of *Esprit* (and a former member of the Resistance) was accused of being a man of the right, the reason being that he had not denounced Le Pen and his (supposedly) flippant references to genocide.[25] The leading semiotician Julia Kristeva caused a scandal when she asked what benefits immigrants expected from *la nation française*, and wondered whether the 'abstract' advantages that were derived from French universalism might not be favourably compared to the 'concrete' advantages of Muslim girls having the right to wear the *tchador* (or veil) in school.[26] It was in this atmosphere that a number of intellectuals launched *un signal d'alarme* and founded a committee of vigilance against the manner in which the right was being legitimised.[27] All this expresses the real fear of the right in present-day France, as exemplified by a leading newspaper which, when reviewing two books on the 'Who's Who' of the extreme right, claimed that reading them caused one to go cold with fright.[28]

Naturally, in this atmosphere the attacks upon the ND have become increasingly fierce. Alain de Benoist has been accused of collaborating with former German Nazis, especially with the publisher Grabert, with the archaeologist (and former SS) Jan Kuhn and the artist Wilhelm Petersen. He has endeavoured to defend himself against these allegations.[29] Certain of his intellectual masters have been attacked, notably Georges Dumézil, the Indo-European specialist, once hailed as *le savant détective*, but recently decried as someone who inspired Hitler.[30] Perhaps the most important allegation is that the ND always had a double discourse, one that was public and harmless, the other that is secret and sinister.[31] The bitterest opponents of Alain de Benoist suggest that he, and the ND, are influenced by symbols of the Nazi past, particularly that which is to be found in the European scout movement and that which is symbolised by Marc Augier, otherwise known as Saint-Loup, the propagandist of the Charlemagne division that fought with the Germans against the Soviet Union.[32] Allegations are also made concerning the considerable funds that appear to be at the disposal of the *Club de l'Horloge*.[33]

Alain de Benoist and his associates have denounced these attacks and allegations as an intellectual persecution, a French version of McCarthyism. However, even when attacking the organisers of this persecution in an ND pamphlet, one notices that photographs of Klaus Barbie, Paul Touvier and René Bousquet (the organiser of the round-up of the Jews in the Vel d'Hiv in 1942) are included.[34]

There is every reason to believe that the ND has become a centre of confusion as well as controversy, and that this reduces its importance. As it denies allegations of anti-Semitism, negationism and Pétainism, it is lost in a welter of self-justification which weakens whatever message it still intends to put forward in the future.

List of abbreviations

GRECE	*Groupement de Recherche et d'Etudes pour une Civilisation Européenne* [Research and Study Group for European Civilisation]
ND	*Nouvelle Droite* [New Right]
PFN	*Parti des Forces Nouvelles* [Party of the New Forces]

Notes

1. H. De Lesquen, *La Politique du Vivant*, Club de l'Horloge, Paris, 1979.

2. It is noticeable that certain prominent members of the *Club de l'Horloge* have recently joined Le Pen's *Front National*, e.g. Jean-Yves le Gallou, who was formerly the Secretary-general of the *Club*, a member of the *Parti Républicain* and assistant to the mayor of Antony, in the southern suburbs of Paris. He explained his position in the *Front National's* weekly paper, *National-Hebdo*, 12 Sept. 1985. Yvan Blot, who was President of the *Club* until 1985 and who was closely associated with Jacques Chirac as mayor of Paris, was elected to the European Parliament as a member of the *Front National* in June 1989. See his interview in *Le Monde*, 2 June 1989, p.15, in which he explains his progressive disappointment with Chirac's party, and *Le Nouvel Observateur*, 7–13 Sept. 1989, p. 28, which describes him as the *maître-à-penser* of Le Pen.

3. The most authoritative work on GRECE is A.-M. Duranton-Crabol, *Visages de la Nouvelle Droite. Le GRECE et son histoire*, Presses de la Fondation Nationale des Sciences Politiques, Paris, 1988. This publication is a version of a thesis which was submitted to the University of Paris-Nanterre in 1987, the full text of which, with a copious bibliography, is deposited in the library of that university. On the subject of the relations between the *Club de l'Horloge* and the ND, see three articles in *Le Matin*, 25, 26, 27 July 1979. A more recent account which surveys the whole history of the ND and provides a biography of Alain de Benoist is P.-A. Taguieff, *Sur la Nouvelle Droite: Jalons d'une Analyse Critique*, La Découverte, Paris, 1994.

4. Alain de Benoist vigorously denied, in an interview with the author, 23 Jan. 1980, any association with 'la droite traditionnelle', and therefore thought the term '*Nouvelle Droite*' inappropriate. He did, however, state, on another occasion, that in the early 1960s he had been a militant in extreme right-wing circles (see Duranton-Crabol, *Visages*, cit., p. 20). Pierre Vial, the Secretary-general of GRECE, claimed that his group was concerned rather with the elaboration of '*une nouvelle culture de droite*' but which, however, felt itself to be nearer to '*une nouvelle gauche*' than to the traditional right (*Le Monde*, 24 August 1979, p. 2).

5. J. Brunn, *La Nouvelle Droite. Le Dossier du Procès*, Nouvelles Editions Oswald, Paris, 1979, is an anthology of these articles. A bibliography of the ND and of kindred movements in Italy is in *Mots*, No. 12, 1986, pp. 204–24.

6. T. Sheehan, 'Paris: Moses and Polytheism', *New York Review of Books*, 24 Jan. 1980, p. 13.

7. A. Fontaine, *Le Monde*, 11 July 1979, p. 1.

8. A. Kriegel, *Le Figaro*, 10 July 1979, p. 2. Several writers in the daily edition of this newspaper, including the editor, Jean d'Ormesson, expressed their disagreement with ideas published in the supplement.

9. *France-Soir*, 10 July 1979.

10. Louis Pauwels, interviewed by Georges Suffert, *Le Point*, 13 Aug. 1979, pp. 28–9. See also L. Pauwels, *Comment devient-on ce que l'on est*, Stock, Paris, 1978, and his preface to the collective work published under the name of Maiastra, *Renaissance de l'Occident*, Plon, Paris, 1979.

11. J.-F. Kahn, *Le Nouvel Observateur*, 13 Aug. 1979, p. 13, makes this point.

12. Author's interview with Alain de Benoist, 23 Jan. 1980.

13. *Le Monde*, 30 July 1979, p. 6. The ideology of the *Parti des Forces Nouvelles* is stated in its pamphlet, *Propositions pour une nation nouvelle*, Paris, 1978 (2nd edn).

14. M. Billig, *L'Internationale raciste. De la psychologie à la science des races*, Maspéro, Paris, 1981, pp. 123–49; G. Seidel, 'Le fascisme dans les textes de la Nouvelle Droite', *Mots*, No. 3, 1981, pp. 47–62.

15. R. Aron, *Mémoires*, Julliard, Paris, 1983, p. 701. He was very anxious that the ND should not be accused of causing the terrorist attack on the synagogue in the rue Copernic in Paris, and he took every opportunity of saying this.

16. R. Rémond, *Les Droites en France*, Aubier, Paris, 1982, pp. 283–5.

17. For the many sources of Alain de Benoist's ideas, see A.-M. Duranton-Crabol, *Visages*, cit.

18. P.-A. Taguieff, 'Alain de Benoist philosophe', *Les Temps Modernes*, Feb. 1984, vol. XIX-XXX, pp. 1439–78, and April 1985, pp. 1780–1842, criticises the nature of the philosophy of the ND and places it in its context in Europe, as well as discussing its attitude towards the controversy over the Holocaust in France.

19. G. Faye, *Les nouveaux enjeux idéologiques*, Editions du Labyrinthe, Paris, 1985.

20. Author's interview with Alain de Benoist, 26 Oct. 1987. On this occasion he said that contrary to press reports, *Nouvelle École* had 10,000 subscribers and that *Éléments* regularly sold between 15,000 and 20,000 copies. In particular it has been suggested that *Nouvelle École* had many fewer subscribers. See, for example, P.-A. Taguieff in 'Vingtième Siècle', *La Nouvelle Droite*, No. 40, Oct.–Dec. 1993, p. 10.

21. R. Reiffel, *La tribu des clercs. Les intellectuels sous la Ve Republique*, Calmann-Lévy, Paris, 1993; O. Corpet, 'La revue', in J.-F. Sirinelli (ed.), *Histoire des droites en France*, Gallimard, Paris, 1992, vol. 2, pp. 161–212.

22. See, for example, *Éléments*, No. 69, Autumn 1990.

23. S. Hoffman, 'France: Keeping the Demons at Bay', *New York Review of Books*, vol. XLI(5), 3 March 1994, p. 12 gives some references.

24. R.-P. Droit, 'La confusion des idées', *Le Monde*, 13 July 1993, pp. 1, 8–9.

25. *Le Nouvel Observateur*, 19 Sept. 1987, p. 34; 16 Oct. 1987, p. 31; Jean-Marie Domenach tells of other accusations made against him as a racist in *Éléments*, No. 78, Sept. 1993, pp. 25–7.

26. J. Kristeva, *Lettre ouverte à Harlem Désir*, Rivages, Paris, 1990.

27. *Le Monde*, 13 July 1993, p. 8 together with a follow-up article discussing the success of this movement, 24 Nov. 1994, p. 2.

28. *Libération*, 9 June 1992, p. 10.

29. R.-P. Droit and A. de Benoist, 'Les Mots et les Faits', *Le Monde*, 17 July 1993, and 31 July 1993, p. 7.

30. D. Lindenberg, *Les années souterraines: 1937–1947*, La Découverte, Paris, 1990. See also the conversation between Dumézil and R.-P. Droit published in the supplement to *Le Monde*, 13–14 July 1986, pp. 16–17.

31. R. Monzat, 'Les masques de la Nouvelle Droite', *Le Monde*, 19 March 1994, p. 4.

32. These allegations are to be found in 'Le rituel nazi de la Nouvelle Droite', *Le Monde*, 3 July 1993, p. 13. A protest was made against these allegations by Bruno Racouchot, director of Le Pen's private office, in *Le Monde*, 5 August 1993, p. 7.

33. *Libération*, 23–24 Oct. 1993, p. 6.

34. *La Nouvelle Inquisition: Ses acteurs, ses méthodes, ses victimes*, Le Labyrinthe, Paris, 1993.

Chapter 13

THE FAR RIGHT IN BELGIUM: THE DOUBLE TRACK
Guy Desolre

One of the principal characteristics of the Belgian far right is a strong difference between the situations prevailing in the Dutch-speaking part of the country and in the French-speaking part. This is why these will be treated separately in this chapter. Both history and the present justify such an approach.

Far right parties and groups define themselves or let themselves be defined (in Belgium as in other countries) by their nationalist xenophobic or (not always avowed) racist attitudes. The Flemish far right defines itself as Flemish Nationalist and independentist, while the French-speaking far right defines itself, generally, as unitarist and anti-federalist.

If the far right groups in French-speaking Belgium have almost always been characterised by royalist positions, the Flemish Bloc [*Vlaams Blok*, VB] defines itself unequivocally as republican.

The Flemish far right is most concentrated around the VB, while the far right in French-speaking Belgium is scattered among a myriad of tendencies and groups of various importance. Both on the organisational and on the parliamentary level, the Flemish far right is much more powerful than its counterpart in French-speaking Belgium.

This difference has, of course, had an electoral impact. In the latest parliamentary elections (on 24 November 1991), the far right received about half a million votes for the whole of Belgium, including less than one hundred thousand in the French-speaking districts.

The present chapter aims to explain the reasons for these differences, without omitting the common points.

The far-right in the Flemish provinces

The Flemish national movement and the nationalist right

The three major Belgian political families were born in the nineteenth century. Although some have suffered significant, albeit temporary, splits, on the whole none generated any rightist fall-out before the First World War. Until 1914, Belgium and its political establishment were essentially French-ruled. Against this French rule, a Flemish national movement developed progressively. But it was during and after the First World War that it took political shape in the Front Movement [*Frontbeweging*, FB] and the Front Party [*Frontpartij*, FP] as a reaction to the fact that the Flemish had often been commanded by French-speaking officers during the First World War.

During that war, Flemish intellectuals and some would-be politicians had tried to take advantage of the German occupation of most Belgian territory to push forward the aims of the Flemish national movement. They were called the 'activists'. Many of these activists and former soldiers joined hands within the FP. This joint bloc won an overwhelming majority in Antwerp during the interim elections of 1928, with 83,000 votes cast for the activist Dr Borms, the candidate of the FP. Between 1919 and 1939 the explicitly Flemish parties increased their electorate almost steadily from 2.6 per cent to 8.27 per cent of the total Belgian electorate.

The FP was a party consisting mainly of Christians, but including many non-Catholics, on the basis of their joint opposition to the war and to French rule. After 1930 and a change of generation it underwent other changes which led to the transformation of the ruins of the party into the Flemish National Confederation [*Vlaams Nationaal Verbond*, VNV], created in 1933 with Staf De Clercq as its main leader. On its right, the VNV had a challenger called Verdinaso, (an extra-parliamentary party), founded in 1931 by Joris van Severen, advocating the annexation of the North of Belgium to the Netherlands, in the framework of a corporatist-organised state.

As a result of the economic recession, the discrediting of the traditional parties and a series of well-exploited political scandals in 1936, the VNV had gained (under the name *Vlaams Blok*) twenty-five seats in the House of Parliament (as against thirty-two for the French-speaking extreme right party REX). In 1939 the VNV representation rose to twenty-six seats. Both parties were violently anti-Semitic and anti-Labour. Both ended up closely collaborating with the Nazi forces after their occupation of Belgian territory.[1]

During the war, the leadership of VNV and REX signed a cooperation agreement to establish a National Socialist 'new order' in Belgium, whose territory was to include a VNV sphere of activity (the Flemish part) and a REX sphere of activity (the Walloon region). Both groups participated in Nazi atrocities till the bitter end. Many of their members were severely sentenced by judicial bodies after the war. However, in 1947 the Parliament voted 'clemency' measures to make it possible for all those who had been sentenced to less than five years imprisonment to regain their rights, on condition that they expressed 'regret' about their conduct. Seven thousand people refused to do so.[2]

The dissatisfaction with the sentences and the demand for an 'amnesty' became the cornerstone around which Flemish nationalists tried to reconstruct a movement.

After the Second World War

The first years after the war have been called the 'catacomb period' for the amnesty movement. In 1949 a party having this demand as its sole programme participated in

246

the elections. The result was a fiasco, although the party's name had been chosen to recall the Flemish Concentration Movement [*Vlaamse Concentratie*, VC], the name of a temporary cooperation agreement that had been concluded in 1937 between the VNV and the Flemish Catholic Party [*Vlaamse Katholieke Partij*, VKP]. It is interesting to note that Karel Dillen, who is the chairman of the *Vlaams Blok* was one of the active members of the *Vlaamse Concentratie* in 1949.

The efforts of the VC and some other groups resulted, in 1954, in the creation of a political party which represented the merger of the former collaboration milieu and some prominent representatives of the Flemish national movement. This movement was the People's Union [*Volksunie*, VU]. Among its seven official founders none had been sentenced for collaborationist activity during the war. In 1957, Karel Dillen joined the new party and immediately became its youth leader in Antwerp. Meanwhile, the Flemish Militants' Organisation [*Vlaamse Militanten Orde*, VMO], a group of activists of the VC which evolved progressively into an uniformed militia, had placed itself at the disposal of the VU. Slowly but steadily, the VU became an important party, whose programme evolved gradually from a right-wing to a centrist one.

The VU and institutional reform

To gain respectability, the VU leadership had already broken all its official ties with the VMO as early as 1963. In practice, collaboration between the two organisations continued until 1976, when the chairman of the VU, Hugo Schiltz, denounced the former as a private militia.

Since its inception, the VU had been an opposition party advocating the transformation of the Belgian state into a federation. In May 1977, however, it participated in negotiations about state reform with the Christian Democrats, the Socialists and the Democratic Front of French Speakers [*Front Démocratique Francophone*, FDF], a centre party. The result of this negotiation is known as the Egmont Pact. It provided for a new state organisation anticipating federalism, but based upon a *sui generis* arrangement of an asymmetrical nature: the country would be divided into three regions (Brussels, the Flemish and the Walloon regions) and three language communities (the French-speaking, the Dutch-speaking and the tiny German-speaking communities). The VU decided, on this basis, to participate in the cabinet.

This led to a revolt of the right-wing and far right elements of the VU. These elements considered the 1977 Egmont Pact as outright treason, because their creed had always been 'federalism based upon two components' (Flanders and Wallonia), excluding Brussels from the construct, out of fear that the weight of the French-speaking Brussels population would outweigh the Flemish. This eventually led to the creation of the VB.

The VU had enjoyed steady electoral growth, from an initial 2.2 per cent in 1954 to 11.1 per cent in 1971. The Egmont Pact of 1977 represented, at the same time, the beginning of collaboration in government and the end of the VU's successes. It sank to 7 per cent in 1978 and to 5.9 per cent in 1991.[3]

One may ask if participation in the institutions did not represent a kiss of death for a party which had been founded as an outright opposition nationalist party. This is the traditional explanation given for the withering away of the VU. However, at the same time, this party has seen a substantial part of its programme implemented.

To preserve a *raison d'être*, the party has radicalised its programme, first to the centre, then to the left. As a result of this, it has lost a number of its MPs to parties belonging to the traditional Belgian political spectrum. The question may therefore be reformulated as follows: Is there a place for a (centre-) left nationalist party in a rich region like Flanders?

The far right groups before the foundation of the Vlaams Blok

Before the foundation of the VB, a myriad of right-wing nationalist groups were created, which eventually became front organisations of the VB.

In July 1971, a new version of the VMO was launched. Among the leaders was Bert Eriksson (former member of the *Hitler Jugend*). It developed as a hard-core Nazi militia. Its publication, *Alarm*, regularly published quotes from Hitler. It did not hesitate to use Nazi methods against political opponents.[4]

The association 'Defend Yourself' [*Were Di*, WD] was created in 1962 as a watchdog for amnesty, traditional 'Flemish values' and a far right ideology. It had a periodical, called *Dietsland-Europa*. Until the creation of the VB, they were led by a group to which Karel Dillen (now European MP and chairman of the VB) and Roeland Raes (now VB senator) belonged. *Were Di* had always strongly defended the South African apartheid system.

Another organisation is Advance Position [*Voorpost*], founded in 1976 as an action group with a uniformed militia.

The Nationalist Student Confederation 1976 [*Nationale Studentenvereniging*, NSV] was a right-wing splinter-group of the Catholic Student Confederation [*Katholieke Studentenvereniging*, KSV]. In 1982 it merged with another organisation into the Nationalist Young Students Confederation [*Nationale Jong-Studenten Vereniging*, NJSV]. It recruits on the basis of a programme against socialism, trade unions, migrants and abortion, and in favour of Nazism and apartheid.

The Vlaams Blok

During the 1950s and the 1960s, the extreme right Flemish nationalists were able to exert an influence upon the VU's political orientation, directly or through organisations like WD and the VMO. In 1971 this influence ceased when the first VMO was dissolved.

The Egmont Pact gave this far right a new chance. In October 1977, Karel Dillen created the Flemish National Party [*Vlaamse Nationale Partij*, VNP] as a whip-party to strive for Flemish independence. One month later, Lode Claes, a banker and a VU senator launched a Flemish People's Party [*Vlaamse Volkspartij*, VVP]. Claes had been, in his youth, a member of the student organisation of the pre-war Fascist extra-parliamentary organisation *Verdinaso*.[5] During the election campaign of December 1978 they formed a coalition, named 'VB'. To everybody's astonishment, this party had one member elected to the Chamber of Deputies: this was Dillen and not Claes. In 1979 both parties merged under the name 'VB' and Claes was left out in the cold.

One of the first far-reaching actions of the VB in parliament was to table a bill to force the unions to accept legal status. This initiative was taken by Dillen, the life-long chairman of the party, in the Chamber of Representatives, in 1983.[6] He proposed the same text again in the Senate in 1988. The only other party to propose action on the same lines is the Liberal party [*Partij voor Vrijheid en Vooruitgang*, PVV; *Parti des Réformes et de la Liberté*, PRL] whose trade union is the smallest in size, and the most conservative in fact.[7]

Belgian trade unions have always refused legal status, although the law permits them to become corporate bodies should they wish to do so. However, at the same time, extensive legislation guarantees the participation of trade union representatives in an impressive series of institutions, including the National Bank, for example. The unions are also in charge of paying unemployment compensation.[8]

Trade union pluralism is also a characteristic of the Belgian system. But the trade unions have close links (although these are loosening in the present period) with the three traditional Belgian political families: the Socialists, the Christian Democrats and the Liberals. The concept of 'the most representative trade union organisation' is central to the Belgian collective-bargaining structure. In the absence of any recognition of its legal existence, this concept, based on union membership and the nationwide importance of the federation, gives certain trade unions the exclusive right to bargain with the public authorities and the private sector.

In the course of a television programme sponsored by his party, broadcast on 15 November 1993, Senator Wim Verreycken went further and denounced the very existence of inter-professional unions, favouring craft unions. The VB also denounces the 'unbridled' right to strike in public and essential services.

During the social upheavals of late 1993, the VB was (as expected) silent about the actual content of the 'global plan' put forward by Prime Minister Jean-Luc Dehaene, who leads the majority cabinet, made up of members of the Christian Social Party [*Christelijke Volkspartij*, CVP; *Parti Social Chrétien*, PSC]. This plan favours wage reductions to ensure the competitiveness of Belgian industry. While favouring capitalist solutions to the crisis, the VB wants to maintain its populist image. Its attacks mainly concerned the social security system. To bridge the gap between expenditure and contributions, Gerolf Annemans, one of its leaders, proposed a variant of its old slogan 'Our own people first' [*Eigen volk eerst*], and advocated the split of the social insurance system into two parts, Flemish and French, and also into 'Belgian cum EU' and 'foreigners' social security systems. (The latter was proclaimed during the VB Congress on social affairs, held in Hasselt on 5 December 1993.) The same meeting demanded that the unions no longer be allowed to pay unemployment compensation allowances.

Pragmatically, the VB does not seem to have a national party line on trade union affiliation, although it appears to favour affiliation to the Liberal unions. Some members of the VB are also members of the Christian unions.[9]

On several occasions (e.g. in the Ghent regional organisation and in the Metalworker's Central Organisation, as well as in the Flemish Socialist Trade Unions

Federation), the Socialist trade unions have declared that simultaneous membership of the extreme right and of the union was not permissible.[10]

The VB also supports membership of some corporativist police officers' unions.[11]

The far right in French-speaking Belgium

The origins: right-wing Catholic militancy

Before 1914, Belgium had no far right party. The Catholics were well-integrated in state institutions and had a party at their disposal. It was in this framework that the most extreme right groups (e.g. those influenced by Charles Maurras and his *Action Française*) acted. It was among the right wing of the Catholic party that the REX publishing house started. Léon Degrelle became its director in 1930. His faction was expelled from the party in early 1936, as a result of the personal attacks it launched against traditional Catholic politicians in the context of its campaign against 'rotten politicians'.

In 1936, REX presented itself as a party in the elections, and got twenty-one members elected to the Lower Chamber (out of 202). Three of the REX representatives had been elected in Flanders. This was largely a result of the disarray of the Labour movement after the Belgian Workers' Party (*Parti Ouvrier Belge, POB; Belgische Werkliechenpartij,* BW) had joined the cabinet, abruptly, after waging a two-year campaign in favour of a 'Labour Plan'. However, in 1939 REX fell back to a mere four members in the lower house and turned increasingly towards Fascism. During the war, Degrelle became a leading SS officer and led the remnants of his party into collaboration.[12]

In Belgium, as elsewhere, the far right had to hide after the Second World War. A number of former REX-ists participated in the pro-Leopold III movement while the 'Royal question' shook Belgium until 1951. Many temporary organisations emerged. The most important was the National Royalist Movement [*Mouvement National Royaliste,* MNR].

A common feature of all these small groups was their monarchist character. None of them, however, had any real social impact. Most of the former REX-ists and collaborators rather gave the impression of jumping on the bandwagon of the CVP/PSC (the new name given to the Catholic Party in 1945) and its pro-Leopold III engagement in order to gain some benefits. Some of them, with J.-R. Debbaudt, a former aide of Léon Degrelle on the Russian front, maintained a tiny Belgian Social Movement [*Mouvement Social Belge,* MSB].

Decolonisation and the avatars of the far right

In 1960, the Belgian Congo (today Zaire) became politically independent. As a result of the incidents following independence, many Belgian colonists came back to Belgium. The overwhelming majority of these colonists were French-speaking. They formed the social basis of several 'ultra' groups, such as the Committee for Action and the Defence of African Belgians [*Comité d'Action et de Défense des Belges d'Afrique*, CADBA] which eventually engendered the Movement for Social Action [*Mouvement d'Action Civique*, MAC], which was closely connected to the French Organisation of the Secret Army [*Organisation de l'Armée Secrète*, OAS].[13]

Another group was the Belgian National Party [*Parti National Belge*, PNB; *Belgische Nationale Partij*, BNP], which presented some candidates, without any success whatsoever, during the 1961 elections. This group developed a programme in favour of national unity around the King and for a strong state. This 'party' ceased to exist in 1972.[14]

The infiltration of the traditional middle-class parties

The French-speaking far right represented only a few hundred scattered people in the early 1970s. It was largely reduced to a few remnants of Second World War collaboration (deprived of the protective umbrella which their Flemish colleagues had in the North of the country), and dispersed rightist activists. Therefore it went partly underground and undertook a 'long march'. It tried to infiltrate traditional middle-class parties and, at the same time, it also tried to penetrate some state security and intelligence bodies.

The organisation that was instrumental in both these attempts to infiltrate was the Youth Front [*Front de la Jeunesse*, FJ]. This had a forerunner: *Nouvel Europe Magazine* [NEM], which had been, with changing titles, an old-timer on the far right scene. Led by Emile Lecerf, a former collaborationist journalist, this magazine created 'discussion groups' in 1972, under the name 'NEM-clubs'.[15] In 1974, these 'clubs' transformed themselves into the FJ. (In parallel, the Party of the New Forces [*Parti des Forces Nouvelles*, PFN] was founded in 1975 on the same ideological basis.)

The first area of infiltration for the FJ was the right-wing French-speaking political tendency of the Christian-Democrats, called Political Centre of the Independants and Christian Cadres [*Centre Politique des Indépendants et Cadres Chrétiens*, CEPIC]. This faction originated in 1972, to counterbalance the influence of the Christian Labour organisations in that party. It soon became a party within a party. The FJ twisted itself into this warm nest, which offered it sympathetic positions: struggle against chaos, despotism, Marxism and materialism, and the defence of Belgians against subversion.

The CEPIC's treasurer, Baron de Bonvoisin, helped the NEM-clubs and the FJ. One of the FJ's leaders, P. Latinus, was designated as a member of the private cabinet of one of the Christian-Democratic ministers. Other members of the French-speaking wing helped FJ members in various ways.[16] Paul Teichman, leader of the MAC, also joined the CEPIC.

In 1981, the administrator of public security presented a note to the parliamentary commission of inquiry concerning the private militias, indicating that the FJ, NEM and CEPIC had close ties.[17] The ministry of justice added a note about the indirect financing of the FN and the PFN by Baron Benoît de Bonvoisin, the CEPIC treasurer.[18]

The CEPIC was dissolved in 1982. While its Christian parliament members remained inside the PSC, its right wing created a new party, the Christian Liberal

Party [*Parti Libéral Chrétien*, PLC] allegedly trying to combine 'Christian fundamental values' with a 'liberal economy'. This formation lasted just a year, after which most of its leaders joined the French-speaking PRL. But in 1985, the PLC was created a second time and polled 0.47 per cent of the votes in Brussels. In 1989, it joined the FN of Dr Féret. The PLC defended the need for an authoritarian regime and an increase in military expenses; it was strongly xenophobic and advocated Belgian unity.[19]

A special mention must be made of the Mayor of Schaerbeek (a district of Brussels), Roger Nols, who distinguished himself for his anti-foreigner attitude, and banned meetings of more than five persons between 10 p.m. and 6 a.m. during Ramadan in 1986. In 1981, he had joined the PRL and served as its vote-catcher in 1983 (with 93,000 preference votes) during the European elections. He did not hesitate to collaborate with extreme right groups and to invite Jean-Marie Le Pen in 1984. However, his attempts to regroup a large, populist far right party failed.[20]

The infiltration of the state apparatus

As well as infiltrating the CEPIC, the FJ has been able – partly with CEPIC's benevolent help – to infiltrate some of the most sensitive institutions of the state. As mentioned, the FN was a paramilitary organisation (a private militia, as the official term has it in Belgium). On three occasions during the 1978–1980 period, it was able to use the premises of the military camps of Marche-les-Dames for its training.[21] The members of the organisation used regularly to train in shooting clubs with members of the police forces.

The various intelligence services were, of course, informed of these activities. They did not try to hinder them. They probably believed that this *modus operandi* was better, as it enabled them to keep some control on the FJ. From this kind of collaboration there is just a step to using the members of the FJ as their auxiliaries. This became a regular practice until the FJ was dissolved as a private militia.

The hard core of the FJ formed, thereupon, an underground organisation, called *Westland New Post* [WNP]. The apparent aim of WNP (many members of which were also members of the army or of the state security) was to spy on left-wing and pacifist groups. Its followers believed that they worked for the State. A 'ritual murder' brought the WNP to the notice of the authorities. In 1984, Latinus (ex-leader of the FJ and of the WNP) was found hanged. The enquiry concluded it was suicide. The WNP was trained by a commissioner of the state security system. It was a neo-Nazi group with a mystical religious Celtic ideology.[22]

General outlook of the French-speaking far right today

The PFN was created in 1975, in the premises of the CEPIC, under the bilingual name New Forces [*Forces Nouvelles – Nieuwe Krachten*] to emphasise its 'national' (i.e. Belgian-wide) character. It remained virtually without public activities between 1975 and 1980, as a result of internal quarrels and also of the competition with the then still more 'respectable' CEPIC and the more 'dynamic' FJ (whose leaders left the party).[23] It tried, during the 1980s, to develop its own identity by establishing ties with the extreme right of the *Movimento Sociale Italiano* and of Le Pen's *Front National*, and through the development of a revisionist (Holocaust denial) ideology. It never received more than 5,000 or 6,000 votes during elections.[24]

In 1989, many activists left the PFN in favour of the National Front [*Front National*, FN]. Among them were Georges Matagne, who became, in 1991, the first (and until now the only) MP of the FN. In 1991, the PFN decided to dissolve and join the FN.[25]

It is no accident that the FN chose the same name as its big French brother. The party was founded in 1985. Its chairman, Dr Daniel Féret, had participated in different right-wing pro-colonialist organisations, favourable to *Algérie française* and the anti-De Gaulle OAS. He was a militant of the right wing of the PRL in the early 1970s, but joined a Union for a New Democracy [*Union pour une nouvelle démocratie*, UND] in 1983, which he united shortly afterwards with other groups into the FN.[26] Although some of the ingredients of the FN are outright racist or look back to the former REX party, the FN has always tried to avoid extremes and follows closely the example of the French *Front National*. It insists that it is neither Nazi nor Fascist, and denies any connection with the British National Front [NF].[27] However, it cannot avoid conflicts between a so-called moderate-populist-liberal wing and an out-and-out far right component. The FN membership is extremely heterogenous and has a high turnover.[28]

Although the FN calls itself a 'Belgian' party, it has never had any foothold in the north of the country. Negotiations with some remnants of the VMO failed in 1987.[29]

In the 1991 elections, the FN polled 33,534 votes in Brussels and 31,559 votes in Wallonia, and elected one MP. During the 1989 regional elections for the Brussels regional parliament, it polled 14,392 votes (3.3 per cent) and obtained two seats.

The group 'To Act' [*Agir*] wants to play more or less the role of a sister-party of the VB in Wallonia. It was founded in Liège in 1989. The main founder, Willy Freson, had been jailed in the early 1980s for participating in a robbery to finance a splinter-group of the FJ. Temporarily 'disconnected' from his 'political scene', he reappeared a few years later.

Freson's first attempt consisted in trying to join his forces with the PFN, but this failed because the PFN had a pro-Nazi and skinhead profile.[30] Negotiations with the FN also failed.

The *Agir* group is the only noteworthy French-speaking far right organisation that distances itself completely from Belgian unitarism. It defines itself as 'Walloon'. It is therefore considered by the VB as its counterpart in the south of the country. This was confirmed by Filip De Winter, VB member of Parliament, for whom the FN is a 'bunch of crooks'.[31] Another difference is that *Agir* is 'pagan', like the French *Nouvelle Droite* [ND], while the FN is often influenced by traditionalist, even fundamentalist, Catholicism. Like the ND, *Agir* is also extremely anti-American.[32] Its leader, Freson, was elected to the Liège provincial council in 1991. The group polled 11,189 votes in the Liège district.[33]

Conclusion

The far right in Belgium moves along two tracks. If we except the *Agir* group in Wallonia, whose area of activity is mainly concentrated around Liège, all the groups in French-speaking Belgium want to keep the kingdom united and express their faith in the monarchy, while refusing the evolution towards a federalisation of the state which began in 1970 and continues with today's constitutional reforms. The VB, on the other hand, defines itself as Flemish, separatist and republican.[34]

This double track can be traced back to the early origins of the far right. Elements were already to be seen just after the First World War, although in 1936 the main far right parties from the two parts of the country realised a short-lived pact not to stand against one another. Except during the Second World War, when both far rights collaborated under a German Nazi command, a common field of stable collaboration has never been found between them.

As far as the future is concerned, one should not, however, dwell on parallels between past and present.

The constitutional evolution of Belgium already permits 'asymmetrical' developments. For example, in 1991, the VB was entitled to receive a seat in the Flemish government, which was to be constituted on a proportional basis. It was only due to the refusal of the VB, which wanted to remain a whip-party and did not want to share responsibilities without the corresponding share of the budget, that this was avoided.[35]

The overall evolution in Europe must also lead us to reject the idea (familiar to many observers ten or even five years ago) that the far right is doomed to play the role of a mere pressure group in favour of a more authoritarian state. As the Flemish example shows (e.g. in Antwerp) we have a far right that bids for power.

Uneasiness, disarray, anxiety and alarm are growing among Democrats and in the Labour movement.[36] Much-needed information about these far right parties, their whereabouts and strategy, is frequently lacking. It has been the aim of this chapter to fill the gap, since knowledge is a prerequisite for action.

List of abbreviations

BNP	*Belgische Nationale Partij* [Belgian National Party]
BW	*Belgische Werkliechenpartij* [Belgian Workers' Party]
CADBA	*Comité d'Action et de Défense des Belges d'Afrique* [Committee for Action and Defence of African Belgians]
CEPIC	*Centre Politique des Indépendants et Cadres Chrétiens* [Political Centre of the Independants and Christian Cadres]
CVP	*Christelijke Volkspartij* [Christian Social Party]
FB	*Frontbeweging* [Front Movement]
FDF	*Front Démocratique Francophone* [Democratic Front of French Speakers]
FJ	*Front de la Jeunesse* [Youth Front]
FN	*Front National* [National Front]
FP	*Frontpartij* [Front Party]

KSV	*Katholieke Studentenvereniging* [Catholic Student Confederation]
MAC	*Mouvement d'Action Civique* [Movement for Social Action]
MNR	*Mouvement National Royaliste* [National Royalist Movement]
MSB	*Mouvement Social Belge* [Belgian Social Movement]
MSI	*Movimento Sociale Italiano* [Italian Social Movement]
NEM	Nouvel Europe Magazine
NJSV	*Nationale Jong-Studenten Vereniging* [National Young Student Confederation]
NSV	*Nationale Studentenvereniging* [National Student Confederation]
PFN	*Parti des Forces Nouvelles* [Party of New Forces]
PLC	*Parti Libéral Chrétien* [Christian Liberal Party]
PNB	*Parti National Belge* [Belgian National Party]
POB	*Parti Ouvrier Belge* [Belgian Workers' Party]
PRL	*Parti des Réformes de la Liberté* [Party of Reforms and Freedom – Liberal Party]
PSC	*Parti Social Chrétien* [Christian Social Party]
PVV	*Partij voor Vrijheid en Vooruitgang* [Party of Reforms and Freedom – Liberal Party]
UND	*Union pour une Nouvelle Démocratie* [Union for a New Democracy]
VB	*Vlaams Blok* [Flemish Bloc]
VC	*Vlaamse Concentratie* [Flemish Concentration Movement]
VKP	*Vlaams Katholieke Partij* [Flemish Catholic Party]
VMO	*Vlaamse Militanten Orde* [Flemish Militants' Organisation]
VNP	*Vlaamse Nationale Partij* [Flemish National Party]
VNV	*Vlaams Nationaal Verbond* [Flemish National Confederation]
VU	*Volksunie* [People's Union]
VVP	*Vlaamse Volkspartij* [Flemish People's Party]
WNP	Westland New Post

Notes

1. See Archief en Museum van de Socialistische Arbeidersbeweging (AMSAB), *De Wereld van Anne Frank in België, 1929–1945. Een dagboek voor de toekomst* [The World of Anne Frank in Belgium 1929–1945. A diary for the future], Hadewijck, Antwerp, 1993.
2. H. Gijsels, *Het Vlaams Blok* [The Flemish Bloc], Kritak, Louvain, 1992, p. 41.
3. Results for the Chamber of Representatives. See F. Elbers and M. Fennema, *Racistische partijen in West-Europa. Tussen nationale traditie en Europese samenwerking* [Racist parties in Western Europe. Between national tradition and European cooperation], Stichting Burgerschapskunde. Nederlands Centrum voor Politieke Vorming, Leiden, 1993, pp. 82–3.
4. There are extensive lists of these actions in J. Cappelle, 'De zwarte schaduw van de Vlaamse burgerij' [The black shadow of the Flemish bourgeoisie], in W. de Bock *et al.*, *Extreem-Rechts en de Staat* [The Far Right and the State], EPO, Berchem, 1981, pp. 81ff.; Gijsels, *Het Vlaams Blok*, cit., pp. 59ff. In 1981, the Antwerp tribunal sentenced 101 VMO members for their membership of a private army.
5. H. Gijsels, *Het Vlaams Blok*, cit., p. 20.

6. Parliamentary Document – Chamber of Representatives, Session 1983–84, No. 766–1, 25 Oct. 1983.

7. See H. Gijsels, *Het Vlaams Blok*, cit., p. 277.

8. See G. Desolre, 'Belgium', in A. A. Blum (ed.), *International Handbook of Industrial Relations*, Greenwood, New York, 1981, pp. 37–48.

9. Since this chapter was written (December 1993) exit polls have shown that the VB was probably able to attract as many as 25 per cent of the votes of Catholic union members and 30 per cent of the votes of Socialist union members in Antwerp, where this party managed to come first in the provincial and municipal elections of 9 October 1994.

10. R. M., 'Een Vakbondsstrategie tegen Extreem-Rechts' [A Union Strategy against the Far Right], in *Verzet* (AFF – info), XII, No. 3, July 1993, p. 24. The same decision has been taken by the statutory congress of the Flemish Socialist trade unions; see *Verzet* (AFF – info), XII, Nos. 5–6, Dec. 1993, p. 39 (and, since this chapter was written, by the Christian trade unions, too).

11. J. Vander Velpen, *Het Vlaams Blok. Daar komen ze aangemarcheerd. Extreem-Rechts in Europa* [The Flemish Bloc. Here they are marching in. The Far Right in Europe], EPO, Berchem, 1992, p. 155.

12. M. Conway, *Collaboration in Belgium. Léon Degrelle and the Rexist Movement, 1940–1944*, Yale University Press, New Haven, CT, 1993, pp. 18ff.

13. F. Balace, 'Le tournant des années soixante. De la droite réactionnaire à l'extrême droite révolutionnaire', in Various Authors, *De l'avant à l'après-guerre. L'extrême droite en Belgique francophone*, De Boeck-Wesmael, Brussels, 1994, p. 210.

14. E. Verhoeyen, *L'extrême droite en Belgique* (I), Courrier hebdomadaire du CRISP (Centre de Recherche et d'Information Socio-Politiques), Brussels, Nos. 642–3, 1974, pp. 16, 20, 31.

15. See P. Brewaeys, in H. de Schampheleire and Y. Thanassekos (eds), *L'Extrême droite en Europe de l'Ouest. Actes du colloque d'Anvers (29 mars 1990)*, VUB-Press, Brussels, 1991, pp. 249–50.

16. S. Dumont, 'Het klavertje vier bij de CEPIC' [CEPIC's four-leaved clover], in W. de Bock *et al.*, *Extreem-Rechts en de Staat* [The Far Right and the State], EPO, Berchem, 1981, pp. 125–39.

17. 'L'Extrême droite en Wallonie et à Bruxelles', special supplement to *Socialisme*, No. 232, July–Aug. 1992, p. 11.

18. P. Brewaeys, V. Dahaut and A. Tolbiac, *L'Extrême droite francophone face aux élections*, Courrier hebdomadaire du CRISP, Brussels, No. 1350, 1992, p. 13.

19. Ibid., p. 17.

20. 'L'Extrême droite en Wallonie et à Bruxelles', cit., pp. 11–2; C. T. Husbands, 'Belgium: Flemish Legions on the March', in P. Hainsworth (ed.), *The Extreme Right in Europe and the USA*, Pinter, London, 1992, p. 133.

21. A. Maesschalk, 'Front de la Jeunesse: een extreem-rechtse privé-militie' [FJ: a far-right private militia], in W. de Bock *et al.*, *Extreem-Rechts*, cit., p. 158.

22. See 'L'Extrême droite en Wallonie', cit., p. 13.

23. Brewaeys, Dahaut and Tolbiac, *L'Extrême droite francophone*, cit., p. 6.

24. Ibid., p. 8.

25. Ibid., pp. 8–9.

26. Ibid., p. 20.

27. Ibid., p. 21.

28. Ibid., p. 23.

29. Ibid., p. 24.

30. Ibid., p. 37.

31. Ibid., pp. 39–40.

32. During the June 1994 European elections, the FN won one seat in the European Parliament (while the VB consolidated its position with a second MEP). The European elections and the provincial and municipal elections of 9 October 1994 represented a breakthrough for both the FN (131,000 votes in October) and *Agir* (36,162 votes in October).

33. This anti-Americanism does not differentiate it from the Belgian and the French FN parties which both took anti-US stances during the Gulf War in 1991. See F. Elbers and M. Fennema, *Racistische partijen*, cit., p. 85.

34. Since the VB wants a Flemish Republic with Brussels as its capital, it distributes propaganda in the French language, too, in Brussels. See *Le Soir*, 3 Dec. 1993.

35. Intervention by Senator W. Verreycken in the VB-sponsored TV programme, 15 Nov. 1993.

36. Especially since a series of scandals have compromised leading members of the French-speaking Socialist Party (and also prominent members of other parties).

Chapter 14

BRITAIN'S NAZI UNDERGROUND
Gerry Gable

On 19 April 1993 Granada Television's *World in Action* devoted a full programme to an investigation of a terrorist group. It was not the IRA or Ulster Defence Association [UDA], nor one of the many groups operating in the Middle East or Latin American revolutionary struggles, but a British group calling itself Combat 18. On the same day the anti-Fascist organisation Searchlight published a special edition of its magazine, to detail the origin, activities and personalities of the group.[1]

A flurry of media interest followed the programme. Shortly afterwards, the parliamentary Home Affairs Committee, which was conducting an inquiry into racially motivated attacks and harassment, asked Searchlight to submit written and, later, oral evidence on the activities and background of this organisation.[2]

The genesis of Combat 18

Since the end of the Second World War, Fascists and Nazis in Britain have made several attempts to organise illegal paramilitary operations. Essentially, they have all failed, either because they were not capable of fulfilling their own aspirations, or because they were exposed by the media, state security organisations or Searchlight.

The best known of these groups, Column 88, was connected with the Gladio networks. These networks were set up after the Second World War, with the support of the US Central Intelligence Agency [CIA], by a number of powers, both within and outside NATO, as anti-Communist resistance bodies. They became a vehicle manipulated by the shadowy world of the intelligence services and the Belgian and Italian sections ran amok, carrying out bombings and killings, before they were exposed by parliamentary inquiries in those countries.[3]

The earliest attempt by neo-Nazis in Britain at setting up a terrorist group was the Spearhead organisation. Formed in 1960, it was an inner core group of the original British National Party [BNP], a party that described itself as 'racial nationalist'. The qualification for probationary membership of Spearhead was six months' membership of the BNP. The leaders of Spearhead were Colin Jordan, often described as Britain's post-war Nazi godfather because of his long association with hardline Nazi groups in Britain and abroad since the war years, and John Tyndall, who now leads the BNP, which he re-formed in April 1982. (The original BNP merged with other Fascist groups to form the National Front [NF] in 1967.)

Spearhead had full dress and field uniforms adorned with sunwheel badges – the sunwheel being an ancient Norse symbol that preceded the swastika. The organisation probably never had more than about sixty members, who were drilled like soldiers and went on training exercises in the New Forest where they practised bombing raids. Special Branch were slow to investigate this group, but one ex-serviceman, John Nicholls, got into it and rose to a position where he was able to gather enough information to tip off the police and the national press about its aims and activities.

In January 1962, Jordan and Tyndall left the BNP to form their own movement, the National Socialist Movement [NSM], which they formally launched on 20 April 1962, the anniversary of Hitler's birthday. They took the Spearhead organisation with them.

Spearhead's activities had become increasingly public in its final days as part of the BNP, through its policy of attacking meetings of its opponents or any meetings of which it disapproved, causing serious injury to members of the audience. At a meeting in St Pancras Town Hall in London, in 1960, the anti-Fascist stewards managed to hold their ground against Spearhead, when the Nazis attacked members of parliament addressing the meeting. Several of the Nazis were injured or arrested.

After the NSM held a rally in Trafalgar Square on 1 July 1962 under the slogan 'Free Britain from Jewish control', the Special Branch stepped up its investigations. Later that year Jordan, Tyndall, Ian Kerr Ritchie and Denis Pirie were arrested under the provisions of the 1936 Public Order Act which forbade the formation of para-military groups for political ends. They were all convicted at the Old Bailey and sent to prison.[4] After their release from prison in 1963 the NSM split. Tyndall left and set up a new Nazi party, the Greater Britain Movement [GMB]. Many members of Spearhead went with him.

In the following seventeen months, thirty-four Jewish properties were attacked in the London area alone. Synagogues and other properties were destroyed, and in a firebomb attack on a *yeshiva* (a Jewish theological college) in Stoke Newington a 19-year-old student was killed and a second youth crippled while jumping from the flames.

The attackers were Nazi action commandos split into at least two sections and drawn from three organisations, the BNP, the NSM and the GBM. They had the three essential ingredients for mounting terror operations of this type: intelligence on their perceived enemies, the ability to analyse the intelligence, and activists willing to risk their liberty for the cause and carry out violent attacks.[5]

The police failed completely to apprehend any of the attackers, but a team of investigative researchers working for Searchlight found one of the Nazis involved and persuaded him to give himself up to the police. The subsequent arrests resulted in three trials at the Old Bailey at which thirteen convictions were secured. Among those convicted were Colin Jordan's estranged wife Françoise Dior, the French perfume heiress; a man called Hugh Hughes, who was a serving soldier in the Welsh Guards; and another man who had just left the parachute regiment.

These convictions, and that of John Tyndall for possession of a firearm and ammunition in 1966, curtailed this type of operation for several years. Half-hearted attempts during the early days of the NF to form a similar terror group were exposed and quickly aborted. Activities by individual members of the NF were also clamped down upon – for example, Ken Matthews, who plotted to bomb trade union offices, received a six-year prison sentence.

A small operation such as the National Socialist Group, a splinter group from the NSM around the time Colin Jordan changed the name of the NSM to British Movement [BM] in 1968, also collapsed following its exposure and joint Special Branch and Searchlight investigations. The police seized bomb-making materials, machine-guns and machine-gun parts.

For the next twenty-four years, only Column 88 filled the vacuum in British far-right paramilitary politics. However, as Column 88 was a state-operated cover organisation, it cannot be considered a genuine Nazi terror group.[6] Individuals who were attracted to terrorist operations went to fight as mercenaries for the illegal regime of Ian Smith in Rhodesia. Many of them also found their way to South Africa and joined units engaged in cross-border raids for covert South African army and special police units.

In Britain both the BM and the NF organised defence units, more correctly termed 'attack units' – the Leader Guard and the Honour Guard respectively. However, these were not intended for terror operations. Many of the members of both groups received training in Britain and abroad in the use of firearms and explosives.

At the same time, the British far right was increasingly forging links with Ulster Loyalist groups like the UDA and its terrorist offshoots, the Ulster Freedom Fighters [UFF] and the Ulster Volunteer Force [UVF]. These groups operate both in Ulster and in mainland Britain, and have proper military structures. An examination of people jailed in Britain for gun-running and other crimes on behalf of these Ulster Loyalist groups over a period of more than twenty years shows evidence of their links with the BM and NF over a long period.

Around 1988–89 it became clear, from intelligence coming from anti-Fascist sources placed inside a number of Nazi groups in Britain and abroad, that moves were afoot to create a new and better organised terror force in Britain. It would have the three prerequisites for a successful terrorist organisation: the ability to gather intelligence, the capacity to analyse that intelligence, and an active and dedicated team of followers to act upon the results of that analysis.

Some people thought this new group might come out of a 400-strong Ku Klux Klan [KKK] operation set up in Britain around that time, but run from the USA. However, the exposure of the KKK in the national press, *Searchlight* and a television documentary made by Television South, between June and October 1990, brought any plans in that direction to an abrupt halt.[7]

Around that time observers of the far right began to see a hard core of older Nazis turning up to protect BNP meetings in London and elsewhere. The same faces were being monitored by the police and anti-Fascists on Ulster Loyalist street protests against pro-Irish Republican marches and rallies in London and Manchester.[8] Many were former members of the BM, which had collapsed as an organised entity around 1982, but had re-formed with a secret inner core calling itself the British National Socialist Movement [BNSM], while others were from the notorious gang of football thugs, the Chelsea Headhunters. Of these, some were in the NF and more were in the BNP, but they appeared as a more or less autonomous grouping.[9]

In summer 1991 Harold Covington, from North Carolina in the USA, travelled to Britain and Europe. He brought with him a plan to set up a network of Nazi terror-style groups linked by common interests and enemies and by modern communications methods such as computer modems and satellite computer links. Whatever the differences between the various factions on the Nazi and Fascist right in Britain, this was a man with a reputation that would enable him to be the catalyst to bring them all together in one organisation.

A meeting in Europe brought Covington into contact with the Swedish group White Aryan Resistance [*Vit Ariskt Motstånd*, VAM], various newly emerging neo-Nazi groups in Germany and Nazi activists from Britain. VAM had a long criminal record for stealing weapons from military arsenals in Sweden and using them to rob banks to raise funds for further operations. Its activities had spread into Norway, where a similar group was set up, and to parts of former East Germany, where its members joined with German and French Nazis in carrying out a series of hold-ups. Covington informed those present of his plan to spread his network across the world, but said he would first go to Britain and set up an operational base there.[10]

Covington's history on the Nazi right in the USA put him in an almost unique position to unify the various factions into one terror group. A middle-aged man, his history in the US Nazi movement and the KKK stretches back to the 1960s. Nearly all the organisations with which he has been associated are violent. In November 1979 he organised a KKK attack on anti-Klan protesters in Greensboro, North Carolina. He personally stayed away from the scene of the crime, but his plan was put into effect, leaving five dead and nine wounded as his henchmen gunned down the protesters in full view of the television cameras. Covington boasted later that it was like killing a snake, and that he had no remorse for the deaths. In the wake of what became known as the Greensboro massacre, Covington left the USA and travelled to the Irish Republic, Britain and Rhodesia, before returning home, having acquired along the way an Irish wife and thus Irish citizenship, making him eligible, under European Community rules, for residence in any member state.

Exploiting his dual nationality, he arrived in Britain in the late summer of 1991, using a study course as cover for his presence. The scene was set for the formation of Combat 18.[11]

The nature of Combat 18 and those who run it

In autumn 1991 an event took place in London that was to breathe life into Combat 18. David Irving, the far-right 'historical revisionist', held a rally at Chelsea Old Town Hall, at which his guest speaker was the US revisionist Fred Leuchter, whom the Home Secretary had banned from entering Britain. It was a long time since Irving had held such a gathering in London, and in the distant past his meetings, under the name the Clarendon Club, had been guarded by thuggish elements drawn from various far right groups. This time he had come to a security arrangement with Nick Griffin, the former chairman of the NF and now the leader of the International Third Position [ITP], a small Strasserite group (i.e. one espousing a 'left' anti-capitalist form of Nazism, as did the Strasser brothers in Germany in the 1920s). Griffin, it appeared, was linked to a newly formed security company, which he used to provide security for Irving's meeting.[12]

The meeting turned into a fiasco when the large body of police guarding it was informed that it was in fact protecting a man who had been banned from entering Britain. After a short delay in the proceedings, Leuchter was led away and two days later deported to the USA. As the police moved in, stewards fled in all directions, leaving the two hundred or more Nazis, anti-Semites and racists, who had come from around the world, in a state of near panic.

The leaders of Nazi organisations like the BNP and their activists resolved that such a disaster could never be allowed to happen again. An effective group of bodyguards and stewards had to be formed.

The embryonic Combat 18 was ready to step into the breach. Old faces and some new ones began to appear at BNP marches and meetings, and in February 1992 a violent attack took place on youngsters leafleting in Tower Hamlets, east London, on behalf of the newly re-formed Anti Nazi League [ANL]. The assault, which put several anti-Fascists in hospital, was carried out by a combined group of key BNP activists and Combat 18 men helped by a group of young Nazi skinheads.

In the run-up to the general election in April 1992, key figures from the old BM were seen alongside some members of the BNP, in particular from its Croydon branch, running the BNP's election rallies and guarding canvassers in east and south-east London. Some were not aligned to any political group, but were known football hooligans belonging to the Chelsea Headhunters gang.

Combat 18 was not a group one could seek to join. It sought out those whom it wanted to recruit, and vetted them to see if they were politically and physically suitable.

Around the time of the election there appeared the first of a series of internal illegal bulletins called *Redwatch*. It carried no British address or post box number, but could be contacted through Harold Covington's box number in North Carolina. He, in turn, would pass on the applications for membership or letters of support and funds to the address in Barnet, north London, of a young criminal called Steven Sargent.

Sargent and his two older brothers, William and Paul David, the latter known as Charlie or Ginger Pig, all had a long record of violence. William had been out of open politics since his days in the NF in the 1970s and had settled down to a life of organising illegal dog fighting from his home near Newmarket in East Anglia. Charlie, who had a list of convictions for international drug smuggling, assault and possession of weapons, had been active in the BM in the late 1970s and early 1980s, as well as engaged in the skinhead music scene. He was well known among the Chelsea Head-hunters as a street fighter in Britain and abroad.

Redwatch contained the usual Nazi political message, but in a sinister new departure it also printed the names, addresses and telephone numbers, sometimes ex-directory, of people from many walks of life whom they perceived as enemies. The list posed a double danger: all the people on it were threatened, but some had no political connection and had been placed on the list by mistake. The targets were drawn not only from the political left, but also from people involved in green and peace politics.

Subsequently, some of the people and organisations listed began to receive death threats and a few were firebombed. Incidents occurred in London and Birmingham, and an elderly woman living in the middle of East Anglia was warned that she would be attacked because she had offered a stay at her guest house as a prize in a Campaign for Nuclear Disarmament raffle. A break-in at the home of Marc Wadsworth, the national secretary of the Anti-Racist Alliance, gave Combat 18 hundreds of names and addresses of anti-racists. Other similar 'fishing expeditions' were being organised.

It was Combat 18's links with the UDA and its London command structure that caused most concern among observers of the far right. Using Fascists who worked inside Royal Mail sorting offices, Combat 18 was tracking down people on the mainland who, it thought, had Republican sympathies. This information was being passed on to men who were stockpiling guns in London, the Midlands and Scotland.

People reporting attacks or threats around the country found that the police treated each incident in isolation. The victims did not, of course, know of Combat 18's existence at this stage, but neither did the police, or if they did, they were not alerting police forces on a national basis.

A small number of other key players on the activist Nazi scene in Britain had now joined the Sargent family in their efforts to enlarge their terror group. One was a former NF member and fanatical Ulster Loyalist called Eddy Whicker, a man in his forties, later to be arrested and freed after he was caught carrying guns and ammunition to the UDA in the Midlands. He is a key link between far-right field intelligence officers and the UDA military command. Another was Paul Ballard, a former member of the BM and the NF. A former civil servant, he is middle-aged and looks more like a 1960s hippy, with long hair and casual dress, than a Nazi in the Combat 18 think-tank. He is possibly the brightest of them intellectually and speaks several languages, but has a reputation for street brawling. He is also a leading member of the BNP and has stood for the party as a candidate in recent elections.

With advice from the USA, John Cato, a young hardline Nazi from Kent, set up a computer system capable of producing Combat 18's internal hate lists as well as international illegal racist and anti-Semitic stickers and leaflets. He was forced to flee with his wife and children from their Kent home to East Anglia, with Special Branch on his trail, after his role in Combat 18 was exposed in summer 1993.

Throughout 1992 it became clear that this rather small group of around seventy to eighty activists was dictating the pace of operations for the much larger BNP, which had around 2,000 paid-up members. It also had a high degree of influence in Blood and Honour, the informal Nazi skinhead organisation. In fact, a year later Combat 18 was running Blood and Honour, after Ian Stuart Donaldson, who led the organisation, handed over control to Charlie Sargent shortly before his death.[13]

Derek Beackon, who was elected as the BNP's first ever local councillor in Tower Hamlets in September 1993, had been the BNP's chief steward, but was seen clearly taking orders from the Sargents on all major events that they attended together. Most of these events during 1992 and 1993 were meetings of David Irving's Clarendon Club in London and Sussex.

By the summer of 1993 it was clear that resistance was growing in the BNP to Combat 18's takeover of nearly all the BNP's street activities. It was clearly not to the liking of the BNP's leaders like John Tyndall and David Bruce. By the time the annual trip to the international rally at Diksmuide in Belgium came around in August, BNP and Combat 18 activists were physically fighting each other. In September and October 1993 in east London, the BNP had a huge anti-Fascist backlash to deal with, and it was being driven off its regular sales pitches by either militant anti-Fascists or the police. Combat 18 refused to come to the BNP's aid, insisting that it now had its own agenda.

Following the attack in Tower Hamlets in February 1992 and another in the summer of the same year, some key Combat 18 street soldiers were arrested, and later released. However, in Nottinghamshire and elsewhere in the Midlands vigorous police action, after multi-agency cooperation, had led to a series of arrests of leading Combat 18 personnel in those parts of the country. One of the arrests furnished proof of the modern terror set-up that Combat 18 had brought to Britain, when the police raiding his home found Nazi hate-lists, drugs for sale and various weapons and ammunition.

The connection between Combat 18 activists and drug and gun dealing gives the group the hallmarks of a twentieth century far-right terror group. Until the 1990s such groups existed in many countries of Europe and America, but had passed Britain by.

Granada Television's 1993 *World in Action* programme exposing the criminality of Combat 18 drew firm links between it, the UDA and Harold Covington. Charlie Sargent threatened on screen to shoot the producer, Andrew Bell, for linking Charlie to the UDA. Eddy Whicker also featured prominently. The programme and the special issue of *Searchlight*, which appeared the same day, were shortly followed by a book, *At War with Society*, in which a young former Nazi described some of Combat 18's activities, naming many names.[14]

Despite all the evidence that Granada Television and Searchlight handed over to the police and the Parliamentary Home Affairs Committee's inquiry into racial attacks and harassment, no comprehensive police investigation had resulted by the end of 1993.

Leaderless resistance

In 1993 the Sargents started producing a regular underground publication: *The Order*. It was named after an American terror group which had robbed payrolls and killed Jews and government agents. The group collapsed when one of its members, Robert J. Mathews, was killed in a shootout with the FBI, and others were sent to prison for 60 to 200 years. The publication carries the same message as the group after which it was named, namely that white people must wage race war in Britain.

The inspiration for The Order (the organisation) was a book written by Dr William Pierce, a one-time university lecturer in physics and a member of the hierarchies of several hardline American Nazi groups since the 1960s. His book, *The Turner Diaries*, written under the pen-name Andrew Macdonald, was about a fictional Nazi underground organisation named 'The Order'. Within two years of the book's publication, Nazis had actually formed an organisation of that name.

Pierce runs the Nationalist Alliance, which has become increasingly adept in recent years at putting its members inside a wide spectrum of far-right organisations in the USA and Canada. Several of them have risen to positions of influence and control.

Since the early 1980s, he had acted as a catalyst for the founding of a series of book-clubs in Britain, which have peddled most of his own extensive book-list, including a dozen or more US special forces manuals on explosive devices, booby-traps and guerrilla warfare. By the end of 1993 John Cato had joined forces with Paul Jeffries to become the British representative of Pierce's group, as well as to run their own book-clubs.

The League of St George [LSG], the smallest but purest of Britain's National Socialist groups, publishes a magazine called *Target*. Hiding behind an offshore address in the USA, like *Redwatch*, it gives home addresses of the Nazis' perceived enemies and suggests they should be harassed and intimidated.

By autumn 1993 the leadership of Combat 18 was telling its followers, through publications like *The Order* and *Forward as Thorwould*, that the BNP was not worthwhile and that they should withdraw their support. Even the election of Derek Beackon as the first post-war Nazi councillor in Tower Hamlets did not appear to provide the necessary encouragement for the two organisations to cooperate.

Combat 18 offered its supporters a new, much more serious, plan of action. Selective targets became the order of the day; and the way these targets are tackled represents a terrifying prospect. For some years, the concept of leaderless resistance has been growing in the US far right. Essentially it takes two forms. One is a murderous cult called the Phineas Priesthood. It is based on a corruption of the biblical story of Phinehas in Numbers 25, who killed two people he perceived as God's enemies and was rewarded by being made the founder of a priesthood. The modern Phineas Priesthood is a cult of individual killers who never come together, but carry out individual acts of murder against perceived enemies. The individual 'Priest' kills once or many times and moves on. He or she does not join any group but strives to protect the 'white race' from its enemies: blacks, Jews, liberals and the left. Gays figure high on the target list. Racists have claimed that the murder in the 1960s of Medgar Evers, a black ex-serviceman and civil rights activist, was such a killing.

The second form of leaderless resistance is undertaken by people who have been involved in organisations such as The Order in the USA, Combat 18 in Britain, or VAM in Sweden. Acting singly or in small groups, they pick a target, destroy it, stand back and wait, and strike again and again. The lack of a formal group with member-ship records, annual general meetings and an organised branch structure makes it very hard for the authorities to react.

One of the people active in promoting this form of action is Louis Beam. Beam, a US Nazi leader, was arrested for his part in The Order. He was acquitted at his trial in Fort Smith, Texas, because the FBI had acted illegally in bringing him and some of his comrades back to the USA from their hide-out in Mexico. A Vietnam war veteran, he is very violent and a passionate orator. His writings on the concept of leaderless resistance are being republished in Combat 18's publication *The Order*.

Once again, though, it has been left to Pierce to lead and inspire the terrorist far right extremists. In a book called *Hunter*, published in the 1980s, Pierce had his hero, who worked alone, indulge in a series of murders of blacks and Jews, especially mixed-race couples. Today Pierce is abandoning the written word in favour of the computer bulletin board and a series of short-wave radio transmitters, which are spreading his message of hate to all parts of the globe, with special emphasis on

Europe. Operating under the name American Dissident Voices, they describe them-selves as being the call-sign for new Aryan Resistance.

The framework for Beam's leaderless resistance concept and Pierce's tactic of infiltration already exists in Britain. Combat 18's followers and a handful of other far right extremists have recently gained military experience fighting as mercenaries in the former Yugoslavia. The BNP's ongoing infiltration of the civil service and armed forces is clear evidence of Pierce's influence.[15]

Is this the path, then, which the far right will tread in Britain up to and beyond the turn of the century? It must be a serious possibility. With Britain's already strong anti-racist laws being further strengthened and used to greater effect, it is likely that most of the old-style groups like the NF and BNP will fade away over the next few years, despite the BNP's small electoral success. The vacuum they leave behind could well be filled by something much more sinister and violent. The vital question is whether or not the British government and its instruments of law and order will step in to end such dangerous operations and to stop those who control them.

Structure of the far right in Britain

The non-terrorist part of the far right in Britain has in some ways become easier to examine since 1979. Membership numbers are down, despite the short-lived success of Beackon, the BNP's chief steward, in winning a council seat after a by-election in Millwall Ward on the Isle of Dogs (east London) in September 1993, by a margin of seven votes. This is an area with exceptional social and political problems, and the result is unlikely to be repeated elsewhere. There is some doubt about whether the seat was won fairly. Thirty voters signed statements claiming that they had been prevented from voting by gangs of BNP supporters around polling stations on polling day.[16]

The BNP is beginning to have a much higher profile as a criminal operation than as a political party. It has around 2,000 members and two monthly publications, the magazine *Spearhead*, edited and published by Tyndall, whose serious criminal past has already been outlined, and a monthly newspaper, *British Nationalist*, edited by John Morse, who has served time in prison for the hate material that the paper has published. Many of the BNP's leading activists have a serious criminal record, and the conviction rate among the party's foot soldiers is also very high.

By late 1993, the BNP's association with Irving appeared to have come to an abrupt halt after Irving's failure to turn up at the BNP's annual 'Party Day' rally. (The BNP does not have annual general meetings, but instead holds a rally, at which overseas Nazis and racists join Tyndall on the platform.) The BNP's relationship with the skinhead Blood and Honour movement has never been stable, and has weakened further. The BNP has treated the movement's 1,400 followers in Britain and thousands more abroad as cannon fodder for street actions rather than as full members of the Party. The death in 1993 of Blood and Honour's leader, Ian Stuart Donaldson[17] and the takeover of the better organised parts of it by Combat 18's Sargent family will go even further to alienate them from the BNP and Tyndall, who has never made any secret of his contempt for them.

Political friction also developed between the BNP and Combat 18 during 1993, coming to a head in December. Combat 18 had just published a glossy magazine, *Combat 18*, no. 1, which contained threats of physical violence and a hit-list of names and addresses in the Bradford and Leeds area. The fact that some of the people on the list were members of parliament was clearly going to add to the pressure on the authorities to take action against the organisation. Tyndall was keen to put as much distance as possible between the BNP and Combat 18.

On 14 December 1993, Tyndall send BNP branch organisers a bulletin, headed 'Combat 18', in which he proscribed Combat 18 on the grounds that it was a hostile organisation. He even suggested that it might be an instrument of the state set up to discredit the BNP. It was clear that the unexpected election of Beackon had put the BNP on its best public behaviour. The bulletin also announced that the BNP must stop being a street gang and emphasis was to be given to canvassing for BNP candidates in the local elections in May 1994.

However, as in the past, Tyndall found it very difficult to distance the party from the criminal elements within it. In the same month that Combat 18 was proscribed, Tyndall shared a platform at a BNP rally in Dagenham, east London, with Anthony Wells, the BNP's Redbridge branch organiser. Wells had, only a few weeks earlier, been released from prison after serving two-thirds of a three-year sentence for assaulting a Jewish teacher. He had previously been convicted for setting off an explosion, and possessing grenades and timing devices, for which he was also sentenced to three years' imprisonment. Tyndall, for reasons that are unclear, decided to stop referring to Wells by that name, under which he had always been known in the BNP, and instead started using his alias, Lecomber.

In the first few months of 1994, it became apparent that Tyndall was having difficulty enforcing the proscription of Combat 18, despite an assault on Wells/Lecomber by members of Combat 18 in east London on 15 January. For example, the first edition of a BNP student paper in Manchester included an advertisement containing the Combat 18 contact address. By spring 1994 several attacks, which the police, Searchlight and John Tyndall himself attributed to Combat 18, had taken place. The targets included BNP candidates and an agent in the local elections; Michael Newland, the national press officer; and Eddy Butler, the national elections officer. A letter bomb that partially exploded inside the BNP's headquarters is still unexplained. What was certain was that the feud between the BNP and Combat 18 was not entirely ideological, but also involved Combat 18's connection with the UDA and the large amounts of money that key Combat 18 activists were making from drug dealing.

In March 1994, a police spokesman from the National Intelligence Squad, which deals with football hooliganism, was interviewed on the BBC Radio 4 programme *File On Four*. He outlined what he said were proven links between BNP members, football violence and non-political crime.

The BNP's policies are simple: repatriation, denial of the Nazi Holocaust, stronger law and order (a little strange coming from an organisation whose members have so many criminal convictions), opposition to Britain's membership of the European Union, and full and open support for the Loyalist paramilitaries in Northern Ireland and their counterparts in mainland Britain. As in many other Nazi groups across Europe, a strong tendency towards pre-Strasserite ideas akin to national Bolshevism has emerged among some key members. Advocates of these ideas believe that Russia and Germany are the keys to the development of a white racial, anti-Semitic bloc in Europe. Often Tyndall appears isolated from his members, but, apart from discontent by BNP members associated with Combat 18, no challenge to his leadership has managed to gather enough momentum to cause him any worry.

Despite the BNP's claim to be a normal political party, it has in the past few years developed much stronger links with far-right and terrorist Nazi groups around the world. John Morse, the BNP's regional leader in the Midlands, has become a star attraction at the Hess memorial rally held in Germany every August. Then a week later he is back on centre stage at the international Nazi and nationalist rally in Diksmuide in Belgium. John Peacock is the British representative of the Odal Ring, a group that started life among members of Belgium's banned Nazi group, the Flemish Militant Order [*Vlaamse Militante Orde*, VMO]. The BNP in turn has played host to speakers and guests from such groups on its platforms in Britain.

Richard Edmonds the BNP's national organiser and a fanatical anti-Semite, was honoured by the New European Order [NEO] with an announcement in 1993 that he was to be its British representative. This group, which has its roots in the SS at the end of the Second World War, had among its top echelons one of the most wanted war criminals: SS general Léon Degrelle, who died in March 1994. Each year a select group of British Nazis and Strasserites travelled to Madrid to meet Degrelle together with Pedro Varella, leader of the Spanish Circle of Friends of Europe [*Circulo Español de Amigos de Europa* – CEDADE], the Spanish section of the NEO. The BNP and ITP were high up on the list of those invited.

Outside the BNP very little far right activity is taking place. The only group causing any concern is the Blood and Honour skinhead network. The NF, sailing aimlessly like an abandoned ship, despite Ian Anderson at its helm, has about 300 members. The occasional appearance of its publication is a non-event even for Nazis and Fascists, as much of the content is somewhere left of hardline Conservative Party racists.

This could explain the flight into the Revolutionary Conservative Caucus [RCC] by long-time Nazis and Fascists from the NF, for example, the NF's former deputy chair Steven Brady and its treasurer Tom Acton. The RCC was set up by former key activists from the Monday Club, a fringe organisation on the right of the Conservative Party, and from Western Goals, a far right group based on the West Coast of the USA. Western Goals was already a thorn in the side of the Conservative Party, after some of its members, most of whom were also in the party, invited foreign Fascist leaders to address fringe meetings at annual conferences in recent years. The RCC and its publishing outlet, the European Book Society, were formed following advice that its leaders received from Le Pen, the leader of the French *Front National*, when he visited London in 1992.

The RCC's key players are Brady and Acton, Stuart Millson, a former member of the BNP, and Jonathan Bowden, formerly in the Monday Club. Gregory Lauder Frost, a former leading light in both the Monday Club and Western Goals, is at present serving a sentence for a fraud against his former employers, the Riverside Health Authority in London. These would-be advocates of law and order cannot be too pleased to have one of their leaders behind bars for stealing from an already ailing National Health Service.

There is a good deal of cross-fertilisation between the RCC and Patrick Harrington's Third Way, a tiny group with large unexplained funding, which is closely linked to developing Third Positionist groups around the world and is rapidly forming links in the former Soviet bloc.

Bowden and Millson espouse the ideas of French New Rightists such as Alain de Benoist. The books advertised in the RCC's publications reflect strong traditional Catholic views as well as anti-Semitism, but a closer look reveals rather harder connections with the extreme right.

Although the RCC is small, the Conservative Party is taking it seriously. After revelations in the *Sunday Express* of 3 October 1993, on the eve of the Conservative Party conference, the party chairman issued a warning to Conservative Party branches not to let RCC members join. However, it appears that the RCC already has a number of key activists in the party. One person with an intimate knowledge of the Monday Club and Western Goals has stated that membership of the Conservative Party was a prerequisite for membership of the RCC.

Three years after Patrick Harrington formed the Third Way came the ITP, run by Nick Griffin, a former chairman of the NF, Colin Todd, a violent former NF regional officer, and Derek Holland, perceived as mentally unbalanced even by members of Colonel Gadaffi's staff.[18] This very small operation, which like Third Way has unexplained funding, has developed connections in Libya, Iraq and Croatia. Its members, especially those who have been in the armed forces, have volunteered to fight for Iraq during the Gulf war and in the civil war in Croatia. While no record of their actually fighting in Iraq has been found, evidence exists of a visit there on the eve of the war. In Croatia, however, they have been very active and are believed to have suffered at least one fatality. The ITP appears to earn some income from producing T-shirts with racist graphics, and to run some form of security company. The membership of Third Way and ITP combined cannot be more than around a hundred.

Anthony Hancock, the Nazi printer and publisher, has maintained his close ties with David Irving and his Clarendon Club, which appears to exist only inside Irving's head. He is also the British representative of the Institute of Historical Review (USA), the world's leading organisation that denies the worst excesses of the Nazi regime, and in particular claims that the Holocaust did not happen. Hancock is seen regularly at various Nazi and anti-Semitic rallies abroad, and services Nazi groups in countries where publication of Nazi material is banned. Despite his convictions for fraud and his involvement in two cases involving drugs and counterfeit money, he appears to live a charmed life, being of use to a wide range of Nazi groups internationally.

Remaining outside the main Nazi organisations are individuals or very tiny groups that see their task mainly as producing and circulating hardline, sometimes pornographic, racist and anti-Semitic material on a substantial level. If the BNP can produce and distribute perhaps four million propaganda items a year, these groups may only do a quarter of that, but are able to distribute it much more strategically. The main people involved are the Dowager Lady Birdwood and Don Martin. They have surrounded themselves with teams of helpers whose main inspiration appears to be the anti-Semitism of the material they publish. Birdwood has already been convicted at the Old Bailey on ten counts of producing and distributing racist material.

The impact of these various Nazi and racist groups and individuals cannot be measured accurately. Clearly, the Home Office's new estimate, drawn from the National Crime Survey, of around 135,000 racial incidents a year in Britain cannot be placed at the door of the BNP alone, no more than can racial murders. These average twelve a year, but the cause and effect of millions of pieces of hate material poisoning people's minds cannot be ignored. A democratic society should not only safeguard itself from the Nazi terrorists of Combat 18, but look seriously at the criminality of groups like the BNP and at the impact of their lawless behaviour.

Many institutions and individuals, including several senior police officers, are now agreed that it is not new legislation which is needed to control the spread of violent racism, but rather the proper use of the existing laws on racism, public order and the communication of hate materials. Past Attorney Generals of both Labour and Conservative administrations have failed conspicuously in their duty by refusing to sanction strategic legal actions against Nazis and racists who break the law. As the law stands at present, no serious case can go ahead without the Attorney General's fiat. Many senior and middle-ranking police officers, members of the judiciary, politicians and anti-racist community workers are demanding that this restriction be removed, and that racist offences be treated as ordinary criminal acts. A change of this nature would result in the police and general public seeing racism being dealt with as crime rather than racist criminals being given democratic rights. In this way, it would both protect and educate.

List of abbreviations

ANL	Anti Nazi League
BM	British Movement
BNP	British National Party
BNSM	British National Socialist Movement
CEDADE	*Circulo Español de Amigos de Europa* [Spanish Circle of Friends of Europe]
CIA	Central Intelligence Agency
GBM	Greater Britain Movement
IRA	Irish Republican Army
ITP	International Third Position
KKK	Ku Klux Klan
LSG	League of St George
NEO	New European Order
NF	National Front
NSM	National Socialist Movement
RCC	Revolutionary Conservative Caucus
UDA	Ulster Defence Association
UFF	Ulster Freedom Fighters
UVF	Ulster Volunteer Force
VAM	*Vit Ariskt Motstånd* [White Aryan Resistance]
VMO	*Vlaamse Militante Orde* [Flemish Militant Order]

Notes

1. *Searchlight*, April 1993, pp. 1–17.
2. Written evidence from Searchlight to the Home Affairs Committee submitted in June 1993, and oral evidence given on 8 Dec. 1993.
3. F. Ferraresi, 'A Secret Structure codenamed Gladio', in S. Hellman and G. Pasquino (eds), *Italian Politics – A Review*, vol. VII, Pinter, London, 1992, pp. 29–49.
4. Court report in *The Times*, 16 Oct. 1962.
5. Reports in the Jewish press, especially the *Jewish Chronicle*, 1965 to 1967.
6. *Searchlight*, July 1985, pp. 3–4.
7. *Searchlight*, July 1990, pp. 3–5; *The Sunday People*, 17 June 1990; TV South documentary, Oct. 1990.
8. *Searchlight*, Aug. 1982, pp. 10–11; Nov. 1986, pp. 3–4; Jan. 1987, pp. 9–12; Sept. 1992, pp. 3–4; April 1993, pp. 2–17.
9. *Searchlight*, Oct. 1983, pp. 5 and 15; July 1986, pp. 8–10; Feb. 1990, pp. 9–12; March 1990, p. 11; April 1993, pp. 2–17.
10. Private German and Swedish sources.
11. *Searchlight*, June 1992, pp. 3–5.
12. On Griffin, see *From Ballots to Bombs*, Searchlight, London, 1989; and G. Gable, 'The far-right in Contemporary Britain', in L. Cheles, R. G. Ferguson and M. Vaughan (eds), *Neo-Fascism in Europe*, Longman, London, 1991, pp. 53–60.
13. *Redwatch* and *Target*, internal bulletins of Combat 18 and the League of St George, 1992–93.
14. T. Hepple and G. Gable, *At War With Society*, Searchlight, London, 1993.
15. For detailed information and analysis of the structure of the order, see K. Flynn and G. Gerhardt, *The Silent Brotherhood*, Collier Macmillan, London, 1989. For primary sources on British Nazi terror groups, see: *The Order*, internal publication of Combat 18; *The Oak*, published by Combat 18 supporters; *Putsch* and *Forward as Thorwould*, published by Combat 18; A. Macdonald (pen-name of William Pierce), *The Turner Diaries*, National Vanguard Books, Hillsboro, WV, 1978; A. Macdonald, *Hunter*, National Vanguard Books, Hillsboro, WV, 1989.
16. Beackon lost the seat at the council elections on 5 May 1994, although he increased his vote by nearly 600. Other BNP candidates did well, polling 10,000 votes in east London. In Newham, a neighbouring borough to Tower Hamlets and an area beset with similar problems, the BNP's results indicated a strong potential for winning seats in future. While the average Fascist vote, in areas in which Fascist candidates stood, in the 1994 local elections in England had risen to 6.8 per cent, the BNP's share of the vote in London averaged 8.4 per cent. Shortly before the local elections John Tyndall announced his decision to fight a parliamentary by-election on 6 June 1994 in Dagenham, following the resignation of the Labour MP Bryan Gould.
17. A. Kershaw, 'The Song Goes On', *Weekend Guardian*, 30 Oct. 1993, pp. 24–27, and *Searchlight*, Nov. 1993, p. 11.
18. Correspondence between the Libyan Ministry of Foreign Affairs and an Australian Nazi in 1989.

Chapter 15

WOMEN AND THE BRITISH EXTREME RIGHT
Martin Durham

The Second World War marked a watershed in the development of the British extreme right. The main Fascist organisation, Sir Oswald Mosley's British Union of Fascists, was banned shortly after the outbreak of hostilities, and attempts to revive the movement in the initial post-war years met with little response. Few joined Mosley's Union Movement, and rival groups – most importantly the League of Empire Loyalists – also proved unsuccessful. However, if neither Empire nor Mosley's new enthusiasm for Europe proved popular, the extreme right was to find an issue with considerably more potential: opposition to black immigration. While the older organisations took up the issue, much of the racist activity from the late 1950s onwards originated from either local anti-immigration groups or splinter groups from the Empire Loyalists. The movement's divisions, however, limited the extent to which the race issue could be exploited, and eventually unity negotiations led to the decision to launch a new organisation, the National Front [NF]. Some on the extreme right, most importantly the NF's future Chairman, John Tyndall, were initially excluded. Others continued with independent organisations. But for the bulk of the movement, the foundation of the NF in 1967 represented at last the bringing together of the forces that stood for race and nation.[1]

This unity, however, was to be short-lived, and, after a period of electoral advance in the early and mid-1970s, it was to suffer a reversal of its fortunes and a succession of bitter rows involving the breakaway of several splinter groups.[2] Nonetheless, it remained the dominant organisation on the British extreme right. During the early 1980s, it underwent a profound process of ideological rethinking which led it to claim fealty to a radical nationalist tradition involving, among others, the dissident Nazis Gregor and Otto Strasser, and the British social critics Hilaire Belloc and G. K. Chesterton.[3] In the mid-1980s, however, disagreements over strategy resulted in a split into two rival groups, both of which laid claim to the name National Front. For the more radical of the two groups, which controlled the party paper, *National Front News*, the search for a 'third way' between capitalism and Communism did not only involve a vision of a largely agrarian society based on a combination of small businesses and workers' co-operatives. It also entailed the creation of an elite of 'political soldiers' and a search for 'anti-Zionist' allies abroad that led it to show a surprising enthusiasm for Libya, Iran and the American Black Muslim leader Louis Farrakhan. For the rival group, which in 1986 launched its own paper, *The Flag*, social radicalism was not in dispute. However, it was not to threaten either the coherence of a race-centred view of world politics or the continuation of the struggle to regain the electoral support achieved, and then lost, during the 1970s.[4]

The bitter rivalry between the two organisations was resolved at the beginning of 1990 by the dissolution of the *National Front News* group, leaving in its wake two minuscule groups: Third Way and Third Position. The self-destruction of one NF, however, did not mean that the other would prosper. The *Flag* group was itself in crisis, and hegemony on the British extreme right was instead passing to an organisation which rejected Strasserite radicalism altogether. Led by the former Chairman of the NF, John Tyndall, the New National Front had broken away in 1980 after unsuccessful efforts to end what was seen as anarchy in the organisation. Changing its name two years later to the British National Party [BNP], Tyndall's organisation saw itself as the continuation of the NF of the 1970s. However, where that organisation had sought to minimise reference to pre-1945 German politics, the BNP appeared more admiring of National Socialism while still falling short of overtly embracing it.[5]

Since the emergence of the National Front, there have been important changes in the British extreme right's ideology, strategy and policy proposals. Although more difficult to delineate, there have also been shifts in its patterns of recruitment, and in the social background, age and geographic concentration of its members and supporters. However, important areas of continuity remain. Just as any exploration of support would be drawn in particular to the East End of London, where the NF achieved high votes in the 1970s and the BNP was to gain its first ever councillor in 1993, so there are a number of persistent ideological themes – above all anti-black racism and anti-Semitism. Yet in exploring what its adherents term 'racial nationalism', how it has been modified over time and within different organisations, and who it appeals to, there is a constant danger of neglecting a vital element both in how it constructs the world ideologically and how it draws support. This element is gender.

Existing studies of the British extreme right have tended to ignore issues of gender and, in particular, the question of the role of women.[6] Yet, as a number of writers have pointed out, the most important form of Fascism, German National Socialism, was deeply concerned with such issues. In its rise to power, it had attacked Weimar society as sexually decadent, called for a revival of the birth-rate and campaigned against the employment of married women. Once in power, the Nazis had largely failed in their efforts to remove women from the labour market, but the regime's emphasis on women's role as mothers was given expression through both propaganda and such measures as marriage loans, increased maternity provision and medals for mothers of large families. The law against abortion was enforced vigorously and birth control clinics were closed as the regime sought to raise the birth-rate of those seen as racially fit. For others, however, it resorted to restrictions on marriage, sterilisation and, ultimately, murder. Nazism had proclaimed the need to raise the white birth-rate and to end sexual confusion, and we might well expect comparable British groups to share these concerns.[7] Furthermore, shifts in gender roles and in sexual values in post-war Britain are exactly of the kind likely to generate anxieties. The extreme right, we would expect, would share and amplify such anxieties, whether it owed its ideological formation to Nazism or to some other form of racist nationalism.

In the discussion that follows, material from different phases of the development of the British extreme right since 1967 will be examined in order to explore the continuities and discontinuities in its views of women. Initially, we will be concerned to examine what we might call the old NF, from 1967 to the breakaway of Tyndall and his supporters at the beginning of 1980. We will then turn our attention both to the NF after the loss of its leading figure and to Tyndall's own organisation. This discussion opens with that most central of questions to racial nationalists: the birth-rate. It is here, in discussing the politics of reproduction and of population, that a racial nationalist view of women can be most clearly understood. We will begin, not inappropriately, with an article written shortly after the inception of the NF in *Spearhead*, a magazine which then supported the NF and now supports the BNP. The author was Tyndall.

Birth controllers, Tyndall argued, believed that all families were to be treated in the same way, yet only some families were of 'absolutely sound stock'. In normal circumstances they would find prosperity and be able to 'have plenty of children to inherit their desirable qualities', while the 'least desirable' would be limited in the number of offspring who might survive. But the Pill was prescribed for anybody, and as a result the most intelligent made the most use of it, while 'the most ignorant and backward' multiplied. Nor did overpopulation justify such an approach. Contraception was not curbing the population explosion and, indeed, some countries were actively pursuing an increase in their birth-rate. The question, therefore, was not whether Britain was overpopulated in relation to its resources, but whether it was overpopulated in relation to other powers. Confronted by 'teeming coloured populations everywhere posing their own special threat to the bastions of white culture and stability', Britain needed an improvement in its birth-rate, both in quantity and quality. To this end, he concluded, 'all ephemeral social considerations should be subordinated'.[8]

Writing almost a decade later, the then editor of *Spearhead*, Richard Verrall, made even clearer the centrality of population to a racial nationalist politics. There was, he argued, no more fundamental question than that of racial survival, and when we looked at the modern world we saw 'a small boat in which the beleaguered White races are slowly sinking as the rising tide of the coloured world population threatens to swamp it'. Decades of Western liberalism had obscured this and worsened the situation by the indiscriminate encouragement of birth control among the very group that was threatened by low fertility. The fact that contraception was promoted among whites, he argued, suggested that the West was 'either in the grip of some peculiar liberal death wish, or at the mercy of forces which are deliberately promoting the progressive reduction of White peoples throughout the world as a dominant racial factor'. Both the numbers and 'the racial quality of the White world' were declining, Verrall claimed, and at some point, 'the White man' would have to take 'unprecedented measures to secure for himself his rightful place on the planet'. In order to do so, a nationalist population policy was vital. Other countries, including Germany and Italy in the 1930s, had pursued a policy of increasing population but, today, population was either neglected or its reduction actually encouraged. Instead, what was needed was 'an education programme which will eliminate the moral and political sensitivity which has surrounded population policy, and has inhibited governments from taking the necessary action'. In such circumstances, government should encourage 'by every means possible, the raising of large families'. This would entail reducing the cost of parenthood, introducing child welfare schemes, repealing the 1967 Abortion Act and ending the 'national and governmental mania' for promoting contraception. 'What is required here', he argued, was 'simply a complete reorientation of government policy where state encouragement to build a family is the priority, instead of state discouragement to build one, as at present.' Through financial incentives such as low-interest mortgages for young couples, increased efforts to lower infant mortality and encouraging woman's role as mother, 'the building of large families' could be brought about.[9]

It was in the light of arguments such as these that the NF discussed 'The family and population' in its 1979 election manifesto.[10] Britain needed a higher birth-rate, it argued, and large families should be made economically feasible. But it was also vital to oppose the levelling-down effects of punitive taxation, egalitarian education and 'racial mixing'. 'Alone among parties', it proclaimed, the NF sought to 'reverse those trends which make for a decline in our population qualitatively as well as quantitatively'.

As we have seen, Verrall had included among his proposals the repeal of the 1967 Abortion Act. Because of the vital need for large families, he declared, it went 'without saying that the present permissive abortion laws should be scrapped'. Indeed, he argued, it could well be that abortion should be completely illegal. His opposition to abortion was expressed exclusively in terms of its effect on the birth-rate: in Communist Romania, he noted, fertility had fallen with lax abortion laws and risen when abortion policy had been reversed.[11] This espousal of a high birth-rate, however, could not be the only factor in deciding NF policy towards abortion, for two very clear reasons. Firstly, potential voters (and even members) could be alienated by a hardline anti-abortion stance. Secondly, opposition to abortion is frequently argued on grounds of 'the right to life', which has very different implications from a concern that it is whites who should be having more children, rather than other racial groupings.

In its address for the October 1974 general election, the NF included the demand 'Repeal Abortion Act'. At its subsequent Annual General Meeting, however, what *Spearhead* called 'very passionate exchanges' occurred before delegates voted to oppose abortion on demand but accepted an amendment permitting abortions on 'special medical grounds'.[12] In the next issue of the magazine, one of the NF's leading figures, Martin Webster, made use of his regular column to reveal that the resolution which the Annual General Meeting had eventually agreed had contained criticism of the NF leadership's decision to include 'unqualified opposition to abortion' in the election address. Most members at the meeting, Webster commented, had recognised that a political party should not 'adopt official policies on questions pertaining to private morality'. This quickly elicited a critical response from another leading activist, Malcolm Skeggs. While agreeing that the NF should not try to turn itself into 'a sort of adjunct of the Festival of Light', he insisted that abortion was not a matter of private morality but was the taking of human life. Shortly after, this was followed in turn by a letter from a prominent woman member, Joan Sandland, arguing that the NF should work for the kind of social conditions that would lessen the demand for abortion rather than driving 'women back to the back street butcher'.[13] Four years later, rejecting the view that abortion was a matter for personal morality, Verrall was the proposer of a successful motion to the NF Annual General Meeting to repeal the Abortion Act and only permit abortion on 'genuine medical grounds'. This is the position which appeared in the NF's manifesto for the 1979 general election.[14]

If there was open dissent within the organisation on whether to oppose abortion, there were also tensions between different arguments against abortion. At times, NF writers sounded exactly like such anti-abortion organisations as Life or the Society for the Protection of Unborn Children [SPUC]. Thus, in the early 1970s, the NF paper, *Britain First*, praised Roman Catholic doctors for refusing to take part in abortions and for taking the view that 'sanctity applies to unborn babies'. In 1980 *Spearhead*, commenting on Liberal leader David Steel's continued support for the 1967 Act, insisted that human life came into existence at the moment of conception and that there was no difference between killing a human being before birth and after.[15] On other occasions, different arguments were espoused. If we look at an article in the late 1970s, we find abortion attacked as the product of liberal permissiveness, compared to 'Herod's massacre of the innocents' and described as debasing and defeminising women – all arguments typical of a 'pro-life' stance. 'For nationalists,' the writer continued, there were 'even more cogent arguments': that most abortions in Britain were of whites, and that, in the face of the 'high coloured birthrate', this represented a racial death wish. Britain, he argued, had already lost more of its young to 'the abortionist's knife' than it had in the two world wars. Abortion did not merely represent selfishness and fear of the future: 'Above all, it is a calculated weapon in the hands of the nation-wreckers, the Final Solution to the problem of European pre-eminence.'[16]

If the NF was bitterly hostile to abortion, and activists could even see it as part of a conspiracy against the white race, what of birth control? Here too, there was tension within the organisation. In 1969, *Spearhead* published a letter claiming to speak 'for a great majority of members' in rejecting Tyndall's views. Birth control, it argued, was vital for women unable to afford to bring up another child. Tyndall, who replied in the same issue, returned to the subject the following year when he complained that student members, seemingly infected by leftist views, had taken to sending letters to the magazine criticising so-called 'reactionary attitudes' towards such issues as contraception.[17] But while often hostile to birth control, the NF did not suggest, as it had done with abortion, that contraception should be banned. In his 1968 article, Tyndall had declared that 'We have no right to dictate to husbands and wives that they should have large families' and that a future nationalist government would leave 'the choice of family size to every husband and wife'.[18] Likewise, the October 1974 election manifesto combined calling for 'a vigorous birth-rate' with the assurance that 'we see it as no part of the function of the State to issue gratuitous advice to families as to how many children they should have. This is a matter for parents alone to decide.'[19] According to Webster, the 1974 Annual General Meeting had been opposed to turning issues of private morality into matters for party policy, and the NF's opposition to abortion was explicitly argued on the grounds that abortion was not purely personal. The same could have been argued about contraception, considering the importance of the birth-rate to the NF, but would have been deeply contentious. To argue against abortion, the NF could talk in terms of the rights of the unborn child; seeking to ban birth control would have been to champion a degree of state intrusion into private lives far more Draconian than members or voters could accept. Its opposition to birth control, then, remained comparatively in the background of NF propaganda, and, however unconvincingly, it assured supporters that a nationalist government would not enforce a population policy.

As we have seen, the population policy envisaged by Verrall in 1977 had emphasised woman's role as mother. What was central, he argued, was 'a society that respected and cherished the feminine role as principally one of wife, mother and home maker'. This, he insisted, was not a male chauvinist view, but a rejection of the 'rebellion against nature' that was displayed in 'the contemporary derision of maternity and domesticity'.[20] The following year, he returned to this theme in a discussion of sociobiology. An examination of 'male dominance and female passivity', of 'male aggression and female domesticity' in the animal world, he suggested, demonstrated their biological basis and discredited feminist claims of sex roles being socially conditioned.[21]

For Tyndall too, the restoration of traditional sex roles was crucial. Most NF members, he declared in 1970, wanted 'a society in which the differentiation between the sexes is clearly marked' and 'the values of real manhood and real womanhood' prioritised.[22] Such views were reiterated later in the 1970s, when the NF received much attention in the media. 'I would like to see real manhood and real womanhood once again valued', he told *The Times* in 1977. In his view, he told another journalist, 'women are of supreme value in the home. As a supportive factor.'[23] The party's 1979 manifesto, while avoiding Tyndall's more pronounced views, denounced values and behaviour which weakened the distinction between masculinity and femininity.[24]

As with race, racial nationalists are fond of resorting to 'scientific evidence' in matters of gender. We have already noted Verrall's use of sociobiology. In 1978, *Spearhead* published an abridged version of an article on 'The Feminine Condition' by Alain de Benoist, a leading figure in the French New Right. The article argued that the sexes were fundamentally different, with men inclined towards aggression and the urge to conquer, while women had such attributes as submissiveness, tenderness and passivity. Quoting from the anti-feminist writer Arianna Stassinopoulos, the psychoanalyst Carl Jung and others, de Benoist argued that the sexes were complementary in their roles. Jung, he noted, had declared that by taking up 'masculine callings', being active in politics and engaging in study, woman had departed from 'her feminine nature'.[25]

If such was the view of women held by leading members of the NF, what of the role of women within the party? One of the most noticeable characteristics of the NF is its overwhelming masculinity. It is not merely that its membership is preponderantly male, a characteristic which it shares with other political parties, or even that its leading figures have been men. As particularly evidenced in its support among football fans and in the 'skinhead' sub-culture, much of the NF's appeal rests on the existence of a virulent machismo. Yet, if less visible, women have been active in the NF since its inception. Women have certainly been a minority of its members and it is likely that their involvement in its most public (and potentially confrontational) activities – marches and street-sales – has been lower still. None the less, photographs and reports in both NF and anti-NF publications show that women have often been involved in such activities, just as there is evidence of their participation in branch meetings and

Annual General Meetings.[26] Unsurprisingly for a male-led movement, women have often been found raising funds or providing refreshments for its events.[27] But while women often played relatively limited roles in NF activities, this was not true for some.

If we look, for instance, at the NF leadership in the 1970s, its character is vividly displayed in a *Spearhead* photograph of an all-male National Directorate.[28] Yet, at times, women had appeared on the Directorate and also stood as general election candidates: one out of ten candidates in 1970, six out of a total of 107 in the two 1974 contests, thirty-six out of 303 in 1979.[29] In local elections, comparable figures have not been compiled, but in these too there have been women candidates. In the 1977 Greater London Council elections, for instance, twenty-one of the ninety-one candidates were women.[30] Women have played a part too in local organisations, often as branch secretary, treasurer or election agent but, on occasion, as branch organiser.[31]

Women activists in the 1970s were, as was true of the movement as a whole, frequently older than those who came to the fore subsequently. Those who appeared by name in *Spearhead* were often presented in terms of their role in the family. Thus Sheila Wright, a general election candidate in 1970, was described as a 'Wolverhampton housewife with two sons aged eight and four', while a 'Mum's Army' of 'six housewives, most of them National Front members', were praised for their pelting of the Labour Home Secretary, Roy Jenkins, with flour 'bombs' in protest against government policy on race.[32]

In the late 1970s, however, the NF decided to launch a youth organisation, the Young National Front [YNF]. As the YNF came to absorb more of its energies, the dominant image of women in the party shifted in both age and tone. Its publications began to carry photographs of young women members modelling NF T-shirts with such captions as 'One good reason for joining the YNF!' or 'Out in Front!'.[33] Soon after the launch of the YNF's paper, *Bulldog*, a woman member had appealed for 'more girls' to join the organisation. The following year it reported a 'large increase' in such members, while in the first issue of *Nationalism Today* it was claimed that, as the YNF had 'moved into 1979, it was noticed that more and more girls were becoming active on NF demonstrations'. This was to be welcomed, the article continued, as until then the vast majority of YNF activists had been male.[34] Racialism was not a male province, as one woman local election candidate, Helena Steven, demonstrated in 1978 with an 'open letter' to voters which declared 'If you are a White woman, then the biggest problem facing you is . . . Black violence'.[35] But the women who were joining the NF were joining an organisation whose racialism was entangled with sexual jealousy and a view of women as a possession in need of protection. 'The enemy within,' *Spearhead* announced, '. . . took our houses, our jobs, our women', a complaint that on other occasions was literally left unspoken but underlay the fondness of the magazine for cover photographs of a white woman and a black man, a pictorial encoding of the male nationalist's belief that the racial alien had access to what was rightfully his.[36] For the NF, the black man was seen less as the lover of a white woman than as her violator. Frequently in the 1970s, *National Front News* carried reports of cases of rapes and other sexual offences allegedly carried out by black men. An early issue of *Bulldog* spelt out the message more clearly still: 'Next time you see a "humane, compassionate" Black just think of the safety of your White womenfolk . . . think of your mother, your sister, your girlfriend.'[37] This concern for white women's sexuality (and for their fertility) did not, as we have seen, preclude their involvement in the NF. Yet, their allegiance was to a party which proved less than welcoming to their initiative. Speaking in 1977, John Tyndall suggested that women's 'intuitive abilities' made them invaluable to the party but incapable of leadership. 'You might say,' he had declared, 'that it is a reflection upon the abilities of the men in the Conservative Party that their present leader is a woman.'[38]

As we have seen, for the NF of the 1960s and the 1970s, population policy was crucial, not only to raise the white birth-rate but to improve the 'quality' of the race. With the departure of Tyndall (and subsequently Verrall) in the early 1980s, this concern has partly receded within the NF. In particular, eugenics has proved problematic in more recent years. Writing shortly before the 1985 split, Steve Brady, subsequently a leading figure in the *Flag* group, wrote a discussion-article in which he proposed shaping 'our evolutionary destiny' by 'a gradual, scientific and humane programme of eugenics'. In response, another leading activist, Paul Matthews, explained why he rejected Brady's vision of the future. 'The imagination reels,' he declared, 'to see how any programme for abortion, euthanasia, the slaughter of the sick and lame of society can be humane; and the practical questions are scarcely less than the moral: who is to have the power of life and death? Who are the unfit?'[39] In raising this argument, two crucial fissures within the extreme right were exposed. Firstly, Matthews was writing explicitly as an advocate of the Distributist stance of Chesterton and Belloc. Within this tradition, a particular form of Roman Catholic social theory underpins an opposition not only to capitalism and to Communism, but to eugenics. However, there is also a class component. Tyndall's and Verrall's arguments about the declining character of the white race appeared to suggest that the white middle class was genetically superior to other whites. As we will see, this has even caused tension within the BNP. It would pose even more problems for a radicalised NF that saw itself as representing the white working class against its exploiters, and favoured radical economic and social policies which sat uncomfortably with any suggestion that poverty is nature's reward for biological inferiority. Writing earlier in the 1980s, another leading radical, Nick Griffin, had argued that Tyndall would be happy to see working class organisations destroyed and workers' birth-rates restricted.[40] When he and others split with Brady in 1986, they created around *National Front News* a group which could not accept a eugenic population policy.

But there was another factor in play too. The radicalisation of the NF involved not only ruralism, but also an enthusiasm for ecology. That this would have an effect on population policy was particularly evident in an article written by Brady himself in the late 1980s. In discussing 'the rising tide of colour', he made no reference to eugenics or to raising the white birth-rate, and even suggested that Britain could, in the future, find a population level 'more in harmony with the capacity of the environment and ecology to support'.[41] More recently, however, enthusiasm for increasing the birth-rate has enjoyed a revival within the *Flag* group, with Brady declaring that only a national revolution could save the white race, but that even under the present system child-bearing can be encouraged through measures to improve maternity leave and provide childcare.[42] In the *National Front News* faction too, concern increased in the late 1980s, with the French government being praised for using financial incentives to increase the birth-rate and the suggestion that in a nationalist society 'tax incentives' could be used to encourage 'large, healthy families'.[43] Such were the strains between ecology and natality, however, that one issue of *National Front News*, published before the split, even managed on one page to call for a 'healthier' white birth-rate, and on another to welcome a Population Concern report that Britain was overpopulated and needed to reduce its numbers to 30 million.[44]

If there was confusion over population, what of abortion? The NF manifesto for the 1983 election envisaged allowing abortion only on grounds of serious danger to the woman's life or health, serious malformation of the foetus or rape.[45] Following the split in the mid-1980s, the *National Front News* faction retained a strongly anti-abortion stance, arguing in late 1987, in 'Abortion: The Nationalist View', that abortion was 'intrinsically evil' and had been brought about by a decadent society which encouraged an attitude of materialistic self-interest. While Life and SPUC campaigned against abortion, it went on, they were unlikely to win against a powerful pro-abortion lobby. Abortion could only be ended by a revolution based on natural laws and values, and the only movement which fully recognised this was the NF.[46] Despite the subsequent appearance of critical letters in the paper, this remained the organisation's position.[47]

The *Flag* group, however, initially appeared more hesitant on the issue. In two separate news reports in one issue of its paper, abortion was described as 'murder'. Yet a subsequent report in its magazine of the defeat in 1988 of the anti-abortion Alton bill, while criticising parliament for failing to debate the issue seriously, merely suggested that whether one supported the bill or not, it should not have been talked out. The clue to this divergence was to be found in the same issue of the magazine, with the appearance of an anti-abortion article under the heading 'Debate'. 'The subject of abortion has traditionally been a very controversial one within Nationalist circles,' the editor noted, and readers' comments would be welcome. Letters duly appeared, both for and against abortion.[48] In time, however, the issue appears to have been settled in favour of the anti-abortion view. Thus in 1990 the *Flag*, in discussing the lowering of the time-limit for abortion from twenty-eight to twenty-four weeks but with exceptions, declared that this allowed even more liberal access to abortion than before. 'Our so-called "pro-family" Government,' it suggested, had 'shown its true face with their record on abortion reform. Sir Geoffrey Howe, Leader of the House, Kenneth Clarke, the Secretary of State, and Virginia Bottomley, the Minister of Health, lead the anti-life campaign in the House of Commons.' An NF administration, it promised, 'would purge our Nation of this terrible scourge'.[49] Its 1992 election manifesto held that abortion could be tolerated only in cases of rape, serious foetal deformity or serious danger to the health of the woman.[50] According to a subsequent article, the availability of contraception, along with 'a greater emphasis on the teaching of moral values in our schools', meant that there was 'no excuse for killing unborn children'.[51]

The NF in the 1980s continued in its concern with the protection of white womanhood. 'Race-mixing destroys our People', declared a cover of *National Front News* in the late 1980s, illustrating the theme with a photo of a white woman and child, while the cover of a pre-split issue carried a picture of a man, woman and child with the caption 'White Man! You Have a Duty to Protect Your Race, Homeland and Family!' Again this concern could easily be sexualised, with *Bulldog* in late 1983 proclaiming in a cover story 'Black pimps force White girls into prostitution'.[52] While this remained a constant, attitudes were more complex concerning women's role itself. In a 1984 article in *Nationalism Today*, leading activist John Field argued that 'many Nationalists' were wrong to see the struggle for women's rights as a 'device with which to divide the White race'. Nationalist men, he claimed, should give protection and aid to 'their racial sisters', but too often they reacted with apathy or even hostility. In ancient times, 'Whites treated their women with respect', but more recently, a women's movement had emerged to fight for economic and social justice in 'reaction against the outrages of the industrial revolution'. The present form of this movement, he claimed, had fallen under Jewish control, but this could be reversed, and already Jewish feminists were complaining of anti-Semitism in the women's movement. Nationalists, he argued, were wrong if they believed that women's place was in the home. In the future society, women would not be forced by economic necessity to 'abandon home and family to get a job', and motherhood would be 'the noblest profession to which any White woman can aspire'. Yet they would still be free to pursue careers and would be rewarded fairly. Furthermore, women now were living in a society in which they had to go out to work and faced such problems as sexual harassment, discrimination and unequal pay. Nationalists, he concluded, should support their struggle.[53] Another activist, Frank Burden, in a letter published shortly afterwards, congratulated Field on his argument. Feminists, he claimed, misrepresented 'our womenfolk' and it was up to racial nationalists to take up women's 'very real and genuine problems'.[54]

Field's 1984 article, although very different from the dominant view of the 1970s, hovered uneasily between the mirage of winning feminists to the NF and calling on white men to 'protect' their womenfolk. Another article of some ambiguity, by woman activist Jackie Griffin, appeared the following year. Too often, she wrote, women were 'found behind the scenes, making cups of tea, addressing envelopes and folding circulars'. However, while she held that NF women had as much right as its men to be 'ideologists' and 'fighters', the main thrust of her argument was to take the most familial aspects of women's struggles as the way forward. Women's support for their families in the miners' strike and mothers' fear of nuclear war, she suggested, were examples for 'a movement which is finding a way to link political matters with home building instincts'.[55] The faction of the NF which both she and Field supported, however, was to dissolve such ambiguities into a far more traditionalist stance. In 1988 *National Front News* expressed the hope that 'true women's groups' would emerge committed to 'the beauty of femininity and the sacred role of motherhood', while a fuller exposition of NF policy on the family was offered in the same period in a two-part article in *Nationalism Today*.[56] The future of the nation, it argued, was threatened by the decline of 'good family life'. The Industrial Revolution had destroyed the economic independence of the family, and capitalists had driven mothers out to work, away from their natural role as child-rearers, home-builders and 'support of the breadwinner'. They women's liberation movement had arisen to promote hostility between the sexes. Nationalists had to resist these developments by reasserting the centrality of 'the organic family' as the basis of the nationalist movement and the future nationalist society. In future society, a mass-propaganda campaign, particularly in the churches and in the media, would be backed up by pro-family legislation.

In an order in which abortion was illegal, family businesses encouraged and commitment favoured over isolation and selfishness, women would find fulfilment. They would be equal, the article insisted, and they would be perfectly free to combine 'a profession and Motherhood' if they so chose, but it would be the latter that would be their vocation and the basis of society.

If traditionalist elements were predominant in one NF, in the other there has been much more of a tension between this strand and a more modernist approach. This was strikingly revealed shortly after the split, when a *Flag* faction pamphlet, *100 Questions and Answers About the National Front*, rejected the suggestion that the NF wanted women confined to the home. The NF fully supported, it declared, 'the changes in society over the last twenty years or so which have allowed women a full and equal role in society'. However, it added, 'some women' did not want a 'full time career and we would make sure that economic and social factors do not force women into careers which they do not want'.[57] To express support for the changes in women's role in recent years was a remarkable statement by any organisation on the extreme right. Other evidence, however, suggested that 'the old Adam' was still alive and well in the *Flag* group. Writing in late 1987, leading NF activist Joe Pearce took the opportunity of reviewing a book by radical feminist Andrea Dworkin to portray feminism as nonsensical and to offer in its place Chesterton's traditionalist views on natural sex differences and the importance of woman's role as mother. The following month, another activist, Tina Denny, replied strongly with a defence of the women's rights movement of the late nineteenth and early twentieth century. Nationalists, she claimed, did not devalue the early labour movement, despite its subsequent development. They should take the same view of the women's rights movement, rejecting present-day feminism, but supporting the historic fight for women's citizenship.[58] In putting forward such an argument, Denny was approaching the issue at a tangent, drawing no direct conclusions for women in the late twentieth century. Following her marriage to another leading activist, Tina Wingfield was elected to the NF's National Directorate. Interviewed in *Vanguard*, she declared that, like other parties, the NF had tended to be male-led, many women having joined through their husbands or boyfriends and not playing a major role. Once again, she was not directly critical of the organisation. The other new woman member of the National Directorate, Caralyn Taylor, however, was less restrained. 'Female members,' she declared, had 'been brainwashed by male members into thinking that running the National Front is a "job for the boys".'[59]

Both Wingfield and Taylor, long active in the NF, have themselves been examples of the complex ways in which NF women can be seen within the movement. Wingfield, at one time described in the *Flag* as 'a housewife and mother', had also been the NF's Administration Officer and a parliamentary by-election candidate, while Taylor, enthused over in one NF publication as a 'lovely blond white girl', had also been a YNF local organiser and an NF branch secretary.[60] Other women have also held seats on the National Directorate, with a peak of four out of eighteen in 1980. The NF has continued its earlier tradition of women candidates at general elections: six out of sixty in 1983, one out of fourteen in 1992.[61] (Neither of the NFs nor, indeed, the BNP had put up candidates in 1987.) And just as the NF of the late 1970s had claimed to be increasing its female membership, so has the *Flag* group more recently. In the late

1980s, it reported that although there were 'more men than women in the movement . . . over the last few years this imbalance has been slowing decreasing and we hope that this will continue to be the case'.[62] Indeed, in 1992 the party Chairman, Ian Anderson, discussing developments since 1986, noted that an article on the future of the NF which had appeared in the first issue of *Vanguard* had ignored the question of recruitment among women. 'We have, however, addressed this question over the past 12–15 months,' he observed, 'and, although we have a long way to go, we are making progress in this direction.'[63] In a report on the General Election of the same year, the NF paper reported an influx of new members. 'To our surprise and delight many of these have been ladies who are now making up an increasing proportion of National Front membership.'[64]

In discussing both wings of the NF during the 1980s, and the surviving group more recently, we have been concerned with the development of organisations which rejected the leadership of John Tyndall. But what of the BNP, the organisation that sought to rival the NF during the 1980s and overshadowed it in the early 1990s? How did the BNP view population, abortion and the role of women? According to its 1983 election manifesto, the BNP believed that 'family size is a private matter to be decided by parents themselves'. However, it continued, it favoured a high birth-rate and advocated the removal of 'all present economic discouragements to British people to have large families – in all cases where the parents are of intelligent, healthy and industrious stock'.[65] Here was undiluted eugenics, encouraging the procreation of the 'fit', discouraging the 'unfit'. But who might be included in such categories and how such a policy might be carried out was less than clear. The previous year Tyndall had characterised those of 'low population quality' as 'in the millions'. The 'inferior strains' within the white population, he argued, had 'for a long time tended to congregate in certain city areas of Britain'. Partly because of religious background, partly because of 'the benevolence of the welfare state', they had tended to have more children than the national average, a trend which needed to be reversed mainly through a lowering of welfare benefits and, where necessary, through sterilisation.[66] Such a stance towards large sections of the white population was, as we have seen, criticised within the organisation Tyndall had left. Nor was the BNP without dissent. As party leader, Tyndall was unlikely to be criticised within its ranks, but this privilege was not extended to those of his supporters who also ventured into print along such lines. Thus, for frequent *Spearhead* contributor Noel A. Hunt, 'the feckless' were being encouraged to 'breed recklessly', while 'the competent, careful, and prudent' were being discouraged from having children. In such a situation, he argued, simple raising of the birth rate was not the answer. What was desperately needed was 'not more babies, but babies of the highest possible quality'. For party activist Eric Brand, however, in a letter which appeared two issues later, 'such Tory arguments' should not have appeared in 'a Nationalist journal'. Hunt's attack on the supposedly feckless, he argued, was really an attack on the low-paid and unemployed.[67]

The views to which Brand objected continued, however, to prosper within the organisation, as was graphically illustrated in a set of discussion-articles by prominent activist Tony Wells, which appeared in the magazine at the end of the 1980s.[68] Attacking 'the familiar claptrap about the "woman's right to control over her own body" ' and advocating the 'strongest possible inducements and encouragements' for the reproduction of the healthy and racially sound, the author suggested that society's maintenance of what he called 'the genetically defective' should be brought to an end. This would entail sterilisation 'or even stronger measures', while positive eugenics should be applied to other sectors of the population. There was, he suggested, a correlation between earning capacity, particularly in the case of men, and genetic quality. Admittedly, he noted, in present society there were many exceptions to this rule, but in the properly ordered racial nationalist community of the future, 'The very poor should be discouraged from breeding', while the 'very wealthy . . . should be given every possible incentive to have large families'. Such views were put forward for discussion rather than as policy statements. Shortly after, however, in the party's 1992 election manifesto, attention was drawn to the 'alarming phenomenon' of 'the more responsible and worthy elements in our society – those whom we should most wish to breed' failing to produce 'enough children even to maintain the population and guarantee national survival'. What was needed, it was suggested, was for social provision to 'be adjusted so as to give the greatest encouragement to larger families among our more valuable people' and 'less encouragement to procreation among our least valuable people'. No doubt by way of reassurance, the manifesto suggested that 'the least valuable' were the minority of the population.[69]

As so often in the extreme right, the impact of a population policy on women had not been a concern. Yet such a stance had the most obvious implications for those who could actually bear the children the BNP wished to see born (let alone those it did not wish for). To render women invisible was far more difficult with the party's stance on abortion. Its 1983 election manifesto noted that the party was 'utterly opposed to Abortion on demand and we are pledged to amend the Abortion Act so as to make Abortion available only to women who can provide evidence of genuine medical need'. During the 1980s, however, the summary of party policy which appeared in its paper called simply for the repeal of abortion legislation. All reference to the issue was dropped from this section in late 1989, only to be reintroduced the following year in an amended form permitting exceptions on 'medical grounds' and also for rape.[70] If there were different views within the organisation, some less restrictive than others, then there were also more authoritarian views expressed within *Spearhead* but excluded from policy pronouncements. In the discussion-articles mentioned earlier, the writer suggested that racial nationalists opposed abortion because of its racial implications. This, he went on, should be distinguished from the approach of 'Right-to-Lifers', who appeared to 'worship anything that pops out of the maternal womb', refusing to recognise the future state's right to abort the unsound.[71]

Opposing access to abortion and what it saw as woefully low and indiscriminate reproduction, the BNP was also opposed to feminism. One effect of this doctrine – readers of the party paper, *British Nationalist*, were told in 1989 – was that 'many women have abandoned belief in the virtues of domesticity and motherhood'. What was needed was a rejection of 'these counsellors of decadence' and a recognition once again of the importance of men and women fulfilling 'their traditional biological roles'. This did not mean, readers were assured, that 'we have to close the career doors to those women who are determined on pursuing careers . . . If a few women want to make careers, let them. But let the majority be encouraged to be housewives and mothers first and foremost.'[72] In an article in *Spearhead* the same year, one writer had seemed more sympathetic to feminism, 'an inevitable reaction to the patriarchal society' which had rightly opposed the male-centredness of the West. But, he went on, it had gone too far in wanting 'liberation from effort and duty' and from femininity itself.[73] In its subsequent election manifesto, the BNP declared that it had 'no wish to withdraw from women those fundamental rights under the law that they have won in the course of their emancipation during the 20th century'. But while no 'legal barriers' would be placed in the way of women who were determined to pursue careers, this was not a social ideal. Instead, the BNP would 'encourage our womenfolk to regard home- and family-making as the highest vocation for their sex'.[74]

The prevalence of such views has not precluded women from joining the BNP. One activist, Isobel Hernon, has been particularly visible in interviews with the press, telling journalists of her fear of alien take-over and her respect for Hitler's achievements. The Jews, she declared, would 'use any means necessary to destroy our race through race mixing'. Hernon has been active as a canvasser and a by-election candidate and, during her earlier involvement in the NF, as a public speaker. But it is as the mother of five that she sees her greatest contribution to the cause: 'That's what we're made for. I'm playing the best part I can in the race war because I'm having children. I'm having the future white race.'[75] Another woman member, Christine Ryan, was reported in *Spearhead* in the mid-1980s giving a speech to the BNP's Stoke-on-Trent branch calling for more women to join the organisation. In part, it was a typically BNP speech, particularly in its admiration for Tyndall as a strong leader. Yet in other respects, it was considerably more surprising. The bearing and rearing of the future generation, she declared, was women's greatest contribution, but those who claimed that women's place was at the kitchen sink were talking 'a load of chauvinistic hogwash!' That women worked outside the home, she held, did not mean they had forsaken their primary role. Both career women and housewives would support the BNP, 'if we could prove ourselves to be a party of roughly equal rights'.[76] Women have not been prominent within the organisation. In 1983, only two of its fifty-four General Election candidates were women, while in 1992 one out of thirteen were.[77] Yet even within such a male-defined organisation, a woman activist can criticise male chauvinism and, as we have seen, party propaganda can go as far as half-heartedly denying that it is opposed to women pursuing careers.

What we have seen, when we examined the NF in the late 1960s and the 1970s, was an organisation that in many ways accords with our expectations. It emphasised a traditionalist notion of gender, it opposed abortion and was troubled by birth control, it talked in eugenic tones of the declining quality of the nation. Above all, the NF put to the fore the birth-rate of the white race, contrasted it with the rates of increase of other ethnic groups and called for a policy that would strengthen the white family and increase its fecundity. But in other ways, it was surprising. Despite its tendency to see women members as mothers or sex objects, it permitted an active role for women within its ranks, was at pains to deny that it would enforce a population policy, and harboured doubts about whether abortion should be opposed, and, if so, why. In the 1980s and early 1990s, the gender politics of the British extreme right was to become more complicated still. The victory of the radicals in the early 1980s and the development of anti-capitalist (and ecological) economic and social policies brought in their wake a move away from the 'selective breeding' views of Tyndall and Verrall, and even claims of a more favourable attitude towards women's equality. But the particular nature of the radicalism expounded in *Nationalism Today* and, to a lesser degree, by the *Flag* group simultaneously pushed the NF towards a traditionalist view of women. The ruralist, medievalist anti-capitalism of Chesterton and Belloc had been hostile to the women's movement of the early twentieth century. When Joe Pearce quotes Chesterton on women or *Nationalism Today* attacks the Industrial Revolution for taking women out of the home, we hear the voice of a back-to-the-land and back-to-the-family politics that is thoroughly antagonistic to feminist claims.

Yet to assume that the post-Tyndall NF is as enthusiastically patriarchal as the NF of the 1970s is to misread the development of the movement. Within the NF, other currents have emerged, and in the same way that it sought to channel opposition to nuclear power or support for the miners' strike in a racial nationalist direction, so too did feminism appear to offer possibilities in the eyes of some racial nationalists. In addition, the NF had recruited women (and men) with diverse attitudes towards male precedence in general and such issues as abortion in particular. The *National Front News* group's adherence to a form of radicalism influenced by Roman Catholic social theory made it particularly prone to a traditionalist view of abortion and of women's role in the family. Within the *Flag* group too traditionalism lives on, but in neither group has it been unchallenged. Most surprisingly, within the BNP, a hard-line stance has not lacked critics.

Even at its most Tyndallesque, the NF of the 1970s had given some women in its ranks the possibility of taking on local and, on occasion, national responsibilities both within the organisation and in election contests. This continued to be the case in later years, and for an NF woman to be portrayed in its press as a housewife or mother – or as a sex object – did not prove incompatible with her playing a role in the public sphere. Within the BNP too, where women have played little part, there are female activists. The NF of the 1970s, like its successor organisations, was suffused with patriarchal values. But if the BNP comes close, all of them diverge from the stereotype – generated by Nazis and anti-Nazis alike – of Fascism as the stormtroops of patriarchy. British racial nationalism has been, and remains, an expression not only of racism, but often of an embattled masculinity. Still, post-war shifts in gender relations and sexual morality have permeated all sections of British society, so that even such a resistant organism as the British extreme right has not been immune.

List of abbreviations

BNP	British National Party
NF	National Front
SPUC	Society for the Protection of Unborn Children
YNF	Young National Front

Notes

1. For the post-war extreme right, see R. Thurlow, *Fascism in Britain*, Blackwell, Oxford, 1987, chs. 10–11.

2. For the early NF, see M. Walker, *The National Front*, Fontana, London, 1977; M. Billig, *Fascists. A Social Psychological View of the National Front*, Harcourt Brace Jovanovitch, New York, 1978; M. Billig and A. Bell, 'Fascist Parties in Post-War Britain', *Race Relations Abstracts*, V, 1980, pp. 7–18; N. Fielding, *The National Front*, Routledge, London, 1981; S. Taylor, *The National Front in English Politics*, Macmillan, London, 1982; C. Husbands, *Racial Exclusionism and the City*, Allen and Unwin, London, 1983.

3. Gregor Strasser, a prominent figure in the German Nazi Party, was murdered on Hitler's orders after the party came to power. His brother Otto had broken with the party earlier. They opposed what they regarded as Hitler's compromises with reactionary forces and betrayal of 'German socialism'. Chesterton and Belloc were early twentieth century advocates of Distributism, a doctrine which held that widespread distribution of property was the only alternative to private or state monopoly. For these and other influences on the modern NF, see *Yesterday and Tomorrow. Roots of the National Revolution*, Rising Press, London, n.d. (c. 1983); D. Baker, 'A. K. Chesterton, the Strasser brothers and the Politics of the National Front', *Patterns of Prejudice*, XIX, 3, 1985, pp. 23–33.

4. On the development of the NF since the 1970s, see Thurlow, *Fascism in Britain*, cit., ch. 12; *From Ballots to Bombs*, Searchlight, London, 1989; L. O'Hara, 'Notes from the underground, part 3; British fascism, 1983–6', *Lobster*, 25, June 1993, pp. 16–20, 26; 'Notes from the Underground part 4: British Fascism, 1983–6 (II)', *Lobster*, 26, Dec. 1993 pp. 13–18; C. Husbands, 'Extreme Right-Wing Politics in Great Britain', *West European Politics*, XI(2), 1988, pp. 65–70; G. Gable, 'The Far Right in Contemporary Britain', in L. Cheles, R. Ferguson and M. Vaughan (eds), *Neo-Fascism in Europe*, Longman, London, 1991, pp. 245–63; R. Eatwell, 'Why has the Extreme Right failed in Britain?' in P. Hainsworth, *The Extreme Right in Europe and the USA*, Pinter, London, 1992, pp. 175–92.

5. Much remains to be written on the BNP, but see e.g. *Searchlight* No. 83, May 1982, pp. 3–5; No. 199, Jan. 1992, p. 14i No. 211, Jan. 1993, pp. 4–5; *The Independent on Sunday Magazine*, 2 Aug. 1992, pp. 8–10; *Time Out*, 22–29 Sept. 1993, pp. 12–13; *Freedom to Hate? Transcript of the Programme Transmitted 13th June 1993*, Broadcasting Support Services, London, 1993. For the BNP's own view, see J. Tyndall, *The Eleventh Hour*, Albion Press, London, 1988.

6. For important exceptions see V. Ware, *Women and the National Front*, Searchlight, London, n.d. (c.1978); Women and Fascism Study Group, *Breeders for Race and Nation*, n.d. (c.1979).

7. See J. Stephenson, *Women in Nazi Society*, Croom Helm, London, 1975; L. J. Rupp, *Mobilizing Women for War*, Princeton University Press, Princeton, NJ. 1978, ch. 2; T. Mason, 'Women in Germany 1925–1940', *History Workshop*, I, 1976, pp. 74–113; II, 1976, pp. 5–32; G. Bock, 'Racism and Sexism in Nazi Germany: Motherhood, Compulsory Sterilization, and the State', in R. Bridenthal, A. Grossmann and M. Kaplan, *When Biology Became Destiny*, Monthly Review Press, New York, 1984, pp. 271–96; C. Koonz, *Mothers in the Fatherland. Women, the Family and Nazi Politics*, Cape, London, 1987.

8. *Spearhead*, No. 21, Nov.–Dec. 1968, pp. 4–6.

9. *Spearhead*, No. 101, Jan. 1977, pp. 6–7, 10.

10. *It's our Country – Let's Win It Back!*, National Front, London, n.d. (1979), p. 57.

11. *Spearhead*, No. 101, Jan. 1977, pp. 7, 10.

12. NF October 1974 election address; *Spearhead*, No. 81, Feb. 1975, p. 18.

13. *Spearhead*, No. 82, March 1975, p. 17, No. 84, May 1975, p. 16; No. 88, Oct. 1975, p. 16.
14. *Spearhead*, No. 126, Feb. 1979, pp. 18, 20; *It's our Country*, cit., p. 56.
15. *Britain First*, No. 15, 25 March–7 April 1972, p. 3; *Spearhead*, No. 135, Jan. 1980, p. 3.
16. *Spearhead*, No. 120, Aug. 1978, p. 5.
17. *Spearhead*, No. 22, Jan.–Feb. 1969, p. 14; No. 31, March 1970, p. 19.
18. *Spearhead*, No. 21, Nov.–Dec. 1968, p. 6.
19. *For a New Britain*, National Front, London, 1974, p. 12.
20. *Spearhead*, No. 101, Jan. 1977, p. 10.
21. *Spearhead*, No. 127, March 1979, p. 10.
22. *Spearhead*, No. 29, Jan. 1970, p. 7.
23. *The Times*, 30 Aug. 1977, p. 10; *Sunday Telegraph Magazine*, 2 Oct. 1977, p. 15.
24. *It's our Country*, cit., p. 13.
25. *Spearhead*, No. 113, Jan. 1978, pp. 8–10.
26. For public activity, see, in particular, the NF's 1981 photo-booklet, *We Are The National Front*. For Annual General Meetings, see, e.g. *Spearhead*, No. 126, Feb. 1979, p. 20. For branch meetings, see, e.g., Fielding, *The National Front*, cit., pp. 33–34, 50–52, 54.
27. See e.g. *Spearhead*, No. 78, Aug. 1974, p. 20. According to Martin Webster, writing on the subject of fundraising, 'Ladies in particular often show a great talent and organising ability in this field (as the other parties know well)'. *Spearhead*, No. 75, May 1974, p. 12.
28. *Spearhead*, No. 103, March 1977, p. 17.
29. For women on the Directorate, see e.g. *Spearhead*, No. 47, Oct. 1971, p. 18; No. 80, Jan. 1975, p. 19. For candidates, see *Spearhead*, No. 34, June 1970, p. 15; F. W. S. Craig, *British Parliamentary Election Results 1974–1983*, Parliamentary Research Services, London, 1984.
30. *Spearhead*, No. 105, May 1977, pp. 18–19; see also, e.g., No. 94, May 1976, pp. 18–19.
31. See, e.g., *Britain First*, No. 33, Oct. 1975, p. 4; *Spearhead*, No. 27, Nov. 1969, p. 12; No. 43, June 1971, p. 11; No. 86, Aug. 1975, p. 20; No. 113, Jan. 1978, p. 18.
32. *Spearhead*, No. 34, June 1970, p. 15; No. 88, Oct. 1975, p. 18. A somewhat younger woman candidate was described as a 'Charming housewife' in *Spearhead*, No. 74, April 1974, p. 19.
33. *Spearhead*, No. 115, March 1978, p. 19; *Anglian News*, No. 12, July 1979, p. 1. *Anglian News* was a local NF publication.
34. *Bulldog*, No. 4, Dec. 1977, p. 4; No. 9, Aug. 1978, p. 1; *Nationalism Today*, No. 1, March 1980, p. 18.
35. Ware, *Women*, cit., p. 14.
36. *Spearhead*, No. 78, Aug. 1974, p. 13; No. 65, June 1973, p. 1; No. 111, Nov. 1977, p. 1; No. 127, March 1979, p. 1.
37. Ware, *Women*, cit., pp. 12–15; *Bulldog*, No. 11, Jan. – Feb. 1979, p. 3.
38. *Sunday Telegraph Magazine*, 2 Oct. 1977, p. 15.
39. *New Nation*, No. 6, Winter 1984, p. 7; No. 7, Summer 1985, p. 16.
40. *Nationalism Today*, No. 10, n.d. (c.1982), p. 9.
41. *Vanguard*, No. 19, June 1988, pp. 6–7.
42. *Flag*, No. 59, Oct. 1991, p. 5.
43. *National Front News*, No. 93, Aug. 1987, p. 1; *Nationalism Today*, No. 44, n.d. (1989), p. 16.
44. *National Front News*, No. 58, July 1984, pp. 6, 2.
45. *Let Britain Live!*, National Front, London, 1983, p. 21.
46. *National Front News*, No. 97, Nov. 1987, p. 4.
47. *National Front News*, No. 102, Feb. 1988, p. 6. See *National Front News*, No. 104, April 1988, p. 6; No. 105, June 1988, p. 6; No. 106, n.d. (1988), p. 6; No. 108, n.d. (1988), p. 6.

48. *Flag*, No. 16, Feb. 1988, pp. 2, 5; *Vanguard*, No. 20, July 1988, pp. 4, 8–9; No. 22, Sept. 1988, p. 18; No. 23, Oct. 1988, p. 18.

49. *Flag*, No. 48, Nov. 1990, p. 6.

50. *Caring For Britain*, National Front, Worthing, 1992, p. 30.

51. *Flag*, No. 72, n.d. (c.1993), p. 4.

52. *National Front News*, No. 93, Aug. 1987, p. 1; No. 35, Aug. 1981, p. 1; *Bulldog*, No. 35, Sept. 1983, p. 1.

53. *Nationalism Today*, No. 25, Nov. 1984, p. 8.

54. *Nationalism Today*, No. 28, April 1985, p. 20.

55. *Nationalism Today*, No. 33, Sept. 1985, p. 15.

56. *National Front News*, No. 105, June 1988, p. 2; *Nationalism Today*, No. 43, n.d. (1988), pp. 14–16; No. 44, n.d. (1989), pp. 14–16.

57. I. Anderson, *100 Questions and Answers About the National Front*, Freedom Books, London, n.d. (c. 1987), p. 28.

58. *Vanguard*, No. 12, Sept. 1987, p. 11; No. 13, Oct. 1987, pp. 12–13.

59. *Vanguard*, No. 28, Nov.–Dec. 1989, pp. 4–5.

60. For Wingfield, see *Flag*, No. 21, July 1988, p. 5; No. 24, Oct. 1988, p. 8 and, for her earlier involvement, *Bulldog*, No. 35, Sept. 1983, p. 4; *National Front News*, No. 58, July 1984, p. 6. For Taylor, previously Caralyn Giles, see *We Are the National Front*, cit., p. 46; *Flag* No. 8, May 1987, p. 7; No. 22, Aug. 1988, p. 6, and, as an early member, *Bulldog*, No. 11, Jan.–Feb. 1979, p. 4.

61. *National Front News*, No. 28, Nov.–Dec. 1980, p. 4; No. 48, July 1983, p. 4; *Flag*, No. 64, n.d. (1992), p. 4.

62. *100 Questions*, cit., p. 29.

63. *Vanguard*, No. 37, n.d. (c. 1992), p. 8.

64. *Flag*, No. 64, n.d. (1992), p. 3.

65. *Vote for Britain*, BNP, n.d. (1983), p. 17.

66. *Spearhead*, No. 161, March 1982, p. 6.

67. *Spearhead*, No. 189, July 1984, p. 7; No. 191, Sept. 1984, p. 16.

68. *Spearhead*, Nos. 240–242, Feb. to April 1989. The quotations are from No. 240, p. 13; No. 241, pp. 12–14.

69. *A New Way Forward*, BNP, Welling, n.d. (1991), p. 11.

70. *Vote for Britain*, cit., p. 17; *British Nationalist*, No. 93, Aug.–Sept. 1989, p. 8; No. 94, Oct. 1989, p. 8; No. 98, Feb. 1990, p. 8.

71. *Spearhead*, No. 241, March 1989, p. 11.

72. *British Nationalist*, No. 96, Dec. 1989, p. 4.

73. *Spearhead*, No. 246, Aug. 1989, p. 10.

74. *A New Way Forward*, cit., p. 12.

75. *The Independent*, 13 Oct. 1993, p. 22; *Elle*, July 1992, pp. 34–36.

76. *Spearhead*, No. 197, March 1985, p. 18.

77. *Spearhead*, No. 176, June 1983, p. 18; No. 278, April 1992, p. 19.

Chapter 16

THE FAR RIGHT IN GERMANY SINCE 1945
David Childs

Was the Nazi seizure of power in 1933 the culmination of long-term trends in German politics and society or was it the result of a series of avoidable accidents? The issue will continue to excite the passions of historians but can have no definitive conclusion. On the one hand, it can certainly be argued that the National Socialist German Workers' Party [*Nationalsozialistische Deutsche Arbeiterpartei*, NSDAP] drew on ideas and emotions – racism, anti-Semitism, imperialism, nationalism, anti-Marxism, opposition to Versailles, anti-capitalism, rejection of the old generation of politicians, acceptance of hierarchy, statism – which were widespread currency in Weimar Germany. On the other hand, support for the Nazis grew rapidly over the brief period 1929–33, which meant that many of its supporters, even members, did not have strong political convictions. In this they were different from the supporters of the Social Democratic Party of Germany [*Sozialdemokratische Partei Deutschlands*, SPD] and the Catholic Centre Party [*Zentrum*, Z], both pillars of the Weimar Republic.

The Nazis seemed to attract the politically inexperienced voters; their vote grew when turnout was high.[1] They achieved their best support in Protestant agricultural areas and in areas where the frontier issue was important (Silesia and the Palatinate). Their support came from all social groups, but the industrial workers were under-represented among their supporters and members, as were Catholics. If we wish to explain the Nazi rise to power, we must conclude that it was the result of certain ideas having widespread currency, but that it needed a particular set of circumstances to turn those holding such views into Nazi supporters. The explosion of support for the Nazis would not have heralded the death of Weimar democracy had not key elements of the bourgeois and aristocratic political and economic establishments lost their nerve and persuaded President Paul von Hindenburg to appoint Hitler Chancellor in 1933. A new party like the Nazi Party needs instant success to maintain the loyalty of its weakly motivated electorate.

After 1933, many foreign observers believed the Nazi regime had immense support. This was first due to the tourist reports of a clean, well-organised Germany where poverty did not seem to exist.[2] Second, it was due to the efforts of Nazi film propaganda. Third, it was the result of the Nazi regime thriving, in spite of the strain of war. Finally, it was later convenient for the wartime allies to stress the support of the Germans for the Nazis because this gave them greater justification for the mass bombing and their plans to dismember Germany once victory was achieved. When one considers the matter more carefully, it becomes clear that this view of over-whelming support for the Nazi regime needs to be modified. First, it is likely that the roughly 20 per cent of the electorate who were SPD supporters and the roughly 12 per cent who were Centre Party supporters did not change their views much after 1933. To a lesser extent we can say the same for the more than 10 per cent of voters who had consistently opted for the Communists.[3] Such a conclusion seems consistent with experience from other countries and with what happened in Germany after 1945. There was probably a weakening of support for these and other non-Nazi parties after 1933, as the regime appeared to be successful. But the outbreak of the war in 1939, predicted by the left, would have strengthened the scepticism of the non-Nazis. German patriotism, Allied mistakes, the *Gestapo*, the efficient rationing system and the exploitation of the occupied states explain how the Nazi regime survived until May 1945.

The early post-war years

At the end of the war, the Allies seriously expected substantial right-wing opposition in occupied Germany. Col. R. L. Frazier, who was then in charge of the investigation of all right and left-wing political, paramilitary and other subversive groups which might in some way threaten the occupation force in the American Zone, from early 1946 to mid-1949, and was also in close touch with British counter-intelligence authorities for all of this period, has described the situation as follows:

> The Americans always considered the possibility of post-war German resistance by right-wing elements as a definite danger. This fear had an effect even on strategy in the last days of the war (e.g. the argument between Churchill, who wanted all effort directed towards Berlin, and Eisenhower, who insisted on moving south-east to prevent the 'National Redoubt' of the Alps being used as a base for long-term resistance). Much of the American (and British) counter-intelligence effort in Germany, from early 1945 onward, was taken up with the investigation of possible Nazi underground organisations which would lead a resistance against the occu-pation. Both the *Gestapo* and the *Hitler Jugend* planned such underground organi-sations, and some effort was made to put them into operation. Both were rolled up by mid-1947, and never really constituted a significant threat, although the *Hitler Jugend* group made a lot of money by turning itself into a haulage firm.[4]

By 1948 ultra right-wing organisations were appearing, ostensibly as embryo political parties. The occupation authorities in the British and American zones took this development seriously and devoted considerable effort to observing the new groups, particularly for indications of any paramilitary activity. Because there was no evidence of the latter, and because the various groups were small and fragmented, no charismatic leader having arisen, it was accepted that there was no real danger, but a watching brief was maintained, even after the *Bundesrepublik* came into existence.

Frazier's statement makes it clear that the Allies expected significant Nazi opposi-tion after the war. Why did such opposition not appear? There can be no final answer to this question, but a number of factors can be mentioned which must have contributed to this situation. First, there was a destruction of the NSDAP leadership and cadres. At the highest level, virtually all of the leading Nazis were either dead or interned. Even at the lower levels, many had either been killed, killed themselves, were interned or were seeking refuge abroad. On the automatic arrest list of the Americans were NSDAP functionaries down to the lowly level of the *Ortsgruppenführer* (local group leader). By December 1945, around 100,000 former members of the Nazi Party, of the SS, of the *Sicherheitsdienst* (the security service responsible for internal surveillance and the monitoring of opinion) and other beneficiaries of Hitler's regime were interned in the American zone.[5] Similar policies were implemented with varying degrees of intensity by the other three occupying powers. Once released, many of the former Nazis were in no psychological or physical state to contemplate opposition and, in any case, had to find ways and means of earning their living. Some former Nazis, it is true, had found employment with their erstwhile foreign enemies, but they probably felt there was no future in biting the hand that fed them. All activity considered by the occupying power to be Nazi, militarist or anti-democratic was of course banned. But even without any ban it would have probably fallen on deaf ears. Germany's defeat was so obvious and total, and National Socialism so obviously a disaster, that few Germans would have been likely to give it a second chance. Germany lay in ruins, on the verge of starvation, had no friends in the international community and, unlike what happened in 1918, was totally occupied by powerful armies. All this represented a devastating psychological blow against Nazism. Michael Balfour, Chief of Information Services, Allied Military Government of Germany, 1945–47, has summed up the position as follow:

> The proportion of those professing to think Nazism 'a good thing badly carried out' never dropped below 42% between November 1945 and January 1946. There is good evidence that 10% of the adult male population remained convinced Nazis – 4 million people. Yet the incontrovertible evidence of total defeat was hard to overlook or excuse away by stories of treachery or corruption . . . Goebbels had left behind a deep scepticism about anything officials said. The Germans may have had a little more faith in us, because, after all, our wartime forecasts had come true.[6]

The occupying powers sought to convince the Germans by 're-education' programmes in the mass media and in the schools. Despite all of the above, it is something of a miracle that a nationalistic, if not directly Nazi, resistance movement of significant proportions did not appear after 1945. The Germans could easily have felt that, as after the 1914–18 war, they were being unjustly treated. First, there was the dismemberment of their country. Germany lost 24.3 per cent of its territory to Poland and the Soviet Union. This territory had been the home of 13.9 per cent of the population of 1937 Germany.[7] Until January 1957, the important industrial region of the Saar was separated from Germany under a pro-French regime. In 1950, 16.7 per cent of the population of West Germany was classified as expellees from the lost territories and a further 3.3 per cent were refugees from the Soviet zone.[8] These could have formed the basis for a dangerous revanchist movement. In fact, many of them supported the relatively moderate League of Expellees from the Homeland and of those without Rights [*Bund der Heimatvertriebenen und Entrechteten*, BHE]. Founded in Kiel in 1950, the party gained 23.4 per cent of the vote in the regional (*Land*) election in Schleswig-Holstein in the same year. There, 38.2 per cent of the population were expellees or refugees. In the national (*Bundestag*) election of 1953, the BHE gained 5.9 per cent (1.6m votes) and joined the government coalition. Splits later destroyed the party. Other factors which could have fuelled a nationalist movement were the dismantling of important industrial plants for reparations, restrictions of the economy and unemployment. It is often forgotten that there was a general strike in the British zone in 1948 against the policy of dismantling. Luckily, the trade unions were firmly in democratic hands. Unemployment stood at 5.5 per cent in the Western zones in 1948. It rose to 8.2 per cent in 1950 and was still 6.4 per cent in 1952, four years after Ludwig Erhard, the economics minister, introduced his famed currency reform. By 1956 it had fallen to 2.2 per cent and in 1960 it was as low as 0.5 per cent.[9] Another potential reserve for a new nationalist movement in the early years were the many displaced ex-officers, civil servants, teachers and others who had lost their jobs and status.

Konrad Adenauer, Chancellor 1949–63, attempted, successfully, to integrate these elements into the new Federal Republic of Germany. Thus, many servants of the Third Reich became servants of the democratic state. In 1952, a *Bundestag* investigation revealed that 184 senior officials out of 542 (34 per cent) in the Foreign Ministry were former members of the Nazi party.[10] The same was true in other parts of the public service, such as the police and the judiciary.[11] Many doctors were also former party members.

The SRP and the DRP

The former members of the NSDAP and of the German National People's Party [*Deutsch-Nationale Volkspartei*, DNVP], who were the coalition partners of the Nazis in 1933, found it difficult to set up a new party. Their efforts to do so were rejected several times by the suspicious French and American occupation authorities. The German Rights Party [*Deutsche Rechtspartei*, DReP], set up in Northern Germany, North Rhine-Westphalia and Hesse in 1946, gained more than local significance. An amalgam of the German Conservatives [*Deutsche Konservative*, DK], the German Construction Party [*Deutsche Aufbaupartei*, DAP], and the German Farmers and Peasants Party [*Deutsche Bauern- und Landvolk-partei*, DB-Lp], it propagated nationalistic and monarchical ideas, and had five representatives in the first *Bundestag*.

In early 1949, the Fellowship of Independent Germans [*Gemeinschaft unabhängiger Deutscher*, GUD] was founded in Bad Godesberg and broke away from the older party. This had been an initiative of Dr Fritz Dorls, who was joined by the former general Otto Ernst Remer. Remer had been promoted by Hitler for his part in crushing the July plot of 1944. On 2 October 1949, Dorls went one step further and founded the Socialist Party of the Reich [*Sozialistische Reichspartei*, SRP], which was joined by a majority of members of the German Rights Party [*Deutsche Rechtspartei*, DReP], sometimes by entire local or district groups. This new party, in contrast to the DRP, had a rather positive attitude towards National Socialism, and made some consider-able gains in former Nazi strongholds. In the Lower Saxony Landtag elections in 1951 it even got 11 per cent of the vote. On the demand of the Federal Government, the Federal Constitutional Court banned the SRP in 1952.

After the ban on the SRP, the German Reich party [*Deutsche Reichspartei*, DRP], formerly DReP, was joined by most of its former supporters. The party's name was taken from a conservative party which existed in Germany between 1871 and the end of the *Kaiserreich*. The party chairman and his three deputies – Otto Hess, Wilhelm Meinberg and Hans Heinrich Kunstmann – had all been members of the NSDAP before 1933. Two others joined the Nazi party after 1933.[12] All in all, these parties of the 'national opposition' remained without significance during the period up to 1964. In the federal election of 1953, the DRP received 1.1 per cent of the vote; in 1957 its vote fell to 1 per cent and in 1961 its percentage fell to 0.8.[13] This was due mainly to three stabilising factors – the years of economic progress, the clear leadership of Konrad Adenauer and the reinstatement of so many potential extreme right-wing voters and activists. Along with this went the integration of the Federal Republic into the Western alliance and building of the German army, the *Bundeswehr*, which in itself was enough to relieve national inferiority complexes.

The success of the DRP in the *Land* election in the Rhineland Palatinate in April 1959 caused great attention. About 90,000 voters, including Catholic voters of the government party, had decided for a party with clear neo-Nazi tendencies. With 5.1 per cent of the vote, the DRP was able to jump the 5 per cent hurdle necessary to win seats in the regional parliament.[14] The DRP put on its last party congress in Bonn in June 1964. There it was decided to found a new union of all 'national democratic forces'. The DRP dissolved itself, thus providing the necessary preconditions for the setting up of the National Democratic Party of Germany [*Nationaldemokratische Partei Deutschlands*, NPD]. Consequently, former functionaries of the DRP provided the nucleus of the NPD.

The 1960s: the rise of the NPD

The foundation of the NPD by Adolf von Thadden, Fritz Thielen and Waldemar Schütz in Hanover on 28 November 1964 as a magnet for all the nationalistic forces did not, at first, seem to bear more fruit than any of their previous efforts had done. Thielen was elected chairman of the new party. He had represented the Christian-Democratic Union [*Christlich-Demokratische Union*, CDU] in the Bremen *Landtag* for eleven years, but joined the conservative German Party [Deutsche Partei, DP] in 1958. Von Thadden had represented the DRP in the first *Bundestag* in 1949. He later became chairman of the DRP and was elected first deputy chairman of the NPD. Schütz was a former NSDAP member and *Waffen* SS officer. A publisher, he joined the NPD's presidium. One source has claimed that, of eighteen members of the first executive committee of the NPD, twelve had been active Nazis before 1945.[15]

In its report for 1968, the West German *Verfassungsschutz*, a body similar to the USA's Federal Bureau of Investigation, commented that 'a democratic formation of opinion from the basis to the leadership cannot be realised in the NPD'. Several NPD district chairmen left the party, claiming that any criticism by party members was being muted by the leadership. The deputy chairman of the Lubeck district of the NPD, Rektor Heinz Willner, said he left the party because 'the individual member is not regarded as a politically mature citizen, but is degraded and becomes a transmitter of party propaganda and opinion'. The speakers, candidates and functionaries were forced 'to publicly defend grotesque slogans coming from the leadership'.

The NPD looked to Salazar's Portugal and the Greece of the right-wing military dictatorship for its version of the German state.[16] The *Verfassungsschutz* characterised the NPD as a party of aggressive nationalism which was against the Bonn system.

At the beginning of 1968, the NPD had about 28,000 members, only 9 per cent of them women. There was a high turnover of members, especially among the young. The refugee community was overrepresented among party members and voters. Members from the middle-class professions provided the backbone of the NPD. Within this group, the proportion of urban and rural self-employed had increased further. It rose from 25 per cent in 1966 to 29 per cent in 1968 of total membership. Party members of this group were least inclined to leave the NPD. Against this, there was a high turnover of employees and workers in family/small- and middle-sized enterprises. The share of industrial workers was about 14 per cent in 1968. Public sector employees, including members of the armed services, made up about 6 per cent of members in 1968. This corresponded to their share of the workforce as a whole.[17]

The 'national opposition' found fertile ground again when political and economic insecurity under Chancellor Erhard (1963–66) and obvious disagreement between Paris and Washington dominated the scene. General de Gaulle was demonstrating quite clearly how crucial it could be to a people to act out of nationalistic motives. The formation of the grand coalition of CDU and SPD in 1966 caused some right-wing voters to feel that their leader had sold out to the left. There was also the feeling that the big party bosses had ganged up against the 'little man' leaving virtually no opposition in Parliament. Some right-of-centre voters wanted to protest against the increasing student unrest, and some farmers wanted to protest against the European Community's agricultural policy. In the federal election of 1965, the NPD gained 664,000 votes (2 per cent). Given the newness of the party, this vote could not be seen as a total failure. The NPD's success in subsequent *Land* elections is given in Table 16.1. The NPD failed to win seats in the Saar, Hamburg and North Rhine Westphalia.

In the federal election of 1969, the NPD gained 1.4m votes (4. 3 per cent). Thus, it failed to reach the 5 per cent minimum required to gain seats in the *Bundestag*. This compared with the liberal FDP's 1.9m votes (5.8 per cent). The FDP has been in government continuously since 1969.

Why did the NPD fail? The *Verfassungsschutz* report for 1968 believed the reasons were as follows:

1. The increasing isolation of the NPD.
2. Factional fights within the party.
3. Improved economic conditions.
4. The fact that there was a limited number of people responsive to the right-wing exploitation of prejudice and emotion.

Table 16.1 NPD's result in *Land* elections

Land	Seats in regional parliament		Election date
Baden-Württemberg	12 out of	127	20/4/1968
Bavaria	14	204	20/11/1966
Bremen	8	100	1/10/1967
Hesse	8	96	6/11/1966
Lower-Saxony	10	149	4/6/1967
Rhineland-Palatinate	4	100	23/4/1967
Schleswig-Holstein	4	73	23/4/1967

Source: *Verfassungsschutz* report for 1968.

5. The increasing radicalisation of the political style of the right-wing extremists, which was rejected in more moderate conservative circles.
6. The increasing understanding by the population of the relationship between right-wing radicalism and foreign policy.
7. The lack of charisma of the representatives of the 'national camp', its functionaries, candidates and (regional) parliamentarians.
8. The lack of tangible parliamentary successes by the representatives of the NPD in local and regional parliaments.
9. The worry of being identified with a party whose banning was demanded by wide sections of the population.

Undoubtedly, the perception that the NPD was harming the Federal Republic's credibility abroad helped to put off potential supporters and spur on its opponents to greater efforts to defeat it.

Table 16.2 Far-right organisation members, 1965–89

1965	1966	1967	1968	1969	1970	1971
26,100	34,500	38,500	36,800	36,300	29,500	27,700
1972	1973	1974	1975	1976	1977	1978
24,500	21,500	21,200	17,300	20,300	18,200	17,800
1979	1980	1981	1982	1983	1984	1985
17,600	19,800	20,300	19,000	20,300	22,100	22,100
1986	1987	1988	1989			
22,100	25,200	28,300	35,900			

Source: *Verfassungsschutz* report for relevant years. These figures include the NPD and DVU; the REP do not appear to have been included.

Like many new parties, the NPD fell to pieces after failing to achieve a quick success. The NPD and other far right groups saw their membership decline after 1969.

Failure in the 1970s

The 1970s were a dismal period for the far right in Germany, as the membership figures in Table 16.2 indicate. Various opinion polls revealed changing attitudes to West Germany's political system and showed increasing, and overwhelming, support for it.[18] One indicator of public attitudes were the replies to a question about great Germans (see Table 16.3 below).

Table 16.3 Responses to question: 'Which great German, in your opinion, has done most for Germany?'

	1950 %	1956 %	1962 %	1967 %	1971 %	1977 %
Adenauer		24	28	60	47	42
Bismarck	35	27	23	17	21	13
Brandt					3	9
Frederick the Great	7	3	3	1	0	1
Hitler	10	8	4	2	2	3

Source: F. Neolle-Neumann (ed.), *The Germans: Public Opinion Polls, 1967–1980*, Westport, CT., 1981.

Migrants: a political factor

In the 1980s, a number of developments helped to create an atmosphere in which far-right parties could be expected to thrive. These were unemployment, especially youth unemployment, the continuing influx of foreigners seeking political asylum or simply work in West Germany, and the migration of ethnic Germans and citizens of the German Democratic Republic to the Federal Republic. There was also a renewal of the discussions about 'the German Question', the Nato alliance and, especially since the collapse of the Communist regimes in Eastern Europe in 1989, Germany's place in Europe.

Unemployment in the Federal Republic was not high by the standards of most of its West European neighbours, but at 7.9 per cent in February 1989 (UK: 6.8 per cent; France: 10.0 per cent; Italy: 16.4 per cent)[19] it caused great anxiety in Germany. It led many to think that the government should find ways and means of stopping the influx from outside which aggravated the difficulties. In 1987, there were 4,630,200 officially recorded foreigners in the Federal Republic. In 1986, the reported figure was

Table 16.4 Influx of political refugees

1980	1981	1982	1983	1984	1985	1986	1987
107,818	49,391	37,423	19,737	35,278	73,832	99,650	57,379

Source: *Statistisches Jahrbuch für die Bundesrepublik Deutschland*, Stuttgart, 1988.

The largest number in each of the above years were as follows:[21]

1980: 57, 913 Turks	1984: 8,063 Sri Lankans
1981: 9,901 Poles	1985: 17,380 Sri Lankans
1982: 6,630 Poles	1986: 21,700 Iranians
1983: 2,645 Sri Lankans	1987: 11,426 Turks

4,512,700. By far the largest number came from Turkey (1,481,400), Yugoslavia (597,600). Italy (544,400) and Greece (279,900). Of these, 2,764,200 – including the majority of the Turks, Yugoslavs and Italians – had lived in the Federal Republic for ten or more years.[20] Like many West European states, West Germany was faced with considerable numbers of foreigners seeking political asylum, as Table 16.4 shows.

Thousands of ethnic Germans (*Aussiedler*) arrived from Eastern Europe: 460,888 in 1968–80, 69,455 in 1981, 48,170 in 1982, 37,925 in 1983, 36,459 in 1984, 38,968 in 1985, 42,788 in 1986, 78,523 in 1987.[22] Finally, every year thousands migrated from the German Democratic Republic to the West (29,459 in 1986, net 26,834).[23] The net increase of German and foreign migrants to the Federal Republic in 1986 appeared to be 188,383, of whom 130,559 were foreigners. Net migration in the 1980s was as follows: 311,900 in 1980, –117,100 in 1983, 151,100 in 1984, 83,400 in 1985.[24] The figures reveal that the Federal Republic had a considerable number of foreigners (like its neighbours), but that the scale of net migration into the Federal Republic was not as great as many Germans believe. The foreign ghettos in some German towns, and the belief that newcomers are a burden, did cause friction and irritation.

The feeling that the threat from the Soviet Union had lessened greatly after Mikhail Gorbachev took over as Soviet leader in 1985 made Germans more aware that their country was still, forty-four years after the Second World War, an occupied and divided land. As in other European Community member states, a minority of Germans feared that the development of the Community in the run-up to 1992 represented an intolerable loss of national identity and sovereignty.

The 1980s: the NPD and the DVU

Given the above-mentioned factors, it was not surprising that the NPD should have improved its position in the 1987 federal elections. In the election of 25 January, the NPD put up candidates in 172 of the 248 constituencies and in ten state lists; it received 227,045 votes on the state lists (0.6 per cent). This was more than twice the number of votes it had in the federal election of 1983 (91,095 = 0.23 per cent). With more than 0.5 per cent of votes on the state lists, it was paid DM 1.3m reimbursements for campaign expenses from public funds.[25] In its campaign, the NPD demanded reunification of Germany and 'all-German neutrality'[26] Dr Gerhard Frey (see below) supported the NPD campaign through his leaflets.

Thus the National Democrats remained the most attractive party to far-right voters at that time. In 1987, they had a membership of around 6,200. With 2,500 members, the German People's Union [*Deutsche Volksunion*, DVU], under its chairman Dr Gerhard Frey, was the second biggest right-wing extremist grouping.[27] In 1987, however, it showed less activity than in previous years because Frey had shifted his activities to the newly founded German People's Union (List D) [*Deutsche Volksunion (Liste D)*, DVU (List D)]. He endeavoured to extend his traditionally good contacts among nationalists in Austria and the South Tyrol to right-wing extremists in France, especially the *Front National* of Jean-Marie Le Pen. Le Pen gave several interviews in Dr Frey's newspapers.[28]

The NPD and DVU (List D) were the two most important of the 69 (1986: 73) right-wing extremist organisations in the Federal Republic in 1987. Allowing for double membership, all these bodies together had a net membership of around 25,200.[29]

The total electoral failure of the far right in West Germany between 1969 and 1988 disguised the fact that there was a far right constituency which was larger than membership of the various right-wing organisations would indicate. This was, to some extent, revealed by the circulation of far-right publications. According to the report of the *Verfassungsschutz* for 1987, the NPD monthly *Deutsche Stimme* had a circulation of over 150,000. This appeared to be the most successful far right publication. A survey carried out by the influential weekly *Der Spiegel* (No. 9, 1989), about attitudes to Adolf Hitler on the centenary of his birth in 1989, also revealed some disturbing tendencies. The first question, 'How is Hitler to be viewed in history?', produced an overall average of −2.7 on a scale between +5 ('absolutely positive') and −5 ('absolutely negative'). To the second question, 'Would you say that without the war and without the holocaust Hitler would have been one of the greatest German statesmen?' 60 per cent replied that 'no, he would not' and 38 per cent that 'yes, he would'. Asked about their view of the Third Reich, 16 per cent thought that it had only bad sides to it, 38 per cent that it had predominantly bad sides to it, 43 per cent thought that it had good and bad sides, and 3 per cent that it had only good sides. In all responses throughout the survey, Green and Republican voters (see below) were at the opposite extremes, while the voters of the CDU and the Christian-Social Union [*Christlich-Soziale Union*, CSU] alliance, those of the SPD and of the Free Democratic Party [*Freie Demokratische Partei*, FDP] held somewhat differing views within the centre.

Die Republikaner

It was also in 1989 that the far right got its biggest boost since the 1960s. This was the success of the Republicans [*Die Republikaner*, REP] in the West Berlin elections of 29 January (see Table 16.5 below).

The REP was set up by Franz Schönhuber in Munich in 1983. A butcher's son, Schönhuber is a native of Bavaria who served in the *Waffen* SS in the Second World War. He established himself as a journalist after the war, moving gradually from the

Table 16.5 1989 and 1985 election results compared

	29 January 1989		10 March 1985	
Turnout:	1,220,524 (79.6%)		1,259,788 (83.6%)	
Party	Votes	%	Votes	%
CDU	453.161	37.8	577.867	46.4
SPD	448,143	37.7	402,875	32.4
AL (Greens)	141,470	11.8	132,484	10.6
REP	90,140	7.5	—	—
FDP	47,129	3.9	105,209	8.5
Others	20,368	1.7	25,180	2.0

Source: Das Parlament, 3–10 February 1989.

far left to the CSU, Bavaria's leading party. Owing to the publication of his war memoirs in 1981, he was forced to give up his job as deputy chief editor of Bavarian television. He subsequently set up the REP with other disgruntled elements of the CSU who felt their leader, Bavarian Prime Minister Franz Josef Strauss, was going too far in his conciliatory policy towards the German Democratic Republic. So far, the public position of Schönhuber has been German nationalist, exploiting discontent about the alleged breakdown of law and order, and the influx of foreigners and ethnic Germans. It is fair to point out that, in an interview with *Der Spiegel* (No. 6, 1989), Schönhuber stated: 'I have no Nazi past, I regard the National Socialist state as absolutely incompatible with the rule of law. Racism and Fascism led us into the most horrible catastrophe in our national history.' He further claimed he was not against foreigners, but wanted to introduce the Swiss system of rotation for foreign workers and an amendment to article 16 of the Basic Law, the article granting the right of political asylum. The editors of *Der Spiegel* were not convinced, pointing out that the Berlin REP used emotional anti-Turkish material in its television advertising campaign. Schönhuber, in the same interview, expressed his doubts about the present European Community, claiming it would cement the division of Germany and lead to the centre of Europe moving to the South-East and the South. Schönhuber went on to say: 'the main reason why I reject this EC is the importation of crime, drugs, the Mafia and Camorra'. He also advocated a united, neutral Germany with its own nuclear weapons.

That the influx of ethnic Germans and foreigners was a key issue in the Berlin campaign is beyond doubt. In an opinion poll, 40 per cent of those asked thought it was 'not in order that there are so many foreigners in Berlin'. There were, in fact, 220,000 foreigners living in West Berlin out of a total of 1.8m. In addition, there were thousands of ethnic Germans and Germans from the GDR. According to *Der Spiegel* (No. 6, 1989), some 20,000 ethnic Germans and Germans from the GDR took up residence in West Berlin in 1988.

One particular feature of the Berlin election which caused alarm was the relatively high number of members of the West Berlin police force who voted for the REP. The police trade union (*Gewerkschaft der Polizei*) was worried that its members in parts of West Germany were also joining the new party. It estimated that 20 per cent of members of the police supported it. In Bavaria, it was possibly over 50 per cent. In Berlin, Baden-Württemberg, Schleswig-Holstein and the Saar, the chairmen or the deputy chairmen of the REP were policemen. The majority of West German policemen and women were dissatisfied over pay, the lack of promotion chances and the effect of police service on their life.[30] Many of them appeared to believe that they had been neglected by the mainstream politicians.

The REP did better than expected in the elections to the European Parliament in June 1989. Franz Schönhuber succeeded in getting elected together with five of his colleagues. The party gained 7.1 per cent of the vote, which compared with 5.6 per cent for the FDP, 8.4 per cent for the Greens, 37.3 per cent for the SPD and 37.8 per cent for the CDU. The CDU vote had fallen from 45.9 per cent in 1984, the SPD vote remained static and the FDP and Greens slightly improved their position. It appeared therefore that the REP had gained mainly at the expense of the CDU. Their best result was in Bavaria where they won 14.6 per cent. Their worst result was in North-Rhine Westphalia where they reached only 4.1 per cent. It seems likely that the Bavarian result was influenced by the recent death of Franz Josef Strauss who had previously managed to attract the bulk of right-wing voters for his CSU. Its vote fell from 57.2 per cent in the 1984 Euro-election to 45.5 per cent. This was the highest percentage loss for the Christian Democrats in any region.

According to the psephologist Joachim Hofmann-Gottig, the REP appeared to be attractive, above all, to young men. This was also true of the NPD. No other party drew such a small percentage of its voters from women. Hofmann-Gottig concluded that the REP was likely to be on the political landscape for some time because of its support among young voters.[31] Another feature of the REP which was causing alarm, were the large numbers of activists, candidates and executive committee members who had NPD backgrounds.

Meanwhile, Dr Frey had been building up support for his organisation. In the last year, Frey's DVU (List D) had grown from 6,000 to over 24,000 members. Frey recruited at least 5,500 of them through a nation-wide mailing campaign to twenty-seven million households.[32]

Although the NPD and the DVU were, up to the 1990s, the largest far right groups, there exist many other, much smaller bodies, which openly proclaim their support for Nazi ideas. Among the more significant is the Free German Workers' Party [*Die Freiheitliche Deutsche Arbeiterpartei*, FAP]. Founded in 1979, it drew many of its early members from the Action Front of National Socialists/National Activists [*Aktionsfront Nationaler Sozialisten/Nationale Aktivisten*, ANS/NA]. The ANS/NA was banned in 1983. Formerly led by Michael Kühnen, who died in 1991, it is now led by 65-year-old Friedheim Busse. After declining for some years from 500 members in 1987 to 150 in 1991, its membership climbed to 220 in 1992 due to recruitment of new members in the former GDR. The FAP would like to win the cooperation of the NPD and sees itself as 'a German people's party' that wants to 'teach fear to the exploiters and oppressors of our beloved German fatherland'. It claims that, 'Too many foreigners endanger the public safety and threaten the existence of the Germans.' Its activities have been limited in recent years, but have included totally unsuccessful attempts to get its candidates elected to regional and local assemblies.

Table 16.6 Infringement of the law by right-wing extremists

	1986	1987	1988	1989
Homicides	0	0	0	1
Bomb/arson attacks	5	8	12	12
Bodily harm	41	38	36	52
Damage to property with use of Force	25	30	25	38
Threats of violence	134	115	83	102
Propaganda offences (daubing Graffiti, etc)	695	1,055	1,222	1,483
Other infringements	381	201	229	165

Source: Verfassungsschutz, report for 1989

Right-wing violence

In 1987, FAP members broke the law in 266 cases; 26 of those involved violence (arson attacks and damages), the rest were related to propaganda and intimidation. In 1987, 327 persons were arrested in connection with FAP activities; 44 per cent of all the offences were committed in North Rhine-Westphalia. In the 1987 federal election, the FAP had two direct candidates and one on a state list; it could not put up candidates in *Land* elections in Hesse and Schleswig-Holstein because it did not manage to collect the necessary number of signatures.

Although disturbing, the figures of right-wing breaches of the law, including the use of violence, provided in Tables 16.6 and 16.7 should not be seen out of context. There have always been such incidents throughout the history of the Federal Republic. These are carefully recorded and open to public scrutiny in a way which is not possible in many other countries where extremist violence is a common occurrence. One other aspect of the extremist scene in Germany which is often neglected is that the number of foreign residents who are members of foreign right-wing extremist organisations far outweighs the number of Germans who are members of German extremist organisations.[33]

Table 16.7 Legal measures against right-wing extremists

	1986	1987	1988	1989
Imprisonment of more than a year	20	12	19	4
Imprisonment of up to a year	36	19	38	45
Fines	35	31	47	20
Other sentences	22	29	39	12

Source: *Verfassungsschutz*, report for 1989

Election 1990

Such was the position of the far right up to 1989, the last year of the division of Germany. In 1990 came the unexpected restoration of German unity. At a stroke, one of the key demands of the far right had been met, not as a result of far right campaigns, not by force and violence, but by the peaceful demonstrations and votes of the East German people, and the diplomacy of democratic politicians. In these circumstances the REP, the NPD and other right-wing contenders were crushed in the first national elections of the newly united Germany, in December 1990. For the moment, Chancellor Helmut Kohl was more popular than he had been at any time since his election as head of government in 1982. At the same time, one other great bugbear of the far right disappeared: Communism. In the election of December 1990, the REP scored 2.3 per cent in the West, and only 1.3 per cent in the East of Germany. The NPD managed only 0.3 per cent in both parts of Germany. Altogether, 1,134,054 Germans had voted for these two parties throughout Germany. As these were the first Germany-wide elections, it is worth reminding ourselves of the percentages gained by the far right from the first West German elections of 1949 onwards.[34]

Apart from the European election of 1989, this is a record of failure. To assess whether this record amounts to a lasting change, we will consider the regional election results, membership of far right organisations, and crimes committed by far right activists, as well as public opinion polls, during the period 1991–94.

Franz Schönhuber and the other right-wingers soon regained their self-confidence and saw the former GDR as a rich source of recruitment. This area has high levels of unemployment, appalling housing conditions and very serious environmental and psychological problems. Some young people hate the older generation, whom they regard as responsible for their present plight. This is in part the explanation for the growth of the radical right among the young. They are attracted to causes and ideas condemned by the hated Communist system. In some cases they are in rebellion against parents who loyally supported the discredited Communist regime. Often, they also suffer from an inferiority complex *vis-à-vis* Western Germany. A 'pride in Germany' is a form of compensation for this by being more 'patriotic' than the more relaxed West Germans.[35]

The problems associated with the continuing influx of foreigners and ethnic Germans seeking residence also present the far right with opportunities. The total number of asylum-seekers runs into seven figures. Germany has more asylum-seekers

Table 16.8 % Votes gained by far right parties, 1949–1990

1949 %	1953 %	1957 %	1961 %	1965 %	1969 %	1972 %	1976 %	1979 E %
5.7	1.0	1.1	0.9	2.2	4.3	0.6	0.4	0

1980 %	1983 %	1984E %	1987 %	1989E %	1990 %
0.2	0.2	0.8	0.6	8.8	2.4

E = European elections

than all the other European Union states together. In 1989 it received 377,055 ethnic Germans and 397,000 in 1990; 221,995 arrived in 1991 and 230,000 in 1992. In the last two years, the great majority of them were from the former Soviet Union.[36] In addition, there are both legal and illegal migrants and asylum-seekers. According to *Das Parlament* (21 January 1994), the numbers of those seeking asylum were: 121,300 in 1989, 193,100 in 1990, 256,100 in 1991, 438,200 in 1992 and 322,800 in 1993. Of those arriving in 1993 the biggest groups were from Romania (73,700), Yugoslavia (72,500), Bulgaria (22,500), Bosnia (21,200) and Turkey (19,100).

Regional elections 1992

This inward migration has continued to be a major theme of German politics since unification. It has provided the far right with a cause: 'Germany for the Germans, the boat is full'. It was this cause which was of decisive importance in the relative success of the right-wing radicals in the regional elections in Baden-Württemberg and Schleswig-Holstein in April 1992. In both cases the results pointed to voter dissatisfaction with the two main parties – the CDU and the SPD. Chancellor Kohl (CDU) had lost the popularity he had at the restoration of German unity. Yet the opposition SPD was not able to turn this to its own advantage. In Baden-Württemberg the REP jumped from 1 per cent of the vote in 1988 to 10.9 in 1992. Most of its gains were from the CDU which dropped from 49 to 39.6 per cent. The SPD vote fell from 32 to 29.4 per cent. Its lost votes went to the Greens (up from 7.9 to 9.5). The Liberals (FDP) remained at 5.9 per cent.

In the northern *Land* of Schleswig-Holstein, it was the DVU which trawled the votes of the dissatisfied right-inclined voters. The DVU vote went up from 2.9 per cent (in 1988) to 6.3 per cent. The Green vote rose from 2.9 per cent to 4.97 and the FDP from 4.4 to 5.6. The CDU hardly moved (33.3 per cent in 1988 and 33.8 in 1992), but the governing SPD vote fell from 54.8 to 46.2 per cent. Here it is important to mention that 1988 was an exceptional year for the SPD in traditionally CDU Schleswig-Holstein. The Social Democrats had expected to lose votes in 1992.

Far right membership and violence

In terms of numbers, excluding the REP, the *Verfassungsschutz* estimated that the members of West German far right organisations were as follows: 35,900 in 1989, 32,200 in 1990, 39,800 in 1991 and 41,900 in 1992. Although these numbers show a marked increase since the 1980s they remain modest. In 1991, one source put REP membership at around 20,000.[37] Far more dramatic has been the violence of fringe neo-Nazi groups especially, but not only, against foreigners. The year 1992 saw an explosion of the use of force by far right groups or individuals.

The two most violent regions, measured according to acts of violence per 10,000 of population, were Mecklenburg and Brandenburg, both in the former GDR. Schleswig-Holstein, in the West, came third, but was well behind. Contrary to its image, Bavaria came fifteenth, out of the sixteen *Länder*, with Bremen having the lowest rate.

It is estimated that in 1992 there were 3,800 far right activists in the former GDR, and 2,600 in Western Germany. Most of them were not members of established political organisations. Often they kept in touch by attending skinhead concerts, where they heard bands such as Radikahl, Wotan, Final Solution and, from Britain, Screwdriver. Over 67 per cent of them were 20 years old or younger. A further 29.9 per cent were between 21 and 30 years old. Only 4.7 per cent were women. In terms of jobs, 43 per cent were either school pupils, students or apprentices, 9 per cent were unemployed, 4 per cent were in the armed forces (often doing compulsory service) and 31 per cent were either skilled workers or craftsmen. A further 9 per cent were white collar employees.

Although the recent public opinion polls gave little comfort to the main parties, they did not indicate any swing to the extremes. In a poll conducted for *Der Spiegel*, in December 1993, the two main parties, the CDU and the SPD, attracted 27 and 30 per cent respectively among those asked. The REP attracted only 3 per cent, the Greens 8, the Party of Democratic Socialism [*Partei des Demokratisch Sozialismus*, PDS] (former Communists) 2 per cent and the FDP 6. The disturbing fact was that 23 per cent said they would not vote. The far right is suffering from many difficulties. There are strong personal rivalries between the various leaders of the parties to the right of the Christian Democrats. Within the REP, Schönhuber faces opposition. He is 70, but he is the nearest the party has to a national leader. He is opposed by those who would wish to push the party in a more pro-Nazi direction. Yet many in the REP know this could be the kiss of death.

Elections in Hamburg and lower Saxony 1993 and 1994

The election in Hamburg in September 1993 saw a divided far right go down in defeat. The REP gained 4.8 per cent, the DVU 2.8. The FDP lost its place in parliament securing only 4.2 per cent. The main feature of that election was the appearance of the Instead Of Party [*Stattpartei*] with 5.6 per cent. It was established in 1993 by a disgruntled former CDU member, Markus Wegner, in protest against what he considered unfair candidate selection procedures. It profited from discontent with the big parties, but went on to form a coalition with the SPD. The FDP failed to regain admission to parliament by falling below 5 per cent of the vote.

The result in the March 1994 regional election in Lower Saxony was very encouraging for the ruling SPD, and for their Alliance 90/Green partners in government. They secured 44.3 per cent (44.2 in 1990) and the Alliance 90/Greens 7.4 per cent (5.5). The CDU won 36.4 per cent (42) and the FDP 4.4 per cent (6). The REP and the two Instead Of parties (two factions of the original party, which stood separately) failed to reach the required 5 per cent to gain entry to parliament. Both the Greens and the REP were able to mobilise some protest voters, who normally did not bother to vote. The REP gained 3.6 per cent (1.5) in 1990. The Instead Of parties received 0.4 and 1.2 per cent respectively. The first of them had flirted with the REP, the second had affinity with the Hamburg party with the same name. For 85 per cent of the voters, unemployment was the main election theme, followed by law and order (84 per cent).

Ecological issues came well behind. The SPD, the Alliance 90 [*Bündis 90*] – Greens [*die Grüne*] pact and the REP benefited from the unemployment theme.

These results reflect dissatisfaction with the Bonn CDU/CSU-FDP coalition. The increase in the REP vote is regarded as a protest vote rather than a sign of pro-Nazi tendencies. Perhaps significantly, the far right challenge has been held in check in Hamburg and Lower Saxony. The Bonn establishment knows, however, that as ever the world's media will be giving a disproportionate amount of time and space to their activities. Meanwhile, attacks on foreigners by skinheads will continue to harm Germany's reputation abroad at a time when there are fears, in some circles, of 'German hegemony' in Europe.

List of abbreviations

ANS/NA	*Aktionsfront Nationaler Sozialisten/Nationale Aktivisten* [Action Front of National Socialists/National Activists]
BHE	*Bund der Heimatvertriebenen und Entrechteten* [League of Expellees from the Homeland and of those without Rights]
CDU	*Christlich-Demokratische Union* [Christian Democratic Union]
DAP	*Deutsche Aufbaupartei* [German Construction Party]
DB-Lp	*Deutsche Bauern-und Landvolk-partei* [German Farmers and Peasants Party]
DK	*Deutsche Konservative* [German Conservatives]
DNVP	*Deutsche-Nationale Volkspartei* [German National People's Party]
DP	*Deutsche Partei* [German Party]
DReP	*Deutsche Rechtspartei* [German Rights Party]
DRP	*Deutsche Reichspartei* [German Reich Party]
DVU	*Deutsche Volksunion* [German People's Union]
DVU (List D)	*Deutsche Volksunion (Liste D)* [German People's Union (List D)]
FAP	*Freiheitliche Deutsche Arbeiterpartei* [Free German Workers' Party]
FDP	*Freie Demokratische Partei* [Free Democratic Party]
GUD	*Gemeinschaft unabhängiger Deutscher* [Fellowship of Independent German]
NPD	*Nationaldemokratische Partei Deutschlands* [National Democratic Party of Germany]
NSDAP	*Nationalsozialistische Deutsche Arbeiterpartei* [National Socialist German Workers' Party]
PDS	*Partei des Demokratischen Sozialismus* [Party of Democratic Socialism]
REP	*Die Republikaner* [The Republicans]
SPD	*Sozialdemokratische Partei Deutschlands* [Social Democratic Party of Germany]
SRP	*Sozialistische Reichspartei* [Socialist Party of the Reich]
Z	*Zentrum* [(Catholic) Centre Party]

Notes

1. For an analysis of voting behaviour at the end of the Weimar Republic, see R. F. Hamilton, *Who voted for Hitler?*, Princeton University Press, Princeton. NJ, 1982.

2. See, for instance, the comments of W. L. Shirer, *The Rise and Fall of the Third Reich*, Book Club Associates, London, 1971. Shirer was a correspondent in Germany at the time.

3. I. Kershaw, *Public Opinion and Political Dissent in the Third Reich. Bavaria 1933–45*, Clarendon, Oxford, 1983, esp. pp. 303, 304 and pp. 313–14. For a discussion on the meaning of National Socialism, see also P. Aycoberry, *The Nazi Question*, Routledge and Kegan Paul, London, 1981.

4. Letter to the author.

5. C. Schick, 'Die Internierungslager', in M. Broszat, K. D. Henke and H. Woller (eds), *Von Stalingrad zu Währungsreform*, Olderbourg, Munich, 1989, p. 306.

6. M. Balfour, 'In Retrospect: Britain's Policy of "Re-Education" ', in N. Pronay and K. Wilson (eds), *The Political Re-Education of Germany and Her Allies*, Croom Helm, London, 1985, p. 148.

7. Press and Information Office of the Federal Government, *Regierung Adenauer, 1949–1963*, Wiesbaden, 1963, p. 190.

8. Ibid., p. 54.

9. Ibid., p. 386.

10. *The Times*, 15 July 1952, p. 4; 43 per cent of senior officials in the German Foreign Ministry were former NSDAP members, 28 per cent had belonged to the old Nazi Foreign Ministry and 16 per cent had suffered political persecution under the Nazis.

11. C. J. Friedrich, *Die Kalte Amnestie. NS Täter in der Bundesrepublik*, Fischer, Frankfurt, 1984.

12. K. Hirsch, *Kommen die Nazis wieder? Gefahren für die Bundesrepublik*, Dokumente zur Zeit in Verlag Kurt Desch, Munich, 1967, p. 54.

13. H.-H. Röhring and K. Sontheimer, *Handbuch des Deutschen Parlamentarismus*, Munich, 1970, p. 118.

14. Hirsch, *Kommen die Nazis wieder?*, cit., p. 36.

15. R. Kühnl, R. Rilling and C. Sager, *Die NPD, Struktur, Ideologie und Funcktion einer Neo-Faschistischen Partei*, Suhrkamp, Frankfurt, 1969, p. 226.

16. Federal Ministry of Interior (*Bundesministerium des Innern*), *Zum Thema, hier: Verfassungsschutz, 1968* (*VSB*), Bonn, 1969, p. 11.

17. Ibid., p. 17.

18. S. Eisel, *Minimalkonsens und Freiheitliche Demokratie*, Paderborn, Munich-Vienna-Zurich, 1986, pp. 230–31.

19. *The Economist*, 1 April 1989, p. 139.

20. Statistisches Bundesamt, *Statistisches Jahrbuch 1988 für die Bundesrepublik Deutschland*, Stuttgart, 1988, p. 82.

21. Ibid., p. 69.

22. Ibid., p. 84.

23. Ibid., p. 80.

24. Ibid., p. 80.

25. *VSB*, 1987, p. 112.

26. Ibid., p. 112.

27. Ibid., p. 117.

28. Ibid., p. 117.

29. Ibid., p. 98.

30. ARD television programme 'Panorama', 16 May 1989.

31. *Die Welt*, 17 May 1989, p. 5. For further information and analysis on the REP until 1989, see *Der Spiegel,* 29 May 1989, and H.-G. Betz, 'Post-Modern Anti-Modernism. The West German "Republikaner" ', *Politics and Society in Germany, Austria and Switzerland*, II(3), summer 1990.

32. *Die Welt*, 19 May 1989, p. 4.

33. *VSB*, 1987, pp. 136–59.

34. R. Stoess, 'Rechtsextremismus und Wahlen in der Bundesrepublik', *Aus Politik und Zeitgeschichte Beilage zur Wochenzeitung Das Parlament*, 12 March 1993, pp. 50–61.

35. U. Backes and P. Moreau, 'The Extreme Right', *German Comments*, No. 33, Jan. 1994, p. 61.

36. B. Koller, 'Aussiedler in Deutschland. Aspekte inhrer sozialen und beruflichen Eingliederung', in *Aus Politik und Zeitgeschichte Beilage zur Wochenzeitung Das Parlament* 26 Nov. 1993. pp. 12–22.

37. T. Assheuer and H. Sarkowicz, *Rechtsradikale in Deutschland. Die alte und die neue Rechte*, Beck, Munich, 1992, p. 53. *Der Spiegel* (8 Nov. 1993) puts REP membership at 23,000, of whom 2,800 were in the former GDR.

Chapter 17

HOW TO REVISE HISTORY (AND INFLUENCE PEOPLE?), NEO-FASCIST STYLE

Roger Eatwell

'For some time the neo-Nazis haven't just been empty heads. At universities, the student clubs are using right-wing views to attract new members with great success.'
(Head of Hamburg Federal Agency for the Protection of the Constitution, quoted in *Der Spiegel*, 3 August 1992, p. 31).

Introduction

For many people the term 'neo-Fascism' must seem a misnomer. The word conjures up images of swastika-bedaubed youths shouting 'Sieg Heil' as the boot goes in, or of ageing SS men listening to David Irving proclaim that there was no 'Holocaust' of the Jews. Surely, it could be argued, the prefix 'neo' should indicate a significant discontinuity in an ideological tradition, which is hardly present in these examples.

I have argued elsewhere that the term 'neo-Fascism' is legitimate.[1] More specifically, I have set out a division between three types of neo-Fascism. First, there is a recidivist form, which looks nostalgically to the past, though in order to avoid proscription it may not always openly proclaim its adherence to past forms of Fascism. Second, there is a radical form of neo-Fascism, which tries to reinterpret the Fascist tradition, sometimes arguing that crucial errors were made in the past. Third, there is a hybrid form, which seeks more a synthesis of Fascism and other ideologies, most notably populism, though the Fascist side is usually largely hidden in order to encourage mass support.

This chapter does not seek to repeat the arguments in favour of this typology. Rather, it seeks to underline both the varieties of neo-Fascism, and its ability to produce relatively sophisticated political discourses, by analysing how neo-Fascists have sought to rewrite Fascist history. Since 1945 Fascism has been a pariah, damned in particular by its genocidal practice. For an alienated minority, this is a psychological attraction. Some may even believe that Jews (substitute: Gypsies, homosexuals, Communists . . .) deserved to be killed: that Fascists were even too lax in this area. Thus Holocaust denial arguments can be turned round to show the need for a true Holocaust! In the words of one, poorly produced, recent pamphlet: 'Let us rid ourselves once and for all of the Jews, the holocaust was a HOAX, lets [*sic*] make it REAL'.[2]

However, the more intelligent neo-Fascists realise that the past is a barrier to future progress. This is clearly revealed in what is probably the best-known of the Holocaust denial publications, *Did Six Million Really Die? The Truth at Last* (Historical Review Press, Southam, 1974). This work, written by Richard Harwood (pseudonym), a leading member of the British National Front [NF], who holds a university degree, notes:

> what happens if a man dares to speak of the race problem, of its biological and political implications? He is branded as that most heinous of creatures, a 'racialist'. And what is racialism, of course, but the very hallmark of a Nazi! They (so everyone is told, anyway) murdered Six Million Jews because of racialism. (Harwood 1974, p. 2)

This quote illustrates an important point to bear in mind when studying neo-Fascism; namely, that there may be a disjunction between its *esoteric* and *exoteric* faces. In other words, what is said in public ('we have been misled about the Holocaust') may not reflect an internal agenda ('come back Hitler and racism').[3] This is especially true in countries where there are bans on the formation of Fascist parties or on the publication of Fascist, racist and/or Holocaust denial literature.

Nevertheless, undue emphasis on the Holocaust denial can create a misleading picture of the more intellectual side of neo-Fascism. The impression gained is that the desire is to revive Fascism in exactly the form in which it existed during the inter-war era. For some, this is precisely the purpose,[4] but among others there has been an ideologically more radical form of revisionism. For this reason two less well-known forms of neo-Fascist revisionism are considered in the second main part of this chapter. These 'left'- and 'right'-wing versions raise a variety of interesting issues.[5] First, they highlight the chameleon-like ideological flexibility of Fascism, and the related long-standing problem of placing Fascism on the left–right spectrum.[6] More importantly in the context of this chapter, they help illustrate that while anti-Semitism and the Holocaust denial are not necessary defining traits of neo-Fascism, they are remarkably common characteristics.

As a final introductory point, it should be noted that the analysis which follows focuses largely on Western European sources. Since the fall of Communism in Eastern Europe, there have been growing attempts to rewrite history, particularly in the case of wartime leaders who collaborated with Fascism. Thus Hungary's Admiral Horthy was re-interred in 1993 at a ceremony attended by several government ministers, and broadcast by the state media (in December 1993 an admirer of Horthy became Prime Minister). Croatia's President Franjo Tudjman, a former historian, offers a particularly notable example of such revisionism. He has tried both to rehabilitate the wartime Croatian Ustashe, and to argue that nowhere near six million Jews died in the 'Holocaust'. Nevertheless, he has stopped short of the claim that there was no systematic policy of genocide. Even more remarkable is Russia's Vladimir Zhirinovsky, whose views have notable similarities with some neo-Fascists. However, in general there has been little revisionism in Eastern Europe which focuses on Fascism *per se.*[7] Zhirinovsky, for example, is concerned with revising, or rather reviving, Russian rather than Fascist traditions. Nevertheless, there are growing contacts between Western and Eastern European groups, and the weak political structures and socioeconomic problems in the East make it a particularly fertile territory for neo-Fascism.

The holocaust denial

The most widely disseminated form of neo-Fascist revisionism is the Holocaust denial.[8] It is also, arguably, the oldest form of widespread neo-Fascist revisionism. By the late 1940s, former Nazis, even those not directly involved in the war, were arguing that there had been no policy of genocide, that Jews were exploiting 'history' in order to legitimise a Jewish state in Palestine, to help stress group identity, and to counter a revival of anti-Semitism.[9]

A growing number of academic works examine various aspects of the Holocaust denial, including the fact that some of its protagonists have held academic posts,[10] and that a $50,000 reward was offered by the Institute for Historical Review (which was set up in the USA in 1979) for anyone who could provide serious proof that a single person had been gassed. Such works usually make clear that the motives of those involved are not necessarily neo-Fascist. Some are mainly anti-Semitic. Some seek to delegitimise the Israeli state, which would almost certainly never have been created without the Holocaust, and which uses the Holocaust legacy to justify its own existence and policies.[11] Nor should the motives of those involved be seen as necessarily deceitful and manipulative. Some clearly believe Holocaust denial arguments.[12]

The point of what follows, therefore, is more to set out briefly the main arguments of those who support the Holocaust denial. 'Historical Revisionists' (as they tend to call themselves) often claim – and with some justice – that their arguments are travestied.[13] The following analysis therefore tries to present the arguments as fairly as possible, in an attempt to show that such arguments can be deceptively convincing.

It is important to begin by noting the usefulness of distinguishing between two types of such material. First, there is a crude, overtly anti-Semitic form of the Holocaust denial.[14] Second, there are arguments presented in more academic fashion, sometimes backed by an array of footnotes or references.[15] In the presentation of Holocaust denial claims which follows, the emphasis is firmly on the latter. This clearly 'sanitises' the argument by making it more believable, but it is important to remember that this chapter focuses on the more intellectual forms of neo-Fascist revisionism. In no way is it being denied here that there is a crude and vicious side to the Holocaust denial. Indeed, there seems to be a dual strategy of using more reasoned arguments to appeal to the educated, and cruder arguments to the appeal to the more stereotypical neo-Fascist activist.[16]

It is also important to begin by setting out what Historical Revisionists claim happened. They usually argue that before 1939 Nazi policy was to rid Germany of Jews through emigration, but that this became impossible with the onset of war. Ghettos and concentration camps were therefore set up specially for Jews, because the international Jewish community had declared war on Germany. Moreover, they point out that such camps were invented by the British in the Boer War, and that large numbers died there. There are variations within 'Historical Revisionist' arguments, but they usually admit that some random atrocities against Jews did take place, especially at the hands of local populations. However, they claim that most deaths in the camps resulted from typhus epidemics, or from the chaos at the end of the war. They estimate such losses in the hundreds of thousands, increasingly citing the latest works of history to justify the claim that most losses resulted from epidemics.[17] Irving especially has tried to use material recently found in Moscow and elsewhere to justify a radically reduced estimate of the number of Jews who died. For example, he claims that the Auschwitz death records, kept secret until recently by the KGB, reveal that 74,000 people died there. This, he notes, was 'of course, bad enough: nearly twice as many as died in the July 1943 RAF attack on Hamburg' (a neat example of the tendency to compare the Holocaust with Allied 'atrocities').[18]

These arguments are backed up by a series of more specific claims about why genocide did not take place. These can usefully be placed under four main headings.

Documentary, trial and confessional evidence

Much play is made of the assertion that, in spite of the Allies capturing vast quantities of German documents, none can be found in which Hitler clearly orders the killing of the Jews, or in which key aspects of the Holocaust are set out.[19] This claim holds that many of the key documents which are alleged to have been part of the planning of the Holocaust are open to different interpretations. For example, at the famous Wannsee conference in January 1942 no reference was made to the experimental gassings which had been carried out during the previous year, nor to future gassings. For 'Historical Revisionists', this constitutes evidence that it was simply a discussion of Jewish population numbers, which is seen as perfectly understandable in view of the Nazi plans to resettle them in camps for the duration of the war.

The American academic Arthur Butz has made a notable effort to show that the language of the Holocaust to be found in documents is open to different interpretations.[20] The term 'final solution' (*Endlösung*), he argues, can be found in contexts where it clearly refers to emigration, or resettlement in Jewish ghettos. The term 'special treatment' (*Sonderbehandlung*), normally seen as designating those to be gassed, can also be found in reference to prominent figures, such as the French Socialist leader Léon Blum, who survived the war. In these cases, 'special treatment' referred to providing better rations or accommodation. This argument maintains that there is a paradox between occasional highly provocative Nazi speeches about the fate of the Jews – for example Hitler's speech in the Reichstag on 30 January 1939 – and the alleged euphemisms of the documents. For 'Historical Revisionists' this poses no fundamental problem. Rhetoric was part of the Nazis' style, part of their social control. Conventional accounts of the Holocaust, it is argued, need a rationale based on an Orwellian double-think: they have to hold that the Nazis in public could be viciously anti-Semitic, but in private dealt only in euphemisms.

Evidence from the post-war trials, especially Nuremberg, is particularly attacked. In part this involves an attack on the very legality of the victors trying the vanquished.

Charge number one (conspiracy to wage aggressive war) could, for example, be seen as applying to one of the judging countries, the Soviet Union, which had invaded both eastern Poland and Finland during 1939–40. More specifically, trial procedure is attacked on two counts. First, much of what was admitted in evidence was not cross-checked. This was hardly surprising in view not only of the presumption of guilt on the part of the accused, but also of the allegedly high percentage of Jews working for the various prosecutors. Second, it is alleged that much testimony was extracted through torture, or various other threats and forms of plea-bargaining. For instance, one recent Holocaust denial work[21] asserts: 'It is now known that [Auschwitz commandant] Hoess was beaten almost to death prior to making the statements relied upon by the Nuremberg Tribunal. His wife and children were threatened with the firing squad.' The work goes on to argue that some of Hoess's claims such as the number killed at Auschwitz are patently wrong – a line of argument which has been used in other cases, especially by the French academic Faurisson.

Jewish and other survivor testimony

Considerable attention is also paid to survivor testimony. It is frequently claimed that there are countless oral and written accounts about gas chambers existing in camps such as Dachau or Ravensbruck which are now accepted as not having been involved in the mass gassing campaign.[22] 'I-too-was-there' evidence has also been used by Germans to counter survivor testimony. A notable example of this genre is Thies Christophersen's pamphlet *Die Auschwitz Lüge* (Kritik Verlag, Mohrkirch, 1973).[23] Great play is made of the fact that the Allies had aerial reconnaissance shots of Auschwitz, which was a major centre of war production. None of these, it is alleged, reveals evidence to support conventional Holocaust-survivor accounts. For example there were no groups waiting for 'selections', or to enter gas chambers; there were no crematoria with constantly smoking chimneys.

One article is especially worth concentrating on. It clearly impresses the Historical Revisionists as it has appeared in the American *Journal of Historical Review*, and in the French *Annales d'histoire révisionniste* (both of which are dedicated primarily to the claim that there was no systematic policy of genocide).[24] Its author is Howard F. Stein, an Associate Professor of Psychiatry at the University of Oklahoma. The editorial of the American journal notes:[25]

Dr Stein is himself of Jewish origin, and believes that forty of his relatives died in Europe during World War Two. His focus is not so much on history as meanings. He feels that it is wrong to label the Holocaust a 'hoax' or 'lie' because the people who are propagating it actually believe in it themselves. It is this phenomenon of self-deception which he addresses in his very fine article.

Stein's own words are:[26]

Whatever did happen in the Holocaust must be made to conform to the group-fantasy of what ought to have happened. For the Jews, the term 'Holocaust' does not simply denote a single catastrophic era in history, but is a grim metaphor for the meaning of Jewish history . . . One is either anxiously awaiting persecution, experiencing persecution, recovering from it, or living in a period that is a temporary reprieve from it.

Thus Stein is arguing that the experiences of camp life were interpreted within a framework of a history of persecution. In camps where families were broken up, where the smells and sounds of industrial production were strong, even repellent, it was easy to imagine all forms of horror. This tendency was fuelled by the fact that some horrific acts did take place within the camps. Limited, non-systematic killings, were therefore incorporated into a collective picture of genocide because of the very nature of Jewish psychology when faced with incarceration in concentration camps.

Holocaust 'myths' and 'lies'

Another major line of attack is to draw parallels with other myths and, especially, to criticise the historiography of the Holocaust. It is often pointed out that the First World War saw a vast number of atrocity stories, including claims that the Germans boiled corpses into soap, or transfixed babies on bayonets. All the major stories later turned out to be fakes. Paradoxically, they featured prominently in First World War propaganda, whereas the Holocaust attracted little attention during the Second World War. Historical Revisionists argue that this points to the conclusion that much of the Holocaust is a post-war fabrication. It is often added that both Allied intelligence services and the Vatican had considerable knowledge of what was happening in occupied Europe; thus if there had been systematic genocide, these sources would have made more of it during the war.

It is noted that there are some fakes relating to the Holocaust which are even admitted by Jewish groups. Many photographs relating to the Holocaust are alleged to have been faked, or presented in a misleading way. Perhaps the most common charge of all, in terms of forgery, is the claim that Anne Frank's diary was clearly written after the war. The argument is based on the claim that parts are in ball-point pen, that the handwriting varies, and that the thoughts are beyond those of a young girl. Although a detailed defence of the validity of the work was published by a Dutch official organisation, Faurisson repeated the forgery claim in 1989.[27] However, the argument is not always used. Butz, while clearly agreeing with the charge, points out that it is irrelevant to proof about the Holocaust as the diary refers to a period of hiding in Amsterdam. Anne Frank subsequently died in a typhoid epidemic in Bergen-Belsen during the closing days of the war.[28]

Historians of the Holocaust are attacked for careless research, even deliberate distortion. Thus Faurisson, in a 1987 *samizdat* circular, claimed that the leading British historian Martin Gilbert had deliberately altered part of the evidence for his book *The Holocaust* (Collins, London, 1986). He also claimed that Gilbert's books were full of manipulation and slipshod scholarship. For example in *Auschwitz and the Allies* Gilbert writes that in 1942 'hundreds of thousands of Jews were being gassed every day at Belzec, Chelmno, Sobibor and Treblinka'.[29] As the hundreds of thousands is in words, not numerals, this cannot be a typographical error. The four million Jews normally considered to have been gassed (rather than killed in other ways), therefore met their end in a month, according to Gilbert. Gilbert is a leading historian, so the fact that such an error can creep into his work is used by the Historical Revisionists to cast doubt on all historical accounts.

Historical Revisionists have put considerable efforts into trying to use population statistics to show that six million Jews cannot possibly have died. Much of this is derived from the works of the French socialist Paul Rassinier, who was imprisoned in Buchenwald concentration camp for resistance activities.[30] Harwood[31] puts the argument concisely when he writes: '*The World Almanac* of 1938 gives the number of Jews in the world as 16,588,259. But after the war the *New York Times*, February 22nd 1948, placed the number of Jews in the world at a minimum of 15,600,000 and a maximum of 18,700,000.' These figures are used to estimate Jewish losses, through epidemics and random killings, as in the hundreds of thousands.

'Scientific' arguments

A final set of arguments can be grouped together under the heading 'scientific'. From his earliest writings, Faurisson tried to show the scientific impossibility of mass gassings.[32] He developed the remarkable claim that gassings, in the way alleged in Holocaust literature, were impossible. He used evidence from the gassing of single prisoners in US executions, and from the commercial use of Zyklon B. He noted that barracks which had been fumigated with Zyklon B were supposed to be left for twenty hours before special teams went in to test them. In American executions, the problem of venting a single small room meant that the acidic vapours were turned into salt, and then flushed out with water. Yet it is alleged that large gas chambers were quickly vented in camps which contained Germans as well as Jews. It is also claimed that teams, usually without masks, went into the chambers within minutes to remove bodies.

This line of argument received major reinforcement when in 1988 an American expert in gas chamber construction, Fred Leuchter, visited Auschwitz, Birkenau and Majdanek.[33] From his study of the design of the installations, he concluded that they could not have been used for mass gassings. Moreover, forensic samples taken in the gas chambers were analysed in the USA, revealing no significant traces of hydrocyanic gas, though comparison samples taken in delousing chambers for clothes revealed significant levels.

This form of argument has now become central to Holocaust denial arguments, and is often used to attack the latest works on the Holocaust. For example, a 1993 *Revisionist Newsletter* specifically attacks the work of the Frenchman Jean-Claude Pressac, author of *Auschwitz: the Technique and Operation of the Gas Chambers* (Beate Klarsfield Foundation, New York, 1989). After quoting Pressac as saying that after the gas chamber doors were opened, hairdressers, dentists and others went in to remove anything of value, it is argued:[34]

Here we are confronted with another technical impossibility. As noted earlier, 15 to 30 minutes of forced draught ventilation could not possible have removed all of the pockets of gas trapped within the hair, mucous membranes and body cavities of the 1,000 to 2,000 victims. Workers assigned to the job of shearing hair and removing gold teeth would have died by HCN poisoning – by inhalation if they weren't wearing gas masks or absorption through the skin, if they were.

The impact of such work seems to have been especially strong on Irving. Before 1988, his public line accepted that Jews had been systematically killed, but he argued that this was not ordered by Hitler: Himmler and the SS were portrayed as the main guilty parties.[35] His conversion to the Holocaust denial position came as a result of Leuchter's work. Or perhaps it would be more accurate to say that the conversion came *allegedly* as a result of the scientific evidence, for Irving provides an excellent example of the need to search for ulterior motives. In particular, he has shown a clear antipathy to Jews on occasion.[36] Moreover, he has very close contacts with a variety of neo-Fascist groups, especially in Germany.[37]

'Left'- and 'right'-wing neo-Fascism

Many of those involved in the Holocaust denial are clearly recidivist neo-Fascists, true to Hitler's final testament in which he called upon his successors to destroy Jewish influence. Their dream is of a fourth Reich, with Hitler's picture in an honoured place on every mantelpiece. Less clear is the extent of Holocaust denial views among the hybrid neo-Fascist groups, which tend to hide their Fascist side in an attempt to court popular support. Le Pen's reference in 1987 to the Holocaust as a 'detail' of history has led many to believe that he held closet Historical Revisionist views. However, it is important to realise that such views are not necessary defining characteristics of neo-Fascism (nor sufficient ones, as some of those involved cannot reasonably be termed 'neo-Fascist'). This can be seen by considering 'left' and 'right' forms of radical neo-Fascist revisionism.

'Left'-wing radical neo-Fascists

There have been three major strands within neo-Fascist 'left' revisionism. One looks mainly to Italian Fascism, the other to Nazism. The third strand can draw on either or both, though Nazism tends to be the model referred to by most neo-Fascists. (Other minor strands consider issues such as whether Fascism was too statist, and whether it is necessarily corporatist).

Some neo-Fascists have looked to the very founding period of Fascism in 1919, or to the final period of Mussolini's rule, the Salò Republic (1943–45), to argue that Fascism was in essence a form of left-wing radicalism, perverted by the compromises of office. Maurice Bardèche, the brother-in-law of the French writer Robert Brasillach, who was executed at the end of the war, provides an excellent example of this form of reasoning.[38] Bardèche was a prolific writer in the post-war era, and edited the important neo-Fascist journal *Défense de l'Occident*. Like most Fascists, he was obsessed with the threat posed by Communism, which he saw as based on false ideals of internationalism and statist egalitarianism. He believed that Fascism was 'the only revolutionary system' which could oppose Communism.[39]

In his book *Qu'est ce que les fascisme?* (Les Sept Couleurs, Paris, 1961), which opened with the remarkable words 'I am a Fascist writer', he argued:[40]

Nothing is more stirring in the history of Italian Fascism than the return to sources achieved under the iron fist of defeat. The programme of the Salò Republic in 1944, this is what Mussolini ought to have fought for twenty years earlier. This is where the real Fascism lies.

On the basis of this radical reading of 'true' Fascism, he went on to reject the notion that Francoism and Latin American dictatorships were 'Fascist', though he was sympathetic to early Peronism on account of its concern for the workers.

The quest for alternative German roots can be seen clearly in 'Strasserism'. Gregor Strasser was one of the 'socialist' Nazis eliminated in the 1934 Night of the Long Knives.[41] His brother Otto survived in exile, and after 1945 was highly active rewriting history, thus helping to sow the seeds of 'Strasserism'.[42] Gregor's views were anti-capitalist rather than socialist; he was also interested in appealing to the important sector of the peasantry. However, by the 1970s Strasserism was seen, particularly within some German groups, as emphasising the need for a radical form of appeal to the working class.[43] Similar views emerged in Britain within the NF: thus, in the bitter 1984–85 miners' strike, the NF sided with the workers, though not with their Marxist leadership.[44] This form of revisionism is sometimes linked to a direct attack on Hitler, not only for killing Gregor, but for betraying the Nazi 'revolution'.

Sir Oswald Mosley serves as an excellent example of the third type of 'left' revisionism – namely 'Europeanism'.[45] Mosley, the leader of the pre-war British Union of Fascists, was imprisoned for much of the war, during which time he read widely (even before the war he had been the Fascist leader most capable of developing a serious level of argument). After 1945, he became a prolific writer, seeking to appeal to a more educated audience than inter-war Fascism.[46] 'Europe, a Nation' and 'European Socialism' now became Mosley's slogans (at least in his more constructive moments, for Mosley could never completely forsake the rabble-rousing tendency).[47] Mosley moved away from some of the statist aspects of Fascism, admitting this had led both to inefficiency and abuse of power. Even more remarkably, in terms of European unity he envisaged a form of full integration, not any 'miserable federal compromise' – with most of Africa linked as a form of colonial appendage. He saw this as a kind of 'third way' bloc between capitalist America and Communist Russia (he often portrayed himself as a centrist rather than as a man of the left). On several occasions he sought to organise a European neo-Fascist federation to promote such views (others involved included Bardèche).[48]

Léon Degrelle serves as another, though somewhat different, example of 'Euro-peanism'.[49] Degrelle was the leader of the 1930s Belgian Rexist Party, who went on to fight with the Waffen SS on the Russian front. He met Hitler on several occasions: the Führer supposedly stated that if he had a son, he would have liked him to be like Degrelle.[50] Degrelle duly worshipped Hitler like a father. After 1945 he lived in exile in Spain, where he kept up a steady output of neo-Fascist literature, and organised meetings with European neo-Fascists. He argued that Italian Fascism was essentially conservative, and pointed to the need for radicals to see Nazism as the role model.[51] This might seem to make Degrelle a recidivist, but his views sought to revise Fascism in major ways. In particular, he sought to portray Fascism as a defence of European rather than national values. One of his books was dedicated to the two thousand five hundred Belgian volunteers who died on the Eastern front fighting Bolshevism 'for Europe and their country'.[52] There was an element of Europeanism in intellectual Nazism (and Fascism), but after 1945 Degrelle added a radical new dimension. As he wrote in one of his books:[53] 'Within six months all the German army had become Russophile. We fraternised everywhere with the peasants . . . Nazi theorists professed violently anti-Slav theories. They would not have lasted ten years in the face of Russo-German compenetration.' Degrelle, like many others, clearly believed that the Germans should have invaded Eastern Europe as liberators, not slave masters, especially as he believed that Fascism could have provided an important counter-appeal to Communism. Slavs were, thus, to be equals in this new Europe, stretching from 'the Pyrenees to the Urals'.[54]

However, it is important to stress that these 'left' forms of revisionism have usually been accompanied by some form of racist politics. For example, Bardèche, Mosley and Degrelle all questioned the Holocaust, though Mosley never went so far as to claim that there was no systematic policy of genocide: his argument was rather that many claims were exaggerated, or not proven, and that there had been Allied atrocities.[55]

'Right'-wing radical neo-Fascists

As with 'left' neo-Fascism, there is an Italian- and German-inspired variant, together with a '*Nouvelle Droite*' [ND], though there is considerable inter-relationship between these positions. (There are also several minor variants, for example the split between those who hold that the 'Faustian' spirit makes technological development inevitable, and those who advocate an almost back-to-the-land, ecologist position).[56]

Julius Evola is arguably the single most important thinker to the 'right' radical neo-Fascist revisionists.[57] Evola was an Italian artist and writer, who before 1945 was not active in the Fascist Party. Evola's thought is obscure and elusive.[58] It is also complicated, after 1945, by a tendency to be guarded at times. Thus, he publicly criticised Hitler, though in private he seems to have been more admiring. The basis of Evola's thought was a form of mystical, anti-egalitarian, elitism. His main criticism of the Nazis was that they sought mass mobilisation and focused too much on economic concerns. He also criticised their biological racism, though his own form of spiritual racism often cited the Jews as the epitome of mercenary and other values deemed to be socially destructive. Evola's Fascist heroes were especially José Antonio, leader of the Spanish Falange, and Corneliu Codreanu, leader of the Romanian Iron Guard (and an anti-Semite). In part, the attraction of these two leaders was that they had died as martyrs. Some of his followers, especially in Italy and Britain, have termed themselves 'political soldiers', a male order selflessly dedicated to the advancement of the cause. In the words of Evola, the vital task is to learn: 'how to love for oneself discipline and limits . . . until a superior and austere vocation . . . stemming from the most intimate and unfathomable roots of life, brings one to knowledge of the vital spirit necessary to go beyond the human condition.'[59] In some cases, the accompanying military terminology has reflected a willingness to see violence, especially terrorism, as the vehicle for the Fascist second coming. However, Evola's thought has also been interpreted as tending to stress the need for spiritual awakening among an elite which withdraws from the everyday concerns of politics into a monastic-like, transcendental existence. Pino Rauti, who broke away from the *Movimento Sociale Italiano* [MSI] to form *Ordine Nuovo* in the 1950s, was the most illustrious follower of this rather confused strategy.[60]

Evola's philosophical starting point was a feeling of total alienation from the modern world, an image of a world in ruins, where integrating values have crumbled. This owed much to the influence of German 'conservative revolutionaries', such as the writers Ernst Jünger, Moeller Van den Bruck and Oswald Spengler.[61] Although these writers are usually seen as having helped prepare the cultural ground for the rise of the Nazis, there were notable differences in ideology. For example, they were not biological racists, tending more to a cultural view of social unity. They were also critical of Nazi mass mobilisation – 'the organisation of the unemployed by the lazy', in Spengler's words. Linked to this was the view that Nazism had made too many compromises in order to come to power, and that it had lost its truly radical social vision. Here the similarities with Evola seem clear. The main differences lie mainly in the absence of the self-actualising, spiritual-violent side: the emphasis is rather on elite, cultural activity, especially to recreate a new national political culture.[62] However, there are other reasons why some neo-Fascists have looked to the 'conservative revolutionaries' rather than to Evola. Probably the main reason is the fact they were not a neatly defined group. It is thus possible to stretch the definition of 'conservatism' to cover both radicals and genuine conservatives, such as Thomas Mann, or those who operated on the fringes of the two categories, such as Carl Schmitt.[63] This has the advantage of helping to make the radicals look more respectable, and thus broadening their appeal.

Similar views can also be found in the misleadingly termed *Nouvelle Droite*. The key country in which such ideas have been developed has been France, though the ND has notable followings, especially in Germany and Italy. Its origins can be traced back to the late 1960s, when various organisations and journals were set up by academics and neo-Fascist activists. Its best known thinker in France is the middle-aged polymath, Alain de Benoist.[64] Benoist openly acknowledges his debt to both Evola and the 'conservative revolutionaries', and his prolific writings clearly show these influences. For example, he argues in his Académie Française prize-winning *Vu de droite* that:[65] 'the "positive nihilism" of Nietzsche has no other sense than this: one can build only in space which has been previously razed to the ground.' However, there are notable differences.

The first concerns Europeanism. Although Evola was more concerned with a defence of European than national values, this was not an aspect of his thought stressed by most of his followers.[66] The ND is essentially Europeanist rather than nationalist, though, like the 'left' neo-Fascist radicals, it has little time for the bureaucratic and capitalist-dominated European Community. Its Europeanism is based more on a sense of decadence stemming from individualistic-commercial values. These are often epitomised by the USA, which before 1989 was often portrayed as a more serious threat to the future of the true Europe than Communism. Communism is also rejected for its egalitarianism and its focus on the material side of life, but Russia is normally seen as part of the future new Europe. The true Russian spirit is seen as disciplined and brave, vital traits from which the rest of Europe could learn, especially in the event of any future war.[67]

The second difference concerns the academic side of the ND. A recurring theme in its writings, especially of its main journal *Nouvelle Ecole*, is the scientific basis of its views. During the 1970s, considerable emphasis was placed on biological and psychological arguments. However, these were used mainly to stress inherent inequalities between people rather than between peoples. The ND's Europeanism is essentially cultural rather than biological. More generally, *Nouvelle Ecole* seeks to create the impression of widespread academic support. For example, among those included in the September 1990 issue's editorial board are figures of world repute, such as the British and American psychologists Hans Eysenck and Arthur Jensen.

The above leads on to the third difference, especially in contrast to Evola. Although the politics of the ND are elitist and anti-egalitarian, it seeks to exert an influence on mass culture. It has advocated what has become known as a 'Gramscism of the right', namely a desire to reconquer the French mind, which has allegedly been captured by left intellectuals who dominated discourse.[68] During the late 1970s and early 1980s several of the ND's leading members pursued this strategy, especially through the columns of *Le Figaro*, which was owned by the right-wing press baron Robert Hersant.

More recently, the ND has faded from public view, though key figures like de Benoist continue to preach their radical views (including a communist-ND *rapprochement*), arguing that they are victims of a McCarthyite ideological witch hunt.[69] One reason for their diminished access to the mainstream media was a belief that the ND was operating on different esoteric and exoteric agendas. In particular, the ND seemed to have a distinctly anti-Semitic side. Its main publications were critical of the 'Judeo-Christian' tradition for its monotheism and alleged egalitarianism, but they did not contain crude anti-Semitic appeals, nor did they feature Holocaust-denial material. However, it is not necessary to probe too far to see another side. The editorial committee of *Nouvelle Ecole*, for example, has included both David Irving and Bernard Notin, a Holocaust-denying lecturer at the University of Lyons III. In addition, two journalists who studied the ND in the 1970s have argued that it acted as a vehicle for circulating Faurisson's works.[70]

Conclusion

It is especially important, in conclusion, to underline what this chapter has *not* done, except occasionally in passing.

First, no attempt has been made to offer a balanced discussion of the content of neo-Fascist publications or public statements. In particular, the focus here on anti-

Semitism must be seen against a broader context where most neo-Fascist propaganda is aimed at 'immigrant' groups. This is especially true of the 'hybrid' groups, which fear that anti-Semitism is largely beyond the pale.[71] The more reasoned revisionist forms of argument considered here should not divert attention either from the frequently crude, and often recidivist, forms of neo-Fascist appeal.

Second, no systematic attempt has been made to point out where neo-Fascist revisionist history is based on gross distortions, or highly debatable interpretations. This is because the main point of this chapter has been typological rather than historiographical. In particular, the purpose has been to illustrate that not all Fascists are clones of the inter-war epoch, nor do they all defend every aspect of inter-war Fascism. Indeed, the discussion shows the dangers of defining Fascism in terms of a mass organised party, willing to use violence, and seeking national grandeur – traits which are usually central to models of 'generic Fascism'. Some neo-Fascists have pointed to different strategies, and to themes which might not be identified by many as Fascist – traits which help broaden their appeal.

This points to a third neglected issue. Some might consider that studying neo-Fascist revisionism is little more than a form of antiquarianism: of no great import other than in its own right. However, such an argument ignores the potential impact of these debates in terms of attracting support for neo-Fascism, or for influencing others. Neo-Fascist revisionism offers a significant potential for sanitising Fascism, for making it less of a pariah. It is important to note here that such revisionism is helped by legitimate academic debates, such as the *Historikerstreit* in Germany which discussed whether the Holocaust was 'merely' one among many forms of genocide, and whether in some ways it was a response to, and imitation of, Communism. The growing academic tendency to see Fascism as a serious ideology, appealing to intellectuals across the political spectrum, also serves indirectly to make Fascism less of a pariah. Moreover, neo-Fascist 'left' and 'right' variants make it particularly adept at finding the political 'space' in which to operate.

Paradoxically, the increasingly-stressed Holocaust denial helps the neo-Fascist revival, but ultimately limits it in Western Europe. There seems little doubt that such material is reaching a rapidly growing audience, and making converts. Recent opinion poll evidence indicates that 50 per cent of British people claim to have heard of the Holocaust denial, and that 7 per cent are willing to accept that there was no Holocaust. This is a small minority, but it is nevertheless a surprising one, especially as people usually will not admit to what are perceived as illegitimate views. Other polls show the persistence of views which could fuel a new popular anti-Semitism. For example, in Germany 39 per cent are willing to admit that they believe that Jews manipulate the Holocaust for their own ends.[72] However, there also seems no question that Holocaust denial views remain beyond the pale for most people, the political equivalent of the 'scientific' claim that the earth is flat. As such, they condemn groups espousing them to political limbo. A major exception to this may be Eastern Europe. Here anti-Semitic views have always had a strong resonance. Moreover, some forms of neo-Fascist revisionism mean that East Europeans, '*Untermenschen*' for many Nazi theorists, can now look to Fascism for lessons.

Nevertheless, the beyond the pale nature of anti-Semitic, and especially Holocaust denial, views in Western Europe raises a final neglected issue: why have such views been common among neo-Fascists? Many would answer this question in mainly psychological terms. The very fact that Fascism has been a pariah since 1945 has meant that it has attracted an alienated fringe, seeking to vent their frustrations, and other feelings, on the Jews – the classic 'outsider' group in European culture.[73] Such approaches are obviously important, but they have limitations. One is that anti-Semitism in both classic and contemporary Fascism had a manipulative side, which did not involve any necessary belief in the arguments put forward. There seems little doubt that one of the reasons why the 'left' neo-Fascists have been tempted by anti-Semitism (and especially anti-immigrant politics) is the belief that such views will have appeal among the 'masses'. A second problem with psychological approaches is that they tend to create the impression that all Fascists/neo-Fascists are anti-Semites, and that the attraction is largely pathological. Both deductions are misleading. There has always been a strand in Fascism which was not anti-Semitic, dating back to the very beginnings of Italian Fascism, which had a notable Jewish following. There has also always been a more rational-intellectual side to Fascism: witness the large number of academics who supported Fascism in both Italy and Germany (such as the major sociologist Robert Michels, or philosopher Martin Heidegger). Although this has been a much less notable feature of neo-Fascism, it is vital not to underestimate the potential of neo-Fascist revisionism to cast an appeal outside the ranks of the alienated – especially at a time when other ideologies seem to be in a crisis which is undermining their intellectual support.[74]

Notes

1. R. Eatwell, 'Towards a New Model of Generic Fascism', *Journal of Theoretical Politics*, 2, 1992, pp. 161–194; R. Eatwell, 'Fascism', in Eatwell and A. W. Wright, *Contemporary Political Ideologies*, Pinter, London, 1993, pp. 169–191. See also R. Griffin, *The Nature of Fascism*, Pinter, London, 1991.

2. From a leaflet printed by 'White working class Nationalists', England, 1992.

3. Thus Ernst Zündel, a leading advocate of the Holocaust denial, recently defended Hitler at a private meeting of David Irving's Clarendon Club, commenting: 'Aryans, if I may use this term that infuriates our enemies, white people . . .', Transcript of meeting in possession of Board of Deputies of British Jews. Zündel was awarded the George Orwell Free Speech prize at the 11th (1992) Congress of the American Institute for Historical Review, whose primary purpose is to disseminate Holocaust denial arguments. Zündel was prevented from entering the USA by immigration officials, and his prize was accepted on his behalf by Ewald Althans – a leading young German neo-Fascist.

4. See, for instance, the publications of the international (Spanish-based) organisation *Círculo Español de Amigos de Europa* [CEDADE]. For example, the June 1979 issue of its journal, *Cedade*, advertises a work on the Holocaust denial, and is full of eulogies to Hitler, pictures of healthy Hitler Youth members and the like.

5. 'Left' and 'right' are notoriously difficult terms to define; they are therefore not discussed here in conceptual terms. For an introduction to the problems see Part One of R. Eatwell and N. O'Sullivan (eds), *The Nature of the Right*, Pinter, London, 1989. Fascists and neo-Fascists have often refused to be placed on the left-right spectrum, arguing that their views are a synthesis of other ideologies.

6. Whilst Fascism is usually regarded as right-wing, several major commentators have viewed

it as having deep left-wing roots. See, for example, A. J. Gregor, *The Fascist Persuasion in Radical Politics*, Free Press, New York, 1969; and Z. Sternhell, M. Sznajder and M. Asheri, *The Birth of Fascist Ideology*, Princeton University Press, Princeton, NJ, 1994.

7. On the recent rise of the extreme right in Eastern Europe see P. Hockenos, *Free to Hate*, Routledge, London, 1993; and Institute of Jewish Affairs, *Anti-Semitism: World Report, 1992* (and subsequent years), IJA, London, 1992–.

8. It is clearly impossible to measure the circulation of neo-Fascist literature with accuracy. However, there is a remarkably large number of Holocaust denial publications, including apparently academic journals relating to it. Moreover, where not banned by law, Holocaust denial publications figure prominently on the booklists of many neo-Fascist groups. For example, see the British National Party's [BNP] *Spearhead*, April 1992; ten of the books it offers for sale relate to the Holocaust denial.

9. One notable non-combatant example is Maurice Bardèche, especially his books: *Nuremberg ou la terre promise*, Les Sept Couleurs, Paris, 1948; and *Nuremberg II ou les faux monnayeurs*, Les Sept Couleurs, Paris, 1950. On Bardèche, see below. This *cui bono?* form of reasoning remains strong in current Holocaust denial arguments.

10. The most notable academics are Professor Arthur Butz, an engineer who teaches at Northwestern University, Illinois; and Dr Robert Faurisson, an expert in French literature who taught at the University of Lyons II.

11. On this see T. Segev, *The Seventh Million*, Hill and Wang, New York, 1993.

12. See especially: G. Seidel, *The Holocaust Denial*, Beyond the Pale, Leeds, 1986; R. Eatwell, 'The Holocaust Denial: a Study in Propaganda Technique', in L. Cheles, R. Ferguson and M. Vaughan (eds), *Neo-Fascism in Europe*, Longman, London, 1991, pp. 120–146; P. Haupt, 'A Universe of Lies', *Patterns of Prejudice*, Summer 1991, pp. 75–85; D. Lipstadt, 'Holocaust Denial and the Compelling Force of Reason', *Patterns of Prejudice*, Nos. 1 and 2, 1992, pp. 64–76; D. Lipstadt, *The Holocaust Denial*, Free Press, New York, 1993; P. Vidal-Naquet, *Assassins of Memory*, Columbia University Press, New York, 1992.

13. For example, The Anne Frank Stichting, *The Extreme Right*, Anne Frank Stichting, Amsterdam, 1985, p. 18, argues: 'The Revisionist propaganda is a reiteration of the forgery . . . *The Protocols of the Elders of Zion*'. In fact, Historical Revisionists may exploit anti-Semitic conspiracy theory, but their main arguments are not based on forgeries. The technique is especially one of selection and distortion. See Eatwell, 'The Holocaust Denial', cit.

14. See, for example, The Committee for Truth in History, *The Six Million Reconsidered*, Historical Review Press, Southam, 1979. Among the chapter titles are: 'The Tsarist Pogrom Myth', 'Jews and Organized Crime' and 'Jews and Communism'. The last of these stresses not just the Jewish nature of Communism, but the appalling nature of Communist atrocities – thus helping to relativise the Holocaust.

15. For example, see C. Mattogno, 'Le mythe de l'extermination des juifs', *Annales d'histoire révisionniste*, 1, 1987, pp. 15–58. Some works sit uneasily between categories, for example A. Butz, *The Hoax of the Twentieth Century*, Historical Review Press, Southam, 1976, which, although replete with an extensive bibliography, more than hints at anti-Semitism.

16. See La Vieille Taupe's samizdat circular, 1986. This organisation, which publishes Faurisson's works, is left-wing anarchist.

17. For example, B. Kulaszka (ed.), *Did Six Million Really Die?*, Samisdat, Toronto, 1992, p. viii, notes: 'The Jewish historian, Arno J. Mayer . . . writes more Jews were killed by so-called "natural" causes than by "unnatural" ones.' The title of the Kulaszka booklet is the same as that of Harwood's 1974 work; this is because the Kulaszka work refers primarily to the trial of Zündel (see note 3), who published Harwood in Canada.

18. Letter in *The Spectator*, 25 November 1989, pp. 32 and 35.

19. For example, Harwood, *Did Six Million Really Die?*, cit., esp. p. 8.
20. Butz, *The Hoax*, cit., esp. pp. 69ff.
21. Kulaszka (ed.), 'Criminal Prosecution of "Holocaust Denial" ', in Kulaszka (ed.), *Did Six Million Really Die?*, cit., p. viii.
22. For example, S. Thion, *Vérité historique ou vérité politique?*, La Vieille Taupe, Paris, 1980, pp. 25ff; and R. Faurisson, *Réponse à Pierre Vidal-Naquet*, La Vieille Taupe, Paris, 1982, pp. 26–8.
23. See also his journal *Kritik, die Stimme des Volkes*, e.g. No. 51, 1980.
24. The American journal was founded in 1980, and is still running. The French journal, which always seemed short of new material, ran from 1987 to 1990.
25. 'The Holocaust, and the Myth of the Past as History', Winter, 1980, p. 296.
26. Ibid., p. 310.
27. 'Les écritures d'Anne Frank', *Annales d'histoire révisionniste*, No. 7, 1989, pp. 45–50.
28. Butz, *The Hoax*, cit., p. 36.
29. Michael Joseph, London, 1981, p. 26.
30. Rassinier's best work in English is the compilation *Debunking the Genocide Myth*, Noontide Press, Torrance, CA, 1978. Among his best works in French are: *Le mensonge d'Ulysse*, Editions Bressanes, Paris, 1950 (reissued by La Vieille Taupe, Paris, 1979); and *Le drame des juifs européens*, Les Sept Couleurs, Paris, 1964 (reissued by La Vieille Taupe, Paris, 1985).
31. *Did Six Million Really Die?*, cit., pp. 6–7.
32. 'The Mechanics of Gassing', *Journal of Historical Review*, 1, 1980.
33. Leuchter was commissioned to make the visit as part of the defence of Zündel (see nn. 3 and 17), in which Faurisson figured prominently. See *The Leuchter Report*, Focal Point, London, 1989.
34. *Revisionist Newsletter*, No. 6, p. 8.
35. *Hitler's War*, Hodder and Stoughton, London, 1977.
36. For example, note his description of a youthful foray to buy a Jaguar sports car in his periodical *Focal Point*, 31 May 1983, p. 21: 'this yellow-waistcoated salesman of unmentionable ethnic origin . . . oozed Levantine charm'. (Irving duly bought a Porsche).
37. His books appear regularly in the book lists of *Deutsche Volks Union* [DVU] and *Republikaner* publications. He has also received prizes from the DVU's publisher, Gerhard Frey.
38. There is little on Bardèche in English. For an introduction, see I. R. Barnes, 'Fascism and Technocratic Elitism', *Wiener Library Bulletin*, No. 34, 1981, pp. 36–41.
39. Bardèche, *Nuremberg ou la terre promise*, cit., p. 258.
40. P. 20. See also his article 'Socialisme et fascisme', *Défense de l'Occident*, No. 146, 1977, pp. 4–12.
41. On Gregor Strasser see P. D. Stachura, *Gregor Strasser and the Rise of Nazism*, George Allen and Unwin, London, 1983.
42. His publications include *Hitler and I*, Jonathan Cape, London, 1940.
43. For a survey of recent developments within German groups, see the annual reports of the Office for the Protection of the Constitution (*Verfassungsschutzberichte*).
44. *National Front News*, No. 62, 1985, p. 5.
45. The best single work on Mosley is R. Skidelsky, *Oswald Mosley*, Macmillan, London, 1975. See also R. Eatwell, 'Metamorphosis and Continuity', in S. Larsen (ed.), *Modern Europe after Fascism, 1945–1989*, Princeton University Press, Princeton, NJ, 1995.
46. The best statements of Mosley's post-war views are: *The Alternative*, Mosley Publications, Ramsbury, 1947; and *Europe: Faith and Plan*, Sanctuary Press, London, 1958.
47. By the late 1950s, signs of growing hostility to immigrants in Britain led Mosley back into active politics and an anti-immigrant platform. His own son broke with him over this,

claiming that with one hand Mosley dealt with great ideas, but with the other he let the rats out of the sewer.

48. In the post-war period, both Italian and German neo-Fascists produced 'Europeanist' journals: especially *Europa Unità* and *Nation Europa*. The latter, which was first published in 1951, continues today as an important vehicle for disseminating ideas.

49. Little has been written on Degrelle in English. For a good account of part of his career see M. Conway, *Collaboration in Belgium: Léon Degrelle and the Rexist Movement*, Yale University Press, New Haven, 1993.

50. L. Degrelle, *Front de l'Est*, La Table Ronde, Paris, 1969, p. 12.

51. L. Degrelle, *Hitler pour 1000 ans*, La Table Ronde, Paris, 1969, pp. 22–3.

52. *Front de l'est*, cit., p. 13.

53. *Hitler pour 1000 ans*, cit., pp. 217–9.

54. Degrelle's views could be considered loyal to Hitler's legacy in the sense that, by the end of the war, Hitler expressed admiration for 'the stronger Eastern nations'. See Nuremberg Documents: Speer 026.

55. For example, see *The Alternative*, pp. 217ff. C. F. Bardèche's *Nuremberg* and *Nuremberg II*; and Degrelle's *Letter to the Pope on his Visit to Auschwitz*, IHR, Torrance, CA, 1987.

56. For an example of the claim that Nazism (though not Italian Fascism) was a form of proto-ecologism, see A. Bramwell, *Ecology in the Twentieth Century*, Yale University Press, London, 1989. The anti-Fascist magazine *Searchlight* (June 1989, p. 4) claimed that Bramwell, who has held academic posts, is associated with neo-Fascists.

57. On Evola, see R. Griffin, 'Revolt against the Modern World', *Literature and History*, XI, Spring 1985, pp. 101–123, and F. Ferraresi, 'Julius Evola: Tradition, Reaction, and the Radical Right', *European Journal of Sociology*, No. 28, 1987, pp. 107–51.

58. Among the key sources are: *Gli uomini e le rovine*, Volpe, Rome, 1951; and *Il Fascismo visto da Destra*, Volpe, Rome, 1964. Much of Evola's work has been translated into French, but little is available in English.

59. *Masques et visages du spiritualisme contemporain*, Editions de l'Homme, Montreal, 1972, p. 307.

60. Rauti re-entered the MSI in 1969 and subsequently became an advocate of the position that Fascism was not right-wing.

61. For an introduction to this group see R. Woods, 'The Radical Right', in Eatwell and O'Sullivan, *The Nature of the Right*, cit., pp. 124–145.

62. See, for example, Jünger's *The Storm of Steel*, Chatto and Windus, London, 1929 (German ed. 1920), or Spengler's *The Decline of the West*, Allen and Unwin, London, 1926 (German ed., 1918).

63. For example, A. Mohler in *Die Konservative Revolution in Deutschland*, Wissenschaftlich Buchgesellschaft, Darmstadt, 1972. Mohler's work is viewed highly favourably by various neo-Fascist groups. See, for instance, the review of his book *Der Nasenring* (1989) by Adolf von Thadden in *Nation Europa*, July 1989, pp. 60–62; Mohler's article on nominalism in *Nouvelle Ecole*, No. 33, June 1979, pp. 13–21; and some of his works published by Edizioni Settimo Sigillo appear in MSI bookshop lists.

64. See the chapter by Douglas Johnson in this volume.

65. Copernic, Paris, 1976, p. 72.

66. For example, see his 'Sur les fondements spirituels et structuraux de l'unité européenne', *Défense de l'occident*, July-August, 1979, pp. 17–28.

67. Some of these themes can be found in J. Cau, *Discours sur la décadence*, Copernic, Paris, 1977, esp. p. 87.

68. See the editorial by Louis Pauwels in *Figaro Magazine*, 7 July 1979, p. 8.

69. See the cover and editorial of *Eléments*, Sept. 1993. For a general critical review of French

revisionism see Ph. Vidolier, 'A peine masqués, s'avancent les falsificateurs du passé', *Le Monde Diplomatique*, January 1994, pp. 16–17.

70. A. Harris and P. Sédouy, *Qui n'est pas de droite?*, Seuil, Paris, 1977, p. 17.

71. For instance, see *Minute La France*, 16–22 August 1992, or *National Hebdo*, 24 August 1992, both of which portrayed the FN's fight against the Maastricht Treaty as part of the battle against immigration. It is important to note that, among periodicals which support the Front, several are not controlled by the party, and these frequently exhibit clear anti-Semitic themes. However, since Le Pen's 'detail' reference to the Holocaust, the national party leadership has clearly tried to distance it from Holocaust denial views. For example, at its 1992 *Bleu-Blanc-Rouge* festival, book-sellers had to sign a declaration that they would not offer books which could fall foul of the Fabius-Gayssot law (making the denial of the Holocaust a criminal offence), and FN stewards checked what was on sale. Information in Pierre Guillaume-La Vieille Taupe circular, 12 Nov. 1992.

72. J. Golub and R. Cohen, *What Do the British Know about the Holocaust?*, AJC, New York, 1993, pp. 27–8; D. A. Jodice, *United Germany and Jewish Concerns*, AJC, New York, 1991, p. 17.

73. For a more sophisticated attempt to use psychology to explain anti-Semitism see M. Billig, 'The Extreme Right: Continuities in Anti-Semitic Conspiracy Theory', in Eatwell and O'Sullivan, *The Nature of the Right*, cit., pp. 146–166.

74. For example, note the loss of support among intellectuals for the German socialist party (SPD). The playwright Botho Strauss offers a particularly good example of someone apparently converted to a synthesis of left and right views, including the defence of national traditions and authority. See his attack on political correctness in *Der Spiegel*, 18 April 1994, pp. 168–170. Ignis Bubis, Chairman of the Jewish Central Council in Germany, held that Strauss was a phenomenon of 'intellectual right-wing radicalism' which had helped the climate for growing neo-Fascist violence.

The author would like to thank the British Academy for grants which made it possible to study various aspects of neo-Fascist ideology.

Chapter 18

MILITANT NEO-NAZISM IN THE FEDERAL REPUBLIC OF GERMANY IN THE 1990s

Christopher T. Husbands

The contribution on militant neo-Nazism in the Federal Republic of Germany in the first edition of this volume[1] discussed the background and characteristics of a group of individuals who were a tiny, ostracised and marginal fragment of the total German social structure and were of course confined to what, since German unification, have come to be called the 'old regions'. At the end of the 1980s the number to be counted as militant neo-Nazis, defined following the usage being employed here, was (by official count, at least) no more than 1,500 individuals and may even have been falling, perhaps because of the undoubted increase in membership of electorally oriented extreme right groups such as the German People s Union [*Deutsche Volksunion*, DVU] and The Republicans [*Die Republikaner*, REP]. The focus in the earlier contribution was on fringe groups who were under the active surveillance of the Federal Office for the Protection of the Constitution [*Bundesamt für Verfassungsschutz*, BfV] – those associated with the notorious Hitler celebrant, Michael Kühnen, for example, or the Free German Workers Party [*Freiheitliche Deutsche Arbeiterpartei*, FAP], or the Nationalist Front [*Nationalistische Front*, NF].

For the reprise volume five years later, the situation is rather different. Most noticeably, but far from exclusively in the 'new regions', there has been an apparent epidemic of violently xenophobic, diffusely organised neo-Nazism directed particularly against foreigners and asylum-seekers and coming especially from sections of the alienated young, especially young men. Well-orchestrated but localised physical attacks by large groups of neo-Nazi youths, some of them skinheads, propelled the Federal Republic of Germany into the international headlines, with uneasy parallels sometimes being drawn between what was happening there to foreigners in the 1990s and what had happened to Jews in the 1930s. Some of these events had their provenance in sociopathological features of the society of the former German Democratic Republic (GDR). However, their extent was more general, as militant neo-Nazis in the old regions – since the early 1980s having been successfully kept within strict bounds by the efficiency of the German state in confronting any threat that they posed – were now encouraged to increase their xenophobic activities, particularly against immigrants (often Turkish ones) and also asylum-seekers.

This chapter considers militant neo-Nazism in the contemporary Federal Republic, examining the following topics:

(a) numbers of groups and individuals;
(b) the extent of neo-Nazi criminality, especially that motivated by xenophobia;
(c) militant neo-Nazism and the German state, including the use of proscriptions against particular organisations;
(d) types of neo-Nazi militance and characteristics of those engaging in it;
(e) theories to explain the growth of militant neo-Nazism during the 1990s; and
(f) in conclusion, scenarios for the future development of militant neo-Nazism.

In contrast with the 1980s, slightly less emphasis needs placing in the present climate upon the actual organisations composing the militant neo-Nazi scene, or upon ideological subtleties that distinguish between particular strains of neo-Nazism. As described later in the chapter, several of the more significant organisations have been proscribed in recent years, and debates about the role of Strasserism,[2] which was an important theme in any description of militant neo-Nazism in the 1980s, have been superseded by the predominating emergence of a crude and often violent xenophobia that makes little claim to ideological or political sophistication. Instead, it is now the extent and nature of the activities in which such groups and those more loosely attached to them engage that go towards establishing the essence of the contemporary movement; this means not only crimes of violence committed and other infractions of public order but the extension of their activities into new domains, such as music (e.g. the followings generated for neo-Nazi skinhead bands), racist and xenophobic computer games, and even electronic networking.

The extent of militant neo-Nazi activism

The marginalised militant neo-Nazi scene of the 1980s in the Federal Republic was transformed after the opening of the Berlin Wall and the abolition of the inner-German frontier in November 1989 and by the unification of October 1990. The centre of gravity of militant neo-Nazism moved eastward, as events in the former GDR revealed the extent to which there was a potential for outbursts that combined xenophobic aggression with neo-Nazi symbolism. What especially distinguished these occurrences from the racist attacks that had long been a feature of the old Federal Republic was their organised scale, their frequent insouciance towards the possibility of intervention by state authorities, the numbers of perpetrators often involved in individual incidents, and the recklessness of their defiance of purportedly constituted authority.

Before the collapse of the GDR regime, militant neo-Nazism in the former Federal Republic had faced a hiatus. The BfV's 1989 report had said that there were twenty-three neo-Nazi groups, with a total of 1,500 members, compared with twenty- three and 1,900 respectively in 1988. This membership number was based upon 1,100 individuals who were members (including some with multiple memberships), and an additional 200 persons classified as neo-Nazis who were not members of any organisation. There were reported to be about 250 neo-Nazi skinheads. 'The Movement', identified in earlier reports from the BfV, continued to be split into two fiercely opposed wings. The FAP had become unambiguously the instrument of one of its wings, having almost everywhere excluded Kühnen's supporters. However, having become more exclusive, it thereupon lost members. Kühnen's supporters established a number of new local groupings in various places in the aftermath of the proscription in March 1989 of his National Assembly [*Nationale Sammlung*, NS]. In May 1989 the German Alternative [*Deutsche Alternative*, DA] had been established in Bremen.[3] A year later, in July 1990, a further break-away group from the FAP, the National Offensive [*Nationale Offensive*, NO], was set up. The collapse of the inner-German frontier led to attempts by Kühnen and other neo-Nazis, as well as by members of the more conventional extreme right, to woo GDR citizens to their cause. On 25 April 1991 Kühnen died an AIDS-related illness.

The situation concerning groups and activists reported by the BfV for the four years from 1990 to 1993 is summarised in Table 18.1. The number of formally structured militant neo-Nazi groups varied between twenty-seven and thirty-three over these years; membership rose to 2,100 in 1991, before settling back to 1,500 in 1993. However, reflecting the changed situation of the 1990s, other right-wing extremist groupings, less formally structured and less purely committed to a neo-Nazi ideology but tending to be more straightforwardly aggressively xenophobic, displayed a different trajectory. Their number remained relatively stable around an average of thirty-eight but their membership significantly increased, by more than 40 per cent between 1990 and 1993, so that more than 4,000 individuals now identified with these groups. Finally, since separate counting was conducted from 1991, there were in 1993 an estimated further 5,600 militant right-wingers, including right-wing skinheads. In addition, the BfV estimated a further 950 neo-Nazi individuals in 1993 who were not members of any group.

Table 18.1 Numbers of militant neo-Nazi groups and activists in the Federal Republic of Germany (old and new regions), 1990–93

	1990	1991	1992	1993
Neo-Nazi groups:				
Number of members	1400	2100	1400	1500
Number of groups	27	30	33	27
Other right-wing extremist groupings:				
Number of members	2900	3950	4000	4100
Number of groups	34	38	41	38
Militant right-wing extremists, especially right-wing skinheads	–[a]	4200	6400	5600
Number of groups	–	–	–	4

Sources: *Verfassungsschutz* reports for 1992 and 1993.

[a] Indicates not available separately

Behind many of these figures is the growth of neo-Nazi activities in the former GDR, although there has been some controversy, as shall be seen, about how far changes after the 1980s are a new-regions phenomenon. The growth of neo-Nazi sentiment in the former GDR (as elsewhere in the former Eastern Bloc) was initially greeted with some surprise by many commentators. Once it became clear that there was indeed a burgeoning neo-Nazi scene in the new regions, mainstream commentary on this performed almost a *volte-face* and interpretations inclined to the purported inevitability of such a development. This may be an exaggeration but, as frequently observed by those writing about neo-Nazism in the new regions, the GDR was not immune from neo-Nazi phenomena, even in its prime. From the early 1980s some disaffected youths, especially working-class males, were attracted to neo-Nazi activities and were often loosely organised around support for certain football clubs. Related court cases were being reported from the late 1980s, and criminologists and students of youth culture in the former GDR were systematically researching the phenomenon.[4] A number of surveys into extreme right sentiments among sections of youth were conducted in the GDR period, especially by the subsequently disbanded Central Institute for Youth Research [*Zentralinstitut für Jugendforschung*, ZIJ], once based in Leipzig.[5]

It is now clear that, even during the 1980s, there were links between neo-Nazis in the west and those in the east. Indeed, several of those purportedly political prisoners who were liberated for cash from GDR gaols by the Federal Government and brought to the west were in fact neo-Nazis, some of whom resumed their activities in the west and were particularly useful as link-persons between west and east, as the old GDR regime was collapsing.[6] Thus, despite attempts by apologists for the former GDR to suggest that the recent neo-Nazism in the new regions was a western import, it is more plausible to argue that it has become a largely self-generated phenomenon with its own character – less exclusive, more anarchistic, more violent, less conventionally ideological, more single-mindedly xenophobic, and indeed more widely supported – than in the west. Indeed, because of the breadth of support, militant neo-Nazism has in some places – such as certain housing estates of Dresden (Saxony), and of Cottbus and Frankfurt an der Oder (both in Brandenburg)[7] – been able to operate with a clear territorial base. Thus, although the contacts between west and east arranged by such people as Kühnen perhaps had some precipitating effect, the GDR regime itself had a number of features that encouraged neo-Nazism among those who became socially alienated. Its authoritarian character, its own particular celebration of the leadership principle, its intolerance of diversity, its ghettoising treatment of its foreign-worker population,[8] its aggressive nationalism in (for example) sport – these characteristics produced a population in which certain marginal groups were attracted to extreme right options when conventional social controls were removed by the collapse of the regime and the consequent Gadarene rush to unification.

A major issue in the early official commentary on neo-Nazis in the GDR had revolved around the question of numbers.[9] At the end of 1990 the General Regional Crime Office [*Gemeinsames Landeskriminalamt*, GLKA] in Berlin had talked of 1,500 neo-Nazis known to the police.[10] This was later increased to 2,000. In September 1991 the BfV was unable to confirm or deny this figure.[11] Later, however, in December 1991, the BfV estimated that the number of 'militant right-wing extremists' (apparently to be understood as those active in the extreme right scene) was at least 4,500 in the whole of Germany,[12] equating reasonably closely with the estimate of the number of activist skinheads. This meant that there were considered to be perhaps twice as many such individuals in the new regions, despite their having only a quarter of the old regions' population. Others have argued that the *potential* for extreme right sympathy, especially concentrated among the young, was in any case much more substantial there, perhaps amounting to 50,000 individuals. One study conducted in the new regions in 1992 among young people aged fourteen to twenty-five years reported that a third of job trainees and a quarter of school pupils held the opinion that 'we should keep pure what is German and prevent interbreeding of different peoples'. Fifty-four per cent of respondents were reported as having a negative attitude to foreigners. Twenty-four per cent of male trainees agreed that 'the Jews are our misfortune'; in December 1990, in an earlier study, the figure had been 7 per cent.[13]

Criminality and militant neo-Nazism

Criminality, especially xenophobic violence, is the feature of militant neo-Nazism that has attracted the most publicity, as well as the most concern, although in recent years the authorities have been monitoring more scrupulously other aspects of extreme right criminality. The BfV's report for 1991, the first comprehensively to cover all sixteen regions, noted sharp increases in violence against foreigners, even in comparison with 1990. Overall, the number of reported individual outrages attributable to the extreme right increased by more than 400 per cent, from 270 in 1990 to 1,483 in 1991.[14] In 1992 the number was 2,584, a 74 per cent increase since the previous year and a twenty-two-fold increase over ten years.[15] Of the 2,283 acts of violence against foreigners in 1992, 681 were attacks by arson or use of explosives against asylum-seekers or their possessions.[16] Arson attacks on asylum-seekers' hostels occurred at a similar per-capita rate of population in east and west Germany; 116 such cases were registered from the east. However, 31 per cent of all extreme right acts of violence occurred in the east, a clear disproportion in per- capita terms. Many such acts were to be laid at the door of the country's 4,200 skinheads, of whom 3,000 were from the new regions.

It would be wrong to suggest that the locus of militant neo-Nazism in the contemporary Federal Republic has moved wholly from the old to the new regions. An increase in racial attacks since February 1991 (especially against asylum-seekers' hostels) has been the most obvious example of militant neo-Nazi influence in both zones of Germany. Still, although many such attacks have undoubtedly been perpetrated by individuals who would not immediately identify with the extremes of militant neo-Nazism, it seems that a higher proportion of perpetrators in the east do self-consciously see themselves as being a part of this phenomenon.

The picture of the contemporary criminality associated with the extreme right may be explored more thoroughly in Table 18.2, which covers the two most recent years for which there are full, publicly available data.[17] Offences have been classified according to whether they involve overt violence against persons or property and whether or not a xenophobic motivation has been imputed. Although two years data do not permit the inference of trends, there are certain patterns, which continued into

1994. The number of death-related offences increased in 1993 but the number of arson attacks was clearly lower, by more than 55 per cent; this reflected the tougher attitude towards prosecution and sentencing against arsonists, including a more frequent readiness to resort to attempted murder charges in arson attacks on inhabited premises, a development to which we shall return in a later section. Attacks against the person in 1993, when directed against foreigners, saw an increase of 24 per cent compared with 1992. However, xenophobically motivated property damage declined by nearly 50 per cent, again perhaps a reflection of prosecutory practice. Overall, xenophobic acts of violence were considerably less in 1993 than in 1992.[18] This pattern of decline continued in 1994, in the first eleven months of which there were 1,233 recorded acts of extreme right-wing violence, a decline of 35 per cent over the corresponding period of 1993.[19]

The picture presented in Table 18.2 by the data on offences other than those involving violence is rather different. Certain types of offence showed dramatic increases between 1992 and 1993; however, given their more peripheral nature in comparison with crimes of violence, these increases seem likely to reflect not only more

Table 18.2 Summary of recorded offences presumed or proven to have been committed by right-wing extremist perpetrators in the Federal Republic of Germany, 1992–93

	1992			1993		
	Xeno-phobic	Other	Total	Xeno-phobic	Other	Total
Offences involving violence						
Crimes resulting in death	6	10	16	20	3	23
Explosions	11	3	14	3	0	3
Arson attacks	656	43	699	284	27	311
Breach of the peace	–[a]	–	–	36	57	93
Attacks against the person	585	173	758	727	172	899
Property damage with extreme violence	1019	133	1152	539	364	903
Subtotals:	2277	362	2639	1609	623	2232
Other offences						
Threatening behaviour	1191	163	1354	1414	285	1699
Graffiti-writing, fly-posting, giving Hitler salute	1211	1914	3125	1437	2437	3874
Others (e.g., incitement, insulting or disparaging behaviour)	329	237	566	2261	495	2756
Subtotals:	2731	2314	5045	5112	3217	8329
Grand totals:	5008	2676	7684	6721	3840	10,561

Source: *Verfassungsschutz* report for 1993.
[a] Indicates not available separately

assiduous recording practices but also perhaps a displacement from more to less serious offences in response to heightened prosecutory deterrence against crimes of violence. This latter change, if true, may reflect favourably on vigorous police responses to extreme right outrages but should not obscure the fact that even 'less serious' xenophobically motivated crime can be highly stressful to its victims. Recorded offences of threatening behaviour increased by 25 per cent, though the increase for those xenophobically classified was rather less. Recorded propaganda-directed offences increased by 24 per cent from 1992 to 1993, with a similar lesser increase in those showing hostility to foreigners. The residual category of non-violent offences shows a huge year-on-year increase, and it would be difficult to deny that greater recording enthusiasm by the authorities was doubtless responsible for much of this change. An increase of nearly 600 per cent in xenophobic offences so classified is difficult to explain in terms of objective circumstances.

As mentioned already, there has been some debate about whether militant neo-Nazi trends since 1990 have been the features particularly or exclusively of the former GDR or rather a country-wide phenomenon. Tables 18.3 and 18.4 enable us to make some observations on this matter. Table 18.3 examines extreme right crimes of violence standardised against population size in each case, using available data from 1992. These data include all offences of violence, whether or not xenophobically motivated, and so may insufficiently control for the availability of the victim population. In the case of all but one of the types of crime listed in Table 18.3, the new regions show a significantly higher per-capita rate; the exception is explosions, for which the case-base is very small. Attacks against the person are particularly higher in the new regions compared with the old ones. An attempt in Table 18.4 is made to control upon the availability of a victim population by examining 1993 data on all 6,721 recorded extreme right offences of a xenophobic character, whether or not involving violence; it must be remembered that these data are those showing the dramatic, mostly

Table 18.3 Offences of violence presumed or proven to have been committed by right-wing extremist perpetrators in old and new regions of the Federal Republic of Germany, 1992

	Old regions		New regions[a]		Whole country	
	Number	Per 1,000,000 non-foreign inhabitants	Number	Per 1,000,000 non-foreign inhabitants	Number	Per 1,000,000 non-foreign inhabitants
Crimes resulting in death	8	0.14	7	0.40	15	0.20
Explosions	13	0.23	1	0.06	14	0.19
Arson attacks	487	8.55	221	12.73	708	9.53
Attacks against the person	418	7.34	307	17.69	725	9.76
Property damage with extreme violence	793	13.92	329	18.96	1122	15.10

Source: Calculated from data on numbers of offences in *Verfassungsschutz* report for 1992.

[a] Though not specified, this apparently includes all Berlin.

Table 18.4 Recorded offences of xenophobic character with presumed or proven extreme right-wing motivation in the old and new regions of the Federal Republic of Germany, 1993

| | Old regions | New regions: | | Whole country |
		Including Berlin	Excluding Berlin	
Number of offences	5831	890	540	6721
Per 1,000,000 non-foreign inhabitants	102.4	51.3	37.8	90.4
Per 100,000 foreigners	101.9	164.0	305.9	107.4
Per 1,000,000 non-foreign inhabitants and 100,000 foreigners	1.8	9.4	21.4	1.4

Source: Calculated from data on numbers of offences and demographic information in *Verfassungsschutz* report for 1993.

recording-related, increases between 1992 and 1993 discussed above. This analysis standardises separately and then together for the non-foreign population (as the 'pool' of potential perpetrators) and also the foreign population (as the 'pool' of potential victims). Controlling merely on non-foreign population seems to imply that the former GDR has a lesser susceptibility to xenophobic outrages; however, given that the old regions have more than 9 per cent of their resident population classified as foreign, whilst the new regions have 3 per cent including all Berlin, and merely 1.2 per cent excluding Berlin, this is not the entire story. Controlling in Table 18.4 on the presence of foreigners already means that the new regions are more inclined to xenophobic activity. Controlling on both non-foreign population and foreign population shows that the new regions are perhaps between five and ten times more likely to be the location for any extreme right xenophobic action. Although control on size of victim population may be particularly stringent in this circumstance, the case seems unexceptionable that there has been a hugely disproportionate amount of xenophobic crime in the new regions, *pace* the fact that in absolute numerical terms violence in the old region of North Rhine-Westphalia far exceeds that in any other region, old or new.[20]

Certain events have become notorious in the development of neo-Nazism in the new regions. Thus, in and around Dresden there was an internationally publicised murder at the end of March 1991 of a Mozambican immigrant who was thrown from a moving tram, and then the shooting in May 1991 of the self-styled neo-Nazi leader and Kühnen associate, Rainer Sonntag, after he had announced his intention of getting rid of a local brothel. The two accused of the crime, coming from the red-light underworld of Mannheim (Baden-Württemberg), were later acquitted after it was decided that they had acted in self-defence. The more jaundiced interpretation of Sonntag's actions was that, far from wanting to cleanse Dresden of brothels, he was attempting to muscle in on this activity. In April 1992 about a thousand neo-Nazis from the whole of Germany demonstrated in Dresden against the outcome of the trial, shouting general slogans against 'murderers, foreigners and pimps'.

In September 1991 in Hoyerswerda, a small town in Saxony, a large assembly of neo-Nazis, including many skinheads but vocally supported by numerous local inhabitants, attacked a hostel for asylum-seekers that housed Romanian gypsies – forcing the authorities to evacuate them from the town and thus making it *ausländerfrei* (free from foreigners), a reprise for contemporary circumstances of the earlier *judenfrei* (free from Jews). An even more serious replication later occurred in Rostock (Mecklenburg-Vorpommern) over a number of nights from 22 to 28 August 1992, as up to 1,200 neo-Nazis and numerous police, including specially trained units subsequently brought in to assist, fought each other around the central reception building for asylum-seekers. Numbers of participants increased over this period due to media publicity and up to 3,000 bystanders offered vocal, if passive, support to the attackers, who succeeded in burning down part of the complex that housed Vietnamese immigrant workers, as well as a temporarily present team of reporters. There was much criticism of the behaviour of certain senior police officials in this matter but, albeit tardily, state authorities did respond and at the end of 1992 over 400 investigations were still pending and some custodial sentences had been handed down but none was for longer than eight months; only in March 1993 was a sentence as long as two-and-a-half years imposed for a conviction for grievous bodily harm, breach of the peace and weapons offences arising from the incidents at Rostock.

Still, some of the perhaps most notorious incidents by neo-Nazi militants actually occurred in the old regions. On 22 March 1992 two drunken neo-Nazi skinheads in Buxtehude (Lower Saxony) beat up and killed a man who had been critical of Adolf Hitler and the Third Reich. The culprits were later sentenced to imprisonment for eight and a half years and six years respectively for homicide. On 23 November 1992 in Mölln (Schleswig-Holstein) arson attacks on two houses inhabited by Turkish families resulted in the deaths of a fifty-one-year-old Turkish women, her ten-year-old granddaughter, and her fourteen-year-old niece. Several other people received injuries in the attack, which had been announced to the local police and fire services by telephone with a 'Heil Hitler' salutation. Two skinheads, one nineteen and the other twenty-five years old, were subsequently convicted of these murders, the latter having been identified as the leader of a group of young men in their early twenties who had been involved in a number of xenophobic attacks in Schleswig-Holstein and Mecklenburg-Vorpommern in September 1992. Later, on 29 May 1993 two women and three children were killed, and seven others were injured, in an arson attack on a Turkish-occupied multi-family dwelling in Solingen (North Rhine-Westphalia); four young neo-Nazis apprehended for this attack were still being tried at the end of 1994. Another phenomenon of the 1990s has been the increased significance of anti-Semitic crimes, as opposed to xenophobic ones, by militant neo-Nazis. In 1993 there were seventy-two acts of violence by the extreme right with presumed anti-Semitic motivation. Some were attacks on the person, but a common crime was the desecration of Jewish cemeteries. For example, the oldest Jewish cemetery in Worms (Rhineland-Palatinate) was twice vandalised in 1993.[21] Perhaps most seriously, a synagogue in Lübeck (Schleswig-Holstein) was fire-bombed on the night of 24–25 March 1994, being about to open for the first time since 1938; eight people living in flats above it managed to escape unhurt. At the end of 1994 four young men were being tried on five charges of attempted murder in connection with the attack.

Militant neo-nazism and the German State

The German state has been subjected to much criticism over alleged half-heartedness in its pursuit of neo-Nazi militants and, although it has been keen to scotch any reputation for complacency, it has to be said that overall the pattern of response is a mixed one, differing between levels and institutions of government and between different types of constituted authority.

National and regional governments and politicians

In April 1991 the then Free Democratic Party [*Freie Demokratische Partei*, FDP] Foreign Minister, Hans-Dietrich Genscher, expressed his concern about rising xenophobia and hostility to foreigners in the new regions, moved particularly by his anxiety for his country s international reputation. Chancellor Kohl, however, was rather more belated in his condemnation, speaking out unequivocally only in June 1991. The former Christian Democratic Union [*Christlich-Demokratische Union*, CDU] Minister of the Interior, Wolfgang Schäuble, expressed his disquiet most publicly in August 1991, when launching the BfV annual report for 1990.[22]

In fact, it has been suggested that the question of how to handle neo-Nazi outrages became an implicit pawn in a bitter inter-party debate about how the Federal Republic should control the arrival of asylum-seekers. The most extreme form of accusations of official laxity was that the events were responded to in such a way as to sharpen the case in favour of a restriction upon the right to political asylum originally guaranteed by Article 16, Paragraph 2, of the Basic Law. Whilst it is certainly hard unequivocally to prove that the Federal Government was slow to act effectively against the mounting tide of violence in order to panic the opposition Social Democratic Party of Germany [*Sozialdemokratische Partei Deutschlands*, SPD] and the governing-partner FDP into giving their approval to such an amendment, it was in August 1992 that the SPD, after officially opposing attempts to restrict the right of asylum, bowed to internal and external pressure and executed a *volte-face* on the issue. Also, although on 13 August 1992 the then Minister of the Interior, Rudolf Seiters, had strongly condemned the growing numbers of attacks on foreigners when presenting to the press the BfV s annual report for 1991, there were suggestions that he failed to act upon received intelligence anticipating the organised attacks against the asylum-seekers' hostel in Rostock less than two weeks later. SPD sources accused both him and his opposite number in the region of Mecklenburg-Vorpommern, Lothar Kupfer, of being less than total in their condemnations of the Rostock events and of allowing the police to use tactics that encouraged the rioters.[23] On the other hand, the BfV, which had earlier been scheduled for a partial run-down in the light of the changing international situation after the end of the Cold War, was instead kept at full complement to monitor the extreme right threat; a new group to counter the extreme right was formed in the Federal Crime Office [*Bundeskriminalamt*, BKA]; and a special service for the reporting of xenophobic violence was also established.

The German authorities were initially hesitant about the use of proscription against neo-Nazi organisations, although of course this weapon had been used on several occasions in the past.[24] However, resort to conspiracy explanations of such hesitancy is not called for; one can fairly accept that pragmatism more than complicity accounted for the reluctance to use proscription, since experience had shown that the memberships of banned organisations often mutate into smaller, more diffuse and localised groupings that are more difficult to monitor than the original banned organisation. However, particularly in the light of the atrocity at Mölln on 23 November 1992, the German government was under considerable domestic and international pressure to be more assertive in its response. It resorted heavily to proscription, largely it must be said as a *faute de mieux* policy. Three neo-Nazi groups were banned by the Federal Minister of the Interior:

(a) on 27 November the Nationalist Front [NF]: founded in November 1985, led by Meinolf Schönborn (born in 1956), with 130 to 150 members, and originally distinctive for its commitment to Strasserism;

(b) in 10 December the German Alternative [DA]: founded at the instigation of Michael Kühnen in May 1989, led by Frank Hübner (born in 1967), and particularly active in the new regions, especially the Cottbus area of Brandenburg;

(c) on 22 December the National Offensive [NO]: founded in July 1990 as a break-away grouping from the FAP, led by Michael Swierczek (born in 1962), with about 140 members, and especially active in Saxony.

All three appealed unsuccessfully against this ban, citing their purported status as political parties. However, Hübner has evaded the proscription by standing in the Brandenburg local elections of December 1993 as candidate for mayor of Cottbus for the REP-break-away German League for People and Homeland [*Deutsche Liga für Volk und Heimat*, DLVH], receiving 3 per cent of votes.[25] On 21 December 1992 the Ministry of the Interior of Lower Saxony proscribed in this region the German Comradeship Association [*Deutscher Kameradschaftsbund*, DKB], a small group with about thirty members, founded in November 1991 in Wilhelmshaven, and particularly virulent and xenophobic. On 9 December 1992 the Federal Government used Article 18 of the Basic Law to petition the Federal Constitutional Court [*Bundesverfassungsgericht*, BVG] for the removal of certain civil rights from two neo-Nazis, Thomas Dienel (born in 1962) and Heinz Reisz (born in 1939).

This proscriptive approach continued in 1993, both nationally and regionally. In September 1993 the Federal Government and the Bundesrat petitioned the BVG for the proscription of the FAP, a procedure differing from proscription by the Ministry of the Interior under the law on associations and thought necessary in this case because of the FAPs presumed status as a political party; anticipating a ban, it had already cut back on its production of written material. In August 1993 the Hamburg Senate petitioned for the outlawing of the neo-Nazi National List [*Nationale Liste*, NL], also considered a political party. This had been founded in Hamburg in March 1989 by two Kühnen followers, Thomas Wulff (born in 1964) and Christian Worch (born in 1957); it was originally intended to be confined to Hamburg, although both men, especially Worch, have been active on the national level, the latter having been a major organiser of a Hess memorial rally at Fulda in August 1993. In a judgement by the

BVG published on 24 February 1995, it rejected the respective motions against the FAP and the NL, stating that neither satisfied its criteria to be regarded as a genuine political party. This pushed the initiative back to the Ministry of the Interior and the Hamburg authorities, who immediately proscribed these groups using their powers under the law on associations. The FAP leader, Friedhelm Busse (born in 1928), had earlier been sentenced to twenty months' imprisonment, suspended for three years, for his use of the FAP to reconstitute the outlawed Action Front of National Socialists/ National Activists [*Aktionsfront Nationaler Sozialisten/Nationale Aktivisten,* ANS/NA], which had been banned by the Federal Government in 1983, and in February 1995 the former FAP general secretary, Jürgen Mosler (born in 1955), was given two years' probation for the same offence, his sentence reduced because of his purported willingness to reveal how the FAP had been infiltrated by former ANS/NA members.

In 1993 three groupings were also banned regionally by the respective interior ministers of Bavaria, Baden-Württemberg and North Rhine-Westphalia:

    (a) on 11 June the National Bloc [*Nationaler Block*, NB]: founded in July 1991 by another supporter of Kühnen and active only in Bavaria;

    (b) on 14 July the Homeland-Loving Union of Germany [*Heimattreue Vereinigung Deutschlands*, HVD]: founded in December 1988 and, with about eighty members, the largest neo-Nazi organisation in Baden-Württemberg;

    (c) on 2 September the Friendship Circle for Freedom for Germany [*Freundeskreis Freiheit für Deutschland*, FFD]: emerged in June 1989 but identical with the Friendship Circle for Independent Intelligence [*Freundeskreis Unabhängige Nachrichten*, FUN] founded in 1969.[26]

More recently, on 10 November 1994, the Federal Minister of the Interior, Manfred Kanther, announced the banning of the youth organisation, Viking Youth [*Wiking-Jugend*, W-J], the largest neo-Nazi youth movement in Germany with 400 members and originally founded in 1952 from, among other groupings, the youth wing of the banned Socialist Reich Party [*Sozialistische Reichspartei*, SRP].[27]

The police

One might be more sanguine about the complete commitment of the German state to fighting neo-Nazi militance if it were conspicuous that all sections were actively opposed to it. However, there have been disturbing suggestions of covert sympathy in some sections, especially the police, and there have been accusations of 'trimming sail', even at the highest levels, in approaches to actual policing against neo-Nazi attacks. These accusations even transcend the suspicions of laxity in the Federal Government's early response that were mentioned above. The accusations occurred particularly in the early years after unification – the background to the Rostock incidents of August 1992 being notorious – but serious examples continue to be reported, especially in the new regions.

In Magdeburg (Saxony-Anhalt) on 12 May 1994 forty or so neo-Nazis attacked five Africans under the eyes of the police and many members of the public. The victims themselves accused the police of encouraging the perpetrators.[28] Forty-nine people were arrested for this crime but all but one were released; the police there were widely criticised for their failure to make prosecutions and to use existing video evidence to assist their enquiry. Recently, three policemen in Gera (Thuringia) were accused of complicity when, in July 1994, they failed to try to establish the culprits concerned after a bus-load of skinheads stopped on their way to the former concentration camp of Buchenwald and threatened and beat up passers-by.[29]

The legitimacy of the police in the eastern regions suffered badly from their association with the previous regime. In addition, they were initially under-equipped and had little sustained experience of handling large-scale riot situations. There were a number of claims that many ordinary police in regions such as Saxony covertly sympathised with much neo-Nazi behaviour, especially against foreigners.[30] Attempts by the Federal Government to improve the training and equipment of the police in the east have necessarily been slow to bear fruit. Moreover, given the findings of innumerable studies in different countries that police officers have a disposition towards authoritarianism, sympathy among some for neo-Nazi actions would not be unexpected.

In any case, the fight against neo-Nazi criminality has met with only indifferent detective success, although this is not always indicative of police laxity. It was admitted in September 1994 that investigation into almost three-quarters of all cases of extreme right criminality in Germany in the first three months of 1994 had been suspended because the perpetrators could not be discovered. Those responsible were undetected in 2,905 of the total of 4,163 cases. In 529 cases there was a conviction, 178 (34 per cent) of these being offences against foreigners.[31]

The courts and prosecuting authorities

In the early years of the neo-Nazi surge there were many suggestions that offences were not being sufficiently seriously prosecuted and that many sentences were inadequate. In the autumn of 1992 there was an extensive discussion as to whether existing laws were adequate and what amendments, if any, were needed. In September 1992 the then Federal Minister of the Interior, Rudolf Seiters, published his Ten-Point Plan against right-wing extremists, which called for the tightening-up of powers of sentencing and detention, more powers to use bugging techniques, and so on.[32] On 20 May 1994 the Bundestag approved measures to counter extreme right violence, which included increased penalties for various crimes (a maximum of five years imprisonment instead of three for assault, for example) and preventive detention without a warrant for up to seven days in certain circumstances.

From early 1993 or so there does seem to have been some modest increase in the severity of sentencing, if only for the more serious crimes. The following examples, though not scientifically sampled, are perhaps reasonably typical. In October 1994 a juvenile court in Weimar (Thuringia) sentenced three of eight youths accused of desecrating a memorial at the former concentration camp at Buchenwald to between six to twenty months' custody, suspended in two cases, after prosecution demands for between ten months' custody suspended and two years' imprisonment.[33] An arson attack on an asylum-seekers hostel in Zwickau (Saxony) by a seventeen-year-old right-wing extremist and his colleagues, accompanied by stone-throwing at the hostel and at the police who had been summoned and by shouting Nazi slogans, produced a fifteen-month sentence for breach of the peace, incitement and displaying the symbols of an unconstitutional organisation. Yet a regional court in Schwerin (Mecklenburg-Vorpommern) sentenced two young men to only two years suspended for attempted murder after an arson attack on accommodation being used by foreigners.[34] Sentences in little-publicised cases do seem appreciably less, despite the gravity of some of the offences, than those in more notorious ones. For example, Michael Peters and Lars Christiansen, who were convicted on 8 December 1993 for the Mölln atrocity a year earlier, received maximum sentences of life imprisonment and ten years respectively, although the latter (aged twenty) was technically a juvenile.[35] None the less, in general there has been some tendency to sharpen charges, say from breach of the peace to attempted murder in the case of arson attacks, and prison sentences for such crimes are often about four years.[36]

However, even in gaol favoured extreme right prisoners often receive the care and attention of extreme right charities, such as the Organisation for the Assistance of National Political Prisoners and Their Dependants [*Hilfsorganisation für nationale politische Gefangene und deren Angehörige*, HNG]; prisoners associated with the FAP have been particularly favoured in this respect. While inside this may mean money, and on release assistance with finding accommodation and work.[37] The HNG was founded in 1979; now led by the neo-Nazi activist Ursula Müller (born in 1933), it has become a focus for a number of older neo-Nazis. As well as attending to the concerns of imprisoned neo-Nazis, it also publishes a professionally produced news letter.[38]

Further types of neo-Nazi militance and characteristics of those engaging in it

Clearly, extreme right criminality is the feature of militant neo-Nazism upon which there is most public attention, partly because of the amorphous manner in which the neo-Nazi scene developed in the new regions. However, it would be wrong to leave the impression that violent xenophobia was the whole story, even if many other activities relate directly or indirectly to this.

The proscriptions since November 1992 have led to a restructuring of the organisational basis of contemporary militant neo-Nazism, involving the actual or attempted formation of new groupings or more informal circles of the former memberships of the banned organisations. Some former members of the DA sought without conspicuous success to reform as the Brandenburg People's Party [*Brandenburgische Volkspartei*, BVP]. More successful was the establishment by the same individuals of a group calling itself the German Nationalists [*Deutsche Nationalisten*, DN]. This was established in Mainz (Rhineland-Palatinate) on 21 July 1993, headed by Michael Petri (born in 1972), formerly head of the DA in Rhineland-Palatinate. It was intended that the DN should participate in elections in order to obviate proscription as a successor organisation of the DA, but a prominent part of its programme is the compulsory repatriation of foreigners. Although not so far banned, the group has attracted the attention of the authorities. For example, on 10 December 1994 a meeting being held in a tavern in Hohenschönhausen, an area of the former East Berlin, was raided by the police. Among the thirty-five participants was Petri, the national leader. Nineteen people were briefly arrested as a grouping of former DA members. Also, the homes of three DN members were searched, leading to the confiscation of propaganda material and weapons.[39]

In 1993 there emerged a group calling itself Direct Action/Central Germany [*Direkte Aktion/Mitteldeutschland*, DA/MD] as a successor to the earlier Support Group of Central German Youth [*Förderwerk Mitteldeutsche Jugend*, FMJ], active particularly in Berlin and Brandenburg.[40] This comprised a group who had been one-time members of the banned NF but, in anticipation of proscription, had left to establish an autonomous group. In January and February 1994 it was the object of police raids.[41] Other groups of longer standing continue to exist. The National Socialist German Workers Party – Overseas Build-up Organisation [*Nationalsozialistische Deutsche Arbeiterpartei – Auslands und Aufbauorganisation*, NSDAP AO] based in Lincoln, Nebraska, in the United States and headed by Gary Rex Lauck (born in 1953), an American citizen, has been active since the early 1980s as a supplier of propaganda to the German neo-Nazi scene, especially his bi-monthly *NS Kampfruf* (*National-Socialist Battle-Cry*); Kühnen himself had reputedly been a member, according to Lauck. The latter is now *persona non grata* in the Federal Republic but this has not seriously affected the distribution of the material that he produces; in fact, as the authorities have increasingly harassed the producers of such material in Germany, the importance of Lauck and other overseas suppliers has increased. In June 1994 the head of the BKA, Hans-Ludwig Zachert, approached the American Federal Bureau of Investigation in a meeting with its representatives in Berlin about prosecution of Lauck but was informed of difficulties under American law of prosecuting for other than criminal *acts*, although the Hamburg State Prosecutor has approached the American authorities about possible prosecution.[42]

Cultural groups such as HNG, mentioned already; those individuals surrounding the Holocaust denier, Thies Christophersen (born in 1918), who fled to Denmark in 1986 to escape prosecution; and Manfred Roeder's (born in 1929) German Citizens Initiative [*Deutsche Bürgerinitiative*, DBI] continue to exist. They are mostly active in producing propaganda material, some of it explicitly anti-Semitic, although Roeder has also associated himself with a so-called German–Russian Community Work – North-east Prussian Support Association [*Deutsch-Russisches Gemeinschaftswerk – Förderverein Nord-Ostpreussen*, DRGW–FNOP], whose stated purpose is to offer material and personal help to ethnic Germans in eastern republics of the former Soviet Union to settle in what was once East Prussia (in Russia).

The trend on the neo-Nazi scene away from organisational structure is seen in the metamorphosis of the once-important New Front Partisan Group [*Gesinnungsgemeinschaft der Neuen Front*, GdNF]. The ideological heir to the Action Front of National Socialists/National Activists [*Aktionsfront Nationaler Sozialisten/Nationale Aktivisten*, ANS/NA], which was banned by the Federal Government in 1983, it was during Kühnen s life-time a real, if amorphous, grouping of his supporters who sought to achieve his national-socialist goals. Since his death it has become little more than a publishing collective, based in The Netherlands, for the publication, *Die Neue Front* (*The New Front*), although on 8 April 1992 Thomas Brehl (born in 1957), a Kühnen loyalist and former ANS/NA leader, was sentenced to a year s imprisonment for having sought through the GdNF to reinstate the banned ANS/NA. During October and November 1994 Christian Worch was charged in Frankfurt am Main with the same offence; he was convicted and sentenced to two years' imprisonment.[43] A further reason for the GdNF s diminished status has been the imprisonment since January 1992 of the Austrian neo-Nazi, Gottfried Küssel (born in 1959), who had been designated by Kühnen as his successor; in September 1993 a Viennese court sentenced Küssel to ten years imprisonment without probation for neo-Nazi activities. He was also well-known to have been a member of the NSDAP–AO since the 1970s.

Many of militant neo-Nazism s current organisational initiatives are elusive and secretive; attempts at public emergence by these small, reclusive, sect-like groups have not infrequently been frustrated by anti-fascist opposition. More impact has been made in other ways. Hitler's birthday (on 23 April) and the anniversary of the death of Rudolf Hess (on 17 August) are notorious for their mobilisation of neo-Nazis of numerous persuasions; the latter is often the commemorative occasion for a single consolidated march under the nose of the authorities. On 17 August 1991 this was held in Bayreuth (Bavaria); on 15 August 1992 it was at Rudolstadt (Thuringia), attended by almost 2,000 domestic and foreign neo-Nazis.[44] A year later, a similar march held in Fulda (Hessen) on 14 August was a particular propaganda coup and attracted considerable attention and publicity, as well as criticism of the authorities for allowing it to take place. The anniversary of the *Kristallnacht* pogrom (on 9 November) also mobilises neo-Nazis; there was a celebratory public march in Halle (Saxony-Anhalt) in 1991, for example; even the Day of German Unity (on 3 October) has been a focus for xenophobic neo-Nazi activity.

Neo-Nazism has attempted to increase its influence by extending itself into aspects of conventional life. Neo-Nazi computer games, for example, have entered circulation and skinhead influence is apparent in certain styles of popular music and culture.[45] Videocassette technology has facilitated the manufacture and distribution of neo-Nazi material; in November 1994, for example, Ewald Bela Althans (born in 1966) went on trial in Munich charged with possession of printed material and videocassettes purveying national-socialist ideology and intended for educational purposes, items that he had produced himself;[46] he was subsequently convicted for these acts of incitement to racial hatred. In fact, it has been thought that technology is increasingly being used by neo-Nazis to overcome recent organisational difficulties and state harassment, by resorting to E-mail, box numbers for computer contact, mobile radios, and so on; the effective policing of the use of such facilities would require considerable resources.[47]

There is, of course, plenty of incidental evidence that those who participate in the more public types of militant neo-Nazism are young and male, a pattern that continues what was seen in the 1980s; as then, this is apparent from pictures of any neo-Nazi public gathering. In the more anarchic parts of the neo-Nazi scene, which are a considerable component of the whole, participants may be as young as their early and middle teens. However, there are subtle differences from the 1980s. Table 18.5 shows some basic social data on those known to have been involved in extreme right acts of

Table 18.5 Some social characteristics of those involved in extreme right offences of violence, 1991–93 (in percentages)[a]

Age (in years)	%	Gender	%	Occupation	%
Less than 18	21	Male	96	School pupils, students, in vocational training	34
18 to 20	44	Female	4	Skilled manual workers	29
21 to 30	31			Unskilled manual workers	11
31 to 40	3			White-collar employees	6
41 or more	1			Military, including those due for call-up	8
				Unemployed	11
				Other occupations	2

Source: *Verfassungsschutz* report for 1993.
[a] Data for age and gender are based upon 763 cases for 1991, 1088 for 1992 and 1397 for 1993. Data on occupation are based upon 494 cases for all three years with available information.

violence from 1991 to 1993. Although this is a particularly violent subset of neo-Nazi activists (small and of unconfirmed representativeness since these are those perpetrators who were detected, and it may even include some from outside the neo-Nazi scene or in other extreme right groupings), it contains some instructive possibilities about the composition of hard-core neo-Nazism. The almost-total male predominance is unsurprising[48] but the age-data are worthy of comment. The median age of these offending activists is less than 19.5 years, which contrasts with the nearly twenty-seven years of those involved in acts of extreme right violence up to 1985.[49] Moreover, it contrasts with the findings on the age of neo-Nazi perpetrators of crimes of violence during an earlier period when there was a neo-Nazi surge, after the December 1959 Cologne synagogue-daubing incident. That incident seemed to mobilise a number of rather older neo-Nazis to emerge 'from the woodwork', many in their thirties who would have experienced significant socialisation during the Hitler years.[50] In the 1990s, on the other hand, the neo-Nazi scene is much more youth-based. Many of those on the fringe, who will not have perpetrated such serious violence, will be even younger. Consistent with this portrayal is the far higher percentage of school pupils, students and those in vocational training than of a comparable group in the early 1980s. Paradoxically, this younger age profile may be one source of longer-term weakness rather than of strength, since youth activists in any movement tend to transitoriness, although their youth does not preclude replacement by their following age-cohort.

Explaining the growth of militant neo-Nazism during the 1990s

There has necessarily been extensive theorisation about the causes of right-wing extremism but much of this, because of a focus on voting behaviour, is of only incidental value in accounting for the far more exclusive and extreme phenomenon of militant neo-Nazism. Thus, the *Modernisierungsverlierer* approach (those losing out from modernisation), variants of which have long been influential in theoretical accounts of extreme right voting in a number of countries including Germany, can be only a very preliminary basis for explaining neo-Nazi militance in the 1990s. Furthermore, the particular subject of interest is not merely what determines how individuals make the transition to neo-Nazism but why in the 1990s a rather larger number (even if still a tiny proportion of the population) have been willing to do so than in the 1980s.

As discussed at greater length elsewhere,[51] despite the plethora of publications in the 1980s on the German extreme right, there was relatively little systematic work on the social psychology of militant neo-Nazis. In the early 1980s Hennig conducted in-depth interviews with a number of young neo-Nazis in the west, from which he was able to construct some elements for a causal model. There was usually a materialist base for their activism, in the sense of a number of economic frustrations consequent upon the state of the economy. However, built upon these not atypical experiences were further personal ones, such as parental problems, difficulties of various sorts at school, with girls, and finally at work, all precipitating the decision to resort to 'political soldiering' and away from a conventional career path; in some cases the male camaraderie and group bonds offered by neo-Nazism were especially attractive.[52] The other major pieces of empirical work with relevance for understanding west German neo-Nazis are those conducted by Heitmeyer and his colleagues, firstly in the mid-1980s with a large survey of 1300 sixteen- and seventeen-year-olds,[53] and then more intensively between 1985 and 1990 with a sample of thirty-one young men between seventeen and twenty-one.[54] However, even though Heitmeyer presents his results less accessibly than those given by Hennig, the former focuses on some of the same factors as determinants. He summarises: 'The research was conducted among young people of whom many found themselves in a difficult position because the basis of their social identity, their professional future, was and remained very threatened.'[55]

This led in some cases to feelings of social exclusion, isolation and inferiority that, when combined with an authoritarian and nationalist disposition, produced an extreme right susceptibility; in other examples, feelings of higher self-worth were associated with this susceptibility. However, in general, rejection of extreme right positions depends on satisfying relationships at work, in the family, and in the immediate social milieu.

The application of such perspectives to militant neo-Nazism in the 1990s, since it took off with such ferocity in the new regions, presents special difficulties, however, even if Heitmeyer himself has sought to present a model appropriate to the new circumstances, whilst recognising the complexities of doing this.[56] For the western situation Heitmeyer, consistent with his 1980s perspective, emphasises feelings of estrangement and isolation, especially when confronted by difficulties and status anxieties from the world of work. For the east he especially notes the consequences of having grown up within an authoritarian state, with the psychological problems of adjustment to its removal, particularly when accompanied by economic uncertainty from 'enforced modernisation', which loosened some bonds and permitted a brutalisation of social perspectives.

Actually applying such perspectives to the known facts about neo-Nazism in the 1990s brings home the difficulty of separating confirmed knowledge from theoretical speculation. Even so, the distinctiveness of the phenomenon in the new regions is undeniable and, despite the many organisational and personnel continuities from the neo-Nazism of the 1980s, the overall character of the 1990s' version has been dramatically affected by events in the east. Those features of GDR society that were mentioned already are a crucial context; but what marks neo-Nazi activity in the east is its banalisation of violence in the youth culture of the new state.[57] Economic uncertainty as the realities of unification were revealed, especially in the light of the large-scale factory closures of the early years, fed a hitherto barely concealed xenophobia, which assumed an especially resentful form because of the forced imposition upon the new regions of their 'fair share' of the country's arriving asylum-seekers.[58] This was a phenomenon for which the new regions were particularly ill-prepared psychologically, given what had been the GDR state's own treatment of foreign workers in the country. The consequent hostility also spilled over against the east's own small foreign-worker population.

The fact that neo-Nazism in the new regions has been so unidimensional in character, marked largely by its xenophobic violence, has contributed some of the organisational anarchy and diffuseness that have been its obvious feature, and still remains so despite suggestions of recently increased networking. This has confined it to simplicities and has militated against the development of subtlety or sophistication in ideology, especially in the younger sections of skinhead culture. Thus, although it has shown a frequent ability at local mobilisation for the purpose of anti-foreigner violence, this with some exceptions has been the limit of its concerted group-based activity, unless numbers have been circumstantially inflated by presence at, say, some sporting gathering.

Scenarios for the future development of militant neo-Nazism

As with the discussion in the previous section of theories to explain the growth of neo-Nazi militance, it is necessary to remember that this does not equate with extreme right party politics, despite some overlap and mutual contagion.

A summary of the present status of militant neo-Nazism in the Federal Republic needs to strike a balance between conflicting trends, especially when assessing implications for the future. Certainly, xenophobic violence attributable to the extreme right has declined somewhat since 1992 and 1993 and the German state has shown itself able to handle the constitutional challenge then posed by the phenomenon. For, two or three years ago, particularly in the period from mid-1992 to early 1993, it would not have been an exaggeration to say that militant neo-Nazism was a serious constitutional threat. This was not because a few thousand skinhead activists had the power to overthrow a democratic constitution, even if they had wanted to do so. They were not a threat even in the sense that they were the on-the-street force of an organised political party, as was the case with Brownshirts in the Weimar period. As discussed already, they had shown themselves almost self-consciously anarchic and deliberately loosely organised beyond their immediate localities. Rather, the threat that they posed came from the pernicious effects upon the quality of life of so many in the country and upon its social institutions if neo-Nazi outrages could be conducted with impunity, remain unpunished or, worse, achieve their objectives. The events at Hoyerswerda in 1991 and Rostock in 1992, for example, had led to arrests and convictions for a few of those involved but this was secondary to the fact that these outrages had achieved their objective. The victims in both cases had been evacuated and dispersed by the regional authorities. The neo-Nazis had confronted the constitutional state and had won: the localities in question were then *ausländerfrei*.

If every foreigner or asylum-seeker on urban public transport has to be constantly on guard against the possibility of physical attack; if passers-by are ready to applaud neo-Nazi violence; if every major mass sporting event offers the likelihood of such violence; if schools or colleges become the locus of xenophobic attacks: a society in which such incidents are commonplace and occur uncontrolled loses any reputation for fairness and decency, even if the great majority of its citizens actively deplore these occurrences.

As was documented above, there has in recent years been a more concerted State response to neo-Nazi outrages, in terms of proscriptions but also in prosecution and sentencing. These initiatives, if not always completely successful, have clearly had an impact. On the other hand, there are some distressing continuities from the past, which seem repeatedly to emerge. The at-best criminally complacent and lax approach of the police in Magdeburg to the attacks on five Africans in May 1994 was mentioned above. In September 1994 Werner Hackmann, the Hamburg official with responsibility for its internal affairs, felt obliged to resign, albeit somewhat quixotically, because of alleged attacks on foreigners by up to twenty-seven Hamburg policemen; seven of them have subsequently been indicted. The German office of Amnesty International said at the time that the Hamburg case was by no means exceptional[59] and similar accusations have been made in Berlin and elsewhere. Such police attitudes do not imply a likely enthusiasm for combating xenophobic violence by neo-Nazis. Moreover, attacks on asylum-seekers and their hostels continue to be reported with depressing frequency, especially but not exclusively from the east, even if the splash factor in the coverage is now generally less and overall numbers of such incidents have declined. Many examples could be cited but one case can suffice: around twenty extreme right youths caused a disturbance and some damage at a hostel in the town of Siedenbrünzow (Mecklenburg-Vorpommern) on 2 October 1994; fourteen of them were briefly held by the police but then released.[60]

Moreover, there is accumulating research evidence that many young people have attitudes that approach, if not equate with, those of neo-Nazism, although it must be said that many such attitudes, if they were to persist into adulthood, would emerge rather in political alienation and perhaps extreme right voting rather than in the much more exclusive phenomenon of neo-Nazi militance. A recent study in Bremen, where the DVU is active, reported, for example, that 25 per cent of older pupils agreed with extreme right positions.[61] In a national survey of young people between fourteen and twenty-seven years in February and March 1993 and published by the Federal Ministry for Women and Youth [*Bundesministerium für Frauen und Jugend*, BMFJ], 8 per cent of those in old regions and 18 per cent of those in new ones said that they had sympathy (*Verständnis*) for people being violent to asylum-seekers; among those with only ordinary secondary education, the figures were 13 and 24 per cent respectively.[62]

In 1993 and 1994 an ongoing debate on the state of the extreme right in the Federal

Republic concerned the extent to which neo-Nazi groups were nationally, even internationally, organised and the nature of such organisation. At the end of 1993 the Regional Crime Office [*Landeskriminalamt, LKA*] in Baden-Württemberg claimed that neo-Nazis in the German south-west were involved in attempts to build a unified national right-wing front, which certainly involved deliberately increased contacts.[63] In March 1994 a meeting of most of the central figures of the neo-Nazi scene (such as Swierczek, Hübner and Worch) met in the resort of Berggiesshübel (Saxony) to discuss the viability of a single group that could avoid state proscriptions, although little concrete has so far emerged from the v enture.[64] Certainly, there is much evidence that neo-Nazis are better organised, or merely more numerous, than in the 1980s; their ability to mobilise significant numbers of supporters at particular events is testimony to this (e.g. locally in the numerous coordinated attacks on asylum-seekers' hostels and nationally in incidents like Hoyerswerda and Rostock or the Hess commemorative rallies). However, despite 'radical' claims of a large-scale, internationally organised conspiracy,[65] the evidence for more than a skeletal national or international network is still not totally compelling. True, in early 1994 a nationwide list of target individuals, computerised into a data-base, was discovered but this is not itself compelling evidence that there exists an explicitly organised network among neo-Nazi groups.[66] More alarming, however, but perhaps more probable, as a result of continued state harassment and proscriptions, is resort to serious and more sustained terrorist actions. Whilst this is not a likely trajectory for the youngest adherents of the neo-Nazi scene, there is a hard core of older neo-Nazis, some with mercenary military experience in Bosnia and elsewhere, who have the requisite knowledge and incentives to take such steps.[67] This then perhaps will be the legacy of militant neo-Nazism's 'golden years' of the early 1990s.

List of Abbreviations

ANS/NA	*Aktionsfront Nationaler Sozialisten/Nationale Aktivisten* [Action Front of National Socialists/National Activists]
BfV	*Bundesamt für Verfassungsschutz* [Federal Office for the Protection of the Constitution]
BKA	*Bundeskriminalamt* [Federal Crime Office]
BMFJ	*Bundesministerium für Frauen und Jugend* [Federal Ministry for Women and Youth]
BVG	*Bundesverfassungsgericht* [Federal Constitutional Court]
BVP	*Brandenburgische Volkspartei* [Brandenburg People's Party]
CDU	*Christlich-Demokratische Union* [Christian Democratic Union]
DA	*Deutsche Alternative* [German Alternative]
DA/MD	*Direkte Aktion/Mitteldeutschland* [Direct Action/Central Germany]
DBI	*Deutsche Bürgerinitiative* [German Citizens' Initiative]
DKB	*Deutscher Kameradschaftsbund* [German Comradeship Association]
DLVH	*Deutsche Liga für Volk und Heimat* [German League for People and Homeland]
DN	*Deutsche Nationalisten* [German Nationalists]

DRGW– FNOP	*Deutsch-Russisches Gemeinschaftswerk – Förderverein Nord-Ostpreußen* [German-Russian Community Work – North-east Prussian Support Association]
DVU	*Deutsche Volksunion* [German People's Union]
FAP	*Freiheitliche Deutsche Arbeiterpartei* [Free German Workers' Party]
FDP	*Freie Demokratische Partei* [Free Democratic Party]
FFD	*Freundeskreis Freiheit für Deutschland* [Friendship Circle for Freedom for Germany]
FMJ	*Förderwerk Mitteldeutsche Jugend* [Support Group of Central German Youth]
FUN	*Freundeskreis Unabhängige Nachrichten* [Friendship Circle for Independent Intelligence]
GdNF	*Gesinnungsgemeinschaft der Neuen Front* [New Front Partisan Group]
GLKA	*Gemeinsames Landeskriminalamt* [General Regional Crime Office]
HNG	*Hilfsorganisation für nationale politische Gefangene und deren Angehörige* [Organisation for the Assistance of National Political Prisoners and Their Dependants]
HVD	*Heimattreue Vereinigung Deutschlands* [Homeland-Loving Union of Germany]
LfV	*Landesamt für Verfassungsschutz* [Regional Office for the Protection of the Constitution]
LKA	*Landeskriminalamt* [Regional Crime Office]
NB	*Nationaler Block* [National Bloc]
NF	*Nationalistische Front* [Nationalist Front]
NL	*Nationale Liste* [National List]
NO	*Nationale Offensive* [National Offensive]
NPD	*Nationaldemokratische Partei Deutschlands* [National Democratic Party of Germany]
NS	*Nationale Sammlung* [National Assembly]
NSDAP	*Nationalsozialistische Deutsche Arbeiterpartei* [National Socialist German Workers' Party]
NSDAP–AO	*Nationalsozialistische Deutsche Arbeiterpartei – Auslands-und Aufbauorganisation* [National Socialist German Workers' Party – Overseas Build-up Organisation]
REP	*Die Republikaner* [The Republicans]
SPD	*Sozialdemokratische Partei Deutschlands* [Social Democratic Party of Germany]
SRP	*Sozialistische Reichspartei* [Socialist Reich Party]
W-J	*Wiking-Jugend* [Viking Youth]
ZIJ	*Zentralinstitut für Jugendforschung* [Central Institute for Youth Research]

Notes

1. See C.T. Husbands, 'Militant Neo-Nazism in the Federal Republic of Germany in the 1980s, in L. Cheles, R. Ferguson and M. Vaughan (eds), *Neo-Fascism in Europe*, Longman,

London, 1991, pp. 86–119. The broad definition of militant neo-Nazism used in the first edition of this book has again been employed. This encompasses groups (and sometimes individuals) who for the most part eschew electoral participation and indulge in activities celebrating various aspects of the Third Reich (although not necessarily Hitler himself) and/or engage in specific other activities (often acts of violence), usually within the confines of small local and highly exclusive groups of dedicated activists. Such other activities are often xenophobic, or anti-Semitic, or directed against left-wing opponents or what are regarded as examples of cultural antinomy (e.g. punks, gays, prostitutes, and fringe artistic groups).

Right-wing extremism, in Germany as elsewhere, has been the focus of a publishing explosion since the 1980s, which has, if anthing, accelerated during the 1990s. However, a large amount of this literature focuses upon the more conventional extreme right that takes a political-party form; militant neo-Nazism receives very little attention in, say, E. Kolinsky, 'A Future for Right Extemism in Germany?', in P. Hainsworth (ed.), *The Extreme Right in Europe and the USA*, Pinter, London, pp. 61–94, nor in E. Zimmermann and T. Saalfeld, 'The Three Waves of West German Right-wing Extremism', in P. H. Merkl and L. Weinberg (eds), *Encounters with the Contemporary Radical Right*, Westview Press, Boulder, Colorado, pp. 50–74, where the principal reference to militant neo-Nazism concerns the 1977–85 period, when extreme right political parties were unsuccessful. Even so, it is usual in some of the general review studies of the extreme right to include a discussion of neo-Nazi militance; see, for example, C. T. Husbands, 'The Other Face of 1992: The Extreme-right Explosion in Western Europe', *Parliamentary Affairs*, Vol. 45, No. 3, July 1992, pp. 267–84.

2. The Strasser brothers, Gregor (1892–1934) and Otto (1897–1974), represented the 'left', anti-capitalist wing of the National Socialist German Workers' Party [*Nationalsozialistische Deutsche Arbeiterpartei*, NSDAP] and were influential in assisting the party's growth in northern Germany during the 1920s. The former was murdered on Hitler's order on the occasion of the so-called Röhm Putsch of June 1934. In the mid- and late-1980s a wing of the German neo-Nazi scene had been particularly attracted to the eponymous Strasserism and even well-known Hitler celebrants such as Michael Kühnen had had to make concessions to the attraction of Strasserism to some neo-Nazi sympathisers.

3. BfV, *Verfassungsschutzbericht 1989*, Bundesministerium des Innern, Bonn, 1990, pp. 108–16. These reports are hereafter cited by the year whose events they describe (e.g. BfV, *Annual Report 1989*); the year of publication is invariably the subsequent one. The BfV's annual report for 1993 was the most recently available when this chapter was being prepared.

4. T. Assheuer and H. Sarkowicz, *Rechtsradikale in Deutschland: Die alte und die neue Rechte*, Verlag C. H. Beck, Munich, 1990, pp. 95–111; P. Ködderitzsch and L. A. Müller, *Rechtsextremismus in der DDR*, Lamuv-Verlag, Göttengen, 1990, pp. 11–23; P. Ködderitzsch, 'Neofaschistische Aktivitäten in der DDR', in K. Bodewig, R. Hesels and D. Mahlberg (eds), *Die schleichende Gefahr: Rechtsextremismus heute*, 2nd ed., Klartext Verlag, Essen, pp. 155–65; C. T. Husbands, 'Neo-Nazis in East Germany: The New Danger?', *Patterns of Prejudice*, Vol. 25, No. 1, Summer 1991, pp. 3–17; B. Siegler, *Auferstanden aus Ruinen . . .: Rechtsextemismus in der DDR*, Tiamat, Berlin, 1991, pp. 61–73; K. Hirsch and P. B. Heim, *Von Links nach Rechts: Rechtsradikale Aktivitäten in den neuen Bundesländern*, Goldmann Verlag, Munich, 1991, pp. 77–89. There is a further extensive literature that could be cited on this aspect of GDR society.

5. Various results from these studies have appeared in a number of different publications, authored or co-authored by Walter Friedrich, who had been head of the ZIJ. See, for example, his 'Einstellungen zu Ausländern in der ehemaligen DDR', pp. 47–62, and his 'Einstellungen ostdeutscher Jugendlichen zu Ausländern', pp. 22–46, both in W. Friedrich (ed.), *Ausländerfeindlichkeit und rechtsextreme Orientierungen bei der ostdeutschen Jugend*, Friedrich-Ebert-Stiftung, Leipzig, 1992.

6. See M. Schmidt, *The New Reich: Violent Extremism in Unified Germany and Beyond*, Hutchinson, London, pp. 59–63.

7. Seigler, *Auferstanden aus Ruinen . . .*, cit., pp. 16–26. For Dresden see, for example, P. Hockenos, *Free to Hate. The Rise of the Right in Post-Communist Eastern Europe*, Routledge, London, 1993, pp. 58–68. For Cottbus see, for example, B. Schröder, *Rechte Kerle: Skinheads, Faschos, Hooligans*, Rowohlt, Reinbek bei Hamburg, 1992, pp. 48–9. Frankfurt an der Oder, being on the German–Polish border, was a particularly useful place for attacking Polish citizens who entered Germany after the visa requirement was removed in April 1991.

8. The numbers of these foreign workers were tiny in comparison with foreign-worker populations in West European countires. In 1989 in the GDR there were 60,000 from Vietnam, 51,000 from Poland, 15,000 from Mozambique, 15,000 from the former Soviet Union (excluding members of the Red Army), 13,000 from Hungary, 8,000 from Cuba, 3,000 from Czechoslovakia, 1,400 from Angola, and 1,200 from Romania. See I. Runge, 'Verschobene Proportionen: Ausländer im Osten', in Friedrich (ed.), *Ausländerfeindlichkeit und rechtsextreme Orientierungen bei der ostdeutschen Jugend*, cit., pp. 76–80.

9. Husbands, 'Neo-Nazis in East Germany', cit., pp. 9–10.

10. Bernd Wagner, the GDR's police specialist on neo-Nazis gave this figure in an interview to the newspaper *Neues Deutschland* in May 1990. See Assheuer and Sarkowicz, *Rechtsradikale in Deutschland*, cit., p. 111.

11. H. Sippel, *Rechtsextremismus im vereinten Deutschland*, Bundesamt für Verfassungsschutz, Bonn, 1991, p. 6.

12. *Süddeutsche Zeitung*, 12 Dec. 1991, p. 2. This chapter is based extensively on material taken from the press, especially but not exclusively the *Süddeutsche Zeitung*. Referencing each individual source is otiose and would have led to a proliferation of newspaper citations. Those instances that would be readily verifiable in other standard sources (such as other newspapers of record or *Keesing's Record of World Events*, Longman, London) have therefore not been referenced; explicit referencing has been reserved only for more esoteric and obscure incidents or facts.

13. *Süddeutsche Zeitung*, 9 July 1992, p. 5.

14. BfV, *Annual Report 1991*, 'Rechtsextremistische Bestrebungen', p. 7.

15. BfV, *Annual Report 1992*, p. 70; this figure for 1992 was increased to 2,639 in BfV, *Annual Report 1993*, pp. 79–80.

16. BfV, *Annual Report 1992*, p. 77.

17. Of course, these data include offences attributable to members of any extreme right groups, not merely those on the militant neo-Nazi fringe. Relevant offences by members of, say, the National Democratic Party of Germany [*Nationaldemokratische Partei Deutschlands*, NPD] will also be covered by these data. Also, like any data on these types of offence, those in Table 18.2 may be susceptible to reporting vagaries.

18. It is obvious that many acts of xenophobia will be committed by individuals who do not belong to the militant neo-Nazi scene, or even to one of the other extreme right groupings. However, it is useful to place the German data in some perspective. Perhaps a larger proportion of xenophobic acts have am extreme right background in Germany than in Great Britian but it is important to emphasise that xenophobic/racist violence is not uniquely nor even predominantly German. In 1993, for example, 9,762 racial incidents were recorded by the police in England and Wales; see *The Guardian*, Tabloid section, 25 Nov. 1994, pp. 4–5.

19. *Süddeutsche Zeitung*, 5/6 Jan. 1995, p. 6.

20. For example, BfV, *Annual Report 1992*, p. 72.

21. BfV, *Annual Report 1993*, p. 88.

22. See Husbands, 'Neo-Nazis in East Germany', cit., pp. 6–7, for further details of the Federal Government's response to the evolving situation in the new regions.

23. *The Guardian*, 26 Aug. 1992, p. 16.

24. See Husbands, 'Militant Neo-Nazism', cit., passim.

25. *Der Spiegel*, 4 April 1994, pp. 53–55.

26. R. Fromm, *Am rechten Rand: Lexikon des Rechtsradikalismus*, 2nd ed., Schüren, Marburg, 1994, p. 85. This book is an excellent source of information about individual neo-Nazi and other extreme right groups or parties in the Federal Republic. The neo-Nazi scene contains its continuities but many aspects change continually; hence, compilations such as this soon become obsolete. For a similar effort describing the late 1980s, see K. Hirsch, *Rechts, REPs, Rechts: Actuelles Handbuch zur rechtsextremen Szene*, Elefanten Press, Berlin, 1990.

27. 'Die "Wiking-Jugend" ', *AVS-Informationsdienst*, Vol. 15, No. 1, Jan. 1995, pp. 9–10.

28. *Frankfurter Rundschau*, 17 May 1994, p. 1.

29. *Süddeutsche Zeitung*, 18 Jan. 1995, p. 6.

30. For a discussion of such reports, see Husbands, 'Neo-Nazis in East Germany', cit., especially pp. 15–16.

31. *Neue Zürcher Zeitung*, 8 Sep. 1994, p. 2.

32. Fuller details are given in C.T. Husbands, 'Racism amd Racist Violence: Some Theories and Policy Perspectives', in T. Björgo and R. Witte (eds), *Racist Violence in Europe*, St. Martin's Press, New York, 1993, pp. 113–27.

33. *Neue Zürcher Zeitung*, 16–17 Oct. 1994, p. 7.

34. *Süddeutsche Zeitung*, 7–8 Jan. 1995, p. 8.

35. It must be remembered that sentencing policy does vary from one country's system of criminal justice to that of another, in terms of length of sentence, use of suspended sentences and probabtion, and use of remission. In 1991 the United Kingdom had the second highest per-captia prison population in the European Union, with almost 100 incarcerated per 100,000 population. The Federal Republic was only sixth highest, although its figure was almost 80 per 100,000; see Central Statistical Office, *Social Trends 24*, HMSO, London, 1994, p. 162. Differences such as these are better explained in terms of vaiations in sentencing policy, rather than by different amounts of crime and differential clear-up and conviction rates. The United Kingdom has a widely known reputation for using incarceration; however, given that the German rate is not far behind, one may wonder whether many of the sentences being imposed by German courts for these types of offence are as stringent as those that would be imposed by British ones. The juvenile status of most offenders is perhaps seen as a mitigating consideration.

36. *Süddeutsche Zeitung*, 2 May 1994, p. 5.

37. *Suddeutsche Zeitung*, 7–8 Jan. 1995, p. 8.

38. See Husbands, 'Militant Neo-Nazism', cit., pp. 100–1.

39. *Süddeutsche Zeitung*, 12 Dec. 1994, p. 5.

40. *Mitteldeutschland* is the name used in many extreme right circles for the former GDR, showing claim to areas of the former German Reich further east that are now in Poland or Russia. The DA, for example, had reacted to the collapse of the GDR by calling more assertively for the restoration of the former Reich, especially in the light of the formalisation by treaty of the frontier between the Federal Republic and Poland as the Oder–Neisse line. 'Not the FRG, not the GDR – we want the Reich', as one of its slogans demanded.

41. *Der Spiegel*, 4 Apr. 1994, pp. 53–5.

42. *Süddeutsche Zeitung*, 30 June 1994, p. 6.

43. *Süddeutsche Zeitung*, 1 Dec. 1994, p. 6.

44. Fromm, *Am rechten Rand*, cit., p. 11.

45. Schröder, *Rechte Kerle*, cit., pp. 91–9.

46. Althans is a neo-Nazi currently associated with no particular group but was once a follower of Kühnen until a disagreement over the latter's overt espousal of homosexuality in a pamphlet on national socialism and homosexuality. Althans was drawn to the German neo-Nazi, Ernst Zündel (born in 1939), who lives in Canada and has financed a number of neo-Nazi initiatives, including an attempted series of radio broadcasts in German sent on various short-wave frequencies from the United States; see *Süddeutsche Zeitung*, 8 Nov. 1994, p. 16, and BfV, *Annual Report 1993*, p. 153.

47. *Süddeutsche Zeitung*, 16 Sept. 1994, p. 2.

48. It must be remembered that these data cover perpetrators of violence. Women do participate in some neo-Nazi groups (say, HNG, for example), where both gender and age distributions are undoubtedly less skewed.

49. See Husbands, 'Militant Neo-Nazism', cit., p. 103. Willems, using data on xenophobic incidents in general collected by questionnaires to regional police forces, found a gender, age and occupation structure very similar to that reported in Table 18.5. Although his data cover not merely those offenders who were overt extreme right sympathisers, it is clear that many were in extreme right or skinhead groups; see H. Willems *et. al.*, *Fremdenfeindliche Gewalt: Einstellungen, Täter, Konflikteskalation*, Leske + Budrich, Opladen, 1993, pp. 110–30.

50. P. Dudek, *Jugendliche Rechtsextremisten: Zwischen Hakenkreuz und Odalsrune, 1945 bis heute*, Bund-Verlag, Cologne, 1985, pp. 87–8.

51. See Husbands, 'Militant Neo-Nazism', cit., esp. pp. 110–11.

52. E. Hennig, 'Neonazistische Militanz und Rechtsextremismus unter Jugendlichen', *Aus Politik und Zeitgeschichte: Beilage zue Wochenzeitung 'Das Parlament'*, 12 June 1982, pp. 23–37, and Bundesministerium des Innern, *Neonazistische Militanz und Rechtsextremismus unter Jugendlichen*, Verlag W. Kohlhammer, Stuttgart, 1982.

53. W. Heitmeyer, *Rechtsextremistische Orientierungen bei Jugendlichen: Empirische Ergebnisse und Erklärungsmuster einer Untersuchung zur politsichen Sozialisation*, 2nd ed., Juventa Verlag, Weinhein, 1988.

54. W. Heitmeyer *et al.*, *Die Bielefelder Rechtsextremismus-Studie: Erste Langzeituntersuchung zur politischen Sozialisation männlicher Jugendlicher*, Juventa Verlag, Weinheim, 1992.

55. Heitmeyer, *Rechtsextremistische Orientierungen bei Jugendlichen*, cit., p. 188.

56. W. Heitmeyer, 'Hostility and Violence towards Foreigners in Germany', in Björgo and Witte (eds), *Racist Violence in Europe*, cit., pp. 17–28. For a statement by Heitmeyer specifically on his views about the new regions, see his 'Die Widerspiegelung von Modernisierungsrücsktänden im Rechsextremismus', in K.-H Heinemann and W. Schubath (eds), *Der antifaschistische Staat entläßt seine Kinder: Jugend und Rechtsextremismus in Ostdeutschland*, Papy Rossa Verlag, Cologne, 1992, pp. 100–15.

For a further discussion that separately considers old and new regions, see R. Merten and H.-U. Otto, 'Rechtsradikale Gewalt im vereinigten Deutschland: Jugend im Kontext von Gewalt, Rassismus und Rechtsextremismus', in H.-U. Otto and R. Merten (eds), *Rechtsradikale Gewalt im vereinigten Deutschland: Jugend im gesellscaftlichen Umbruch*, Leske + Budrich, Opladen, 1993, pp. 13–33.

The following discussion draws in part upon all these sources.

57. This aspect is particularly emphasised by H. Lynen von Berg, 'Rechtsextremismus in Ostdeutschland seit der Wende', in W. Kowalsky and W. Schroeder (eds), *Rechtsextremismus: Einführung und Forschungsbilanz*, Westdeutscher Verlag, Opladen, 1994, pp. 103–26.

58. For some further details, see Husbands, 'Neo-Nazis in East Germany', cit., p. 5.

59. *Süddeutsche Zeitung*, 15 Sep. 1994, p. 2.

60. *Süddeutsche Zeitung*, 4 Oct. 1994, p. 6.

61. *Süddeutsche Zeitung*, 14–15 Jan. 1995, p.6.

62. Institut für Praxisorientierte Sozialforschung, *Jugendliche und junge Erwachsene in Deutschland*, Bundesministerium für Frauen und Jugend, Bonn, June 1993, p. 84.

63. *Süddeutsche Zeitung*, 9 Dec. 1993, p. 6.

64. *Der Spiegel*, 4 Apr. 1994, pp. 53–5.

65. This is a major theme of, for example, Schmidt, *The New Reich*, cit.

66. In early 1994 there were reports about a neo-Nazi telephone line disseminating information about anti-Fascists; see *Süddeutsche Zeitung*, 12 Jan. 1994, p.5.

67. This possibility has been expressed by Michael Wolf, head of the Regional Office for the Protection of the Constitution [*Landesamt für Verfassungsschutz*] in Schleswig-Holstein; see *Süddeutsche Zeitung*, 14–15 Jan. 1995, p. 6.

SELECT BIBLIOGRAPHY

General

T. Björgo and R. Witte (eds) — *Racist Violence in Europe*, St Martin's Press, New York, 1993.

M. Blinkhorn (ed.) — *Fascists and Conservatives. The Radical Right and the Establishment in Twentieth Century Europe,* Unwin Hyman, London, 1990.

F. L. Carsten — *The Rise of Fascism*, Batsford, London, 1967.

H. de Schampheleire and Y. Thanassekos (eds) — *L'Extrême droite en Europe de l'Ouest. Actes du Colloque d'Anvers (29 mars 1990)*, VUP-Press, Brussels 1991.

A. M. Duranton-Crabol — *L'Europe de l'Extrême Droite*, Complexe, Brussels, 1991.

F. Elbers and M. Fennema — *Racistische partijen in West-Europa. Tussen nationale traditie en Europese samenwerking* [Racist parties in Western Europe. Between national tradition and European co-operation], Stichting Burgerschapskunde. Nederlands Centrum voor Politieke Vorming, Leiden, 1993.

European Parliament — *Committee of Inquiry into the Rise of Fascism and Racism in Europe. Report on the Findings of the Inquiry,* Luxembourg, 1985.

R. Griffin — *The Nature of Fascism*, Pinter, London, 1991.

R. Grimm and J. Hermand — *Faschismus und Avantgarde*, Athenäum, Königstein/Ts., 1980.

P. Hainsworth (ed.) — *The Extreme Right in Europe and the USA*, Pinter, London, 1992.

A. C. Hargreaves and J. Leaman (eds) — *Race, Ethnicity and Politics in Contemporary Europe*, Edward Elgar, London, 1995.

G. Harris — *The Dark Side of Europe. The Extreme Right Today*, Edinburgh University Press, Edinburgh, 1990.

P. M. Hayes — *Fascism*, Allen and Unwin, London, 1973.

P. Ignazi — *L'Estrema Destra in Europa*, Il Mulino, Bologna, 1994.

M. Kitchen — *Fascism*, Macmillan, London, 1982.

J. Krejčí and V. Velímský — *Ethnic and Political Nations in Europe*, Croom Helm, London, and St. Martin's Press, New York, 1972.

M. A. Ledeen — *Universal Fascism. The Theory and Practice of the Fascist International, 1928–1936,* Fertig, New York, 1972.

C. Ó Maoláin — *The Radical Right. A World Directory*, Longman, London, 1987.

P. H. Merkl and L. Weinberg (eds) — *Encounters with the Contemporary Radical Right*, Westview, Boulder, CO, 1993.

J. Milfull (ed.) — *The Attractions of Fascism. Social Psychology and Aesthetics of the 'Triumph of the Right',* Berg, Oxford, 1990.

354

G. L. Mosse   *International Fascism. New Thoughts and New Approaches,* Sage, London, 1979.

A. Pravda (ed.)   *The End of the Outer Empire,* Royal Institute of International Affairs, Sage, London, 1992.

H. A. Turner, Jr. (ed.)   *Reappraisals of Fascism,* New Viewpoints, New York, 1975.

Various Authors   *Extreme Right in Europe,* special issue of *Parliamentary Affairs,* XLV (3), 1992.

K. von Beyme (ed.)   *Right-Wing Extremism in Western Europe,* special issue of *West European Politics,* XI (2), 1988.

S. J. Woolf (ed.)   *Fascism in Europe,* Methuen, London, 1981.

Nationalism

B. Anderson   *Imagined Communities: Reflections on the Origins and Spread of Nationalism,* Verso, London, 1983.

J. Armstrong   *Nations Before Nationalism,* University of North Carolina Press, Chapel Hill, NC, 1982.

W. Connor   'A nation is a nation, is a state, is an ethnic group, is a . . .', *Ethnic and Racial Studies,* I (4), 1978, pp. 377–400.

E. Gellner   *Nations and Nationalism,* Blackwell, Oxford, 1983.

E. Hobsbawm   *Nations and Nationalism Since 1780,* Cambridge University Press, Cambridge, 1990.

E. Kedourie   *Nationalism,* Hutchinson, London, 1960.

H. Kohn   *Prelude to Nation-States: The French and German Experience, 1789–1815,* Van Nostrand, Princeton, NJ, 1967.

J. Krejčí   'Ethnic Problems in Europe', in S. Giner and M. S. Archer (eds), *Contemporary Europe. Social Structures and Cultural Patterns,* Routledge and Kegan Paul, London, 1978, pp. 124–71.

G. Mosse   *The Crisis of German Ideology,* Grosset and Dunlap, New York, 1964.

A. D. Smith   *The Ethnic Origins of Nations,* Blackwell, Oxford, 1986.

A. D. Smith   *National Identity,* Penguin, Harmondsworth, 1991.

P. Sugar and I. Lederer (eds)   *Nationalism in Eastern Europe,* University of Washington Press, Seattle, 1969.

Italy

L. Cheles   '"Dolce Stil Nero?" Images of Women in the Graphic Propaganda of the Italian Neo-Fascist Party', in Z. G. Barański and S. W. Vinall (eds), *Women and Italy. Essays*

	on *Gender, Culture and History*, Macmillan, London, 1991, pp. 64–94.
L. Cheles	'The Italian Far Right: Nationalist Attitudes and Views on Ethnicity and Immigration', in A. C. Hargreaves and J. Leaman (eds), *Race, Ethnicity and Politics in Contemporary Europe*, Edward Elgar, London, 1995.
R. Chiarini and P. Corsini	*Da Salò a Piazza della Loggia*, Franco Angeli, Milan, 1985.
G. Cianflone and D. Scafoglio	*Fascismo sui muri*, Guida, Naples, 1976.
S. Di Michele and A. Galiani	*Mal di Destra*, Sperling and Kupfer, Milan, 1995.
R. H. Drake	'Julius Evola and the Ideological Origins of the Radical Right in Contemporary Italy', in P. H. Merkl (ed.), *Political Violence and Terror. Motifs and Motivations*, University of California Press, Los Angeles, 1986, pp. 161–89.
F. Ferraresi	'The Radical Right in Post-War Italy', *Politics and Society*, XVI, 1988, pp. 71–119.
F. Ferraresi	'A Secret Structure Codenamed Gladio', in S. Hellman and G. Pasquino (eds), *Italian Politics – A Review*, vol. 7, Pinter, London, 1992, pp. 29–49.
P. Furlong	'The Extreme Right in Italy: Old Orders and Dangerous Novelties', in *Extreme Right in Europe*, special issue of *Parliamentary Affairs*, XLV (3), 1992, pp. 345–56.
R. Griffin	'Revolts Against the Modern World', *Literature and History*, XI, Spring 1985, pp. 101–23.
P. Ignazi	*Il polo escluso. Profilo del Movimento Sociale Italiano*, Il Mulino, Bologna, 1989.
P. Ignazi	'The Changing Profile of the Italian Social Movement', in P. H. Merkl and L. Weinberg (eds), *Encounters with the Contemporary Radical Right*, Westview, Boulder, CO, 1993; pp. 75–92, 240–2.
P. Ignazi	*Postfascisti? Dal Movimento Sociale ad Alleanza Nazionale,* Il Mulino, Bologna, 1994.
G. Locatelli and D. Martini	*Duce, addio. La biografia di Gianfranco Fini,* Longanesi, Milan, 1994.
F. Sidoti	'The Extreme Right in Italy: Ideological Orphans and Countermobilization', in P. Hainsworth (ed.), *The Extreme Right in Europe and the USA*, Pinter, London, 1992, pp. 151–74.
G. Tassani	'The Italian Social Movement: from Almirante to Fini', in R. Nanetti and R. Catanzaro (eds), *Italian Politics – A Review*, vol. IV, Pinter, London, 1990, pp. 124–45.
C. Valentini	'Alleanza Nazionale: la componente "storica" del Polo delle Libertà', in P. Ginsborg (ed.), *Stato dell'Italia*, Il Saggiatore-Bruno Mondadori, Milan, 1994, pp. 677–81.

Various Authors   *Fascismo oggi. Nuova destra e cultura reazionaria negli anni ottanta,* special issue of *Notiziario dell'Istituto Storico della Resistenza in Cuneo e Provincia,* No. 23, June 1983.

Spain

S. Ellwood   'Falange y franquismo' in J. Fontana (ed.), *España bajo el franquismo,* Crítica, Barcelona, 1986, pp. 39–59.

S. Ellwood   'Not so Much a Programme, More a Way of Life: Oral History and Spanish Fascism', *Oral History,* XVI (2), 1988, pp. 57–66.

S. Ellwood   *Spanish Fascism in the Franco Era,* Macmillan, London, 1987.

S. Ellwood   'The Extreme Right in Post-Francoist Spain', *Parliamentary Affairs,* XLV (3), 1992, pp. 373–385.

J. Gilmour   'The Extreme Right in Spain: Blas Piñar and the Spirit of the Nationalist Uprising', in P. Hainsworth (ed.), *The Extreme Right in Europe and the USA,* Pinter, London, 1992, pp. 206–31.

P. Preston   'General Franco's Rearguard', *New Society,* 29 Nov. 1973, pp. 519–21.

P. Preston   'Spain', in S. J. Woolf (ed.), *Fascism in Europe,* Methuen, London, 1981, pp. 329–51.

P. Preston   'Populism and Parasitism: the Falange and the Spanish Establishment, 1939–75, in M. Blinkhorn (ed.), *Fascists and Conservatives,* Unwin Hyman, London, 1990, pp. 138–56.

P. Preston   *The Politics of Revenge,* Unwin Hyman, London, 1990.

J. Rodríguez Puértolas   *Literatura fascista española,* Akal, Madrid, 1986, 2 vols.

M. Sánchez Soler,   *Los hijos del 20N,* Temas de Hoy, Madrid, 1994.

Portugal

M. Braga da Cruz   *O Partido e o Estado no Salazarismo,* Presença, Lisbon, 1988.

A. Costa Pinto   *Salazarism and European Fascism. Problems and Perspectives of Interpretation,* Columbia University Press, New York, 1995.

A. Costa Pinto   *Os Camisas Azuis. Ideologia, elites e movimentos fascistas em Portugal, 1914–1945,* Estampa, Lisbon, 1994.

A. Costa Pinto   'Dealing with the Legacy of Authoritarianism: Political Purge and Radical Right Movements in Portugal's Transition to Democracy (1974–90s)', in S. U. Larsen *et al.* (eds), *Modern Europe After Fascism, 1945–1980s,* Columbia University Press, New York, 1995.

M. de Lucena	*A Evolução do Sistema Corporativo Português,* vol. I – *O Salazarismoi,* vol. II – *O Marcelismo,* Perspectivas e Realidades, Lisbon, 1976.
T. Gallagher	'Portugal: The Marginalization of the Extreme Right', in P. Hainsworth (ed.), *The Extreme Right in Europe and the USA,* Pinter, London, 1992, pp. 232–45.

Greece

M. Blinkhorn and Th. Veremis (eds)	*Modern Greece: Nationalism and Nationality,* Sage-ELLIAMEP, Athens, 1990.
R. Clogg and L. Yannopoulos (eds)	*Greece Under Military Rule,* Secker and Warburg, London, 1972.
R. Clogg	*Parties and Elections in Greece,* C. Hurst, London, 1988.
R. Clogg	*A Concise History of Greece,* Cambridge University Press, Cambridge, 1992.
D. Close	'Conservatism, Authoritarianism and Fascism in Greece, 1915–45', in M. Blinkhorn (ed.), *Fascists and Conservatives,* Unwin Hyman, London, 1990, pp. 200–217.
P. E. Dimitras	'Greece: The Virtual Absence of an Extreme Right', in P. Hainsworth (ed.), *The Extreme Right in Europe and the USA,* Pinter, London, 1992, pp. 246–68.
K. Featherston and D. Katsoudas (eds)	*Political Change in Greece: Before and After the Colonels,* Croom Helm, London, 1988.
R. Higham and Th. Veremis (eds)	*Aspects of Greece: 1936–40, The Metaxas Dictatorship,* ELIAMEP-Vryonis Centre, Athens, 1993.
V. Kapetanyannis	'Socio-political Conflicts and Military Intervention – The Case of Greece: 1950–1967,' Ph.D. thesis, University of London, 1986.
S. Lanardatos	*Pos ftasame sten 4e Avgoustou* [How we reached the 4th of August], Themelio, Athens, 1965.
S. Linardatos	*H 4e Avgoustou* [The Fourth of August], Themelio Athens, 1966.
Th. Veremis	'Veto and Impasse, 1967–74', in C. Clapham and G. Philip (eds), *The Political Dilemmas of Military Regimes,* Croom Helm, London, 1985.
C. M. Woodhouse	*The Rise and Fall of the Greek Colonels,* Granada, St Albans, 1985.
C. M. Woodhouse	*Modern Greece. A Short History,* Faber and Faber, London, 1986, 4th edn.

Yugoslavia

I. Banac	*The National Question in Yugoslavia. Origins, History, Politics,* Cornell University Press, Ithaca, NY, 1988.

L. J. Cohen   *Broken Bonds. The Disintegration of Yugoslavia*, Westview, Boulder, CO, 1993.

A. Djilas   *The Contested Country. Yugoslav Unity and Communist Revolution, 1919–1953*, Harvard University Press, Cambridge, MA, 1991.

F. Dvornik   *The Slavs in European History and Civilisation*, The State University, Rutgers, 1962.

M. Glenny   *The Fall of Yugoslavia. The Third Balkan War*, Penguin, Harmondsworth, 1992.

J. A. Irvine   *The Croat Question. Partisan Politics in the Formation of the Yugoslav Socialist State*, Westview, Boulder, CO, 1993.

B. Magas   *The Destruction of Yugoslavia. Tracking the Break-Up, 1980–92*, Verso, London, 1993.

S. Ramet   *Nationalism and Federalism in Yugoslavia, 1962–1991*, Indiana University Press, Bloomington, IN, 1992.

I. Siber   'Strengthening of the Right and Social Changes in Croatia and Yugoslavia', in J. Held, *Democracy and Right-Wing Politics in Eastern Europe in the 1990s*, East European Monographs, Boulder, CO (Distributed by Cornell University Press, Ithaca, NY), 1988.

M. Thompson   *A Paper House. The Ending of Yugoslavia*, Pantheon, New York, 1992.

Former Soviet Union

A. Barsenkov, A. Vdovin and V. Koretsky (eds)   *Russky Vopros v Natsionalnoi Politike XXV* [The Russian Question in National Politics], Moskovsky Rabochy, Moscow, 1993.

S. Carter   *Russian Nationalism – Yesterday, Today, Tomorrow*, Pinter, London, 1990.

M. Cox   'After Stalinism. The Extreme Right in Russia, East Germany and Eastern Europe', in P. Hainsworth (ed.), *The Extreme Right in Europe and the USA*, Pinter, London, 1992, pp. 269–85.

K. Dawisha and B. Parrott   *Russia and the New States of Eurasia*, Cambridge University Press, Cambridge, 1994.

J. Dunlop   *The New Russian Nationalism*, Praeger, New York, 1985.

D. Hammer   *Russian Nationalism and Soviet Politics*, Westview, Boulder, CO, 1989.

P. Hockenos   *Free to Hate. The Rise of the Right in Post-Communist Eastern Europe*, Routledge, London, 1993.

V. Krasnov   '*Pamiat*: Russian Right-Wing Radicalism', in P. H. Merkl and L. Weinberg (eds), *Encounters with the Contemporary Radical Right*, Westview, Boulder, CO, 1993, pp. 111–31.

G. Lapidus, V. Zaslavsky and P. Goldman (eds)	*From Union to Commonwealth*, Cambridge University Press, Cambridge, 1992.
W. Laqueur	*Black Hundred. The Rise of the Extreme Right in Russia*, Harper Collins, New York, 1993.
A. Shtromas and M. A. Kaplan (eds)	*The Soviet Union and the Challenge of the Future*, Paragon House, New York, 1988 and 1989, 2 vols.
S. White	*After Gorbachev*, Cambridge University Press, Cambridge, 1993.

Poland

N. Ascherson	*The Struggles for Poland*, Michael Joseph, London, 1987.
N. Ascherson	*The Polish August, The Self-limiting Revolution*, Penguin, Harmondsworth, 1981.
N. Davies	*God's Playground. A History of Poland*, vol. 2, Columbia University Press, New York, 1982.
N. Davies	*Heart of Europe. A Short History of Poland*, Oxford University Press, Oxford, 1986.
M. K. Dziewanowski	*The Communist Party of Poland*, 2nd edn, Harvard University Press, Cambridge, MA, 1976.
D. S. Mason	*Public Opinion and Political Change in Poland, 1980–1982*, Cambridge University Press, Cambridge, 1989.
M. Mushkat	*Philo-Semitism and anti-Jewish attitudes in Post-Holocaust Poland*, Edwin Hellen, Lewiston, NY, 1992.
A. Polonsky (ed.)	*My Brother's Keeper? Recent Polish Debates on the Holocaust*, Routledge, London, in association with the Institute of Polish-Jewish Studies, Oxford, 1990.

France

J.-P. Apparu	*La droite d'aujourd'hui*, A. Michel, Paris, 1979.
G. Birenbaum	*Le Front National en politque*, Balland. Paris, 1992.
G. Bresson and C. Lionet	*Le Pen. Biographie*, Seuil, Paris, 1994.
J.-Y. Camus and R. Monzat	*Les droites nationales et radicales en France*, Presses Universitaires de Lyon, Lyons, 1992.
A. Chebel D'Appolonia	*L'Extrême-Droite en France, de Maurras à Le Pen*, Complexe, Brussels, 1986.
A. M. Duranton-Crabol	*Visages de la Nouvelle Droite. Le GRECE et son histoire*, Presses de la Fondation Nationale des Sciences Politiques, Paris, 1988.
G. Faye	*Les nouveaux enjeux idéologiques*, Editions du Labyrinthe, Paris, 1985.

P. Fysh and J. Wolfreys	'Le Pen, the National Front and the Extreme Right in France', in *Extreme Right in Europe*, special issue of *Parliamentary Affairs*, XLV (3), 1992, pp. 309–26.
J. Marcilly	*Le Pen sans bandeau*, Grancher, Paris, 1984.
T. Maricourt	*Les nouvelles passerelles de l'extrême droite*, Manya, Paris, 1993.
N. Mayer and Perrineau	*Le Front National à découvert*, Presses de la Fondation Nationale des Sciences Politiques, Paris, 1989.
P. Milza	*Le fascisme français: passé et présent*, Flammarion, Paris, 1987.
A. Monzat	*Enquêtes sur la droite extrême*, Le Monde-Editions, Paris, 1992.
B. Orfali	*L'adhésion au Front National. De la minorité active au mouvement social*, Kimé, Paris, 1990.
E. Plenel and A. Rollat	*L'effet Le Pen*, Le Monde – La Découverte, Paris, 1984.
R. Rémond	*Les droites en France*, Aubier, Paris, 1985.
A. Rollat	*Les hommes de l'extrême droite*, Calmann-Lévy, Paris, 1985.
W. Safran	'The National Front in France: from Lunatic Fringe to Limited Respectability', in P. H. Merkl and L. Weinberg (eds), *Encounters with the Contemporary Radical Right*, Westview, Boulder, CO, 1993, pp. 19–49.
T. Sheehan	'Myth and Violence. The Fascism of Julius Evola and Alain de Benoist', *Social Research*, XLVIII (1), spring 1981, pp. 45–73.
J.-F. Sirinelli (ed.)	*Histoire des droites en France*, Gallimard, Paris, 1992, 3 vols.
Z. Sternhell	*Neither Left nor Right*, University of California Press, Berkely, CA, 1986.
P.-A. Taguieff	*Sur la Nouvelle Droite. Jalons d'une analyse critique*, La Découverte, Paris, 1994.
M. Winock	*Histoire de l'extrême droite en France*, Seuil, Paris, 1993.

Belgium

Archief en Museum van de Socialistische Arbeidersbeweging (AMSAB)	*De Wereld van Anne Frank in België, 1929–1945. Een dagboek voor de toekomst* [The World of Anne Frank in Belgium, 1929–1945. A diary for the future], Hadewijck, Antwerp, 1993.
F. Balace	'Le tournant des années soixante. De la droite réactionnaire à l'extrême droite révolutionnaire', in Various Authors, *De l'avant à l'après-guerre. L'extrême droite en Belgique francophone*, De Boeck-Wesmael, Brussels, 1994.
G. Braes	*L'affront national. Le nouveau visage de l'extrême droite en Belgique*, EPO, Berchem, 1991.
Ph. Brewaeys	'L'Extrême droite en Belgique francophone', in H. de Schampheleire and Y. Thanassekos (eds), *L'Extrême*

	droite en Europe de l'Ouest. Actes du colloque d'Anvers (*29 mars 1990*), VUB-Press, Brussels, 1991, pp. 247–54.
Ph. Brewaeys, V. Dahaut and A. Tolbiac	*L'Extrême droite francophone face aux élections*, Courrier hebdomadaire du CRISP (Centre de Recherche et d'Information Socio-Politiques), Brussels, No. 1350, 1992.
M. Conway	*Collaboration in Belgium. Léon Degrelle and the Rexist Movement, 1940–1944*, Yale University Press, New Haven, CT, 1993.
S. Dumont	*Les brigades noires. L'extrême droite en France et en Belgique francophone de 1944 à nos jours*, EPO, Berchem, 1983, 2nd edn.
F. Elbers and M. Fennema	*Racistische partijen in West-Europa. Tussen nationale traditie en Europese samenwerking* [Racist parties in Western Europe. Between national tradition and European cooperation], Stichting Burgerschapskunde. Nederlands Centrum voor Politieke Vorming, Leiden, 1993, pp. 80–96.
J. Fitzmaurice	'The Extreme Right in Belgium: Recent Developments', in *Extreme Right in Europe*, special issue of *Parliamentary Affairs*, XLV (3), 1992, pp. 300–308.
H. Gijsels	*Het Vlaams Blok* [The Flemish Bloc], Kritak, Louvain, 1992.
C. T. Husbands	'Belgium: Flemish Legions on the March', in P. Hainsworth (ed.), *The Extreme Right in Europe and the USA*, Pinter, London, 1992.
M. Swyngedouw	'Het Vlaams Blok in Antwerpen. Een analyse van de verkiezingsuitslagen sinds 1985' [The Flemish Bloc in Antwerp. An analysis of the electoral results since 1985], in H. de Schampheleire and Y. Thanassekos (eds), *L'Extrême droite en Europe de l'Ouest. Actes du Colloque d'Anvers* (*29 mars 1990*), VUB-Press, Brussels, 1991, pp. 93–114.
M. Swyngedouw and L. de Winter	'Het Vlaams Blok in de Europese Verkiezingen van 1984 en 1989' [The Flemish Bloc during the European Elections of 1984 and 1989], in de Schampheleire and Thanassekos (eds), *L'Extrême droite*, cit., pp. 115–27.
J. Vander Velpen	*Het Vlaams Blok. Daar komen ze aangemarcheerd. Extreem-Rechts in Europa* [The Flemish Bloc. Here they are marching in. The Far-Right in Europe], EPO, Berchem, 1992, pp. 103–55.
Various Authors	*L'Extrême droite en Wallonie et à Bruxelles*, special supplement to *Socialisme*, No. 232, July–Aug. 1992.
P. Verlinden	'Morfologie van Extreem-Rechts binnen het Vlaams-Nationalisme' [Morphology of the Far Right in the framework of Flemish Nationalism], in de Schampheleire and Thanassekos (eds), *L'Extrême droite*, cit., pp. 235–45.

Great Britain

D. Baker	'A. K. Chesterton, the Strasser Brothers and the Politics of the National Front', *Patterns of Prejudice*, No. 19, 1985, pp. 23–33.
M. Billig	*Fascists. A Social Psychological View of the National Front*, Harcourt Brace Jovanovitch, New York, 1978.
M. Billig and A. Bell	'Fascist Parties in Post-War Britain', *Race Relations Abstracts*, V, 1980, pp. 7–18.
R. Eatwell	'Why Has the Extreme Right Failed in Britain?', in P. Hainsworth (ed.), *The Extreme Right in Europe and the USA*, Pinter, London, 1992, pp. 175–92.
N. Fielding	*The National Front*, Routledge, London, 1981.
G. Gable	'The Far Right in Contemporary Britain', in L. Cheles, R. Ferguson and M. Vaughan (eds), *Neo-Fascism in Europe*, Longman, London, 1991, pp. 245–63.
R. Hill with A. Bell	*The Other Face of Terror*, Grafton Books, London, 1988.
C. Husbands	*Racial Exclusionism and the City*, Allen and Unwin, London, 1983.
C. Husbands	'Extreme Right-Wing Politics in Great Britain', in *Right-Wing Extremism in Western Europe*, special issue of *West European Politics*, XI (2), 1988, pp. 65–79.
T. Kushner and K. Lunn	*The Politics of Marginality. Race, the Radical Right and Minorities in Twentieth Century Britain*, Frank Cass, London, 1990.
L. O'Hara	'Notes from the Underground. Part 3: British Fascism 1983–96', *Lobster*, No. 25, June 1993, pp. 16–20, 26.
L. O'Hara	'Notes from the Underground. Part 4: British Fascism 1983–86 (II)', *Lobster*, No. 26. Dec. 1993, pp. 13–18.
Searchlight	*From Ballots to Bombs*, Searchlight, London, 1989.
S. Taylor	*The National Front in English Politics*, Macmillan, London, 1982.
R. Thurlow	*Fascism in Britain*, Blackwell, Oxford, 1987.
N. Toczek	*The Bigger Tory Vote*, A. K. Press, Stirling, 1992.
M. Walker	*The National Front*, Fontana, London, 1977.

Germany

T. Assheuer and H. Sarkowicz	*Rechtsradikale in Deutschland. Die alte und die neue Rechte*, Beck, Munich, 1992.
U. Backes and P. Moreau	'The Extreme Right', *German Comments*, No. 33, Jan. 1994.
W. Benz (ed.)	*Rechtsextremismus in der Bundesrepublik*, Fischer, Frankfurt, 1989.
H-G. Betz	'Post-Modern Anti-Modernism: the West German

Republikaner', in *Politics and Society in Germany, Austria and Switzerland*, II (3), Summer 1990, pp. 1–22.

R. Fromm — *Am rechten Rand: Lexikon des Rechtsradikalismus*, Schüren, Marburg, 1994 (2nd edn).

K. Hirsch — *Rechts, REPs, Rechts: Aktuelles Handbuch zur rechtsextremen Szene*, Elefanten Press, Berlin, 1990.

C.T. Husbands — "Neo-Nazis in East Germany: The New Danger?", *Patterns of Prejudice*, XXV (1), 1991, pp. 3–17.

P. Ködderitzsch and L.A. Müller — *Rechtsextremismus in der DDR*, Lamuv, Göttingen, 1990.

W. Kowalsky and W. Schroeder (eds) — *Rechtsextremismus: Einführung und Forschungsbilanz*, Westdeutscher, Opladen, 1994.

R. Kühnl, R. Rilling, C. Sager — *Die NPD. Struktur, Ideologie and Funktion einer neofaschistischen Partei*, Suhrkamp, Frankfurt, 1969.

G. K. Roberts — 'Right-Wing Radicalism in the New Germany', in *Extreme Right in Europe*, special issue of *Parliamentary Affairs*, XLV (3), 1992, pp. 327–44.

P. Reif-Spirek (ed.) — *Rechtsextremismus in den neuen Bundesländern*, Landszentrale für politische Bildung Thuringen, Erfurt, 1992.

T. Saalfeld — 'The Politics of National Populism. Ideological Politics of the German Republikaner Party', in *German Politics*, II, 2 Aug. 1993.

D. Schoenbaum — *Hitler's Social Revolution. Class and Status in Nazi Germany, 1933–39*, Weidenfeld and Nicolson, London, 1967.

B. Schröder — *Rechte Kerle: Skinheads, Faschos, Hooligans*, Rowohlt, Reinbek bei Hamburg, 1992.

H. J. Schwagerl — *Rechtsextremes Denken Merkmale und Methoden*, Fischer, Frankfurt, 1993.

H-J. Veen, N. Lepszy and P. Mnich — *The Republikaner Party in Germany*, Centre for Strategic and International Studies, Washington DC, Praeger, Westport, CT, 1993.

E. Zimmermann and T. Saalfeld — 'The Three Waves of West German Right-Wing Extremism', in H. Merkl and L. Weinberg (eds), *Encounters with the Contemporary Radical Right*, Westview, Boulder, CO, 1993, pp. 50–74.

Holocaust Denial

R. Eatwell — 'The Holocaust Denial: A Study in Propaganda Technique', in L. Cheles, R. Ferguson and M. Vaughan (eds), *Neo-Fascism in Europe*, Longman, London, 1991, pp. 129–46.

P. Haupt — 'A Universe of Lies', *Patterns of Prejudice*, Summer 1991, pp. 75–85.

D. Lipstadt	'Holocaust Denial and the Compelling Force of Reason', *Patterns of Prejudice*, Nos. 1–2, 1992, pp. 64–76.
D. Lipstadt	*The Holocaust Denial*, Free Press, New York, 1993.
G. Seidel	*The Holocaust Denial*, Beyond the Pale, Leeds, 1986.
P. Vidal-Naquet	*Assassins of Memory*, Basic Books, New York, 1993.
Ph. Videlier	'A peine masqués, s'avancent les falsificateurs du passé', *Le Monde Diplomatique*, Jan. 1994, pp. 16–17.

INDEX